WHO'S WHO IN CONGRESS 1999
106th CONGRESS

Who's Who in Congress 1999

106th Congress

Congressional Quarterly Inc.
Washington, D.C.

Congressional Quarterly

Congressional Quarterly Inc., an editorial research service and publishing company, serves clients in the fields of news, education, business, and government. It combines the specific coverage of Congress, government, and politics contained in the *CQ Weekly* with the more general subject range of an affiliated publication, the *CQ Researcher*.

Congressional Quarterly also publishes a variety of books, including college political science textbooks under the CQ Press imprint and public affairs paperbacks on developing issues and events. CQ also publishes information directories and reference books on the federal government, national elections, and politics, including the *Guide to the Presidency,* the *Guide to Congress,* the *Guide to the U.S. Supreme Court,* the *Guide to U.S. Elections,* and *Politics in America. CQ's Encyclopedia of American Government* is a four-volume reference work providing essential information about the U.S. government and elections. The *CQ Almanac,* a compendium of legislation for one session of Congress, is published each year. *Congress and the Nation,* a record of government for a presidential term, is published every four years.

CQ also publishes the *CQ Daily Monitor,* a daily report on current and future activities of congressional committees. An electronic online information system, CQ.com, provides immediate access to CQ's databases of legislative action, votes, schedules, profiles, and analyses.

Project managers   Talia Greenberg, Peter Roybal, Anne Perra
Researchers   Kristin Brainerd, Rebecca Marquis, Elizabeth A. Urbauer
Members data conversion   Kevin Shanley
Vote studies   Derek Willis
Interns   Jordan Brenner, Christine Justice, Sandhya Somashekhar
Committee information   Ian McCaleb, Anthony L. Porretta
Interior and cover design   Kachergis Book Design
Electronic composition   Paul P. Pressau
Cover photo   Air Photographics, Inc.

ISBN 1-56802-080-5   ISSN 1054-9234

All rights reserved. No part of this publication may be reproduced or transmitted in any form or by any means, electronic or mechanical, including photocopy, recording, or any information storage and retrieval system, without permission in writing from the publisher.

Printed in the United States of America

Copyright © 1999 Congressional Quarterly Inc.
1414 22nd Street, N.W., Washington, D.C. 20037   (202) 887-8500

CQ Books on the Web: http://books.cq.com
CQ Books customer service: (202) 822-1475; (800) 638-1710

Table of Contents

Preface vii

U.S. Senators, 106th Congress 1
U.S. Representatives, 106th Congress 53

Appendixes
State Delegations, 106th Congress 277
Congressional Leadership 282
Senate Committees, 106th Congress 283
House Committees, 106th Congress 296
Key Senate Votes, 1998 319
Key House Votes, 1998 324
Senate Terms of Office 334
TV Guide to Senate Floor Action 335
TV Guide to House Floor Action 337
Congressional Bell System 339
Glossary 340

Preface

Congressional Quarterly, the preeminent source of information on Congress, captures in these pages the most succinct and reliable information available on the 106th Congress. *Who's Who in Congress 1999* — a pocket guide to the facts behind the faces of our nation's lawmakers — provides brief biographies and photographs of all members of the Senate and the House.

Each profile includes the information CQ's readers request most often. The biographical data — including date of birth, education, military service, religion, family, previous occupations, and political career — were obtained through CQ surveys and staff reporting. Also included is a pronunciation guide for some of the most-often mispronounced names of members of Congress. Fax numbers and Internet addresses also are included when available.

CQ researchers gathered information on congressional staffs in April 1999. Listed for each member is his or her chief aide, press secretary, appointments secretary, and legislative director; but not all members employ a person in each of those positions. Committee and subcommittee assignments, current as of April 12, are also included with every profile; committee chairmen and ranking members are identified.

Election results are provided for the previous two cycles for incumbent members and for 1998 for freshmen. The symbol "u/o" indicates that a member was unopposed in an election or did not appear on the ballot. Special and runoff elections also are noted. All election percentages were calculated from official election returns received from each state.

Election procedures in four states deserve special note.

Washington has a "jungle" primary, in which candidates of all parties appear on the same ballot; the candidate in each party with the most votes advances to the general election.

California adopted the "jungle" primary process in 1998.

In Alaska's "jungle" primary, all Republicans appear on one primary ballot; Democrats and all other candidates appear on a separate ballot. The candidate with the most votes in each party advances to the general election.

Before 1998, Louisiana held its primary before national election day. It was an open primary, with candidates from all parties on the ballot. Any candidate who received more than half the votes was elected, and no general election was held for that post. Likewise, a candidate with no opposition was declared elected and did not appear on the final ballot. If no candidate received more than half the votes, the top two vote-getters, regardless of political party, participated in a runoff election on national election day in November.

As a result, candidates in Louisiana could be elected to Congress before their counterparts throughout the nation. In December 1997, the Supreme Court ruled that this procedure violated an 1872 federal statute that sets a nationwide biennial date for the election of federal officers. Following the ruling, in 1998, Louisiana moved its primary election to Nov. 3.

Although the election was referred to as the primary, it was essentially the general election, and this book lists it as such. If there were contests in which no candidate received more than half the vote, there would have been a runoff election on Dec. 5. No runoffs were required, however.

Each member's profile also includes scores from CQ's vote studies for 1997 and 1998. The presidential support score is the percentage of recorded floor votes on which President Clinton took a position and on which a member voted "yea" or "nay" in agreement with the president's position. Party-unity scores represent the percentage of recorded votes on which a member voted "yea" or "nay" in agreement with a majority of his or her party. Party-unity roll calls are those on which a majority of voting Democrats opposed a majority of voting Republicans. (Failure to vote on presidential support or party-unity roll calls may lower a member's score.) Voting participation is the percentage of recorded floor votes on which a member voted "yea" or "nay." Participation in quorum calls is not reflected.

Members who served in 1997 and 1998 are given annual ratings for those years by four interest groups: the Americans for Democratic Action (ADA), the American Conservative Union (ACU), the AFL-CIO, and the Chamber of Commerce of the United States (CCUS). Freshmen do not have scores for CQ vote studies or interest group ratings.

The appendixes and other ancillary materials include information useful in navigating around Capitol Hill. Inside the front cover is a list of frequently called legislative phone numbers; a map of Capitol Hill is inside the back cover. The appendix contains state delegations, congressional leadership, committee and subcommittee rosters for the House and Senate, CQ key votes for 1998, Senate terms of office, guides to the televised proceedings of the Senate and House floor action, an explanation of the congressional bell system, and a glossary of legislative terms.

All of the facts and statistics found in *Who's Who in Congress 1999* are included and expanded upon in its parent publication, *Politics in America*.

U.S. SENATORS

Spencer Abraham (R–Mich.)
Of Auburn Hills • Elected 1994

Born: June 12, 1952, Lansing, Mich.
Education: Michigan State U., B.A. 1974; Harvard U., J.D. 1979.
Occupation: Lawyer; vice presidential aide.
Family: Wife, Jane; three children.
Religion: Eastern Orthodox.
Political Career: Mich. Republican Party chairman, 1983–90.

Capitol Office: 329 Dirksen Senate Office Building 20510; 224-4822; (fax) 224-8834; (e-mail) michigan@abraham.senate.gov; (web) www.senate.gov/~abraham.
Office Staff: Admin. Asst., Joseph P. McMonigle; Legis. Dir., Cesar Conda; Communications Dir., Joe McMonigle; Office Mgr., Jim Neill.
Committees: Budget; Commerce, Science & Transportation (Aviation; Communications; Consumer Affairs, Foreign Commerce & Tourism; Manufacturing & Competitiveness — chairman; Science, Technology & Space; Surface Transportation & Merchant Marine); Judiciary (Administrative Oversight & the Courts; Immigration — chairman; Criminal Justice Oversight); Small Business.

Michigan — The statewide vote for Bill Clinton was 52% in 1996.

CQ Voting Studies

	1997	1998
Presidential	60%	46%
Party	93%	91%
Participation	100%	100%

Interest Groups

	1997	1998
ADA	15%	5%
ACU	76%	76%
AFL-CIO	14%	n/a
CCUS	90%	83%

Elections

	1994
General	52%
Primary	52%

Daniel K. Akaka (D–Hawaii)
Of Honolulu • Elected 1990
Appointed to the Senate 1990

Born: Sept. 11, 1924, Honolulu, Hawaii.
Education: U. of Hawaii, B.Ed. 1952, M.Ed. 1966.
Military Career: Army Corps of Engineers, 1945–47.
Occupation: State economic grants official; elementary school teacher and principal.
Family: Wife, Mary Mildred Chong; five children.
Religion: Congregationalist.
Political Career: Sought Democratic nomination for lieutenant governor, 1974; U.S. House, 1977–90.

Capitol Office: 720 Hart Senate Office Building 20510; 224-6361; (fax) 224-2126; (e-mail) senator@akaka.senate.gov; (web) www.senate.gov/~akaka.
Office Staff: Admin. Asst., James Sakai; Legis. Dir., Patrick McGarey; Press Secy., Paul Kardus; Personal Secy./Office Mgr., Patricia Hill.
Committees: Energy & Natural Resources (Energy Research, Development, Production & Regulation; Forests & Public Land Management; National Parks, Historic Preservation & Recreation — ranking member); Governmental Affairs (International Security, Proliferation & Federal Services — ranking member; Investigations); Indian Affairs; Veterans' Affairs.

Hawaii — The statewide vote for Bill Clinton was 57% in 1996.

CQ Voting Studies

	1997	1998
Presidential	90%	81%
Party	95%	89%
Participation	98%	93%

Interest Groups

	1997	1998
ADA	95%	85%
ACU	4%	10%
AFL-CIO	71%	n/a
CCUS	60%	41%

Elections

	1990	1994
General	54%	72%
Primary	91%	u/o

SENATE • Allard / Ashcroft

Wayne Allard (R–Colo.)
Of Loveland • Elected 1996

Born: Dec. 2, 1943, Fort Collins, Colo.
Education: Colorado State U., D.V.M. 1968.
Occupation: Veterinarian.
Family: Wife, Joan; two children.
Religion: Protestant.
Political Career: Colo. Senate, 1983–91; U.S. House, 1991–97.

Capitol Office: 513 Hart Senate Office Building 20510; 224-5941; (fax) 225-8630; (e-mail) www.senate.gov/~allard/webform.html; (web) www.senate.gov/~allard.
Office Staff: Admin. Asst., Mike Bennett; Press Secy., Sean Conway; Scheduler, Wendy Evans.
Committees: Armed Services (Airland Forces; Personnel — chairman; Strategic Forces); Banking, Housing & Urban Affairs (Financial Institutions; Housing & Transportation — chairman; Securities); Select Intelligence.

Colorado — The statewide vote for Bill Clinton was 44% in 1996.

CQ Voting Studies

	1997	1998
Presidential	48%	28%
Party	98%	96%
Participation	100%	99%

Interest Groups

	1997	1998
ADA	0%	5%
ACU	100%	100%
AFL-CIO	0%	n/a
CCUS	80%	83%

Elections

	1996
General	51%
Primary	57%

John Ashcroft (R–Mo.)
Of Springfield • Elected 1994

Born: May 9, 1942, Chicago, Ill.
Education: Yale U., A.B. 1964; U. of Chicago, J.D. 1967.
Occupation: Lawyer.
Family: Wife, Janet; three children.
Religion: Assembly of God.
Political Career: Republican nominee for U.S. House, 1972; Mo. auditor, 1973–75; Mo. assistant attorney general, 1975–76; Mo. attorney general, 1976–85; Mo. governor, 1985–93.

Capitol Office: 316 Hart Senate Office Building 20510; 224-6154; (fax) 228-0998; (e-mail) john_ashcroft@ashcroft.senate.gov; (web) www.senate.gov/~ashcroft.
Office Staff: Chief of Staff, David T. Ayres; Legis. Dir., Kris Ardizzone; Communications Dir., Greg Harris; Scheduler, Andy Beach.
Committees: Commerce, Science & Transportation (Aviation; Communications; Consumer Affairs, Foreign Commerce & Tourism — chairman; Manufacturing & Competitiveness; Surface Transportation & Merchant Marine); Foreign Relations (European Affairs; Near Eastern & South Asian Affairs; Western Hemisphere); Judiciary (Constitution, Federalism & Property Rights — chairman; Youth Violence; Criminal Justice Oversight).

Missouri — The statewide vote for Bill Clinton was 48% in 1996.

CQ Voting Studies

	1997	1998
Presidential	51%	24%
Party	99%	98%
Participation	99%	99%

Interest Groups

	1997	1998
ADA	0%	5%
ACU	100%	100%
AFL-CIO	0%	n/a
CCUS	70%	78%

Elections

	1994
General	60%
Primary	83%

Max Baucus (D–Mont.)
Of Helena • Elected 1978

Born: Dec. 11, 1941, Helena, Mont.
Education: Stanford U., A.B. 1964, LL.B. 1967.
Occupation: Lawyer.
Family: Wife, Wanda Minge; one child.
Religion: United Church of Christ.
Political Career: Mont. House, 1973–75; U.S. House, 1975–78.

Capitol Office: 511 Hart Senate Office Building 20510; 224-2651; (e-mail) max@baucus.senate.gov; (web) www.senate.gov/~baucus.
Office Staff: Chief of Staff, Christine M. Niedermeier; Legis. Dir., Brian Cavey; Deputy Press Secy., Giano Cromley; Scheduler, Julie Wirkkala.
Committees: Joint Taxation; Agriculture, Nutrition & Forestry (Forestry, Conservation & Rural Revitalization; Marketing, Inspection & Product Promotion — ranking member); Environment & Public Works — ranking member (Transportation & Infrastructure — ranking member); Finance (Health Care; International Trade; Taxation & IRS Oversight — ranking member); Select Intelligence.

Montana — The statewide vote for Bill Clinton was 41% in 1996.

CQ Voting Studies

	1997	1998
Presidential	87%	71%
Party	72%	80%
Participation	99%	95%

Interest Groups

	1997	1998
ADA	65%	80%
ACU	4%	5%
AFL-CIO	29%	n/a
CCUS	70%	56%

Elections

	1990	1996
General	68%	50%
Primary	83%	u/o

Evan Bayh (D–Ind.)
Of Indianapolis • Elected 1998
Pronounced: BY

Born: Dec. 26, 1955, Shirkieville, Ind.
Education: Indiana U., B.S. 1978; U. of Virginia, J.D. 1982.
Occupation: Lawyer.
Family: Wife, Susan; two children.
Religion: Episcopalian.
Political Career: Ind. secretary of state, 1986–89; governor, 1989–97.

Capitol Office: 717 Hart Senate Office Building 20510; 224-5623; (fax) 228-1377.
Office Staff: Chief of Staff, Tom Sugar; Legis. Dir., Andrew Lowenthal; Press Secy., Mary Magher; Scheduler, Angie Koons.
Committees: Special Aging; Banking, Housing & Urban Affairs (Financial Institutions; International Trade & Finance; Securities); Energy & Natural Resources (Energy Research, Development, Production & Regulation; Forests & Public Land Management; National Parks, Historic Preservation & Recreation).

Indiana — The statewide vote for Bill Clinton was 42% in 1996.

Elections

	1998
General	64%
Primary	u/o

Robert F. Bennett (R–Utah)
Of Salt Lake City • Elected 1992

Born: Sept. 18, 1933, Salt Lake City, Utah.
Education: U. of Utah, B.S. 1957.
Occupation: Management consultant.
Family: Wife, Joyce; six children.
Religion: Mormon.
Political Career: No previous office.

Capitol Office: 431 Dirksen Senate Office Building 20510; 224-5444; (fax) 224-4908; (e–mail) senator@bennett.senate.gov; (web) www.senate.gov/~bennett.
Office Staff: Chief of Staff, James C. Barker; Legis. Dir., Chip Yost; Press Secy., Mary Jane Collipriest; Exec. Asst., Trish Kent.
Committees: Joint Economic; Appropriations (Energy & Water Development; Foreign Operations; Interior; Legislative Branch — chairman; Transportation); Banking, Housing & Urban Affairs (Financial Institutions — chairman; Economic Policy; Securities); Environment & Public Works (Clean Air, Wetlands, Private Property & Nuclear Safety; Fisheries, Wildlife & Drinking Water); Small Business; Year 2000 Technology Problem — chairman.

Utah — The statewide vote for Bill Clinton was 33% in 1996.

CQ Voting Studies

	1997	1998
Presidential	60%	47%
Party	85%	81%
Participation	97%	95%

Interest Groups

	1997	1998
ADA	10%	10%
ACU	68%	64%
AFL-CIO	0%	n/a
CCUS	100%	89%

Elections

	1992	1998
General	55%	64%
Primary	51%	u/o

Joseph R. Biden Jr. (D–Del.)
Of Wilmington • Elected 1972

Born: Nov. 20, 1942, Scranton, Pa.
Education: U. of Delaware, B.A. 1965; Syracuse U., J.D. 1968.
Occupation: Lawyer.
Family: Wife, Jill; three children.
Religion: Roman Catholic.
Political Career: New Castle County Council, 1970–72.

Capitol Office: 221 Russell Senate Office Building 20510; 224-5042; (fax) 224-0139; (e–mail) senator@biden.senate.gov; (web) www.senate.gov/~biden.
Office Staff: Admin. Asst., Alan L. Hoffman; Legis. Dir., Jane Woodfin; Communications Dir., Chris Madison; Exec. Asst., Marianne Baker.
Committees: Foreign Relations — ranking member (European Affairs — ranking member); Judiciary (Technology, Terrorism & Government Information; Youth Violence — ranking member; Criminal Justice Oversight).

Delaware — The statewide vote for Bill Clinton was 52% in 1996.

CQ Voting Studies

	1997	1998
Presidential	76%	83%
Party	81%	85%
Participation	96%	96%

Interest Groups

	1997	1998
ADA	70%	85%
ACU	16%	4%
AFL-CIO	57%	n/a
CCUS	70%	56%

Elections

	1990	1996
General	63%	60%
Primary	u/o	u/o

Jeff Bingaman (D-N.M.)
Of Santa Fe • Elected 1982

Born: Oct. 3, 1943, El Paso, Texas.
Education: Harvard U., A.B. 1965; Stanford U., J.D. 1968.
Military Career: Army Reserve, 1968–74.
Occupation: Lawyer.
Family: Wife, Anne Kovacovich; one child.
Religion: Methodist.
Political Career: N.M. attorney general, 1979–83.

Capitol Office: 703 Hart Senate Office Building 20510; 224-5521; (fax) 224-5521; (e–mail) senator_bingaman@bingaman.senate.gov; (web) www.senate.gov/~bingaman.
Office Staff: Chief of Staff, Bernard R. Toon; Legis. Dir., Trudy Vincent; Press Secy., Kristen Ludecke; Personal Asst., Virginia White.
Committees: Joint Economic — ranking member; Armed Services (Emerging Threats & Capabilities — ranking member; Readiness & Management Support; Strategic Forces); Energy & Natural Resources — ranking member; Health, Education, Labor & Pensions (Children & Families; Public Health); Year 2000 Technology Problem.

New Mexico — The statewide vote for Bill Clinton was 49% in 1996.

CQ Voting Studies

	1997	1998
Presidential	92%	81%
Party	87%	83%
Participation	96%	95%

Interest Groups

	1997	1998
ADA	90%	85%
ACU	0%	0%
AFL-CIO	57%	n/a
CCUS	60%	56%

Elections

	1988	1994
General	63%	54%
Primary	u/o	u/o

Christopher S. Bond (R–Mo.)
Of Mexico • Elected 1986

Born: Mar. 6, 1939, St. Louis, Mo.
Education: Princeton U., A.B. 1960; U. of Virginia, LL.B. 1963.
Occupation: Lawyer.
Family: Divorced; one child.
Religion: Presbyterian.
Political Career: Republican nominee for U.S. House, 1968; Mo. assistant attorney general, 1969–70; Mo. auditor, 1971–73; governor, 1973–77; Republican nominee for governor, 1976; governor, 1981–85.

Capitol Office: 274 Russell Senate Office Building 20510; 224-5721; (fax) 224-8149; (e–mail) kit_bond@bond.senate.gov; (web) www.senate.gov/~bond.
Office Staff: Chief of Staff/Legis. Dir., Julie Dammann; Communications Dir., Dan Hubbard; Scheduler, Samantha Hamilton.
Committees: Appropriations (Agriculture, Rural Development & Related Agencies; Defense; Foreign Operations; Transportation; VA, HUD & Independent Agencies — chairman); Budget; Environment & Public Works (Fisheries, Wildlife & Drinking Water; Transportation & Infrastructure); Small Business — chairman.

Missouri — The statewide vote for Bill Clinton was 48% in 1996.

CQ Voting Studies

	1997	1998
Presidential	60%	38%
Party	87%	86%
Participation	99%	98%

Interest Groups

	1997	1998
ADA	15%	15%
ACU	76%	72%
AFL-CIO	0%	n/a
CCUS	100%	89%

Elections

	1992	1998
General	52%	53%
Primary	83%	87%

SENATE

Barbara Boxer (D–Calif.)
Of Greenbrae • Elected 1992

Born: Nov. 11, 1940, Brooklyn, N.Y.
Education: Brooklyn College, B.A. 1962.
Occupation: Congressional aide; journalist; stockbroker.
Family: Husband, Stewart; two children.
Religion: Jewish.
Political Career: Candidate for Marin County Board of Supervisors, 1972; Marin County Board of Supervisors, 1977–83; U.S. House, 1983–93.

Capitol Office: 112 Hart Senate Office Building 20510; 224-3553; (e–mail) senator@boxer.senate.gov; (web) www.senate.gov/~boxer.
Office Staff: Admin. Asst., Karen Olick; Legis. Dir., Liz Tankersley; Communications Dir., David Sandretti; Exec. Asst., Jay Rosenthal.
Committees: Budget; Environment & Public Works (Clean Air, Wetlands, Private Property & Nuclear Safety; Fisheries, Wildlife & Drinking Water; Superfund, Waste Control & Risk Assessment); Foreign Relations (International Economic Policy, Export & Trade Promotion; International Operations — ranking member; Western Hemisphere).

California — The statewide vote for Bill Clinton was 51% in 1996.

CQ Voting Studies

	1997	1998
Presidential	89%	85%
Party	95%	88%
Participation	99%	97%

Interest Groups

	1997	1998
ADA	100%	95%
ACU	0%	4%
AFL-CIO	86%	n/a
CCUS	50%	59%

Elections

	1992	1998
General	48%	53%
Primary	44%	*44%

*Open primary

John B. Breaux (D–La.)
Of Crowley • Elected 1986
Pronounced: BRO

Born: Mar. 1, 1944, Crowley, La.
Education: U. of Southwestern Louisiana, B.A. 1964; Louisiana State U., J.D. 1967.
Occupation: Lawyer; congressional aide.
Family: Wife, Lois; four children.
Religion: Roman Catholic.
Political Career: U.S. House, 1972–87.

Capitol Office: 516 Hart Senate Office Building 20510; 224-4623; (fax) 228-2577; (e–mail) senator@breaux.senate.gov; (web) www.senate.gov/~breaux.
Office Staff: Chief of Staff, Fred Hatfield; Legis. Dir., Darla Romfo; Communications Dir., Bette Phelan; Exec. Asst./Scheduler, Susie Owens.
Committees: Special Aging — ranking member; Commerce, Science & Transportation (Aviation; Communications; Consumer Affairs, Foreign Commerce & Tourism; Oceans & Fisheries; Science, Technology & Space — ranking member; Surface Transportation & Merchant Marine); Finance (Health Care; International Trade; Social Security & Family Policy — ranking member).

Louisiana — The statewide vote for Bill Clinton was 52% in 1996.

CQ Voting Studies

	1997	1998
Presidential	81%	78%
Party	65%	73%
Participation	99%	99%

Interest Groups

	1997	1998
ADA	55%	75%
ACU	20%	20%
AFL-CIO	14%	n/a
CCUS	70%	59%

Elections

	1992	1998
General	u/o	64%
Primary	73%	

Sam Brownback (R–Kan.)
Of Topeka • Elected 1996

Born: Sept. 12, 1956, Garnett, Kan.
Education: Kansas State U., B.S. 1979; U. of Kansas, J.D. 1982.
Occupation: Teacher; lawyer; White House fellow; broadcaster.
Family: Wife, Mary; three children.
Religion: Methodist.
Political Career: Kan. secretary of Agriculture, 1986–93; U.S. House, 1995–96.

Capitol Office: 303 Hart Senate Office Building 20510; 224-6521; (fax) 228-1265; (e-mail) sam_brownback@brownback.senate.gov; (web) www.senate.gov/~brownback.
Office Staff: Chief of Staff, Heather Wyngate; Legis. Dir., Karen Knutson; Press Secy., Erik Hotmire; Scheduler, Emily Wellman.
Committees: Joint Economic; Commerce, Science & Transportation (Aviation; Communications; Consumer Affairs, Foreign Commerce & Tourism; Manufacturing & Competitiveness; Surface Transportation & Merchant Marine); Foreign Relations (African Affairs; International Operations; Near Eastern & South Asian Affairs — chairman); Health, Education, Labor & Pensions (Children & Families; Public Health).

Kansas — The statewide vote for Bill Clinton was 36% in 1996.

CQ Voting Studies

	1997	1998
Presidential	56%	36%
Party	96%	96%
Participation	100%	99%

Interest Groups

	1997	1998
ADA	0%	0%
ACU	100%	92%
AFL-CIO	0%	n/a
CCUS	100%	94%

Elections

	1996	1998
General	*54%	65%
Primary	*55%	u/o

*Special election

Richard H. Bryan (D–Nev.)
Of Las Vegas • Elected 1988

Born: July 16, 1937, Washington, D.C.
Education: U. of Nevada, B.A. 1959; U. of California, Hastings College of the Law, LL.B. 1963.
Military Career: Army, 1959–60.
Occupation: Lawyer.
Family: Wife, Bonnie; three children.
Religion: Episcopalian.
Political Career: Nev. Assembly, 1968–72; Nev. Senate, 1972–78; Democratic nominee for Nev. attorney general, 1974; Nev. attorney general, 1978–82; governor, 1982–88.

Capitol Office: 269 Russell Senate Office Building 20510; 224-6244; (fax) 224-1867; (e-mail) senator@bryan.senate.gov; (web) www.senate.gov/~bryan.
Office Staff: Admin. Asst., Jean Marie Neal; Legis. Dir., Andy Vermilye; Communications Dir., Dave Lemmon; Scheduler, Kari Beckett.
Committees: Special Aging; Banking, Housing & Urban Affairs (Financial Institutions — ranking member; Housing & Transportation; Securities); Commerce, Science & Transportation (Aviation; Consumer Affairs, Foreign Commerce & Tourism — ranking member; Manufacturing & Competitiveness; Surface Transportation & Merchant Marine); Finance (Health Care; Long-Term Growth & Debt Reduction; Taxation & IRS Oversight); Select Intelligence.

Nevada — The statewide vote for Bill Clinton was 44% in 1996.

CQ Voting Studies

	1997	1998
Presidential	89%	88%
Party	71%	90%
Participation	99%	99%

Interest Groups

	1997	1998
ADA	70%	95%
ACU	4%	8%
AFL-CIO	29%	n/a
CCUS	70%	50%

Elections

	1988	1994
General	50%	51%
Primary	79%	u/o

Jim Bunning (R–Ky.)
Of Southgate • Elected 1998

Born: Oct. 23, 1931, Campbell County, Ky.
Education: Xavier U., B.S. 1953.
Occupation: Investment broker; sports agent; professional baseball player.
Family: Wife, Mary; nine children.
Religion: Roman Catholic.
Political Career: Fort Thomas City Council, 1977–79; Ky. Senate, 1979–83; Republican nominee for governor, 1983; U.S. House, 1987–99.

Capitol Office: 502 Hart Senate Office Building 20510; 224-4343; (fax) 228-1373; (e-mail) jim_bunning@bunning.senate.gov.
Office Staff: Chief of Staff/Press Secy., David A. York; Legis. Dir., Jon Deuser; Office Mgr./Exec. Secy., Joan L. Manning.
Committees: Special Aging; Banking, Housing & Urban Affairs (Financial Institutions; Economic Policy; Securities); Energy & Natural Resources (Energy Research, Development, Production & Regulation; National Parks, Historic Preservation & Recreation; Water & Power).

Elections

	1998
General	50%
Primary	74%

Kentucky — The statewide vote for Bill Clinton was 46% in 1996.

Conrad Burns (R–Mont.)
Of Billings • Elected 1988

Born: Jan. 25, 1935, Gallatin, Mo.
Education: U. of Missouri, attended 1952–54.
Military Career: Marine Corps, 1955–57.
Occupation: Radio and television broadcaster.
Family: Wife, Phyllis; two children.
Religion: Lutheran.
Political Career: Yellowstone County Commission, 1987–89.

Capitol Office: 187 Dirksen Senate Office Building 20510; 224-2644; (fax) 224-8594; (e-mail) conrad_burns@burns.senate.gov; (web) www.senate.gov/~burns.
Office Staff: Chief of Staff, Leo Giacometto; Legis. Dir., Ric Molen; Press Secy., Matt Raymond; Scheduler, Jennifer Parson.
Committees: Special Aging; Appropriations (Agriculture, Rural Development & Related Agencies; Energy & Water Development; Interior; Military Construction — chairman; VA, HUD & Independent Agencies); Commerce, Science & Transportation (Aviation; Communications — chairman; Consumer Affairs, Foreign Commerce & Tourism; Science, Technology & Space; Surface Transportation & Merchant Marine); Energy & Natural Resources (Forests & Public Land Management; National Parks, Historic Preservation & Recreation); Small Business.

CQ Voting Studies

	1997	1998
Presidential	54%	38%
Party	92%	94%
Participation	96%	99%

Interest Groups

	1997	1998
ADA	15%	0%
ACU	88%	84%
AFL-CIO	14%	n/a
CCUS	78%	100%

Elections

	1988	1994
General	52%	62%
Primary	85%	u/o

Montana — The statewide vote for Bill Clinton was 41% in 1996.

Robert C. Byrd (D–W.Va.)
Of Sophia • Elected 1958

Born: Nov. 20, 1917, North Wilkesboro, N.C.
Education: American U., J.D. 1963; Marshall U., B.A. 1994.
Occupation: Lawyer.
Family: Wife, Erma Ora Byrd; two children.
Religion: Baptist.
Political Career: W.Va. House, 1947–51; W.Va. Senate, 1951–53; U.S. House, 1953–59.

Capitol Office: 311 Hart Senate Office Building 20510; 224-3954; (fax) 228-0002; (e–mail) senator_byrd@byrd.senate.gov; (web) www.senate.gov/~byrd.
Office Staff: Admin. Asst., Lisa Tuite; Legis. Dir., Peter Kiefhaber; Press Secy., Ann Adler; Appts. Secy., Martha Anne McIntosh.
Committees: Appropriations — ranking member (Defense; Energy & Water Development; Interior — ranking member; Transportation; VA, HUD & Independent Agencies); Armed Services (Emerging Threats & Capabilities; Readiness & Management Support; Strategic Forces); Rules & Administration.

West Virginia — The statewide vote for Bill Clinton was 51% in 1996.

CQ Voting Studies

	1997	1998
Presidential	81%	74%
Party	81%	72%
Participation	99%	100%

Interest Groups

	1997	1998
ADA	70%	80%
ACU	16%	16%
AFL-CIO	100%	n/a
CCUS	40%	44%

Elections

	1988	1994
General	65%	69%
Primary	81%	85%

Ben Nighthorse Campbell
(R–Colo.)
Of Ignacio • Elected 1992

Born: Apr. 13, 1933, Auburn, Calif.
Education: San Jose State U., B.A. 1957; Meiji U. (Tokyo, Japan), attended 1960–64.
Military Career: Air Force, 1951–53.
Occupation: Jewelry designer; rancher; horse trainer; teacher.
Family: Wife, Linda; two children.
Religion: Unspecified.
Political Career: Colo. House, 1983–87, served as a Democrat; U.S. House, 1987–93, served as a Democrat.

Capitol Office: 380 Russell Senate Office Building 20510; 224-5852; (fax) 224-1933; (web) www.senate.gov/~campbell.
Office Staff: Chief of Staff, Ginnie Kontnik; Deputy Chief of Staff, Mike Russell; Press Secy., Audrey Hudson; Scheduler, Michelle Hoeft.
Committees: Appropriations (Commerce, Justice, State & Judiciary; Foreign Operations; Interior; Transportation; Treasury & General Government — chairman); Energy & Natural Resources (Forests & Public Land Management; National Parks, Historic Preservation & Recreation; Water & Power); Indian Affairs — chairman; Veterans' Affairs.

Colorado — The statewide vote for Bill Clinton was 44% in 1996.

CQ Voting Studies

	1997	1998
Presidential	65%	47%
Party	83%	82%
Participation	99%	99%

Interest Groups

	1997	1998
ADA	25%	25%
ACU	72%	76%
AFL-CIO	29%	n/a
CCUS	60%	83%

Elections

	1992	1998
General	52%	62%
Primary	u/o	71%

John H. Chafee (R–R.I.)
Of Warwick • Elected 1976

Born: Oct. 22, 1922, Providence, R.I.
Education: Yale U., B.A. 1947; Harvard U., LL.B. 1950.
Military Career: Marine Corps, 1942–45, 1951–52.
Occupation: Lawyer.
Family: Wife, Virginia; five children.
Religion: Episcopalian.
Political Career: R.I. House, 1957–63, minority leader, 1959–63; governor, 1963–69; defeated for re-election as governor, 1968; secretary of the Navy, 1969–72; Republican nominee for U.S. Senate, 1972.

Capitol Office: 505 Dirksen Senate Office Building 20510; 224-2921; (e mail) senator_chafee@chafee.senate.gov; (web) www.senate.gov/~chafee.
Office Staff: Chief of Staff, David A. Griswold; Legis. Dir., David Sloane; Press Secy., Nicholas J. Graham; Scheduler, Kathy Wilmoth.
Committees: Joint Taxation; Environment & Public Works — chairman; Finance (Health Care — chairman; International Trade; Long-Term Growth & Debt Reduction; Social Security & Family Policy); Select Intelligence.

Rhode Island — The statewide vote for Bill Clinton was 60% in 1996.

CQ Voting Studies

	1997	1998
Presidential	73%	76%
Party	60%	57%
Participation	98%	99%

Interest Groups

	1997	1998
ADA	55%	45%
ACU	24%	32%
AFL-CIO	14%	n/a
CCUS	100%	89%

Elections

	1988	1994
General	55%	65%
Primary	u/o	69%

Max Cleland (D–Ga.)
Of Lithonia • Elected 1996
Pronounced: CLEE-lend

Born: Aug. 24, 1942, Atlanta, Ga.
Education: Stetson U., B.A. 1964; Emory U., M.A. 1968.
Military Career: Army, 1965–68.
Occupation: Veterans administration official; congressional aide.
Family: Single.
Religion: Methodist.
Political Career: Ga. Senate, 1971–75; sought Democratic nomination for lieutenant governor, 1974; U.S. administrator of Veterans Affairs, 1977–81; Ga. secretary of state, 1983–96.

Capitol Office: 461 Dirksen Senate Office Building 20510; 224-3521; (fax) 224-0072; (e-mail) senator_max_cleland@cleland.senate.gov; (web) www.senate.gov/~cleland.
Office Staff: Admin. Asst., Wayne Howell; Legis. Dir., Bill Johnstone; Press Secy., Jennifer Wardrep; Scheduler, Farrar Johnston.
Committees: Armed Services (Airland Forces; Personnel — ranking member; Readiness & Management Support); Commerce, Science & Transportation (Aviation; Communications; Surface Transportation & Merchant Marine); Governmental Affairs (International Security, Proliferation & Federal Services; Investigations); Small Business.

Georgia — The statewide vote for Bill Clinton was 46% in 1996.

CQ Voting Studies

	1997	1998
Presidential	87%	86%
Party	84%	87%
Participation	100%	99%

Interest Groups

	1997	1998
ADA	75%	85%
ACU	8%	0%
AFL-CIO	57%	n/a
CCUS	80%	56%

Elections

	1996
General	49%
Primary	u/o

Thad Cochran (R–Miss.)
Of Jackson • Elected 1978

Born: Dec. 7, 1937, Pontotoc, Miss.
Education: U. of Mississippi, B.A. 1959; Trinity College (U. of Dublin, Ireland), attended 1963–64; U. of Mississippi, J.D. 1965.
Military Career: Navy, 1959–61.
Occupation: Lawyer.
Family: Wife, Rose; two children.
Religion: Baptist.
Political Career: U.S. House, 1973–78.

Capitol Office: 326 Russell Senate Office Building 20510; 224-5054; (e–mail) senator@cochran.senate.gov; (web) www.senate.gov/~cochran.
Office Staff: Chief of Staff, Mark Keenum; Legis. Dir., James Lofton; Press Secy., Beth Day; Exec. Asst., Doris Wagley.
Committees: Joint Library; Joint Printing; Agriculture, Nutrition & Forestry (Marketing, Inspection & Product Promotion; Production & Price Competitiveness); Appropriations (Agriculture, Rural Development & Related Agencies — chairman; Defense; Energy & Water Development; Interior; Labor, Health & Human Services & Education); Governmental Affairs (International Security, Proliferation & Federal Services — chairman; Investigations); Rules & Administration.

Mississippi — The statewide vote for Bill Clinton was 44% in 1996.

CQ Voting Studies

	1997	1998
Presidential	67%	53%
Party	81%	86%
Participation	99%	100%

Interest Groups

	1997	1998
ADA	15%	0%
ACU	56%	76%
AFL-CIO	0%	n/a
CCUS	90%	100%

Elections

	1990	1996
General	u/o	71%
Primary	u/o	95%

Susan Collins (R–Maine)
Of Bangor • Elected 1996

Born: Dec. 7, 1952, Caribou, Maine.
Education: St. Lawrence U., B.A. 1975.
Occupation: Business center director; congressional aide.
Family: Single.
Religion: Roman Catholic.
Political Career: Maine commissioner of financial regulation, 1987–91; Small Business Administration official, 1992–93; Maine deputy treasurer, 1993; Republican nominee for governor, 1994.

Capitol Office: 172 Russell Senate Office Building 20510; 224-2523; (fax) 224-2693; (e–mail) senator@collins.senate.gov; (web) www.senate.gov/~collins.
Office Staff: Chief of Staff, Steve Abbott; Legis. Dir., Don Green; Communications Dir., Felicia Knight; D.C. Scheduler, Cynthia Bailey.
Committees: Special Aging; Governmental Affairs (International Security, Proliferation & Federal Services; Investigations — chairman); Health, Education, Labor & Pensions (Children & Families; Public Health); Year 2000 Technology Problem.

Maine — The statewide vote for Bill Clinton was 52% in 1996.

CQ Voting Studies

	1997	1998
Presidential	76%	63%
Party	61%	67%
Participation	100%	100%

Interest Groups

	1997	1998
ADA	50%	35%
ACU	48%	36%
AFL-CIO	14%	n/a
CCUS	80%	78%

Elections

	1996
General	49%
Primary	55%

Kent Conrad (D-N.D.)
Of Bismarck • Elected 1986

Born: Mar. 12, 1948, Bismarck, N.D.
Education: U. of Missouri, attended 1967; Stanford U., A.B. 1971; George Washington U., M.B.A. 1975.
Occupation: Management and personnel director.
Family: Wife, Lucy Calautti; one child.
Religion: Unitarian.
Political Career: Candidate for N.D. auditor, 1976; N.D. tax commissioner, 1981–87.
Capitol Office: 530 Hart Senate Office Building 20510; 224-2043; (fax) 224-7776; (e-mail) senator@conrad.senate.gov; (web) www.senate.gov/~conrad.
Office Staff: Acting Chief of Staff, Bob Van Heuvelen; Legis. Dir., Bob Foust; Press Secy., Aileen Pincus; Exec. Asst./Scheduling Dir., Joyce Power.
Committees: Agriculture, Nutrition & Forestry (Forestry, Conservation & Rural Revitalization — ranking member; Marketing, Inspection & Product Promotion); Budget; Select Ethics; Finance (Health Care; International Trade; Taxation & IRS Oversight); Indian Affairs.

North Dakota — The statewide vote for Bill Clinton was 40% in 1996.

CQ Voting Studies

	1997	1998
Presidential	81%	75%
Party	79%	87%
Participation	99%	99%

Interest Groups

	1997	1998
ADA	65%	90%
ACU	16%	16%
AFL-CIO	57%	n/a
CCUS	50%	61%

Elections

	1992	1994
General	*63%	58%
Primary		u/o

*Special election

Paul Coverdell (R-Ga.)
Of Atlanta • Elected 1992

Born: Jan. 20, 1939, Des Moines, Iowa.
Education: U. of Missouri, B.A. 1961.
Military Career: Army, 1962–64.
Occupation: Financial executive; Peace Corps director.
Family: Wife, Nancy.
Religion: Methodist.
Political Career: Ga. Senate, 1971–89, minority leader, 1975–89; candidate for U.S. House (special election), 1977; Ga. Republican Party chairman, 1985–87.

Capitol Office: 200 Russell Senate Office Building 20510; 224-3643; (fax) 228-3783; (e-mail) senator_coverdell@coverdell.senate.gov; (web) www.senate.gov/~coverdell.
Office Staff: Admin. Asst., Molly Dye; Legis. Dir., Alex Albert; Communications Dir., Laura L. Cox; Scheduler, Tucker Shumack.
Committees: Agriculture, Nutrition & Forestry (Forestry, Conservation & Rural Revitalization; Marketing, Inspection & Product Promotion — chairman); Foreign Relations (East Asian & Pacific Affairs; European Affairs; Western Hemisphere — chairman); Small Business.

Georgia — The statewide vote for Bill Clinton was 46% in 1996.

CQ Voting Studies

	1997	1998
Presidential	56%	39%
Party	93%	90%
Participation	100%	97%

Interest Groups

	1997	1998
ADA	10%	0%
ACU	92%	92%
AFL-CIO	29%	n/a
CCUS	90%	89%

Elections

	1992	1998
General	*51%	52%
Primary	*50%	u/o

*Runoff election

Larry E. Craig (R–Idaho)
Of Payette • Elected 1990

Born: July 20, 1945, Council, Idaho.
Education: U. of Idaho, B.A. 1969; George Washington U., attended 1969–70.
Military Career: Idaho National Guard, 1970–71.
Occupation: Farmer; rancher.
Family: Wife, Suzanne; three children.
Religion: Methodist.
Political Career: Idaho Senate, 1975–81; U.S. House, 1981–91.

Capitol Office: 313 Hart Senate Office Building 20510; 224-2752; (fax) 228-1067; (e-mail) larry_craig@craig.senate.gov; (web) www.senate.gov/~craig.
Office Staff: Chief of Staff, Michael O. Ware; Legis. Counsel, Brooke Roberts; Communications Dir., Will Hart; Exec. Asst., Bess Conway.
Committees: Special Aging; Agriculture, Nutrition & Forestry (Forestry, Conservation & Rural Revitalization — chairman; Production & Price Competitiveness); Appropriations (Energy & Water Development; Labor, Health & Human Services & Education; Legislative Branch; Military Construction; VA, HUD & Independent Agencies); Energy & Natural Resources (Energy Research, Development, Production & Regulation; Forests & Public Land Management — chairman; Water & Power); Veterans' Affairs.

CQ Voting Studies

	1997	1998
Presidential	54%	29%
Party	97%	99%
Participation	100%	100%

Interest Groups

	1997	1998
ADA	5%	5%
ACU	84%	84%
AFL-CIO	0%	n/a
CCUS	100%	100%

Elections

	1990	1996
General	61%	57%
Primary	59%	u/o

Idaho — The statewide vote for Bill Clinton was 34% in 1996.

Michael D. Crapo (R–Idaho)
Of Idaho Falls • Elected 1998
Pronounced: CRAY-poe

Born: May 20, 1951, Idaho Falls, Idaho.
Education: Brigham Young U., B.A. 1973; Harvard U., J.D. 1977.
Occupation: Lawyer.
Family: Wife, Susan; five children.
Religion: Mormon.
Political Career: Idaho Senate, 1985–93, president pro tempore, 1989–93; U.S. House, 1993–99.

Capitol Office: 111 Russell Senate Office Building 20510; 224-6142.
Office Staff: Chief of Staff, John Hoehne; Admin. Asst./Communications Dir., Susan Wheeler; Legis. Dir., Ken Flanz; Office Mgr./Exec. Asst., Dorothy Boger.
Committees: Banking, Housing & Urban Affairs (Financial Institutions; International Trade & Finance; Securities); Environment & Public Works (Fisheries, Wildlife & Drinking Water — chairman; Superfund, Waste Control & Risk Assessment); Small Business.

Elections

	1998
General	70%
Primary	87%

Idaho — The statewide vote for Bill Clinton was 34% in 1996.

Tom Daschle (D–S.D.)
Of Aberdeen • Elected 1986
Pronounced: DASH-el

Born: Dec. 9, 1947, Aberdeen, S.D.
Education: South Dakota State U., B.A. 1969.
Military Career: Air Force, 1969–72.
Occupation: Congressional aide.
Family: Wife, Linda Hall; three children.
Religion: Roman Catholic.
Political Career: U.S. House, 1979–87.

Capitol Office: 509 Hart Senate Office Building 20510; 224-2321; (fax) 224-2047; (e-mail) tom_daschle@daschle.senate.gov; (web) www.senate.gov/~daschle.

Office Staff: Chief of Staff, Peter Rouse; Admin. Asst., Jeff Lane; National Press Secy., Ranit Schmeltzer; Scheduler, Stephanie Peterson.

Committees: Agriculture, Nutrition & Forestry (Forestry, Conservation & Rural Revitalization; Production & Price Competitiveness).

South Dakota — The statewide vote for Bill Clinton was 43% in 1996.

CQ Voting Studies

	1997	1998
Presidential	90%	90%
Party	91%	90%
Participation	97%	100%

Interest Groups

	1997	1998
ADA	80%	90%
ACU	4%	4%
AFL-CIO	71%	n/a
CCUS	60%	61%

Elections

	1992	1998
General	65%	62%
Primary	u/o	u/o

Mike DeWine (R–Ohio)
Of Cedarville • Elected 1994

Born: Jan. 5, 1947, Springfield, Ohio.
Education: Miami U. (Ohio), B.S. 1969; Ohio Northern U., J.D. 1972.
Occupation: Lawyer.
Family: Wife, Frances Struewing; eight children.
Religion: Roman Catholic.
Political Career: Greene County prosecuting attorney, 1977–81; Ohio Senate, 1981–83; U.S. House, 1983–91; lieutenant governor, 1991–95; Republican nominee for U.S. Senate, 1992.

Capitol Office: 140 Russell Senate Office Building 20510; 224-2315; (fax) 224-6519; (e-mail) senator_dewine@dewine.senate.gov; (web) www.senate.gov/~dewine.

Office Staff: Chief of Staff, Laurel Pressler; Legis. Dir., Robert Hoffman; Press Secy., Charlie Boesel; Scheduler, Amy Mitchell.

Committees: Select Intelligence; Judiciary (Antitrust, Business Rights & Competition — chairman; Technology, Terrorism & Government Information; Criminal Justice Oversight); Health, Education, Labor & Pensions (Aging — chairman; Children & Families).

Ohio — The statewide vote for Bill Clinton was 47% in 1996.

CQ Voting Studies

	1997	1998
Presidential	62%	51%
Party	81%	82%
Participation	100%	100%

Interest Groups

	1997	1998
ADA	15%	10%
ACU	68%	64%
AFL-CIO	0%	n/a
CCUS	80%	89%

Elections

	1994
General	53%
Primary	52%

Christopher J. Dodd (D–Conn.)
Of East Haddam • Elected 1980

Born: May 27, 1944, Willimantic, Conn.
Education: Providence College, B.A. 1966; U. of Louisville, J.D. 1972.
Military Career: Army Reserve, 1969–75.
Occupation: Lawyer.
Family: Divorced.
Religion: Roman Catholic.
Political Career: U.S. House, 1975–81.

Capitol Office: 444 Russell Senate Office Building 20510; 224-2823; (e–mail) sen_dodd@dodd.senate.gov; (web) www.senate.gov/~dodd.
Office Staff: Chief of Staff, Stephenie Foster; Legis. Dir., Shawn Maher; Press Secy., Marvin Fast; Scheduler, Adria Deasy.
Committees: Joint Library; Joint Printing — ranking member; Banking, Housing & Urban Affairs (Economic Policy; Housing & Transportation; Securities — ranking member); Foreign Relations (European Affairs; Near Eastern & South Asian Affairs; Western Hemisphere — ranking member); Health, Education, Labor & Pensions (Aging; Children & Families — ranking member; Employment, Safety & Training); Rules & Administration — ranking member; Year 2000 Technology Problem — ranking member.

Connecticut — The statewide vote for Bill Clinton was 52% in 1996.

CQ Voting Studies

	1997	1998
Presidential	92%	93%
Party	87%	90%
Participation	98%	99%

Interest Groups

	1997	1998
ADA	90%	95%
ACU	4%	4%
AFL-CIO	57%	n/a
CCUS	50%	61%

Elections

	1992	1998
General	59%	65%
Primary	u/o	u/o

Pete V. Domenici (R–N.M.)
Of Albuquerque • Elected 1972
Pronounced: da-MEN-ih-chee

Born: May 7, 1932, Albuquerque, N.M.
Education: U. of Albuquerque, attended 1950–52; U. of New Mexico, B.S. 1954; U. of Denver, LL.B. 1958.
Occupation: Lawyer.
Family: Wife, Nancy; eight children.
Religion: Roman Catholic.
Political Career: Albuquerque City Commission, 1966–70, chairman and ex–officio mayor, 1967–70; Republican nominee for governor, 1970.

Capitol Office: 328 Hart Senate Office Building 20510; 224-6621; (fax) 224-7371; (e–mail) senator_domenici@domenici.senate.gov; (web) www.senate.gov/~domenici.
Office Staff: Admin. Asst., Steve Bell; Legis. Dir., Denise Ramonas; Press Secy., Chris Gallegos; Personal Secy., Audrey Clifford.
Committees: Appropriations (Commerce, Justice, State & Judiciary; Defense; Energy & Water Development — chairman; Interior; Transportation); Budget — chairman; Energy & Natural Resources (Energy Research, Development, Production & Regulation; Forests & Public Land Management); Governmental Affairs (International Security, Proliferation & Federal Services; Investigations); Indian Affairs.

New Mexico — The statewide vote for Bill Clinton was 49% in 1996.

CQ Voting Studies

	1997	1998
Presidential	67%	53%
Party	84%	81%
Participation	99%	95%

Interest Groups

	1997	1998
ADA	25%	5%
ACU	60%	70%
AFL-CIO	0%	n/a
CCUS	100%	100%

Elections

	1990	1996
General	73%	65%
Primary	u/o	u/o

Byron L. Dorgan (D–N.D.)
Of Bismarck • Elected 1992

Born: May 14, 1942, Regent, N.D.
Education: U. of North Dakota, B.S. 1965; U. of Denver, M.B.A. 1966.
Occupation: Public official.
Family: Wife, Kimberly Olson; three children.
Religion: Lutheran.
Political Career: N.D. tax commissioner, 1969–80; Democratic nominee for U.S. House, 1974; U.S. House, 1981–93.

Capitol Office: 713 Hart Senate Office Building 20510; 224-2551; (fax) 224-1193; (e-mail) senator@dorgan.senate.gov; (web) www.senate.gov/~dorgan.
Office Staff: Chief of Staff, Lucy Calautti; Legis. Dir., Doug Norell; Communications Dir., Barry Piatt; Exec. Asst., Sylvia Oliver.
Committees: Appropriations (Agriculture, Rural Development & Related Agencies; Defense; Energy & Water Development; Interior; Treasury & General Government — ranking member); Commerce, Science & Transportation (Aviation; Communications; Manufacturing & Competitiveness — ranking member; Science, Technology & Space; Surface Transportation & Merchant Marine); Energy & Natural Resources (Energy Research, Development, Production & Regulation; Water & Power — ranking member); Indian Affairs.

CQ Voting Studies

	1997	1998
Presidential	81%	75%
Party	84%	87%
Participation	98%	99%

Interest Groups

	1997	1998
ADA	80%	90%
ACU	16%	12%
AFL-CIO	86%	n/a
CCUS	50%	61%

Elections

	1992	1998
General	59%	63%
Primary	u/o	u/o

North Dakota — The statewide vote for Bill Clinton was 40% in 1996.

Richard J. Durbin (D–Ill.)
Of Springfield • Elected 1996

Born: Nov. 21, 1944, East St. Louis, Ill.
Education: Georgetown U., B.S.F.S. 1966, J.D. 1969.
Occupation: Lawyer; congressional and legislative aide.
Family: Wife, Loretta Schaefer Durbin; three children.
Religion: Roman Catholic.
Political Career: Democratic nominee for Ill. Senate, 1976; Democratic nominee for lieutenant governor, 1978; U.S. House, 1983–97.

Capitol Office: 364 Russell Senate Office Building 20510; 224-2152; (fax) 228-0400; (e-mail) dick@durbin.senate.gov; (web) www.senate.gov/~durbin.
Office Staff: Admin. Asst., Ed Greelegs; Legis. Dir., Tom Faletti; Press Secy., Melissa Merz; Scheduler, Cynthia Bowie.
Committees: Appropriations (Agriculture, Rural Development & Related Agencies; Defense; District of Columbia — ranking member; Legislative Branch); Budget; Select Ethics; Governmental Affairs (Oversight of Government Management — ranking member; Investigations).

CQ Voting Studies

	1997	1998
Presidential	92%	86%
Party	96%	94%
Participation	99%	98%

Interest Groups

	1997	1998
ADA	100%	95%
ACU	4%	8%
AFL-CIO	100%	n/a
CCUS	40%	50%

Elections

	1996
General	56%
Primary	65%

Illinois — The statewide vote for Bill Clinton was 54% in 1996.

John Edwards (D-N.C.)
Of Raleigh • Elected 1998

Born: June 10, 1953, Seneca, S.C.
Education: North Carolina State U., B.S. 1974; U. of North Carolina, J.D. 1977.
Occupation: Lawyer.
Family: Wife, Elizabeth; two children.
Religion: Methodist.
Political Career: No previous office.

Capitol Office: 825 Hart Senate Office Building 20510; 224-3154; (fax) 228-1374; (e-mail) senator@edwards.senate.gov.
Office Staff: Chief of Staff, Vacant; Legis. Dir., Victoria Bassetti; Scheduler, Julianna Smoot.
Committees: Banking, Housing & Urban Affairs (Financial Institutions; Housing & Transportation; Securities); Governmental Affairs (International Security, Proliferation & Federal Services; Investigations); Small Business.

Elections

	1998
General	51%
Primary	51%

North Carolina — The statewide vote for Bill Clinton was 44% in 1996.

Michael B. Enzi (R-Wyo.)
Of Gillette • Elected 1996
Pronounced: EN-zee

Born: Feb. 1, 1944, Bremerton, Wash.
Education: George Washington U., B.S. 1966; U. of Denver, M.A. 1968.
Military Career: Wyo. Air National Guard, 1968–73.
Occupation: Accountant; shoe store owner.
Family: Wife, Diana; three children.
Religion: Presbyterian.
Political Career: Mayor of Gillette, 1975–83; Wyo. House, 1987–91; Wyo. Senate, 1991–96.

Capitol Office: 290 Russell Senate Office Building 20510; 224-3424; (fax) 228-0359; (e-mail) senator@enzi.senate.gov; (web) www.senate.gov/~enzi.
Office Staff: Chief of Staff, Flip McConnaughey; Legis. Dir., Kathryn Brunett McGuire; Press Secy., Coy Knobel; Scheduler, Evora Williams.
Committees: Special Aging; Banking, Housing & Urban Affairs (Financial Institutions; Economic Policy; International Trade & Finance — chairman); Health, Education, Labor & Pensions (Employment, Safety & Training — chairman; Public Health); Small Business.

CQ Voting Studies

	1997	1998
Presidential	51%	31%
Party	97%	96%
Participation	99%	99%

Interest Groups

	1997	1998
ADA	10%	0%
ACU	88%	92%
AFL-CIO	14%	n/a
CCUS	70%	94%

Wyoming — The statewide vote for Bill Clinton was 37% in 1996.

Elections

	1996
General	54%
Primary	32%

Russell D. Feingold (D–Wis.)
Of Middleton • Elected 1992
Pronounced: FINE-gold

Born: Mar. 2, 1953, Janesville, Wis.
Education: U. of Wisconsin, B.A. 1975; Oxford U., B.A. 1977; Harvard U., J.D. 1979.
Occupation: Lawyer.
Family: Wife, Mary; two children, two stepchildren.
Religion: Jewish.
Political Career: Wis. Senate, 1983–93.

Capitol Office: 716 Hart Senate Office Building 20510; 224-5323; (fax) 224-2725; (e-mail) senator@feingold.senate.gov; (web) www.senate.gov/~feingold.
Office Staff: Admin. Asst., Mary Murphy; Legis. Dir., Tom Walls; Press Secy., Mary Bottari; Scheduler, Tom McCormick.
Committees: Special Aging; Budget; Foreign Relations (African Affairs — ranking member; East Asian & Pacific Affairs; International Operations); Judiciary (Administrative Oversight & the Courts; Constitution, Federalism & Property Rights — ranking member).

Wisconsin — The statewide vote for Bill Clinton was 49% in 1996.

CQ Voting Studies

	1997	1998
Presidential	86%	83%
Party	86%	86%
Participation	100%	100%

Interest Groups

	1997	1998
ADA	95%	90%
ACU	8%	12%
AFL-CIO	86%	n/a
CCUS	20%	28%

Elections

	1992	1998
General	53%	51%
Primary	70%	u/o

Dianne Feinstein (D–Calif.)
Of San Francisco • Elected 1992
Pronounced: FINE-stine

Born: June 22, 1933, San Francisco, Calif.
Education: Stanford U., A.B. 1955.
Occupation: Public official.
Family: Husband, Richard Blum; one child; three stepchildren.
Religion: Jewish.
Political Career: San Francisco Board of Supervisors, 1970–78, president, 1970–71, 1974–75, 1978; mayor of San Francisco, 1978–89; Democratic nominee for governor, 1990.

Capitol Office: 331 Hart Senate Office Building 20510; 224-3841; (fax) 228-3954; (e-mail) senator@feinstein.senate.gov; (web) www.senate.gov/~feinstein.
Office Staff: Chief of Staff, Mike McGill; Legis. Dir., Mark Kadesh; Communications Dir., Howard Gantman; Scheduler, Trevor Daley.
Committees: Appropriations (Agriculture, Rural Development & Related Agencies; Interior; Labor, Health & Human Services & Education; Legislative Branch — ranking member; Judiciary (Immigration; Technology, Terrorism & Government Information — ranking member; Youth Violence); Rules & Administration.

California — The statewide vote for Bill Clinton was 51% in 1996.

CQ Voting Studies

	1997	1998
Presidential	89%	88%
Party	85%	87%
Participation	99%	99%

Interest Groups

	1997	1998
ADA	85%	90%
ACU	4%	4%
AFL-CIO	57%	n/a
CCUS	50%	61%

Elections

	1992	1994
General	*54%	47%
Primary	*58%	74%

*Special election

Peter G. Fitzgerald (R–Ill.)
Of Inverness • Elected 1998

Born: Oct. 20, 1960, Elgin, Ill.
Education: Dartmouth College, A.B. 1982; Aristotelian U. (Greece), attended 1983; U. of Michigan, J.D. 1986.
Occupation: Lawyer.
Family: Wife, Nina; one child.
Religion: Roman Catholic.
Political Career: Ill. Senate, 1993–99; sought Republican nomination for U.S. House, 1994.

Capitol Office: 555 Dirksen Senate Office Building 20510; 224-2854; (fax) 228-1372; (e–mail) senator_fitzgerald@fitzgerald.senate.gov.
Office Staff: Chief of Staff, Richard A. Hertling; Legis. Dir., Gregg Rickman; Communications Dir., Mike Cys; Scheduler, Lanae Denny.
Committees: Agriculture, Nutrition & Forestry (Forestry, Conservation & Rural Revitalization; Research, Nutrition & General Legislation — chairman); Energy & Natural Resources (Energy Research, Development, Production & Regulation; Forests & Public Land Management); Small Business.

Illinois — The statewide vote for Bill Clinton was 54% in 1996.

Elections

	1998
General	50%
Primary	52%

Bill Frist (R–Tenn.)
Of Nashville • Elected 1994

Born: Feb. 22, 1952, Nashville, Tenn.
Education: Princeton U., B.A. 1974; Harvard U., M.D. 1978.
Occupation: Surgeon.
Family: Wife, Karyn; three children.
Religion: Presbyterian.
Political Career: No previous office.

Capitol Office: 567 Dirksen Senate Office Building 20510; 224-3344; (fax) 228-1264; (e–mail) senator_frist@frist.senate.gov; (web) www.senate.gov/~frist.
Office Staff: Admin. Asst., Lee Rawls; Legis. Counsel, Gus Puryear; Press Secy., Margaret Camp; Exec. Asst., Ramona Lessen.
Committees: Budget; Commerce, Science & Transportation (Aviation; Communications; Manufacturing & Competitiveness; Science, Technology & Space — chairman; Surface Transportation & Merchant Marine); Foreign Relations (African Affairs — chairman; International Economic Policy, Export & Trade Promotion; International Operations); Health, Education, Labor & Pensions (Children & Families; Public Health — chairman).

Tennessee — The statewide vote for Bill Clinton was 48% in 1996.

CQ Voting Studies

	1997	1998
Presidential	59%	44%
Party	89%	94%
Participation	100%	99%

Interest Groups

	1997	1998
ADA	10%	5%
ACU	72%	80%
AFL-CIO	0%	n/a
CCUS	100%	94%

Elections

	1994
General	56%
Primary	44%

Slade Gorton (R-Wash.)
Of Seattle • Elected 1980
Did not serve 1987–89

Born: Jan. 8, 1928, Chicago, Ill.
Education: Dartmouth College, A.B. 1950; Columbia U., LL.B. 1953.
Military Career: Army, 1946–47; Air Force, 1953–56; Air Force Reserve, 1956–81.
Occupation: Lawyer.
Family: Wife, Sally Jean Clark; three children.
Religion: Episcopalian.
Political Career: Wash. House, 1959–69, majority leader, 1967–69; Wash. attorney general, 1969–81; defeated for re-election to U.S. Senate, 1986.
Capitol Office: 730 Hart Senate Office Building 20510; 224-3441; (fax) 224-9393; (e-mail) senator_gorton@gorton.senate.gov; (web) www.senate.gov/~gorton.
Office Staff: Chief of Staff, Tony Williams; Legis. Dir., Sam Spina; Communications Dir., Rob Nichols; Office Mgr./Scheduler, Vickie McQuade.
Committees: Appropriations (Agriculture, Rural Development & Related Agencies; Energy & Water Development; Interior — chairman; Labor, Health & Human Services & Education; Transportation); Budget; Commerce, Science & Transportation (Aviation — chairman; Communications; Consumer Affairs, Foreign Commerce & Tourism; Oceans & Fisheries); Energy & Natural Resources (Energy Research, Development, Production & Regulation; National Parks, Historic Preservation & Recreation; Water & Power); Indian Affairs.

CQ Voting Studies

	1997	1998
Presidential	67%	49%
Party	83%	83%
Participation	100%	99%

Interest Groups

	1997	1998
ADA	20%	0%
ACU	60%	72%
AFL-CIO	0%	n/a
CCUS	100%	89%

Elections

	1988	1994
General	51%	56%
Primary	*36%	*53%

*Open primary

Washington — The statewide vote for Bill Clinton was 51% in 1996.

Bob Graham (D-Fla.)
Of Miami Lakes • Elected 1986

Born: Nov. 9, 1936, Miami Lakes, Fla.
Education: U. of Florida, B.A. 1959; Harvard U., LL.B. 1962.
Occupation: Real estate developer; cattle rancher.
Family: Wife, Adele Khoury Graham; four children.
Religion: United Church of Christ.
Political Career: Fla. House, 1967–71; Fla. Senate, 1971–79; governor, 1979–87.
Capitol Office: 524 Hart Senate Office Building 20510; 224-3041; (fax) 224-2237; (e-mail) bob_graham@graham.senate.gov; (web) www.senate.gov/~graham.
Office Staff: Admin. Asst., Ken Klein; Legis. Dir., Russell Sullivan; Press Secy., Kimberly James; Exec. Asst./D.C. Scheduler, Allison Jackson.
Committees: Energy & Natural Resources (Energy Research, Development, Production & Regulation — ranking member; National Parks, Historic Preservation & Recreation; Water & Power); Environment & Public Works (Clean Air, Wetlands, Private Property & Nuclear Safety — ranking member; Fisheries, Wildlife & Drinking Water; Transportation & Infrastructure); Finance (Health Care; International Trade; Long-Term Growth & Debt Reduction — ranking member); Select Intelligence; Veterans' Affairs.

CQ Voting Studies

	1997	1998
Presidential	84%	83%
Party	71%	85%
Participation	99%	100%

Interest Groups

	1997	1998
ADA	60%	85%
ACU	8%	4%
AFL-CIO	29%	n/a
CCUS	80%	61%

Elections

	1992	1998
General	65%	62%
Primary	84%	u/o

Florida — The statewide vote for Bill Clinton was 48% in 1996.

Phil Gramm (R–Texas)
Of College Station • Elected 1984

Born: July 8, 1942, Fort Benning, Ga.
Education: U. of Georgia, B.B.A. 1964, Ph.D. 1967.
Occupation: Professor.
Family: Wife, Wendy Lee Gramm; two children.
Religion: Episcopalian.
Political Career: Sought Democratic nomination for U.S. Senate, 1976; U.S. House, 1979–85; sought Republican nomination for president, 1996.

Capitol Office: 370 Russell Senate Office Building 20510; 224-2934; (fax) 228-2856; (web) www.senate.gov/~gramm.
Office Staff: Chief of Staff, Ruth Cymber; Legis. Dir., Richard L. Ribbentrop; Press Secy., Larry Neal; Scheduler, Zodie Dempsey.
Committees: Banking, Housing & Urban Affairs — chairman (Housing & Transportation); Budget; Finance (Health Care; International Trade; Social Security & Family Policy).

Texas — The statewide vote for Bill Clinton was 44% in 1996.

CQ Voting Studies

	1997	1998
Presidential	56%	32%
Party	99%	97%
Participation	100%	99%

Interest Groups

	1997	1998
ADA	0%	0%
ACU	100%	96%
AFL-CIO	14%	n/a
CCUS	80%	94%

Elections

	1990	1996
General	60%	55%
Primary	u/o	85%

Rod Grams (R–Minn.)
Of Anoka • Elected 1994

Born: Feb. 4, 1948, Princeton, Minn.
Education: Anoka-Ramsey Community College, attended 1970–72; Carroll College, attended 1974–75.
Occupation: Contractor; television journalist.
Family: Divorced; four children.
Religion: Lutheran.
Political Career: U.S. House, 1993–95.

Capitol Office: 257 Dirksen Senate Office Building 20510; 224-3244; (fax) 228-0956; (e–mail) mail_grams@grams.senate.gov; (web) www.senate.gov/~grams.
Office Staff: Chief of Staff, Christine Gunhus; Legis. Dir., Pat Eveland; Press Secy., Steven Behm; Scheduler, Cindy Waters.
Committees: Joint Economic; Banking, Housing & Urban Affairs (International Trade & Finance; Housing & Transportation; Securities — chairman); Budget; Foreign Relations (African Affairs; International Operations — chairman; Near Eastern & South Asian Affairs).

Minnesota — The statewide vote for Bill Clinton was 51% in 1996.

CQ Voting Studies

	1997	1998
Presidential	52%	39%
Party	94%	97%
Participation	98%	99%

Interest Groups

	1997	1998
ADA	0%	0%
ACU	100%	88%
AFL-CIO	14%	n/a
CCUS	80%	94%

Elections

	1994
General	49%
Primary	58%

Charles E. Grassley (R–Iowa)
Of New Hartford • Elected 1980

Born: Sept. 17, 1933, New Hartford, Iowa.
Education: U. of Northern Iowa, B.A. 1955, M.A. 1956; U. of Iowa, attended 1957–58.
Occupation: Farmer.
Family: Wife, Barbara; five children.
Religion: Baptist.
Political Career: Republican nominee for Iowa House, 1956; Iowa House, 1959–75; U.S. House, 1975–81.

Capitol Office: 135 Hart Senate Office Building 20510; 224-3744; (fax) 224-6020; (e-mail) chuck_grassley@grassley.senate.gov; (web) www.senate.gov/~grassley.
Office Staff: Chief of Staff, Kenneth C. Cunningham; Legis. Dir., Jim Jochum; Press Secy., Jill Kozeny; Scheduler, Rebecca Shimkus.
Committees: Joint Taxation; Special Aging — chairman; Agriculture, Nutrition & Forestry (Forestry, Conservation & Rural Revitalization; Production & Price Competitiveness); Budget; Finance (Health Care; International Trade — chairman; Taxation & IRS Oversight); Judiciary (Administrative Oversight & the Courts — chairman; Immigration; Technology, Terrorism & Government Information).

CQ Voting Studies

	1997	1998
Presidential	60%	39%
Party	91%	86%
Participation	100%	100%

Interest Groups

	1997	1998
ADA	5%	5%
ACU	80%	80%
AFL-CIO	0%	n/a
CCUS	100%	83%

Elections

	1992	1998
General	70%	68%
Primary	u/o	u/o

Iowa — The statewide vote for Bill Clinton was 50% in 1996.

Judd Gregg (R–N.H.)
Of Rye • Elected 1992

Born: Feb. 14, 1947, Nashua, N.H.
Education: Columbia U., A.B. 1969; Boston U., J.D. 1972, LL.M. 1975.
Occupation: Lawyer.
Family: Wife, Kathleen; three children.
Religion: Congregationalist.
Political Career: N.H. Governor's Executive Council, 1979–81; U.S. House, 1981–89; governor, 1989–93.

Capitol Office: 393 Russell Senate Office Building 20510; 224-3324; (fax) 224-4952; (e-mail) mailbox@gregg.senate.gov; (web) www.senate.gov/~gregg.
Office Staff: Admin. Asst., Townsend Lange McNitt; Legis. Dir., Alyssa Shooshan; Press Secy., Edmund Amorosi; Appts. Secy., Sharon Clifford.
Committees: Appropriations (Commerce, Justice, State & Judiciary — chairman; Defense; Foreign Operations; Interior; Labor, Health & Human Services & Education); Budget; Governmental Affairs (International Security, Proliferation & Federal Services; Oversight of Government Management); Health, Education, Labor & Pensions (Aging; Children & Families — chairman; Public Health).

CQ Voting Studies

	1997	1998
Presidential	63%	42%
Party	87%	90%
Participation	99%	98%

Interest Groups

	1997	1998
ADA	10%	5%
ACU	76%	76%
AFL-CIO	0%	n/a
CCUS	100%	89%

Elections

	1992	1998
General	48%	68%
Primary	50%	86%

New Hampshire — The statewide vote for Bill Clinton was 50% in 1996.

Chuck Hagel (R–Neb.)
Of Omaha • Elected 1996

Born: Oct. 4, 1946, North Platte, Neb.
Education: U. of Nebraska, Omaha, B.A. 1971.
Military Career: Army, 1967–68.
Occupation: Investment bank executive; cell phone company founder; lobbyist; congressional aide; radio talk show host.
Family: Wife, Lilibet; two children.
Religion: Episcopalian.
Political Career: Veterans Administration deputy administrator, 1981–82.

Capitol Office: 346 Russell Senate Office Building 20510; 224-4224; (fax) 224-5213; (e–mail) chuck_hagel@hagel.senate.gov; (web) www.senate.gov/~hagel.
Office Staff: Deputy Chief of Staff, Kent Bonham; Legis. Dir., Derek Schmidt; Press Secy., Deb Fiddelke; Scheduler, Brenda Hart.
Committees: Special Aging; Banking, Housing & Urban Affairs (Financial Institutions; International Trade & Finance; Securities); Foreign Relations (East Asian & Pacific Affairs; European Affairs; International Economic Policy, Export & Trade Promotion — chairman); Health, Education, Labor & Pensions (Children & Families; Employment, Safety & Training).

Nebraska — The statewide vote for Bill Clinton was 35% in 1996.

CQ Voting Studies

	1997	1998
Presidential	59%	42%
Party	92%	89%
Participation	100%	99%

Interest Groups

	1997	1998
ADA	5%	0%
ACU	80%	72%
AFL-CIO	0%	n/a
CCUS	100%	94%

Elections

	1996
General	56%
Primary	62%

Tom Harkin (D–Iowa)
Of Cumming • Elected 1984

Born: Nov. 19, 1939, Cumming, Iowa.
Education: Iowa State U., B.S. 1962; Catholic U., J.D. 1972.
Military Career: Navy, 1962–67; Naval Reserve, 1968–74.
Occupation: Lawyer; congressional aide.
Family: Wife, Ruth; two children.
Religion: Roman Catholic.
Political Career: Democratic nominee for U.S. House, 1972; U.S. House, 1975–85; sought Democratic nomination for president, 1992.

Capitol Office: 731 Hart Senate Office Building 20510; 224-3254; (fax) 224-9369; (e–mail) tom_harkin@harkin.senate.gov; (web) www.senate.gov/~harkin.
Office Staff: Admin. Asst., Jeff Link; Legis. Dir., Peter Reinecke; Press Secy., Patrick Dorton; Scheduler, Carrie Nelson.
Committees: Agriculture, Nutrition & Forestry — ranking member; Appropriations (Agriculture, Rural Development & Related Agencies; Defense; Foreign Operations; Labor, Health & Human Services & Education — ranking member; VA, HUD & Independent Agencies); Health, Education, Labor & Pensions (Employment, Safety & Training; Public Health); Small Business.

Iowa — The statewide vote for Bill Clinton was 50% in 1996.

CQ Voting Studies

	1997	1998
Presidential	83%	81%
Party	90%	92%
Participation	95%	96%

Interest Groups

	1997	1998
ADA	85%	95%
ACU	12%	5%
AFL-CIO	71%	n/a
CCUS	70%	50%

Elections

	1990	1996
General	54%	52%
Primary	u/o	u/o

Orrin G. Hatch (R–Utah)
Of Salt Lake City • Elected 1976

Born: Mar. 22, 1934, Pittsburgh, Pa.
Education: Brigham Young U., B.S. 1959; U. of Pittsburgh, J.D. 1962.
Occupation: Lawyer.
Family: Wife, Elaine; six children.
Religion: Mormon.
Political Career: No previous office.

Capitol Office: 131 Russell Senate Office Building 20510; 224-5251; (fax) 224-6331; (e–mail) senator_hatch@hatch.senate.gov; (web) www.senate.gov/~hatch.
Office Staff: Chief of Staff, Patricia Knight; Legis. Dir., Kristine Iverson; Press Secy., Paul Smith; Personal Secy./Scheduler, Ruth Montoya.
Committees: Finance (Health Care; International Trade; Taxation & IRS Oversight — chairman); Indian Affairs; Select Intelligence; Judiciary — chairman (Antitrust, Business Rights & Competition; Constitution, Federalism & Property Rights; Technology, Terrorism & Government Information).

Utah — The statewide vote for Bill Clinton was 33% in 1996.

CQ Voting Studies

	1997	1998
Presidential	63%	47%
Party	86%	87%
Participation	99%	99%

Interest Groups

	1997	1998
ADA	15%	5%
ACU	68%	80%
AFL-CIO	0%	n/a
CCUS	100%	94%

Elections

	1988	1994
General	67%	69%
Primary	u/o	u/o

Jesse Helms (R–N.C.)
Of Raleigh • Elected 1972

Born: Oct. 18, 1921, Monroe, N.C.
Education: Wingate College, attended 1938–39; Wake Forest U., attended 1939–40.
Military Career: Navy, 1942–45.
Occupation: Journalist; broadcasting executive; banking executive; congressional aide.
Family: Wife, Dorothy; three children.
Religion: Baptist.
Political Career: Raleigh City Council, 1957–61.

Capitol Office: 403 Dirksen Senate Office Building 20510; 224-6342; (fax) 228-1339; (e–mail) jesse_helms@helms.senate.gov; (web) www.senate.gov/~helms.
Office Staff: Admin. Asst., Jimmy Broughton; Press Secy., Walter Price; Scheduler, Anne Chitwood.
Committees: Agriculture, Nutrition & Forestry (Marketing, Inspection & Product Promotion; Production & Price Competitiveness); Foreign Relations — chairman (East Asian & Pacific Affairs; International Operations; Western Hemisphere); Rules & Administration.

North Carolina — The statewide vote for Bill Clinton was 44% in 1996.

CQ Voting Studies

	1997	1998
Presidential	44%	25%
Party	98%	75%
Participation	98%	78%

Interest Groups

	1997	1998
ADA	0%	0%
ACU	100%	100%
AFL-CIO	14%	n/a
CCUS	70%	88%

Elections

	1990	1996
General	53%	53%
Primary	84%	u/o

Ernest F. Hollings (D–S.C.)
Of Charleston • Elected 1966

Born: Jan. 1, 1922, Charleston, S.C.
Education: The Citadel, B.A. 1942; U. of South Carolina, LL.B. 1947.
Military Career: Army, 1942–45.
Occupation: Lawyer.
Family: Wife, Rita "Peatsy" Liddy; four children.
Religion: Lutheran.
Political Career: S.C. House, 1949–55; lieutenant governor, 1955–59; governor, 1959–63; sought Democratic nomination for U.S. Senate, 1962; sought Democratic nomination for president, 1984.

Capitol Office: 125 Russell Senate Office Building 20510; 224-6121; (fax) 224-4293; (e-mail) senator@hollings.senate.gov; (web) www.senate.gov/~hollings.
Office Staff: Chief of Staff, Joey Lesesne; Press Secy., Maury Lane; Appts. Secy., Robin McCain.
Committees: Appropriations (Commerce, Justice, State & Judiciary — ranking member; Defense; Energy & Water Development; Interior; Labor, Health & Human Services & Education); Budget; Commerce, Science & Transportation — ranking member (Aviation; Communications — ranking member; Manufacturing & Competitiveness).

South Carolina — The statewide vote for Bill Clinton was 44% in 1996.

CQ Voting Studies

	1997	1998
Presidential	75%	67%
Party	72%	74%
Participation	97%	89%

Interest Groups

	1997	1998
ADA	75%	55%
ACU	8%	33%
AFL-CIO	83%	n/a
CCUS	20%	71%

Elections

	1992	1998
General	50%	53%
Primary	u/o	u/o

Tim Hutchinson (R–Ark.)
Of Bentonville • Elected 1996

Born: Aug. 11, 1949, Bentonville, Ark.
Education: Bob Jones U., B.A. 1971; U. of Arkansas, M.A. 1990.
Occupation: Minister; college instructor; radio station executive.
Family: Wife, Donna Jean King; three children.
Religion: Baptist.
Political Career: Ark. House, 1985–93; U.S. House, 1993–97.

Capitol Office: 245 Dirksen Senate Office Building 20510; 224-2353; (fax) 228-3973; (e-mail) senator.hutchinson@hutchinson.senate.gov; (web) www.senate.gov/~hutchinson.
Office Staff: Chief of Staff, Todd Deatherage; Legis. Dir., Steve Carey; Press Secy., Sue Hensley; Scheduler, Heather Larrison.
Committees: Special Aging; Armed Services (Airland Forces; Readiness & Management Support; Strategic Forces); Health, Education, Labor & Pensions (Aging; Employment, Safety & Training); Veterans' Affairs.

Arkansas — The statewide vote for Bill Clinton was 54% in 1996.

CQ Voting Studies

	1997	1998
Presidential	59%	24%
Party	92%	94%
Participation	98%	95%

Interest Groups

	1997	1998
ADA	0%	5%
ACU	100%	100%
AFL-CIO	0%	n/a
CCUS	80%	89%

Elections

	1996
General	53%

Kay Bailey Hutchison (R–Texas)
Of Dallas • Elected 1993

Born: July 22, 1943, Galveston, Texas.
Education: U. of Texas, B.A. 1992, J.D. 1967.
Occupation: Broadcast journalist; lawyer; banking executive; candy manufacturer.
Family: Husband, Ray Hutchison.
Religion: Episcopalian.
Political Career: Texas House, 1973–77; sought Republican nomination for U.S. House, 1982; Texas state treasurer, 1991–93.

Capitol Office: 284 Russell Senate Office Building 20510; 224-5922; (fax) 224-0776; (e–mail) senator@hutchison.senate.gov; (web) www.senate.gov/~hutchison.
Office Staff: Chief of Staff, Mark Franz; Legis. Dir., Larry DiRita; Communications Dir., Barry Bitzer; Personal Secy., Hollen Johnson.
Committees: Appropriations (Commerce, Justice, State & Judiciary; Defense; District of Columbia — chairman; Labor, Health & Human Services & Education; Military Construction; VA, HUD & Independent Agencies); Commerce, Science & Transportation (Aviation; Communications; Oceans & Fisheries; Science, Technology & Space; Surface Transportation & Merchant Marine — chairman); Environment & Public Works (Clean Air, Wetlands, Private Property & Nuclear Safety; Fisheries, Wildlife & Drinking Water); Rules & Administration.

CQ Voting Studies

	1997	1998
Presidential	62%	35%
Party	95%	89%
Participation	99%	96%

Interest Groups

	1997	1998
ADA	5%	0%
ACU	92%	88%
AFL-CIO	0%	n/a
CCUS	100%	100%

Elections

	1993	1994
General	*†67%	61%
Primary		84%

*Runoff election
†Special election

Texas — The statewide vote for Bill Clinton was 44% in 1996.

James M. Inhofe (R–Okla.)
Of Tulsa • Elected 1994
Pronounced: IN-hoff

Born: Nov. 17, 1934, Des Moines, Iowa.
Education: U. of Tulsa, B.A. 1959.
Military Career: Army, 1956–58.
Occupation: Real estate developer; insurance executive.
Family: Wife, Kay; four children.
Religion: Presbyterian.
Political Career: Okla. House, 1967–69; Okla. Senate, 1969–77; Republican nominee for governor, 1974; Republican nominee for U.S. House, 1976; mayor of Tulsa, 1978–84; defeated for re-election as mayor of Tulsa, 1984; U.S. House, 1987–94.

Capitol Office: 453 Russell Senate Office Building 20510; 224-4721; (fax) 228-0380; (web) www.senate.gov/~inhofe.
Office Staff: Admin. Asst., Vacant; Legis. Dir., Ruth Van Mark; Press Secy., Gary Hoitsma; Exec. Asst., Phyllis Kreis.
Committees: Armed Services (Airland Forces; Readiness & Management Support — chairman; Strategic Forces); Environment & Public Works (Clean Air, Wetlands, Private Property & Nuclear Safety — chairman; Superfund, Waste Control & Risk Assessment; Transportation & Infrastructure); Indian Affairs; Select Intelligence.

CQ Voting Studies

	1997	1998
Presidential	49%	13%
Party	96%	95%
Participation	98%	95%

Interest Groups

	1997	1998
ADA	5%	5%
ACU	100%	100%
AFL-CIO	14%	n/a
CCUS	50%	76%

Elections

	1994	1996
General	*55%	57%
Primary	*78%	75%

*Special election

Oklahoma — The statewide vote for Bill Clinton was 40% in 1996.

Daniel K. Inouye (D–Hawaii)
Of Honolulu • Elected 1962
Pronounced: in-NO-ay

Born: Sept. 7, 1924, Honolulu, Hawaii.
Education: U. of Hawaii, A.B. 1950; George Washington U., J.D. 1952.
Military Career: Army, 1943–47.
Occupation: Lawyer.
Family: Wife, Margaret Shinobu Awamura; one child.
Religion: Methodist.
Political Career: Hawaii Territorial House, 1954–58, majority leader; Hawaii Territorial Senate, 1958–59; U.S. House, 1959–63.

Capitol Office: 722 Hart Senate Office Building 20510; 224-3934; (fax) 224-6747; (e–mail) senator@inouye.senate.gov; (web) www.senate.gov/~inouye.
Office Staff: Admin. Asst., Patrick DeLeon; Legis. Dir., Margaret Cummisky; Press Secy., Michele Konishi; Personal Secy., Sally Watanabe.
Committees: Joint Printing; Appropriations (Commerce, Justice, State & Judiciary; Defense — ranking member; Foreign Operations; Labor, Health & Human Services & Education; Military Construction); Commerce, Science & Transportation (Aviation; Communications; Oceans & Fisheries; Surface Transportation & Merchant Marine — ranking member); Indian Affairs — ranking member; Rules & Administration.

Hawaii — The statewide vote for Bill Clinton was 57% in 1996.

CQ Voting Studies

	1997	1998
Presidential	83%	75%
Party	85%	79%
Participation	95%	85%

Interest Groups

	1997	1998
ADA	75%	80%
ACU	4%	9%
AFL-CIO	83%	n/a
CCUS	50%	44%

Elections

	1992	1998
General	57%	79%
Primary	76%	93%

James M. Jeffords (R–Vt.)
Of Shrewsbury • Elected 1988

Born: May 11, 1934, Rutland, Vt.
Education: Yale U., B.S.I.A. 1956; Harvard U., LL.B. 1962.
Military Career: Navy, 1956–59; Naval Reserve, 1959–90.
Occupation: Lawyer.
Family: Wife, Elizabeth Daley; two children.
Religion: Congregationalist.
Political Career: Vt. Senate, 1967–69; Vt. attorney general, 1969–73; sought Republican nomination for governor, 1972; U.S. House, 1975–89.

Capitol Office: 728 Hart Senate Office Building 20510; 224-5141; (e–mail) vermont@jeffords.senate.gov; (web) www.senate.gov/~jeffords.
Office Staff: Chief of Staff, Susan Boardman Russ; Legis. Dir., Ken Connolly; Press Secy., Erik Smulson; Scheduler, Trecia McEvoy.
Committees: Special Aging; Finance (Health Care; International Trade; Social Security & Family Policy); Health, Education, Labor & Pensions — chairman (Aging; Employment, Safety & Training); Veterans' Affairs.

Vermont — The statewide vote for Bill Clinton was 54% in 1996.

CQ Voting Studies

	1997	1998
Presidential	75%	68%
Party	51%	49%
Participation	97%	99%

Interest Groups

	1997	1998
ADA	45%	55%
ACU	21%	24%
AFL-CIO	0%	n/a
CCUS	100%	89%

Elections

	1988	1994
General	68%	50%
Primary	61%	u/o

Tim Johnson (D-S.D.)
Of Vermillion • Elected 1996

Born: Dec. 28, 1946, Canton, S.D.
Education: U. of South Dakota, B.A. 1969, M.A. 1970; Michigan State U., attended 1970–71; U. of South Dakota, J.D. 1975.
Military Career: Army, 1969.
Occupation: Lawyer.
Family: Wife, Barbara; three children.
Religion: Lutheran.
Political Career: S.D. House, 1979–83; S.D. Senate, 1983–87; Clay County deputy state's attorney, 1985; U.S. House, 1987–97.

Capitol Office: 502 Hart Senate Office Building 20510; 224-5842; (fax) 228-5765; (e-mail) tim@johnson.senate.gov; (web) www.senate.gov/~johnson.
Office Staff: Admin. Asst., Greg Billings; Legis. Dir., Dwight Fettig; Communications Dir., Lisa Gruenloh; Scheduler, Cindy Reesman.
Committees: Agriculture, Nutrition & Forestry (Production & Price Competitiveness; Research, Nutrition & General Legislation); Banking, Housing & Urban Affairs (Financial Institutions; International Trade & Finance — ranking member; Securities); Budget; Energy & Natural Resources (Energy Research, Development, Production & Regulation; Forests & Public Land Management).

South Dakota — The statewide vote for Bill Clinton was 43% in 1996.

CQ Voting Studies

	1997	1998
Presidential	84%	89%
Party	86%	93%
Participation	98%	100%

Interest Groups

	1997	1998
ADA	80%	90%
ACU	12%	4%
AFL-CIO	71%	n/a
CCUS	70%	56%

Elections

	1996
General	51%
Primary	u/o

Edward M. Kennedy (D-Mass.)
Of Boston • Elected 1962

Born: Feb. 22, 1932, Boston, Mass.
Education: Harvard U., B.A. 1956; International Law School, The Hague (The Netherlands), attended 1958; U. of Virginia, LL.B. 1959.
Military Career: Army, 1951–53.
Occupation: Lawyer.
Family: Wife, Victoria Reggie Kennedy; three children, two stepchildren.
Religion: Roman Catholic.
Political Career: Suffolk County assistant district attorney, 1961–62; sought Democratic nomination for president, 1980.

Capitol Office: 315 Russell Senate Office Building 20510; 224-4543; (fax) 224-2417; (e-mail) senator@kennedy.senate.gov; (web) www.senate.gov/~kennedy.
Office Staff: Chief of Staff, Gerry Kavanaugh; Legis. Dir., Carey Parker; Press Secy., Jim Manley; Scheduler, Soo Han.
Committees: Joint Economic; Armed Services (Emerging Threats & Capabilities; Personnel; Seapower — ranking member); Judiciary (Constitution, Federalism & Property Rights; Immigration — ranking member); Health, Education, Labor & Pensions — ranking member (Employment, Safety & Training; Public Health — ranking member).

Massachusetts — The statewide vote for Bill Clinton was 62% in 1996.

CQ Voting Studies

	1997	1998
Presidential	84%	92%
Party	96%	98%
Participation	97%	97%

Interest Groups

	1997	1998
ADA	100%	95%
ACU	4%	0%
AFL-CIO	100%	n/a
CCUS	40%	47%

Elections

	1988	1994
General	65%	58%
Primary	u/o	u/o

Bob Kerrey (D–Neb.)
Of Lincoln • Elected 1988

Born: Aug. 27, 1943, Lincoln, Neb.
Education: U. of Nebraska, B.S. 1966.
Military Career: Navy, 1966–69.
Occupation: Restaurateur.
Family: Divorced; two children.
Religion: Congregationalist.
Political Career: Governor, 1983–87; sought Democratic nomination for president, 1992.

Capitol Office: 141 Hart Senate Office Building 20510; 224-6551; (fax) 224-7645; (e-mail) bob@kerrey.senate.gov; (web) www.senate.gov/~kerrey.
Office Staff: Chief of Staff, Shelia Nix; Legis. Dir., Anne Urban; Communications Dir., Greg Weiner; Scheduler, Cindy Dwyer.
Committees: Agriculture, Nutrition & Forestry (Marketing, Inspection & Product Promotion; Production & Price Competitiveness — ranking member); Finance (Health Care; International Trade; Social Security & Family Policy); Select Intelligence — ranking member.

Nebraska — The statewide vote for Bill Clinton was 35% in 1996.

CQ Voting Studies

	1997	1998
Presidential	87%	89%
Party	78%	88%
Participation	99%	98%

Interest Groups

	1997	1998
ADA	75%	95%
ACU	4%	0%
AFL-CIO	43%	n/a
CCUS	60%	56%

Elections

	1988	1994
General	57%	55%
Primary	91%	u/o

John Kerry (D–Mass.)
Of Boston • Elected 1984

Born: Dec. 11, 1943, Denver, Colo.
Education: Yale U., B.A. 1966; Boston College, J.D. 1976.
Military Career: Navy, 1966–70.
Occupation: Lawyer.
Family: Wife, Teresa Heinz; two children, three stepchildren.
Religion: Roman Catholic.
Political Career: Democratic nominee for U.S. House, 1972; lieutenant governor, 1983–85.

Capitol Office: 421 Russell Senate Office Building 20510; 224-2742; (fax) 224-8525; (e-mail) john_kerry@kerry.senate.gov; (web) www.senate.gov/~kerry.
Office Staff: Chief of Staff, David McKean; Policy Dir., Jim Jones; Press Secy., Jim Jordan; Scheduler, Ayanna Pressley.
Committees: Banking, Housing & Urban Affairs (Economic Policy; International Trade & Finance; Housing & Transportation — ranking member); Commerce, Science & Transportation (Communications; Oceans & Fisheries — ranking member; Science, Technology & Space); Foreign Relations (East Asian & Pacific Affairs — ranking member; International Economic Policy, Export & Trade Promotion; International Operations); Select Intelligence; Small Business — ranking member.

Massachusetts — The statewide vote for Bill Clinton was 62% in 1996.

CQ Voting Studies

	1997	1998
Presidential	87%	90%
Party	97%	95%
Participation	99%	98%

Interest Groups

	1997	1998
ADA	95%	95%
ACU	0%	4%
AFL-CIO	71%	n/a
CCUS	50%	50%

Elections

	1990	1996
General	57%	52%
Primary	u/o	u/o

Herb Kohl (D–Wis.)
Of Milwaukee • Elected 1988

Born: Feb. 7, 1935, Milwaukee, Wis.
Education: U. of Wisconsin, B.A. 1956; Harvard U., M.B.A. 1958.
Military Career: Army Reserve, 1958–64.
Occupation: Professional basketball team owner; department and grocery store owner.
Family: Single.
Religion: Jewish.
Political Career: Wis. Democratic Party chairman, 1975–77.

Capitol Office: 330 Hart Senate Office Building 20510; 224-5653; (fax) 224-9787; (e-mail) senator_kohl@kohl.senate.gov; (web) www.senate.gov/ kohl.
Office Staff: Chief of Staff, Paul Bock; Legis. Dir., Kate Sparks; Press Secy., Lynn Becker; Exec. Asst., Arlene Branca.
Committees: Special Aging; Appropriations (Agriculture, Rural Development & Related Agencies — ranking member; Energy & Water Development; Interior; Labor, Health & Human Services & Education; Transportation); Judiciary (Antitrust, Business Rights & Competition — ranking member; Technology, Terrorism & Government Information; Youth Violence).

Wisconsin — The statewide vote for Bill Clinton was 49% in 1996.

CQ Voting Studies

	1997	1998
Presidential	90%	85%
Party	74%	87%
Participation	100%	99%

Interest Groups

	1997	1998
ADA	70%	85%
ACU	20%	4%
AFL-CIO	29%	n/a
CCUS	80%	44%

Elections

	1988	1994
General	52%	58%
Primary	47%	90%

Jon Kyl (R–Ariz.)
Of Phoenix • Elected 1994

Born: Apr. 25, 1942, Oakland, Neb.
Education: U. of Arizona, B.A. 1962–64, LL.B. 1966.
Occupation: Lawyer.
Family: Wife, Caryll Collins; two children.
Religion: Presbyterian.
Political Career: U.S. House, 1987–95.

Capitol Office: 724 Hart Senate Office Building 20510; 224-4521; (fax) 224-2207; (e-mail) info@kyl.senate.gov; (web) www.senate.gov/~kyl.
Office Staff: Chief of Staff, Laurie Fenton; Senior Policy Adviser, Jeanine V. Esperne; Press Secy., Vince Sollitto; Scheduler, Christine Gilligan.
Committees: Appropriations (District of Columbia; Labor, Health & Human Services & Education; Military Construction; Treasury & General Government; VA, HUD & Independent Agencies); Select Intelligence; Judiciary (Immigration; Technology, Terrorism & Government Information — chairman; Youth Violence); Year 2000 Technology Problem.

Arizona — The statewide vote for Bill Clinton was 47% in 1996.

CQ Voting Studies

	1997	1998
Presidential	57%	31%
Party	98%	93%
Participation	99%	94%

Interest Groups

	1997	1998
ADA	0%	0%
ACU	96%	96%
AFL-CIO	0%	n/a
CCUS	70%	76%

Elections

	1994
General	54%
Primary	u/o

Mary L. Landrieu (D–La.)
Of Baton Rouge • Elected 1996
Pronounced: LAN-drew

Born: Nov. 23, 1955, Arlington, Va.
Education: Louisiana State U., B.A. 1977.
Occupation: Real estate agent.
Family: Husband, Frank E. Snellings; two children.
Religion: Roman Catholic.
Political Career: La. House, 1980–88; La. treasurer, 1988–96; candidate for governor, 1995.

Capitol Office: 702 Hart Senate Office Building 20510; 224-5824; (e–mail) senator@landrieu.senate.gov; (web) www.senate.gov/~landrieu.
Office Staff: Chief of Staff, Norma Jane Sabiston; Legis. Dir., Ben Cannon; Communications Dir., Rich Masters; Scheduler, Kay LaFrance.
Committees: Armed Services (Airland Forces; Readiness & Management Support; Strategic Forces — ranking member); Energy & Natural Resources (Energy Research, Development, Production & Regulation; Forests & Public Land Management; National Parks, Historic Preservation & Recreation); Small Business.

Louisiana — The statewide vote for Bill Clinton was 52% in 1996.

CQ Voting Studies

	1997	1998
Presidential	87%	85%
Party	76%	88%
Participation	99%	99%

Interest Groups

	1997	1998
ADA	70%	90%
ACU	16%	8%
AFL-CIO	29%	n/a
CCUS	70%	67%

Elections

	1996
General	50%
Primary	22%

Frank R. Lautenberg (D–N.J.)
Of Cliffside Park • Elected 1982

Born: Jan. 23, 1924, Paterson, N.J.
Education: Columbia U., B.S. 1949.
Military Career: Army, 1942–46.
Occupation: Computer firm executive.
Family: Divorced; four children.
Religion: Jewish.
Political Career: No previous office.

Capitol Office: 506 Hart Senate Office Building 20510; 224-4744; (fax) 224-9707; (e–mail) frank_lautenberg@lautenberg.senate.gov; (web) www.senate.gov/~lautenberg.
Office Staff: Chief of Staff, Eve Lubalin; Legis. Dir., Sander Lurie; Communications Dir., Retha Sherrod; Scheduler, Lisa Baranello.
Committees: Appropriations (Commerce, Justice, State & Judiciary; Defense; Foreign Operations; Transportation — ranking member; VA, HUD & Independent Agencies); Budget — ranking member; Environment & Public Works (Fisheries, Wildlife & Drinking Water; Superfund, Waste Control & Risk Assessment — ranking member); Select Intelligence.

New Jersey — The statewide vote for Bill Clinton was 53% in 1996.

CQ Voting Studies

	1997	1998
Presidential	83%	90%
Party	94%	97%
Participation	99%	99%

Interest Groups

	1997	1998
ADA	95%	95%
ACU	0%	4%
AFL-CIO	71%	n/a
CCUS	60%	50%

Elections

	1988	1994
General	54%	50%
Primary	78%	81%

Patrick J. Leahy (D-Vt.)
Of Middlesex • Elected 1974

Born: Mar. 31, 1940, Montpelier, Vt.
Education: St. Michael's College, B.A. 1961; Georgetown U., J.D. 1964.
Occupation: Lawyer.
Family: Wife, Marcelle; three children.
Religion: Roman Catholic.
Political Career: Chittenden County state's attorney, 1967–75.

Capitol Office: 433 Russell Senate Office Building 20510; 224-4242; (e–mail) senator_leahy@leahy.senate.gov; (web) www.senate.gov/~leahy.
Office Staff: Chief of Staff, Luke Albee; Legis. Dir., John P. Dowd; Press Secy., David Carle; Scheduler, Kevin McDonald.
Committees: Agriculture, Nutrition & Forestry (Forestry, Conservation & Rural Revitalization; Research, Nutrition & General Legislation — ranking member); Appropriations (Commerce, Justice, State & Judiciary; Defense; Foreign Operations — ranking member; Interior; VA, HUD & Independent Agencies); Judiciary — ranking member (Antitrust, Business Rights & Competition; Constitution, Federalism & Property Rights; Criminal Justice Oversight).

Vermont — The statewide vote for Bill Clinton was 54% in 1996.

CQ Voting Studies

	1997	1998
Presidential	87%	81%
Party	89%	86%
Participation	98%	99%

Interest Groups

	1997	1998
ADA	80%	90%
ACU	13%	12%
AFL-CIO	67%	n/a
CCUS	60%	56%

Elections

	1992	1998
General	54%	72%
Primary	u/o	97%

Carl Levin (D-Mich.)
Of Detroit • Elected 1978

Born: June 28, 1934, Detroit, Mich.
Education: Swarthmore College, B.A. 1956; Harvard U., LL.B. 1959.
Occupation: Lawyer.
Family: Wife, Barbara; three children.
Religion: Jewish.
Political Career: Michigan Civil Rights Commission general counsel, 1964–67; Detroit chief appellate defender, 1968–69; Detroit City Council, 1970–77, president, 1974–77.

Capitol Office: 459 Russell Senate Office Building 20510; 224-6221; (fax) 224-1388; (e–mail) senator@levin.senate.gov; (web) www.senate.gov/~levin.
Office Staff: Chief of Staff, Gordon Kerr; Legis. Dir., Rich Arenberg; Press Secy., John Brennan; Exec. Secy., Helen Galen.
Committees: Armed Services — ranking member; Governmental Affairs (International Security, Proliferation & Federal Services; Investigations — ranking member); Select Intelligence; Small Business.

Michigan — The statewide vote for Bill Clinton was 52% in 1996.

CQ Voting Studies

	1997	1998
Presidential	90%	88%
Party	95%	95%
Participation	100%	97%

Interest Groups

	1997	1998
ADA	95%	90%
ACU	0%	0%
AFL-CIO	86%	n/a
CCUS	50%	44%

Elections

	1990	1996
General	57%	58%
Primary	u/o	u/o

Joseph I. Lieberman (D–Conn.)
Of New Haven • Elected 1988

Born: Feb. 24, 1942, Stamford, Conn.
Education: Yale U., B.A. 1964, LL.B. 1967.
Occupation: Lawyer.
Family: Wife, Hadassah; four children.
Religion: Jewish.
Political Career: Conn. Senate, 1971–81, majority leader, 1975–81; Democratic nominee for U.S. House, 1980; Conn. attorney general, 1983–89.

Capitol Office: 706 Hart Senate Office Building 20510; 224-4041; (fax) 224-9750; (e–mail) senator_lieberman@lieberman.senate.gov; (web) www.senate.gov/~lieberman.
Office Staff: Admin. Asst., William G. Andresen; Legis. Dir./Chief Counsel, William B. Bonvillian; Press Secy., Vacant; Exec. Asst., Melissa Winter.
Committees: Armed Services (Airland Forces — ranking member; Emerging Threats & Capabilities; Strategic Forces); Environment & Public Works (Clean Air, Wetlands, Private Property & Nuclear Safety; Transportation & Infrastructure); Governmental Affairs — ranking member; Small Business.

Connecticut — The statewide vote for Bill Clinton was 52% in 1996.

CQ Voting Studies

	1997	1998
Presidential	90%	83%
Party	76%	80%
Participation	99%	100%

Interest Groups

	1997	1998
ADA	75%	80%
ACU	20%	16%
AFL-CIO	29%	n/a
CCUS	60%	56%

Elections

	1988	1994
General	50%	67%
Primary	u/o	u/o

Blanche Lincoln (D–Ark.)
Of Hughes • Elected 1998

Born: Sept. 30, 1960, Helena, Ark.
Education: Randolph-Macon Woman's College, B.A. 1982.
Occupation: Lobbyist; congressional aide.
Family: Husband, Steve; two children.
Religion: Episcopalian.
Political Career: U.S. House, 1993–97.

Capitol Office: 359 Dirksen Senate Office Building 20510; 224-4843; (fax) 228-1371; (e–mail) blanche_lincoln@lincoln.senate.gov.
Office Staff: Chief of Staff, Steve Patterson; Legis. Dir., Kelly Rucker; Press Secy., Jennifer Greeson; Scheduler, Beth Overman.
Committees: Special Aging; Agriculture, Nutrition & Forestry (Production & Price Competitiveness; Research, Nutrition & General Legislation); Energy & Natural Resources (Forests & Public Land Management; National Parks, Historic Preservation & Recreation; Water & Power).

Arkansas — The statewide vote for Bill Clinton was 54% in 1996.

Elections

	1998
General	55%
Primary	*62%

*Runoff election

Trent Lott (R–Miss.)
Of Pascagoula • Elected 1988

Born: Oct. 9, 1941, Grenada County, Miss.
Education: U. of Mississippi, B.P.A. 1963, J.D. 1967.
Occupation: Lawyer; congressional aide.
Family: Wife, Patricia Elizabeth Lott; two children.
Religion: Baptist.
Political Career: U.S. House, 1973–89.

Capitol Office: 487 Russell Senate Office Building 20510; 224-6253; (fax) 224-2262; (e–mail) senatorlott@lott.senate.gov; (web) www.senate.gov/~lott.
Office Staff: Chief of Staff, William Gottshall; Legis. Dir., Carl Biersack; Press Secy., John Czwartacki; Scheduler, Hardy Lott.
Committees: Commerce, Science & Transportation (Aviation; Communications); Finance (International Trade; Social Security & Family Policy; Taxation & IRS Oversight); Rules & Administration.

Mississippi — The statewide vote for Bill Clinton was 44% in 1996.

CQ Voting Studies

	1997	1998
Presidential	56%	39%
Party	94%	94%
Participation	100%	98%

Interest Groups

	1997	1998
ADA	5%	0%
ACU	72%	92%
AFL-CIO	0%	n/a
CCUS	90%	94%

Elections

	1988	1994
General	54%	69%
Primary	u/o	95%

Richard G. Lugar (R–Ind.)
Of Indianapolis • Elected 1976

Born: Apr. 4, 1932, Indianapolis, Ind.
Education: Denison U., B.A. 1954; Oxford U., B.A. 1956, M.A. 1956.
Military Career: Navy, 1957–60.
Occupation: Farm manager; manufacturing executive.
Family: Wife, Charlene; four children.
Religion: Methodist.
Political Career: Indianapolis School Board, 1964–67; mayor of Indianapolis, 1968–75; Republican nominee for U.S. Senate, 1974.

Capitol Office: 306 Hart Senate Office Building 20510; 224-4814; (e–mail) senator_lugar@lugar.senate.gov; (web) www.senate.gov/~lugar.
Office Staff: Chief of Staff, Marty Morris; Legis. Dir., Dan Diller; Press Secy., Andy Fisher; Scheduler, Jeff Hilliker.
Committees: Agriculture, Nutrition & Forestry — chairman; Foreign Relations (European Affairs; International Economic Policy, Export & Trade Promotion; Western Hemisphere); Select Intelligence.

Indiana — The statewide vote for Bill Clinton was 42% in 1996.

CQ Voting Studies

	1997	1998
Presidential	62%	54%
Party	83%	84%
Participation	100%	100%

Interest Groups

	1997	1998
ADA	30%	0%
ACU	64%	68%
AFL-CIO	0%	n/a
CCUS	90%	94%

Elections

	1988	1994
General	68%	67%
Primary	u/o	u/o

Connie Mack (R-Fla.)
Of Cape Coral • Elected 1988

Born: Oct. 29, 1940, Philadelphia, Pa.
Education: U. of Florida, B.S. 1966.
Occupation: Banker.
Family: Wife, Priscilla; two children.
Religion: Roman Catholic.
Political Career: U.S. House, 1983–89.

Capitol Office: 517 Hart Senate Office Building 20510; 224-5274; (fax) 224-8022; (e-mail) connie@mack.senate.gov; (web) www.senate.gov/~mack.
Office Staff: Chief of Staff, John Reich; Legis. Dir., Wendy Grubbs; Communications Dir., Nancy Segerdahl; Scheduler, Suzanne Schaffrath.
Committees: Joint Economic — chairman; Banking, Housing & Urban Affairs (Financial Institutions; Economic Policy — chairman; International Trade & Finance); Finance (Long-Term Growth & Debt Reduction; Taxation & IRS Oversight).

Florida — The statewide vote for Bill Clinton was 48% in 1996.

CQ Voting Studies

	1997	1998
Presidential	57%	50%
Party	86%	86%
Participation	98%	99%

Interest Groups

	1997	1998
ADA	0%	0%
ACU	88%	80%
AFL-CIO	0%	n/a
CCUS	80%	89%

Elections

	1988	1994
General	50%	70%
Primary	62%	u/o

John McCain (R-Ariz.)
Of Phoenix • Elected 1986

Born: Aug. 29, 1936, Panama Canal Zone, Panama.
Education: U.S. Naval Academy, B.S. 1958; National War College, attended 1973–74.
Military Career: Navy, 1958–81.
Occupation: Navy officer; Senate Navy liaison; beer distributor.
Family: Wife, Cindy; seven children.
Religion: Episcopalian.
Political Career: U.S. House, 1983–87.

Capitol Office: 241 Russell Senate Office Building 20510; 224-2235; (fax) 228-2862; (e-mail) senator_mccain@mccain.senate.gov; (web) www.senate.gov/~mccain.
Office Staff: Admin. Asst., Mark Salter; Legis. Dir., Ann Sauer; Press Secy., Nancy Ives; Scheduler, Ellen Cahill.
Committees: Armed Services (Personnel; Readiness & Management Support; Seapower); Commerce, Science & Transportation — chairman; Indian Affairs.

Arizona — The statewide vote for Bill Clinton was 47% in 1996.

CQ Voting Studies

	1997	1998
Presidential	68%	46%
Party	83%	81%
Participation	98%	94%

Interest Groups

	1997	1998
ADA	5%	20%
ACU	80%	68%
AFL-CIO	14%	n/a
CCUS	100%	76%

Elections

	1992	1998
General	56%	69%
Primary	u/o	u/o

Mitch McConnell (R–Ky.)
Of Louisville • Elected 1984

Born: Feb. 20, 1942, Sheffield, Ala.
Education: U. of Louisville, B.A. 1964; U. of Kentucky, J.D. 1967.
Occupation: Lawyer; Justice Department official; congressional aide.
Family: Wife, Elaine Chao; three children.
Religion: Baptist.
Political Career: Jefferson County judge/executive, 1978–85.

Capitol Office: 361A Russell Senate Office Building 20510; 224-2541; (fax) 224-2499; (e–mail) senator@mcconnell.senate.gov; (web) www.senate.gov/~mcconnell.
Office Staff: Admin. Asst./Legis. Dir., Kyle Simmons; Press Secy., Robert Steurer; Scheduler, Nan Mosher.
Committees: Joint Library; Joint Printing; Agriculture, Nutrition & Forestry (Marketing, Inspection & Product Promotion; Research, Nutrition & General Legislation); Appropriations (Agriculture, Rural Development & Related Agencies; Commerce, Justice, State & Judiciary; Defense; Energy & Water Development; Foreign Operations — chairman); Rules & Administration — chairman.

Kentucky — The statewide vote for Bill Clinton was 46% in 1996.

CQ Voting Studies

	1997	1998
Presidential	59%	39%
Party	97%	95%
Participation	99%	99%

Interest Groups

	1997	1998
ADA	5%	0%
ACU	88%	92%
AFL-CIO	0%	n/a
CCUS	100%	94%

Elections

	1990	1996
General	52%	55%
Primary	89%	89%

Barbara A. Mikulski (D–Md.)
Of Baltimore • Elected 1986

Born: July 20, 1936, Baltimore, Md.
Education: Mount Saint Agnes College, B.A. 1958; U. of Maryland, M.S.W. 1965.
Occupation: Social worker.
Family: Single.
Religion: Roman Catholic.
Political Career: Baltimore City Council, 1971–77; Democratic nominee for U.S. Senate, 1974; U.S. House, 1977–87.

Capitol Office: 709 Hart Senate Office Building 20510; 224-4654; (fax) 224-8858; (e–mail) senator@mikulski.senate.gov; (web) www.senate.gov/~mikulski.
Office Staff: Chief of Staff, Shaila Aery; Legis. Dir., Julia Fritfield; Communications Dir., Mona Miller; Scheduler, Debbie Frantz.
Committees: Appropriations (Commerce, Justice, State & Judiciary; Foreign Operations; Transportation; Treasury & General Government; VA, HUD & Independent Agencies — ranking member); Health, Education, Labor & Pensions (Aging — ranking member; Public Health).

Maryland — The statewide vote for Bill Clinton was 54% in 1996.

CQ Voting Studies

	1997	1998
Presidential	79%	86%
Party	87%	94%
Participation	92%	96%

Interest Groups

	1997	1998
ADA	95%	90%
ACU	4%	4%
AFL-CIO	86%	n/a
CCUS	44%	53%

Elections

	1992	1998
General	71%	71%
Primary	77%	84%

Daniel Patrick Moynihan
(D-N.Y.)
Of Pindars Corners • Elected 1976

Born: Mar. 16, 1927, Tulsa, Okla.
Education: City U. of New York, City College, attended 1943; Tufts U., B.N.S. 1946, B.A. 1948; Fletcher School of Law and Diplomacy, M.A. 1949; London School of Economics, attended 1950–51; Fletcher School of Law and Diplomacy, Ph.D. 1961.
Military Career: Navy, 1944–47; Naval Reserve, 1947–66.
Occupation: Professor; writer.
Family: Wife, Elizabeth Brennan Moynihan; three children.
Religion: Roman Catholic.
Political Career: Sought Democratic nomination for N.Y. City Council president, 1965.

Capitol Office: 464 Russell Senate Office Building 20510; 224-4451; (fax) 228-0406; (e-mail) senator@dpm.senate.gov; (web) www.senate.gov/~moynihan.
Office Staff: Admin. Asst., Tony Bullock; Legis. Dir., Gray Maxwell; Press Secy., Mike Waterman; Personal Secy., Vicki Dodson.
Committees: Joint Library; Joint Taxation — ranking member; Environment & Public Works (Superfund, Waste Control & Risk Assessment; Transportation & Infrastructure); Finance — ranking member (International Trade — ranking member; Social Security & Family Policy; Taxation & IRS Oversight); Rules & Administration; Year 2000 Technology Problem.

CQ Voting Studies

	1997	1998
Presidential	81%	71%
Party	77%	83%
Participation	99%	93%

Interest Groups

	1997	1998
ADA	60%	95%
ACU	12%	8%
AFL-CIO	29%	n/a
CCUS	50%	44%

Elections

	1988	1994
General	67%	55%
Primary	u/o	75%

New York — The statewide vote for Bill Clinton was 59% in 1996.

Frank H. Murkowski (R–Alaska)
Of Fairbanks • Elected 1980

Born: Mar. 28, 1933, Seattle, Wash.
Education: U. of Santa Clara, attended 1951–53; Seattle U., B.A. 1955.
Military Career: Coast Guard, 1955–56.
Occupation: Banker.
Family: Wife, Nancy Gore; six children.
Religion: Roman Catholic.
Political Career: Alaska commissioner of economic development, 1966–70; Republican nominee for U.S. House, 1970.

Capitol Office: 322 Hart Senate Office Building 20510; 224-6665; (fax) 224-5301; (e-mail) email@murkowski.senate.gov; (web) www.senate.gov/~murkowski.
Office Staff: Chief of Staff, David Garman; Legis. Dir., Alexander Polinsky; Press Secy., Chuck Kleeschulte; Exec. Asst./Scheduler, Janet Klinger.
Committees: Energy & Natural Resources — chairman; Finance (International Trade; Long-Term Growth & Debt Reduction — chairman; Taxation & IRS Oversight); Indian Affairs; Veterans' Affairs.

CQ Voting Studies

	1997	1998
Presidential	59%	38%
Party	91%	91%
Participation	97%	96%

Interest Groups

	1997	1998
ADA	10%	5%
ACU	68%	78%
AFL-CIO	0%	n/a
CCUS	100%	100%

Elections

	1992	1998
General	53%	74%
Primary	81%	92%

Alaska — The statewide vote for Bill Clinton was 33% in 1996.

Patty Murray (D–Wash.)
Of Seattle • Elected 1992

Born: Oct. 11, 1950, Seattle, Wash.
Education: Washington State U., B.A. 1972.
Occupation: Parenting class instructor.
Family: Husband, Rob; two children.
Religion: Roman Catholic.
Political Career: Shoreline School Board, 1983–89; Wash. Senate, 1989–93.

Capitol Office: 111 Russell Senate Office Building 20510; 224-2621; (fax) 224-0238; (e-mail) senator_murray@murray.senate.gov; (web) www.senate.gov/~murray.

Office Staff: Chief of Staff, Patricia Akiyama; Legis. Dir., Ric Ilgenfritz; Press Secy., Rex Carney; Exec. Asst., Kristin Hochswinder.

Committees: Appropriations (Energy & Water Development; Foreign Operations; Labor, Health & Human Services & Education; Military Construction — ranking member; Transportation); Budget; Health, Education, Labor & Pensions (Aging; Children & Families); Veterans' Affairs.

Washington — The statewide vote for Bill Clinton was 51% in 1996.

CQ Voting Studies

	1997	1998
Presidential	87%	82%
Party	93%	91%
Participation	99%	99%

Interest Groups

	1997	1998
ADA	90%	90%
ACU	0%	4%
AFL-CIO	71%	n/a
CCUS	70%	56%

Elections

	1992	1998
General	54%	58%
Primary	*28%	*46%

*Open primary

Don Nickles (R–Okla.)
Of Ponca City • Elected 1980

Born: Dec. 6, 1948, Ponca City, Okla.
Education: Oklahoma State U., B.B.A. 1971.
Military Career: Okla. National Guard, 1970–76.
Occupation: Machine company executive.
Family: Wife, Linda; four children.
Religion: Roman Catholic.
Political Career: Okla. Senate, 1979–81.

Capitol Office: 133 Hart Senate Office Building 20510; 224-5754; (fax) 224-6008; (e-mail) senator@nickles.senate.gov; (web) www.senate.gov/~nickles.

Office Staff: Admin. Asst., Bret Bernhardt; Legis. Dir., Diane Moery; Communications Dir., Brook Simmons; Scheduler, Erin Hickman.

Committees: Joint Printing; Budget; Energy & Natural Resources (Energy Research, Development, Production & Regulation — chairman; National Parks, Historic Preservation & Recreation); Finance (Health Care; Social Security & Family Policy — chairman; Taxation & IRS Oversight); Rules & Administration.

Oklahoma — The statewide vote for Bill Clinton was 40% in 1996.

CQ Voting Studies

	1997	1998
Presidential	59%	22%
Party	97%	98%
Participation	100%	99%

Interest Groups

	1997	1998
ADA	0%	0%
ACU	96%	96%
AFL-CIO	0%	n/a
CCUS	100%	83%

Elections

	1992	1998
General	59%	66%
Primary	u/o	u/o

Jack Reed (D-R.I.)
Of Cranston • Elected 1996

Born: Nov. 12, 1949, Providence, R.I.
Education: U.S. Military Academy, B.S. 1971; Harvard U., M.P.P. 1973, J.D. 1982.
Military Career: Army, 1967–79; Army Reserve, 1979–91.
Occupation: Lawyer.
Family: Single.
Religion: Roman Catholic.
Political Career: R.I. Senate, 1985–91; U.S. House, 1991–97.

Capitol Office: 320 Hart Senate Office Building 20510; 224-4642; (fax) 224-4680; (e-mail) jack@reed.senate.gov; (web) www.senate.gov/~reed.
Office Staff: Admin. Asst., J.B. Poersch; Legis. Dir., Neil Campbell; Press Secy., Vacant; Scheduler, Roseanne Haroian.
Committees: Special Aging; Armed Services (Airland Forces; Personnel; Seapower); Banking, Housing & Urban Affairs (Financial Institutions; Economic Policy — ranking member; Securities); Health, Education, Labor & Pensions (Children & Families; Public Health).

Rhode Island — The statewide vote for Bill Clinton was 60% in 1996.

CQ Voting Studies

	1997	1998
Presidential	86%	90%
Party	98%	98%
Participation	99%	100%

Interest Groups

	1997	1998
ADA	100%	95%
ACU	0%	0%
AFL-CIO	100%	n/a
CCUS	44%	56%

Elections

	1996
General	63%
Primary	86%

Harry Reid (D–Nev.)
Of Searchlight • Elected 1986

Born: Dec. 2, 1939, Searchlight, Nev.
Education: Southern Utah State College, A.S. 1959; Utah State U., B.A. 1961; George Washington U., J.D. 1964; U. of Nevada, Las Vegas, attended 1969–70.
Occupation: Lawyer.
Family: Wife, Landra; five children.
Religion: Mormon.
Political Career: Nev. Assembly, 1969–71; lieutenant governor, 1971–75; Democratic nominee for U.S. Senate, 1974; candidate for mayor of Las Vegas, 1975; Nevada Gaming Commission chairman, 1977–81; U.S. House, 1983–87.

Capitol Office: 528 Hart Senate Office Building 20510; 224-3542; (fax) 224-7327; (e-mail) senator_reid@reid.senate.gov; (web) www.senate.gov/~reid.
Office Staff: Chief of Staff, Susan McCue; Legis. Dir., Jim Ryan; Press Secy., Jenny Backus; Scheduler, Sheila Brown.
Committees: Special Aging; Appropriations (Energy & Water Development — ranking member; Interior; Labor, Health & Human Services & Education; Military Construction; Transportation); Environment & Public Works (Fisheries, Wildlife & Drinking Water — ranking member; Transportation & Infrastructure); Select Ethics — vice chairman; Indian Affairs.

Nevada — The statewide vote for Bill Clinton was 44% in 1996.

CQ Voting Studies

	1997	1998
Presidential	84%	76%
Party	83%	78%
Participation	99%	98%

Interest Groups

	1997	1998
ADA	85%	90%
ACU	8%	20%
AFL-CIO	86%	n/a
CCUS	50%	56%

Elections

	1992	1998
General	51%	48%
Primary	53%	u/o

Charles S. Robb (D–Va.)
Of McLean • Elected 1988

Born: June 26, 1939, Phoenix, Ariz.
Education: Cornell U., attended 1957–58; U. of Wisconsin, B.B.A. 1961; U. of Virginia, J.D. 1973.
Military Career: Marine Corps, 1961–70; Marine Corps Reserve, 1970–91.
Occupation: Lawyer.
Family: Wife, Lynda; three children.
Religion: Episcopalian.
Political Career: Lieutenant governor, 1978–82; governor, 1982–86.

Capitol Office: 154 Russell Senate Office Building 20510; 224-4024; (fax) 224-8689; (e-mail) senator@robb.senate.gov; (web) www.senate.gov/~robb.
Office Staff: Chief of Staff, Thomas Lehner; Legis. Dir., C. Ridge Schuyler; Press Secy., John DiBiase; Scheduler, Jennifer Ney.
Committees: Armed Services (Readiness & Management Support — ranking member; Seapower; Strategic Forces); Finance (International Trade; Social Security & Family Policy; Taxation & IRS Oversight); Select Intelligence.

Virginia — The statewide vote for Bill Clinton was 45% in 1996.

CQ Voting Studies

	1997	1998
Presidential	87%	90%
Party	71%	83%
Participation	100%	100%

Interest Groups

	1997	1998
ADA	60%	80%
ACU	4%	12%
AFL-CIO	43%	n/a
CCUS	70%	72%

Elections

	1988	1994
General	71%	46%
Primary	u/o	58%

Pat Roberts (R–Kan.)
Of Dodge City • Elected 1996

Born: Apr. 20, 1936, Topeka, Kan.
Education: Kansas State U., B.A. 1958; Arizona State U., attended 1962–64.
Military Career: Marine Corps, 1958–62.
Occupation: Journalist; congressional aide.
Family: Wife, Franki; three children.
Religion: Methodist.
Political Career: U.S. House, 1981–97.

Capitol Office: 302 Hart Senate Office Building 20510; 224-4774; (fax) 224-3514; (e-mail) pat_roberts@roberts.senate.gov; (web) www.senate.gov/~roberts.
Office Staff: Chief of Staff, Leroy Towns; Legis. Dir., Heide Cashman; Press Secy., Betsy Holahan; Scheduler, Maggie Ward.
Committees: Agriculture, Nutrition & Forestry (Production & Price Competitiveness — chairman; Research, Nutrition & General Legislation); Armed Services (Airland Forces; Emerging Threats & Capabilities — chairman; Readiness & Management Support); Select Ethics; Select Intelligence.

Kansas — The statewide vote for Bill Clinton was 36% in 1996.

CQ Voting Studies

	1997	1998
Presidential	59%	35%
Party	87%	94%
Participation	97%	99%

Interest Groups

	1997	1998
ADA	15%	0%
ACU	68%	84%
AFL-CIO	0%	n/a
CCUS	90%	100%

Elections

	1996
General	62%
Primary	78%

John D. Rockefeller IV (D–W.Va.)
Of Charleston • Elected 1984

Born: June 18, 1937, New York, N.Y.
Education: International Christian U. (Tokyo), attended 1957–60; Harvard U., A.B. 1961.
Occupation: College president; public official.
Family: Wife, Sharon Percy; four children.
Religion: Presbyterian.
Political Career: W.Va. House, 1967–69; W.Va. secretary of state, 1969–73; Democratic nominee for governor, 1972; governor, 1977–85.

Capitol Office: 531 Hart Senate Office Building 20510; 224-6472; (fax) 224-7665; (e–mail) senator@rockefeller.senate.gov; (web) www.senate.gov/~rockefeller.
Office Staff: Chief of Staff, Tamera Luzzatto; Legis. Dir., Ellen Doneski; Communications Dir., Don Marshall; Scheduler, Shelby Brown.
Committees: Commerce, Science & Transportation (Aviation — ranking member; Communications; Manufacturing & Competitiveness; Science, Technology & Space); Finance (Health Care — ranking member; International Trade; Social Security & Family Policy); Veterans' Affairs — ranking member.

West Virginia — The statewide vote for Bill Clinton was 51% in 1996.

CQ Voting Studies

	1997	1998
Presidential	79%	82%
Party	83%	88%
Participation	95%	93%

Interest Groups

	1997	1998
ADA	70%	90%
ACU	8%	0%
AFL-CIO	71%	n/a
CCUS	67%	56%

Elections

	1990	1996
General	68%	77%
Primary	85%	88%

William V. Roth Jr. (R–Del.)
Of Wilmington • Elected 1970

Born: July 22, 1921, Great Falls, Mont.
Education: U. of Oregon, B.A. 1944; Harvard U., M.B.A. 1947, LL.B. 1949.
Military Career: Army, 1943–46.
Occupation: Lawyer.
Family: Wife, Jane Richards; two children.
Religion: Episcopalian.
Political Career: Republican nominee for lieutenant governor, 1960; Del. Republican Party chairman, 1961–64; U.S. House, 1967–70.

Capitol Office: 104 Hart Senate Office Building 20510; 224-2441; (e–mail) comments@roth.senate.gov; (web) www.senate.gov/~roth.
Office Staff: Admin. Asst./Legis. Dir., John M. Duncan; Press Secy., Brian Tassinari; Appts. Secy., Susie Cohen.
Committees: Joint Economic; Joint Taxation — vice chairman; Finance — chairman (Health Care; International Trade; Taxation & IRS Oversight); Governmental Affairs (Oversight of Government Management; Investigations).

Delaware — The statewide vote for Bill Clinton was 52% in 1996.

CQ Voting Studies

	1997	1998
Presidential	62%	58%
Party	79%	75%
Participation	98%	96%

Interest Groups

	1997	1998
ADA	10%	15%
ACU	64%	65%
AFL-CIO	0%	n/a
CCUS	100%	78%

Elections

	1988	1994
General	62%	56%
Primary	u/o	u/o

Rick Santorum (R–Pa.)
Of Pittsburgh • Elected 1994
Pronounced: san-TORE-um

Born: May 10, 1958, Winchester, Va.
Education: Pennsylvania State U., B.A. 1980; U. of Pittsburgh, M.B.A. 1981; Dickinson School of Law, J.D. 1986.
Occupation: Lawyer; legislative aide.
Family: Wife, Karen Garver Santorum; four children.
Religion: Roman Catholic.
Political Career: U.S. House, 1991–95.

Capitol Office: 120 Russell Senate Office Building 20510; 224-6324; (fax) 228-0604; (e–mail) senator@santorum.senate.gov; (web) www.senate.gov/~santorum.
Office Staff: Chief of Staff, Mark D. Rodgers; Legis. Dir., Mike Hershey; Communications Dir., Melissa Sabatine; Scheduler, Ramona Ely.
Committees: Special Aging; Agriculture, Nutrition & Forestry (Forestry, Conservation & Rural Revitalization; Research, Nutrition & General Legislation); Armed Services (Airland Forces — chairman; Emerging Threats & Capabilities; Readiness & Management Support); Banking, Housing & Urban Affairs (Financial Institutions; Housing & Transportation; Securities); Rules & Administration.

Pennsylvania — The statewide vote for Bill Clinton was 49% in 1996.

CQ Voting Studies

	1997	1998
Presidential	60%	40%
Party	90%	91%
Participation	99%	99%

Interest Groups

	1997	1998
ADA	15%	0%
ACU	84%	84%
AFL-CIO	14%	n/a
CCUS	90%	89%

Elections

	1994
General	49%
Primary	82%

Paul S. Sarbanes (D–Md.)
Of Baltimore • Elected 1976

Born: Feb. 3, 1933, Salisbury, Md.
Education: Princeton U., A.B. 1954; Oxford U., B.A. 1957; Harvard U., LL.B. 1960.
Occupation: Lawyer.
Family: Wife, Christine Dunbar; three children.
Religion: Greek Orthodox.
Political Career: Md. House, 1967–71; U.S. House, 1971–77.

Capitol Office: 309 Hart Senate Office Building 20510; 224-4524; (fax) 224-1651; (e–mail) senator@sarbanes.senate.gov; (web) www.senate.gov/~sarbanes.
Office Staff: Chief of Staff, Peter Marudas; Legis. Dir./Deputy Chief of Staff, Julie Kehrli; Press Secy., Jesse Jacobs; Appts. Secy., Elise Gillette.
Committees: Joint Economic; Banking, Housing & Urban Affairs — ranking member (Financial Institutions); Budget; Foreign Relations (African Affairs; European Affairs; International Economic Policy, Export & Trade Promotion — ranking member; Near Eastern & South Asian Affairs).

Maryland — The statewide vote for Bill Clinton was 54% in 1996.

CQ Voting Studies

	1997	1998
Presidential	87%	92%
Party	97%	99%
Participation	99%	99%

Interest Groups

	1997	1998
ADA	100%	95%
ACU	0%	4%
AFL-CIO	100%	n/a
CCUS	30%	44%

Elections

	1988	1994
General	62%	59%
Primary	86%	79%

Charles E. Schumer (D-N.Y.)
Of Brooklyn • Elected 1998

Born: Nov. 23, 1950, Brooklyn, N.Y.
Education: Harvard U., B.A. 1971, J.D. 1974.
Occupation: Lawyer.
Family: Wife, Iris Weinshall; two children.
Religion: Jewish.
Political Career: N.Y. Assembly, 1975–81; U.S. House, 1981–99.

Capitol Office: 313 Hart Senate Office Building 20510; 224-6542; (fax) 228-3027.
Office Staff: Chief of Staff, Josh Isay.
Committees: Banking, Housing & Urban Affairs (Financial Institutions; International Trade & Finance; Securities); Judiciary (Administrative Oversight & the Courts; Immigration; Criminal Justice Oversight — ranking member); Rules & Administration.

New York — The statewide vote for Bill Clinton was 59% in 1996.

Elections

	1998
General	55%
Primary	51%

Jeff Sessions (R-Ala.)
Of Mobile • Elected 1996

Born: Dec. 24, 1946, Hybart, Ala.
Education: Huntingdon College, B.A. 1969; U. of Alabama, J.D. 1973.
Military Career: Army Reserve, 1973–86.
Occupation: Lawyer.
Family: Wife, Mary Blackshear Sessions; three children.
Religion: Methodist.
Political Career: Assistant U.S. attorney, 1975–77; U.S. Attorney, 1981–93; Ala. attorney general, 1995–97.

Capitol Office: 495 Russell Senate Office Building 20510; 224-4124; (fax) 224-3149; (e-mail) senator@sessions.senate.gov; (web) www.senate.gov/~sessions.
Office Staff: Chief of Staff, Armand DeKeyser; Legis. Dir., Rick Dearborn; Press Secy., John Cox; Scheduler, Kate Hollis.
Committees: Joint Economic; Armed Services (Emerging Threats & Capabilities; Seapower; Strategic Forces); Judiciary (Administrative Oversight & the Courts; Youth Violence — chairman); Health, Education, Labor & Pensions (Employment, Safety & Training; Public Health).

Alabama — The statewide vote for Bill Clinton was 43% in 1996.

CQ Voting Studies

	1997	1998
Presidential	56%	28%
Party	99%	98%
Participation	99%	97%

Interest Groups

	1997	1998
ADA	0%	0%
ACU	100%	100%
AFL-CIO	0%	n/a
CCUS	70%	89%

Elections

	1996
General	52%
Primary	*59%

*Runoff election

Richard C. Shelby (R–Ala.)
Of Tuscaloosa • Elected 1986

Born: May 6, 1934, Birmingham, Ala.
Education: U. of Alabama, A.B. 1957, LL.B. 1963.
Occupation: Lawyer.
Family: Wife, Annette Nevin Shelby; two children.
Religion: Presbyterian.
Political Career: Ala. Senate, 1971–79, served as a Democrat; U.S. House, 1979–87, served as a Democrat.

Capitol Office: 110 Hart Senate Office Building 20510; 224-5744; (fax) 224-3416; (e-mail) senator@shelby.senate.gov; (web) www.senate.gov/~shelby.
Office Staff: Chief of Staff, Tom Young; Legis. Dir., Kathy Casey; Press Secy., Laura Cox; Office Mgr./Scheduler, Anne Caldwell.
Committees: Special Aging; Appropriations (Defense; Foreign Operations; Transportation — chairman; Treasury & General Government; VA, HUD & Independent Agencies); Banking, Housing & Urban Affairs (Financial Institutions; Housing & Transportation; Securities); Select Intelligence — chairman.

Alabama — The statewide vote for Bill Clinton was 43% in 1996.

CQ Voting Studies

	1997	1998
Presidential	57%	33%
Party	93%	91%
Participation	100%	98%

Interest Groups

	1997	1998
ADA	5%	5%
ACU	92%	92%
AFL-CIO	14%	n/a
CCUS	90%	78%

Elections

	1992	1998
General	65%	63%
Primary	u/o	u/o

Gordon H. Smith (R–Ore.)
Of Pendleton • Elected 1996

Born: May 25, 1952, Pendleton, Ore.
Education: Brigham Young U., B.A. 1976; Southwestern U., J.D. 1979.
Occupation: Frozen food company executive; lawyer.
Family: Wife, Sharon; three children.
Religion: Mormon.
Political Career: Ore. Senate, 1993–97, Senate president, 1995–97; Republican nominee for U.S. Senate, 1996, special election.

Capitol Office: 359 Dirksen Senate Office Building 20510; 224-3753; (fax) 228-3997; (e-mail) oregon@gsmith.senate.gov; (web) www.senate.gov/~gsmith.
Office Staff: Chief of Staff, Kurt Pfotenhauer; Legis. Dir., Penny Schiller; Press Secy., Mary Healy; Scheduler, Sue Keenom.
Committees: Budget; Energy & Natural Resources (Energy Research, Development, Production & Regulation; Forests & Public Land Management; Water & Power — chairman); Foreign Relations (East Asian & Pacific Affairs; European Affairs — chairman; Near Eastern & South Asian Affairs); Year 2000 Technology Problem.

Oregon — The statewide vote for Bill Clinton was 47% in 1996.

CQ Voting Studies

	1997	1998
Presidential	65%	54%
Party	83%	85%
Participation	99%	99%

Interest Groups

	1997	1998
ADA	25%	5%
ACU	72%	72%
AFL-CIO	0%	n/a
CCUS	100%	94%

Elections

	1996
General	50%
Primary	78%

Robert C. Smith (R-N.H.)
Of Tuftonboro • Elected 1990

Born: Mar. 30, 1941, Trenton, N.J.
Education: Trenton Junior College, A.A. 1963; Lafayette College, B.A. 1965; California State U., Long Beach, attended 1968–69.
Military Career: Naval Reserve, 1962–65; Navy, 1965–67; Naval Reserve, 1967–69.
Occupation: Real estate broker; high school teacher.
Family: Wife, Mary Jo; three children.
Religion: Roman Catholic.
Political Career: Gov. Wentworth Regional School Board (Wolfeboro, N.H.), 1978–84; sought Republican nomination for U.S. House, 1980; Republican nominee for U.S. House, 1982; U.S. House, 1985–91.

Capitol Office: 307 Dirksen Senate Office Building 20510; 224-2841; (fax) 224-1353; (e-mail) opinion@smith.senate.gov; (web) www.senate.gov/~smith.
Office Staff: Chief of Staff, Patrick Pettey; Legis. Dir./General Counsel, Rick Valentine; Press Secy., Lisa Harrison; Scheduler, Alexandra Johnson.
Committees: Armed Services (Emerging Threats & Capabilities; Seapower; Strategic Forces — chairman); Environment & Public Works (Superfund, Waste Control & Risk Assessment — chairman; Transportation & Infrastructure); Select Ethics — chairman; Judiciary (Constitution, Federalism & Property Rights; Youth Violence).

New Hampshire — The statewide vote for Bill Clinton was 50% in 1996.

CQ Voting Studies

	1997	1998
Presidential	51%	19%
Party	97%	98%
Participation	100%	99%

Interest Groups

	1997	1998
ADA	5%	5%
ACU	96%	100%
AFL-CIO	14%	n/a
CCUS	50%	78%

Elections

	1990	1996
General	65%	49%
Primary	65%	u/o

Olympia J. Snowe (R–Maine)
Of Falmouth • Elected 1994

Born: Feb. 21, 1947, Augusta, Maine.
Education: U. of Maine, B.A. 1969.
Occupation: Public official.
Family: Husband, John R. McKernan Jr.
Religion: Greek Orthodox.
Political Career: Maine House, 1973–77; Maine Senate, 1977–79; U.S. House, 1979–95.

Capitol Office: 250 Russell Senate Office Building 20510; 224-5344; (fax) 224-1946; (e-mail) olympia@snowe.senate.gov; (web) www.senate.gov/~snowe.
Office Staff: Chief of Staff, Kevin Raye; Legis. Dir., Jane Calderwood; Communications Dir., Dave Lackey; Exec. Asst./Scheduler, Marilyn Abel.
Committees: Armed Services (Emerging Threats & Capabilities; Personnel; Seapower — chairman); Budget; Commerce, Science & Transportation (Aviation; Manufacturing & Competitiveness; Oceans & Fisheries — chairman; Surface Transportation & Merchant Marine); Small Business.

Maine — The statewide vote for Bill Clinton was 52% in 1996.

CQ Voting Studies

	1997	1998
Presidential	78%	54%
Party	59%	65%
Participation	100%	99%

Interest Groups

	1997	1998
ADA	55%	35%
ACU	44%	40%
AFL-CIO	43%	n/a
CCUS	70%	78%

Elections

	1994
General	60%
Primary	u/o

Arlen Specter (R–Pa.)
Of Philadelphia • Elected 1980

Born: Feb. 12, 1930, Wichita, Kan.
Education: U. of Pennsylvania, B.A. 1951; Yale U., LL.B. 1956.
Military Career: Air Force, 1951–53.
Occupation: Lawyer; professor.
Family: Wife, Joan; two children.
Religion: Jewish.
Political Career: Philadelphia district attorney, 1966–74; Republican nominee for mayor of Philadelphia, 1967; defeated for re-election as district attorney, 1973; sought Republican nomination for U.S. Senate, 1976; sought Republican nomination for governor, 1978.
Capitol Office: 711 Hart Senate Office Building 20510; 224-4254; (fax) 228-1229; (e-mail) senator_specter@specter.senate.gov; (web) www.senate.gov/~specter.
Office Staff: Chief of Staff, David Urban; Legis. Dir., Dan Renberg; Press Secy., John Ullyot; Scheduler, Patricia Haag.
Committees: Appropriations (Agriculture, Rural Development & Related Agencies; Defense; Foreign Operations; Labor, Health & Human Services & Education — chairman; Transportation); Governmental Affairs (International Security, Proliferation & Federal Services; Investigations); Judiciary (Antitrust, Business Rights & Competition; Constitution, Federalism & Property Rights; Immigration); Veterans' Affairs — chairman.

Pennsylvania — The statewide vote for Bill Clinton was 49% in 1996.

CQ Voting Studies

	1997	1998
Presidential	71%	49%
Party	50%	41%
Participation	99%	86%

Interest Groups

	1997	1998
ADA	70%	45%
ACU	32%	33%
AFL-CIO	57%	n/a
CCUS	50%	60%

Elections

	1992	1998
General	49%	61%
Primary	65%	67%

Ted Stevens (R–Alaska)
Of Girdwood • Elected 1970
Appointed to the Senate 1968

Born: Nov. 18, 1923, Indianapolis, Ind.
Education: U. of California, Los Angeles, B.A. 1947; Harvard U., LL.B. 1950.
Military Career: Army Air Corps, 1943–46.
Occupation: Lawyer.
Family: Wife, Catherine Chandler; six children.
Religion: Episcopalian.
Political Career: U.S. attorney for Alaska, 1953–56; Republican nominee for U.S. Senate, 1962; Alaska House, 1965–68, majority leader and speaker pro tempore, 1967–68; sought Republican nomination for U.S. Senate, 1968.
Capitol Office: 522 Hart Senate Office Building 20510; 224-3004; (fax) 224-2354; (e-mail) senator_stevens@stevens.senate.gov; (web) www.senate.gov/~stevens.
Office Staff: Chief of Staff, Mitch Rose; Legis. Dir., Trevor McCabe; Press Secy., Connie Godwin; Scheduler, DeLynn Henry.
Committees: Joint Library — chairman; Appropriations — chairman (Commerce, Justice, State & Judiciary; Defense — chairman; Interior; Labor, Health & Human Services & Education; Legislative Branch); Commerce, Science & Transportation (Aviation; Communications; Oceans & Fisheries; Science, Technology & Space; Surface Transportation & Merchant Marine); Governmental Affairs (International Security, Proliferation & Federal Services; Investigations); Rules & Administration.

Alaska — The statewide vote for Bill Clinton was 33% in 1996.

CQ Voting Studies

	1997	1998
Presidential	71%	53%
Party	78%	82%
Participation	99%	99%

Interest Groups

	1997	1998
ADA	30%	20%
ACU	58%	56%
AFL-CIO	14%	n/a
CCUS	80%	94%

Elections

	1990	1996
General	66%	77%
Primary	*59%	68%

*Open primary

Craig Thomas (R–Wyo.)
Of Casper • Elected 1994

Born: Feb. 17, 1933, Cody, Wyo.
Education: U. of Wyoming, B.A. 1955; La Salle U., LL.B. 1963.
Military Career: Marine Corps, 1955–59.
Occupation: Power company executive.
Family: Wife, Susan; four children.
Religion: Methodist.
Political Career: Sought Republican nomination for Wyo. treasurer, 1978, 1982; Wyo. House, 1985–89; U.S. House, 1989–95.

Capitol Office: 109 Hart Senate Office Building 20510; 224-6441; (fax) 224-1724; (e-mail) craig@thomas.senate.gov; (web) www.senate.gov/~thomas.
Office Staff: Chief of Staff, Dan Naatz; Legis. Dir., Chris Jahn; Press Secy., Dan Kunsman; Scheduler, Kathi Wise.
Committees: Energy & Natural Resources (Forests & Public Land Management; National Parks, Historic Preservation & Recreation — chairman); Environment & Public Works (Fisheries, Wildlife & Drinking Water; Transportation & Infrastructure); Foreign Relations (East Asian & Pacific Affairs — chairman; International Economic Policy, Export & Trade Promotion; Near Eastern & South Asian Affairs); Indian Affairs.

Wyoming — The statewide vote for Bill Clinton was 37% in 1996.

CQ Voting Studies

	1997	1998
Presidential	57%	39%
Party	98%	94%
Participation	99%	99%

Interest Groups

	1997	1998
ADA	10%	5%
ACU	84%	84%
AFL-CIO	0%	n/a
CCUS	90%	89%

Elections

	1994
General	59%
Primary	u/o

Fred Thompson (R–Tenn.)
Of Nashville • Elected 1994

Born: Aug. 19, 1942, Sheffield, Ala.
Education: Memphis State U., B.S. 1964; Vanderbilt U., J.D. 1967.
Occupation: Lawyer; actor.
Family: Divorced; three children.
Religion: Protestant.
Political Career: Assistant U.S. attorney, 1969–72.

Capitol Office: 523 Dirksen Senate Office Building 20510; 224-4944; (fax) 228-3679; (e-mail) kelley_hankins@thompson.senate.gov; (web) www.senate.gov/~thompson.
Office Staff: Chief of Staff, Powell A. Moore; Legis. Dir., Libby Wood; Press Secy., Harvey Valentine; Exec. Asst., Bonnie Sansonetti.
Committees: Finance (Health Care; International Trade; Social Security & Family Policy; Taxation & IRS Oversight); Governmental Affairs — chairman.

Tennessee — The statewide vote for Bill Clinton was 48% in 1996.

CQ Voting Studies

	1997	1998
Presidential	59%	42%
Party	89%	87%
Participation	100%	100%

Interest Groups

	1997	1998
ADA	0%	10%
ACU	88%	84%
AFL-CIO	0%	n/a
CCUS	60%	89%

Elections

	1994	1996
General	*60%	61%
Primary	*64%	94%

*Special election

Strom Thurmond (R–S.C.)
Of Aiken • Elected 1954
Did not serve April-Nov. 1956

Born: Dec. 5, 1902, Edgefield, S.C.
Education: Clemson U., B.S. 1923.
Military Career: Army Reserve, 1924–41; Army, 1942–46; Army Reserve, 1947–65.
Occupation: Lawyer; teacher.
Family: Separated; three children.
Religion: Baptist.
Political Career: Edgefield superintendent of education, 1929–33; S.C. Senate, 1933–38; S.C. Circuit Court of Appeals, 1938–46; governor, 1947–51; States' Rights nominee for president, 1948; sought Democratic nomination for U.S. Senate, 1950.

Capitol Office: 217 Russell Senate Office Building 20510; 224-5972; (fax) 224-1300; (e-mail) senator@thurmond.senate.gov; (web) www.senate.gov/~thurmond.
Office Staff: Chief of Staff, R.J. Duke Short; Legis. Dir., Vacant; Press Secy., John DeCrosta; Exec. Asst., Holly Richardson.
Committees: Armed Services (Personnel; Readiness & Management Support; Strategic Forces); Judiciary (Administrative Oversight & the Courts; Antitrust, Business Rights & Competition; Constitution, Federalism & Property Rights; Criminal Justice Oversight — chairman); Veterans' Affairs.

South Carolina — The statewide vote for Bill Clinton was 44% in 1996.

CQ Voting Studies

	1997	1998
Presidential	57%	44%
Party	95%	91%
Participation	99%	99%

Interest Groups

	1997	1998
ADA	5%	0%
ACU	96%	76%
AFL-CIO	14%	n/a
CCUS	80%	94%

Elections

	1990	1996
General	64%	53%
Primary	u/o	60%

Robert G. Torricelli (D–N.J.)
Of Englewood • Elected 1996
Pronounced: tor–uh-SELL-ee

Born: Aug. 26, 1951, Paterson, N.J.
Education: Rutgers U., A.B. 1974, J.D. 1977; Harvard U., M.P.A. 1980.
Occupation: Lawyer; campaign aide.
Family: Divorced.
Religion: Methodist.
Political Career: U.S. House, 1983–97.

Capitol Office: 113 Dirksen Senate Office Building 20510; 224-3224; (fax) 224-8567; (e-mail) senator_torricelli@torricelli.senate.com; (web) www.senate.gov/~torricelli.
Office Staff: Admin. Asst., James P. Fox; Legis. Dir., Eric Shuffler; Communications Dir., Joy Howell; Scheduler, Lona Valmoro.
Committees: Foreign Relations (East Asian & Pacific Affairs; Near Eastern & South Asian Affairs; Western Hemisphere); Governmental Affairs (International Security, Proliferation & Federal Services; Oversight of Government Management); Judiciary (Administrative Oversight & the Courts — ranking member; Antitrust, Business Rights & Competition; Criminal Justice Oversight); Rules & Administration.

New Jersey — The statewide vote for Bill Clinton was 53% in 1996.

CQ Voting Studies

	1997	1998
Presidential	89%	75%
Party	90%	83%
Participation	100%	98%

Interest Groups

	1997	1998
ADA	80%	85%
ACU	16%	8%
AFL-CIO	86%	n/a
CCUS	40%	47%

Elections

	1996
General	53%
Primary	u/o

George V. Voinovich (R–Ohio)
Of Cleveland • Elected 1998

Born: July 15, 1936, Collinwood, Ohio.
Education: Ohio U., B.A. 1958; Ohio State U., J.D. 1961.
Occupation: Lawyer.
Family: Wife, Janet; three children.
Religion: Roman Catholic.
Political Career: Ohio assistant attorney general, 1963–64; Ohio House, 1967–71; Cuyahoga County auditor, 1971–76; Cuyahoga County Commission, 1977–78; lieutenant governor, 1979; mayor of Cleveland, 1979–90; Republican nominee for U.S. Senate, 1988; governor, 1991–99.

Capitol Office: 317 Hart Senate Office Building 20510; 224-3353; (fax) 228-1382; (e-mail) senator_voinovich@voinovich.senate.gov.
Office Staff: Chief of Staff, Ted Hollingsworth; Legis. Dir., Wayne Palmer; Press Secy., Mike Dawson; Scheduler, Abbey Fox.
Committees: Environment & Public Works (Clean Air, Wetlands, Private Property & Nuclear Safety; Transportation & Infrastructure — chairman); Select Ethics; Governmental Affairs (Oversight of Government Management — chairman; Investigations); Small Business.

Elections

	1998
General	56%
Primary	72%

Ohio — The statewide vote for Bill Clinton was 47% in 1996.

John W. Warner (R–Va.)
Of Alexandria • Elected 1978

Born: Feb. 18, 1927, Washington, D.C.
Education: Washington and Lee U., B.S. 1949; U. of Virginia, LL.B. 1953.
Military Career: Navy, 1944–46; Marine Corps, 1950–52; Marine Corps Reserve, 1952–64.
Occupation: Lawyer; farmer.
Family: Divorced; three children.
Religion: Episcopalian.
Political Career: Assistant U.S. attorney, 1956–60; under secretary of the Navy, 1969–72; secretary of the Navy, 1972–74.

Capitol Office: 225 Russell Senate Office Building 20510; 224-2023; (fax) 224-6295; (e-mail) senator@warner.senate.gov; (web) www.senate.gov/~warner.
Office Staff: Chief of Staff, Susan Magill; Legis. Dir., Ann Loomis; Communications Dir., Carter Cornick; Personal Asst./Scheduler, Eileen Mandel.
Committees: Armed Services — chairman; Environment & Public Works (Fisheries, Wildlife & Drinking Water; Superfund, Waste Control & Risk Assessment; Transportation & Infrastructure); Rules & Administration.

CQ Voting Studies

	1997	1998
Presidential	63%	38%
Party	88%	83%
Participation	98%	97%

Interest Groups

	1997	1998
ADA	10%	20%
ACU	80%	79%
AFL-CIO	0%	n/a
CCUS	100%	100%

Elections

	1990	1996
General	81%	52%
Primary	u/o	65%

Virginia — The statewide vote for Bill Clinton was 45% in 1996.

Paul Wellstone (D–Minn.)
Of St. Paul • Elected 1990

Born: July 21, 1944, Washington, D.C.
Education: U. of North Carolina, B.A. 1965, Ph.D. 1969.
Occupation: Professor.
Family: Wife, Sheila Ison; three children.
Religion: Jewish.
Political Career: Democratic nominee for Minn. auditor, 1982; Democratic National Committee, 1984–91.

Capitol Office: 136 Hart Senate Office Building 20510; 224-5641; (fax) 224-8438; (e-mail) senator@wellstone.senate.gov; (web) www.senate.gov/~wellstone.
Office Staff: Chief of Staff, Colin McGinnis; Legis. Dir., Mike Epstein; Communications Dir., Jim Farrell; Scheduler, Jennifer Lambert-O'Keefe.
Committees: Foreign Relations (East Asian & Pacific Affairs; European Affairs; Near Eastern & South Asian Affairs — ranking member); Indian Affairs; Health, Education, Labor & Pensions (Children & Families; Employment, Safety & Training — ranking member); Small Business; Veterans' Affairs.

Minnesota — The statewide vote for Bill Clinton was 51% in 1996.

CQ Voting Studies

	1997	1998
Presidential	83%	85%
Party	91%	98%
Participation	96%	97%

Interest Groups

	1997	1998
ADA	100%	100%
ACU	4%	4%
AFL-CIO	100%	n/a
CCUS	10%	22%

Elections

	1990	1996
General	50%	50%
Primary	60%	86%

Ron Wyden (D–Ore.)
Of Portland • Elected 1996

Born: May 3, 1949, Wichita, Kan.
Education: U. of California, Santa Barbara, attended 1967–69; Stanford U., A.B. 1971; U. of Oregon, J.D. 1974.
Occupation: Lawyer; professor.
Family: Wife, Laurie; two children.
Religion: Jewish.
Political Career: U.S. House, 1981–96.

Capitol Office: 717 Hart Senate Office Building 20510; 224-5244; (fax) 228-2717; (e-mail) senator@wyden.senate.gov; (web) www.senate.gov/~wyden.
Office Staff: Chief of Staff, Josh R. Kardon; Legis. Dir., Carole Grunberg; Communications Dir., David Seldin; Scheduler, Bruce Ehrle.
Committees: Special Aging; Budget; Commerce, Science & Transportation (Aviation; Communications; Surface Transportation & Merchant Marine); Energy & Natural Resources (Forests & Public Land Management — ranking member; Water & Power); Environment & Public Works (Fisheries, Wildlife & Drinking Water).

Oregon — The statewide vote for Bill Clinton was 47% in 1996.

CQ Voting Studies

	1997	1998
Presidential	81%	79%
Party	83%	86%
Participation	99%	96%

Interest Groups

	1997	1998
ADA	80%	100%
ACU	8%	4%
AFL-CIO	71%	n/a
CCUS	70%	56%

Elections

	1996	1998
General	*48%	61%
Primary		92%

*Special election

U.S. REPRESENTATIVES

Neil Abercrombie (D–Hawaii)
Of Honolulu • *Elected 1990*
Also served Sept. 1986–Jan. 1987

Born: June 26, 1938, Buffalo, N.Y.
Education: Union College, B.A. 1959; U. of Hawaii, M.A. 1964, Ph.D. 1974.
Occupation: Educator.
Family: Wife, Nancie Caraway.
Religion: Unspecified.
Political Career: Sought Democratic nomination for U.S. Senate, 1970; Hawaii House, 1975–79; Hawaii Senate, 1979–86; sought Democratic nomination for U.S. House, 1986; U.S. House, 1986–87; Honolulu City Council, 1988–90.

Capitol Office: 1502 Longworth House Office Building 20515; 225-2726; (fax) 225-4580; (e–mail) neil.abercrombie@mail.house.gov; (web) www.house.gov/abercrombie.
Office Staff: Chief of Staff, Alan Yamamoto; Legis. Dir., Tom Wanley; Communications Dir., Michael Slackman; Scheduler, Patti Itamoto.
Committees: Armed Services (Military Installations & Facilities; Military Personnel — ranking member); Resources (Fisheries Conservation, Wildlife & Oceans).

Hawaii 1st — Honolulu — Pearl City. The district vote for Bill Clinton was 57% in 1996.

CQ Voting Studies

	1997	1998
Presidential	72%	82%
Party	85%	91%
Participation	98%	99%

Interest Groups

	1997	1998
ADA	95%	95%
ACU	20%	12%
AFL-CIO	100%	n/a
CCUS	30%	22%

Elections

	1996	1998
General	50%	62%
Primary	72%	91%

Gary L. Ackerman (D–N.Y.)
Of Queens • *Elected 1983*

Born: Nov. 19, 1942, Brooklyn, N.Y.
Education: Queens College, B.A. 1965.
Occupation: Teacher; publisher and editor; advertising executive.
Family: Wife, Rita; three children.
Religion: Jewish.
Political Career: Sought Democratic nomination for N.Y. City Council at large, 1977; N.Y. Senate, 1979–83.

Capitol Office: 2243 Rayburn House Office Building 20515; 225-2601; (fax) 225-1589; (e–mail) www.house.gov/writerep; (web) www.house.gov/ackerman.
Office Staff: Admin. Asst., Jedd Moskowitz; Legis. Dir., Jonathan Berger; Press Secy., Jordan Goldes; Scheduler, Seth Applebaum.
Committees: Banking & Financial Services (Capital Markets & Securities; Financial Institutions & Consumer Credit); International Relations (Asia & the Pacific; Western Hemisphere — ranking member).

New York 5th — Northeast Queens; northern Nassau and Suffolk counties. The district vote for Bill Clinton was 60% in 1996.

CQ Voting Studies

	1997	1998
Presidential	79%	82%
Party	86%	94%
Participation	91%	92%

Interest Groups

	1997	1998
ADA	80%	100%
ACU	13%	0%
AFL-CIO	100%	n/a
CCUS	33%	35%

Elections

	1996	1998
General	64%	65%
Primary	u/o	u/o

Robert B. Aderholt (R–Ala.)
Of Haleyville • Elected 1996
Pronounced: ADD-er–holt

Born: July 22, 1965, Haleyville, Ala.
Education: Birmingham Southern U., B.A. 1987; Samford U., J.D. 1990.
Occupation: Municipal judge; lawyer; gubernatorial aide.
Family: Wife, Caroline.
Religion: Congregationalist Baptist.
Political Career: Republican nominee for Ala. House, 1990.

Capitol Office: 1007 Longworth House Office Building 20515; 225-4876; (fax) 225-5587; (e–mail) www.house.gov/writerep; (web) www.house.gov/aderholt.

Office Staff: Chief of Staff, Mark Busching; Legis. Dir., Mark Zelden; Press Secy., Laura Woolfrey; Scheduler, Alison Klukas.

Committees: Appropriations (District of Columbia; Military Construction; Transportation).

Alabama 4th — North Central — Gadsden. The district vote for Bill Clinton was 43% in 1996.

CQ Voting Studies

	1997	1998
Presidential	24%	21%
Party	97%	90%
Participation	99%	99%

Interest Groups

	1997	1998
ADA	0%	10%
ACU	96%	96%
AFL-CIO	0%	n/a
CCUS	80%	83%

Elections

	1996	1998
General	50%	56%
Primary	49%	u/o

Tom Allen (D–Maine)
Of Portland • Elected 1996

Born: Apr. 16, 1945, Portland, Maine.
Education: Bowdoin College, B.A. 1967; Oxford U., B.Phil. 1970; Harvard U., J.D. 1974.
Occupation: Policy consultant; lawyer; congressional aide.
Family: Wife, Diana; two children.
Religion: Protestant.
Political Career: Portland City Council, 1989–95; mayor of Portland, 1991–92; sought Democratic nomination for governor, 1994.

Capitol Office: 1717 Longworth House Office Building 20515; 225-6116; (fax) 225-5590; (e–mail) rep.tomallen@mail.house.gov; (web) www.house.gov/allen.

Office Staff: Chief of Staff, Jackie Potter; Legis. Dir., Stella Livanios; Communications Dir., Mark Sullivan; Scheduler, Jean Waskow.

Committees: Armed Services (Military Procurement; Military Research & Development); Government Reform (Civil Service; National Security & Veterans Affairs).

Maine 1st — South — Portland; Augusta. The district vote for Bill Clinton was 52% in 1996.

CQ Voting Studies

	1997	1998
Presidential	81%	82%
Party	94%	91%
Participation	99%	98%

Interest Groups

	1997	1998
ADA	95%	100%
ACU	8%	0%
AFL-CIO	100%	n/a
CCUS	50%	39%

Elections

	1996	1998
General	55%	60%
Primary	52%	u/o

Robert E. Andrews (D–N.J.)
Of Haddon Heights • Elected 1990

Born: Aug. 4, 1957, Camden, N.J.
Education: Bucknell U., B.A. 1979; Cornell U., J.D. 1982.
Occupation: Professor.
Family: Wife, Camille Spinella; two children.
Religion: Episcopalian.
Political Career: Camden County Board of Chosen Freeholders, 1987–90, director, 1988–90; sought Democratic nomination for governor, 1997.

Capitol Office: 2439 Rayburn House Office Building 20515; 225-6501; (fax) 225-6583; (e–mail) rob.andrews@mail.house.gov.
Office Staff: Chief of Staff, David Socolow; Scheduler, Joanne Rising.
Committees: Armed Services (Military Research & Development); Education & Workforce (Employer-Employee Relations — ranking member; Postsecondary Education, Training & Life-Long Learning).

New Jersey 1st — Southwest — Camden. The district vote for Bill Clinton was 59% in 1996.

CQ Voting Studies

	1997	1998
Presidential	60%	77%
Party	77%	84%
Participation	86%	98%

Interest Groups

	1997	1998
ADA	85%	95%
ACU	22%	12%
AFL-CIO	100%	n/a
CCUS	33%	44%

Elections

	1996	1998
General	76%	73%
Primary	u/o	u/o

Bill Archer (R–Texas)
Of Houston • Elected 1970

Born: Mar. 22, 1928, Houston, Texas.
Education: Rice U., attended 1945–46; U. of Texas, B.B.A. 1949, LL.B. 1951.
Military Career: Air Force, 1951–53.
Occupation: Lawyer; feed company executive.
Family: Wife, Sharon Sawyer; five children, two stepchildren.
Religion: Roman Catholic.
Political Career: Hunters Creek Village Council, 1955–62; Texas House, 1967–71.

Capitol Office: 1236 Longworth House Office Building 20515; 225-2571; (fax) 225-4381; (e–mail) www.house.gov/writerep; (web) www.house.gov/archer.
Office Staff: Chief of Staff, Don Carlson; Legis. Dir., Gary Bartlett; Press Secy., Sean Rushton; Exec. Asst., Linda Figura.
Committees: Ways & Means — chairman; Joint Taxation — chairman.

Texas 7th — Western Houston; northwestern suburbs. The district vote for Bill Clinton was 28% in 1996.

CQ Voting Studies

	1997	1998
Presidential	29%	21%
Party	93%	95%
Participation	96%	97%

Interest Groups

	1997	1998
ADA	5%	0%
ACU	80%	92%
AFL-CIO	0%	n/a
CCUS	100%	100%

Elections

	1996	1998
General	81%	93%
Primary		97%

Dick Armey (R–Texas)
Of Irving • Elected 1984

Born: July 7, 1940, Cando, N.D.
Education: Jamestown College, B.A. 1963; U. of North Dakota, M.A. 1964; U. of Oklahoma, Ph.D. 1969.
Occupation: Economist; professor.
Family: Wife, Susan Byrd; five children.
Religion: Presbyterian.
Political Career: No previous office.
Capitol Office: 301 Cannon House Office Building 20515; 225-7772; (fax) 226-8101; (e–mail) www.house.gov/writerep; (web) armey.house.gov.
Office Staff: Admin. Asst., Paul Morrell; Legis. Dir., Gayland Barksdale; Press Secy., Richard Diamond; Scheduler, Leah Leavy.
Committees: Majority Leader (no committee assignments)

Texas 26th — Suburban Dallas; part of Irving. The district vote for Bill Clinton was 30% in 1996.

CQ Voting Studies

	1997	1998
Presidential	25%	22%
Party	94%	94%
Participation	97%	97%

Interest Groups

	1997	1998
ADA	0%	0%
ACU	88%	100%
AFL-CIO	0%	n/a
CCUS	100%	100%

Elections

	1996	1998
General	74%	88%
Primary		u/o

Spencer Bachus (R–Ala.)
Of Birmingham • Elected 1992
Pronounced: BACK-us

Born: Dec. 28, 1947, Birmingham, Ala.
Education: Auburn U., B.A. 1969; U. of Alabama, J.D. 1972.
Military Career: National Guard, 1969–71.
Occupation: Lawyer; manufacturer.
Family: Wife, Linda; three children, two stepchildren.
Religion: Baptist.
Political Career: Ala. Senate, 1983; Ala. House, 1983–87; Ala. Board of Education, 1987–91; candidate for Ala. attorney general, 1990; Ala. Republican Party chairman, 1991–92.

Capitol Office: 442 Cannon House Office Building 20515; 225-4921; (fax) 225-2082; (e–mail) sbachus@mail.house.gov; (web) www.house.gov/bachus.
Office Staff: Chief of Staff/Press Secy., Jeff Emerson; Legis. Dir., Shayne Gill; Scheduler, Gerry Cashin.
Committees: Banking & Financial Services (Domestic & International Monetary Policy — chairman; General Oversight & Investigations); Judiciary (Commercial & Administrative Law; Constitution); Transportation & Infrastructure (Aviation; Ground Transportation; Health).

Alabama 6th — Part of Birmingham and suburbs. The district vote for Bill Clinton was 28% in 1996.

CQ Voting Studies

	1997	1998
Presidential	25%	20%
Party	93%	89%
Participation	99%	99%

Interest Groups

	1997	1998
ADA	0%	5%
ACU	96%	84%
AFL-CIO	13%	n/a
CCUS	90%	89%

Elections

	1996	1998
General	71%	72%
Primary	u/o	u/o

Brian Baird (D-Wash.)
Of Olympia • Elected 1998

Born: Mar. 7, 1956, Chama, N.M.
Education: U. of Utah, B.S. 1977; U. of Wyoming, M.S. 1980, Ph.D. 1984.
Occupation: Professor; psychologist.
Family: Divorced.
Religion: Protestant.
Political Career: Democratic nominee for U.S. House, 1996.

Capitol Office: 1721 Longworth House Office Building 20515; 225-3536; (fax) 225-3478; (e-mail) www.house.gov/writerep.
Office Staff: Chief of Staff, Joe Shoemaker; Legis. Dir., Beth Osborne; Press Secy., Megan Sather; Scheduler, Colleen Hazlett; Scheduler, Cindy Gipson.
Committees: Small Business (Rural Enterprises); Transportation & Infrastructure (Coast Guard & Maritime Transportation; Water Resources & Environment).

Washington 3rd — Southwest — Olympia; Vancouver. The district vote for Bill Clinton was 49% in 1996.

Elections

	1998
General	55%
Primary	*48%

*Open primary

Richard H. Baker (R-La.)
Of Baton Rouge • Elected 1986

Born: May 22, 1948, New Orleans, La.
Education: Louisiana State U., B.A. 1971.
Occupation: Real estate broker.
Family: Wife, Kay; two children.
Religion: Methodist.
Political Career: La. House, 1972–86, served as a Democrat, 1972–85.

Capitol Office: 434 Cannon House Office Building 20515; 225-3901; (fax) 225-7313; (e-mail) www.house.gov/writerep; (web) www.house.gov/baker.
Office Staff: Admin. Asst., Christy Casteel; Press Secy./Legis. Dir., Paul Sawyer; Exec. Asst., Lynn Ann Kirk.
Committees: Banking & Financial Services (Capital Markets & Securities — chairman; Housing & Community Opportunity); Transportation & Infrastructure (Ground Transportation; Water Resources & Environment); Veterans' Affairs.

Louisiana 6th — South Central — Baton Rouge. The district vote for Bill Clinton was 50% in 1996.

CQ Voting Studies

	1997	1998
Presidential	24%	20%
Party	90%	92%
Participation	94%	95%

Interest Groups

	1997	1998
ADA	0%	0%
ACU	92%	100%
AFL-CIO	0%	n/a
CCUS	100%	100%

Elections

	1996	1998
General	u/o	51%
Primary	69%	—

John Baldacci (D–Maine)
Of Bangor • Elected 1994
Pronounced: Ball-DATCH-ee

Born: Jan. 30, 1955, Bangor, Maine.
Education: U. of Maine, B.A. 1986.
Occupation: Restaurant owner.
Family: Wife, Karen; one child.
Religion: Roman Catholic.
Political Career: Bangor City Council, 1978–81; Maine Senate, 1982–94.

Capitol Office: 1740 Longworth House Office Building 20515; 225-6306; (fax) 225-2943; (e–mail) baldacci@me02.house.gov; (web) www.house.gov/baldacci.

Office Staff: Admin. Asst., Larry Benoit; Legis. Dir., Ashley Abbott; Press Secy., Doug Dunbar; Scheduler, Liz Smagala.

Committees: Agriculture (General Farm Commodities; Risk Management, Research & Specialty Crops); Transportation & Infrastructure (Aviation; Water Resources & Environment).

Maine 2nd — North — Lewiston; Auburn; Bangor. The district vote for Bill Clinton was 51% in 1996.

CQ Voting Studies

	1997	1998
Presidential	83%	79%
Party	88%	91%
Participation	99%	99%

Interest Groups

	1997	1998
ADA	95%	95%
ACU	8%	4%
AFL-CIO	100%	n/a
CCUS	60%	39%

Elections

	1996	1998
General	72%	76%
Primary	u/o	u/o

Tammy Baldwin (D–Wis.)
Of Madison • Elected 1998

Born: Feb. 11, 1962, Madison, Wis.
Education: Smith College, A.B. 1984; U. of Wisconsin, J.D. 1989.
Occupation: Lawyer; public policy analyst.
Family: Single.
Religion: Unspecified.
Political Career: Madison City Council, 1986; Dane County Board, 1986–94; Wis. Assembly, 1993–99.

Capitol Office: 1020 Longworth House Office Building 20515; 225-2906; (fax) 225-6942; (e–mail) www.house.gov/writerep.

Office Staff: Chief of Staff, Brad Fitch; Legis. Dir., Kris Pratt.

Committees: Budget; Judiciary (Commercial & Administrative Law).

Wisconsin 2nd — South — Madison. The district vote for Bill Clinton was 55% in 1996.

Elections

	1998
General	52%
Primary	37%

Cass Ballenger (R–N.C.)
Of Hickory • Elected 1986

Born: Dec. 6, 1926, Hickory, N.C.
Education: U. of North Carolina, attended 1944–45; Amherst College, B.A. 1948.
Military Career: Naval Air Corps, 1944–45.
Occupation: Plastics company executive.
Family: Wife, Donna; three children.
Religion: Episcopalian.
Political Career: Catawba County Board of Commissioners, 1966–74, chairman, 1970–74; N.C. House, 1975–77; N.C. Senate, 1977–86.

Capitol Office: 2182 Rayburn House Office Building 20515; 225-2576; (fax) 225-0316; (e–mail) cass.ballenger@mail.house.gov; (web) www.house.gov/ballenger.
Office Staff: Chief of Staff/Press Secy., Patrick Murphy; Legis. Dir., Roberta Myers; Scheduler, Caroline Brown.
Committees: Education & Workforce (Employer-Employee Relations; Workforce Protections — chairman); International Relations (International Operations & Human Rights; Western Hemisphere).

North Carolina 10th — Northwest — Hickory. The district vote for Bill Clinton was 35% in 1996.

CQ Voting Studies

	1997	1998
Presidential	27%	22%
Party	90%	92%
Participation	95%	97%

Interest Groups

	1997	1998
ADA	10%	5%
ACU	83%	91%
AFL-CIO	0%	n/a
CCUS	100%	82%

Elections

	1996	1998
General	70%	86%
Primary	u/o	u/o

James A. Barcia (D–Mich.)
Of Bay City • Elected 1992
Pronounced: BAR-sha

Born: Feb. 25, 1952, Bay City, Mich.
Education: Saginaw Valley State U., B.A. 1974.
Occupation: Congressional aide.
Family: Wife, Vicki Bartlett; two stepchildren.
Religion: Roman Catholic.
Political Career: Mich. House, 1977–83, majority whip, 1979–83; Mich. Senate, 1983–93.

Capitol Office: 2419 Rayburn House Office Building 20515; 225-8171; (fax) 225-2168; (e–mail) jim.barcia–pub@mail.house.gov; (web) www.house.gov/barcia.
Office Staff: Admin. Asst./Scheduler, Roger Szemraj; Legis. Dir., John D. Ferrera; Acting Press Secy., Roger Szemraj.
Committees: Science (Energy & Environment; Technology — ranking member); Transportation & Infrastructure (Ground Transportation; Water Resources & Environment).

Michigan 5th — East — Saginaw; Bay City. The district vote for Bill Clinton was 53% in 1996.

CQ Voting Studies

	1997	1998
Presidential	45%	60%
Party	60%	66%
Participation	97%	98%

Interest Groups

	1997	1998
ADA	50%	90%
ACU	64%	40%
AFL-CIO	88%	n/a
CCUS	60%	50%

Elections

	1996	1998
General	70%	71%
Primary	u/o	u/o

Bob Barr (R–Ga.)
Of Smyrna • Elected 1994

Born: Nov. 5, 1948, Iowa City, Iowa.
Education: U. of Southern California, B.A. 1970; George Washington U., M.A. 1972; Georgetown U., J.D. 1977.
Occupation: Lawyer; CIA analyst.
Family: Wife, Jeri; four children.
Religion: Methodist.
Political Career: Sought Republican nomination for Ga. House, 1984; U.S. attorney, 1986–90; sought Republican nomination for U.S. Senate, 1992.

Capitol Office: 1207 Longworth House Office Building 20515; 225-2931; (fax) 225-2944; (e–mail) barr.ga@mail.house.gov; (web) www.house.gov/barr.
Office Staff: Chief of Staff, Vacant; Legis. Dir., Jonathan Blyth; Press Secy., Chip Walker; Scheduler/Office Mgr., Catherine Gabrysh.
Committees: Banking & Financial Services (Financial Institutions & Consumer Credit; General Oversight & Investigations; Housing & Community Opportunity); Government Reform (Criminal Justice, Drug Policy & Human Resources; National Economic Growth); Judiciary (Constitution; Crime).

Georgia 7th — Northwest — Rome; part of Marietta. The district vote for Bill Clinton was 40% in 1996.

CQ Voting Studies

	1997	1998
Presidential	21%	20%
Party	97%	90%
Participation	98%	95%

Interest Groups

	1997	1998
ADA	5%	5%
ACU	96%	100%
AFL-CIO	0%	n/a
CCUS	80%	72%

Elections

	1996	1998
General	58%	55%
Primary	u/o	u/o

Bill Barrett (R–Neb.)
Of Lexington • Elected 1990

Born: Feb. 9, 1929, Lexington, Neb.
Education: Hastings College, B.A. 1951.
Military Career: Navy, 1951–52.
Occupation: Real estate and insurance broker.
Family: Wife, Elsie Carlson Barrett; four children.
Religion: Presbyterian.
Political Career: Neb. Republican Party chairman, 1973–75; Neb. Legislature, 1979–91, speaker, 1987–91.

Capitol Office: 2458 Rayburn House Office Building 20515; 225-6435; (e–mail) barrett.ntouch@mail.house.gov; (web) www.house.gov/billbarrett.
Office Staff: Chief of Staff, Jeri Finke; Legis. Dir., Mark Whitacre; Press Secy., Julie Ryan; Scheduler, Adele Brophy.
Committees: Agriculture (General Farm Commodities — chairman; Risk Management, Research & Specialty Crops); Education & Workforce (Postsecondary Education, Training & Life-Long Learning; Workforce Protections).

Nebraska 3rd — Rural West — Grand Island; North Platte. The district vote for Bill Clinton was 29% in 1996.

CQ Voting Studies

	1997	1998
Presidential	33%	27%
Party	88%	87%
Participation	97%	99%

Interest Groups

	1997	1998
ADA	5%	15%
ACU	79%	76%
AFL-CIO	25%	n/a
CCUS	100%	89%

Elections

	1996	1998
General	77%	84%
Primary	u/o	u/o

Thomas M. Barrett (D–Wis.)
Of Milwaukee • Elected 1992

Born: Dec. 8, 1953, Milwaukee, Wis.
Education: U. of Wisconsin, B.A. 1976, J.D. 1980.
Occupation: Lawyer.
Family: Wife, Kristine; four children.
Religion: Roman Catholic.
Political Career: Candidate for Wis. Assembly, 1982; Wis. Assembly, 1984–89; Wis. Senate, 1989–93.

Capitol Office: 1214 Longworth House Office Building 20515; 225-3571; (fax) 225-2185; (e–mail) telltom@mail.house.gov; (web) www.house.gov/barrett.
Office Staff: Chief of Staff, Sharon Robinson; Legis. Dir., Tama Mattocks; Press Secy., David DiMartino; Scheduler, Jodie Leu.
Committees: Commerce (Finance & Hazardous Materials; Health & Environment).

Wisconsin 5th — Northern Milwaukee, Milwaukee County suburbs. The district vote for Bill Clinton was 63% in 1996.

CQ Voting Studies

	1997	1998
Presidential	84%	88%
Party	91%	93%
Participation	99%	99%

Interest Groups

	1997	1998
ADA	90%	95%
ACU	20%	4%
AFL-CIO	100%	n/a
CCUS	40%	17%

Elections

	1996	1998
General	73%	78%
Primary	u/o	u/o

Roscoe G. Bartlett (R–Md.)
Of Frederick • Elected 1992

Born: June 3, 1926, Moreland, Ky.
Education: Columbia Union College, B.S. 1947; U. of Maryland, M.S. 1948, Ph.D. 1952.
Occupation: Real estate developer; scientific research company owner; farmer; biomedical engineer.
Family: Wife, Ellen Louise Baldwin; ten children.
Religion: Seventh-Day Adventist.
Political Career: Republican nominee for U.S. House, 1982.

Capitol Office: 2412 Rayburn House Office Building 20515; 225-2721; (fax) 225-2193; (e-mail) www.house.gov/writerep; (web) www.house.gov/bartlett.
Office Staff: Chief of Staff, Jim Backlin; Legis. Dir., Scott Plecs; Press Secy., Lisa Wright; Scheduler, Sallie Taylor.
Committees: Armed Services (Military Personnel; Military Research & Development); Science (Space & Aeronautics; Technology); Small Business (Government Programs & Oversight — chairman).

Maryland 6th — Central and West — Frederick; Hagerstown. The district vote for Bill Clinton was 38% in 1996.

CQ Voting Studies

	1997	1998
Presidential	27%	18%
Party	96%	94%
Participation	99%	99%

Interest Groups

	1997	1998
ADA	5%	5%
ACU	100%	100%
AFL-CIO	0%	n/a
CCUS	90%	78%

Elections

	1996	1998
General	57%	63%
Primary	85%	u/o

Joe L. Barton (R–Texas)
Of Ennis • Elected 1984

Born: Sept. 15, 1949, Waco, Texas.
Education: Texas A&M U., B.S. 1972; Purdue U., M.S. 1973.
Occupation: Engineering consultant.
Family: Wife, Janet Sue Barton; three children.
Religion: Methodist.
Political Career: Sought Republican nomination for U.S. Senate (special election), 1993.

Capitol Office: 2264 Rayburn House Office Building 20515; 225-2002; (fax) 225-3052; (e–mail) rep.barton@mail.house.gov; (web) www.house.gov/barton.
Office Staff: Chief of Staff, Heather Stansell; Legis. Dir., Beth Hall; Communications Dir., Samantha Jordan; Scheduler, Anne Marie Synnott.
Committees: Commerce (Energy & Power — chairman; Oversight & Investigations); Science (Energy & Environment; Space & Aeronautics).

Texas 6th — Suburban Dallas — Part of Fort Worth; part of Arlington. The district vote for Bill Clinton was 33% in 1996.

CQ Voting Studies

	1997	1998
Presidential	24%	20%
Party	86%	92%
Participation	93%	97%

Interest Groups

	1997	1998
ADA	10%	5%
ACU	92%	100%
AFL-CIO	0%	n/a
CCUS	78%	78%

Elections

	1996	1998
General	77%	73%
Primary		73%

Charles Bass (R–N.H.)
Of Peterborough • Elected 1994

Born: Jan. 8, 1952, Boston, Mass.
Education: Dartmouth College, A.B. 1974.
Occupation: Congressional aide; architectural products executive.
Family: Wife, Lisa L. Bass; two children.
Religion: Episcopalian.
Political Career: Sought Republican nomination for U.S. House, 1980; N.H. House, 1983–89; N.H. Senate, 1989–93.

Capitol Office: 218 Cannon House Office Building 20515; 225-5206; (fax) 225-2946; (e–mail) cbass@mail.house.gov; (web) www.house.gov/bass.
Office Staff: Staff Dir., David B. Leland; Legis. Dir., Annette O'Connor; Press Secy., Jana Nuzum; Scheduler, Kelly Grant.
Committees: Budget; Select Intelligence (Human Intelligence, Analysis & Counterintelligence; Technical & Tactical Intelligence); Transportation & Infrastructure (Aviation; Ground Transportation).

New Hampshire 2nd — West — Concord; Nashua. The district vote for Bill Clinton was 50% in 1996.

CQ Voting Studies

	1997	1998
Presidential	39%	33%
Party	86%	78%
Participation	99%	99%

Interest Groups

	1997	1998
ADA	15%	10%
ACU	80%	63%
AFL-CIO	0%	n/a
CCUS	90%	94%

Elections

	1996	1998
General	50%	53%
Primary	66%	83%

Herbert H. Bateman (R–Va.)
Of Newport News • Elected 1982

Born: Aug. 7, 1928, Elizabeth City, N.C.
Education: College of William and Mary, B.A. 1949; Georgetown U., J.D. 1956.
Military Career: Air Force, 1951–53.
Occupation: Lawyer.
Family: Wife, Laura; two children.
Religion: Protestant.
Political Career: Va. Senate, 1968–82; sought Republican nomination for U.S. House, 1976; sought Republican nomination for lieutenant governor, 1981.

Capitol Office: 2211 Rayburn House Office Building 20515; 225-4261; (fax) 225-4382; (e-mail) www.house.gov/writerep; (web) www.house.gov/bateman.
Office Staff: Admin. Asst./Press Secy., Dan Scandling; Legis. Dir., Paul D. McClung; Exec. Asst., Peggy Haar.
Committees: Armed Services (Military Readiness — chairman; Military Research & Development); Transportation & Infrastructure (Ground Transportation; Water Resources & Environment).

Virginia 1st — East — Parts of Newport News and Hampton; Fredericksburg. The district vote for Bill Clinton was 41% in 1996.

CQ Voting Studies

	1997	1998
Presidential	35%	21%
Party	87%	77%
Participation	98%	81%

Interest Groups

	1997	1998
ADA	15%	5%
ACU	64%	86%
AFL-CIO	25%	n/a
CCUS	100%	100%

Elections

	1996	1998
General	u/o	76%
Primary	80%	u/o

Xavier Becerra (D–Calif.)
Of Los Angeles • Elected 1992
Pronounced: HAH-vee–air beh-SEH-ra

Born: Jan. 26, 1958, Sacramento, Calif.
Education: Stanford U., A.B. 1980, J.D. 1984.
Occupation: Lawyer.
Family: Wife, Dr. Carolina Reyes; three children.
Religion: Roman Catholic.
Political Career: Calif. Assembly, 1990–92.

Capitol Office: 1119 Longworth House Office Building 20515; 225-6235; (fax) 225-2202; (e-mail) www.house.gov/writerep; (web) www.house.gov/becerra.
Office Staff: Chief of Staff, Krista Atteberry; Legis. Dir., Deidre Martinez; Press Secy., Magaly Rivas; Exec. Asst., Joseph Ortega.
Committees: Ways & Means (Trade).

California 30th — Central, East and Southeast Los Angeles. The district vote for Bill Clinton was 71% in 1996.

CQ Voting Studies

	1997	1998
Presidential	80%	82%
Party	93%	90%
Participation	93%	92%

Interest Groups

	1997	1998
ADA	90%	90%
ACU	0%	0%
AFL-CIO	100%	n/a
CCUS	30%	35%

Elections

	1996	1998
General	72%	81%
Primary	u/o	*80%

*Open primary

Ken Bentsen (D–Texas)
Of Houston • Elected 1994

Born: June 3, 1959, Houston, Texas.
Education: U. of St. Thomas, B.A. 1982; American U., M.P.A. 1985.
Occupation: Investment banker; congressional aide.
Family: Wife, Tamra; two children.
Religion: Presbyterian.
Political Career: Harris County Democratic Party chairman, 1990–93.

Capitol Office: 326 Cannon House Office Building 20515; 225-7508; (fax) 225-2947; (e–mail) www.house.gov/writerep; (web) www.house.gov/bentsen.
Office Staff: Chief of Staff, Patti M. Strong; Admin. Asst./Press Secy., Vince Willmore; Legis. Dir., Bradley Edgell; Exec. Asst., Brenda O'Lenick.
Committees: Banking & Financial Services (Capital Markets & Securities; Financial Institutions & Consumer Credit); Budget.

Texas 25th — South Houston and suburbs. The district vote for Bill Clinton was 51% in 1996.

CQ Voting Studies

	1997	1998
Presidential	80%	78%
Party	84%	85%
Participation	99%	99%

Interest Groups

	1997	1998
ADA	75%	95%
ACU	13%	4%
AFL-CIO	88%	n/a
CCUS	60%	50%

Elections

	1996	1998
General	*57%	58%
Primary		u/o

*Runoff election

Doug Bereuter (R–Neb.)
Of Cedar Bluffs • Elected 1978
Pronounced: BEE-right–er

Born: Oct. 6, 1939, York, Neb.
Education: U. of Nebraska, B.A. 1961; Harvard U., M.C.P. 1966, M.P.A. 1973.
Military Career: Army, 1963–65.
Occupation: City planner; professor; state official.
Family: Wife, Louise; two children.
Religion: Lutheran.
Political Career: Neb. Legislature, 1975–79.

Capitol Office: 2184 Rayburn House Office Building 20515; 225-4806; (e–mail) www.house.gov/writerep; (web) www.house.gov/bereuter.
Office Staff: Chief of Staff, Susan Olson; Legis. Dir., Jodi Smith; Communications Dir./Legis. Asst., Carol Lawrence; Personal Secy., Sue Plessman.
Committees: Banking & Financial Services (Financial Institutions & Consumer Credit; Housing & Community Opportunity); International Relations (Asia & the Pacific — chairman; International Economic Policy & Trade); China Investigation; Transportation & Infrastructure (Ground Transportation; Water Resources & Environment).

Nebraska 1st — East — Lincoln; Norfolk. The district vote for Bill Clinton was 38% in 1996.

CQ Voting Studies

	1997	1998
Presidential	40%	28%
Party	84%	83%
Participation	98%	99%

Interest Groups

	1997	1998
ADA	20%	5%
ACU	68%	64%
AFL-CIO	29%	n/a
CCUS	90%	100%

Elections

	1996	1998
General	70%	73%
Primary	u/o	u/o

Shelley Berkley (D–Nev.)
Of Las Vegas • Elected 1998

Born: Jan. 20, 1951, New York, N.Y.
Education: U. of Nevada, Las Vegas, B.A. 1972; U. of San Diego, J.D. 1976.
Occupation: Lawyer; university regent.
Family: Husband, Dr. Larry Lehrner; two children.
Religion: Jewish.
Political Career: Nev. Assembly, 1983–85.

Capitol Office: 1505 Longworth House Office Building 20515; 225-5965; (fax) 225-3119; (e-mail) www.house.gov/writerep.
Office Staff: Chief of Staff, Richard Urey; Legis. Dir., Mark Guiton; Press Secy., Laura K. Chapin.
Committees: Transportation & Infrastructure (Oversight & Investigations; Ground Transportation); Veterans' Affairs (Benefits).

Elections

	1998
General	49%
Primary	81%

Nevada 1st — South — Las Vegas. The district vote for Bill Clinton was 51% in 1996.

Howard L. Berman (D–Calif.)
Of North Hollywood • Elected 1982

Born: Apr. 15, 1941, Los Angeles, Calif.
Education: U. of California, Los Angeles, B.A. 1962, LL.B. 1965.
Occupation: Lawyer.
Family: Wife, Janis; one child, one stepchild.
Religion: Jewish.
Political Career: Calif. Assembly, 1973–83.

Capitol Office: 2330 Rayburn House Office Building 20515; 225-4695; (e-mail) www.house.gov/writerep; (web) www.house.gov/berman.
Office Staff: Chief of Staff/Press Secy., Gene Smith; Legis. Dir., Bari L. Schwartz; Exec. Asst., Nancy Milburn.
Committees: International Relations (Asia & the Pacific); Judiciary (Courts & Intellectual Property — ranking member; Immigration & Claims); Standards of Official Conduct — ranking member.

California 26th — San Fernando Valley. The district vote for Bill Clinton was 65% in 1996.

CQ Voting Studies

	1997	1998
Presidential	81%	76%
Party	81%	83%
Participation	91%	87%

Interest Groups

	1997	1998
ADA	80%	90%
ACU	9%	5%
AFL-CIO	100%	n/a
CCUS	33%	36%

Elections

	1996	1998
General	66%	82%
Primary	84%	*61%

*Open primary

Marion Berry (D–Ark.)
Of Gillett • Elected 1996

Born: Aug. 27, 1942, Stuttgart, Ark.
Education: U. of Arkansas, attended 1960–62; U. of Arkansas, Little Rock, B.S. 1965.
Occupation: Farmer; White House aide; pharmacist.
Family: Wife, Carolyn; two children.
Religion: Methodist.
Political Career: Gillett City Council, 1976–80; Ark. Soil and Water Conservation Commission, 1986–94, chairman, 1992.

Capitol Office: 1113 Longworth House Office Building 20515; 225-4076; (fax) 225-5602; (e–mail) www.house.gov/writerep; (web) www.house.gov/berry.
Office Staff: Admin. Asst., Bruce Harris; Legis. Dir., Courtenay McKinnon Dusenbury; Press Secy., Nicole Dueffer; Scheduler, Courtney Clabaugh.
Committees: Agriculture (Department Operations, Oversight, Nutrition & Forestry; Livestock & Horticulture); Transportation & Infrastructure (Aviation; Ground Transportation).

Arkansas 1st — Northeast — Jonesboro; West Memphis. The district vote for Bill Clinton was 58% in 1996.

CQ Voting Studies

	1997	1998
Presidential	59%	61%
Party	72%	68%
Participation	99%	98%

Interest Groups

	1997	1998
ADA	75%	70%
ACU	44%	28%
AFL-CIO	100%	n/a
CCUS	60%	67%

Elections

	1996	1998
General	53%	u/o
Primary	*52%	u/o

*Runoff election

Judy Biggert (R–Ill.)
Of Hinsdale • Elected 1998

Born: Aug. 15, 1937, Chicago, Ill.
Education: Stanford U., B.A. 1959; Northwestern U., J.D. 1963.
Occupation: Lawyer.
Family: Husband, Rody; four children.
Religion: Episcopalian.
Political Career: Ill. House, 1993–99.

Capitol Office: 508 Cannon House Office Building 20515; 225-3515; (fax) 225-9420; (e–mail) www.house.gov/writerep.
Office Staff: Chief of Staff, Kathy Lydon; Legis. Dir., Kristin Wolgemuth; Press Secy., Kathy Lydon; Scheduler, Sue Geibel.
Committees: Banking & Financial Services (Capital Markets & Securities; Domestic & International Monetary Policy); Government Reform (Government Management, Information & Technology; National Security & Veterans Affairs); Science (Basic Research; Energy & Environment).

Illinois 13th — Southwest Chicago suburbs — Naperville. The district vote for Bill Clinton was 41% in 1996.

Elections

	1998
General	61%
Primary	45%

Brian P. Bilbray (R–Calif.)
Of San Diego • Elected 1994

Born: Jan. 28, 1951, Coronado, Calif.
Education: Southwestern College, attended 1970–74.
Occupation: Tax firm owner.
Family: Wife, Karen; two children, three stepchildren.
Religion: Roman Catholic.
Political Career: Imperial Beach City Council, 1977–79; mayor of Imperial Beach, 1979–85; San Diego County Board of Supervisors, 1985–95.

Capitol Office: 1530 Longworth House Office Building 20515; 225-2040; (fax) 225-2948; (e-mail) brian.bilbray@mail.house.gov; (web) www.house.gov/bilbray.
Office Staff: Chief of Staff, John Woodard; Legis. Dir., David Schroeder; Communications Dir., Ion Valaskakis; Office Mgr./Scheduler, Suzanne Michel.
Committees: Commerce (Finance & Hazardous Materials; Health & Environment; Oversight & Investigations).

California 49th — North San Diego; Coronado; Imperial Beach. The district vote for Bill Clinton was 49% in 1996.

CQ Voting Studies

	1997	1998
Presidential	35%	34%
Party	87%	73%
Participation	97%	97%

Interest Groups

	1997	1998
ADA	15%	20%
ACU	76%	64%
AFL-CIO	13%	n/a
CCUS	80%	61%

Elections

	1996	1998
General	53%	49%
Primary	u/o	*53%

*Open primary

Michael Bilirakis (R–Fla.)
Of Palm Harbor • Elected 1982
Pronounced: bil–lee-RACK-us

Born: July 16, 1930, Tarpon Springs, Fla.
Education: U. of Pittsburgh, B.S. 1959; George Washington U., attended 1959–60; U. of Florida, J.D. 1963.
Military Career: Air Force, 1951–55.
Occupation: Lawyer; restaurateur; engineer.
Family: Wife, Evelyn Miaoulis; two children.
Religion: Greek Orthodox.
Political Career: No previous office.

Capitol Office: 2369 Rayburn House Office Building 20515; 225-5755; (fax) 225-4085; (e-mail) www.house.gov/writerep; (web) www.house.gov/bilirakis.
Office Staff: Admin. Asst., Patricia DeLoatche; Legis. Dir., Rebecca Hyder; Communications Dir., Jerry White; Scheduler, Doug Menorca; Scheduler, Patti Caccamo.
Committees: Commerce (Energy & Power; Health & Environment — chairman); Veterans' Affairs (Health).

Florida 9th — West — Northern Pinellas and Hillsborough counties; central Pasco County; Clearwater. The district vote for Bill Clinton was 45% in 1996.

CQ Voting Studies

	1997	1998
Presidential	28%	20%
Party	92%	89%
Participation	99%	97%

Interest Groups

	1997	1998
ADA	10%	5%
ACU	84%	92%
AFL-CIO	14%	n/a
CCUS	100%	89%

Elections

	1996	1998
General	69%	u/o
Primary	80%	u/o

Sanford D. Bishop Jr. (D-Ga.)
Of Albany • Elected 1992

Born: Feb. 4, 1947, Mobile, Ala.
Education: Morehouse College, B.A. 1968; Emory U., J.D. 1971.
Military Career: Army, 1971.
Occupation: Lawyer.
Family: Divorced.
Religion: Baptist.
Political Career: Ga. House, 1977–91; Ga. Senate, 1991–93.

Capitol Office: 1433 Longworth House Office Building 20515; 225-3631; (fax) 225-2203; (e–mail) www.house.gov/writerep; (web) www.house.gov/bishop.
Office Staff: Chief of Staff, Beverly Gilyard; Legis. Dir., Ken Keck; Communications Dir., Selby McCash; Scheduler, Dee Sims.
Committees: Agriculture (General Farm Commodities; Risk Management, Research & Specialty Crops); Select Intelligence (Technical & Tactical Intelligence — ranking member).

Georgia 2nd — Southwest — Parts of Macon, Columbus, Albany and Valdosta. The district vote for Bill Clinton was 49% in 1996.

CQ Voting Studies

	1997	1998
Presidential	57%	57%
Party	75%	70%
Participation	99%	99%

Interest Groups

	1997	1998
ADA	75%	70%
ACU	29%	44%
AFL-CIO	88%	n/a
CCUS	60%	61%

Elections

	1996	1998
General	54%	57%
Primary	59%	u/o

Rod R. Blagojevich (D-Ill.)
Of Chicago • Elected 1996
Pronounced: bla-GOY-a-vich

Born: Dec. 10, 1956, Chicago, Ill.
Education: Northwestern U., B.A. 1979; Pepperdine U., J.D. 1983.
Occupation: Lawyer.
Family: Wife, Patricia; one child.
Religion: Eastern Orthodox.
Political Career: Assistant Cook County state's attorney, 1986–88; Ill. House, 1993–97.

Capitol Office: 331 Cannon House Office Building 20515; 225-4061; (fax) 225-5603; (e–mail) www.house.gov/writerep; (web) www.house.gov/blagojevich.
Office Staff: Chief of Staff, John Wyma; Legis. Dir., Tod Preston; Press Secy., Matt Devine; Exec. Asst., Mary Kate McGivern.
Committees: Armed Services (Military Procurement; Military Readiness); Government Reform (Criminal Justice, Drug Policy & Human Resources; National Security & Veterans Affairs — ranking member).

Illinois 5th — Chicago — North Side. The district vote for Bill Clinton was 63% in 1996.

CQ Voting Studies

	1997	1998
Presidential	80%	74%
Party	87%	85%
Participation	98%	95%

Interest Groups

	1997	1998
ADA	90%	100%
ACU	16%	8%
AFL-CIO	100%	n/a
CCUS	40%	39%

Elections

	1996	1998
General	64%	74%
Primary	50%	u/o

Thomas J. Bliley Jr. (R-Va.)
Of Richmond • Elected 1980

Born: Jan. 28, 1932, Chesterfield County, Va.
Education: Georgetown U., B.A. 1952.
Military Career: Navy, 1952–55.
Occupation: Funeral director.
Family: Wife, Mary Virginia Bliley; two children.
Religion: Roman Catholic.
Political Career: Richmond City Council, 1968–77, vice mayor, 1968–70, mayor, 1970–77 (served as a Democrat).

Capitol Office: 2409 Rayburn House Office Building 20515; 225-2815; (fax) 225-0011; (e–mail) www.house.gov/writerep; (web) www.house.gov/bliley.
Office Staff: Chief of Staff/Scheduler, Linda Pedigo; Legis. Dir./Press Secy., Bill Dolbow.
Committees: Commerce — chairman.

Virginia 7th — Central — Part of Richmond and suburbs. The district vote for Bill Clinton was 34% in 1996.

CQ Voting Studies

	1997	1998
Presidential	29%	23%
Party	90%	93%
Participation	98%	99%

Interest Groups

	1997	1998
ADA	5%	0%
ACU	75%	100%
AFL-CIO	0%	n/a
CCUS	100%	100%

Elections

	1996	1998
General	75%	79%
Primary	u/o	u/o

Earl Blumenauer (D-Ore.)
Of Portland • Elected 1996
Pronounced: BLUM-men–hour

Born: Aug. 16, 1948, Portland, Ore.
Education: Lewis and Clark College, B.A. 1970, J.D. 1976.
Occupation: Lawyer; public official.
Family: Divorced; two children.
Religion: Unspecified.
Political Career: Ore. House, 1973–77; Multnomah County Commission, 1978–86; candidate for Portland City Council, 1980; Portland City Council, 1986–96; candidate for mayor of Portland, 1992.

Capitol Office: 1406 Longworth House Office Building 20515; 225-4811; (e–mail) write.earl@mail.house.gov; (web) www.house.gov/blumenauer.
Office Staff: Senior Counsel, Bob Crane; Staff Dir., Stephanie D. Vance; Press Secy., Shannon Jacobs; Scheduler, Stephanie Henley.
Committees: Transportation & Infrastructure (Ground Transportation; Water Resources & Environment).

Oregon 3rd — East and North Portland and eastern suburbs. The district vote for Bill Clinton was 57% in 1996.

CQ Voting Studies

	1997	1998
Presidential	80%	83%
Party	88%	91%
Participation	95%	98%

Interest Groups

	1997	1998
ADA	95%	95%
ACU	4%	4%
AFL-CIO	100%	n/a
CCUS	40%	41%

Elections

	1996	1998
General	*70%	84%
Primary	*72%	u/o

*Special election

Roy Blunt (R–Mo.)
Of Bolivar • Elected 1996

Born: Jan. 10, 1950, Niangua, Mo.
Education: Southwest Baptist U., B.A. 1970; Southwest Missouri State U., M.A. 1972.
Occupation: University president; teacher.
Family: Wife, Roseann; three children.
Religion: Baptist.
Political Career: Greene County clerk, 1973–84; Republican nominee for lieutenant governor, 1980; Mo. secretary of state, 1985–93; sought Republican nomination for governor, 1992.

Capitol Office: 217 Cannon House Office Building 20515; 225-6536; (fax) 225-5604; (e-mail) www.house.gov/writerep; (web) www.house.gov/blunt.
Office Staff: Chief of Staff, Gregg Hartley; Press Secy., Dan Wadlington; Scheduler, Jared Craighead.
Committees: Commerce (Finance & Hazardous Materials; Oversight & Investigations; Telecommunications, Trade & Consumer Protection).

Missouri 7th — Southwest — Springfield; Joplin. The district vote for Bill Clinton was 37% in 1996.

CQ Voting Studies

	1997	1998
Presidential	24%	17%
Party	93%	93%
Participation	98%	96%

Interest Groups

	1997	1998
ADA	10%	0%
ACU	80%	100%
AFL-CIO	25%	n/a
CCUS	90%	82%

Elections

	1996	1998
General	65%	73%
Primary	56%	u/o

Sherwood Boehlert (R–N.Y.)
Of New Hartford • Elected 1982
Pronounced: BO-lert

Born: Sept. 28, 1936, Utica, N.Y.
Education: Utica College, A.B. 1961.
Military Career: Army, 1956–58.
Occupation: Congressional aide; public relations executive.
Family: Wife, Marianne Willey; four children.
Religion: Roman Catholic.
Political Career: Sought Republican nomination for U.S. House, 1972; Oneida County executive, 1979–82.

Capitol Office: 2246 Rayburn House Office Building 20515; 225-3665; (fax) 225-1891; (e-mail) rep.boehlert@mail.house.gov; (web) www.house.gov/boehlert.
Office Staff: Chief of Staff, Dean D'Amore; Legis. Dir., David Goldston; Press Secy., Jim Philipps; Exec. Secy., Julie Phillips.
Committees: Select Intelligence (Technical & Tactical Intelligence); Science (Basic Research); Transportation & Infrastructure (Ground Transportation; Water Resources & Environment — chairman).

New York 23rd — Central — Utica; Rome. The district vote for Bill Clinton was 46% in 1996.

CQ Voting Studies

	1997	1998
Presidential	57%	60%
Party	69%	58%
Participation	99%	99%

Interest Groups

	1997	1998
ADA	55%	60%
ACU	32%	24%
AFL-CIO	63%	n/a
CCUS	67%	61%

Elections

	1996	1998
General	64%	81%
Primary	65%	u/o

John A. Boehner (R–Ohio)
Of West Chester • Elected 1990
Pronounced: BAY-ner

Born: Nov. 17, 1949, Cincinnati, Ohio.
Education: Xavier U., B.S. 1977.
Military Career: Navy, 1968.
Occupation: Plastics and packaging executive.
Family: Wife, Debbie; two children.
Religion: Roman Catholic.
Political Career: Ohio House, 1985–91.

Capitol Office: 1011 Longworth House Office Building 20515; 225-6205; (fax) 225-0704; (e–mail) www.house.gov/writerep; (web) www.house.gov/boehner.
Office Staff: Chief of Staff, Barry Jackson; Legis. Dir., George Canty; Press Secy., Dave Schnittger; Scheduler, Mike Sommers.
Committees: House Administration; Agriculture (General Farm Commodities; Livestock & Horticulture); Education & Workforce (Early Childhood, Youth & Families; Employer-Employee Relations — chairman; Workforce Protections); Joint Library; Joint Printing.

Ohio 8th — Southwest — Hamilton; Middletown. The district vote for Bill Clinton was 37% in 1996.

CQ Voting Studies

	1997	1998
Presidential	25%	24%
Party	93%	95%
Participation	98%	99%

Interest Groups

	1997	1998
ADA	0%	0%
ACU	87%	96%
AFL-CIO	0%	n/a
CCUS	100%	89%

Elections

	1996	1998
General	70%	71%
Primary	u/o	u/o

Henry Bonilla (R–Texas)
Of San Antonio • Elected 1992
Pronounced: bo-NEE-uh

Born: Jan. 2, 1954, San Antonio, Texas.
Education: U. of Texas, Austin, B.A. 1976.
Occupation: Television reporter, producer and executive; gubernatorial aide.
Family: Wife, Deborah Knapp; two children.
Religion: Baptist.
Political Career: No previous office.

Capitol Office: 1427 Longworth House Office Building 20515; 225-4511; (fax) 225-2237; (e–mail) www.house.gov/writerep; (web) www.house.gov/bonilla.
Office Staff: Chief of Staff, Steve Ruhlen; Legis. Dir., Marcus Lubin; Press Secy., Susan Phalen; Scheduler, Carolyn Hensarling.
Committees: Appropriations (Agriculture, Rural Development, FDA & Related Agencies; Labor, Health & Human Services & Education; Defense).

Texas 23rd — Southwest — Laredo; San Antonio suburbs. The district vote for Bill Clinton was 50% in 1996.

CQ Voting Studies

	1997	1998
Presidential	33%	29%
Party	84%	83%
Participation	89%	98%

Interest Groups

	1997	1998
ADA	5%	10%
ACU	95%	92%
AFL-CIO	0%	n/a
CCUS	90%	88%

Elections

	1996	1998
General	62%	64%
Primary	u/o	u/o

David E. Bonior (D–Mich.)
Of Mount Clemens • Elected 1976
Pronounced: BON-yer

Born: June 6, 1945, Detroit, Mich.
Education: U. of Iowa, B.A. 1967; Chapman College, M.A. 1972.
Military Career: Air Force, 1968–72.
Occupation: Probation officer; adoption caseworker.
Family: Wife, Judy; three children.
Religion: Roman Catholic.
Political Career: Mich. House, 1973–77.

Capitol Office: 2207 Rayburn House Office Building 20515; 225-2106; (fax) 226-1169; (e–mail) david.bonior@mail.house.gov; (web) davidbonior.house.gov.
Office Staff: Admin. Asst., Sarah Dufendach; Press Secy., Fred Clarke; Exec. Secy., Paula Short.
Committees: Minority Whip (no committee assignments)

Michigan 10th — Southeast — Macomb County; Port Huron. The district vote for Bill Clinton was 48% in 1996.

CQ Voting Studies

	1997	1998
Presidential	71%	80%
Party	91%	94%
Participation	96%	99%

Interest Groups

	1997	1998
ADA	85%	95%
ACU	12%	16%
AFL-CIO	100%	n/a
CCUS	40%	22%

Elections

	1996	1998
General	54%	52%
Primary	u/o	u/o

Mary Bono (R–Calif.)
Of Palm Springs • Elected 1998

Born: Oct. 24, 1961, Cleveland, Ohio.
Education: U. of Southern California, B.F.A. 1984.
Occupation: Homemaker; restaurateur.
Family: Widowed; two children.
Religion: Protestant.
Political Career: No previous office.

Capitol Office: 516 Cannon House Office Building 20515; 225-5330; (fax) 225-2961; (e–mail) www.house.gov/writerep.
Office Staff: Chief of Staff, Brian Nestande; Legis. Dir., Chris Katopis; Press Secy., Frank Cullen; Exec. Asst., Majida Dandy.
Committees: Armed Services (Military Personnel; Military Procurement); Judiciary (Commercial & Administrative Law; Courts & Intellectual Property); Small Business (Government Programs & Oversight).

California 44th — Eastern Riverside County. The district vote for Bill Clinton was 44% in 1996.

CQ Voting Studies

	1998
Presidential	23%
Party	92%
Participation	99%

Interest Groups

	1998
ADA	0%
ACU	95%
AFL-CIO	n/a
CCUS	93%

Elections

	1998	1998
General	*64%	60%
Primary		†58%

*Special election
†Open primary

Robert A. Borski (D–Pa.)
Of Philadelphia • Elected 1982

Born: Oct. 20, 1948, Philadelphia, Pa.
Education: U. of Baltimore, B.A. 1972.
Occupation: Stockbroker.
Family: Wife, Karen Lloyd; five children.
Religion: Roman Catholic.
Political Career: Pa. House, 1977–83.

Capitol Office: 2267 Rayburn House Office Building 20515; 225-8251; (fax) 225-4628; (e-mail) www.house.gov/writerep.
Office Staff: Admin. Asst./Legis. Dir., Mark Vieth; Press Secy., Karen Peck; Scheduler, Kevin Gallagher.
Committees: Transportation & Infrastructure (Ground Transportation; Water Resources & Environment — ranking member).

Pennsylvania 3rd — Northeast Philadelphia. The district vote for Bill Clinton was 61% in 1996.

CQ Voting Studies

	1997	1998
Presidential	60%	78%
Party	82%	89%
Participation	98%	97%

Interest Groups

	1997	1998
ADA	75%	90%
ACU	17%	12%
AFL-CIO	100%	n/a
CCUS	30%	22%

Elections

	1996	1998
General	69%	59%
Primary	91%	87%

Leonard L. Boswell (D–Iowa)
Of Davis City • Elected 1996

Born: Jan. 10, 1934, Harrison County, Mo.
Education: Graceland College, B.A. 1969.
Military Career: Army, 1956–76.
Occupation: Farmer.
Family: Wife, Dody; three children.
Religion: Mormon.
Political Career: Iowa Senate, 1985–97, president, 1992–97; sought Democratic nomination for U.S. House, 1986; Iowa Democratic Central Committee, 1992–96; Democratic nominee for lieutenant governor, 1994.

Capitol Office: 1029 Longworth House Office Building 20515; 225-3806; (fax) 225-5608; (e-mail) www.house.gov/writerep; (web) www.house.gov/boswell.
Office Staff: Chief of Staff, Jeani Murray; Legis. Dir., E.H. "Ned" Michalek; Press Asst., Seth Boffeli; Scheduler, Sandy Carter.
Committees: Agriculture (Livestock & Horticulture; Risk Management, Research & Specialty Crops); Transportation & Infrastructure (Aviation; Water Resources & Environment).

Iowa 3rd — South Central — Ames; Burlington. The district vote for Bill Clinton was 50% in 1996.

CQ Voting Studies

	1997	1998
Presidential	73%	65%
Party	72%	65%
Participation	99%	99%

Interest Groups

	1997	1998
ADA	65%	65%
ACU	28%	36%
AFL-CIO	75%	n/a
CCUS	70%	83%

Elections

	1996	1998
General	49%	57%
Primary	58%	u/o

Rick Boucher (D-Va.)
Of Abingdon • Elected 1982
Pronounced: BOUGH-cher

Born: Aug. 1, 1946, Abingdon, Va.
Education: Roanoke College, B.A. 1968; U. of Virginia, J.D. 1971.
Occupation: Lawyer.
Family: Single.
Religion: Methodist.
Political Career: Va. Senate, 1976–82.

Capitol Office: 2329 Rayburn House Office Building 20515; 225-3861; (fax) 225-0442; (e-mail) ninthnet@mail.house.gov; (web) www.house.gov/boucher.
Office Staff: Chief of Staff, Becky Coleman; Legis. Dir./Press Secy., Sharon Ringley; Scheduler, Lauren Frazier.
Committees: Commerce (Energy & Power; Telecommunications, Trade & Consumer Protection); Judiciary (Courts & Intellectual Property).

Virginia 9th — Southwest — Blacksburg; Bristol. The district vote for Bill Clinton was 46% in 1996.

CQ Voting Studies

	1997	1998
Presidential	72%	77%
Party	76%	78%
Participation	93%	94%

Interest Groups

	1997	1998
ADA	85%	95%
ACU	8%	4%
AFL-CIO	100%	n/a
CCUS	40%	35%

Elections

	1996	1998
General	65%	61%
Primary	u/o	u/o

Allen Boyd (D-Fla.)
Of Monticello • Elected 1996

Born: June 6, 1945, Valdosta, Ga.
Education: North Florida Junior College, A.A. 1966; Florida State U., B.S. 1969.
Military Career: Army, 1969–71.
Occupation: Farmer.
Family: Wife, Stephanie A. Roush; three children.
Religion: Methodist.
Political Career: Fla. House, 1989–97.

Capitol Office: 107 Cannon House Office Building 20515; 225-5235; (fax) 225-5615; (e-mail) www.house.gov/writerep; (web) www.house.gov/boyd.
Office Staff: Admin. Asst./Chief of Staff, Jennifer Cannon; Legis. Dir., Jason Quaranto; Press Secy., Diane Pratt; Scheduler, Ingrid Norgaard.
Committees: Appropriations (Agriculture, Rural Development, FDA & Related Agencies; Military Construction).

Florida 2nd — Panhandle — Tallahassee; part of Panama City. The district vote for Bill Clinton was 48% in 1996.

CQ Voting Studies

	1997	1998
Presidential	61%	61%
Party	68%	68%
Participation	99%	99%

Interest Groups

	1997	1998
ADA	55%	65%
ACU	44%	32%
AFL-CIO	75%	n/a
CCUS	80%	65%

Elections

	1996	1998
General	59%	95%
Primary	*64%	u/o

*Runoff election

Kevin Brady (R–Texas)
Of The Woodlands • Elected 1996

Born: Apr. 11, 1955, Vermillion, S.D.
Education: U. of South Dakota, B.S. 1990.
Occupation: Chamber of commerce executive.
Family: Wife, Cathy.
Religion: Roman Catholic.
Political Career: Texas House, 1991–96.

Capitol Office: 1531 Longworth House Office Building 20515; 225-4901; (fax) 225-5524; (e–mail) www.house.gov/writerep; (web) www.house.gov/brady.
Office Staff: Chief of Staff, Doug Centilli; Legis. Dir., Barry Brown; Press Secy., Doug Larkin; Scheduler, Drake McGraw.
Committees: International Relations (International Economic Policy & Trade; Western Hemisphere); Resources (Energy & Mineral Resources); Science (Space & Aeronautics; Technology).

Texas 8th — Northern Houston Suburbs; College Station. The district vote for Bill Clinton was 27% in 1996.

CQ Voting Studies

	1997	1998
Presidential	28%	20%
Party	96%	90%
Participation	99%	95%

Interest Groups

	1997	1998
ADA	5%	0%
ACU	100%	96%
AFL-CIO	0%	n/a
CCUS	100%	94%

Elections

	1996	1998
General	*59%	93%
Primary		89%

*Runoff election

Robert A. Brady (D–Pa.)
Of Philadelphia • Elected 1998

Born: Apr. 7, 1945, Philadelphia, Pa.
Education: St. Thomas More H.S., graduated 1963.
Occupation: Union lobbyist; carpenter.
Family: Wife, Debra; two children.
Religion: Roman Catholic.
Political Career: 34th Ward Democratic Executive Committee, 1967–present, leader, 1980–present; candidate for Philadelphia City Council, 1983; Philadelphia Democratic Party chairman, 1986–present.

Capitol Office: 216 Cannon House Office Building 20515; 225-4731; (fax) 225-0088; (e–mail) www.house.gov/writerep.
Office Staff: Chief of Staff, Stan White; Press Secy., Karen Warrington; Scheduler, Kim Williams.
Committees: Armed Services (Military Installations & Facilities; Military Procurement); Small Business (Regulatory Reform & Paperwork Reduction).

Pennsylvania 1st — South and central Philadelphia; part of Chester. The district vote for Bill Clinton was 83% in 1996.

CQ Voting Studies

	1998
Presidential	83%
Party	92%
Participation	96%

Interest Groups

	1998
ADA	50%
ACU	0%
AFL-CIO	n/a
CCUS	25%

Elections

	1998	1998
General	*74%	81%
Primary		64%

*Special election

Corrine Brown (D–Fla.)
Of Jacksonville • Elected 1992

Born: Nov. 11, 1946, Jacksonville, Fla.
Education: Florida A&M U., B.S. 1969, M.A. 1971; U. of Florida, Ed.S. 1974.
Occupation: College guidance counselor; travel agency owner.
Family: Divorced; one child.
Religion: Baptist.
Political Career: Candidate for Fla. House, 1980; Fla. House, 1983–93.

Capitol Office: 2444 Rayburn House Office Building 20515; 225-0123; (fax) 225-2256; (e-mail) www.house.gov/writerep; (web) www.house.gov/corrinebrown.
Office Staff: Admin. Asst., Elias Ronnie Simmons; Legis. Dir., Tom McDaniels; Press Secy., Gretchen Hitchner; Exec. Asst., Darla Smallwood.
Committees: Transportation & Infrastructure (Aviation; Ground Transportation); Veterans' Affairs (Oversight & Investigations — ranking member).

Florida 3rd — North — parts of Jacksonville and Orlando. The district vote for Bill Clinton was 60% in 1996.

CQ Voting Studies

	1997	1998
Presidential	69%	77%
Party	84%	89%
Participation	94%	93%

Interest Groups

	1997	1998
ADA	90%	95%
ACU	17%	4%
AFL-CIO	100%	n/a
CCUS	44%	31%

Elections

	1996	1998
General	61%	55%
Primary	u/o	u/o

George E. Brown Jr. (D–Calif.)
Of San Bernardino • Elected 1962
Did not serve 1971–73

Born: Mar. 6, 1920, Holtville, Calif.
Education: El Centro Junior College, attended 1938; U. of California, Los Angeles, B.A. 1946.
Military Career: Army, 1942–46.
Occupation: Management consultant; physicist.
Family: Wife, Marta Macias; two children, five stepchildren.
Religion: Methodist.
Political Career: Monterey Park City Council, 1954–55; mayor of Monterey Park, 1955–56; Calif. Assembly, 1959–63; sought Democratic nomination for U.S. Senate, 1970.

Capitol Office: 2300 Rayburn House Office Building 20515; 225-6161; (fax) 225-8671; (e-mail) talk2geb@mail.house.gov; (web) www.house.gov/georgebrown.
Office Staff: Admin. Asst., Bill Grady; Legis. Dir., Bill Grady; Acting Press Secy., Marta Brown; Acting Scheduler, Marta Brown.
Committees: Agriculture (Department Operations, Oversight, Nutrition & Forestry; Risk Management, Research & Specialty Crops); Science — ranking member.

California 42nd — San Bernardino County — San Bernardino. The district vote for Bill Clinton was 54% in 1996.

CQ Voting Studies

	1997	1998
Presidential	88%	77%
Party	88%	90%
Participation	93%	96%

Interest Groups

	1997	1998
ADA	100%	100%
ACU	4%	0%
AFL-CIO	100%	n/a
CCUS	30%	29%

Elections

	1996	1998
General	50%	55%
Primary	78%	*54%

*Open primary

Sherrod Brown (D–Ohio)
Of Lorain • Elected 1992

Born: Nov. 9, 1952, Mansfield, Ohio.
Education: Yale U., B.A. 1974; Ohio State U., M.A. 1979, M.A. 1981.
Occupation: Teacher.
Family: Divorced; two children.
Religion: Lutheran.
Political Career: Ohio House, 1975–83; Ohio secretary of state, 1983–91; defeated for re-election as Ohio secretary of state, 1990.

Capitol Office: 201 Cannon House Office Building 20515; 225-3401; (fax) 225-2266; (e–mail) www.house.gov/writerep; (web) www.house.gov/sherrodbrown.
Office Staff: Chief of Staff, Donna Pignatelli; Legis. Dir., Kevin Brennan; Press Secy., Kenneth H. Berlack; Scheduler, Annmarie Tirpak.
Committees: Commerce (Energy & Power; Health & Environment — ranking member); International Relations (Asia & the Pacific).

Ohio 13th — Northeast — Suburbs of Cleveland, Akron and Youngstown. The district vote for Bill Clinton was 46% in 1996.

CQ Voting Studies

	1997	1998
Presidential	81%	82%
Party	94%	94%
Participation	97%	97%

Interest Groups

	1997	1998
ADA	100%	100%
ACU	12%	4%
AFL-CIO	100%	n/a
CCUS	22%	17%

Elections

	1996	1998
General	60%	62%
Primary	u/o	u/o

Ed Bryant (R–Tenn.)
Of Henderson • Elected 1994

Born: Sept. 7, 1948, Jackson, Tenn.
Education: U. of Mississippi, B.A. 1970, J.D. 1972.
Military Career: Army, 1970–78.
Occupation: Lawyer.
Family: Wife, Cynthia; three children.
Religion: Protestant.
Political Career: Republican nominee for U.S. House, 1988; U.S. Attorney, 1991–93.

Capitol Office: 408 Cannon House Office Building 20515; 225-2811; (fax) 225-2989; (e–mail) www.house.gov/writerep; (web) www.house.gov/bryant.
Office Staff: Chief of Staff, P.K. Rehbein; Legis. Dir., Drew Maloney; Press Secy., Steven Susens; Scheduler, Polly Payne.
Committees: Commerce (Energy & Power; Health & Environment; Oversight & Investigations); Judiciary (Commercial & Administrative Law).

Tennessee 7th — West Central — Clarksville; part of Shelby County. The district vote for Bill Clinton was 41% in 1996.

CQ Voting Studies

	1997	1998
Presidential	25%	20%
Party	94%	95%
Participation	98%	99%

Interest Groups

	1997	1998
ADA	5%	0%
ACU	100%	100%
AFL-CIO	0%	n/a
CCUS	100%	100%

Elections

	1996	1998
General	64%	u/o
Primary	u/o	u/o

Richard M. Burr (R–N.C.)
Of Winston-Salem • Elected 1994

Born: Nov. 30, 1955, Charlottesville, Va.
Education: Wake Forest U., B.A. 1978.
Occupation: Marketing manager.
Family: Wife, Brooke; two children.
Religion: Methodist.
Political Career: Republican nominee for U.S. House, 1992.

Capitol Office: 1513 Longworth House Office Building 20515; 225-2071; (fax) 225-2995; (e–mail) richard.burrnc05@mail.house.gov; (web) www.house.gov/burr.
Office Staff: Admin. Asst., Alicia Peterson; Press Secy., John Versaggi; Scheduler, Jim Ray.
Committees: Commerce (Energy & Power; Health & Environment; Oversight & Investigations); International Relations (Asia & the Pacific; International Economic Policy & Trade).

North Carolina 5th — North Central — Part of Winston-Salem. The district vote for Bill Clinton was 36% in 1996.

CQ Voting Studies

	1997	1998
Presidential	28%	23%
Party	92%	89%
Participation	96%	97%

Interest Groups

	1997	1998
ADA	10%	5%
ACU	92%	92%
AFL-CIO	13%	n/a
CCUS	90%	82%

Elections

	1996	1998
General	62%	68%
Primary	u/o	u/o

Dan Burton (R–Ind.)
Of Indianapolis • Elected 1982

Born: June 21, 1938, Indianapolis, Ind.
Education: Indiana U., attended 1958–59; Cincinnati Bible College, attended 1959–60.
Military Career: Army, 1956–57; Army Reserve, 1957–62.
Occupation: Real estate and insurance agent.
Family: Wife, Barbara Logan; three children.
Religion: Christian.
Political Career: Ind. House, 1967–69; Ind. Senate, 1969–71; Republican nominee for U.S. House, 1970; sought Republican nomination for U.S. House, 1972; Ind. House, 1977–81; Ind. Senate, 1981–83.

Capitol Office: 2185 Rayburn House Office Building 20515; 225-2276; (fax) 225-0016; (e–mail) www.house.gov/writerep; (web) www.house.gov/burton.
Office Staff: Chief of Staff, Mark Walker; Press Secy., John Williams; Personal Secy., Claudia Keller.
Committees: Government Reform — chairman; International Relations (International Operations & Human Rights; Western Hemisphere).

Indiana 6th — Central — Suburban Indianapolis. The district vote for Bill Clinton was 28% in 1996.

CQ Voting Studies

	1997	1998
Presidential	25%	20%
Party	92%	86%
Participation	97%	92%

Interest Groups

	1997	1998
ADA	5%	5%
ACU	96%	96%
AFL-CIO	13%	n/a
CCUS	80%	93%

Elections

	1996	1998
General	75%	72%
Primary	u/o	84%

Steve Buyer (R–Ind.)
Of Monticello • Elected 1992
Pronounced: BOO-yer

Born: Nov. 26, 1958, Rensselaer, Ind.
Education: The Citadel, B.S. 1980; Valparaiso U., J.D. 1984.
Military Career: Army Reserve, 1980–84; Army, 1984–87; Army Reserve, 1987–present.
Occupation: Lawyer.
Family: Wife, Joni; two children.
Religion: Methodist.
Political Career: No previous office.

Capitol Office: 227 Cannon House Office Building 20515; 225-5037; (fax) 225-2267; (e-mail) www.house.gov/writerep; (web) www.house.gov/buyer.
Office Staff: Chief of Staff, Kelly Craven; Legis. Dir., Myrna Dugan; Press Secy., Mike Copher; Scheduler, Danelle Bowsher.
Committees: Armed Services (Military Installations & Facilities; Military Personnel — chairman); Veterans' Affairs (Oversight & Investigations).

Indiana 5th — Northern Rural — Kokomo. The district vote for Bill Clinton was 37% in 1996.

CQ Voting Studies

	1997	1998
Presidential	24%	23%
Party	86%	85%
Participation	94%	92%

Interest Groups

	1997	1998
ADA	0%	15%
ACU	83%	88%
AFL-CIO	0%	n/a
CCUS	100%	94%

Elections

	1996	1998
General	65%	63%
Primary	u/o	u/o

Sonny Callahan (R–Ala.)
Of Mobile • Elected 1984

Born: Sept. 11, 1932, Mobile, Ala.
Education: McGill H.S., graduated 1950; U. of Alabama, attended 1959–60.
Military Career: Navy, 1952–54.
Occupation: Moving and storage company executive.
Family: Wife, Karen; six children (one deceased).
Religion: Roman Catholic.
Political Career: Ala. House, 1971–79, served as a Democrat; Ala. Senate, 1979–83, served as a Democrat; sought Democratic nomination for lieutenant governor, 1982.

Capitol Office: 2466 Rayburn House Office Building 20515; 225-4931; (fax) 225-0562; (e-mail) sonny.callahan@mail.house.gov; (web) www.house.gov/callahan.
Office Staff: Chief of Staff/Press Secy., Jo Bonner; Legis. Dir., Nancy E. Tippins; Exec. Asst., Helen Vulevich.
Committees: Appropriations (Energy & Water Development; Foreign Operations & Export Financing — chairman; Transportation).

Alabama 1st — Southwest — Mobile. The district vote for Bill Clinton was 39% in 1996.

CQ Voting Studies

	1997	1998
Presidential	27%	23%
Party	90%	89%
Participation	97%	95%

Interest Groups

	1997	1998
ADA	5%	0%
ACU	88%	96%
AFL-CIO	14%	n/a
CCUS	90%	100%

Elections

	1996	1998
General	64%	u/o
Primary	u/o	u/o

Ken Calvert (R–Calif.)
Of Riverside • Elected 1992

Born: June 8, 1953, Corona, Calif.
Education: Chaffey College, A.A. 1973; San Diego State U., B.A. 1975.
Occupation: Real estate executive.
Family: Divorced.
Religion: Protestant.
Political Career: Sought Republican nomination for U.S. House, 1982; Riverside County Republican Party chairman, 1984–88.

Capitol Office: 2201 Rayburn House Office Building 20515; 225-1986; (fax) 225-2004; (e-mail) www.house.gov/writerep; (web) www.house.gov/calvert.
Office Staff: Chief of Staff, Dave Ramey; Legis. Dir., Chris Pedigo; Press Secy., Kathy Besser; Appts. Secy., Linda Ulrich.
Committees: Agriculture (Livestock & Horticulture); Resources (Water & Power); Science (Energy & Environment — chairman; Space & Aeronautics).

California 43rd — Riverside County — western suburbs. The district vote for Bill Clinton was 43% in 1996.

CQ Voting Studies

	1997	1998
Presidential	27%	24%
Party	93%	93%
Participation	98%	99%

Interest Groups

	1997	1998
ADA	0%	0%
ACU	92%	92%
AFL-CIO	0%	n/a
CCUS	100%	100%

Elections

	1996	1998
General	55%	56%
Primary	74%	*39%

*Open primary

Dave Camp (R–Mich.)
Of Midland • Elected 1990

Born: July 9, 1953, Midland, Mich.
Education: Albion College, B.A. 1975; U. of California, San Diego, J.D. 1978.
Occupation: Lawyer.
Family: Wife, Nancy Keil; two children.
Religion: Roman Catholic.
Political Career: Mich. House, 1989–91.

Capitol Office: 137 Cannon House Office Building 20515; 225-3561; (fax) 225-9679; (e-mail) davecamp@mail.house.gov; (web) www.house.gov/camp.
Office Staff: Chief of Staff, John Guzik; Legis. Dir., Behrends Foster; Press Secy., Margaret Murphy; Exec. Asst., Cheryl Montgomery.
Committees: Standards of Official Conduct; Ways & Means (Health; Human Resources; Trade).

Michigan 4th — North Central — Midland. The district vote for Bill Clinton was 47% in 1996.

CQ Voting Studies

	1997	1998
Presidential	32%	27%
Party	92%	91%
Participation	99%	99%

Interest Groups

	1997	1998
ADA	20%	10%
ACU	84%	96%
AFL-CIO	13%	n/a
CCUS	100%	100%

Elections

	1996	1998
General	65%	91%
Primary	u/o	u/o

Tom Campbell (R–Calif.)
Of Campbell • Elected 1988
Did not serve 1993–95

Born: Aug. 14, 1952, Chicago, Ill.
Education: U. of Chicago, B.A. 1973, M.A. 1973; Harvard U., J.D. 1976; U. of Chicago, Ph.D. 1980.
Occupation: Economics professor; federal official; lawyer.
Family: Wife, Susanne Martin Campbell.
Religion: Roman Catholic.
Political Career: U.S. House, 1989–93; sought Republican nomination for U.S. Senate, 1992; Calif. Senate, 1993–95.

Capitol Office: 2442 Rayburn House Office Building 20515; 225-2631; (fax) 225-6788; (e-mail) campbell@mail.house.gov; (web) www.house.gov/campbell.
Office Staff: Admin. Asst., Jackie Benditt; Legis. Dir., Charlie DeWitt; Press Secy., Suhail Khan; Scheduler, Annabelle Romero.
Committees: Banking & Financial Services (Financial Institutions & Consumer Credit; Housing & Community Opportunity); International Relations (Africa; International Economic Policy & Trade).

California 15th — Santa Clara and Santa Cruz counties. The district vote for Bill Clinton was 53% in 1996.

CQ Voting Studies

	1997	1998
Presidential	51%	51%
Party	75%	64%
Participation	99%	99%

Interest Groups

	1997	1998
ADA	50%	35%
ACU	68%	52%
AFL-CIO	38%	n/a
CCUS	80%	72%

Elections

	1996	1998
General	59%	61%
Primary	u/o	*66%

*Open primary

Charles T. Canady (R–Fla.)
Of Lakeland • Elected 1992
Pronounced: CAN-uh–dee

Born: June 22, 1954, Lakeland, Fla.
Education: Haverford College, B.A. 1976; Yale U., J.D. 1979.
Occupation: Lawyer.
Family: Wife, Jennifer Houghton.
Religion: Presbyterian.
Political Career: Fla. House, 1984–90, majority whip 1986–88; Republican nominee for Fla. Senate, 1990.

Capitol Office: 2432 Rayburn House Office Building 20515; 225-1252; (fax) 225-2279; (e-mail) rep.charles.canady@mail.house.gov; (web) www.house.gov/canady.
Office Staff: Chief of Staff, Stacey Windham; Legis. Dir., Zack Moore; Press Secy., Bridget Bustillos; Scheduler, Athena Buonome.
Committees: Agriculture (Department Operations, Oversight, Nutrition & Forestry); Judiciary (Constitution — chairman; Crime; Immigration & Claims).

Florida 12th — Central — Polk County; Lakeland; parts of Hillsborough County. The district vote for Bill Clinton was 43% in 1996.

CQ Voting Studies

	1997	1998
Presidential	29%	22%
Party	93%	93%
Participation	99%	99%

Interest Groups

	1997	1998
ADA	10%	5%
ACU	92%	88%
AFL-CIO	13%	n/a
CCUS	100%	89%

Elections

	1996	1998
General	62%	u/o
Primary	u/o	u/o

Christopher B. Cannon (R–Utah)
Of Mapleton • Elected 1996

Born: Oct. 20, 1950, Salt Lake City, Utah.
Education: Brigham Young U., B.S. 1968–74, J.D. 1980.
Occupation: Venture capital executive; steel company executive; cabinet department lawyer; lawyer.
Family: Wife, Claudia Fox Cannon; seven children.
Religion: Mormon.
Political Career: Utah Republican Party finance chairman, 1992–94.

Capitol Office: 118 Cannon House Office Building 20515; 225-7751; (fax) 225-5629; (e–mail) cannon.ut03@mail.house.gov; (web) www.house.gov/cannon.
Office Staff: Admin. Asst., Mark Emerson; Legis. Dir., Claudia A. Hrvatin; Communications Dir., Rusty Payne; Scheduler, Courtney Chapman.
Committees: Judiciary (Courts & Intellectual Property; Immigration & Claims); Resources (Energy & Mineral Resources; National Parks & Public Lands); Science (Space & Aeronautics; Technology).

Utah 3rd — East — Provo; Orem; rural Utah. The district vote for Bill Clinton was 29% in 1996.

CQ Voting Studies

	1997	1998
Presidential	31%	17%
Party	93%	87%
Participation	98%	89%

Interest Groups

	1997	1998
ADA	10%	5%
ACU	96%	95%
AFL-CIO	13%	n/a
CCUS	90%	100%

Elections

	1996	1998
General	51%	77%
Primary	56%	76%

Lois Capps (D–Calif.)
Of Santa Barbara • Elected 1998

Born: Jan. 10, 1938, Ladysmith, Wis.
Education: Pacific Lutheran U., B.S. 1959; Yale U., M.A. 1964; U. of California, Santa Barbara, M.A. 1990.
Occupation: Elementary school nurse; college instructor.
Family: Widowed; three children.
Religion: Lutheran.
Political Career: No previous office.

Capitol Office: 1118 Longworth House Office Building 20515; 225-3601; (fax) 225-5632; (e–mail) lois.capps@mail.house.gov; (web) www.house.gov/capps.
Office Staff: Chief of Staff, Jeremy Rabinovitz; Legis. Dir., Randolph Harrison; Press Secy., Lisa Finkel; Scheduler, Alishya Mayfield.
Committees: Commerce (Finance & Hazardous Materials; Health & Environment).

California 22nd — Santa Barbara; Santa Maria; San Luis Obispo. The district vote for Bill Clinton was 44% in 1996.

CQ Voting Studies

	1998
Presidential	73%
Party	90%
Participation	99%

Interest Groups

	1998
ADA	85%
ACU	18%
AFL-CIO	n/a
CCUS	71%

Elections

	1998	1998
General	*54%	55%
Primary	*45%	†52%

*Special election
†Open primary

Michael E. Capuano (D–Mass.)
Of Somerville • Elected 1998
Pronounced: CAP-oo-ON-oh

Born: Jan. 9, 1952, Somerville, Mass.
Education: Dartmouth College, B.A. 1973; Boston College, J.D. 1977.
Occupation: Lawyer; Mass. legislature aide.
Family: Wife, Barbara Teebagy; two children.
Religion: Roman Catholic.
Political Career: Somerville alderman, 1977–79; candidate for Somerville mayor, 1979, 1981; Somerville alderman–at–large, 1985–89; mayor of Somerville, 1990–99; sought Democratic nomination for Mass. secretary of state, 1994.

Capitol Office: 1232 Longworth House Office Building 20515; 225-5111; (fax) 225-9322; (e–mail) www.house.gov/writerep.
Office Staff: Admin. Asst., Dan Muroff; Legis. Dir., Robert Primus; Scheduler, Geoff Mackler.
Committees: Banking & Financial Services (Capital Markets & Securities; Housing & Community Opportunity); Science (Technology).

Massachusetts 8th — Parts of Boston and suburbs — Cambridge; Somerville. The district vote for Bill Clinton was 77% in 1996.

Elections

	1998
General	82%
Primary	23%

Benjamin L. Cardin (D–Md.)
Of Baltimore • Elected 1986

Born: Oct. 5, 1943, Baltimore, Md.
Education: U. of Pittsburgh, B.A. 1964; U. of Maryland, LL.B. 1967.
Occupation: Lawyer.
Family: Wife, Myrna Edelman Cardin; two children.
Religion: Jewish.
Political Career: Md. House, 1967–87, speaker, 1979–87.

Capitol Office: 104 Cannon House Office Building 20515; 225-4016; (fax) 225-9219; (e–mail) rep.cardin@mail.house.gov; (web) www.house.gov/cardin.
Office Staff: Admin. Asst., David Koshgarian; Legis. Dir., Michael Enright; Press Secy., Susan Sullam; Office Mgr./Scheduler, Debbie Yamada.
Committees: Ways & Means (Human Resources — ranking member; Social Security).

Maryland 3rd — Downtown and ethnic Baltimore; Columbia. The district vote for Bill Clinton was 58% in 1996.

CQ Voting Studies

	1997	1998
Presidential	83%	74%
Party	85%	86%
Participation	98%	95%

Interest Groups

	1997	1998
ADA	85%	95%
ACU	12%	8%
AFL-CIO	88%	n/a
CCUS	40%	25%

Elections

	1996	1998
General	67%	78%
Primary	90%	90%

Julia Carson (D–Ind.)
Of Indianapolis • Elected 1996

Born: July 8, 1938, Louisville, Ky.
Education: Martin U., attended 1994–95.
Occupation: Clothing store owner; human resources manager; congressional aide.
Family: Divorced; two children.
Religion: Baptist.
Political Career: Ind. House, 1973–77; Ind. Senate, 1977–91; Center Township trustee, 1991–97.

Capitol Office: 1541 Longworth House Office Building 20515; 225-4011; (fax) 225-5633; (e-mail) rep.carson@mail.house.gov; (web) www.house.gov/carson.
Office Staff: Chief of Staff, Sarge Visher; Legis. Dir., Susan Role; Press Secy., Steve Cook; Scheduler, Arline Flournoy.
Committees: Banking & Financial Services (Domestic & International Monetary Policy; Housing & Community Opportunity); Veterans' Affairs (Health).

Indiana 10th — Central — Indianapolis. The district vote for Bill Clinton was 54% in 1996.

CQ Voting Studies

	1997	1998
Presidential	72%	83%
Party	84%	92%
Participation	87%	93%

Interest Groups

	1997	1998
ADA	90%	95%
ACU	9%	0%
AFL-CIO	100%	n/a
CCUS	30%	22%

Elections

	1996	1998
General	53%	58%
Primary	49%	87%

Michael N. Castle (R–Del.)
Of Wilmington • Elected 1992

Born: July 2, 1939, Wilmington, Del.
Education: Hamilton College, B.A. 1961; Georgetown U., LL.B. 1964.
Occupation: Lawyer.
Family: Wife, Jane DiSabatino.
Religion: Roman Catholic.
Political Career: Del. deputy attorney general, 1965–66; Del. House, 1967–69; Del. Senate, 1969–77, minority leader, 1976–77; lieutenant governor, 1981–85; governor, 1985–93.

Capitol Office: 1227 Longworth House Office Building 20515; 225-4165; (fax) 225-2291; (e-mail) delaware@mail.house.gov; (web) www.house.gov/castle.
Office Staff: Admin. Asst., Paul Leonard; Legis. Dir., Booth Jameson; Press Secy., Ronald Bonjean; Scheduler, Helen Prince.
Committees: Banking & Financial Services (Domestic & International Monetary Policy; Financial Institutions & Consumer Credit); Education & Workforce (Early Childhood, Youth & Families — chairman; Postsecondary Education, Training & Life-Long Learning); Select Intelligence (Technical & Tactical Intelligence — chairman).

Delaware — At large. The district vote for Bill Clinton was 52% in 1996.

CQ Voting Studies

	1997	1998
Presidential	55%	51%
Party	72%	63%
Participation	99%	99%

Interest Groups

	1997	1998
ADA	50%	30%
ACU	56%	42%
AFL-CIO	38%	n/a
CCUS	90%	67%

Elections

	1996	1998
General	70%	66%
Primary	u/o	u/o

Steve Chabot (R–Ohio)
Of Cincinnati • Elected 1994
Pronounced: SHAB-butt

Born: Jan. 22, 1953, Cincinnati, Ohio.
Education: College of William and Mary, B.A. 1975; Northern Kentucky U., J.D. 1978.
Occupation: Lawyer.
Family: Wife, Donna; two children.
Religion: Roman Catholic.
Political Career: Independent candidate for Cincinnati City Council, 1979; Republican candidate for Cincinnati City Council, 1983; Cincinnati City Council, 1985–90; Republican nominee for U.S. House, 1988; Hamilton County commissioner, 1990–95.

Capitol Office: 129 Cannon House Office Building 20515; 225-2216; (fax) 225-3012; (e–mail) www.house.gov/writerep; (web) www.house.gov/chabot.
Office Staff: Admin. Asst./Press Secy., Gary Lindgren; Legis. Dir., Kevin W. Fitzpatrick; Scheduler/Exec. Asst., Cynthia Keegan.
Committees: International Relations (Africa; International Economic Policy & Trade); Judiciary (Commercial & Administrative Law; Crime); Small Business (Tax, Finance & Exports).

Ohio 1st — Hamilton County — Western Cincinnati and suburbs. The district vote for Bill Clinton was 50% in 1996.

CQ Voting Studies

	1997	1998
Presidential	27%	27%
Party	87%	91%
Participation	99%	99%

Interest Groups

	1997	1998
ADA	20%	0%
ACU	96%	96%
AFL-CIO	0%	n/a
CCUS	100%	83%

Elections

	1996	1998
General	54%	53%
Primary	u/o	u/o

Saxby Chambliss (R–Ga.)
Of Moultrie • Elected 1994
Pronounced: SAX-bee CHAM-bliss

Born: Nov. 10, 1943, Warrenton, N.C.
Education: Louisiana Tech U., attended 1961–62; U. of Georgia, B.B.A. 1966; U. of Tennessee, J.D. 1968.
Occupation: Lawyer; hotel owner.
Family: Wife, Julianne; two children.
Religion: Episcopalian.
Political Career: Sought Republican nomination for U.S. House, 1992.

Capitol Office: 1019 Longworth House Office Building 20515; 225-6531; (fax) 225-3013; (e–mail) saxby@mail.house.gov; (web) www.house.gov/chambliss.
Office Staff: Chief of Staff, Rob Leebern; Legis. Dir., Krister Holiday; Press Secy., Matthew Strawn; Scheduler, Priscilla Jones.
Committees: Agriculture (Department Operations, Oversight, Nutrition & Forestry; General Farm Commodities; Risk Management, Research & Specialty Crops); Armed Services (Military Readiness; Military Research & Development); Budget.

Georgia 8th — South Central — Macon; Warner Robins. The district vote for Bill Clinton was 47% in 1996.

CQ Voting Studies

	1997	1998
Presidential	25%	22%
Party	93%	94%
Participation	97%	99%

Interest Groups

	1997	1998
ADA	5%	0%
ACU	88%	96%
AFL-CIO	0%	n/a
CCUS	88%	94%

Elections

	1996	1998
General	53%	62%
Primary	u/o	u/o

Helen Chenoweth (R–Idaho)
Of Boise • Elected 1994
Pronounced: CHEN-o-weth

Born: Jan. 27, 1938, Topeka, Kan.
Education: Whitworth College, attended 1955–58.
Occupation: Public affairs and policy consultant; congressional aide.
Family: Divorced; two children.
Religion: Christian.
Political Career: Idaho Republican Party executive director, 1975–77.

Capitol Office: 1727 Longworth House Office Building 20515; 225-6611; (fax) 225-3029; (e–mail) askhelen@mail.house.gov; (web) www.house.gov/chenoweth.
Office Staff: Chief of Staff, Keith Lee Rupp; Legis. Dir., Gregory Peek; Communications Dir., Chad Hyslop; Exec. Asst., Lisa Staker.
Committees: Agriculture (Livestock & Horticulture); Government Reform (National Economic Growth; National Security & Veterans Affairs); Resources (Forests & Forest Health — chairman; Water & Power); Veterans' Affairs (Health).

Idaho 1st — West — Boise; Nampa; Panhandle. The district vote for Bill Clinton was 35% in 1996.

CQ Voting Studies

	1997	1998
Presidential	24%	29%
Party	90%	88%
Participation	96%	98%

Interest Groups

	1997	1998
ADA	0%	20%
ACU	96%	92%
AFL-CIO	0%	n/a
CCUS	70%	67%

Elections

	1996	1998
General	50%	55%
Primary	68%	71%

William L. Clay (D–Mo.)
Of St. Louis • Elected 1968

Born: Apr. 30, 1931, St. Louis, Mo.
Education: St. Louis U., B.S. 1953.
Military Career: Army, 1953–55.
Occupation: Real estate and insurance broker.
Family: Wife, Carol Ann Johnson; three children.
Religion: Roman Catholic.
Political Career: St. Louis Board of Aldermen, 1959–64; St. Louis Democratic Committee, 1964–67.

Capitol Office: 2306 Rayburn House Office Building 20515; 225-2406; (fax) 225-1725; (e–mail) www.house.gov/writerep; (web) www.house.gov/clay.
Office Staff: Chief of Staff/Press Secy., Harriet Pritchett Grigsby; Legis. Dir., Michelle Bogdanovich; Secy., Eunice McCall.
Committees: Education & Workforce — ranking member.

Missouri 1st — North St. Louis; Northeast St. Louis County. The district vote for Bill Clinton was 74% in 1996.

CQ Voting Studies

	1997	1998
Presidential	75%	73%
Party	86%	83%
Participation	90%	87%

Interest Groups

	1997	1998
ADA	95%	85%
ACU	9%	5%
AFL-CIO	100%	n/a
CCUS	20%	19%

Elections

	1996	1998
General	70%	73%
Primary	78%	u/o

Eva Clayton (D-N.C.)
Of Littleton • Elected 1992

Born: Sept. 16, 1934, Savannah, Ga.
Education: Johnson C. Smith U., B.S. 1955; North Carolina Central U., M.S. 1962; U. of North Carolina, attended 1967.
Occupation: Consulting firm owner; nonprofit executive; state official; university official.
Family: Husband, Theaoseus; four children.
Religion: Presbyterian.
Political Career: Sought Democratic nomination for U.S. House, 1968; N.C. assistant secretary of natural resources, 1977–81; Warren County Commission, 1982–92, chairman 1982–90.

Capitol Office: 2440 Rayburn House Office Building 20515; 225-3101; (fax) 225-3354; (e-mail) eclayton1@mail.house.gov; (web) www.house.gov/clayton.
Office Staff: Admin. Asst./Press Secy., Johnny Barnes; Legis. Dir., Corliss Clemonts-James; Exec. Asst., Jean R. Chippel.
Committees: Agriculture (Department Operations, Oversight, Nutrition & Forestry — ranking member; General Farm Commodities); Budget.

North Carolina 1st — Northeast — Parts of Goldsboro, Greenville and Rocky Mount. The district vote for Bill Clinton was 58% in 1996.

CQ Voting Studies

	1997	1998
Presidential	71%	80%
Party	88%	90%
Participation	95%	94%

Interest Groups

	1997	1998
ADA	100%	100%
ACU	4%	0%
AFL-CIO	100%	n/a
CCUS	40%	39%

Elections

	1996	1998
General	66%	62%
Primary	u/o	67%

Bob Clement (D-Tenn.)
Of Nashville • Elected 1988

Born: Sept. 23, 1943, Nashville, Tenn.
Education: U. of Tennessee, B.S. 1967; Memphis State U., M.B.A. 1968.
Military Career: Army, 1969–71; National Guard, 1971–present.
Occupation: College president; marketing, management and real estate executive.
Family: Wife, Mary; two children, two stepchildren.
Religion: Methodist.
Political Career: Tenn. Public Service Commission, 1973–79; sought Democratic nomination for governor, 1978; Democratic nominee for U.S. House, 1982.

Capitol Office: 2229 Rayburn House Office Building 20515; 225-4311; (fax) 226-1035; (e-mail) bob.clement@mail.house.gov; (web) www.house.gov/clement.
Office Staff: Chief of Staff, Alex Haught; Legis. Dir., Caroline Neilson; Press Secy., Christi Ray; Exec. Asst., Carolyn Waugh.
Committees: Budget; Transportation & Infrastructure (Ground Transportation; Water Resources & Environment).

Tennessee 5th — Nashville. The district vote for Bill Clinton was 55% in 1996.

CQ Voting Studies

	1997	1998
Presidential	64%	65%
Party	71%	74%
Participation	97%	97%

Interest Groups

	1997	1998
ADA	55%	85%
ACU	25%	24%
AFL-CIO	75%	n/a
CCUS	80%	72%

Elections

	1996	1998
General	72%	83%
Primary	u/o	u/o

James E. Clyburn (D-S.C.)
Of Columbia • Elected 1992

Born: July 21, 1940, Sumter, S.C.
Education: South Carolina State College, B.S. 1962.
Occupation: State official; teacher.
Family: Wife, Emily England; three children.
Religion: African Methodist Episcopal.
Political Career: S.C. Human Affairs commissioner, 1974–92; sought Democratic nomination for S.C. secretary of state, 1978, 1986.
Capitol Office: 319 Cannon House Office Building 20515; 225-3315; (fax) 225-2313; (e-mail) jclyburn@mail.house.gov; (web) www.house.gov/clyburn.
Office Staff: Chief of Staff, Yelberton Watkins; Legis. Dir., Danny Cromer; Legis. Asst./Press Asst., Lindy Birch; Scheduler, Jennie Chaplin.
Committees: Appropriations (Energy & Water Development; Transportation).

South Carolina 6th — Central and South — Florence; parts of Columbia and Charleston. The district vote for Bill Clinton was 66% in 1996.

CQ Voting Studies

	1997	1998
Presidential	75%	83%
Party	87%	93%
Participation	98%	97%

Interest Groups

	1997	1998
ADA	90%	95%
ACU	16%	4%
AFL-CIO	100%	n/a
CCUS	30%	28%

Elections

	1996	1998
General	69%	73%
Primary	88%	83%

Howard Coble (R-N.C.)
Of Greensboro • Elected 1984

Born: Mar. 18, 1931, Greensboro, N.C.
Education: Appalachian State U., attended 1949–50; Guilford College, A.B. 1958; U. of North Carolina, J.D. 1962.
Military Career: Coast Guard, 1952–56; Coast Guard Reserve, 1960–82; Coast Guard, 1977–78.
Occupation: Lawyer; insurance claims supervisor.
Family: Single.
Religion: Presbyterian.
Political Career: N.C. House, 1969; assistant U.S. attorney, 1969–73; N.C. Department of Revenue secretary, 1973–77; Republican nominee for N.C. treasurer, 1976; N.C. House, 1979–83.

Capitol Office: 2468 Rayburn House Office Building 20515; 225-3065; (fax) 225-8611; (e-mail) repcoble@mail.house.gov; (web) www.house.gov/coble.
Office Staff: Admin. Asst./Press Secy., Edward McDonald; Legis. Dir., Missy Branson; Exec. Asst., Carolyn Williams.
Committees: Judiciary (Courts & Intellectual Property — chairman; Crime); Transportation & Infrastructure (Coast Guard & Maritime Transportation; Ground Transportation).

North Carolina 6th — Central — Greensboro and High Point. The district vote for Bill Clinton was 42% in 1996.

CQ Voting Studies

	1997	1998
Presidential	24%	16%
Party	93%	91%
Participation	98%	96%

Interest Groups

	1997	1998
ADA	5%	10%
ACU	88%	96%
AFL-CIO	0%	n/a
CCUS	90%	89%

Elections

	1996	1998
General	73%	89%
Primary	u/o	u/o

Tom Coburn (R–Okla.)
Of Muskogee • Elected 1994

Born: Mar. 14, 1948, Casper, Wyo.
Education: Oklahoma State U., B.S. 1970; Oklahoma U., M.D. 1983.
Occupation: Physician; optical firm manager.
Family: Wife, Carolyn; three children.
Religion: Baptist.
Political Career: No previous office.

Capitol Office: 429 Cannon House Office Building 20515; 225-2701; (fax) 225-3038; (e–mail) rep.coburn@mail.house.gov; (web) www.house.gov/coburn.
Office Staff: Chief of Staff/Press Secy., Karl E. Ahlgren; Press Secy., John Hart; Scheduler, Melissa James; Scheduler, Gwen Coburn.
Committees: Commerce (Energy & Power; Health & Environment).

Oklahoma 2nd — Northeast — Muskogee. The district vote for Bill Clinton was 47% in 1996.

CQ Voting Studies

	1997	1998
Presidential	23%	16%
Party	85%	91%
Participation	92%	97%

Interest Groups

	1997	1998
ADA	5%	5%
ACU	95%	100%
AFL-CIO	0%	n/a
CCUS	78%	71%

Elections

	1996	1998
General	55%	58%
Primary	u/o	u/o

Mac Collins (R–Ga.)
Of Hampton • Elected 1992

Born: Oct. 15, 1944, Jackson, Ga.
Education: Jackson H.S., graduated 1962.
Military Career: National Guard, 1964–70.
Occupation: Trucking company owner.
Family: Wife, Julie; four children.
Religion: Methodist.
Political Career: Butts County Commission chairman, 1977–81; Flovilla City Council, 1977–81; candidate for Ga. Senate, 1984, 1986; Ga. Senate, 1989–93.

Capitol Office: 1131 Longworth House Office Building 20515; 225-5901; (fax) 225-2515; (e–mail) mac.collins@mail.house.gov; (web) www.house.gov/maccollins.
Office Staff: Admin. Asst., Betty Monro; Legis. Dir., Bo Bryant; Press Secy., Sari Greenberg; Scheduler, Anne Jasien.
Committees: Budget; Ways & Means (Social Security).

Georgia 3rd — West Central — Columbus; Atlanta suburbs. The district vote for Bill Clinton was 43% in 1996.

CQ Voting Studies

	1997	1998
Presidential	27%	12%
Party	90%	93%
Participation	95%	97%

Interest Groups

	1997	1998
ADA	5%	0%
ACU	83%	100%
AFL-CIO	13%	n/a
CCUS	80%	83%

Elections

	1996	1998
General	61%	u/o
Primary	u/o	u/o

Larry Combest (R–Texas)
Of Lubbock • Elected 1984

Born: Mar. 20, 1945, Memphis, Texas.
Education: West Texas State U., B.B.A. 1969.
Occupation: Electronics wholesaler; congressional aide; farmer.
Family: Wife, Sharon; two children.
Religion: Methodist.
Political Career: No previous office.

Capitol Office: 1026 Longworth House Office Building 20515; 225-4005; (e–mail) www.house.gov/writerep; (web) www.house.gov/combest.
Office Staff: Admin. Asst., Rob Lehman; Press Secy., Becca Underwood; Office Mgr., Lynn Cowart.
Committees: Agriculture — chairman; Small Business (Regulatory Reform & Paperwork Reduction).

Texas 19th — Western Panhandle — Parts of Lubbuck and Amarillo. The district vote for Bill Clinton was 26% in 1996.

CQ Voting Studies

	1997	1998
Presidential	29%	22%
Party	94%	95%
Participation	98%	99%

Interest Groups

	1997	1998
ADA	10%	0%
ACU	92%	100%
AFL-CIO	0%	n/a
CCUS	100%	94%

Elections

	1996	1998
General	80%	84%
Primary	u/o	u/o

Gary A. Condit (D–Calif.)
Of Ceres • Elected 1989

Born: Apr. 21, 1948, Salina, Okla.
Education: California State U., Stanislaus, B.A. 1972.
Occupation: Public official.
Family: Wife, Carolyn Berry; two children.
Religion: Baptist.
Political Career: Ceres City Council, 1972–76, mayor, 1974–76; Stanislaus County Board of Supervisors, 1976–82, chairman, 1980; Calif. Assembly, 1983–89.

Capitol Office: 2234 Rayburn House Office Building 20515; 225-6131; (fax) 225-0819; (e–mail) gary.condit@mail.house.gov; (web) www.house.gov/gcondit.
Office Staff: Admin. Asst./Scheduler, Mike Dayton; Press Secy., Randy Groves; Scheduler, Ashley Newell.
Committees: Agriculture (Livestock & Horticulture; Risk Management, Research & Specialty Crops — ranking member); Select Intelligence (Human Intelligence, Analysis & Counterintelligence; Technical & Tactical Intelligence).

California 18th — Central Valley — Modesto; Merced. The district vote for Bill Clinton was 46% in 1996.

CQ Voting Studies

	1997	1998
Presidential	53%	50%
Party	60%	62%
Participation	99%	99%

Interest Groups

	1997	1998
ADA	60%	60%
ACU	52%	56%
AFL-CIO	75%	n/a
CCUS	60%	67%

Elections

	1996	1998
General	66%	87%
Primary	u/o	*89%

*Open primary

John Conyers Jr. (D–Mich.)
Of Detroit • Elected 1964

Born: May 16, 1929, Detroit, Mich.
Education: Wayne State U., B.A. 1957, LL.B. 1958.
Military Career: National Guard, 1948–50; Army, 1950–54; Army Reserve, 1954–57.
Occupation: Lawyer; congressional aide.
Family: Wife, Monica; two children.
Religion: Baptist.
Political Career: Candidate for mayor of Detroit, 1989, 1993.

Capitol Office: 2426 Rayburn House Office Building 20515; 225-5126; (fax) 225-0072; (e-mail) john.conyers@mail.house.gov; (web) www.house.gov/conyers.
Office Staff: Chief of Staff, Greg Moore; Legis. Dir., Carl LeVan; Press Secy., Andrea McCombs; Scheduler, Kathryn Baer.
Committees: Judiciary — ranking member (Constitution; Courts & Intellectual Property).

Michigan 14th — Parts of Detroit; Harper Woods; Highland Park. The district vote for Bill Clinton was 86% in 1996.

CQ Voting Studies

	1997	1998
Presidential	77%	79%
Party	90%	84%
Participation	91%	90%

Interest Groups

	1997	1998
ADA	95%	80%
ACU	4%	0%
AFL-CIO	100%	n/a
CCUS	30%	20%

Elections

	1996	1998
General	86%	87%
Primary	u/o	u/o

Merrill Cook (R–Utah)
Of Salt Lake City • Elected 1996

Born: May 6, 1946, Philadelphia, Pa.
Education: U. of Utah, B.A. 1969; Harvard U., M.B.A. 1971.
Occupation: Explosives company executive; radio talk show host; management consultant.
Family: Wife, Camille; five children.
Religion: Mormon.
Political Career: Candidate for Utah Board of Education, 1984; candidate for mayor of Salt Lake City, 1985; Republican nominee for Salt Lake County Commission, 1986; Independent candidate for governor, 1988, 1992; Independent candidate for U.S. House, 1994.

Capitol Office: 1431 Longworth House Office Building 20515; 225-3011; (fax) 225-5638; (e-mail) cong.merrill.cook@mail.house.gov; (web) www.house.gov/cook.
Office Staff: Admin. Asst., Connie Humphrey; Press Secy., Ginger Lowe.
Committees: Banking & Financial Services (Capital Markets & Securities; Financial Institutions & Consumer Credit); Science (Space & Aeronautics; Technology); Transportation & Infrastructure (Aviation; Ground Transportation).

Utah 2nd — Central — Parts of Salt Lake City. The district vote for Bill Clinton was 41% in 1996.

CQ Voting Studies

	1997	1998
Presidential	24%	18%
Party	92%	87%
Participation	100%	97%

Interest Groups

	1997	1998
ADA	5%	15%
ACU	88%	84%
AFL-CIO	0%	n/a
CCUS	80%	89%

Elections

	1996	1998
General	55%	53%
Primary	52%	u/o

John Cooksey (R–La.)
Of Monroe • Elected 1996

Born: Aug. 20, 1941, Alexandria, La.
Education: Louisiana State U., B.A. 1962, M.D. 1966; U. of Texas, M.B.A. 1994.
Military Career: Air Force, 1967–69; Air National Guard, 1969–72.
Occupation: Physician.
Family: Wife, Ann; three children.
Religion: Methodist.
Political Career: No previous office.

Capitol Office: 317 Cannon House Office Building 20515; 225-8490; (fax) 225-5639; (e–mail) congressman.cooksey@mail.house.gov; (web) www.house.gov/cooksey.
Office Staff: Admin. Asst., Lee Fletcher; Legis. Dir., Jim Phalen; Press Secy., Bob Anderson; Scheduler, Ali de Jongh.
Committees: Agriculture (Department Operations, Oversight, Nutrition & Forestry); International Relations (Asia & the Pacific; International Economic Policy & Trade); Transportation & Infrastructure (Aviation; Economic Development & Public Buildings).

Louisiana 5th — Northeast and central — Monroe; Alexandria. The district vote for Bill Clinton was 47% in 1996.

CQ Voting Studies

	1997	1998
Presidential	28%	23%
Party	90%	88%
Participation	93%	91%

Interest Groups

	1997	1998
ADA	10%	0%
ACU	91%	96%
AFL-CIO	0%	n/a
CCUS	100%	100%

Elections

	1996	1998
General	58%	u/o
Primary	34%	—

Jerry F. Costello (D–Ill.)
Of Belleville • Elected 1988

Born: Sept. 25, 1949, East St. Louis, Ill.
Education: Belleville Area College, A.A. 1970; Maryville College of the Sacred Heart, B.A. 1972.
Occupation: Law enforcement official.
Family: Wife, Georgia Cockrum Costello; three children.
Religion: Roman Catholic.
Political Career: St. Clair County Board chairman, 1980–88.

Capitol Office: 2454 Rayburn House Office Building 20515; 225-5661; (fax) 225-0285; (e–mail) jfc.il12@mail.house.gov; (web) www.house.gov/costello.
Office Staff: Admin. Asst./Press Secy., Brian Lott; Legis. Dir., Elizabeth Pile; Scheduler, Cindy O'Flaherty-Dolasinski.
Committees: Science (Energy & Environment — ranking member); Transportation & Infrastructure (Aviation; Water Resources & Environment).

Illinois 12th — Southwest — Carbondale; East St. Louis. The district vote for Bill Clinton was 56% in 1996.

CQ Voting Studies

	1997	1998
Presidential	57%	67%
Party	73%	75%
Participation	97%	98%

Interest Groups

	1997	1998
ADA	85%	90%
ACU	25%	25%
AFL-CIO	100%	n/a
CCUS	40%	28%

Elections

	1996	1998
General	72%	60%
Primary	u/o	87%

Christopher Cox (R–Calif.)
Of Newport Beach • Elected 1988

Born: Oct. 16, 1952, St. Paul, Minn.
Education: U. of Southern California, B.A. 1973; Harvard U., M.B.A. 1977, J.D. 1977.
Occupation: White House counsel; lawyer; professor.
Family: Wife, Rebecca; three children.
Religion: Roman Catholic.
Political Career: No previous office.

Capitol Office: 2402 Rayburn House Office Building 20515; 225-5611; (fax) 225-9177; (e-mail) christopher.cox@mail.house.gov; (web) www.house.gov/chriscox.
Office Staff: Chief of Staff, C. Dean McGrath; Legis. Dir., Peter Uhlmann; Press Secy., Paul Wilkinson; Appts. Secy., Lance Larson.
Committees: Commerce (Finance & Hazardous Materials; Oversight & Investigations; Telecommunications, Trade & Consumer Protection); China Investigation — chairman.

California 47th — Coastal — Central Orange County; Irvine. The district vote for Bill Clinton was 36% in 1996.

CQ Voting Studies

	1997	1998
Presidential	23%	26%
Party	87%	89%
Participation	91%	95%

Interest Groups

	1997	1998
ADA	10%	0%
ACU	96%	100%
AFL-CIO	0%	n/a
CCUS	75%	89%

Elections

	1996	1998
General	66%	68%
Primary	u/o	*71%

*Open primary

William J. Coyne (D–Pa.)
Of Pittsburgh • Elected 1980

Born: Aug. 24, 1936, Pittsburgh, Pa.
Education: Robert Morris College, B.S. 1965.
Military Career: Army, 1955–57.
Occupation: Accountant.
Family: Single.
Religion: Roman Catholic.
Political Career: Pa. House, 1971–73; sought Democratic nomination for Pa. Senate, 1972; Pittsburgh City Council, 1974–81.

Capitol Office: 2455 Rayburn House Office Building 20515; 225-2301; (fax) 225-1844; (e-mail) www.house.gov/writerep; (web) www.house.gov/coyne.
Office Staff: Admin. Asst./Legis. Dir., Coleman J. Conroy; Press Secy., Matt Dinkel; Appts. Secy./Receptionist, Elisa Howie.
Committees: Ways & Means (Human Resources; Oversight — ranking member).

Pennsylvania 14th — Pittsburgh and suburbs. The district vote for Bill Clinton was 59% in 1996.

CQ Voting Studies

	1997	1998
Presidential	83%	82%
Party	97%	95%
Participation	99%	99%

Interest Groups

	1997	1998
ADA	100%	80%
ACU	0%	4%
AFL-CIO	100%	n/a
CCUS	20%	22%

Elections

	1996	1998
General	61%	61%
Primary	66%	u/o

Robert E. "Bud" Cramer (D–Ala.)
Of Huntsville • Elected 1990

Born: Aug. 22, 1947, Huntsville, Ala.
Education: U. of Alabama, B.A. 1969, J.D. 1972.
Military Career: Army, 1972; Army Reserve, 1976–78.
Occupation: Lawyer.
Family: Widowed; one child.
Religion: Methodist.
Political Career: Madison County district attorney, 1981–91.

Capitol Office: 2350 Rayburn House Office Building 20515; 225-4801; (e-mail) budmail@mail.house.gov; (web) www.house.gov/cramer.
Office Staff: Admin. Asst., Jeff Murray; Legis. Dir., Shar Hendrick; Press Secy., David Butler; Exec. Asst., Samantha Smith.
Committees: Appropriations (Interior; VA, HUD & Independent Agencies).

Alabama 5th — North — Huntsville. The district vote for Bill Clinton was 43% in 1996.

CQ Voting Studies

	1997	1998
Presidential	52%	52%
Party	58%	58%
Participation	99%	98%

Interest Groups

	1997	1998
ADA	45%	65%
ACU	48%	44%
AFL-CIO	75%	n/a
CCUS	80%	78%

Elections

	1996	1998
General	56%	70%
Primary	u/o	u/o

Philip M. Crane (R–Ill.)
Of Wauconda • Elected 1969

Born: Nov. 3, 1930, Chicago, Ill.
Education: DePauw U., attended 1948–50; Hillsdale College, B.A. 1952; U. of Michigan, attended 1952–54; U. of Vienna (Austria), attended 1953, attended 1956; Indiana U., M.A. 1961, Ph.D. 1963.
Military Career: Army, 1954–56.
Occupation: Professor; author; advertising executive.
Family: Wife, Arlene Catherine Crane; eight children.
Religion: Protestant.
Political Career: Sought Republican nomination for president, 1980.

Capitol Office: 233 Cannon House Office Building 20515; 225-3711; (fax) 225-7830; (e-mail) www.house.gov/writerep; (web) www.house.gov/crane.
Office Staff: Chief of Staff, Jim Thacker; Legis. Dir., Christopher J. Myers; Scheduler, Amata Radewagen.
Committees: Ways & Means (Health; Trade — chairman); Joint Taxation.

Illinois 8th — Northwest Cook County — Schaumburg; Palatine. The district vote for Bill Clinton was 41% in 1996.

CQ Voting Studies

	1997	1998
Presidential	23%	23%
Party	92%	93%
Participation	95%	94%

Interest Groups

	1997	1998
ADA	5%	0%
ACU	96%	96%
AFL-CIO	0%	n/a
CCUS	80%	81%

Elections

	1996	1998
General	62%	69%
Primary	75%	65%

Joseph Crowley (D–N.Y.)
Of Elmhurst • Elected 1998
Pronounced: KRAU-lee

Born: Mar. 16, 1962, Elmhurst, N.Y.
Education: Queens College, B.A. 1985.
Occupation: State legislator.
Family: Wife, Kasey.
Religion: Roman Catholic.
Political Career: N.Y. Assembly, 1986–99.

Capitol Office: 1517 Longworth House Office Building 20515; 225-3965; (fax) 225-1909; (e-mail) www.house.gov/writerep.
Office Staff: Admin. Asst., Chris McCannell; Press Secy., Josh Straka.
Committees: International Relations (International Economic Policy & Trade); Resources (Forests & Forest Health; National Parks & Public Lands).

New York 7th — Parts of Queens and the Bronx — Long Island City. The district vote for Bill Clinton was 69% in 1996.

Elections

	1998
General	69%
Primary	u/o

Barbara Cubin (R–Wyo.)
Of Casper • Elected 1994
Pronounced: CUE-bin

Born: Nov. 30, 1946, Salinas, Calif.
Education: Creighton U., B.S. 1969; Casper College, attended 1993.
Occupation: Medical office manager; realtor; chemist.
Family: Husband, Frederick William Cubin III; two children.
Religion: Episcopalian.
Political Career: Wyo. House, 1987–93; Wyo. Senate, 1993–95.

Capitol Office: 1114 Longworth House Office Building 20515; 225-2311; (fax) 225-3057; (e-mail) barbara.cubin@mail.house.gov; (web) www.house.gov/cubin.
Office Staff: Admin. Asst., Patty McDonald; Legis. Dir., Marian Marshall; Press Secy., Tom Wiblemo; Scheduler, Susan Sherwood.
Committees: Commerce (Health & Environment; Telecommunications, Trade & Consumer Protection); Resources (Energy & Mineral Resources — chairman).

Wyoming — At large. The district vote for Bill Clinton was 37% in 1996.

CQ Voting Studies

	1997	1998
Presidential	21%	21%
Party	75%	95%
Participation	78%	98%

Interest Groups

	1997	1998
ADA	0%	5%
ACU	100%	100%
AFL-CIO	0%	n/a
CCUS	71%	94%

Elections

	1996	1998
General	55%	58%
Primary	u/o	u/o

Elijah E. Cummings (D–Md.)
Of Baltimore • Elected 1996

Born: Jan. 18, 1951, Baltimore, Md.
Education: Howard U., B.A. 1973; U. of Maryland, J.D. 1976.
Occupation: Lawyer.
Family: Separated; two children.
Religion: Baptist.
Political Career: Md. House, 1983–96, speaker pro tempore, 1995.

Capitol Office: 1632 Longworth House Office Building 20515; 225-4741; (fax) 225-3178; (e–mail) rep.cummings@mail.house.gov; (web) www.house.gov/cummings.

Office Staff: Chief of Staff, Darleen Taylor; Scheduler, Mattie Barrow.

Committees: Government Reform (Civil Service — ranking member; Criminal Justice, Drug Policy & Human Resources); Transportation & Infrastructure (Aviation; Ground Transportation).

Maryland 7th — Inner-City Baltimore; Western Baltimore County. The district vote for Bill Clinton was 81% in 1996.

CQ Voting Studies

	1997	1998
Presidential	76%	82%
Party	93%	95%
Participation	98%	99%

Interest Groups

	1997	1998
ADA	100%	100%
ACU	4%	4%
AFL-CIO	100%	n/a
CCUS	30%	28%

Elections

	1996	1998
General	*81%	86%
Primary	*37%	91%

*Special election

Randy "Duke" Cunningham
(R–Calif.)
Of San Diego • Elected 1990

Born: Dec. 8, 1941, Los Angeles, Calif.
Education: U. of Missouri, B.A. 1964, M.A. 1965; National U., M.B.A. 1985.
Military Career: Navy, 1966–87.
Occupation: Computer software executive; Top Gun flight school instructor.
Family: Wife, Nancy; three children.
Religion: Christian.
Political Career: No previous office.

Capitol Office: 2238 Rayburn House Office Building 20515; 225-5452; (fax) 225-2558; (e–mail) www.house.gov/writerep; (web) www.house.gov/cunningham.

Office Staff: Chief of Staff, Patrick McSwain; Legis. Dir., Frank Purcell; Press Secy., Julie Pope; Exec. Asst., Susan Woodworth.

Committees: Appropriations (District of Columbia; Labor, Health & Human Services & Education; Defense).

California 51st — San Diego area — North county suburbs. The district vote for Bill Clinton was 39% in 1996.

CQ Voting Studies

	1997	1998
Presidential	28%	22%
Party	95%	82%
Participation	99%	91%

Interest Groups

	1997	1998
ADA	0%	0%
ACU	92%	100%
AFL-CIO	0%	n/a
CCUS	100%	100%

Elections

	1996	1998
General	65%	61%
Primary	86%	*67%

*Open primary

Pat Danner (D–Mo.)
Of Kansas City • Elected 1992

Born: Jan. 13, 1934, Louisville, Ky.
Education: Northeast Missouri State U., B.A. 1972.
Occupation: Congressional aide; federal official.
Family: Husband, Mark Meyer; four children.
Religion: Roman Catholic.
Political Career: Sought Democratic nomination for U.S. House, 1976; Mo. Senate, 1983–93.

Capitol Office: 2262 Rayburn House Office Building 20515; 225-7041; (fax) 225-8221; (e–mail) www.house.gov/writerep.
Office Staff: Chief of Staff/Exec. Asst., Cathie McCarley; Legis. Dir., Amy Perlik; Press Secy., Rich West.
Committees: International Relations (International Economic Policy & Trade); Transportation & Infrastructure (Aviation; Ground Transportation).

Missouri 6th — Northwest — St. Joseph. The district vote for Bill Clinton was 46% in 1996.

CQ Voting Studies

	1997	1998
Presidential	41%	45%
Party	60%	58%
Participation	98%	97%

Interest Groups

	1997	1998
ADA	50%	60%
ACU	56%	52%
AFL-CIO	75%	n/a
CCUS	70%	67%

Elections

	1996	1998
General	69%	71%
Primary	77%	u/o

Danny K. Davis (D–Ill.)
Of Chicago • Elected 1996

Born: Sept. 6, 1941, Parkdale, Ark.
Education: Arkansas A.M.&N. College, B.A. 1961; Chicago State U., M.A. 1968; Union Institute, Ph.D. 1977.
Occupation: Health care consultant; teacher.
Family: Wife, Vera; two children.
Religion: Baptist.
Political Career: Chicago City Council, 1979–90; sought Democratic nomination for U.S. House, 1984, 1986; Cook County Commission, 1990–97; candidate for Chicago mayor, 1991.

Capitol Office: 1222 Longworth House Office Building 20515; 225-5006; (fax) 225-5641; (e–mail) www.house.gov/writerep.
Office Staff: Chief of Staff, Richard Boykin; Legis. Dir., Courtni Pew; Press Secy., Ira Cohen; Exec. Asst., Cullen Davis.
Committees: Government Reform (Census; Postal Service); Small Business (Government Programs & Oversight — ranking member).

Illinois 7th — Chicago — Downtown; West Side. The district vote for Bill Clinton was 82% in 1996.

CQ Voting Studies

	1997	1998
Presidential	76%	84%
Party	92%	93%
Participation	98%	96%

Interest Groups

	1997	1998
ADA	100%	95%
ACU	8%	8%
AFL-CIO	100%	n/a
CCUS	10%	28%

Elections

	1996	1998
General	82%	93%
Primary	33%	85%

Jim Davis (D–Fla.)
Of Tampa • Elected 1996

Born: Oct. 11, 1957, Tampa, Fla.
Education: Washington and Lee U., B.A. 1979; U. of Florida, J.D. 1982.
Occupation: Lawyer.
Family: Wife, Peggy Bessent Davis; two children.
Religion: Episcopalian.
Political Career: Fla. House, 1988–97, majority leader, 1994–97.

Capitol Office: 418 Cannon House Office Building 20515; 225-3376; (fax) 225-5652; (e–mail) www.house.gov/writerep; (web) www.house.gov/jimdavis.
Office Staff: Chief of Staff, Suzanne Farmer; Legis. Dir., Tricia Barrentine; Press Secy., Brian Edwards; Scheduler, Joan Hall.
Committees: House Administration; Budget; International Relations (Asia & the Pacific; Western Hemisphere); Joint Library.

Florida 11th — West — Southern Hillsborough County; Tampa. The district vote for Bill Clinton was 52% in 1996.

CQ Voting Studies

	1997	1998
Presidential	80%	73%
Party	83%	80%
Participation	98%	99%

Interest Groups

	1997	1998
ADA	75%	85%
ACU	16%	16%
AFL-CIO	88%	n/a
CCUS	60%	67%

Elections

	1996	1998
General	58%	65%
Primary	*56%	u/o

*Runoff election

Thomas M. Davis III (R–Va.)
Of Falls Church • Elected 1994

Born: Jan. 5, 1949, Minot, N.D.
Education: Amherst College, B.A. 1971; U. of Virginia, J.D. 1975.
Military Career: Army, 1971–72; National Guard, 1972–79; Army Reserve, 1972–79.
Occupation: Lawyer; professional services firm executive; state legislative aide.
Family: Wife, Margaret "Peggy"; three children.
Religion: Christian Scientist.
Political Career: Fairfax County Board of Supervisors, 1980–94, chairman, 1991–94.

Capitol Office: 224 Cannon House Office Building 20515; 225-1492; (fax) 225-3071; (e–mail) tom.davis@mail.house.gov; (web) www.house.gov/tomdavis.
Office Staff: Chief of Staff/Legis. Dir./Press Secy., Mike Hettinger; Appts. Secy., Hana Brilliant.
Committees: Government Reform (Census; District of Columbia — chairman; Government Management, Information & Technology).

Virginia 11th — D.C. Suburbs — Parts of Fairfax and Prince William counties. The district vote for Bill Clinton was 48% in 1996.

CQ Voting Studies

	1997	1998
Presidential	39%	33%
Party	81%	80%
Participation	99%	98%

Interest Groups

	1997	1998
ADA	25%	15%
ACU	72%	64%
AFL-CIO	38%	n/a
CCUS	100%	100%

Elections

	1996	1998
General	64%	82%
Primary	u/o	u/o

Nathan Deal (R–Ga.)
Of Gainesville • Elected 1992

Born: Aug. 25, 1942, Millen, Ga.
Education: Mercer U., B.A. 1964, J.D. 1966.
Military Career: Army, 1966–68.
Occupation: Lawyer.
Family: Wife, Sandra Dunagan Deal; four children.
Religion: Baptist.
Political Career: Assistant district attorney, 1970–71; juvenile court judge, 1971–72; Hall County attorney, 1977–79; Ga. Senate, 1981–93, president pro tempore, 1991–93.

Capitol Office: 2437 Rayburn House Office Building 20515; 225-5211; (fax) 225-8272; (e-mail) www.house.gov/writerep; (web) www.house.gov/deal.
Office Staff: Chief of Staff/Press Secy., Mark Maddox; Legis. Dir., Jennifer Rich; Scheduler, Rick Story.
Committees: Commerce (Health & Environment; Telecommunications, Trade & Consumer Protection); Education & Workforce (Postsecondary Education, Training & Life-Long Learning).

Georgia 9th — North — Dalton; Gainesville; Toccoa. The district vote for Bill Clinton was 35% in 1996.

CQ Voting Studies

	1997	1998
Presidential	23%	16%
Party	96%	93%
Participation	99%	98%

Interest Groups

	1997	1998
ADA	0%	10%
ACU	96%	88%
AFL-CIO	0%	n/a
CCUS	90%	67%

Elections

	1996	1998
General	66%	u/o
Primary	u/o	u/o

Peter A. DeFazio (D–Ore.)
Of Springfield • Elected 1986
Pronounced: da-FAH-zee–o

Born: May 27, 1947, Needham, Mass.
Education: Tufts U., B.A. 1969; U. of Oregon, attended 1969–71, M.S. 1977.
Military Career: Air Force, 1967–71.
Occupation: Congressional aide.
Family: Wife, Myrnie L. Daut.
Religion: Roman Catholic.
Political Career: Lane County Commission, 1982–86; sought Democratic nomination for U.S. Senate (special election), 1996.

Capitol Office: 2134 Rayburn House Office Building 20515; 225-6416; (fax) 225-0373; (e-mail) peter.defazio@mail.house.gov; (web) www.house.gov/defazio.
Office Staff: Admin. Asst., Penny Dodge; Legis. Dir., Jeff Stier; Press Secy., Kathie Eastman; Scheduler, Aaron Deas.
Committees: Resources (Fisheries Conservation, Wildlife & Oceans; Water & Power); Transportation & Infrastructure (Aviation; Coast Guard & Maritime Transportation — ranking member).

Oregon 4th — Southwest — Eugene. The district vote for Bill Clinton was 45% in 1996.

CQ Voting Studies

	1997	1998
Presidential	67%	77%
Party	88%	89%
Participation	97%	95%

Interest Groups

	1997	1998
ADA	85%	95%
ACU	28%	16%
AFL-CIO	100%	n/a
CCUS	20%	12%

Elections

	1996	1998
General	66%	70%
Primary	u/o	u/o

Diana DeGette (D–Colo.)
Of Denver • Elected 1996
Pronounced: de-GET

Born: July 29, 1957, Tachikawa, Japan.
Education: Colorado College, B.A. 1979; New York U., J.D. 1982.
Occupation: Lawyer.
Family: Husband, Lino Lipinsky; two children.
Religion: Presbyterian.
Political Career: Colo. House, 1993–97.

Capitol Office: 1339 Longworth House Office Building 20515; 225-4431; (fax) 225-5657; (e-mail) degette@mail.house.gov; (web) www.house.gov/degette.
Office Staff: Admin. Asst., Lisa Cohen; Legis. Dir., Elizabeth Mullin; Press Secy., Jamin Spitzer; Scheduler, Chaundini Bachman.

Committees: Commerce (Finance & Hazardous Materials; Health & Environment; Oversight & Investigations).

Colorado 1st — Denver. The district vote for Bill Clinton was 61% in 1996.

CQ Voting Studies

	1997	1998
Presidential	80%	85%
Party	94%	96%
Participation	96%	99%

Interest Groups

	1997	1998
ADA	100%	95%
ACU	13%	4%
AFL-CIO	100%	n/a
CCUS	22%	22%

Elections

	1996	1998
General	57%	67%
Primary	56%	u/o

Bill Delahunt (D–Mass.)
Of Quincy • Elected 1996
Pronounced: DELL-a-hunt

Born: July 18, 1941, Quincy, Mass.
Education: Middlebury College, B.A. 1963; Boston College, J.D. 1967.
Military Career: Coast Guard, 1963; Coast Guard Reserve, 1963–71.
Occupation: Lawyer.
Family: Divorced; two children.
Religion: Roman Catholic.
Political Career: Quincy City Council, 1971–73; Mass. House, 1973–76; Norfolk County district attorney, 1976–97.

Capitol Office: 1317 Longworth House Office Building 20515; 225-3111; (fax) 225-5658; (e-mail) william.delahunt@mail.house.gov; (web) www.house.gov/delahunt.
Office Staff: Admin. Asst./Press Secy., Steve Schwadron; Legis. Dir., Mark Agrast; Scheduler, Miriam Wolfe.
Committees: International Relations (International Economic Policy & Trade; International Operations & Human Rights); Judiciary (Commercial & Administrative Law; Courts & Intellectual Property).

Massachusetts 10th — South Shore — Cape Cod; islands. The district vote for Bill Clinton was 56% in 1996.

CQ Voting Studies

	1997	1998
Presidential	76%	83%
Party	92%	95%
Participation	98%	99%

Interest Groups

	1997	1998
ADA	95%	100%
ACU	0%	8%
AFL-CIO	100%	n/a
CCUS	20%	28%

Elections

	1996	1998
General	54%	70%
Primary	38%	u/o

Rosa DeLauro (D–Conn.)
Of New Haven • Elected 1990
Pronounced: da-LAUR-o

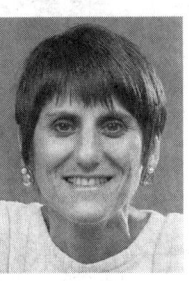

Born: Mar. 2, 1943, New Haven, Conn.
Education: London School of Economics, attended 1962–63; Marymount College, B.A. 1964; Columbia U., M.A. 1966.
Occupation: Political activist.
Family: Husband, Stanley Greenberg; three stepchildren.
Religion: Roman Catholic.
Political Career: No previous office.

Capitol Office: 436 Cannon House Office Building 20515; 225-3661; (fax) 225-4890; (e-mail) delauro. ct03@mail.house.gov; (web) www.house.gov/delauro.
Office Staff: Admin. Asst., Maura Keefe; Legis. Dir., Catriona MacDonald; Press Secy., Jim Papa; Exec. Asst., Nancy Mulry.
Committees: Appropriations (Agriculture, Rural Development, FDA & Related Agencies; Labor, Health & Human Services & Education).

Connecticut 3rd — South — New Haven. The district vote for Bill Clinton was 57% in 1996.

CQ Voting Studies

	1997	1998
Presidential	83%	82%
Party	96%	96%
Participation	99%	99%

Interest Groups

	1997	1998
ADA	95%	100%
ACU	13%	8%
AFL-CIO	100%	n/a
CCUS	30%	28%

Elections

	1996	1998
General	71%	71%
Primary	u/o	u/o

Tom DeLay (R–Texas)
Of Sugarland • Elected 1984

Born: Apr. 8, 1947, Laredo, Texas.
Education: Baylor U., attended 1965–67; U. of Houston, B.S. 1970.
Occupation: Pest control executive.
Family: Wife, Christine; one child.
Religion: Baptist.
Political Career: Texas House, 1979–85.

Capitol Office: 341 Cannon House Office Building 20515; 225-5951; (fax) 225-5241; (e-mail) thewhip@ mail.house.gov; (web) www.majoritywhip.house.gov.
Office Staff: Chief of Staff, Susan Hirschmann; Legis. Dir., Dan Flynn; Press Secy., Mike Scanlon; Scheduler, Maryellen Wright.
Committees: Appropriations (Transportation; VA, HUD & Independent Agencies).

Texas 22nd — Southwest Houston and suburbs; Fort Bend and Brazoria counties. The district vote for Bill Clinton was 38% in 1996.

CQ Voting Studies

	1997	1998
Presidential	27%	20%
Party	94%	93%
Participation	98%	96%

Interest Groups

	1997	1998
ADA	0%	0%
ACU	88%	96%
AFL-CIO	0%	n/a
CCUS	100%	100%

Elections

	1996	1998
General	68%	65%
Primary		u/o

Jim DeMint (R-S.C.)
Of Greenville • Elected 1998

Born: Sept. 2, 1951, Greenville, S.C.
Education: U. of Tennessee, B.S. 1973; Clemson U., M.B.A. 1981.
Occupation: Market research company owner.
Family: Wife, Debbie; four children.
Religion: Presbyterian.
Political Career: No previous office.

Capitol Office: 507 Cannon House Office Building 20515; 225-6030; (fax) 226-1177; (e–mail) www. house.gov/writerep.
Office Staff: Chief of Staff, Marie Wheat.
Committees: Education & Workforce (Early Childhood, Youth & Families; Employer-Employee Relations); Small Business (Empowerment; Rural Enterprises); Transportation & Infrastructure (Aviation; Ground Transportation).

South Carolina 4th — Northwest — Greenville; Spartanburg. The district vote for Bill Clinton was 37% in 1996.

Elections

	1998
General	58%
Primary	*53%

*Runoff election

Peter Deutsch (D–Fla.)
Of Fort Lauderdale • Elected 1992
Pronounced: DOYCH

Born: Apr. 1, 1957, Bronx, N.Y.
Education: Swarthmore College, B.A. 1979; Yale U., J.D. 1982.
Occupation: Lawyer; nonprofit executive.
Family: Wife, Lori Ann Coffino; two children.
Religion: Jewish.
Political Career: Fla. House, 1983–93.

Capitol Office: 204 Cannon House Office Building 20515; 225-7931; (fax) 225-8456; (e–mail) www. house.gov/writerep.
Office Staff: Chief of Staff, Robin Rorapaugh; Legis. Dir., Fritz Hirst; Press Secy., Ray Krauze; Scheduler, Victoria Cervantes.
Committees: Commerce (Energy & Power; Finance & Hazardous Materials; Health & Environment).

Florida 20th — South — Southern and western Broward County; Hollywood; the Keys. The district vote for Bill Clinton was 59% in 1996.

CQ Voting Studies

	1997	1998
Presidential	75%	79%
Party	82%	84%
Participation	95%	93%

Interest Groups

	1997	1998
ADA	80%	95%
ACU	21%	4%
AFL-CIO	100%	n/a
CCUS	60%	35%

Elections

	1996	1998
General	65%	u/o
Primary	u/o	u/o

Lincoln Diaz-Balart (R–Fla.)
Of Miami • Elected 1992
Pronounced: DEE-az baa-LART

Born: Aug. 13, 1954, Havana, Cuba.
Education: U. of South Florida, B.A. 1976; Case Western Reserve U., J.D. 1979.
Occupation: Lawyer.
Family: Wife, Cristina; two children.
Religion: Roman Catholic.
Political Career: Democratic nominee for Fla. House, 1982; Fla. House, 1987–89; Fla. Senate, 1989–92.

Capitol Office: 404 Cannon House Office Building 20515; 225-4211; (fax) 225-8576; (e–mail) www.house.gov/writerep; (web) www.house.gov/diaz–balart.
Office Staff: Admin. Asst., Stephen Vermillion; Legis. Dir., Elizabeth Humphrey; Press Secy., Yanik Fenton; Scheduler, Christine DelPortillo.
Committees: Rules (Rules & Organization of the House).

Florida 21st — Southeast — Part of Dade County; Hialeah. The district vote for Bill Clinton was 45% in 1996.

CQ Voting Studies

	1997	1998
Presidential	29%	32%
Party	82%	79%
Participation	95%	96%

Interest Groups

	1997	1998
ADA	20%	25%
ACU	72%	68%
AFL-CIO	63%	n/a
CCUS	70%	72%

Elections

	1996	1998
General	u/o	75%
Primary	u/o	u/o

Jay Dickey (R–Ark.)
Of Pine Bluff • Elected 1992

Born: Dec. 14, 1939, Pine Bluff, Ark.
Education: U. of Arkansas, B.A. 1961, J.D. 1963.
Occupation: Lawyer; restaurateur.
Family: Divorced; four children.
Religion: Methodist.
Political Career: Pine Bluff city attorney, 1968–70.

Capitol Office: 2453 Rayburn House Office Building 20515; 225-3772; (fax) 225-1314; (e–mail) talk2jay@mail.house.gov; (web) www.house.gov/dickey.
Office Staff: Chief of Staff, Allen W. Maxwell; Admin. Asst./Press Secy., Rob Johnson; Legis. Dir., Brian Casal; Scheduler, Jennifer Weems.
Committees: Appropriations (Agriculture, Rural Development, FDA & Related Agencies; Labor, Health & Human Services & Education; Defense).

Arkansas 4th — South — Pine Bluff; Hot Springs. The district vote for Bill Clinton was 60% in 1996.

CQ Voting Studies

	1997	1998
Presidential	20%	24%
Party	91%	91%
Participation	98%	97%

Interest Groups

	1997	1998
ADA	5%	5%
ACU	88%	96%
AFL-CIO	0%	n/a
CCUS	80%	94%

Elections

	1996	1998
General	64%	58%
Primary	u/o	u/o

Norm Dicks (D–Wash.)
Of Bremerton • Elected 1976

Born: Dec. 16, 1940, Bremerton, Wash.
Education: U. of Washington, B.A. 1963, J.D. 1968.
Occupation: Congressional aide.
Family: Wife, Suzanne; two children.
Religion: Lutheran.
Political Career: No previous office.

Capitol Office: 2467 Rayburn House Office Building 20515; 225-5916; (fax) 226-1176; (e-mail) www.house.gov/writerep.
Office Staff: Legis. Dir., Pete Modaff; Press Secy., George Behan; Office Mgr., Donna Taylor; Scheduler, Sara Crumb.
Committees: Appropriations (Interior — ranking member; Military Construction; Defense); China Investigation — ranking member.

Washington 6th — West — Bremerton. The district vote for Bill Clinton was 50% in 1996.

CQ Voting Studies

	1997	1998
Presidential	77%	84%
Party	78%	84%
Participation	97%	98%

Interest Groups

	1997	1998
ADA	70%	95%
ACU	17%	0%
AFL-CIO	88%	n/a
CCUS	60%	39%

Elections

	1996	1998
General	66%	68%
Primary	*67%	*71%

*Open primary

John D. Dingell (D–Mich.)
Of Dearborn • Elected 1955

Born: July 8, 1926, Colorado Springs, Colo.
Education: Georgetown U., B.S. 1949, J.D. 1952.
Military Career: Army, 1944–46.
Occupation: Lawyer.
Family: Wife, Deborah; four children.
Religion: Roman Catholic.
Political Career: Wayne County assistant prosecutor, 1953–55.

Capitol Office: 2328 Rayburn House Office Building 20515; 225-4071; (e-mail) www.house.gov/writerep; (web) www.house.gov/dingell.
Office Staff: Admin. Asst., Marda Robillard; Legis. Dir., Dan Beattie; Communications Dir., Mike Greene; Scheduler, Beth Siniawski.
Committees: Commerce — ranking member.

Michigan 16th — Southeast Wayne County; Monroe County. The district vote for Bill Clinton was 54% in 1996.

CQ Voting Studies

	1997	1998
Presidential	77%	77%
Party	83%	82%
Participation	95%	94%

Interest Groups

	1997	1998
ADA	80%	85%
ACU	8%	8%
AFL-CIO	100%	n/a
CCUS	50%	28%

Elections

	1996	1998
General	62%	67%
Primary	u/o	u/o

Julian C. Dixon (D–Calif.)
Of Los Angeles • Elected 1978

Born: Aug. 8, 1934, Washington, D.C.
Education: California State U., Los Angeles, B.S. 1962; Southwestern U., LL.B. 1967.
Military Career: Army, 1957–60.
Occupation: Legislative aide; lawyer.
Family: Wife, Betty Lee Dixon; one child.
Religion: Episcopalian.
Political Career: Calif. Assembly, 1973–79.

Capitol Office: 2252 Rayburn House Office Building 20515; 225-7084; (fax) 225-3073; (e–mail) www.house.gov/writerep.
Office Staff: Admin. Asst./Press Secy., Andrea Tracy Holmes; Legis. Dir., Paul Cunningham; Personal Secy., Deanne Samuels.
Committees: Appropriations (Commerce, Justice, State & Judiciary; District of Columbia; Defense); Select Intelligence — ranking member.

California 32nd — West Los Angeles; Culver City. The district vote for Bill Clinton was 81% in 1996.

CQ Voting Studies

	1997	1998
Presidential	76%	76%
Party	86%	85%
Participation	95%	89%

Interest Groups

	1997	1998
ADA	90%	100%
ACU	12%	0%
AFL-CIO	100%	n/a
CCUS	30%	29%

Elections

	1996	1998
General	82%	87%
Primary	u/o	*86%

*Open primary

Lloyd Doggett (D–Texas)
Of Austin • Elected 1994

Born: Oct. 6, 1946, Austin, Texas.
Education: U. of Texas, Austin, B.B.A. 1967, J.D. 1970.
Occupation: Lawyer.
Family: Wife, Libby Belk; two children.
Religion: Methodist.
Political Career: Texas Senate, 1973–85; Democratic nominee for U.S. Senate, 1984; Texas Supreme Court, 1989–94.

Capitol Office: 328 Cannon House Office Building 20515; 225-4865; (fax) 225-3073; (e–mail) lloyd.doggett@mail.house.gov; (web) www.house.gov/doggett.
Office Staff: Admin. Asst., Leo Coco; Legis. Asst., Sean E. O'Reilly; Press Secy., Audrey Duff.
Committees: Ways & Means (Social Security).

Texas 10th — Central — Austin. The district vote for Bill Clinton was 53% in 1996.

CQ Voting Studies

	1997	1998
Presidential	79%	80%
Party	91%	91%
Participation	99%	99%

Interest Groups

	1997	1998
ADA	95%	100%
ACU	16%	8%
AFL-CIO	100%	n/a
CCUS	40%	39%

Elections

	1996	1998
General	56%	85%
Primary	u/o	u/o

Cal Dooley (D–Calif.)
Of Visalia • Elected 1990

Born: Jan. 11, 1954, Visalia, Calif.
Education: U. of California, Davis, B.S. 1977; Stanford U., M.A. 1987.
Occupation: Farmer.
Family: Wife, Linda; two children.
Religion: Protestant.
Political Career: No previous office.

Capitol Office: 1201 Longworth House Office Building 20515; 225-3341; (fax) 225-9308; (e–mail) www.house.gov/writerep; (web) www.house.gov/dooley.
Office Staff: Chief of Staff, Lisa Quigley; Legis. Dir., Emily Beizer; Press Secy., Lori Denham; Scheduler, Marla Kowalski.
Committees: Agriculture (Livestock & Horticulture; Risk Management, Research & Specialty Crops); Resources (Energy & Mineral Resources; Water & Power — ranking member).

California 20th — Parts of Kern, Kings and Fresno counties. The district vote for Bill Clinton was 52% in 1996.

CQ Voting Studies

	1997	1998
Presidential	75%	80%
Party	75%	79%
Participation	98%	99%

Interest Groups

	1997	1998
ADA	65%	85%
ACU	12%	4%
AFL-CIO	50%	n/a
CCUS	90%	67%

Elections

	1996	1998
General	57%	61%
Primary	u/o	*44%

*Open primary

John T. Doolittle (R–Calif.)
Of Rocklin • Elected 1990

Born: Oct. 30, 1950, Glendale, Calif.
Education: U. of California, Santa Cruz, B.A. 1972; U. of the Pacific, J.D. 1978.
Occupation: Lawyer.
Family: Wife, Julie Harlow; two children.
Religion: Mormon.
Political Career: Calif. Senate, 1981–91.

Capitol Office: 1526 Longworth House Office Building 20515; 225-2511; (fax) 225-5444; (e–mail) doolittle@mail.house.gov; (web) www.house.gov/doolittle.
Office Staff: Chief of Staff, David Lopez; District Dir./Press Secy., Richard Robinson; Legis. Dir., Peter Evich; Exec. Asst., Terra Awalt.
Committees: Government Reform (Census; National Economic Growth); Resources (Forests & Forest Health; Water & Power — chairman); Transportation & Infrastructure (Aviation; Oversight & Investigations; Water Resources & Environment); Joint Economic.

California 4th — Northeast Central. The district vote for Bill Clinton was 38% in 1996.

CQ Voting Studies

	1997	1998
Presidential	24%	16%
Party	91%	91%
Participation	96%	95%

Interest Groups

	1997	1998
ADA	0%	5%
ACU	96%	100%
AFL-CIO	0%	n/a
CCUS	80%	89%

Elections

	1996	1998
General	60%	63%
Primary	u/o	*65%

*Open primary

Mike Doyle (D–Pa.)
Of Swissvale • Elected 1994

Born: Aug. 5, 1953, Pittsburgh, Pa.
Education: Pennsylvania State U., B.S. 1975.
Occupation: Insurance company executive; state legislative aide.
Family: Wife, Susan; four children.
Religion: Roman Catholic.
Political Career: Swissvale Borough Council, 1977–81.

Capitol Office: 133 Cannon House Office Building 20515; 225-2135; (fax) 225-3084; (e-mail) rep.doyle@mail.house.gov; (web) www.house.gov/doyle.
Office Staff: Chief of Staff/Press Secy., David Lucas; Legis. Dir., Sharon Grant; Scheduler, Judy Wolford.
Committees: Science (Basic Research; Energy & Environment); Veterans' Affairs (Health).

Pennsylvania 18th — Pittsburgh suburbs; Clairton; McKeesport. The district vote for Bill Clinton was 52% in 1996.

CQ Voting Studies

	1997	1998
Presidential	61%	66%
Party	67%	76%
Participation	99%	97%

Interest Groups

	1997	1998
ADA	65%	80%
ACU	36%	25%
AFL-CIO	88%	n/a
CCUS	70%	50%

Elections

	1996	1998
General	56%	68%
Primary	74%	65%

David Dreier (R–Calif.)
Of San Dimas • Elected 1980

Born: July 5, 1952, Kansas City, Mo.
Education: Claremont McKenna College, B.A. 1975; Claremont Graduate U., M.A. 1976.
Occupation: Real estate developer and property manager.
Family: Single.
Religion: Christian Scientist.
Political Career: Republican nominee for U.S. House, 1978.

Capitol Office: 237 Cannon House Office Building 20515; 225-2305; (fax) 225-7018; (e-mail) www.house.gov/writerep; (web) www.house.gov/dreier.
Office Staff: Staff Dir./Press Secy., Brad Smith; Legis. Dir., Brian Faughnan; Scheduler, Janice McKinney.
Committees: Rules — chairman (Legislative & Budget Process; Rules & Organization of the House).

California 28th — Northeastern Los Angeles suburbs. The district vote for Bill Clinton was 45% in 1996.

CQ Voting Studies

	1997	1998
Presidential	27%	26%
Party	93%	90%
Participation	98%	99%

Interest Groups

	1997	1998
ADA	0%	0%
ACU	88%	92%
AFL-CIO	0%	n/a
CCUS	100%	100%

Elections

	1996	1998
General	61%	58%
Primary	u/o	*60%

*Open primary

John J. "Jimmy" Duncan Jr.
(R–Tenn.)
Of Knoxville • Elected 1988

Born: July 21, 1947, Lebanon, Tenn.
Education: U. of Tennessee, B.S. 1969; George Washington U., J.D. 1973.
Military Career: Tenn. National Guard and Army Reserve, 1970–87.
Occupation: Judge; lawyer.
Family: Wife, Lynn; four children.
Religion: Presbyterian.
Political Career: Knox County Criminal Court judge, 1981–88.

Capitol Office: 2400 Rayburn House Office Building 20515; 225-5435; (fax) 225-6440; (e-mail) jjduncan@mail.house.gov; (web) www.house.gov/duncan.
Office Staff: Chief of Staff, Judy Whitbred; Legis. Dir., Don Walker; Communications Dir., David Balloff; Scheduler, Victoria Peroulas.
Committees: Resources (Forests & Forest Health; National Parks & Public Lands); Transportation & Infrastructure (Aviation — chairman; Ground Transportation).

Tennessee 2nd — East — Knoxville. The district vote for Bill Clinton was 42% in 1996.

CQ Voting Studies

	1997	1998
Presidential	29%	22%
Party	89%	88%
Participation	99%	99%

Interest Groups

	1997	1998
ADA	10%	15%
ACU	88%	84%
AFL-CIO	0%	n/a
CCUS	80%	78%

Elections

	1996	1998
General	71%	89%
Primary	u/o	u/o

Jennifer Dunn (R–Wash.)
Of Bellevue • Elected 1992

Born: July 29, 1941, Seattle, Wash.
Education: Stanford U., attended 1959; U. of Washington, attended 1960–62; Stanford U., B.A. 1963.
Occupation: State party official.
Family: Divorced; two children.
Religion: Episcopalian.
Political Career: Wash. Republican Party chairwoman, 1980–92.

Capitol Office: 432 Cannon House Office Building 20515; 225-7761; (fax) 225-8673; (e-mail) dunnwa08@mail.house.gov; (web) www.house.gov/dunn.
Office Staff: Chief of Staff, T.J. Petrizzo; Legis. Dir., Doug Badger; Press Secy., Kara Kinderman; Scheduler, Natalie Zoll.
Committees: Ways & Means (Oversight; Trade).

Washington 8th — Puget Sound (East) — King County suburbs; Bellevue. The district vote for Bill Clinton was 47% in 1996.

CQ Voting Studies

	1997	1998
Presidential	31%	23%
Party	94%	93%
Participation	99%	98%

Interest Groups

	1997	1998
ADA	0%	0%
ACU	92%	96%
AFL-CIO	0%	n/a
CCUS	100%	100%

Elections

	1996	1998
General	65%	60%
Primary	*65%	*66%

*Open primary

Chet Edwards (D–Texas)
Of Waco • Elected 1990

Born: Nov. 24, 1951, Corpus Christi, Texas.
Education: Texas A&M U., B.A. 1974; Harvard U., M.B.A. 1981.
Occupation: Radio station executive; congressional aide.
Family: Wife, Lea Ann Edwards; two children.
Religion: Methodist.
Political Career: Sought Democratic nomination for U.S. House, 1978; Texas Senate, 1983–91.

Capitol Office: 2459 Rayburn House Office Building 20515; 225-6105; (fax) 225-0350; (e–mail) www.house.gov/writerep; (web) www.house.gov/edwards.
Office Staff: Admin. Asst., Chris Chwastyk; Legis. Dir., Vacant; Press Secy., Vance Gore; Exec. Asst., Renata Middleton.
Committees: Appropriations (Energy & Water Development; Military Construction).

Texas 11th — Central — Waco. The district vote for Bill Clinton was 42% in 1996.

CQ Voting Studies

	1997	1998
Presidential	72%	80%
Party	76%	83%
Participation	96%	99%

Interest Groups

	1997	1998
ADA	60%	90%
ACU	28%	8%
AFL-CIO	88%	n/a
CCUS	70%	44%

Elections

	1996	1998
General	57%	82%
Primary	u/o	u/o

Vernon J. Ehlers (R–Mich.)
Of Grand Rapids • Elected 1993
Pronounced: AY-lurz

Born: Feb. 6, 1934, Pipestone, Minn.
Education: Calvin College, attended 1952–55; U. of California, Berkeley, A.B. 1956, Ph.D. 1960.
Occupation: Professor; physicist.
Family: Wife, Johanna Meulink; four children.
Religion: Christian Reformed Church.
Political Career: Kent County Commission, 1975–83, chairman, 1979–82; Mich. House, 1983–85, assistant Republican floor leader; Mich. Senate, 1985–93, president pro tempore.

Capitol Office: 1714 Longworth House Office Building 20515; 225-3831; (fax) 225-5144; (e–mail) rep.ehlers@mail.house.gov; (web) www.house.gov/ehlers.
Office Staff: Chief of Staff, Bill McBride; Legis. Dir., Will Plaster; Press Secy., Christopher Barbee; Scheduler, Lorraine Kehl.
Committees: House Administration; Education & Workforce (Postsecondary Education, Training & LifeLong Learning); Science (Energy & Environment; Space & Aeronautics); Transportation & Infrastructure (Aviation; Water Resources & Environment); Joint Library.

Michigan 3rd — West Central — Grand Rapids. The district vote for Bill Clinton was 39% in 1996.

CQ Voting Studies

	1997	1998
Presidential	41%	33%
Party	80%	77%
Participation	97%	98%

Interest Groups

	1997	1998
ADA	35%	25%
ACU	67%	56%
AFL-CIO	13%	n/a
CCUS	90%	89%

Elections

	1996	1998
General	69%	73%
Primary	u/o	u/o

HOUSE • Ehrlich / Emerson

Robert L. Ehrlich Jr. (R–Md.)
Of Lutherville • Elected 1994
Pronounced: ER-lick

Born: Nov. 25, 1957, Baltimore, Md.
Education: Princeton U., B.A. 1979; Wake Forest U., J.D. 1982.
Occupation: Lawyer; football coach.
Family: Wife, Kendel Sibiski Ehrlich.
Religion: Methodist.
Political Career: Md. House, 1987–95.

Capitol Office: 315 Cannon House Office Building 20515; 225-3061; (fax) 225-3094; (e-mail) ehrlich@mail.house.gov; (web) www.house.gov/ehrlich.
Office Staff: Chief of Staff/Legis. Dir., Steven Kreseski; Press Asst., Jill Homan; Exec. Asst., Terry King.
Committees: Commerce (Energy & Power; Finance & Hazardous Materials; Telecommunications, Trade & Consumer Protection).

Maryland 2nd — Baltimore and Harford counties. The district vote for Bill Clinton was 40% in 1996.

CQ Voting Studies

	1997	1998
Presidential	33%#	24%
Party	89%	85%
Participation	99%	95%

Interest Groups

	1997	1998
ADA	0%	5%
ACU	72%	92%
AFL-CIO	0%	n/a
CCUS	90%	94%

Elections

	1996	1998
General	62%	69%
Primary	83%	u/o

Jo Ann Emerson (R–Mo.)
Of Cape Girardeau • Elected 1996

Born: Sept. 16, 1950, Washington, D.C.
Education: Ohio Wesleyan U., B.A. 1972.
Occupation: Public affairs executive; lobbyist.
Family: Widowed; four children.
Religion: Presbyterian.
Political Career: No previous office.

Capitol Office: 132 Cannon House Office Building 20515; 225-4404; (fax) 226-0326; (e-mail) joann.emerson@mail.house.gov; (web) www.house.gov/emerson.
Office Staff: Legis. Dir., Seaver Sowers; Communications Dir., Kristen Kruger; Scheduler, Kacky Garner.
Committees: Appropriations (Agriculture, Rural Development, FDA & Related Agencies; District of Columbia; Treasury, Postal Service & General Government).

Missouri 8th — Southeast — Cape Girardeau. The district vote for Bill Clinton was 45% in 1996.

CQ Voting Studies

	1997	1998
Presidential	27%	22%
Party	95%	91%
Participation	98%	99%

Interest Groups

	1997	1998
ADA	5%	5%
ACU	88%	92%
AFL-CIO	0%	n/a
CCUS	90%	83%

Elections

	1996	1998
General	50%	63%
Primary	51%	u/o

HOUSE • Engel / English   113

Eliot L. Engel   (D–N.Y.)
Of Bronx • Elected 1988

Born: Feb. 18, 1947, Bronx, N.Y.
Education: Hunter-Lehman College, B.A. 1969; City U. of New York, Lehman College, M.A. 1973; New York Law School, J.D. 1987.
Occupation: Teacher; guidance counselor.
Family: Wife, Patricia Ennis Engel; three children.
Religion: Jewish.
Political Career: Bronx Democratic district leader, 1974–77; N.Y. Assembly, 1977–88.

Capitol Office: 2303 Rayburn House Office Building 20515; 225-2464; (fax) 225-5513; (e-mail) www.house.gov/writerep; (web) www.house.gov/engel.
Office Staff: Admin. Asst., John Calvelli; Legis. Dir., Jason Steinbaum; Communications Dir., Joseph O'Brien; Office Mgr., Pamela Segal.
Committees: Commerce (Finance & Hazardous Materials; Telecommunications, Trade & Consumer Protection).

New York 17th — North Bronx; parts of southern Westchester. The district vote for Bill Clinton was 85% in 1996.

CQ Voting Studies

	1997	1998
Presidential	71%	79%
Party	91%	93%
Participation	95%	93%

Interest Groups

	1997	1998
ADA	100%	95%
ACU	8%	4%
AFL-CIO	100%	n/a
CCUS	30%	24%

Elections

	1996	1998
General	85%	88%
Primary	77%	80%

Phil English   (R–Pa.)
Of Erie • Elected 1994

Born: June 20, 1956, Erie, Pa.
Education: U. of Pennsylvania, B.A. 1978.
Occupation: State legislative aide.
Family: Wife, Christiane.
Religion: Roman Catholic.
Political Career: Erie County Controller, 1986–89; Republican nominee for Pa. treasurer, 1988.

Capitol Office: 1410 Longworth House Office Building 20515; 225-5406; (fax) 225-3103; (e-mail) www.house.gov/writerep; (web) www.house.gov/english.
Office Staff: Chief of Staff, Robert Holste; Legis. Dir., Laura Eugster; Press Secy., Kate Pulley; Exec. Asst./Scheduler, Annette Car.
Committees: Small Business (Empowerment; Tax, Finance & Exports); Ways & Means (Health; Human Resources).

Pennsylvania 21st — Northwest — Erie. The district vote for Bill Clinton was 49% in 1996.

CQ Voting Studies

	1997	1998
Presidential	37%	35%
Party	85%	81%
Participation	98%	98%

Interest Groups

	1997	1998
ADA	20%	35%
ACU	76%	68%
AFL-CIO	75%	n/a
CCUS	70%	89%

Elections

	1996	1998
General	51%	63%
Primary	u/o	u/o

Anna G. Eshoo (D–Calif.)
Of Atherton • Elected 1992
Pronounced: EH-shoo

Born: Dec. 13, 1942, New Britain, Conn.
Education: Canada College, A.A. 1975.
Occupation: Legislative aide.
Family: Divorced; two children.
Religion: Roman Catholic.
Political Career: Democratic National Committee, 1980–92; San Mateo County Board of Supervisors, 1982–92; Democratic nominee for U.S. House, 1988.

Capitol Office: 205 Cannon House Office Building 20515; 225-8104; (fax) 225-8890; (e–mail) annagram@mail.house.gov; (web) www–eshoo.house.gov.
Office Staff: Chief of Staff, John Flaherty; Legis. Dir., Stacey Rampy; Communications Dir., Tracey Warren; Exec. Asst., Megan O'Reilly.
Committees: Commerce (Health & Environment; Telecommunications, Trade & Consumer Protection).

California 14th — Southern San Mateo and northern Santa Clara counties. The district vote for Bill Clinton was 58% in 1996.

CQ Voting Studies

	1997	1998
Presidential	87%	87%
Party	91%	92%
Participation	97%	96%

Interest Groups

	1997	1998
ADA	100%	90%
ACU	8%	0%
AFL-CIO	100%	n/a
CCUS	40%	39%

Elections

	1996	1998
General	65%	69%
Primary	u/o	*66%

*Open primary

Bob Etheridge (D–N.C.)
Of Lillington • Elected 1996

Born: Aug. 7, 1941, Sampson County, N.C.
Education: Campbell U., B.S. 1965.
Military Career: Army, 1965–67.
Occupation: Hardware store owner; tobacco farmer.
Family: Wife, Faye Cameron Etheridge; three children.
Religion: Presbyterian.
Political Career: Harnett County Commission, 1973–77, chairman, 1975–77; N.C. House, 1979–87; superintendent of public instruction, 1989–96.

Capitol Office: 1641 Longworth House Office Building 20515; 225-4531; (e–mail) bob.etheridge@mail.house.gov; (web) www.house.gov/etheridge.
Office Staff: Chief of Staff, Julie Dwyer; Legis. Dir., Patrick J. Devlin; Press Secy., Mark Hilpert; Scheduler, Kim Williams.
Committees: Agriculture (Livestock & Horticulture; Risk Management, Research & Specialty Crops); Science (Basic Research; Space & Aeronautics).

North Carolina 2nd — Central — Parts of Raleigh and Rocky Mount. The district vote for Bill Clinton was 45% in 1996.

CQ Voting Studies

	1997	1998
Presidential	63%	71%
Party	78%	79%
Participation	98%	98%

Interest Groups

	1997	1998
ADA	65%	80%
ACU	32%	28%
AFL-CIO	88%	n/a
CCUS	70%	65%

Elections

	1996	1998
General	53%	57%
Primary	u/o	u/o

Lane Evans (D–Ill.)
Of Rock Island • Elected 1982

Born: Aug. 4, 1951, Rock Island, Ill.
Education: Augustana College (Ill.), B.A. 1974; Georgetown U., J.D. 1978.
Military Career: Marine Corps, 1969–71.
Occupation: Lawyer.
Family: Single.
Religion: Roman Catholic.
Political Career: No previous office.

Capitol Office: 2335 Rayburn House Office Building 20515; 225-5905; (fax) 225-5396; (e–mail) lane. evans@mail.house.gov; (web) www.house.gov/evans.
Office Staff: Admin. Asst., Dennis J. King; Legis. Dir., Tom O'Donnell; Press Secy., Steve Vetzner; Scheduler, Eda S. Robinson.
Committees: Armed Services (Military Procurement); Veterans' Affairs — ranking member.

Illinois 17th — West — Rock Island; Moline. The district vote for Bill Clinton was 51% in 1996.

CQ Voting Studies

	1997	1998
Presidential	73%	82%
Party	93%	91%
Participation	99%	99%

Interest Groups

	1997	1998
ADA	100%	90%
ACU	16%	16%
AFL-CIO	100%	n/a
CCUS	20%	22%

Elections

	1996	1998
General	52%	52%
Primary	u/o	u/o

Terry Everett (R–Ala.)
Of Enterprise • Elected 1992

Born: Feb. 15, 1937, Dothan, Ala.
Education: Enterprise State Junior College, attended.
Military Career: Air Force, 1955–59.
Occupation: Newspaper executive; construction company owner; farm owner; real estate developer.
Family: Wife, Barbara.
Religion: Baptist.
Political Career: No previous office.

Capitol Office: 2312 Rayburn House Office Building 20515; 225-2901; (e–mail) terry.everett@mail.house. gov; (web) www.house.gov/everett.
Office Staff: Admin. Asst., H. Clay Swanzy; Legis. Dir., Wade Heck; Press Secy., Mike Lewis; Scheduler, Joanna Buchanan.
Committees: Agriculture (Livestock & Horticulture; Risk Management, Research & Specialty Crops); Armed Services (Military Procurement; Military Readiness); Veterans' Affairs (Oversight & Investigations — chairman).

Alabama 2nd — Southeast — Part of Montgomery; Dothan. The district vote for Bill Clinton was 37% in 1996.

CQ Voting Studies

	1997	1998
Presidential	27%	20%
Party	95%	94%
Participation	99%	99%

Interest Groups

	1997	1998
ADA	0%	5%
ACU	96%	100%
AFL-CIO	0%	n/a
CCUS	80%	89%

Elections

	1996	1998
General	63%	69%
Primary	u/o	u/o

Thomas W. Ewing (R–Ill.)
Of Pontiac • Elected 1991

Born: Sept. 19, 1935, Atlanta, Ill.
Education: Millikin U., B.S. 1957; John Marshall Law School (Chicago), J.D. 1968.
Military Career: Army, 1957; Army Reserve, 1957–63.
Occupation: Lawyer.
Family: Wife, Connie; three children; three stepchildren.
Religion: Methodist.
Political Career: Ill. House, 1975–91, deputy Republican leader, 1990–91.

Capitol Office: 2417 Rayburn House Office Building 20515; 225-2371; (fax) 225-8071; (e–mail) www.house.gov/writerep; (web) www.house.gov/ewing.
Office Staff: Admin. Asst./Legis. Dir., Brad Close; Communications Dir., Maria Gemskie; Scheduler, Karen Kaumeier.
Committees: House Administration; Agriculture (Department Operations, Oversight, Nutrition & Forestry; Risk Management, Research & Specialty Crops — chairman); Science (Basic Research; Technology); Transportation & Infrastructure (Aviation; Economic Development & Public Buildings); Joint Economic.

Illinois 15th — East Central — Champaign; Kankakee. The district vote for Bill Clinton was 45% in 1996.

CQ Voting Studies

	1997	1998
Presidential	36%	27%
Party	91%	86%
Participation	98%	95%

Interest Groups

	1997	1998
ADA	20%	0%
ACU	84%	91%
AFL-CIO	25%	n/a
CCUS	80%	100%

Elections

	1996	1998
General	57%	62%
Primary	u/o	u/o

Sam Farr (D–Calif.)
Of Carmel • Elected 1993

Born: July 4, 1941, San Francisco, Calif.
Education: Willamette U., B.S. 1963.
Occupation: State legislative aide.
Family: Wife, Shary Baldwin Farr; one child.
Religion: Episcopalian.
Political Career: Monterey County Board of Supervisors, 1975–81; Calif. Assembly, 1981–93.

Capitol Office: 1221 Longworth House Office Building 20515; 225-2861; (fax) 225-6791; (e–mail) samfarr@mail.house.gov; (web) www.house.gov/farr.
Office Staff: Admin. Asst., Rochelle Dornatt; Legis. Dir., Debbie Merrill; Press Secy., Naomi Seligman; Exec. Asst., Amy Slavin.
Committees: Appropriations (Agriculture, Rural Development, FDA & Related Agencies; Military Construction).

California 17th — Monterey, San Benito and Santa Cruz counties — Santa Cruz. The district vote for Bill Clinton was 55% in 1996.

CQ Voting Studies

	1997	1998
Presidential	73%	84%
Party	85%	90%
Participation	91%	95%

Interest Groups

	1997	1998
ADA	95%	100%
ACU	4%	0%
AFL-CIO	100%	n/a
CCUS	40%	44%

Elections

	1996	1998
General	59%	65%
Primary	88%	*60%

*Open primary

Chaka Fattah (D–Pa.)
Of Philadelphia • Elected 1994
Pronounced: SHOCK-ah fa-TAH

Born: Nov. 21, 1956, Philadelphia, Pa.
Education: Community College of Philadelphia, A.A. 1976; U. of Pennsylvania, M.A. 1986.
Occupation: Public official.
Family: Wife, Patricia Renfroe; three children.
Religion: Baptist.
Political Career: Democratic candidate for Philadelphia City commissioner, 1978; Pa. House, 1983–89; Pa. Senate, 1989–95; Consumer Party nominee for U.S. House (special election), 1991.

Capitol Office: 1205 Longworth House Office Building 20515; 225-4001; (fax) 225-5392; (e–mail) www.house.gov/writerep; (web) www.house.gov/fattah.
Office Staff: Chief of Staff, Claudia Pharis; Legis. Dir., Neil A. Snyder; Press Secy., Rebecca Kirszner; Exec. Asst., Michelle Anderson.
Committees: House Administration; Education & Workforce (Early Childhood, Youth & Families; Postsecondary Education, Training & Life-Long Learning); Government Reform (Postal Service — ranking member); Standards of Official Conduct; Joint Printing.

Pennsylvania 2nd — West Philadelphia; Chestnut Hill; Yeadon. The district vote for Bill Clinton was 86% in 1996.

CQ Voting Studies

	1997	1998
Presidential	85%	80%
Party	91%	91%
Participation	94%	92%

Interest Groups

	1997	1998
ADA	100%	95%
ACU	0%	0%
AFL-CIO	100%	n/a
CCUS	50%	25%

Elections

	1996	1998
General	88%	87%
Primary	u/o	u/o

Bob Filner (D–Calif.)
Of San Diego • Elected 1992

Born: Sept. 4, 1942, Pittsburgh, Pa.
Education: Cornell U., B.A. 1963; U. of Delaware, M.A. 1969; Cornell U., Ph.D. 1973.
Occupation: Public official; college professor.
Family: Wife, Jane Merrill; two children.
Religion: Jewish.
Political Career: San Diego School Board, 1979–83, president, 1982; candidate for San Diego City Council, 1983; San Diego City Council, 1987–92, deputy mayor, 1991.

Capitol Office: 2463 Rayburn House Office Building 20515; 225-8045; (fax) 225-9073; (e–mail) TalktoBobFilner@mail.house.gov.
Office Staff: Chief of Staff, Stewart Durst; Legis. Dir., Richard Patrick; Press Secy., Kelly Werner; Exec. Asst., Kim Messineo.
Committees: Transportation & Infrastructure (Aviation; Ground Transportation); Veterans' Affairs (Benefits — ranking member).

California 50th — Central and south San Diego; Chula Vista; National City. The district vote for Bill Clinton was 60% in 1996.

CQ Voting Studies

	1997	1998
Presidential	72%	84%
Party	93%	94%
Participation	97%	98%

Interest Groups

	1997	1998
ADA	95%	100%
ACU	8%	4%
AFL-CIO	100%	n/a
CCUS	30%	22%

Elections

	1996	1998
General	62%	u/o
Primary	55%	u/o

Ernie Fletcher (R-Ky.)
Of Lexington • Elected 1998

Born: Nov. 12, 1952, Mount Sterling, Ky.
Education: U. of Kentucky, B.S 1974, M.D. 1984.
Military Career: Air Force, 1974–80.
Occupation: Physician.
Family: Wife, Glenna; two children.
Religion: Baptist.
Political Career: Ky. House, 1995–96; Republican nominee for U.S House, 1996.

Capitol Office: 1117 Longworth House Office Building 20515; 225-4706; (fax) 225-2122; (e–mail) ernest.fletcher@mail.house.gov.
Office Staff: Chief of Staff, Daniel Groves; Press Secy., Wes Irwin; Scheduler, Pamela Maddux.
Committees: Agriculture (Risk Management, Research & Specialty Crops); Budget; Education & Workforce (Employer-Employee Relations; Oversight & Investigations).

Kentucky 6th — East central — Lexington; Frankfort. The district vote for Bill Clinton was 46% in 1996.

Elections

	1998
General	53%
Primary	76%

Mark Foley (R–Fla.)
Of West Palm Beach • Elected 1994

Born: Sept. 8, 1954, Newton, Mass.
Education: Palm Beach Community College, attended 1973–75.
Occupation: Catering company founder; real estate broker; restaurant chain owner.
Family: Single.
Religion: Roman Catholic.
Political Career: Lake Worth City Council, 1977–79; sought Democratic nomination for Fla. House, 1980; Lake Worth city commissioner, 1982–84; sought Democratic nomination for Palm Beach County Commission, 1984; Republican nominee for Fla. House, 1986; Fla. House, 1991–93; Fla. Senate, 1993–95.

Capitol Office: 113 Cannon House Office Building 20515; 225-5792; (fax) 225-3132; (e–mail) mark.foley@mail.house.gov; (web) www.house.gov/foley.
Office Staff: Admin. Asst., Kirk Fordham; Legis. Dir., Liz Nicolson; Communications Dir., Sean Spicer; Scheduler, Meredith Smalley.
Committees: Ways & Means (Human Resources).

Florida 16th — Central — Coastal Martin, Palm Beach and St. Lucie counties. The district vote for Bill Clinton was 47% in 1996.

CQ Voting Studies

	1997	1998
Presidential	36%	38%
Party	88%	82%
Participation	98%	96%

Interest Groups

	1997	1998
ADA	30%	20%
ACU	84%	80%
AFL-CIO	25%	n/a
CCUS	100%	100%

Elections

	1996	1998
General	64%	u/o
Primary	u/o	u/o

Michael P. Forbes (R–N.Y.)
Of Quogue • Elected 1994

Born: July 16, 1952, Riverhead, N.Y.
Education: State U. of New York at Albany, B.A. 1983.
Occupation: Chamber of commerce manager; Small Business Administration regional administrator; congressional aide.
Family: Wife, Barbara; two children.
Religion: Roman Catholic.
Political Career: No previous office.

Capitol Office: 125 Cannon House Office Building 20515; 225-3826; (fax) 225-3143; (e-mail) mike.forbes@mail.house.gov; (web) www.house.gov/forbes.
Office Staff: Chief of Staff, Diana Weir; Legis. Dir., Dave Silverstein; Press Secy., Anthony J. Howard; Appts. Secy., Kate Rea.
Committees: Appropriations (Energy & Water Development; Foreign Operations & Export Financing; Treasury, Postal Service & General Government); Small Business (Government Programs & Oversight; Tax, Finance & Exports).

New York 1st — Eastern Suffolk County — Brookhaven; Smithtown. The district vote for Bill Clinton was 51% in 1996.

CQ Voting Studies

	1997	1998
Presidential	28%	41%
Party	63%	63%
Participation	88%	96%

Interest Groups

	1997	1998
ADA	30%	65%
ACU	70%	46%
AFL-CIO	50%	n/a
CCUS	60%	61%

Elections

	1996	1998
General	55%	64%
Primary	u/o	u/o

Harold E. Ford Jr. (D–Tenn.)
Of Memphis • Elected 1996

Born: May 11, 1970, Memphis, Tenn.
Education: U. of Pennsylvania, B.A. 1992; U. of Michigan, J.D. 1996.
Occupation: Law clerk; congressional aide.
Family: Single.
Religion: Baptist.
Political Career: No previous office.

Capitol Office: 325 Cannon House Office Building 20515; 225-3265; (fax) 225-5663; (e-mail) rep.harold.ford.jr@mail.house.gov; (web) www.house.gov/ford.
Office Staff: Chief of Staff, Jarvis Stewart; Legis. Dir., Beverly Fields; Communications Dir., Mark Schuermann; Scheduler, Rebecca Aaron.
Committees: Education & Workforce (Early Childhood, Youth & Families; Oversight & Investigations); Government Reform (Census; National Economic Growth).

Tennessee 9th — Memphis. The district vote for Bill Clinton was 71% in 1996.

CQ Voting Studies

	1997	1998
Presidential	79%	61%
Party	91%	76%
Participation	98%	85%

Interest Groups

	1997	1998
ADA	85%	80%
ACU	8%	14%
AFL-CIO	100%	n/a
CCUS	60%	62%

Elections

	1996	1998
General	61%	79%
Primary	60%	u/o

Vito J. Fossella (R–N.Y.)
Of Great Kills • Elected 1997
Pronounced: VEE-toe Fuh-SELL-ah

Born: Mar. 9, 1965, Staten Island, N.Y.
Education: U. of Pennsylvania, B.S. 1987; Fordham U., J.D. 1993.
Occupation: Management consultant.
Family: Wife, Mary Pat; two children.
Religion: Roman Catholic.
Political Career: N.Y. City Council, 1994–97.

Capitol Office: 431 Cannon House Office Building 20515; 225-3371; (fax) 226-1272; (e-mail) vito.fossella@mail.house.gov; (web) www.house.gov/fossella.
Office Staff: Chief of Staff, Tom Quaadman; Legis. Dir., Jennifer Prazmark; Press Secy., Craig Donner; Office Mgr./Scheduler, Vicki Hook.
Committees: Commerce (Energy & Power; Finance & Hazardous Materials; Telecommunications, Trade & Consumer Protection).

New York 13th — Staten Island; part of southwest Brooklyn. The district vote for Bill Clinton was 51% in 1996.

CQ Voting Studies

	1997	1998
Presidential	13%	23%
Party	100%	90%
Participation	100%	98%

Interest Groups

	1998
ADA	0%
ACU	96%
AFL-CIO	n/a
CCUS	100%

Elections

	1997	1998
General	*61%	65%
Primary		u/o

*Special election

Tillie Fowler (R–Fla.)
Of Jacksonville • Elected 1992

Born: Dec. 23, 1942, Milledgeville, Ga.
Education: Emory U., A.B. 1964, J.D. 1967.
Occupation: White House aide; congressional aide; lawyer.
Family: Husband, L. Buck; two children.
Religion: Episcopalian.
Political Career: Jacksonville City Council, 1985–92, president, 1989–90.

Capitol Office: 106 Cannon House Office Building 20515; 225-2501; (fax) 225-9318; (e-mail) www.house.gov/writerep; (web) www.house.gov/fowler.
Office Staff: Admin. Asst., David Gilliland; Legis. Dir., Bill Klein; Press Secy., Kristin Accipiter; Scheduler, Lynn Miller.
Committees: Armed Services (Military Installations & Facilities; Military Readiness); Transportation & Infrastructure (Oversight & Investigations — chairman; Ground Transportation).

Florida 4th — Northeast — Part of Jacksonville. The district vote for Bill Clinton was 37% in 1996.

CQ Voting Studies

	1997	1998
Presidential	31%	26%
Party	91%	87%
Participation	97%	95%

Interest Groups

	1997	1998
ADA	5%	5%
ACU	84%	88%
AFL-CIO	0%	n/a
CCUS	90%	94%

Elections

	1996	1998
General	u/o	u/o
Primary	89%	u/o

Barney Frank (D–Mass.)
Of Newton • Elected 1980

Born: Mar. 31, 1940, Bayonne, N.J.
Education: Harvard U., B.A. 1962, J.D. 1977.
Occupation: Lawyer.
Family: Single.
Religion: Jewish.
Political Career: Mass. House, 1973–81.

Capitol Office: 2210 Rayburn House Office Building 20515; 225-5931; (fax) 225-0182; (e–mail) www.house.gov/writerep; (web) www.house.gov/frank.
Office Staff: Chief of Staff/Press Secy., Peter Kovar; Scheduler, Maria Giesta.
Committees: Banking & Financial Services (Domestic & International Monetary Policy; Housing & Community Opportunity — ranking member); Judiciary (Constitution; Immigration & Claims).

Massachusetts 4th — Boston suburbs — Newton; New Bedford; part of Fall River. The district vote for Bill Clinton was 64% in 1996.

CQ Voting Studies

	1997	1998
Presidential	77%	80%
Party	91%	90%
Participation	96%	95%

Interest Groups

	1997	1998
ADA	100%	100%
ACU	4%	4%
AFL-CIO	100%	n/a
CCUS	30%	33%

Elections

	1996	1998
General	72%	u/o
Primary	u/o	u/o

Bob Franks (R–N.J.)
Of Berkeley Heights • Elected 1992

Born: Sept. 21, 1951, Hackensack, N.J.
Education: DePauw U., B.A. 1973; Southern Methodist U., J.D. 1976.
Occupation: Newspaper owner.
Family: Wife, Fran; one child.
Religion: Methodist.
Political Career: N.J. Assembly, 1980–92; N.J. Republican Party chairman, 1988–92.

Capitol Office: 225 Cannon House Office Building 20515; 225-5361; (fax) 225-9460; (e–mail) franksnj@mail.house.gov; (web) www.house.gov/bobfranks.
Office Staff: Chief of Staff, Bill Ulrey; Legis. Dir., Doug Tansey; Deputy Chief of Staff/Press Secy., Janet M. Thompson; Scheduler, Karen Cologne.
Committees: Budget; Transportation & Infrastructure (Economic Development & Public Buildings — chairman; Ground Transportation; Water Resources & Environment).

New Jersey 7th — North and Central — Parts of Woodbridge and Union. The district vote for Bill Clinton was 51% in 1996.

CQ Voting Studies

	1997	1998
Presidential	45%	38%
Party	74%	72%
Participation	99%	99%

Interest Groups

	1997	1998
ADA	40%	25%
ACU	64%	52%
AFL-CIO	38%	n/a
CCUS	90%	83%

Elections

	1996	1998
General	55%	53%
Primary	u/o	u/o

Rodney Frelinghuysen (R-N.J.)
Of Morristown • Elected 1994
Pronounced: FREE-ling–high–zen

Born: Apr. 29, 1946, New York, N.Y.
Education: Hobart College, B.A. 1969; Trinity College (Hartford, Conn.), attended 1971.
Military Career: Army, 1969–71.
Occupation: Public official.
Family: Wife, Virginia T. Frelinghuysen; two children.
Religion: Episcopalian.
Political Career: Morris County freeholder, 1974–83, director, 1980; sought Republican nomination for U.S. House, 1982; N.J. Assembly, 1983–95; sought Republican nomination for U.S. House, 1990.

Capitol Office: 228 Cannon House Office Building 20515; 225-5034; (fax) 225-3186; (e-mail) rodney.frelinghuysen@mail.house.gov; (web) www.house.gov/frelinghuysen.
Office Staff: Admin. Asst., Donna F. Mullins; Legis. Dir., Ed Krenik; Press Secy., Mark Broadhurst; Scheduler, Nancy Fox.
Committees: Appropriations (Energy & Water Development; Defense; VA, HUD & Independent Agencies).

New Jersey 11th — North — Morris County. The district vote for Bill Clinton was 42% in 1996.

CQ Voting Studies

	1997	1998
Presidential	48%	37%
Party	78%	76%
Participation	99%	99%

Interest Groups

	1997	1998
ADA	40%	10%
ACU	52%	52%
AFL-CIO	25%	n/a
CCUS	90%	83%

Elections

	1996	1998
General	66%	68%
Primary	u/o	u/o

Martin Frost (D-Texas)
Of Dallas • Elected 1978

Born: Jan. 1, 1942, Glendale, Calif.
Education: U. of Missouri, B.A., B.J. 1964; Georgetown U., J.D. 1970.
Military Career: Army Reserve, 1966–72.
Occupation: Lawyer.
Family: Wife, Kathy George Frost; three children.
Religion: Jewish.
Political Career: Sought Democratic nomination for U.S. House, 1974.

Capitol Office: 2256 Rayburn House Office Building 20515; 225-3605; (fax) 225-4951; (e-mail) martin.frost@mail.house.gov; (web) www.house.gov/frost.
Office Staff: Admin. Asst., Ronnie P. Carleton; Chief of Staff, Matt Angle; Legis. Dir., Susan McAvoy; Press Secy., Greg Speed; Exec. Asst., Vera Lou Durigon.
Committees: Rules (Legislative & Budget Process — ranking member).

Texas 24th — Parts of Dallas and Tarrant counties. The district vote for Bill Clinton was 53% in 1996.

CQ Voting Studies

	1997	1998
Presidential	77%	71%
Party	83%	80%
Participation	97%	94%

Interest Groups

	1997	1998
ADA	80%	95%
ACU	20%	8%
AFL-CIO	100%	n/a
CCUS	60%	56%

Elections

	1996	1998
General	56%	57%
Primary		u/o

Elton Gallegly (R–Calif.)
Of Simi Valley • Elected 1986
Pronounced: GAL-uh–glee

Born: Mar. 7, 1944, Huntington Park, Calif.
Education: California State U., Los Angeles, attended 1962–63.
Occupation: Real estate broker.
Family: Wife, Janice; four children.
Religion: Protestant.
Political Career: Simi Valley City Council, 1979–80; mayor of Simi Valley, 1980–86.

Capitol Office: 2427 Rayburn House Office Building 20515; 225-5811; (fax) 225-1100; (e–mail) www.house.gov/writerep; (web) www.house.gov/gallegly.
Office Staff: Admin. Asst., Joel Kassiday; Legis. Dir., Richard Mereu; Press Secy., Tom Pfeifer; Scheduler, Pat Koch.
Committees: International Relations (Western Hemisphere — chairman); Judiciary (Courts & Intellectual Property; Immigration & Claims); Resources (National Parks & Public Lands).

California 23rd — Most of Ventura County; Oxnard; Ventura; Simi Valley. The district vote for Bill Clinton was 46% in 1996.

CQ Voting Studies

	1997	1998
Presidential	29%	21%
Party	88%	90%
Participation	96%	99%

Interest Groups

	1997	1998
ADA	5%	15%
ACU	80%	76%
AFL-CIO	0%	n/a
CCUS	100%	83%

Elections

	1996	1998
General	60%	60%
Primary	u/o	*63%

*Open primary

Greg Ganske (R–Iowa)
Of Des Moines • Elected 1994
Pronounced: GAN-skee

Born: Mar. 31, 1949, New Hampton, Iowa.
Education: U. of Iowa, B.A. 1972, M.D. 1976.
Military Career: Army Reserve, 1986–present.
Occupation: Plastic surgeon.
Family: Wife, Corrine; three children.
Religion: Roman Catholic.
Political Career: No previous office.

Capitol Office: 1108 Longworth House Office Building 20515; 225-4426; (fax) 225-3193; (e–mail) rep.ganske@mail.house.gov; (web) www.house.gov/ganske.
Office Staff: Chief of Staff, John Barnes; Legis. Dir., Jonathan G. Traub; Press Secy., Barbara Levering; Exec. Asst., Erica Hanson.
Committees: Commerce (Finance & Hazardous Materials; Health & Environment; Oversight & Investigations).

Iowa 4th — Southwest — Des Moines; Council Bluffs. The district vote for Bill Clinton was 49% in 1996.

CQ Voting Studies

	1997	1998
Presidential	32%	33%
Party	86%	75%
Participation	99%	98%

Interest Groups

	1997	1998
ADA	30%	5%
ACU	76%	64%
AFL-CIO	13%	n/a
CCUS	70%	81%

Elections

	1996	1998
General	52%	65%
Primary	u/o	u/o

Sam Gejdenson (D–Conn.)
Of Bozrah • Elected 1980
Pronounced: GAY-den-son

Born: May 20, 1948, Eschwege, Germany.
Education: Mitchell College, A.S. 1968; U. of Connecticut, B.A. 1970.
Occupation: Dairy farmer.
Family: Wife, Betsy Henley-Cohn; two children; two stepchildren.
Religion: Jewish.
Political Career: Conn. House, 1975–79.

Capitol Office: 2304 Rayburn House Office Building 20515; 225-2076; (fax) 225-4977; (e-mail) bozrah@mail.house.gov; (web) www.house.gov/gejdenson.
Office Staff: Chief of Staff/Legis. Dir., Scott Kovarovics; Press Secy., Jonathan Lenzner.
Committees: International Relations — ranking member.

Connecticut 2nd — East — New London. The district vote for Bill Clinton was 53% in 1996.

CQ Voting Studies

	1997	1998
Presidential	83%	83%
Party	93%	93%
Participation	98%	98%

Interest Groups

	1997	1998
ADA	95%	100%
ACU	12%	9%
AFL-CIO	100%	n/a
CCUS	40%	28%

Elections

	1996	1998
General	52%	61%
Primary	u/o	u/o

George W. Gekas (R–Pa.)
Of Harrisburg • Elected 1982

Born: Apr. 14, 1930, Harrisburg, Pa.
Education: Dickinson College, B.A. 1952; Dickinson School of Law, LL.B. 1958, J.D. 1958.
Military Career: Army, 1953–55.
Occupation: Lawyer.
Family: Wife, Evangeline Charas Gekas.
Religion: Greek Orthodox.
Political Career: Dauphin County assistant district attorney, 1960–66; Pa. House, 1967–75; Republican nominee for Pa. House, 1974; Pa. Senate, 1977–83.

Capitol Office: 2410 Rayburn House Office Building 20515; 225-4315; (fax) 225-8440; (e-mail) www.house.gov/writerep; (web) www.house.gov/gekas.
Office Staff: Chief of Staff/Legis. Dir., Allan Cagnoli; Press Secy., Carey Voigt Dearnley; Exec. Asst., Matt Zonarich.
Committees: Judiciary (Commercial & Administrative Law — chairman; Crime).

Pennsylvania 17th — South Central — Harrisburg. The district vote for Bill Clinton was 37% in 1996.

CQ Voting Studies

	1997	1998
Presidential	29%	21%
Party	88%	90%
Participation	97%	97%

Interest Groups

	1997	1998
ADA	15%	10%
ACU	88%	84%
AFL-CIO	25%	n/a
CCUS	100%	100%

Elections

	1996	1998
General	72%	u/o
Primary	u/o	u/o

Richard A. Gephardt (D–Mo.)
Of St. Louis • Elected 1976

Born: Jan. 31, 1941, St. Louis, Mo.
Education: Northwestern U., B.S. 1962; U. of Michigan, J.D. 1965.
Military Career: Air National Guard, 1965–71.
Occupation: Lawyer.
Family: Wife, Jane Byrnes Gephardt; three children.
Religion: Baptist.
Political Career: St. Louis Board of Aldermen, 1971–76; sought Democratic nomination for president, 1988.

Capitol Office: 1226 Longworth House Office Building 20515; 225-2671; (fax) 225-7452; (e-mail) gephardt@mail.house.gov; (web) www.house.gov/gephardt.
Office Staff: Chief of Staff, Steve A. Elmendorf; Legis. Dir., Cathy Dente; Communications Dir., Laura Nichols; Scheduler, Sharon Daniels.
Committees: Minority Leader (no committee assignments)

Missouri 3rd — South St. Louis; southeast St. Louis County; Jefferson and Ste. Genevieve counties. The district vote for Bill Clinton was 49% in 1996.

CQ Voting Studies

	1997	1998
Presidential	69%	73%
Party	80%	85%
Participation	87%	90%

Interest Groups

	1997	1998
ADA	80%	90%
ACU	14%	12%
AFL-CIO	100%	n/a
CCUS	11%	24%

Elections

	1996	1998
General	59%	56%
Primary	75%	74%

Jim Gibbons (R–Nev.)
Of Reno • Elected 1996

Born: Dec. 16, 1944, Sparks, Nev.
Education: U. of Nevada, Reno, B.S. 1967, M.S. 1973; Southwestern U., J.D. 1979.
Military Career: Air Force, 1967–71; Nev. Air National Guard, 1975–95.
Occupation: Airline pilot; lawyer; geologist.
Family: Wife, Dawn; three children.
Religion: Protestant.
Political Career: Nev. Assembly, 1989–93, minority whip, 1993; Republican nominee for governor, 1994.

Capitol Office: 100 Cannon House Office Building 20515; 225-6155; (fax) 225-5629; (e-mail) mail.gibbons@mail.house.gov; (web) www.house.gov/gibbons.
Office Staff: Chief of Staff, Mike Dayton; Legis. Dir., Jack Victory; Communications Dir., Jay Cranford; Scheduler, Lynne Kasko.
Committees: Armed Services (Military Procurement; Military Readiness); Select Intelligence (Human Intelligence, Analysis & Counterintelligence; Technical & Tactical Intelligence); Resources (Energy & Mineral Resources; National Parks & Public Lands); Veterans' Affairs (Benefits).

Nevada 2nd — Reno, the Cow Counties and part of Clark County. The district vote for Bill Clinton was 40% in 1996.

CQ Voting Studies

	1997	1998
Presidential	29%	22%
Party	88%	93%
Participation	96%	99%

Interest Groups

	1997	1998
ADA	0%	20%
ACU	91%	92%
AFL-CIO	0%	n/a
CCUS	80%	89%

Elections

	1996	1998
General	59%	81%
Primary	42%	u/o

Wayne T. Gilchrest (R-Md.)
Of Kennedyville • Elected 1990

Born: Apr. 15, 1946, Rahway, N.J.
Education: Wesley College, A.A. 1971; Delaware State U., B.A. 1973; Loyola College (Baltimore, Md.), attended 1990.
Military Career: Marine Corps, 1964–68.
Occupation: High school teacher.
Family: Wife, Barbara; three children.
Religion: Methodist.
Political Career: Republican nominee for U.S. House, 1988.

Capitol Office: 2245 Rayburn House Office Building 20515; 225-5311; (fax) 225-0254; (e-mail) www.house.gov/writerep; (web) www.house.gov/gilchrest.
Office Staff: Admin. Asst., Tony Caligiuri; Legis. Dir., Eric Webster; Press Secy./Scheduler, Cathy Bassett.
Committees: Resources (Fisheries Conservation, Wildlife & Oceans; Forests & Forest Health); Transportation & Infrastructure (Coast Guard & Maritime Transportation — chairman; Water Resources & Environment).

Maryland 1st — Cross Bay — Eastern Shore; Annapolis; Glen Burnie. The district vote for Bill Clinton was 43% in 1996.

CQ Voting Studies

	1997	1998
Presidential	44%	37%
Party	80%	71%
Participation	99%	97%

Interest Groups

	1997	1998
ADA	20%	35%
ACU	71%	44%
AFL-CIO	0%	n/a
CCUS	90%	89%

Elections

	1996	1998
General	62%	69%
Primary	65%	u/o

Paul E. Gillmor (R-Ohio)
Of Old Fort • Elected 1988

Born: Feb. 1, 1939, Tiffin, Ohio.
Education: Ohio Wesleyan U., B.A. 1961; U. of Michigan, J.D. 1964.
Military Career: Air Force, 1965–66.
Occupation: Lawyer.
Family: Wife, Karen L. Gillmor; five children.
Religion: Methodist.
Political Career: Ohio Senate, 1967–89, minority leader, 1978–80, 1983–84, president, 1981–82, 1985–88; sought Republican nomination for governor, 1986.

Capitol Office: 1203 Longworth House Office Building 20515; 225-6405; (e-mail) www.house.gov/writerep; (web) www.house.gov/gillmor.
Office Staff: Admin. Asst., Mark Wellman; Legis. Dir., Jim Steen; Press Secy., Christopher Slagle; Exec. Asst., Kelley Kurtz.
Committees: Commerce (Finance & Hazardous Materials; Telecommunications, Trade & Consumer Protection); International Relations (Asia & the Pacific; Western Hemisphere).

Ohio 5th — Northwest — Bowling Green; Sandusky. The district vote for Bill Clinton was 42% in 1996.

CQ Voting Studies

	1997	1998
Presidential	31%	28%
Party	88%	85%
Participation	96%	98%

Interest Groups

	1997	1998
ADA	10%	5%
ACU	84%	68%
AFL-CIO	13%	n/a
CCUS	89%	100%

Elections

	1996	1998
General	61%	67%
Primary		u/o

Benjamin A. Gilman (R–N.Y.)
Of Middletown • Elected 1972

Born: Dec. 6, 1922, Poughkeepsie, N.Y.
Education: U. of Pennsylvania, B.S. 1946; New York Law School, LL.B. 1950.
Military Career: Army, 1943–45.
Occupation: Lawyer.
Family: Wife, Georgia Nickles Tingus; three children; two stepchildren.
Religion: Jewish.
Political Career: Assistant N.Y. attorney general, 1953–55; N.Y. Assembly, 1967–73.

Capitol Office: 2449 Rayburn House Office Building 20515; 225-3776; (fax) 225-2541; (e-mail) ben@mail.house.gov; (web) www.house.gov/gilman.
Office Staff: Admin. Asst., Robert Becker; Legis. Dir., P. Todd Burger; Press Secy., Andrew Zarutskie; Appts. Secy., Ellen Pentland.
Committees: Government Reform (Criminal Justice, Drug Policy & Human Resources; Postal Service); International Relations — chairman.

New York 20th — Rockland and parts of Westchester, Orange and Sullivan counties. The district vote for Bill Clinton was 54% in 1996.

CQ Voting Studies

	1997	1998
Presidential	49%	45%
Party	69%	61%
Participation	98%	99%

Interest Groups

	1997	1998
ADA	50%	45%
ACU	40%	38%
AFL-CIO	75%	n/a
CCUS	60%	71%

Elections

	1996	1998
General	57%	58%
Primary	u/o	u/o

Charlie Gonzalez (D–Texas)
Of San Antonio • Elected 1998

Born: May 5, 1945, San Antonio, Texas.
Education: U. of Texas, Austin, B.A. 1969; St. Mary's U. (San Antonio), J.D. 1972.
Military Career: Texas Air National Guard, 1969–75.
Occupation: Lawyer.
Family: Wife, Becky Whetstone; one child.
Religion: Roman Catholic.
Political Career: Bexar County judge, 1982–87; Texas District Court judge, 1988–97.

Capitol Office: 327 Cannon House Office Building 20515; 225-3236; (fax) 225-1915; (e-mail) www.house.gov/writerep.
Office Staff: Chief of Staff, Kevin Kimble; Press Secy., Rochelle Tafolla; Exec. Asst./Scheduler, Laura Flores.
Committees: Banking & Financial Services (Financial Institutions & Consumer Credit; General Oversight & Investigations); Small Business (Government Programs & Oversight; Tax, Finance & Exports).

Texas 20th — Downtown San Antonio. The district vote for Bill Clinton was 59% in 1996.

Elections

	1998
General	63%
Primary	*62%

*Runoff election

Virgil H. Goode Jr. (D–Va.)
Of Rocky Mount • Elected 1996
Pronounced: GOOD (rhymes with "food")

Born: Oct. 17, 1946, Richmond, Va.
Education: U. of Richmond, B.A. 1969; U. of Virginia, J.D. 1973.
Military Career: Va. National Guard, 1969–75.
Occupation: Lawyer.
Family: Wife, Lucy D. Goode; one child.
Religion: Baptist.
Political Career: Va. Senate, 1973–97; sought Democratic nomination for U.S. Senate, 1982, 1994.

Capitol Office: 1520 Longworth House Office Building 20515; 225-4711; (fax) 225-5681; (e-mail) rep.goode@mail.house.gov; (web) www.house.gov/goode.
Office Staff: Admin. Asst., Vacant; Scheduler, Judy Epperly.
Committees: Agriculture (Department Operations, Oversight, Nutrition & Forestry; Risk Management, Research & Specialty Crops); Banking & Financial Services (General Oversight & Investigations; Housing & Community Opportunity).

Virginia 5th — South — Danville; Charlottesville. The district vote for Bill Clinton was 43% in 1996.

CQ Voting Studies

	1997	1998
Presidential	28%	26%
Party	37%	27%
Participation	98%	98%

Interest Groups

	1997	1998
ADA	25%	30%
ACU	84%	83%
AFL-CIO	13%	n/a
CCUS	80%	72%

Elections

	1996	1998
General	60%	u/o
Primary	u/o	u/o

Robert W. Goodlatte (R–Va.)
Of Roanoke • Elected 1992
Pronounced: GOOD-lat

Born: Sept. 22, 1952, Holyoke, Mass.
Education: Bates College, B.A. 1974; Washington and Lee U., J.D. 1977.
Occupation: Lawyer; congressional aide.
Family: Wife, Maryellen; two children.
Religion: Christian Scientist.
Political Career: Roanoke City Republican Committee chairman, 1980–83; 6th Congressional District Republican Party chairman, 1983–88.

Capitol Office: 2240 Rayburn House Office Building 20515; 225-5431; (fax) 225-9681; (e-mail) talk2bob@mail.house.gov; (web) www.house.gov/goodlatte.
Office Staff: Chief of Staff, David Lehman; Legis. Dir., Ben Cline; Press Secy., Ellen Stroud; Scheduler, Rachel Palmer.
Committees: Agriculture (Department Operations, Oversight, Nutrition & Forestry — chairman; Livestock & Horticulture); Judiciary (Constitution; Courts & Intellectual Property; Immigration & Claims).

Virginia 6th — West — Roanoke; Lynchburg. The district vote for Bill Clinton was 41% in 1996.

CQ Voting Studies

	1997	1998
Presidential	29%	23%
Party	94%	92%
Participation	99%	99%

Interest Groups

	1997	1998
ADA	10%	0%
ACU	80%	100%
AFL-CIO	13%	n/a
CCUS	100%	100%

Elections

	1996	1998
General	67%	69%
Primary	u/o	u/o

Bill Goodling (R–Pa.)
Of Seven Valleys • Elected 1974

Born: Dec. 5, 1927, Loganville, Pa.
Education: U. of Maryland, B.S. 1953; Western Maryland College, M.Ed. 1956; Pennsylvania State U., attended 1960–62.
Military Career: Army, 1946–48.
Occupation: Public school superintendent.
Family: Wife, Hilda; two children.
Religion: Methodist.
Political Career: Dallastown School Board president, 1964–67.

Capitol Office: 2107 Rayburn House Office Building 20515; 225-5836; (fax) 226-1000; (e–mail) www.house.gov/writerep; (web) www.house.gov/goodling.
Office Staff: Chief of Staff, Kimberly Strycharz; Legis. Dir., Christine O'Connor; Press Secy., Greg Englert; Scheduler, Anne Sluck.
Committees: Education & Workforce — chairman (Early Childhood, Youth & Families; Employer-Employee Relations; Postsecondary Education, Training & Life-Long Learning); International Relations (International Operations & Human Rights).

Pennsylvania 19th — South Central — York. The district vote for Bill Clinton was 38% in 1996.

CQ Voting Studies

	1997	1998
Presidential	27%	18%
Party	90%	90%
Participation	98%	95%

Interest Groups

	1997	1998
ADA	10%	5%
ACU	88%	92%
AFL-CIO	13%	n/a
CCUS	90%	88%

Elections

	1996	1998
General	63%	68%
Primary	55%	68%

Bart Gordon (D–Tenn.)
Of Murfreesboro • Elected 1984

Born: Jan. 24, 1949, Murfreesboro, Tenn.
Education: Middle Tennessee State U., B.S. 1971; U. of Tennessee, J.D. 1973.
Military Career: Army Reserve, 1971–72.
Occupation: Lawyer.
Family: Wife, Leslie.
Religion: Methodist.
Political Career: Tenn. Democratic Party chairman, 1981–83.

Capitol Office: 2368 Rayburn House Office Building 20515; 225-4231; (fax) 225-6887; (e–mail) bart.gordon@mail.house.gov; (web) www.house.gov/gordon.
Office Staff: Admin. Asst., Chuck Atkins; Legis. Dir., Louis Finkel; Press Secy., Karen Sloane; Exec. Asst., Amy Ridings.
Committees: Commerce (Energy & Power; Telecommunications, Trade & Consumer Protection); Science (Space & Aeronautics — ranking member; Technology).

Tennessee 6th — North Central — Murfreesboro. The district vote for Bill Clinton was 45% in 1996.

CQ Voting Studies

	1997	1998
Presidential	63%	61%
Party	68%	72%
Participation	98%	97%

Interest Groups

	1997	1998
ADA	60%	90%
ACU	36%	36%
AFL-CIO	75%	n/a
CCUS	70%	72%

Elections

	1996	1998
General	54%	55%
Primary	89%	u/o

Porter J. Goss (R–Fla.)
Of Sanibel • Elected 1988

Born: Nov. 26, 1938, Waterbury, Conn.
Education: Yale U., B.A. 1960.
Military Career: Army, 1960–62.
Occupation: Newspaper founder; CIA agent.
Family: Wife, Mariel; four children.
Religion: Presbyterian.
Political Career: Sanibel City Council, 1974–82, mayor, 1975–77, 1982; Lee County Commission, 1983–88, chairman, 1985–86.

CQ Voting Studies

	1997	1998
Presidential	31%	28%
Party	90%	84%
Participation	97%	89%

Interest Groups

	1997	1998
ADA	10%	5%
ACU	88%	91%
AFL-CIO	0%	n/a
CCUS	80%	86%

Elections

	1996	1998
General	73%	u/o
Primary	u/o	u/o

Capitol Office: 108 Cannon House Office Building 20515; 225-2536; (fax) 225-6820; (e-mail) www.house.gov/writerep; (web) www.house.gov/goss.
Office Staff: Chief of Staff, Sheryl V. Wooley; Legis. Dir., Darren Willcox; Press Secy., Jennifer Millerwise; Office Mgr./Appts. Secy., Maggie Knutson.
Committees: Select Intelligence — chairman; China Investigation; Rules (Legislative & Budget Process — chairman).

Florida 14th — Southwest — Lee and Collier counties; Cape Coral; Fort Myers; Naples. The district vote for Bill Clinton was 38% in 1996.

Lindsey Graham (R–S.C.)
Of Seneca • Elected 1994

Born: July 9, 1955, Seneca, S.C.
Education: U. of South Carolina, B.A. 1977, M.P.A. 1978, J.D. 1981.
Military Career: Air Force, 1982–88, 1990; Air National Guard, 1989–present.
Occupation: Lawyer.
Family: Single.
Religion: Southern Baptist.
Political Career: S.C. assistant attorney, 1988–92; S.C. House, 1992–95.

CQ Voting Studies

	1997	1998
Presidential	25%	22%
Party	93%	89%
Participation	98%	95%

Interest Groups

	1997	1998
ADA	5%	15%
ACU	92%	88%
AFL-CIO	0%	n/a
CCUS	90%	76%

Elections

	1996	1998
General	60%	u/o
Primary	u/o	u/o

Capitol Office: 1429 Longworth House Office Building 20515; 225-5301; (fax) 225-3216; (e-mail) www.house.gov/writerep; (web) www.house.gov/graham.
Office Staff: Chief of Staff, Richard Perry; Legis. Dir., Alex Jarvis; Press Secy., Kevin Bishop; Personal Secy., Ellen Bradley.
Committees: Armed Services (Military Personnel; Military Procurement); Education & Workforce (Early Childhood, Youth & Families; Postsecondary Education, Training & Life-Long Learning; Workforce Protections); Judiciary (Commercial & Administrative Law; Constitution).

South Carolina 3rd — West — Anderson; Aiken. The district vote for Bill Clinton was 39% in 1996.

Kay Granger (R–Texas)
Of Fort Worth • Elected 1996

Born: Jan. 18, 1943, Greenville, Texas.
Education: Texas Wesleyan U., B.S. 1965.
Occupation: Insurance agent; teacher.
Family: Divorced; three children.
Religion: Methodist.
Political Career: Fort Worth City Council, 1989–91; Fort Worth mayor, 1991–95.

Capitol Office: 435 Cannon House Office Building 20515; 225-5071; (fax) 225-5683; (e-mail) texas.granger@mail.house.gov; (web) www.house.gov/granger.
Office Staff: Chief of Staff, Ken Mehlman; Legis. Dir., Bruce Butler; Press Secy., Kasey Pipes; Scheduler, Nancy Scott.
Committees: Appropriations (Legislative Branch; Military Construction; Transportation).

Texas 12th — Northwest Tarrant County; part of Fort Worth. The district vote for Bill Clinton was 46% in 1996.

CQ Voting Studies

	1997	1998
Presidential	29%	28%
Party	91%	90%
Participation	96%	98%

Interest Groups

	1997	1998
ADA	0%	5%
ACU	92%	84%
AFL-CIO	0%	n/a
CCUS	100%	100%

Elections

	1996	1998
General	58%	62%
Primary	69%	u/o

Gene Green (D–Texas)
Of Houston • Elected 1992

Born: Oct. 17, 1947, Houston, Texas.
Education: U. of Houston, B.B.A. 1971; Bates College of Law, attended 1971–77.
Occupation: Lawyer.
Family: Wife, Helen Albers Green; two children.
Religion: Methodist.
Political Career: Texas House, 1973–85; Texas Senate, 1985–92.

Capitol Office: 2429 Rayburn House Office Building 20515; 225-1688; (fax) 225-9903; (e-mail) ask.gene@mail.house.gov; (web) www.house.gov/green.
Office Staff: Admin. Asst., Marc Gonzales; Legis. Dir., Adam Gluck; Press Secy./Scheduler, Cindy Jimenz.
Committees: Commerce (Health & Environment; Oversight & Investigations; Telecommunications, Trade & Consumer Protection).

Texas 29th — Parts of Houston. The district vote for Bill Clinton was 61% in 1996.

CQ Voting Studies

	1997	1998
Presidential	61%	68%
Party	75%	81%
Participation	97%	94%

Interest Groups

	1997	1998
ADA	75%	95%
ACU	42%	16%
AFL-CIO	100%	n/a
CCUS	60%	47%

Elections

	1996	1998
General	68%	93%
Primary		u/o

Mark Green (R-Wis.)
Of Green Bay • Elected 1998

Born: June 1, 1960, Boston, Mass.
Education: U. of Wisconsin, Eau Claire, B.A. 1983; U. of Wisconsin, Madison, J.D. 1987.
Occupation: Lawyer; teacher.
Family: Wife, Susan; three children.
Religion: Roman Catholic.
Political Career: Wis. Assembly, 1993–99.

Capitol Office: 1218 Longworth House Office Building 20515; 225-5665; (fax) 225-5729; (e-mail) www.house.gov/writerep.
Office Staff: Chief of Staff, Mark Graul; Legis. Dir., Gina Elmore; Communications Dir., Chris Tuttle; Scheduler/Office Mgr., Nicole Vernon.
Committees: Banking & Financial Services (Domestic & International Monetary Policy; Housing & Community Opportunity); Budget; Science (Space & Aeronautics; Technology).

Wisconsin 8th — Northeast — Green Bay; Appleton. The district vote for Bill Clinton was 46% in 1996.

Elections

	1998
General	55%
Primary	80%

James C. Greenwood (R-Pa.)
Of Erwinna • Elected 1992

Born: May 4, 1951, Philadelphia, Pa.
Education: Dickinson College, B.A. 1973.
Occupation: Social services agency caseworker; state legislative aide.
Family: Wife, Christina; three children.
Religion: Presbyterian.
Political Career: Pa. House, 1981–87; Pa. Senate, 1987–93.

Capitol Office: 2436 Rayburn House Office Building 20515; 225-4276; (fax) 225-9511; (e-mail) www.house.gov/writerep; (web) www.house.gov/greenwood.
Office Staff: Chief of Staff, Jordan "Pete" Krauss; Legis. Dir., Judy Borger; Communications Dir., Niko Yen; Scheduler/Exec. Asst., Mary Corcoran.
Committees: Commerce (Finance & Hazardous Materials; Health & Environment); Education & Workforce (Early Childhood, Youth & Families; Postsecondary Education, Training & Life-Long Learning).

Pennsylvania 8th — Northern Philadelphia suburbs — Bucks County. The district vote for Bill Clinton was 45% in 1996.

CQ Voting Studies

	1997	1998
Presidential	48%	35%
Party	76%	64%
Participation	96%	94%

Interest Groups

	1997	1998
ADA	55%	25%
ACU	50%	48%
AFL-CIO	13%	n/a
CCUS	90%	94%

Elections

	1996	1998
General	59%	63%
Primary	60%	67%

Luis V. Gutierrez (D–Ill.)
Of Chicago • Elected 1992
Pronounced: loo-EES goo–tee-AIR-ez

Born: Dec. 10, 1953, Chicago, Ill.
Education: Northeastern Illinois U., B.A. 1975.
Occupation: Teacher; social worker.
Family: Wife, Soraida Arocho; two children.
Religion: Roman Catholic.
Political Career: Chicago City Council, 1986–93.

Capitol Office: 2438 Rayburn House Office Building 20515; 225-8203; (fax) 225-7810; (e-mail) luisg@gutierrez.house.gov.
Office Staff: Chief of Staff, Doug Scofield; Legis. Dir., Jennice Fuentes; Press Secy., Bill Weinberg; Exec. Asst., Lisa Esquivel.
Committees: Banking & Financial Services (Financial Institutions & Consumer Credit; General Oversight & Investigations); Veterans' Affairs (Health — ranking member).

Illinois 4th — Chicago — Parts of North Side, southwest side. The district vote for Bill Clinton was 80% in 1996.

CQ Voting Studies

	1997	1998
Presidential	68%	80%
Party	86%	92%
Participation	95%	96%

Interest Groups

	1997	1998
ADA	95%	90%
ACU	13%	16%
AFL-CIO	100%	n/a
CCUS	13%	28%

Elections

	1996	1998
General	94%	82%
Primary	71%	u/o

Gil Gutknecht (R–Minn.)
Of Rochester • Elected 1994
Pronounced: GOOT-neck

Born: Mar. 20, 1951, Cedar Falls, Iowa.
Education: U. of Northern Iowa, B.A. 1973.
Occupation: Real estate broker; school supplies salesman; auctioneer; computer software salesman.
Family: Wife, Mary; three children.
Religion: Roman Catholic.
Political Career: Minn. House, 1983–95, floor leader.

Capitol Office: 425 Cannon House Office Building 20515; 225-2472; (fax) 225-3246; (e-mail) gil.gutknecht@mail.house.gov; (web) www.house.gov/gutknecht.
Office Staff: Admin. Asst., Brent R. Orrell; Legis. Counsel, Jeff Harrison; Press Secy./Scheduler, Sarah Derrick.
Committees: Agriculture (Livestock & Horticulture; Risk Management, Research & Specialty Crops); Budget; Science (Basic Research; Technology).

Minnesota 1st — Southeast — Rochester; part of Mankato. The district vote for Bill Clinton was 48% in 1996.

CQ Voting Studies

	1997	1998
Presidential	28%	24%
Party	92%	91%
Participation	99%	98%

Interest Groups

	1997	1998
ADA	15%	5%
ACU	92%	92%
AFL-CIO	0%	n/a
CCUS	100%	94%

Elections

	1996	1998
General	53%	55%
Primary	u/o	u/o

Ralph M. Hall (D–Texas)
Of Rockwall • Elected 1980

Born: May 3, 1923, Fate, Texas.
Education: Texas Christian U., attended 1943; U. of Texas, attended 1946–47; Southern Methodist U., LL.B. 1951.
Military Career: Navy, 1942–45.
Occupation: Lawyer; aluminum company president.
Family: Wife, Mary Ellen Hall; three children.
Religion: Methodist.
Political Career: Rockwall County judge, 1951–63; Texas Senate, 1963–73; sought Democratic nomination for lieutenant governor, 1972.

Capitol Office: 2221 Rayburn House Office Building 20515; 225-6673; (fax) 225-3332; (e-mail) www.house.gov/writerep; (web) www.house.gov/ralphhall.
Office Staff: Chief of Staff/Communications Dir., Janet Perry; Legis. Dir., Grace Warren; Scheduler, Elizabeth Kowal.
Committees: Commerce (Energy & Power — ranking member; Finance & Hazardous Materials; Health & Environment); Science (Energy & Environment; Space & Aeronautics).

Texas 4th — Northeast — Sherman; part of Tyler. The district vote for Bill Clinton was 35% in 1996.

CQ Voting Studies

	1997	1998
Presidential	27%	29%
Party	38%	23%
Participation	99%	99%

Interest Groups

	1997	1998
ADA	10%	15%
ACU	96%	96%
AFL-CIO	25%	n/a
CCUS	80%	76%

Elections

	1996	1998
General	64%	58%
Primary	u/o	u/o

Tony P. Hall (D–Ohio)
Of Dayton • Elected 1978

Born: Jan. 16, 1942, Dayton, Ohio.
Education: Denison U., A.B. 1964.
Occupation: Real estate broker.
Family: Wife, Janet; one child.
Religion: Presbyterian.
Political Career: Ohio House, 1969–73; Ohio Senate, 1973–79; Democratic nominee for Ohio secretary of state, 1974.

Capitol Office: 1436 Longworth House Office Building 20515; 225-6465; (fax) 225-9272; (e-mail) www.house.gov/writerep; (web) www.house.gov/tonyhall.
Office Staff: Chief of Staff, Rick Carne; Legis. Dir., David Goldberg; Exec. Asst./Press Secy., Michael D. Gessel; Scheduler, Eric Humpert.
Committees: Rules (Rules & Organization of the House — ranking member).

Ohio 3rd — Southwest — Dayton. The district vote for Bill Clinton was 50% in 1996.

CQ Voting Studies

	1997	1998
Presidential	63%	65%
Party	68%	74%
Participation	95%	96%

Interest Groups

	1997	1998
ADA	70%	75%
ACU	21%	21%
AFL-CIO	88%	n/a
CCUS	50%	44%

Elections

	1996	1998
General	64%	69%
Primary	u/o	u/o

James V. Hansen (R–Utah)
Of Farmington • Elected 1980

Born: Aug. 14, 1932, Salt Lake City, Utah.
Education: U. of Utah, B.S. 1960.
Military Career: Navy, 1951–53.
Occupation: Insurance executive; developer.
Family: Wife, Ann; five children.
Religion: Mormon.
Political Career: Farmington City Council, 1960–72; Utah House, 1973–81, speaker, 1979–81.

Capitol Office: 242 Cannon House Office Building 20515; 225-0453; (fax) 225-5857; (e-mail) www.house.gov/writerep; (web) www.house.gov/hansen.
Office Staff: Chief of Staff/Press Secy./Scheduler, Nancee W. Blockinger; Legis. Dir., Bill Johnson.
Committees: Armed Services (Military Procurement; Military Readiness); China Investigation; Resources (Fisheries Conservation, Wildlife & Oceans; National Parks & Public Lands — chairman); Veterans' Affairs (Benefits).

Utah 1st — West — Salt Lake City suburbs; Ogden; Logan; rural Utah. The district vote for Bill Clinton was 29% in 1996.

CQ Voting Studies

	1997	1998
Presidential	27%	18%
Party	91%	92%
Participation	96%	96%

Interest Groups

	1997	1998
ADA	0%	5%
ACU	91%	100%
AFL-CIO	0%	n/a
CCUS	90%	100%

Elections

	1996	1998
General	68%	68%
Primary	u/o	u/o

J. Dennis Hastert (R–Ill.)
Of Yorkville • Elected 1986

Born: Jan. 2, 1942, Aurora, Ill.
Education: Wheaton College, A.B. 1964; Northern Illinois U., M.A. 1967.
Occupation: Teacher; restaurateur.
Family: Wife, Jean; two children.
Religion: Methodist.
Political Career: Ill. House, 1981–86.

Capitol Office: 2263 Rayburn House Office Building 20515; 225-2976; (fax) 225-0697; (e-mail) dhastert@mail.house.gov; (web) dennyhastert.house.gov.
Office Staff: Chief of Staff, Scott B. Palmer; Legis. Dir., Bill Koetzle; Press Secy., John Feehery; Communications Dir., Pete Jeffries; Scheduler, Helen Morrell.
Committees: Speaker of the House (no committee assignments)

Illinois 14th — North Central — Aurora; Elgin; De Kalb. The district vote for Bill Clinton was 41% in 1996.

CQ Voting Studies

	1997	1998
Presidential	32%	21%
Party	95%	95%
Participation	98%	98%

Interest Groups

	1997	1998
ADA	0%	0%
ACU	88%	100%
AFL-CIO	0%	n/a
CCUS	100%	100%

Elections

	1996	1998
General	64%	70%
Primary	u/o	u/o

Alcee L. Hastings (D–Fla.)
Of Miramar • Elected 1992

Born: Sept. 5, 1936, Altamonte Springs, Fla.
Education: Fisk U., B.A. 1958; Howard U., attended 1958–60; Florida A&M U., J.D. 1963.
Occupation: Judge; lawyer.
Family: Divorced; three children.
Religion: African Methodist Episcopal.
Political Career: U.S. District Court judge, 1979–89; Democratic nominee for Fla. secretary of state, 1990.

Capitol Office: 2235 Rayburn House Office Building 20515; 225-1313; (fax) 226-0690; (e–mail) www.house.gov/alceehastings/guestbook.html; (web) www.house.gov/alceehastings.
Office Staff: Admin. Asst./Legis. Dir., Ann Jacobs; Communications Dir./Scheduler, Lillian German.
Committees: International Relations (Africa; Asia & the Pacific); Select Intelligence (Human Intelligence, Analysis & Counterintelligence — ranking member); Science (Energy & Environment; Space & Aeronautics).

Florida 23rd — Southeast — Parts of St. Lucie, Martin, Broward and Palm Beach counties. The district vote for Bill Clinton was 75% in 1996.

CQ Voting Studies

	1997	1998
Presidential	69%	84%
Party	84%	85%
Participation	90%	91%

Interest Groups

	1997	1998
ADA	80%	80%
ACU	19%	5%
AFL-CIO	100%	n/a
CCUS	20%	22%

Elections

	1996	1998
General	73%	u/o
Primary	u/o	u/o

Richard "Doc" Hastings
(R–Wash.)
Of Pasco • Elected 1994

Born: Feb. 7, 1941, Spokane, Wash.
Education: Columbia Basin College, attended 1959–61; Central Washington U., attended 1964.
Military Career: Army Reserve, 1964–69.
Occupation: Paper company executive.
Family: Wife, Claire; three children.
Religion: Roman Catholic.
Political Career: Wash. House, 1979–87; Republican nominee for U.S. House, 1992.

Capitol Office: 1323 Longworth House Office Building 20515; 225-5816; (fax) 225-3251; (e–mail) www.house.gov/writerep; (web) www.house.gov/hastings.
Office Staff: Chief of Staff, Ed Cassidy; Legis. Dir., Craig Kennedy; Deputy Chief of Staff/Press Secy., Jennifer Scott; Scheduler/Office Mgr., Holly Thompson.
Committees: Rules (Legislative & Budget Process).

Washington 4th — Central — Yakima and Tri-Cities. The district vote for Bill Clinton was 40% in 1996.

CQ Voting Studies

	1997	1998
Presidential	28%	22%
Party	96%	97%
Participation	98%	99%

Interest Groups

	1997	1998
ADA	0%	0%
ACU	92%	100%
AFL-CIO	0%	n/a
CCUS	100%	94%

Elections

	1996	1998
General	53%	69%
Primary	*55%	*69%

*Open primary

Robin Hayes (R-N.C.)
Of Concord • Elected 1998

Born: Aug. 14, 1945, Concord, N.C.
Education: Duke U., B.A. 1967.
Occupation: Hosiery mill owner.
Family: Wife, Barbara; two children.
Religion: Presbyterian.
Political Career: N.C. House, 1993–97; Republican nominee for governor, 1996.

Capitol Office: 130 Cannon House Office Building 20515; 225-3715; (fax) 225-4036; (e–mail) www.house.gov/writerep.
Office Staff: Chief of Staff, Chris Cox; Legis. Dir., Alex Mistri; Communications Dir., Andrew Duke; Scheduler, Bonner Meade.
Committees: Agriculture (General Farm Commodities; Risk Management, Research & Specialty Crops); Armed Services (Military Personnel; Military Procurement); Resources (Fisheries Conservation, Wildlife & Oceans; Forests & Forest Health).

North Carolina 8th — South Central — Parts of Kannapolis and Fayetteville. The district vote for Bill Clinton was 46% in 1996.

Elections

	1998
General	51%
Primary	u/o

J.D. Hayworth (R–Ariz.)
Of Scottsdale • Elected 1994

Born: July 12, 1958, High Point, N.C.
Education: North Carolina State U., B.A. 1980.
Occupation: Sports broadcaster; public relations consultant; insurance agent.
Family: Wife, Mary; three children.
Religion: Baptist.
Political Career: No previous office.

Capitol Office: 1023 Longworth House Office Building 20515; 225-2190; (fax) 225-3263; (e–mail) www.house.gov/writerep; (web) www.house.gov/hayworth.
Office Staff: Chief of Staff, Joseph Eule; Legis. Dir., Katharine Mottley; Press Secy., Jim Heath; Exec. Asst./Scheduler, Tricia Evans.
Committees: Veterans' Affairs (Benefits); Ways & Means (Oversight; Social Security).

Arizona 6th — Northeast — Flagstaff; Navajo reservation. The district vote for Bill Clinton was 47% in 1996.

CQ Voting Studies

	1997	1998
Presidential	29%	23%
Party	97%	94%
Participation	99%	99%

Interest Groups

	1997	1998
ADA	5%	0%
ACU	96%	100%
AFL-CIO	0%	n/a
CCUS	90%	89%

Elections

	1996	1998
General	48%	53%
Primary	u/o	u/o

Joel Hefley (R–Colo.)
Of Colorado Springs • Elected 1986

Born: Apr. 18, 1935, Ardmore, Okla.
Education: Oklahoma Baptist U., B.A. 1957; Oklahoma State U., M.S. 1962.
Occupation: Community planner; management consultant.
Family: Wife, Lynn Christian; three children.
Religion: Presbyterian.
Political Career: Colo. House, 1977–79; Colo. Senate, 1979–87, assistant majority leader, 1981–86.

Capitol Office: 2230 Rayburn House Office Building 20515; 225-4422; (fax) 225-1942; (e–mail) www.house.gov/writerep.
Office Staff: Legis. Dir., Larry Hojo; Press Secy., Leigh LaMora; Exec. Asst./Scheduler, Michelle Spear.
Committees: Armed Services (Military Installations & Facilities — chairman; Military Research & Development); Resources (National Parks & Public Lands); Small Business; Standards of Official Conduct.

Colorado 5th — South Central — Colorado Springs. The district vote for Bill Clinton was 33% in 1996.

CQ Voting Studies

	1997	1998
Presidential	25%	21%
Party	94%	91%
Participation	99%	98%

Interest Groups

	1997	1998
ADA	5%	0%
ACU	96%	100%
AFL-CIO	0%	n/a
CCUS	80%	75%

Elections

	1996	1998
General	72%	73%
Primary	77%	u/o

Wally Herger (R–Calif.)
Of Marysville • Elected 1986

Born: May 20, 1945, Sutter County, Calif.
Education: American River College, A.A. 1967; California State U., Sacramento, attended 1969.
Occupation: Rancher; gas company executive.
Family: Wife, Pamela; eight children.
Religion: Mormon.
Political Career: Calif. Assembly, 1981–87.

Capitol Office: 2433 Rayburn House Office Building 20515; 225-3076; (e–mail) www.house.gov/writerep; (web) www.house.gov/herger.
Office Staff: Admin. Asst., John P. Magill; Legis. Dir., Steve Thompson; Press Secy., Ron Shinn; Scheduler, Katy-Duke Chamberlin.
Committees: Budget; Ways & Means (Trade).

California 2nd — North and East — Chico; Redding. The district vote for Bill Clinton was 36% in 1996.

CQ Voting Studies

	1997	1998
Presidential	27%	22%
Party	93%	93%
Participation	95%	96%

Interest Groups

	1997	1998
ADA	5%	0%
ACU	96%	100%
AFL-CIO	0%	n/a
CCUS	90%	88%

Elections

	1996	1998
General	61%	63%
Primary	84%	*63%

*Open primary

Baron P. Hill (D-Ind.)
Of Seymour • Elected 1998

Born: June 23, 1953, Seymour, Ind.
Education: Furman U., B.A. 1975.
Occupation: Financial adviser; insurance company manager.
Family: Wife, Betty; three children.
Religion: Christian Church.
Political Career: Ind. House, 1983–91; Democratic nominee for U.S. Senate, 1990.

Capitol Office: 1208 Longworth House Office Building 20515; 225-5315; (fax) 225-1101; (e-mail) www.house.gov/writerep.
Office Staff: Chief of Staff, Matt Pierce; Interim Press Secy., Angela Belden; Scheduler, Ryan Guthrie.
Committees: Agriculture (Department Operations, Oversight, Nutrition & Forestry; General Farm Commodities); Armed Services (Military Research & Development).

Indiana 9th — Southeast Hill Country — New Albany. The district vote for Bill Clinton was 44% in 1996.

Elections

	1998
General	51%
Primary	70%

Rick Hill (R-Mont.)
Of Helena • Elected 1996

Born: Dec. 30, 1946, Grand Rapids, Mich.
Education: St. Cloud State U., B.A. 1968.
Occupation: Surety bonding and insurance company owner.
Family: Wife, Betti; three children.
Religion: Assembly of God.
Political Career: Mont. Republican Party chairman, 1991–92; Mont. Workmen's Compensation Board chairman, 1993–95.

Capitol Office: 1609 Longworth House Office Building 20515; 225-3211; (fax) 225-5687; (e-mail) rick.hill@mail.house.gov; (web) www.house.gov/hill.
Office Staff: Chief of Staff, Larry Akey; Legis. Dir., Robert E. Hobart IV; Communications Dir., Dan DuBray; Scheduler, Shane Hedges.
Committees: Banking & Financial Services (Financial Institutions & Consumer Credit; Housing & Community Opportunity); Resources (Forests & Forest Health; National Parks & Public Lands); Small Business (Regulatory Reform & Paperwork Reduction; Rural Enterprises).

Montana — At large. The district vote for Bill Clinton was 41% in 1996.

CQ Voting Studies

	1997	1998
Presidential	24%	27%
Party	94%	87%
Participation	99%	96%

Interest Groups

	1997	1998
ADA	0%	10%
ACU	92%	79%
AFL-CIO	13%	n/a
CCUS	80%	83%

Elections

	1996	1998
General	52%	53%
Primary	44%	u/o

Van Hilleary (R–Tenn.)
Of Spring City • Elected 1994
Pronounced: HILL-ary

Born: June 20, 1959, Dayton, Tenn.
Education: U. of Tennessee, B.S. 1981, attended 1985–87; Samford U., J.D. 1990.
Military Career: Air Force, 1982; Air Force Reserve, 1982–present.
Occupation: Textile industry executive.
Family: Single.
Religion: Presbyterian.
Political Career: Republican nominee for Tenn. Senate, 1992.

Capitol Office: 114 Cannon House Office Building 20515; 225-6831; (fax) 225-3272; (e-mail) van.hilleary@mail.house.gov; (web) www.house.gov/hilleary.

Office Staff: Chief of Staff, Elaine Robinson; Legis. Dir., Roger Morse; Press Secy., Ed Frank; Scheduler, Mary Sumpter-Johnson.

Committees: Armed Services (Military Installations & Facilities; Military Research & Development); Budget; Education & Workforce (Early Childhood, Youth & Families; Oversight & Investigations).

Tennessee 4th — Northeast and south central. The district vote for Bill Clinton was 46% in 1996.

CQ Voting Studies

	1997	1998
Presidential	20%	20%
Party	95%	91%
Participation	99%	99%

Interest Groups

	1997	1998
ADA	5%	5%
ACU	100%	96%
AFL-CIO	0%	n/a
CCUS	90%	83%

Elections

	1996	1998
General	58%	60%
Primary	u/o	u/o

Earl F. Hilliard (D–Ala.)
Of Birmingham • Elected 1992

Born: Apr. 9, 1942, Birmingham, Ala.
Education: Morehouse College, B.A. 1964; Howard U., J.D. 1967; Atlanta U., M.B.A. 1970.
Occupation: Lawyer; insurance broker.
Family: Wife, Mary Franklin Hilliard; two children.
Religion: Baptist.
Political Career: Ala. House, 1975–81; Ala. Senate, 1981–93.

Capitol Office: 1314 Longworth House Office Building 20515; 225-2665; (fax) 226-0772; (e-mail) callearl@mail.house.gov; (web) www.house.gov/hilliard.

Office Staff: Chief of Staff, Phyllis Hallmon; Legis. Dir., Matthew Lyons; Press Secy., Robert James; Scheduler, Hannah Ramsey.

Committees: Agriculture (Risk Management, Research & Specialty Crops); International Relations (International Economic Policy & Trade; International Operations & Human Rights).

Alabama 7th — West Central — Parts of Birmingham, Montgomery and Tuscaloosa. The district vote for Bill Clinton was 73% in 1996.

CQ Voting Studies

	1997	1998
Presidential	67%	84%
Party	83%	90%
Participation	93%	94%

Interest Groups

	1997	1998
ADA	80%	100%
ACU	10%	8%
AFL-CIO	100%	n/a
CCUS	44%	28%

Elections

	1996	1998
General	71%	u/o
Primary	u/o	u/o

Maurice D. Hinchey (D–N.Y.)
Of Saugerties • Elected 1992

Born: Oct. 27, 1938, New York, N.Y.
Education: State U. of New York, New Paltz, B.S., B.A. 1968, M.A. 1970.
Military Career: Navy, 1956–59.
Occupation: State employee.
Family: Wife, Ilene Marder; three children.
Religion: Roman Catholic.
Political Career: Democratic nominee for N.Y. Assembly, 1972; N.Y. Assembly, 1975–93.

Capitol Office: 2431 Rayburn House Office Building 20515; 225-6335; (fax) 226-0774; (e-mail) maurice.hinchey@mail.house.gov; (web) www.house.gov/hinchey.
Office Staff: Chief of Staff, Kiersten Stewart; Legis. Dir., Dianne Miller; Press Secy., Wendy Darwell; Exec. Asst., Dan Ahouse.
Committees: Appropriations (Agriculture, Rural Development, FDA & Related Agencies; Interior).

New York 26th — South — Kingston; Binghamton; Ithaca. The district vote for Bill Clinton was 51% in 1996.

CQ Voting Studies

	1997	1998
Presidential	80%	82%
Party	94%	94%
Participation	95%	98%

Interest Groups

	1997	1998
ADA	95%	100%
ACU	8%	4%
AFL-CIO	100%	n/a
CCUS	20%	22%

Elections

	1996	1998
General	55%	62%
Primary	u/o	u/o

Ruben Hinojosa (D–Texas)
Of Mercedes • Elected 1996
Pronounced: ru-BEN ee–na-HO-suh

Born: Aug. 20, 1940, Edcouch, Texas.
Education: U. of Texas, B.B.A. 1962; U. of Texas, Pan American, M.B.A. 1980.
Occupation: Food processing executive.
Family: Wife, Martha; five children.
Religion: Roman Catholic.
Political Career: Texas State Board of Education, 1974–84, chairman of special populations.

Capitol Office: 1032 Longworth House Office Building 20515; 225-2531; (fax) 225-5688; (e-mail) rep.hinojosa@mail.house.gov; (web) www.house.gov/hinojosa.
Office Staff: Chief of Staff, Rita Jaramillo; Legis. Dir./Press Secy., Anton Papich; Scheduler, Diana Rodriguez.
Committees: Education & Workforce (Early Childhood, Youth & Families; Postsecondary Education, Training & Life-Long Learning); Small Business (Government Programs & Oversight; Tax, Finance & Exports).

Texas 15th — South — Bee, Brooks, Hidalgo and San Patricio counties; McAllen. The district vote for Bill Clinton was 60% in 1996.

CQ Voting Studies

	1997	1998
Presidential	71%	76%
Party	83%	85%
Participation	98%	95%

Interest Groups

	1997	1998
ADA	75%	95%
ACU	29%	16%
AFL-CIO	100%	n/a
CCUS	60%	59%

Elections

	1996	1998
General	62%	58%
Primary	*52%	u/o

*Runoff election

David L. Hobson (R–Ohio)
Of Springfield • Elected 1990

Born: Oct. 17, 1936, Cincinnati, Ohio.
Education: Ohio Wesleyan U., B.A. 1958; Ohio State U., J.D. 1963.
Military Career: Ohio Air National Guard, 1958–63.
Occupation: Financial executive.
Family: Wife, Carolyn; three children.
Religion: Methodist.
Political Career: Candidate for Ohio House, 1982; Ohio Senate, 1982–90, majority whip, 1986–88, president pro tempore, 1988–90.
Capitol Office: 1514 Longworth House Office Building 20515; 225-4324; (e-mail) www.house.gov/writerep; (web) www.house.gov/hobson.
Office Staff: Chief of Staff, Mary Beth Carozza; Legis. Dir., Kenny Kraft; Press Secy., Mike Catanzaro; Exec. Asst., Ginny Gano.
Committees: Appropriations (Military Construction — chairman; Defense; VA, HUD & Independent Agencies).

Ohio 7th — West central — Springfield; Lancaster. The district vote for Bill Clinton was 41% in 1996.

CQ Voting Studies

	1997	1998
Presidential	33%	28%
Party	90%	90%
Participation	99%	99%

Interest Groups

	1997	1998
ADA	5%	5%
ACU	80%	88%
AFL-CIO	13%	n/a
CCUS	90%	82%

Elections

	1996	1998
General	68%	67%
Primary	86%	86%

Joseph M. Hoeffel (D–Pa.)
Of Abington • Elected 1998
Pronounced: HUFF-ull

Born: Sept. 3, 1950, Philadelphia, Pa.
Education: Boston U., B.S. 1972; Temple U., J.D. 1986.
Military Career: Army Reserve, 1970–76.
Occupation: Lawyer.
Family: Wife, Francesca; two children.
Religion: Protestant.
Political Career: Pa. House, 1977–85; Democratic nominee for U.S. House, 1984, 1986; Montgomery County Commission, 1992–98; Democratic nominee for U.S. House, 1996.
Capitol Office: 1229 Longworth House Office Building 20515; 225-6111; (fax) 226-0611; (e-mail) www.house.gov/writerep.
Office Staff: Chief of Staff, Beryl Hall; Legis. Dir., Joshua Shapiro; Press Secy., Frank Custer; Scheduler, Mel Gipprich.
Committees: Budget; International Relations (International Economic Policy & Trade).

Pennsylvania 13th — Northwest Philadelphia suburbs — The Main Line. The district vote for Bill Clinton was 50% in 1996.

Elections

	1998
General	52%
Primary	u/o

Peter Hoekstra (R–Mich.)
Of Holland • Elected 1992
Pronounced: HOKE-struh

Born: Oct. 30, 1953, Groningen, Netherlands.
Education: Hope College, B.A. 1975; U. of Michigan, M.B.A. 1977.
Occupation: Furniture company executive.
Family: Wife, Diane; three children.
Religion: Christian Reformed Church.
Political Career: No previous office.

Capitol Office: 1124 Longworth House Office Building 20515; 225-4401; (fax) 226-0779; (e-mail) tellhoek@mail.house.gov; (web) www.house.gov/hoekstra.
Office Staff: Chief of Staff, Jon Vanden Heuvel; Legis. Dir., Chris LaGrand; Press Secy., Jon Brandt; Exec. Asst., Dawn Konynduik.
Committees: Budget; Education & Workforce (Employer-Employee Relations; Oversight & Investigations — chairman; Workforce Protections).

Michigan 2nd — West — Holland; Muskegon. The district vote for Bill Clinton was 41% in 1996.

CQ Voting Studies

	1997	1998
Presidential	27%	24%
Party	90%	93%
Participation	97%	99%

Interest Groups

	1997	1998
ADA	15%	5%
ACU	88%	100%
AFL-CIO	0%	n/a
CCUS	100%	82%

Elections

	1996	1998
General	65%	69%
Primary	u/o	u/o

Tim Holden (D–Pa.)
Of St. Clair • Elected 1992

Born: Mar. 5, 1957, St. Clair, Pa.
Education: Bloomsburg U., B.A. 1980.
Occupation: Sheriff; probation officer.
Family: Wife, Gwen.
Religion: Roman Catholic.
Political Career: Schuylkill County sheriff, 1985–93.

Capitol Office: 1421 Longworth House Office Building 20515; 225-5546; (fax) 226-0996; (e-mail) www.house.gov/writerep; (web) www.house.gov/holden.
Office Staff: Chief of Staff/Press Secy., Trish Reilly; Legis. Dir., Paul Giuliano; Scheduler, Kristie Greco.
Committees: Agriculture (General Farm Commodities; Livestock & Horticulture); Transportation & Infrastructure (Aviation; Ground Transportation).

Pennsylvania 6th — Southeast — Reading. The district vote for Bill Clinton was 42% in 1996.

CQ Voting Studies

	1997	1998
Presidential	49%	61%
Party	61%	73%
Participation	98%	99%

Interest Groups

	1997	1998
ADA	50%	70%
ACU	54%	24%
AFL-CIO	86%	n/a
CCUS	70%	56%

Elections

	1996	1998
General	59%	61%
Primary	u/o	u/o

Rush D. Holt (D–N.J.)
Of Hopewell • Elected 1998

Born: Oct. 15, 1948, Weston, W.Va.
Education: Carleton College, B.A. 1966–70; New York U., M.S. 1972–80, Ph.D. 1972–81.
Occupation: University research assistant director; physics professor.
Family: Wife, Margaret Lancefield; three children.
Religion: Quaker.
Political Career: Sought Democratic nomination for U.S. House, 1996.

Capitol Office: 1630 Longworth House Office Building 20515; 225-5801; (fax) 225-0625; (e–mail) rush.holt@mail.house.gov.
Office Staff: Admin. Asst., Steve Mavigilio; Legis. Dir., Chris Davis.
Committees: Budget; Education & Workforce (Employer-Employee Relations; Postsecondary Education, Training & Life-Long Learning).

New Jersey 12th — North and central — Flemington; Princeton. The district vote for Bill Clinton was 48% in 1996.

Elections

	1998
General	50%
Primary	64%

Darlene Hooley (D–Ore.)
Of West Linn • Elected 1996

Born: Apr. 4, 1939, Williston, N.D.
Education: Pasadena Nazarene College, attended 1957–59; Oregon State U., B.S. 1961.
Occupation: Teacher.
Family: Divorced; two children.
Religion: Lutheran.
Political Career: West Linn City Council, 1977–81; Ore. House, 1981–87; Clackamas County Commission, 1987–97.

Capitol Office: 1130 Longworth House Office Building 20515; 225-5711; (fax) 225-5699; (e–mail) darlene@mail.house.gov; (web) www.house.gov/hooley.
Office Staff: Chief of Staff, Joan Mooney; Legis. Dir./Press Secy., David Danzig; Exec. Asst., Margaret Ellis.
Committees: Banking & Financial Services (Capital Markets & Securities; Housing & Community Opportunity); Budget.

Oregon 5th — Willamette Valley, Pacific Coast — Salem; Corvallis. The district vote for Bill Clinton was 47% in 1996.

CQ Voting Studies

	1997	1998
Presidential	80%	77%
Party	88%	88%
Participation	99%	97%

Interest Groups

	1997	1998
ADA	90%	95%
ACU	16%	12%
AFL-CIO	88%	n/a
CCUS	50%	59%

Elections

	1996	1998
General	51%	55%
Primary	51%	u/o

Steve Horn (R–Calif.)
Of Long Beach • Elected 1992

Born: May 31, 1931, San Juan Bautista, Calif.
Education: Stanford U., A.B. 1953; Harvard U., M.P.A. 1955; Stanford U., Ph.D. 1958.
Military Career: Army Reserve, 1954–62.
Occupation: Professor; college president; congressional aide.
Family: Wife, Nini; two children.
Religion: Protestant.
Political Career: U.S. Commission on Civil Rights vice chairman/member, 1969–82; sought Republican nomination for U.S. House, 1988.

Capitol Office: 2331 Rayburn House Office Building 20515; 225-6676; (fax) 226-1012; (e-mail) steve.horn@mail.house.gov; (web) www.house.gov/horn.
Office Staff: Chief of Staff, David Bartel; Legis. Dir., Eric Swedlund; Press Secy., Matthew Phillips; Scheduler, Katherine Leonard.
Committees: Government Reform (District of Columbia; Government Management, Information & Technology — chairman); Transportation & Infrastructure (Ground Transportation; Water Resources & Environment).

California 38th — Long Beach; Downey; Lakewood. The district vote for Bill Clinton was 53% in 1996.

CQ Voting Studies

	1997	1998
Presidential	47%	34%
Party	71%	73%
Participation	99%	99%

Interest Groups

	1997	1998
ADA	50%	20%
ACU	44%	56%
AFL-CIO	50%	n/a
CCUS	60%	83%

Elections

	1996	1998
General	53%	53%
Primary	u/o	*53%

*Open primary

John Hostettler (R–Ind.)
Of Wadesville • Elected 1994
Pronounced: HO-stet–lur

Born: July 19, 1961, Evansville, Ind.
Education: Rose-Hulman Institute of Technology, B.S.M.E. 1983.
Occupation: Mechanical engineer.
Family: Wife, Elizabeth Ann Hamman; four children.
Religion: General Baptist.
Political Career: No previous office.

Capitol Office: 1507 Longworth House Office Building 20515; 225-4636; (fax) 225-3284; (e-mail) john.hostettler@mail.house.gov; (web) www.house.gov/hostettler.
Office Staff: Admin. Asst., Tom Washburn; Legis. Dir., Carl Little; Press Secy., Michael Jahr; Appts. Secy., Katie Stusrud.
Committees: Agriculture (Department Operations, Oversight, Nutrition & Forestry; Livestock & Horticulture); Armed Services (Military Installations & Facilities; Military Research & Development).

Indiana 8th — Southwest — Evansville; Bloomington. The district vote for Bill Clinton was 45% in 1996.

CQ Voting Studies

	1997	1998
Presidential	25%	24%
Party	96%	91%
Participation	98%	99%

Interest Groups

	1997	1998
ADA	5%	10%
ACU	88%	92%
AFL-CIO	0%	n/a
CCUS	80%	78%

Elections

	1996	1998
General	50%	52%
Primary	82%	u/o

Amo Houghton (R-N.Y.)
Of Corning • Elected 1986
Pronounced: HO-tun

Born: Aug. 7, 1926, Corning, N.Y.
Education: Harvard U., A.B. 1950, M.B.A. 1952.
Military Career: Marine Corps, 1945–46.
Occupation: Glassworks company executive.
Family: Wife, Priscilla; four children, three stepchildren.
Religion: Episcopalian.
Political Career: No previous office.

Capitol Office: 1110 Longworth House Office Building 20515; 225-3161; (fax) 225-5574; (e–mail) houghton@mail.house.gov; (web) www.house.gov/houghton.
Office Staff: Chief of Staff, Brian Fitzpatrick; Legis. Dir., Robert W. Van Wicklin; Communications Dir., Chet Lunner; Scheduler, Francesca Tedesco.
Committees: International Relations (Africa); Ways & Means (Oversight — chairman; Trade).

New York 31st — Southern Tier — Jamestown; Elmira; Corning. The district vote for Bill Clinton was 44% in 1996.

CQ Voting Studies

	1997	1998
Presidential	56%	44%
Party	64%	63%
Participation	91%	94%

Interest Groups

	1997	1998
ADA	45%	30%
ACU	33%	29%
AFL-CIO	50%	n/a
CCUS	90%	100%

Elections

	1996	1998
General	72%	68%
Primary	u/o	u/o

Steny H. Hoyer (D–Md.)
Of Mechanicsville • Elected 1981

Born: June 14, 1939, New York, N.Y.
Education: U. of Maryland, B.S. 1963; Georgetown U., J.D. 1966.
Occupation: Lawyer.
Family: Widowed; three children.
Religion: Baptist.
Political Career: Md. Senate, 1967–79, president, 1975–79; sought Democratic nomination for lieutenant governor, 1978; Md. Board of Higher Education, 1978–81.

Capitol Office: 1705 Longworth House Office Building 20515; 225-4131; (fax) 225-4300; (e–mail) www.house.gov/writerep; (web) www.house.gov/hoyer.
Office Staff: Admin. Asst., Betsy Bossart; Legis. Dir., Cory Alexander; Press Secy., Deborah Deshong; Appts. Secy., Kathleen May.
Committees: House Administration — ranking member; Appropriations (Labor, Health & Human Services & Education; Legislative Branch; Treasury, Postal Service & General Government — ranking member); Joint Library — ranking member; Joint Printing.

Maryland 5th — Outer Prince George's; Southern Maryland. The district vote for Bill Clinton was 52% in 1996.

CQ Voting Studies

	1997	1998
Presidential	75%	80%
Party	84%	88%
Participation	98%	98%

Interest Groups

	1997	1998
ADA	85%	95%
ACU	12%	4%
AFL-CIO	100%	n/a
CCUS	40%	28%

Elections

	1996	1998
General	57%	65%
Primary	84%	86%

Kenny Hulshof (R-Mo.)
Of Columbia • Elected 1996
Pronounced: HULLZ-hoff

Born: May 22, 1958, Sikeston, Mo.
Education: U. of Missouri, B.S. 1980; U. of Mississippi, J.D. 1983.
Occupation: State and city prosecutor; public defender.
Family: Wife, Renee.
Religion: Roman Catholic.
Political Career: Sought Republican nomination for Boone County prosecutor, 1992; Republican nominee for U.S. House, 1994.

Capitol Office: 412 Cannon House Office Building 20515; 225-2956; (fax) 225-5712; (e-mail) www.house.gov/writerep; (web) www.house.gov/hulshof.
Office Staff: Admin. Asst., Matt Miller; Legis. Dir., Manning Feraci; Press Secy., Lara Kennedy; Scheduler, Sara Kennedy.
Committees: Ways & Means (Oversight; Social Security).

Missouri 9th — Northeast — Columbia. The district vote for Bill Clinton was 44% in 1996.

CQ Voting Studies

	1997	1998
Presidential	29%	24%
Party	93%	87%
Participation	99%	98%

Interest Groups

	1997	1998
ADA	15%	15%
ACU	92%	88%
AFL-CIO	13%	n/a
CCUS	90%	100%

Elections

	1996	1998
General	49%	62%
Primary	50%	u/o

Duncan Hunter (R-Calif.)
Of El Cajon • Elected 1980

Born: May 31, 1948, Riverside, Calif.
Education: U. of Montana, attended 1966–67; U. of California, Santa Barbara, attended 1967–68; Western State U., B.S.L. 1976, J.D. 1976.
Military Career: Army, 1969–71.
Occupation: Lawyer.
Family: Wife, Lynne; two children.
Religion: Baptist.
Political Career: No previous office.

Capitol Office: 2265 Rayburn House Office Building 20515; 225-5672; (fax) 225-0235; (e-mail) www.house.gov/writerep; (web) www.house.gov/hunter.
Office Staff: Chief of Staff, Victoria J. Middleton; Press Secy., Harald Stavenas; Appts. Secy., Melinda Patterson.
Committees: Armed Services (Military Procurement — chairman; Military Readiness).

California 52nd — Inland San Diego and Imperial counties. The district vote for Bill Clinton was 41% in 1996.

CQ Voting Studies

	1997	1998
Presidential	24%	20%
Party	93%	91%
Participation	94%	95%

Interest Groups

	1997	1998
ADA	0%	5%
ACU	88%	100%
AFL-CIO	0%	n/a
CCUS	80%	71%

Elections

	1996	1998
General	65%	76%
Primary	u/o	*78%

*Open primary

Asa Hutchinson (R–Ark.)
Of Fort Smith • Elected 1996

Born: Dec. 3, 1950, Bentonville, Ark.
Education: Bob Jones U., B.S. 1972; U. of Arkansas, J.D. 1975.
Occupation: Lawyer.
Family: Wife, Susan; four children.
Religion: Baptist.
Political Career: City attorney of Bentonville, 1977–78; U.S. attorney, 1982–85; Republican nominee for U.S. Senate, 1986; Republican nominee for Ark. attorney general, 1990; Ark. Republican Party chairman, 1990–95.

Capitol Office: 1535 Longworth House Office Building 20515; 225-4301; (fax) 225-5713; (e-mail) asa.hutchinson@mail.house.gov; (web) www.house.gov/hutchinson.
Office Staff: Chief of Staff, West Doss; Legis. Dir., Stacey Shrader; Communications Dir., Christopher Battle; Scheduler, Diana Ludlow.
Committees: Government Reform (Civil Service; Criminal Justice, Drug Policy & Human Resources); Judiciary (Constitution; Crime); Transportation & Infrastructure (Aviation; Water Resources & Environment).

Arkansas 3rd — Northwest — Fort Smith; Fayetteville. The district vote for Bill Clinton was 44% in 1996.

CQ Voting Studies

	1997	1998
Presidential	27%	26%
Party	93%	85%
Participation	98%	94%

Interest Groups

	1997	1998
ADA	10%	5%
ACU	88%	92%
AFL-CIO	25%	n/a
CCUS	90%	94%

Elections

	1996	1998
General	56%	81%
Primary		u/o

Henry J. Hyde (R–Ill.)
Of Bensenville • Elected 1974

Born: Apr. 18, 1924, Chicago, Ill.
Education: Duke U., attended 1943–44; Georgetown U., B.S. 1947; Loyola U., J.D. 1949.
Military Career: Navy, 1944–46; Naval Reserve, 1946–68.
Occupation: Lawyer.
Family: Widowed; four children.
Religion: Roman Catholic.
Political Career: Republican nominee for U.S. House, 1962; Ill. House, 1967–75, majority leader, 1971–73.

Capitol Office: 2110 Rayburn House Office Building 20515; 225-4561; (fax) 225-1166; (e-mail) www.house.gov/writerep; (web) www.house.gov/hyde.
Office Staff: Chief of Staff/Legis. Dir., Judy Wolverton; Press Secy., Sam Stratman; Personal Secy., Ann Kelly.
Committees: International Relations (International Operations & Human Rights); Judiciary — chairman (Constitution).

Illinois 6th — Northwest and west Chicago suburbs. The district vote for Bill Clinton was 43% in 1996.

CQ Voting Studies

	1997	1998
Presidential	28%	20%
Party	89%	91%
Participation	97%	95%

Interest Groups

	1997	1998
ADA	20%	0%
ACU	68%	92%
AFL-CIO	25%	n/a
CCUS	70%	88%

Elections

	1996	1998
General	64%	67%
Primary	84%	u/o

Jay Inslee (D–Wash.)
Of Bainbridge Island • Elected 1998
Also served 1993–95

Born: Feb. 9, 1951, Seattle, Wash.
Education: Stanford U., attended 1969–70; U. of Washington, B.A. 1973; Willamette U., J.D. 1976.
Occupation: Lawyer.
Family: Wife, Trudi; three children.
Religion: Protestant.
Political Career: Wash. House, 1989–93; sought Democratic nomination for governor, 1996.

Capitol Office: 308 Cannon House Office Building 20515; 225-6311; (fax) 226-1606; (e-mail) www.house.gov/writerep.
Office Staff: Chief of Staff, Joby Shimomura; Legis. Dir., Jake Johnston; Press Secy., Sara O'Connell; Scheduler, Mike Greenle.
Committees: Banking & Financial Services (Domestic & International Monetary Policy; Financial Institutions & Consumer Credit); Resources (Energy & Mineral Resources; National Parks & Public Lands).

Elections

	1998
General	50%
Primary	*44%

*Open primary

Washington 1st — Puget Sound (west and east) — North Seattle suburbs; Kitsap Peninsula. The district vote for Bill Clinton was 51% in 1996.

Johnny Isakson (R–Ga.)
Of Marietta • Elected 1999

Born: Dec. 27, 1944, Atlanta, Ga.
Education: U. of Georgia, B.B.A. 1966.
Military Career: Air National Guard, 1966–72.
Occupation: Real estate company president.
Family: Wife, Dianne; three children.
Religion: Methodist.
Political Career: Candidate for Cobb County Commission, 1974; Ga. House, 1975–90, Republican leader, 1983–90; Republican nominee for governor, 1990; Ga. Senate, 1994–96; sought Republican nomination for U.S. Senate, 1996; Ga. Board of Education chairman, 1996–99.

Capitol Office: 2428 Rayburn House Office Building 20515; 225-4501; (fax) 225-4656.
Office Staff: Chief of Staff, Heath Garrett; Admin. Asst., Dave Heil.
Committees: Education & Workforce (Postsecondary Education, Training & Life-Long Learning; Workforce Protections); Transportation & Infrastructure (Aviation; Oversight & Investigations).

Elections

	1999
General	*65%

*Special election

Georgia 6th — Atlanta Suburbs — Roswell; part of Marietta. The district vote for Bill Clinton was 33% in 1996.

Ernest Istook (R–Okla.)
Of Oklahoma City • Elected 1992
Pronounced: IZ-took

Born: Feb. 11, 1950, Fort Worth, Texas.
Education: Baylor U., B.A. 1971; Oklahoma City U., J.D. 1976.
Occupation: Lawyer; gubernatorial aide; journalist.
Family: Wife, Judy Lee Istook; five children.
Religion: Mormon.
Political Career: Warr Acres City Council, 1983–87; Okla. House, 1987–93.

Capitol Office: 2404 Rayburn House Office Building 20515; 225-2132; (fax) 226-1463; (e–mail) istook@mail.house.gov; (web) www.house.gov/istook.
Office Staff: Admin. Asst./Legis. Dir., John Albaugh; Press Secy., Micah Swafford; Scheduler, Kim Rubin.
Committees: Appropriations (District of Columbia — chairman; Labor, Health & Human Services & Education; Defense).

Oklahoma 5th — North Central — Part of Oklahoma City. The district vote for Bill Clinton was 31% in 1996.

CQ Voting Studies

	1997	1998
Presidential	17%	16%
Party	93%	89%
Participation	95%	93%

Interest Groups

	1997	1998
ADA	5%	0%
ACU	100%	95%
AFL-CIO	0%	n/a
CCUS	89%	94%

Elections

	1996	1998
General	70%	68%
Primary	u/o	u/o

Jesse L. Jackson Jr. (D–Ill.)
Of Chicago • Elected 1995

Born: Mar. 11, 1965, Greenville, S.C.
Education: North Carolina A&T U., B.S. 1987; Chicago Theological Seminary, M.A. 1990; U. of Illinois, J.D. 1993.
Occupation: Lawyer.
Family: Wife, Sandra.
Religion: Baptist.
Political Career: No previous office.

Capitol Office: 313 Cannon House Office Building 20515; 225-0773; (fax) 225-0899; (e–mail) comments@jessejacksonjr.org.
Office Staff: Chief of Staff, Kenneth Edmonds; Legis. Dir., George H. Seymore Jr.; Communications Dir., Frank Watkins; Scheduler, Deborah Posey.
Committees: Appropriations (Foreign Operations & Export Financing; Labor, Health & Human Services & Education).

Illinois 2nd — Chicago — Far South Side; south suburbs; Chicago Heights. The district vote for Bill Clinton was 85% in 1996.

CQ Voting Studies

	1997	1998
Presidential	79%	83%
Party	95%	96%
Participation	100%	100%

Interest Groups

	1997	1998
ADA	100%	100%
ACU	4%	8%
AFL-CIO	100%	n/a
CCUS	20%	22%

Elections

	1996	1998
General	94%	89%
Primary	u/o	u/o

Sheila Jackson-Lee (D–Texas)
Of Houston • Elected 1994

Born: Jan. 12, 1950, Jamaica, N.Y.
Education: Yale U., B.A. 1972; U. of Virginia, J.D. 1975.
Occupation: Lawyer; congressional aide.
Family: Husband, Elwyn; two children.
Religion: Seventh-Day Adventist.
Political Career: Houston municipal judge, 1987–89; Houston City Council, 1990–95.

Capitol Office: 410 Cannon House Office Building 20515; 225-3816; (fax) 225-3317; (e–mail) tx.18@mail.house.gov; (web) www.house.gov/jacksonlee.
Office Staff: Chief of Staff, Kathi Wilkes; Legis. Dir., Diego Alavarez; Communications Dir., Devona Dolli-ole; Scheduler, Suzanne James.
Committees: Judiciary (Crime; Immigration & Claims — ranking member); Science (Space & Aeronautics).

Texas 18th — Downtown Houston. The district vote for Bill Clinton was 73% in 1996.

CQ Voting Studies

	1997	1998
Presidential	75%	78%
Party	90%	90%
Participation	98%	97%

Interest Groups

	1997	1998
ADA	80%	95%
ACU	13%	4%
AFL-CIO	100%	n/a
CCUS	44%	44%

Elections

	1996	1998
General	77%	90%
Primary		u/o

William J. Jefferson (D–La.)
Of New Orleans • Elected 1990

Born: Mar. 14, 1947, Lake Providence, La.
Education: Southern U. and A&M College, B.A. 1969; Harvard U., J.D. 1972; Georgetown U., LL.M. 1996.
Military Career: Army, 1969–75.
Occupation: Lawyer.
Family: Wife, Andrea Green; five children.
Religion: Baptist.
Political Career: La. Senate, 1980–91; candidate for mayor of New Orleans, 1982, 1986.

Capitol Office: 240 Cannon House Office Building 20515; 225-6636; (fax) 225-1988; (e–mail) www.house.gov/writerep.
Office Staff: Chief of Staff/Legis. Dir., Lionel Collins; Communications Dir., Jean LaPlace; Scheduler, Christopher D. Becnel.
Committees: Ways & Means (Human Resources; Trade).

Louisiana 2nd — East — New Orleans. The district vote for Bill Clinton was 78% in 1996.

CQ Voting Studies

	1997	1998
Presidential	61%	73%
Party	83%	82%
Participation	92%	88%

Interest Groups

	1997	1998
ADA	75%	80%
ACU	17%	13%
AFL-CIO	100%	n/a
CCUS	50%	43%

Elections

	1996	1998
General	u/o	86%
Primary	u/o	u/o

Bill Jenkins (R–Tenn.)
Of Rogersville • Elected 1996

Born: Nov. 29, 1936, Detroit, Mich.
Education: Tennessee Technological U., B.B.A.; U. of Tennessee, J.D. 1961.
Military Career: Army, 1960–62.
Occupation: Lawyer; farmer.
Family: Wife, Kathryn; four children.
Religion: Baptist.
Political Career: Tenn. House, 1963–71, speaker, 1969–1971; sought Republican nomination for governor, 1970; circuit court judge, 1990–96.

Capitol Office: 1708 Longworth House Office Building 20515; 225-6356; (fax) 225-5714; (e-mail) rep.jenkins@mail.house.gov; (web) www.house.gov/jenkins.

Office Staff: Chief of Staff, Jeff Anderson; Legis. Dir., Brenda Otterson; Press Secy., Richard Vaughn; Scheduler, Beth Point.

Committees: Agriculture (General Farm Commodities; Risk Management, Research & Specialty Crops); Judiciary (Constitution; Courts & Intellectual Property).

Tennessee 1st — Northeast — Tri–cities. The district vote for Bill Clinton was 37% in 1996.

CQ Voting Studies

	1997	1998
Presidential	29%	20%
Party	93%	94%
Participation	99%	98%

Interest Groups

	1997	1998
ADA	5%	5%
ACU	88%	100%
AFL-CIO	13%	n/a
CCUS	100%	89%

Elections

	1996	1998
General	64%	69%
Primary	18%	u/o

Chris John (D–La.)
Of Crowley • Elected 1996

Born: Jan. 5, 1960, Crowley, La.
Education: Louisiana State U., B.A. 1982.
Occupation: Trucking company owner.
Family: Wife, Payton; two children.
Religion: Roman Catholic.
Political Career: Crowley City Council, 1984–88; La. House, 1988–96; candidate for lieutenant governor, 1995.

Capitol Office: 1504 Longworth House Office Building 20515; 225-2031; (fax) 225-5724; (e-mail) chrisjohn@mail.house.gov; (web) www.house.gov/john.

Office Staff: Chief of Staff, Lynn Hershey; Legis. Dir., Gordon Taylor; Press Secy., Alisha Prather; Scheduler, Monica Taylor.

Committees: Agriculture (Risk Management, Research & Specialty Crops); Resources (Energy & Mineral Resources).

Louisiana 7th — Southwest — Lake Charles; Lafayette. The district vote for Bill Clinton was 51% in 1996.

CQ Voting Studies

	1997	1998
Presidential	51%	43%
Party	59%	48%
Participation	97%	86%

Interest Groups

	1997	1998
ADA	40%	50%
ACU	64%	45%
AFL-CIO	38%	n/a
CCUS	100%	76%

Elections

	1996	1998
General	53%	u/o
Primary	26%	

Eddie Bernice Johnson (D–Texas)
Of Dallas • Elected 1992

Born: Dec. 3, 1935, Waco, Texas.
Education: Texas Christian U., B.S. 1967; Southern Methodist U., M.P.A. 1976.
Occupation: Business relocation company owner; nurse.
Family: Divorced; one child.
Religion: Baptist.
Political Career: Texas House, 1973–77; Texas Senate, 1987–93.

Capitol Office: 1511 Longworth House Office Building 20515; 225-8885; (fax) 226-1477; (e-mail) ejohnson@mail.house.gov; (web) www.house.gov/ebjohnson.
Office Staff: Chief of Staff, Solange Bitol; Legis. Dir., John George; Communications Dir., Eric K. Foster; Scheduler, Kim Placek.
Committees: Science (Basic Research — ranking member; Energy & Environment); Transportation & Infrastructure (Aviation; Ground Transportation).

Texas 30th — Downtown Dallas; part of Irving. The district vote for Bill Clinton was 69% in 1996.

CQ Voting Studies

	1997	1998
Presidential	79%	79%
Party	88%	87%
Participation	99%	94%

Interest Groups

	1997	1998
ADA	85%	90%
ACU	16%	4%
AFL-CIO	100%	n/a
CCUS	40%	47%

Elections

	1996	1998
General	55%	72%
Primary		u/o

Nancy L. Johnson (R–Conn.)
Of New Britain • Elected 1982

Born: Jan. 5, 1935, Chicago, Ill.
Education: Radcliffe College, B.A. 1957; U. of London, attended 1957–58.
Occupation: Civic leader.
Family: Husband, Theodore; three children.
Religion: Unitarian.
Political Career: Republican candidate for New Britain Common Council, 1975; Conn. Senate, 1977–83.

Capitol Office: 2113 Rayburn House Office Building 20515; 225-4476; (fax) 225-4488; (e-mail) njohnson@mail.house.gov; (web) www.house.gov/nancyjohnson.
Office Staff: Chief of Staff, Dave Karvelas; Press Secy., David White; Scheduler/Deputy Chief of Staff, Margo Smith.
Committees: Ways & Means (Health; Human Resources — chairman).

Connecticut 6th — Northwest — New Britain. The district vote for Bill Clinton was 50% in 1996.

CQ Voting Studies

	1997	1998
Presidential	60%	57%
Party	67%	62%
Participation	99%	99%

Interest Groups

	1997	1998
ADA	55%	55%
ACU	36%	16%
AFL-CIO	50%	n/a
CCUS	80%	83%

Elections

	1996	1998
General	50%	58%
Primary	u/o	u/o

Sam Johnson (R–Texas)
Of Plano • Elected 1991

Born: Oct. 11, 1930, San Antonio, Texas.
Education: Southern Methodist U., B.B.A. 1951; George Washington U., M.S.I.A. 1974.
Military Career: Air Force, 1951–79.
Occupation: Home builder.
Family: Wife, Shirley Melton; three children.
Religion: Methodist.
Political Career: Texas House, 1985–91.

Capitol Office: 1030 Longworth House Office Building 20515; 225-4201; (fax) 225-1485; (e–mail) sam.tx03@mail.house.gov; (web) www.house.gov/samjohnson.
Office Staff: Chief of Staff, Michael Hanson; Legis. Dir., Kristan Mack; Communications Dir., Jeanie Mamo; Scheduler, Lesley Gilbert.
Committees: Education & Workforce (Early Childhood, Youth & Families; Workforce Protections); Ways & Means (Health; Social Security).

Texas 3rd — Northeast Dallas suburbs; Plano. The district vote for Bill Clinton was 32% in 1996.

CQ Voting Studies

	1997	1998
Presidential	28%	20%
Party	88%	91%
Participation	93%	92%

Interest Groups

	1997	1998
ADA	10%	0%
ACU	96%	100%
AFL-CIO	0%	n/a
CCUS	100%	88%

Elections

	1996	1998
General	73%	91%
Primary		u/o

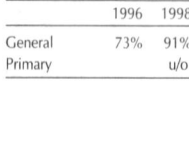

Stephanie Tubbs Jones (D–Ohio)
Of Cleveland • Elected 1998

Born: Sept. 10, 1949, Cleveland, Ohio.
Education: Case Western Reserve U., B.A. 1971, J.D. 1974.
Occupation: Lawyer.
Family: Husband, Mervyn; one child.
Religion: Baptist.
Political Career: Cuyahoga County judge, 1983–91; Cuyahoga County prosecutor, 1991–99.

Capitol Office: 1516 Longworth House Office Building 20515; 225-7032; (fax) 225-1339; (e–mail) www.house.gov/writerep.
Office Staff: Chief of Staff, Marcia Fudge; Legis. Dir., Vacant; Press Secy./Scheduler, Vercilla Brown.
Committees: Banking & Financial Services (Capital Markets & Securities; Housing & Community Opportunity); Small Business (Empowerment).

Ohio 11th — Cleveland — East Side and suburbs. The district vote for Bill Clinton was 79% in 1996.

Elections

	1998
General	80%
Primary	51%

Walter B. Jones Jr. (R–N.C.)
Of Farmville • Elected 1994

Born: Feb. 10, 1943, Farmville, N.C.
Education: North Carolina State U., attended 1962–65; Atlantic Christian College, B.A. 1967.
Military Career: N.C. National Guard, 1967–71.
Occupation: Lighting company executive; insurance benefits company executive.
Family: Wife, Joe Anne Jones; one child.
Religion: Roman Catholic.
Political Career: N.C. House, 1983–93; sought Democratic nomination for U.S. House, 1992.

Capitol Office: 422 Cannon House Office Building 20515; 225-3415; (fax) 225-3286; (e–mail) www.house.gov/writerep; (web) www.house.gov/jones.
Office Staff: Admin. Asst., Glen Downs; Legis. Dir., Katie Podlesak; Press Secy., Kimberly Nielson; Appts. Secy., Dena Cruz.
Committees: Armed Services (Military Readiness; Military Research & Development); Banking & Financial Services (Capital Markets & Securities; Housing & Community Opportunity); Resources (Fisheries Conservation, Wildlife & Oceans; National Parks & Public Lands).

North Carolina 3rd — East — Parts of Greenville and Goldsboro; Outer Banks. The district vote for Bill Clinton was 39% in 1996.

CQ Voting Studies

	1997	1998
Presidential	24%	21%
Party	93%	92%
Participation	99%	99%

Interest Groups

	1997	1998
ADA	5%	5%
ACU	100%	100%
AFL-CIO	0%	n/a
CCUS	80%	72%

Elections

	1996	1998
General	63%	62%
Primary	u/o	u/o

Paul E. Kanjorski (D–Pa.)
Of Nanticoke • Elected 1984

Born: Apr. 2, 1937, Nanticoke, Pa.
Education: Temple U., attended 1957–62; Dickinson School of Law, attended 1962–65.
Military Career: Army, 1960–61.
Occupation: Lawyer.
Family: Wife, Nancy; one child.
Religion: Roman Catholic.
Political Career: Sought Democratic nomination for U.S. House (special election), 1980; sought Democratic nomination for U.S. House, 1980.

Capitol Office: 2353 Rayburn House Office Building 20515; 225-6511; (e–mail) paul.kanjorski@mail.house.gov; (web) www.house.gov/kanjorski.
Office Staff: Chief of Staff, Karen Feather; Legis. Dir., Todd Harper; Press Secy., J.J. Balaban; Scheduler, Donna Giobbi.
Committees: Banking & Financial Services (Capital Markets & Securities — ranking member; Domestic & International Monetary Policy); Government Reform (Government Management, Information & Technology; National Economic Growth).

Pennsylvania 11th — Northeast — Wilkes-Barre. The district vote for Bill Clinton was 48% in 1996.

CQ Voting Studies

	1997	1998
Presidential	68%	82%
Party	78%	86%
Participation	99%	99%

Interest Groups

	1997	1998
ADA	90%	85%
ACU	12%	12%
AFL-CIO	100%	n/a
CCUS	40%	22%

Elections

	1996	1998
General	68%	67%
Primary	u/o	u/o

Marcy Kaptur (D–Ohio)
Of Toledo • Elected 1982

Born: June 17, 1946, Toledo, Ohio.
Education: U. of Wisconsin, B.A. 1968; U. of Michigan, M.U.P. 1974; Massachusetts Institute of Technology, attended 1981.
Occupation: Urban planner; White House aide.
Family: Single.
Religion: Roman Catholic.
Political Career: No previous office.
Capitol Office: 2366 Rayburn House Office Building 20515; 225-4146; (fax) 225-7711; (e–mail) rep.kaptur@mail.house.gov; (web) www.house.gov/kaptur.
Office Staff: Admin. Asst., Steve Katich; Staff Dir., Bobbi Jeanquart; Press Secy., Susan DiLiddo; Scheduler, Norma Olsen.
Committees: Appropriations (Agriculture, Rural Development, FDA & Related Agencies — ranking member; VA, HUD & Independent Agencies).

Ohio 9th — Northwest — Toledo. The district vote for Bill Clinton was 55% in 1996.

CQ Voting Studies

	1997	1998
Presidential	45%	67%
Party	73%	80%
Participation	91%	94%

Interest Groups

	1997	1998
ADA	75%	80%
ACU	32%	28%
AFL-CIO	100%	n/a
CCUS	22%	17%

Elections

	1996	1998
General	77%	81%
Primary	u/o	u/o

John R. Kasich (R–Ohio)
Of Westerville • Elected 1982
Pronounced: KAY-sick

Born: May 13, 1952, McKees Rocks, Pa.
Education: Ohio State U., B.A. 1974.
Occupation: Legislative aide.
Family: Wife, Karen.
Religion: Christian.
Political Career: Ohio Senate, 1979–83.
Capitol Office: 1111 Longworth House Office Building 20515; 225-5355; (e–mail) www.house.gov/writerep; (web) www.house.gov/kasich.
Office Staff: Chief of Staff, Don Thibaut; Legis. Dir., Ron Christie; Press Secy., Bruce Cuthbertson; Exec. Asst., Lise Middleton.
Committees: Armed Services (Military Research & Development); Budget — chairman.

Ohio 12th — Central — Eastern Columbus and suburbs. The district vote for Bill Clinton was 47% in 1996.

CQ Voting Studies

	1997	1998
Presidential	31%	24%
Party	88%	92%
Participation	97%	98%

Interest Groups

	1997	1998
ADA	20%	0%
ACU	88%	96%
AFL-CIO	0%	n/a
CCUS	80%	82%

Elections

	1996	1998
General	64%	67%
Primary	88%	91%

Sue W. Kelly (R–N.Y.)
Of Katonah • Elected 1994

Born: Sept. 26, 1936, Lima, Ohio.
Education: Denison U., B.A. 1958; Sarah Lawrence College, M.A. 1985.
Occupation: Professor; teacher; hospital administrative aide; medical researcher; retailer.
Family: Husband, Edward W. Kelly; four children.
Religion: Presbyterian.
Political Career: No previous office.

Capitol Office: 1122 Longworth House Office Building 20515; 225-5441; (fax) 225-3289; (e-mail) dearsue@mail.house.gov; (web) www.house.gov/suekelly.
Office Staff: Chief of Staff, Steve Hall; Legis. Dir., Al Garesche; Press Secy., Drew Cantor; Office Mgr., Sally Collins.
Committees: Banking & Financial Services (Financial Institutions & Consumer Credit; Housing & Community Opportunity); Small Business (Regulatory Reform & Paperwork Reduction — chairman); Transportation & Infrastructure (Ground Transportation; Water Resources & Environment).

New York 19th — Hudson Valley — Poughkeepsie. The district vote for Bill Clinton was 48% in 1996.

CQ Voting Studies

	1997	1998
Presidential	41%	41%
Party	79%	66%
Participation	98%	99%

Interest Groups

	1997	1998
ADA	40%	45%
ACU	64%	48%
AFL-CIO	38%	n/a
CCUS	70%	83%

Elections

	1996	1998
General	46%	62%
Primary	53%	u/o

Patrick J. Kennedy (D–R.I.)
Of Providence • Elected 1994

Born: July 14, 1967, Brighton, Mass.
Education: Providence College, B.A. 1991.
Occupation: Public official.
Family: Single.
Religion: Roman Catholic.
Political Career: R.I. House, 1989–95.

Capitol Office: 312 Cannon House Office Building 20515; 225-4911; (fax) 225-3290; (e-mail) www.house.gov/writerep; (web) www.house.gov/patrickkennedy.
Office Staff: Chief of Staff, Anthony C. Marcella; Legis. Dir., Bill Burke; Press Secy., Larry Berman; Scheduler, Terri Alford.
Committees: Armed Services (Military Personnel; Military Research & Development); Resources (Energy & Mineral Resources; Forests & Forest Health — ranking member).

Rhode Island 1st — East — Part of Providence; Pawtucket; Newport. The district vote for Bill Clinton was 61% in 1996.

CQ Voting Studies

	1997	1998
Presidential	76%	79%
Party	91%	90%
Participation	97%	99%

Interest Groups

	1997	1998
ADA	80%	95%
ACU	17%	12%
AFL-CIO	100%	n/a
CCUS	20%	33%

Elections

	1996	1998
General	69%	67%
Primary	u/o	u/o

Dale E. Kildee (D–Mich.)
Of Flint • Elected 1976

Born: Sept. 16, 1929, Flint, Mich.
Education: Sacred Heart Seminary, B.A. 1952; U. of Detroit, attended 1954; U. of Peshawar (Pakistan), attended 1958–59; U. of Michigan, M.A. 1961.
Occupation: Teacher.
Family: Wife, Gayle Heyn; three children.
Religion: Roman Catholic.
Political Career: Mich. House, 1965–75; Mich. Senate, 1975–77.

Capitol Office: 2187 Rayburn House Office Building 20515; 225-3611; (fax) 225-6393; (e–mail) dale.kildee@mail.house.gov; (web) www.house.gov/kildee.
Office Staff: Admin. Asst./Press Secy., Christopher Mansour; Legis. Dir., Callie Coffman; Scheduler, Greta Moore.
Committees: Education & Workforce (Early Childhood, Youth & Families — ranking member; Employer-Employee Relations); Resources (Forests & Forest Health; National Parks & Public Lands).

Michigan 9th — East Central — Flint; Pontiac. The district vote for Bill Clinton was 52% in 1996.

CQ Voting Studies

	1997	1998
Presidential	63%	74%
Party	77%	84%
Participation	100%	99%

Interest Groups

	1997	1998
ADA	80%	95%
ACU	24%	16%
AFL-CIO	100%	n/a
CCUS	40%	33%

Elections

	1996	1998
General	59%	56%
Primary	u/o	u/o

Carolyn Cheeks Kilpatrick (D–Mich.)
Of Detroit • Elected 1996

Born: June 25, 1945, Detroit, Mich.
Education: Ferris State U., A.A. 1965; Western Michigan U., B.S. 1968; U. of Michigan, M.S. 1972.
Occupation: Teacher.
Family: Divorced; two children.
Religion: Baptist.
Political Career: Mich. House, 1979–97; sought Democratic nomination for Mich. Senate, 1994.

Capitol Office: 503 Cannon House Office Building 20515; 225-2261; (fax) 225-5730; (e–mail) www.house.gov/writerep; (web) www.house.gov/kilpatrick.
Office Staff: Admin. Asst., Beverlyn C. Hilton; Legis. Dir., James Williams Jr.; Press Secy., Kimberly Trent; Exec. Asst., Gerri Houston.
Committees: Appropriations (Foreign Operations & Export Financing; Transportation).

Michigan 15th — Parts of Detroit; Grosse Pointe; Hamtramck; River Rouge. The district vote for Bill Clinton was 86% in 1996.

CQ Voting Studies

	1997	1998
Presidential	73%	77%
Party	95%	90%
Participation	97%	90%

Interest Groups

	1997	1998
ADA	100%	90%
ACU	12%	0%
AFL-CIO	100%	n/a
CCUS	30%	28%

Elections

	1996	1998
General	88%	87%
Primary	51%	89%

Ron Kind (D–Wis.)
Of La Crosse • Elected 1996

Born: Mar. 16, 1963, La Crosse, Wis.
Education: Harvard U., B.A. 1985; London School of Economics, M.A. 1986; U. of Minnesota, J.D. 1990.
Occupation: Lawyer.
Family: Wife, Tawni Zappa; two children.
Religion: Lutheran.
Political Career: No previous office.

Capitol Office: 1713 Longworth House Office Building 20515; 225-5506; (fax) 225-5739; (e-mail) ron.kind@mail.house.gov; (web) www.house.gov/kind.
Office Staff: Admin. Asst., Alan MacCleod; Legis. Dir., Sylvia Gaudette; Press Secy., Mike Fahey; Scheduler, Karen Miller.
Committees: Education & Workforce (Oversight & Investigations; Postsecondary Education, Training & Life-Long Learning); Resources (Forests & Forest Health; National Parks & Public Lands).

Wisconsin 3rd — West — Eau Claire; La Crosse. The district vote for Bill Clinton was 50% in 1996.

CQ Voting Studies

	1997	1998
Presidential	79%	77%
Party	89%	84%
Participation	99%	99%

Interest Groups

	1997	1998
ADA	85%	85%
ACU	28%	20%
AFL-CIO	100%	n/a
CCUS	50%	56%

Elections

	1996	1998
General	52%	71%
Primary	46%	u/o

Peter T. King (R–N.Y.)
Of Seaford • Elected 1992

Born: Apr. 5, 1944, Manhattan, N.Y.
Education: St. Francis College, B.A. 1965; U. of Notre Dame, J.D. 1968.
Military Career: National Guard, 1968–73.
Occupation: Lawyer.
Family: Wife, Rosemary; two children.
Religion: Roman Catholic.
Political Career: Hempstead Town Council, 1978–81; Nassau County comptroller, 1981–93.

Capitol Office: 403 Cannon House Office Building 20515; 225-7896; (fax) 226-2279; (e-mail) pete.king@mail.house.gov; (web) www.house.gov/king.
Office Staff: Chief of Staff, Robert O'Connor; Legis. Dir., Jenny McCulloch; Communications Dir., Kevin Fogarty; Exec. Asst., Carolyn Radcliff.
Committees: Banking & Financial Services (Capital Markets & Securities; General Oversight & Investigations — chairman); International Relations (Asia & the Pacific; International Operations & Human Rights).

New York 3rd — Eastern Nassau County — Oyster Bay. The district vote for Bill Clinton was 53% in 1996.

CQ Voting Studies

	1997	1998
Presidential	32%	30%
Party	82%	80%
Participation	98%	97%

Interest Groups

	1997	1998
ADA	25%	10%
ACU	64%	76%
AFL-CIO	75%	n/a
CCUS	40%	82%

Elections

	1996	1998
General	55%	64%
Primary	88%	78%

Jack Kingston (R–Ga.)
Of Savannah • Elected 1992

Born: Apr. 24, 1955, Bryan, Texas.
Education: U. of Georgia, B.A. 1978.
Occupation: Insurance broker.
Family: Wife, Libby; four children.
Religion: Episcopalian.
Political Career: Ga. House, 1984–92.

Capitol Office: 1034 Longworth House Office Building 20515; 225-5831; (fax) 226-2269; (e–mail) www.house.gov/writerep; (web) www.house.gov/kingston.
Office Staff: Chief of Staff, Grace Cummings; Legis. Dir., Adam J. Sullivan; Communications Dir., Robyn K. Ridgley; Scheduler, Karleen Mahn.
Committees: Appropriations (Agriculture, Rural Development, FDA & Related Agencies; Foreign Operations & Export Financing; Interior).

Georgia 1st — Southeast — Savannah; Brunswick. The district vote for Bill Clinton was 45% in 1996.

CQ Voting Studies

	1997	1998
Presidential	21%	20%
Party	89%	94%
Participation	98%	99%

Interest Groups

	1997	1998
ADA	5%	0%
ACU	96%	100%
AFL-CIO	0%	n/a
CCUS	80%	82%

Elections

	1996	1998
General	68%	u/o
Primary	u/o	u/o

Gerald D. Kleczka (D–Wis.)
Of Milwaukee • Elected 1984
Pronounced: KLETCH-kuh

Born: Nov. 26, 1943, Milwaukee, Wis.
Education: U. of Wisconsin, attended 1961–62, attended 1967, attended 1970.
Military Career: Air National Guard, 1963–69.
Occupation: Accountant.
Family: Wife, Bonnie.
Religion: Roman Catholic.
Political Career: Wis. Assembly, 1969–74; Wis. Senate, 1975–84.

Capitol Office: 2301 Rayburn House Office Building 20515; 225-4572; (fax) 225-8135; (e–mail) jerry.4wi@mail.house.gov; (web) www.house.gov/kleczka.
Office Staff: Admin. Asst./Legis. Dir., Winfield Boerckel; Communications Dir., Dave de Felice; Scheduler, Tanya Hughes.
Committees: Budget; Ways & Means (Health).

Wisconsin 4th — Southern Milwaukee and Milwaukee County suburbs; southeast Waukesha County. The district vote for Bill Clinton was 49% in 1996.

CQ Voting Studies

	1997	1998
Presidential	64%	74%
Party	79%	84%
Participation	98%	99%

Interest Groups

	1997	1998
ADA	70%	90%
ACU	25%	20%
AFL-CIO	88%	n/a
CCUS	50%	39%

Elections

	1996	1998
General	58%	58%
Primary	85%	89%

Ron Klink (D–Pa.)
Of Murrysville • Elected 1992

Born: Sept. 23, 1951, Canton, Ohio.
Education: Meyersdale H.S., graduated 1969.
Occupation: Television journalist.
Family: Wife, Linda; two children.
Religion: United Church of Christ.
Political Career: No previous office.

Capitol Office: 2448 Rayburn House Office Building 20515; 225-2565; (fax) 226-2274; (e–mail) www.house.gov/writerep; (web) www.house.gov/klink.
Office Staff: Admin. Asst., Mary Kiernan; Legis. Dir., Emmet O'Keefe; Press Secy., Charles Territo; Scheduler, Krissy Dobies.
Committees: Commerce (Energy & Power; Oversight & Investigations — ranking member; Telecommunications, Trade & Consumer Protection).

Pennsylvania 4th — West — Beaver County; part of Westmoreland County. The district vote for Bill Clinton was 47% in 1996.

CQ Voting Studies

	1997	1998
Presidential	60%	70%
Party	68%	80%
Participation	99%	97%

Interest Groups

	1997	1998
ADA	65%	80%
ACU	32%	13%
AFL-CIO	100%	n/a
CCUS	33%	22%

Elections

	1996	1998
General	64%	64%
Primary	u/o	u/o

Joe Knollenberg (R–Mich.)
Of Bloomfield Township • Elected 1992

Born: Nov. 28, 1933, Mattoon, Ill.
Education: Eastern Illinois U., B.S. 1955.
Military Career: Army, 1955–57.
Occupation: Insurance broker.
Family: Wife, Sandie; two children.
Religion: Roman Catholic.
Political Career: Oakland County Republican Party chairman, 1978–86.

Capitol Office: 2349 Rayburn House Office Building 20515; 225-5802; (fax) 226-2356; (e–mail) www.house.gov/writerep; (web) www.house.gov/knollenberg.
Office Staff: Chief of Staff, Paul Welday; Legis. Dir., David Cherington; Press Secy., Trent Wisecup; Scheduler, Lidie Rodriguez-Hupp; Scheduler, Julie Pulgini-Fagan.
Committees: Appropriations (Energy & Water Development; Foreign Operations & Export Financing; VA, HUD & Independent Agencies); Budget; Standards of Official Conduct.

Michigan 11th — Southeast — Part of Oakland County. The district vote for Bill Clinton was 47% in 1996.

CQ Voting Studies

	1997	1998
Presidential	31%	24%
Party	89%	94%
Participation	99%	99%

Interest Groups

	1997	1998
ADA	10%	0%
ACU	76%	96%
AFL-CIO	13%	n/a
CCUS	100%	100%

Elections

	1996	1998
General	61%	64%
Primary	u/o	u/o

Jim Kolbe (R–Ariz.)
Of Tucson • Elected 1984
Pronounced: COLE-bee

Born: June 28, 1942, Evanston, Ill.
Education: Northwestern U., B.A. 1965; Stanford U., M.B.A. 1967.
Military Career: Navy, 1967–69.
Occupation: Real estate consultant.
Family: Divorced.
Religion: Methodist.
Political Career: Ariz. Senate, 1977–83; Republican nominee for U.S. House, 1982.

Capitol Office: 2266 Rayburn House Office Building 20515; 225-2542; (fax) 225-0378; (e-mail) www.house.gov/writerep; (web) www.house.gov/kolbe.
Office Staff: Chief of Staff, Frances McNaught; Legis. Dir., Everett Eissenstat; Press Secy., Keith Rosenblum; Exec. Asst., Patrick Baugh.
Committees: Appropriations (Commerce, Justice, State & Judiciary; Interior; Treasury, Postal Service & General Government — chairman).

Arizona 5th — Southeast — Tucson. The district vote for Bill Clinton was 47% in 1996.

CQ Voting Studies

	1997	1998
Presidential	52%	40%
Party	79%	80%
Participation	98%	98%

Interest Groups

	1997	1998
ADA	25%	15%
ACU	64%	72%
AFL-CIO	0%	n/a
CCUS	100%	89%

Elections

	1996	1998
General	69%	52%
Primary	70%	77%

Dennis J. Kucinich (D–Ohio)
Of Cleveland • Elected 1996
Pronounced: ku-SIN-itch

Born: Oct. 8, 1946, Cleveland, Ohio.
Education: Case Western Reserve U., B.A. 1973, M.A. 1973.
Occupation: Video producer; public power consultant.
Family: Divorced; one child.
Religion: Roman Catholic.
Political Career: Cleveland City Council, 1969–75; mayor of Cleveland, 1977–79; Cleveland City Council, 1983; Democratic nominee for U.S. House, 1972; independent candidate for U.S. House, 1974; sought Democratic nomination for U.S. House, 1988, 1992; Ohio Senate, 1995–97.

Capitol Office: 1730 Longworth House Office Building 20515; 225-5871; (fax) 225-5745; (e-mail) www.house.gov/writerep.
Office Staff: Admin. Asst./Press Secy., John Edgell; Legis. Dir., Dan Marschall; Scheduler, Michael Yarbrough.
Committees: Education & Workforce (Early Childhood, Youth & Families; Workforce Protections); Government Reform (Criminal Justice, Drug Policy & Human Resources; National Economic Growth — ranking member).

Ohio 10th — Cleveland — West Side and suburbs. The district vote for Bill Clinton was 51% in 1996.

CQ Voting Studies

	1997	1998
Presidential	65%	78%
Party	80%	83%
Participation	99%	99%

Interest Groups

	1997	1998
ADA	90%	90%
ACU	16%	20%
AFL-CIO	100%	n/a
CCUS	20%	22%

Elections

	1996	1998
General	49%	67%
Primary	77%	88%

Steven T. Kuykendall (R–Calif.)
Of San Pedro • Elected 1998
Pronounced: KY-ken-doll

Born: Jan. 27, 1947, McAlester, Okla.
Education: Oklahoma City U., B.S. 1968; California State U., San Diego, M.B.A. 1974.
Military Career: Marine Corps, 1968–73.
Occupation: Real estate executive.
Family: Wife, Jan; three children.
Religion: Presbyterian.
Political Career: Rancho Palos Verdes City Council, 1991–94, mayor, 1994; Calif. Assembly, 1994–99.

Capitol Office: 512 Cannon House Office Building 20515; 225-8220; (fax) 225-8220; (e-mail) www.house.gov/writerep; (web) www.house.gov/kuykendall.
Office Staff: Chief of Staff/Legis. Dir., Katherine Hahn; District Dir./Press Secy., Adam Medelsohn; Scheduler, Leslie Schindel.
Committees: Armed Services (Military Personnel; Military Research & Development); Science (Space & Aeronautics; Technology); Transportation & Infrastructure (Aviation; Water Resources & Environment).

California 36th — West Los Angeles County; Manhattan Beach; Torrance. The district vote for Bill Clinton was 47% in 1996.

Elections

	1998
General	49%
Primary	*23%

*Open primary

John J. LaFalce (D–N.Y.)
Of Tonawanda • Elected 1974

Born: Oct. 6, 1939, Buffalo, N.Y.
Education: Canisius College, B.S. 1961; Villanova U., J.D. 1964.
Military Career: Army, 1965–67.
Occupation: Lawyer.
Family: Wife, Patricia; one child.
Religion: Roman Catholic.
Political Career: N.Y. Senate, 1971–72; N.Y. Assembly, 1973–74.

Capitol Office: 2310 Rayburn House Office Building 20515; 225-3231; (fax) 225-8693; (e-mail) www.house.gov/writerep; (web) www.house.gov/lafalce.
Office Staff: Admin. Asst., Roy Dye; Legis. Dir., Vacant; Communications Dir., Gary Luczak; Personal Secy., Jane Mulliken.
Committees: Banking & Financial Services — ranking member.

New York 29th — Northwest — Part of Buffalo; Niagara Falls. The district vote for Bill Clinton was 51% in 1996.

CQ Voting Studies

	1997	1998
Presidential	76%	82%
Party	82%	88%
Participation	96%	98%

Interest Groups

	1997	1998
ADA	85%	85%
ACU	16%	8%
AFL-CIO	100%	n/a
CCUS	40%	41%

Elections

	1996	1998
General	62%	57%
Primary	u/o	u/o

164 HOUSE • LaHood / Lampson

Ray LaHood (R–Ill.)
Of Peoria • Elected 1994

Born: Dec. 6, 1945, Peoria, Ill.
Education: Spoon River Community College, attended 1963–65; Bradley U., B.S. 1971.
Occupation: Congressional aide; youth bureau director; urban planning commission director; teacher.
Family: Wife, Kathleen; four children.
Religion: Roman Catholic.
Political Career: Ill. House, 1982–83.

Capitol Office: 329 Cannon House Office Building 20515; 225-6201; (fax) 225-9249; (e–mail) www.house.gov/writerep; (web) www.house.gov/lahood.
Office Staff: Chief of Staff, Diane R. Liesman; Legis. Dir., Chris Guidry; Press Secy., Tim Butler; Scheduler, Joan E. Mitchell.
Committees: Agriculture (Department Operations, Oversight, Nutrition & Forestry; Risk Management, Research & Specialty Crops); Select Intelligence (Human Intelligence, Analysis & Counterintelligence; Technical & Tactical Intelligence); Transportation & Infrastructure (Aviation; Ground Transportation); Veterans' Affairs (Benefits).

Illinois 18th — Central — Peoria; part of Springfield. The district vote for Bill Clinton was 44% in 1996.

CQ Voting Studies

	1997	1998
Presidential	31%	28%
Party	91%	83%
Participation	99%	99%

Interest Groups

	1997	1998
ADA	20%	20%
ACU	64%	60%
AFL-CIO	38%	n/a
CCUS	80%	83%

Elections

	1996	1998
General	59%	73%
Primary	u/o	u/o

Nick Lampson (D–Texas)
Of Beaumont • Elected 1996

Born: Feb. 14, 1945, Beaumont, Texas.
Education: Lamar U., B.S. 1968, M.Ed. 1971.
Occupation: Teacher; tax assessor.
Family: Wife, Susan; two children.
Religion: Roman Catholic.
Political Career: Jefferson County tax assessor, 1977–95.

Capitol Office: 417 Cannon House Office Building 20515; 225-6565; (fax) 225-5547; (e–mail) www.house.gov/writerep; (web) www.house.gov/lampson.
Office Staff: Chief of Staff, Tom Combs; Legis. Dir., Abby Hochberg; Press Secy., Monette Goodrich; Scheduler, Courtney Young.
Committees: Science (Space & Aeronautics); Transportation & Infrastructure (Aviation; Water Resources & Environment).

Texas 9th — Southeast — Beaumont; Galveston. The district vote for Bill Clinton was 48% in 1996.

CQ Voting Studies

	1997	1998
Presidential	77%	80%
Party	85%	84%
Participation	99%	95%

Interest Groups

	1997	1998
ADA	75%	90%
ACU	24%	16%
AFL-CIO	88%	n/a
CCUS	50%	33%

Elections

	1996	1998
General	*53%	64%
Primary		u/o

*Runoff election

Tom Lantos (D–Calif.)
Of San Mateo • Elected 1980

Born: Feb. 1, 1928, Budapest, Hungary.
Education: U. of Washington, B.A. 1949, M.A. 1950; U. of California, Berkeley, Ph.D. 1953.
Occupation: Professor.
Family: Wife, Annette; two children.
Religion: Jewish.
Political Career: Millbrae Board of Education, 1958–66.

Capitol Office: 2217 Rayburn House Office Building 20515; 225-3531; (e–mail) talk2tom@mail.house.gov; (web) www.house.gov/lantos.
Office Staff: Chief of Staff/Press Secy., Robert R. King; Legis. Dir., Chris Walker; Exec. Secy., Helena Anderson.
Committees: Government Reform (National Economic Growth; National Security & Veterans Affairs); International Relations (Asia & the Pacific — ranking member).

California 12th — Most of San Mateo County; southwest San Francisco. The district vote for Bill Clinton was 64% in 1996.

CQ Voting Studies

	1997	1998
Presidential	69%	80%
Party	87%	92%
Participation	92%	96%

Interest Groups

	1997	1998
ADA	95%	100%
ACU	8%	8%
AFL-CIO	100%	n/a
CCUS	33%	33%

Elections

	1996	1998
General	72%	74%
Primary	u/o	*72%

*Open primary

Steve Largent (R–Okla.)
Of Tulsa • Elected 1994

Born: Sept. 28, 1954, Tulsa, Okla.
Education: U. of Tulsa, B.S. 1976.
Occupation: Marketing consultant; professional football player.
Family: Wife, Terry; four children.
Religion: Christian.
Political Career: No previous office.

Capitol Office: 426 Cannon House Office Building 20515; 225-2211; (fax) 225-9187; (e–mail) ok01. largent@mail.house.gov; (web) www.house.gov/largent.
Office Staff: Chief of Staff, Terry Allen; Legis. Dir., Scott Bensing; Communications Dir., Brad Keena; Scheduler, Lucy Elkins.
Committees: Commerce (Energy & Power; Finance & Hazardous Materials; Telecommunications, Trade & Consumer Protection).

Oklahoma 1st — Tulsa; part of Wagoner County. The district vote for Bill Clinton was 37% in 1996.

CQ Voting Studies

	1997	1998
Presidential	23%	26%
Party	88%	87%
Participation	94%	94%

Interest Groups

	1997	1998
ADA	5%	10%
ACU	96%	92%
AFL-CIO	0%	n/a
CCUS	90%	82%

Elections

	1996	1998
General	68%	62%
Primary	u/o	u/o

John B. Larson (D–Conn.)
Of East Hartford • Elected 1998

Born: July 22, 1948, Hartford, Conn.
Education: Central Connecticut State U., B.S. 1971.
Occupation: Insurance company owner; high school teacher.
Family: Wife, Leslie; three children.
Religion: Roman Catholic.
Political Career: East Hartford Board of Education, 1978–79; East Hartford Town Council, 1979–83; Conn. Senate, 1983–94, president pro tempore, 1986–94; sought Democratic nomination for governor, 1994.

Capitol Office: 1419 Longworth House Office Building 20515; 225-2265; (fax) 225-1031; (e–mail) www.house.gov/writerep.
Office Staff: Admin. Asst./Legis. Dir., George Shevlin; Press Secy., Beth Bellizzi; Scheduler, Mary McHugh.
Committees: Armed Services (Military Personnel; Military Research & Development); Science (Basic Research; Space & Aeronautics).

Connecticut 1st — Central — Hartford. The district vote for Bill Clinton was 59% in 1996.

Elections

	1998
General	58%
Primary	46%

Tom Latham (R–Iowa)
Of Alexander • Elected 1994

Born: July 14, 1948, Hampton, Iowa.
Education: Wartburg College, attended 1967; Iowa State U., attended 1967–70.
Occupation: Seed company executive; insurance agency marketing representative; insurance agent; bank teller.
Family: Wife, Kathy; three children.
Religion: Lutheran.
Political Career: Franklin County Republican chairman, 1984–91.

Capitol Office: 324 Cannon House Office Building 20515; 225-5476; (fax) 225-3301; (e–mail) www.house.gov/writerep; (web) www.house.gov/latham.
Office Staff: Washington Operations Dir./Press Secy., James D. Carstensen; Legis. Dir., Mike Gruber; Scheduler, Rachel Sarno.
Committees: Appropriations (Agriculture, Rural Development, FDA & Related Agencies; Commerce, Justice, State & Judiciary; Energy & Water Development).

Iowa 5th — Northwest — Sioux City; Fort Dodge. The district vote for Bill Clinton was 44% in 1996.

CQ Voting Studies

	1997	1998
Presidential	28%	24%
Party	93%	94%
Participation	99%	99%

Interest Groups

	1997	1998
ADA	10%	0%
ACU	76%	92%
AFL-CIO	0%	n/a
CCUS	100%	100%

Elections

	1996	1998
General	65%	u/o
Primary	u/o	u/o

Steven C. LaTourette (R-Ohio)
Of Madison • Elected 1994
Pronounced: la-TUR-et

Born: July 22, 1954, Cleveland, Ohio.
Education: U. of Michigan, B.A. 1976; Cleveland State U., J.D. 1979.
Occupation: Lawyer.
Family: Wife, Susan; four children.
Religion: Methodist.
Political Career: Candidate for Lake County prosecutor, 1984; Lake County prosecutor, 1989–94.

Capitol Office: 1224 Longworth House Office Building 20515; 225-5731; (fax) 225-3307; (e-mail) www.house.gov/writerep; (web) www.house.gov/latourette.
Office Staff: Chief of Staff, Jennifer Laptook; Legis. Dir., Kathy Donahue; Communications Dir., Debbie Winston; Exec. Asst., Kathy Kato.
Committees: Banking & Financial Services (Financial Institutions & Consumer Credit; General Oversight & Investigations); Government Reform (Criminal Justice, Drug Policy & Human Resources; Postal Service); Transportation & Infrastructure (Economic Development & Public Buildings; Ground Transportation; Water Resources & Environment).

Ohio 19th — Cleveland suburbs — Ashtabula and Lake counties. The district vote for Bill Clinton was 48% in 1996.

CQ Voting Studies

	1997	1998
Presidential	33%	38%
Party	82%	78%
Participation	96%	99%

Interest Groups

	1997	1998
ADA	30%	40%
ACU	71%	52%
AFL-CIO	50%	n/a
CCUS	90%	78%

Elections

	1996	1998
General	55%	66%
Primary	u/o	u/o

Rick A. Lazio (R–N.Y.)
Of Brightwaters • Elected 1992
Pronounced: LAZZ-ee–o

Born: Mar. 13, 1958, West Islip, N.Y.
Education: Vassar College, B.A. 1980; American U., J.D. 1983.
Occupation: Lawyer.
Family: Wife, Patricia; two children.
Religion: Roman Catholic.
Political Career: Suffolk County Legislature, 1990–93.

Capitol Office: 2244 Rayburn House Office Building 20515; 225-3335; (fax) 225-4669; (e-mail) lazio@mail.house.gov; (web) www.house.gov/lazio.
Office Staff: Chief of Staff, David Horne; Legis. Dir., Andrew Ehrlich; Press Secy., Mollie Conkey; Office Mgr., Jessica Lynch.
Committees: Banking & Financial Services (Housing & Community Opportunity — chairman); Commerce (Finance & Hazardous Materials; Health & Environment).

New York 2nd — Western Suffolk County; Islip; Babylon. The district vote for Bill Clinton was 54% in 1996.

CQ Voting Studies

	1997	1998
Presidential	44%	37%
Party	76%	72%
Participation	97%	99%

Interest Groups

	1997	1998
ADA	30%	40%
ACU	65%	52%
AFL-CIO	50%	n/a
CCUS	80%	89%

Elections

	1996	1998
General	64%	66%
Primary	u/o	u/o

Jim Leach (R–Iowa)
Of Davenport • Elected 1976

Born: Oct. 15, 1942, Davenport, Iowa.
Education: Princeton U., B.A. 1964; Johns Hopkins U., M.A. 1966; London School of Economics, attended 1966–68.
Occupation: Propane gas company executive; foreign service officer; congressional aide.
Family: Wife, Elisabeth Ann "Deba" Leach; two children.
Religion: Episcopalian.
Political Career: Republican nominee for U.S. House, 1974.

Capitol Office: 2186 Rayburn House Office Building 20515; 225-6576; (fax) 226-1278; (e–mail) talk2jim@mail.house.gov; (web) www.house.gov/leach.
Office Staff: Admin. Asst., Bill Tate; Press Secy., Doug Wagner; Appts. Secy., Sarah Morgan.
Committees: Banking & Financial Services — chairman; International Relations (Asia & the Pacific).

Iowa 1st — East — Cedar Rapids; Davenport; Iowa City. The district vote for Bill Clinton was 54% in 1996.

CQ Voting Studies

	1997	1998
Presidential	48%	51%
Party	71%	62%
Participation	97%	98%

Interest Groups

	1997	1998
ADA	45%	45%
ACU	60%	32%
AFL-CIO	50%	n/a
CCUS	100%	89%

Elections

	1996	1998
General	53%	57%
Primary	u/o	u/o

Barbara Lee (D–Calif.)
Of Oakland • Elected 1998

Born: July 16, 1946, El Paso, Texas.
Education: Mills College, B.A. 1973; U. of California, Berkeley, M.S.W. 1975.
Occupation: Congressional aide.
Family: Husband, Michael Millben; two children.
Religion: Baptist.
Political Career: Calif. Assembly, 1991–97; Calif. Senate, 1997–98.

Capitol Office: 414 Cannon House Office Building 20515; 225-2661; (fax) 225-9817; (e–mail) www.house.gov/writerep.
Office Staff: Admin. Asst., Carlottia Scott; Legis. Dir., Ying Lee; Press Secy., John Newsome; Office Mgr./Scheduler, Gena Tapscott.
Committees: Banking & Financial Services (Domestic & International Monetary Policy; Housing & Community Opportunity); International Relations (Africa).

California 9th — Alameda County — Oakland; Berkeley. The district vote for Bill Clinton was 75% in 1996.

CQ Voting Studies

	1998
Presidential	85%
Party	98%
Participation	99%

Interest Groups

	1998
ADA	75%
ACU	5%
AFL-CIO	n/a
CCUS	14%

Elections

	1998	1998
General	*67%	83%
Primary		†70%

*Special election
†Open primary

Sander M. Levin (D–Mich.)
Of Royal Oak • Elected 1982

Born: Sept. 6, 1931, Detroit, Mich.
Education: U. of Chicago, B.A. 1952; Columbia U., M.A. 1954; Harvard U., LL.B. 1957.
Occupation: Lawyer.
Family: Wife, Victoria; four children.
Religion: Jewish.
Political Career: Oakland Board of Supervisors, 1961–64; Mich. Senate, 1965–71, minority leader, 1969–70; Democratic nominee for governor, 1970, 1974.

Capitol Office: 2268 Rayburn House Office Building 20515; 225-4961; (fax) 226-1033; (e-mail) slevin@mail.house.gov; (web) www.house.gov/levin.
Office Staff: Chief of Staff, Hilarie Chambers; Legis. Dir., Daniel Jourdan; Press Secy., Julie Piscitelli; Office Mgr./Scheduler, Carol Ertel.
Committees: Ways & Means (Social Security; Trade — ranking member).

Michigan 12th — Suburban Detroit — Warren; Sterling Heights. The district vote for Bill Clinton was 53% in 1996.

CQ Voting Studies

	1997	1998
Presidential	84%	83%
Party	92%	93%
Participation	99%	99%

Interest Groups

	1997	1998
ADA	100%	100%
ACU	4%	8%
AFL-CIO	100%	n/a
CCUS	50%	33%

Elections

	1996	1998
General	57%	56%
Primary	u/o	u/o

Jerry Lewis (R–Calif.)
Of Redlands • Elected 1978

Born: Oct. 21, 1934, Seattle, Wash.
Education: U. of California, Los Angeles, B.A. 1956.
Occupation: Insurance executive.
Family: Wife, Arlene; four children, three stepchildren.
Religion: Presbyterian.
Political Career: San Bernardino School Board, 1965–68; Calif. Assembly, 1969–79; Republican nominee for Calif. Senate, 1973.

Capitol Office: 2112 Rayburn House Office Building 20515; 225-5861; (fax) 225-6498; (e-mail) www.house.gov/writerep; (web) www.house.gov/jerrylewis.
Office Staff: Admin. Asst., Arlene Willis; Legis. Dir., Jeff Shockey; Press Secy./Deputy Chief of Staff, David LesStrang; Exec. Asst., Julie Hooks.
Committees: Appropriations (Foreign Operations & Export Financing; Legislative Branch; Defense — chairman); Select Intelligence (Human Intelligence, Analysis & Counterintelligence).

California 40th — San Bernardino County — Redlands. The district vote for Bill Clinton was 38% in 1996.

CQ Voting Studies

	1997	1998
Presidential	33%	32%
Party	83%	86%
Participation	96%	97%

Interest Groups

	1997	1998
ADA	20%	10%
ACU	63%	75%
AFL-CIO	38%	n/a
CCUS	80%	100%

Elections

	1996	1998
General	65%	65%
Primary	77%	*61%

*Open primary

John Lewis (D–Ga.)
Of Atlanta • Elected 1986

Born: Feb. 21, 1940, Troy, Ala.
Education: American Baptist Theological Seminary, B.A. 1961; Fisk U., B.A. 1963.
Occupation: Civil rights activist.
Family: Wife, Lillian; one child.
Religion: Baptist.
Political Career: Sought Democratic nomination for U.S. House (special election), 1977; Atlanta City Council, 1982–86.

Capitol Office: 343 Cannon House Office Building 20515; 225-3801; (fax) 225-0351; (e-mail) www.house.gov/writerep; (web) www.house.gov/johnlewis.
Office Staff: Chief of Staff, Robert H. Bassin; Legis. Dir., George Dusenbury; Press Secy., Jack Pannell; Scheduler, Lacretia Hill.
Committees: Ways & Means (Health; Oversight).

Georgia 5th — Parts of Atlanta. The district vote for Bill Clinton was 74% in 1996.

CQ Voting Studies

	1997	1998
Presidential	77%	74%
Party	96%	82%
Participation	98%	81%

Interest Groups

	1997	1998
ADA	95%	90%
ACU	4%	0%
AFL-CIO	100%	n/a
CCUS	20%	13%

Elections

	1996	1998
General	u/o	79%
Primary	u/o	u/o

Ron Lewis (R–Ky.)
Of Cecilia • Elected 1994

Born: Sept. 14, 1946, Greenup County, Ky.
Education: Morehead State U., attended; U. of Kentucky, B.A. 1969; Morehead State U., M.A. 1981.
Military Career: Navy, 1972.
Occupation: Christian bookstore owner; minister; college instructor.
Family: Wife, Kayi; two children.
Religion: Baptist.
Political Career: Sought Republican nomination for Ky. House, 1971.

Capitol Office: 223 Cannon House Office Building 20515; 225-3501; (fax) 226-2019; (e-mail) www.house.gov/writerep; (web) www.house.gov/ronlewis.
Office Staff: Admin. Asst., Greg Van Tatenhove; Legis. Dir., Helen McCarthy; Communications Dir., Shawn Pinkston; Appts. Secy./Personal Secy., Jane Riddleberger.
Committees: Ways & Means (Human Resources).

Kentucky 2nd — West central — Owensboro. The district vote for Bill Clinton was 41% in 1996.

CQ Voting Studies

	1997	1998
Presidential	25%	20%
Party	94%	93%
Participation	97%	99%

Interest Groups

	1997	1998
ADA	0%	0%
ACU	95%	100%
AFL-CIO	0%	n/a
CCUS	78%	100%

Elections

	1996	1998
General	58%	64%
Primary	u/o	u/o

John Linder (R–Ga.)
Of Tucker • Elected 1992

Born: Sept. 9, 1942, Deer River, Minn.
Education: U. of Minnesota, Duluth, B.S. 1963; U. of Minnesota, D.D.S. 1967.
Military Career: Air Force, 1967–69.
Occupation: Financial executive; dentist.
Family: Wife, Lynne; two children.
Religion: Presbyterian.
Political Career: Ga. House, 1975–81; Republican nominee for Ga. Senate, 1980; Ga. House, 1983–91; Republican nominee for U.S. House, 1990.

Capitol Office: 2447 Rayburn House Office Building 20515; 225-4272; (fax) 225-4696; (e-mail) john.linder@mail.house.gov; (web) www.house.gov/linder.
Office Staff: Admin. Asst., Henry Plaster; Legis. Dir., Rob Woodall; Press Secy., Bill Evans; Scheduler, Ginny Gilman.
Committees: Rules (Rules & Organization of the House — chairman).

Georgia 11th — Northeast — Part of Gwinnett County; Athens. The district vote for Bill Clinton was 37% in 1996.

CQ Voting Studies

	1997	1998
Presidential	31%	20%
Party	91%	92%
Participation	97%	96%

Interest Groups

	1997	1998
ADA	0%	0%
ACU	87%	100%
AFL-CIO	0%	n/a
CCUS	100%	100%

Elections

	1996	1998
General	64%	69%
Primary	u/o	u/o

William O. Lipinski (D–Ill.)
Of Chicago • Elected 1982

Born: Dec. 22, 1937, Chicago, Ill.
Education: Loras College, attended 1956–57.
Military Career: Army Reserve, 1961–67.
Occupation: Parks supervisor.
Family: Wife, Rose Marie Lipinski; two children.
Religion: Roman Catholic.
Political Career: Chicago City Council, 1975–83.

Capitol Office: 1501 Longworth House Office Building 20515; 225-5701; (fax) 225-1012; (e-mail) www.house.gov/writerep.
Office Staff: Admin. Asst., Colleen Corr; Legis. Dir., Michael McLaughlin; Communications Dir., Jason Tai; Exec. Asst., Jennifer Murer.
Committees: Transportation & Infrastructure (Aviation — ranking member; Ground Transportation).

Illinois 3rd — Chicago — Southwest Side; south and west suburbs. The district vote for Bill Clinton was 53% in 1996.

CQ Voting Studies

	1997	1998
Presidential	40%	48%
Party	59%	55%
Participation	92%	93%

Interest Groups

	1997	1998
ADA	40%	45%
ACU	46%	48%
AFL-CIO	75%	n/a
CCUS	40%	50%

Elections

	1996	1998
General	65%	72%
Primary	u/o	u/o

Frank A. LoBiondo (R-N.J.)
Of Vineland • Elected 1994
Pronounced: lo–bee–ON–dough

Born: May 12, 1946, Bridgeton, N.J.
Education: St. Joseph's U., B.S. 1968.
Occupation: Trucking company operations manager.
Family: Wife, Jan; two children.
Religion: Roman Catholic.
Political Career: Cumberland County Board of Freeholders, 1985–88; N.J. Assembly, 1988–94; Republican nominee for U.S. House, 1992.

Capitol Office: 222 Cannon House Office Building 20515; 225-6572; (fax) 225-3318; (e–mail) lobiondo@mail.house.gov; (web) www.house.gov/lobiondo.
Office Staff: Chief of Staff, Mary Annie Harper; Press Secy., John Scofield; Exec. Asst., Vacant.
Committees: Small Business (Rural Enterprises — chairman); Transportation & Infrastructure (Aviation; Coast Guard & Maritime Transportation; Water Resources & Environment).

New Jersey 2nd — South — Atlantic City; Vineland. The district vote for Bill Clinton was 50% in 1996.

CQ Voting Studies

	1997	1998
Presidential	36%	35%
Party	83%	75%
Participation	99%	99%

Interest Groups

	1997	1998
ADA	35%	30%
ACU	68%	68%
AFL-CIO	63%	n/a
CCUS	67%	78%

Elections

	1996	1998
General	60%	66%
Primary	u/o	u/o

Zoe Lofgren (D-Calif.)
Of San Jose • Elected 1994
Pronounced: ZO

Born: Dec. 21, 1947, Palo Alto, Calif.
Education: Stanford U., B.A. 1970; U. of Santa Clara, J.D. 1975.
Occupation: Lawyer; professor; congressional aide.
Family: Husband, John Marshall Collins; two children.
Religion: Unspecified.
Political Career: Santa Clara County Board of Supervisors, 1981–95.

Capitol Office: 318 Cannon House Office Building 20515; 225-3072; (fax) 225-3336; (e–mail) zoegram@logfren.house.gov; (web) www.house.gov/lofgren.
Office Staff: Legis. Dir., Jason Mahler; Press Secy., Michele Heller; Staff Asst., Lily Toton.
Committees: Judiciary (Courts & Intellectual Property; Immigration & Claims); Science (Energy & Environment; Space & Aeronautics); Standards of Official Conduct.

California 16th — Santa Clara County — San Jose. The district vote for Bill Clinton was 61% in 1996.

CQ Voting Studies

	1997	1998
Presidential	88%	84%
Party	92%	90%
Participation	99%	95%

Interest Groups

	1997	1998
ADA	95%	95%
ACU	8%	0%
AFL-CIO	100%	n/a
CCUS	40%	47%

Elections

	1996	1998
General	66%	73%
Primary	u/o	*72%

*Open primary

Nita M. Lowey (D–N.Y.)
Of Harrison • Elected 1988
Pronounced: LOW-ee

Born: July 5, 1937, Bronx, N.Y.
Education: Mount Holyoke College, B.A. 1959.
Occupation: Public official; homemaker.
Family: Husband, Stephen; three children.
Religion: Jewish.
Political Career: N.Y. assistant secretary of state, 1985–87.

Capitol Office: 2421 Rayburn House Office Building 20515; 225-6506; (fax) 225-0546; (e-mail) nita.lowey@mail.house.gov; (web) www.house.gov/lowey.
Office Staff: Chief of Staff/Press Secy., Howard Wolfson; Legis. Dir., Matt Traub; Exec. Asst., Randy Stokes.
Committees: Appropriations (Foreign Operations & Export Financing; Labor, Health & Human Services & Education).

New York 18th — Parts of Westchester — Bronx and Queens counties. The district vote for Bill Clinton was 58% in 1996.

CQ Voting Studies

	1997	1998
Presidential	83%	82%
Party	92%	93%
Participation	95%	97%

Interest Groups

	1997	1998
ADA	95%	100%
ACU	8%	8%
AFL-CIO	100%	n/a
CCUS	40%	35%

Elections

	1996	1998
General	64%	83%
Primary	u/o	u/o

Frank D. Lucas (R–Okla.)
Of Cheyenne • Elected 1994

Born: Jan. 6, 1960, Cheyenne, Okla.
Education: Oklahoma State U., B.S. 1982.
Occupation: Farmer; rancher.
Family: Wife, Lynda; three children.
Religion: Baptist.
Political Career: Republican nominee for Okla. House, 1984, 1986; Okla. House, 1989–94.

Capitol Office: 438 Cannon House Office Building 20515; 225-5565; (fax) 225-8698; (e-mail) www.house.gov/writerep; (web) www.house.gov/lucas.
Office Staff: Chief of Staff, Randy Swanson; Legis. Dir., Nicole Scott; Press Secy., Natalie Rule; Scheduler, Susan McMurry.
Committees: Agriculture (General Farm Commodities; Livestock & Horticulture; Risk Management, Research & Specialty Crops); Banking & Financial Services (Capital Markets & Securities; Domestic & International Monetary Policy); Science (Basic Research; Space & Aeronautics).

Oklahoma 6th — West and Panhandle — part of Oklahoma City. The district vote for Bill Clinton was 41% in 1996.

CQ Voting Studies

	1997	1998
Presidential	29%	22%
Party	97%	95%
Participation	99%	100%

Interest Groups

	1997	1998
ADA	0%	0%
ACU	92%	100%
AFL-CIO	0%	n/a
CCUS	90%	100%

Elections

	1996	1998
General	64%	65%
Primary	u/o	u/o

Ken Lucas (D–Ky.)
Of Richwood • Elected 1998

Born: Aug. 22, 1933, Covington, Ky.
Education: U. of Kentucky, B.S. 1955; Xavier U., M.B.A. 1970.
Military Career: Air Force, 1955–57; Air National Guard, 1957–67.
Occupation: Banking executive; university regent; financial planner.
Family: Wife, Mary; five children.
Religion: Christian Church.
Political Career: Florence City Council, 1967–74; Boone County Commission, 1974–82; Boone County judge-executive, 1992–98.

Capitol Office: 1237 Longworth House Office Building 20515; 225-3465; (fax) 225-8698; (e–mail) write.kenlucas@mail.house.gov.
Office Staff: Chief of Staff, John Lapp; Legis. Dir., Cheryl Brownell; Press Secy., John Lapp; Exec. Asst., Angie Dixon.
Committees: Agriculture (Livestock & Horticulture; Risk Management, Research & Specialty Crops); Budget.

Kentucky 4th — North and East — Covington; Ashland. The district vote for Bill Clinton was 41% in 1996.

Elections

	1998
General	53%
Primary	66%

Bill Luther (D–Minn.)
Of Stillwater • Elected 1994

Born: June 27, 1945, Fergus Falls, Minn.
Education: U. of Minnesota, B.S. 1967, J.D. 1970.
Occupation: Lawyer.
Family: Wife, Darlene; two children.
Religion: Roman Catholic.
Political Career: Minn. House, 1975–77; Minn. Senate, 1977–95, assistant majority leader, 1982–95.

Capitol Office: 117 Cannon House Office Building 20515; 225-2271; (fax) 225-3368; (e–mail) tell.bill@mail.house.gov; (web) www.house.gov/luther.
Office Staff: Admin. Asst., Bob Decheine; Legis. Dir., Steve Heuer; Exec. Asst., Romayne Houle.
Committees: Commerce (Finance & Hazardous Materials; Telecommunications, Trade & Consumer Protection).

Minnesota 6th — Eastern, Southern Twin Cities suburbs. The district vote for Bill Clinton was 51% in 1996.

CQ Voting Studies

	1997	1998
Presidential	77%	71%
Party	83%	85%
Participation	99%	96%

Interest Groups

	1997	1998
ADA	85%	90%
ACU	24%	4%
AFL-CIO	88%	n/a
CCUS	60%	56%

Elections

	1996	1998
General	56%	50%
Primary	u/o	u/o

Carolyn B. Maloney (D–N.Y.)
Of Manhattan • Elected 1992

Born: Feb. 19, 1948, Greensboro, N.C.
Education: Greensboro College, A.B. 1968.
Occupation: Legislative aide; teacher.
Family: Husband, Clifton H.W. Maloney; two children.
Religion: Presbyterian.
Political Career: N.Y. City Council, 1982–93.

Capitol Office: 2430 Rayburn House Office Building 20515; 225-7944; (fax) 225-4709; (e-mail) rep.carolyn.maloney@mail.house.gov; (web) www.house.gov/maloney.
Office Staff: Admin. Asst., Ben Chevat; Press Secy., Terese Schlachter; Scheduler, Kate Spangler.
Committees: Banking & Financial Services (Capital Markets & Securities; Financial Institutions & Consumer Credit); Government Reform (Census — ranking member; District of Columbia; Government Management, Information & Technology); Joint Economic.

New York 14th — East Side Manhattan; parts of Queens and Brooklyn. The district vote for Bill Clinton was 71% in 1996.

CQ Voting Studies

	1997	1998
Presidential	77%	79%
Party	93%	91%
Participation	97%	94%

Interest Groups

	1997	1998
ADA	95%	100%
ACU	8%	8%
AFL-CIO	100%	n/a
CCUS	50%	33%

Elections

	1996	1998
General	72%	77%
Primary	u/o	u/o

Jim Maloney (D–Conn.)
Of Danbury • Elected 1996

Born: Sept. 17, 1948, Quincy, Mass.
Education: Harvard U., B.A. 1972; Boston U., J.D. 1980.
Occupation: Lawyer.
Family: Wife, Mary; three children.
Religion: Roman Catholic.
Political Career: Conn. Senate, 1987–95; Democratic nominee for U.S. House, 1994.

Capitol Office: 1213 Longworth House Office Building 20515; 225-3822; (fax) 225-5746; (e-mail) www.house.gov/writerep; (web) www.house.gov/jimmaloney.
Office Staff: Chief of Staff, Jim Hart; Legis. Dir., Alex Sternhell; Press Secy., Lisa Sohn; Exec. Asst., Isabel Corte-Real.
Committees: Armed Services (Military Procurement; Military Readiness); Banking & Financial Services (Capital Markets & Securities; Housing & Community Opportunity).

Connecticut 5th — West — Waterbury; Danbury. The district vote for Bill Clinton was 48% in 1996.

CQ Voting Studies

	1997	1998
Presidential	68%	66%
Party	84%	79%
Participation	99%	97%

Interest Groups

	1997	1998
ADA	75%	85%
ACU	32%	32%
AFL-CIO	75%	n/a
CCUS	60%	56%

Elections

	1996	1998
General	52%	50%
Primary	u/o	u/o

Donald Manzullo (R–Ill.)
Of Egan • Elected 1992
Pronounced: man-ZOO-low

Born: Mar. 24, 1944, Rockford, Ill.
Education: American U., B.A. 1967; Marquette U., J.D. 1970.
Occupation: Lawyer.
Family: Wife, Freda; three children.
Religion: Baptist.
Political Career: Sought Republican nomination for U.S. House, 1990.

Capitol Office: 409 Cannon House Office Building 20515; 225-5676; (fax) 225-5284; (e–mail) www.house.gov/writerep; (web) www.house.gov/manzullo.
Office Staff: Chief of Staff, J. Douglas Thomas; Legis. Dir., Kurt Markva; Scheduler, Suzanne Hartzell.
Committees: Banking & Financial Services (Capital Markets & Securities); International Relations (Asia & the Pacific; International Economic Policy & Trade); Small Business (Tax, Finance & Exports — chairman).

Illinois 16th — Northwest — Rockford; McHenry. The district vote for Bill Clinton was 42% in 1996.

CQ Voting Studies

	1997	1998
Presidential	23%	21%
Party	95%	95%
Participation	99%	98%

Interest Groups

	1997	1998
ADA	5%	0%
ACU	100%	92%
AFL-CIO	0%	n/a
CCUS	90%	94%

Elections

	1996	1998
General	60%	u/o
Primary	u/o	u/o

Edward J. Markey (D–Mass.)
Of Malden • Elected 1976

Born: July 11, 1946, Malden, Mass.
Education: Boston College, B.A. 1968, J.D. 1972.
Military Career: Army Reserve, 1968–73.
Occupation: Lawyer.
Family: Wife, Susan Blumenthal.
Religion: Roman Catholic.
Political Career: Mass. House, 1973–77.

Capitol Office: 2108 Rayburn House Office Building 20515; 225-2836; (e–mail) www.house.gov/writerep; (web) www.house.gov/markey.
Office Staff: Chief of Staff/Press Secy., David Moulton; Legis. Dir., Jeff Duncan; Scheduler/Exec. Asst., Nancy Morrissey.
Committees: Budget; Commerce (Energy & Power; Finance & Hazardous Materials; Telecommunications, Trade & Consumer Protection — ranking member).

Massachusetts 7th — Northwest suburbs — Woburn; Framingham; Revere. The district vote for Bill Clinton was 64% in 1996.

CQ Voting Studies

	1997	1998
Presidential	76%	76%
Party	94%	85%
Participation	97%	91%

Interest Groups

	1997	1998
ADA	100%	90%
ACU	8%	4%
AFL-CIO	100%	n/a
CCUS	20%	31%

Elections

	1996	1998
General	70%	71%
Primary	u/o	u/o

Matthew G. Martinez (D–Calif.)
Of Monterey Park • Elected 1982

Born: Feb. 14, 1929, Walsenburg, Colo.
Education: Los Angeles Trade-Technical College, attended 1958–59.
Military Career: Marine Corps, 1947–50.
Occupation: Upholstery company owner.
Family: Separated; five children.
Religion: Roman Catholic.
Political Career: Monterey Park City Council, 1974–80, mayor, 1976, 1980; Calif. Assembly, 1981–82.

Capitol Office: 2269 Rayburn House Office Building 20515; 225-5464; (fax) 225-5467; (e-mail) www.house.gov/writerep; (web) www.house.gov/martinez.
Office Staff: Chief of Staff/Legis. Dir./Press Secy., Maxine Grant; Scheduler/Exec. Asst., Lynnette Sarhardian.
Committees: Education & Workforce (Postsecondary Education, Training & Life-Long Learning — ranking member; Workforce Protections); International Relations (Asia & the Pacific; Western Hemisphere).

California 31st — Eastern Los Angeles County; El Monte; Alhambra; Azusa. The district vote for Bill Clinton was 65% in 1996.

CQ Voting Studies

	1997	1998
Presidential	72%	77%
Party	80%	77%
Participation	94%	88%

Interest Groups

	1997	1998
ADA	70%	75%
ACU	22%	29%
AFL-CIO	88%	n/a
CCUS	60%	41%

Elections

	1996	1998
General	67%	70%
Primary	u/o	*67%

*Open primary

Frank R. Mascara (D–Pa.)
Of Charleroi • Elected 1994

Born: Jan. 19, 1930, Belle Vernon, Pa.
Education: California University of Pennsylvania, B.S. 1972.
Military Career: Army, 1946–47.
Occupation: Accountant; educator.
Family: Wife, Dolores; four children.
Religion: Roman Catholic.
Political Career: Washington County Controller, 1974–79; Washington County Commission chairman, 1980–95; sought Democratic nomination for U.S. House, 1992.

Capitol Office: 314 Cannon House Office Building 20515; 225-4665; (fax) 225-3377; (e-mail) www.house.gov/writerep; (web) www.house.gov/mascara.
Office Staff: Admin. Asst., Bill Sember; Legis. Dir., Jonathan Godfrey; Press Secy., Stephanie Kang; Exec. Asst./Office Mgr., Brenda Connolly.
Committees: Banking & Financial Services (Capital Markets & Securities; Financial Institutions & Consumer Credit); Transportation & Infrastructure (Ground Transportation; Water Resources & Environment).

Pennsylvania 20th — Southwest — The Mon Valley; Washington. The district vote for Bill Clinton was 50% in 1996.

CQ Voting Studies

	1997	1998
Presidential	61%	73%
Party	71%	80%
Participation	99%	100%

Interest Groups

	1997	1998
ADA	65%	85%
ACU	32%	20%
AFL-CIO	100%	n/a
CCUS	50%	33%

Elections

	1996	1998
General	54%	u/o
Primary	u/o	u/o

Robert T. Matsui (D–Calif.)
Of Sacramento • Elected 1978

Born: Sept. 17, 1941, Sacramento, Calif.
Education: U. of California, Berkeley, A.B. 1963, J.D. 1966.
Occupation: Lawyer.
Family: Wife, Doris; one child.
Religion: Methodist.
Political Career: Sacramento City Council, 1971–78, vice mayor, 1977.

Capitol Office: 2308 Rayburn House Office Building 20515; 225-7163; (fax) 225-0566; (e–mail) www.house.gov/writerep; (web) www.house.gov/matsui.
Office Staff: Admin. Asst., Tom Keaney; Press Secy./Legis. Dir., Jim Bonham; Exec. Asst., Shirley Queja.
Committees: Ways & Means (Human Resources; Social Security — ranking member).

California 5th — Sacramento. The district vote for Bill Clinton was 57% in 1996.

CQ Voting Studies

	1997	1998
Presidential	72%	82%
Party	89%	92%
Participation	97%	99%

Interest Groups

	1997	1998
ADA	90%	95%
ACU	20%	4%
AFL-CIO	100%	n/a
CCUS	40%	39%

Elections

	1996	1998
General	70%	72%
Primary	u/o	*71%

*Open primary

Carolyn McCarthy (D–N.Y.)
Of Mineola • Elected 1996

Born: Jan. 5, 1944, Brooklyn, N.Y.
Education: Glen Cove Nursing School, L.P.N. 1964.
Occupation: Nurse.
Family: Widowed; one child.
Religion: Roman Catholic.
Political Career: No previous office.

Capitol Office: 1725 Longworth House Office Building 20515; 225-5516; (fax) 225-5758; (e–mail) www.house.gov/writerep; (web) www.house.gov/carolynmccarthy.
Office Staff: Chief of Staff, Beneva Schulte; Legis. Dir., Sean McDonough; Press Secy., Stacey Winograd; Exec. Asst., Christopher Hoven.
Committees: Education & Workforce (Early Childhood, Youth & Families; Employer-Employee Relations); Small Business (Tax, Finance & Exports — ranking member).

New York 4th — Southwest Nassau County — Hempstead; Mineola. The district vote for Bill Clinton was 56% in 1996.

CQ Voting Studies

	1997	1998
Presidential	69%	68%
Party	83%	82%
Participation	98%	99%

Interest Groups

	1997	1998
ADA	80%	90%
ACU	16%	24%
AFL-CIO	86%	n/a
CCUS	50%	61%

Elections

	1996	1998
General	57%	53%
Primary	u/o	u/o

Karen McCarthy (D–Mo.)
Of Kansas City • Elected 1994

Born: Mar. 18, 1947, Haverhill, Mass.
Education: U. of Kansas, B.S. 1969; U. of Birmingham, England, attended 1974; U. of Missouri, Kansas City, M.A. 1976; U. of Kansas, M.B.A. 1986.
Occupation: Teacher.
Family: Divorced.
Religion: Roman Catholic.
Political Career: Mo. House, 1977–95.

Capitol Office: 1330 Longworth House Office Building 20515; 225-4535; (fax) 225-4403; (e-mail) www.house.gov/writerep.
Office Staff: Legis. Dir., Fred Turner; Press Secy., Amy Shollenberger; Scheduler, Judy Wright.
Committees: Commerce (Energy & Power; Oversight & Investigations; Telecommunications, Trade & Consumer Protection).

Missouri 5th — Kansas City and eastern suburbs; Independence. The district vote for Bill Clinton was 58% in 1996.

CQ Voting Studies

	1997	1998
Presidential	81%	80%
Party	88%	88%
Participation	97%	96%

Interest Groups

	1997	1998
ADA	80%	100%
ACU	16%	0%
AFL-CIO	88%	n/a
CCUS	60%	56%

Elections

	1996	1998
General	67%	66%
Primary	u/o	79%

Bill McCollum (R–Fla.)
Of Longwood • Elected 1980

Born: July 12, 1944, Brooksville, Fla.
Education: U. of Florida, B.A. 1965, J.D. 1968.
Military Career: Navy, 1969–72; Naval Reserve, 1972–92.
Occupation: Lawyer.
Family: Wife, Ingrid; three children.
Religion: Episcopalian.
Political Career: Seminole County Republican Executive Committee chairman, 1976–80.

Capitol Office: 2109 Rayburn House Office Building 20515; 225-2176; (fax) 225-0999; (e-mail) www.house.gov/writerep; (web) www.house.gov/mccollum.
Office Staff: Chief of Staff, John Ariale; Legis. Dir., Karl Kaufmann; Press Secy., Shannon Gravitte; Office Mgr./Exec. Asst., Lisa Smith.
Committees: Banking & Financial Services (Domestic & International Monetary Policy; Financial Institutions & Consumer Credit); Select Intelligence (Human Intelligence, Analysis & Counterintelligence — chairman); Judiciary (Crime — chairman; Immigration & Claims).

Florida 8th — Central — Orange County; part of Orlando. The district vote for Bill Clinton was 43% in 1996.

CQ Voting Studies

	1997	1998
Presidential	27%	26%
Party	91%	90%
Participation	97%	97%

Interest Groups

	1997	1998
ADA	5%	5%
ACU	88%	84%
AFL-CIO	0%	n/a
CCUS	90%	94%

Elections

	1996	1998
General	67%	66%
Primary	u/o	u/o

Jim McCrery (R–La.)
Of Shreveport • Elected 1988

Born: Sept. 18, 1949, Shreveport, La.
Education: Louisiana Tech U., B.A. 1971; Louisiana State U., J.D. 1975.
Occupation: Lawyer; congressional aide; government relations executive.
Family: Wife, Johnette; two children.
Religion: Methodist.
Political Career: Candidate for Leesville City Council, 1978.
Capitol Office: 2104 Rayburn House Office Building 20515; 225-2777; (fax) 225-8039; (e–mail) jim.mccrery@mail.house.gov; (web) www.house.gov/mccrery.
Office Staff: Chief of Staff, Richard Hunt; Legis. Dir., Chris King; Press Secy., Chris Downing; Office Mgr./Scheduler, Leah Hill.
Committees: Ways & Means (Health; Human Resources; Social Security); Joint Economic.

Louisiana 4th — Northwest and west — Shreveport; Bossier City. The district vote for Bill Clinton was 52% in 1996.

CQ Voting Studies

	1997	1998
Presidential	29%	24%
Party	90%	90%
Participation	95%	92%

Interest Groups

	1997	1998
ADA	20%	5%
ACU	83%	96%
AFL-CIO	0%	n/a
CCUS	100%	100%

Elections

	1996	1998
General	u/o	u/o
Primary	71%	

Jim McDermott (D–Wash.)
Of Seattle • Elected 1988

Born: Dec. 28, 1936, Chicago, Ill.
Education: Wheaton College, B.S. 1958; U. of Illinois, M.D. 1963.
Military Career: Navy Medical Corps, 1968–70.
Occupation: Psychiatrist.
Family: Wife, Therese Hansen; two children.
Religion: Episcopalian.
Political Career: Wash. House, 1971–73; sought Democratic nomination for governor, 1972; Wash. Senate, 1975–87; Democratic nominee for governor, 1980; sought Democratic nomination for governor, 1984.

Capitol Office: 1035 Longworth House Office Building 20515; 225-3106; (e–mail) www.house.gov/writerep; (web) www.house.gov/mcdermott.
Office Staff: Admin. Asst./Legis. Dir., Charles M. Williams; Press Secy., Jennifer Crider; Exec. Asst., Wilda Chisolm.
Committees: Budget; Ways & Means (Health; Oversight).

Washington 7th — Seattle and suburbs. The district vote for Bill Clinton was 69% in 1996.

CQ Voting Studies

	1997	1998
Presidential	80%	89%
Party	92%	92%
Participation	95%	96%

Interest Groups

	1997	1998
ADA	90%	90%
ACU	4%	0%
AFL-CIO	100%	n/a
CCUS	20%	38%

Elections

	1996	1998
General	81%	88%
Primary	*79%	*84%

*Open primary

Jim McGovern (D–Mass.)
Of Worcester • Elected 1996

Born: Nov. 20, 1959, Worcester, Mass.
Education: American U., B.A. 1981, M.P.A. 1984.
Occupation: Congressional aide.
Family: Wife, Lisa; one child.
Religion: Roman Catholic.
Political Career: Sought Democratic nomination for U.S. House, 1994.

Capitol Office: 416 Cannon House Office Building 20515; 225-6101; (fax) 225-5759; (e–mail) www.house.gov/writerep; (web) www.house.gov/mcgovern.
Office Staff: Chief of Staff, Ed Augustus; Legis. Dir., Cindy Buhl; Press Secy., Michael Mershon; Scheduler, Daniel Holt.
Committees: Transportation & Infrastructure (Aviation; Water Resources & Environment).

Massachusetts 3rd — Central and Southeast — Worcester; coastal towns. The district vote for Bill Clinton was 60% in 1996.

CQ Voting Studies

	1997	1998
Presidential	84%	78%
Party	96%	93%
Participation	99%	96%

Interest Groups

	1997	1998
ADA	100%	100%
ACU	4%	4%
AFL-CIO	100%	n/a
CCUS	30%	39%

Elections

	1996	1998
General	53%	57%
Primary	u/o	u/o

John M. McHugh (R–N.Y.)
Of Pierrepont Manor • Elected 1992

Born: Sept. 29, 1948, Watertown, N.Y.
Education: Utica College of Syracuse U., B.A. 1970; State U. of New York, Albany, M.P.A. 1977.
Occupation: City official; legislative aide; insurance broker.
Family: Divorced.
Religion: Roman Catholic.
Political Career: N.Y. Senate, 1985–93.

Capitol Office: 2441 Rayburn House Office Building 20515; 225-4611; (fax) 226-0621; (e–mail) www.house.gov/writerep; (web) www.house.gov/mchugh.
Office Staff: Chief of Staff, Cary Brick; Senior Legis. Asst., Judith M. Brewer; Press Secy., Dana Johnson; Admin. Secy., Donna Bell.
Committees: Armed Services (Military Installations & Facilities; Military Research & Development); Government Reform (National Security & Veterans Affairs; Postal Service — chairman); International Relations (Asia & the Pacific).

New York 24th — North Country — Plattsburgh; Watertown; Oswego. The district vote for Bill Clinton was 49% in 1996.

CQ Voting Studies

	1997	1998
Presidential	32%	34%
Party	83%	78%
Participation	97%	98%

Interest Groups

	1997	1998
ADA	15%	25%
ACU	60%	68%
AFL-CIO	50%	n/a
CCUS	80%	89%

Elections

	1996	1998
General	71%	79%
Primary	u/o	u/o

Scott McInnis (R–Colo.)
Of Grand Junction • Elected 1992

Born: May 9, 1953, Glenwood Springs, Colo.
Education: Fort Lewis College, B.A. 1975; St. Mary's U. of San Antonio, J.D. 1980.
Occupation: Lawyer; police officer; firefighter.
Family: Wife, Lori; three children.
Religion: Roman Catholic.
Political Career: Colo. House, 1983–93, majority leader, 1991–93.

Capitol Office: 320 Cannon House Office Building 20515; 225-4761; (fax) 226-0622; (e–mail) www.house.gov/writerep; (web) www.house.gov/mcinnis.
Office Staff: Chief of Staff, Mike Hesse; Legis. Dir., Christopher Atcher; Press Secy., Will Bos; Scheduler/Office Mgr., Karen Paulson.
Committees: Ways & Means (Human Resources; Oversight).

Colorado 3rd — Western Slope; Pueblo. The district vote for Bill Clinton was 43% in 1996.

CQ Voting Studies

	1997	1998
Presidential	27%	26%
Party	87%	89%
Participation	94%	96%

Interest Groups

	1997	1998
ADA	0%	5%
ACU	91%	96%
AFL-CIO	0%	n/a
CCUS	90%	100%

Elections

	1996	1998
General	69%	66%
Primary	u/o	u/o

David M. McIntosh (R–Ind.)
Of Muncie • Elected 1994

Born: June 8, 1958, Oakland, Calif.
Education: Yale U., B.A. 1980; U. of Chicago, J.D. 1983.
Occupation: Lawyer; White House aide; national security and public policy analyst.
Family: Wife, Elizabeth Ruth McIntosh; one child.
Religion: Episcopalian.
Political Career: No previous office.

Capitol Office: 1610 Longworth House Office Building 20515; 225-3021; (fax) 225-3382; (e–mail) www.house.gov/writerep; (web) www.house.gov/mcintosh.
Office Staff: Chief of Staff, Jeff Taylor; Legis. Dir., John Steele; Communications Dir., Chris Jones; Exec. Asst., Meredith Rasmussen.
Committees: Education & Workforce (Early Childhood, Youth & Families; Postsecondary Education, Training & Life-Long Learning); Government Reform (National Economic Growth — chairman; National Security & Veterans Affairs); Small Business (Regulatory Reform & Paperwork Reduction).

Indiana 2nd — East Central — Muncie; Anderson; Columbus. The district vote for Bill Clinton was 42% in 1996.

CQ Voting Studies

	1997	1998
Presidential	25%	23%
Party	83%	91%
Participation	89%	96%

Interest Groups

	1997	1998
ADA	15%	0%
ACU	100%	100%
AFL-CIO	14%	n/a
CCUS	67%	94%

Elections

	1996	1998
General	58%	61%
Primary	86%	u/o

Mike McIntyre (D–N.C.)
Of Lumberton • Elected 1996

Born: Aug. 6, 1956, Lumberton, N.C.
Education: U. of North Carolina, B.A. 1978, J.D. 1981.
Occupation: Lawyer.
Family: Wife, Dee; two children.
Religion: Presbyterian.
Political Career: No previous office.

Capitol Office: 1605 Longworth House Office Building 20515; 225-2731; (fax) 225-5773; (e-mail) congmcintyre@mail.house.gov; (web) www.house.gov/mcintyre.
Office Staff: Chief of Staff/Press Secy., Dean Mitchell; Legis. Dir., Bill Bondshu; Exec. Asst., Audrey Lesesne.
Committees: Agriculture (Livestock & Horticulture; Risk Management, Research & Specialty Crops); Armed Services (Military Procurement; Military Readiness).

North Carolina 7th — Southeast — Wilmington; part of Fayetteville. The district vote for Bill Clinton was 47% in 1996.

CQ Voting Studies

	1997	1998
Presidential	43%	51%
Party	53%	60%
Participation	98%	97%

Interest Groups

	1997	1998
ADA	40%	60%
ACU	60%	52%
AFL-CIO	50%	n/a
CCUS	80%	72%

Elections

	1996	1998
General	53%	91%
Primary	*52%	94%

*Runoff election

Howard P. "Buck" McKeon
(R–Calif.)
Of Santa Clarita • Elected 1992

Born: Sept. 9, 1939, Los Angeles, Calif.
Education: Brigham Young U., B.S. 1985.
Occupation: Clothing store owner.
Family: Wife, Patricia; six children.
Religion: Mormon.
Political Career: William S. Hart School Board, 1978–87; Santa Clarita City Council, 1987–92, mayor, 1987–88.

Capitol Office: 2242 Rayburn House Office Building 20515; 225-1956; (fax) 226-0683; (e-mail) tellbuck@mail.house.gov; (web) www.house.gov/mckeon.
Office Staff: Chief of Staff, Bob Cochran; Legis. Dir., Greg Campbell; Press Secy./District Dir., David Foy; Exec. Asst., Maggie Giammarco.
Committees: Armed Services (Military Installations & Facilities; Military Research & Development); Education & Workforce (Employer-Employee Relations; Postsecondary Education, Training & Life-Long Learning — chairman); Veterans' Affairs (Health).

California 25th — Northern Los Angeles County; Lancaster; Palmdale. The district vote for Bill Clinton was 41% in 1996.

CQ Voting Studies

	1997	1998
Presidential	29%	23%
Party	97%	94%
Participation	99%	99%

Interest Groups

	1997	1998
ADA	0%	5%
ACU	92%	96%
AFL-CIO	0%	n/a
CCUS	90%	100%

Elections

	1996	1998
General	62%	75%
Primary	85%	*79%

*Open primary

Cynthia A. McKinney (D–Ga.)
Of Lithonia • Elected 1992

Born: Mar. 17, 1955, Atlanta, Ga.
Education: U. of Southern California, B.A. 1978.
Occupation: Professor.
Family: Divorced; one child.
Religion: Roman Catholic.
Political Career: Democratic nominee for Ga. House, 1986; Ga. House, 1989–93.

Capitol Office: 124 Cannon House Office Building 20515; 225-1605; (fax) 226-0691; (e-mail) cymck@mail.house.gov; (web) www.house.gov/mckinney.
Office Staff: Chief of Staff, Gary Cox; Legis. Dir., Merwyn Scott; Press Secy., Scott Southward; Scheduler, James Romano.
Committees: Armed Services (Military Personnel; Military Procurement); International Relations (International Operations & Human Rights — ranking member).

Georgia 4th — Atlanta Suburbs — Parts of De Kalb and Gwinnett Counties. The district vote for Bill Clinton was 64% in 1996.

CQ Voting Studies

	1997	1998
Presidential	72%	87%
Party	83%	92%
Participation	92%	99%

Interest Groups

	1997	1998
ADA	100%	100%
ACU	13%	8%
AFL-CIO	100%	n/a
CCUS	30%	22%

Elections

	1996	1998
General	58%	61%
Primary	67%	u/o

Michael R. McNulty (D–N.Y.)
Of Green Island • Elected 1988

Born: Sept. 16, 1947, Troy, N.Y.
Education: College of the Holy Cross, A.B. 1969.
Occupation: Public official.
Family: Wife, Nancy Ann; four children.
Religion: Roman Catholic.
Political Career: Green Island supervisor, 1970–77; Democratic nominee for N.Y. Assembly, 1976; mayor of Green Island, 1977–83; N.Y. Assembly, 1983–89.

Capitol Office: 2161 Rayburn House Office Building 20515; 225-5076; (fax) 225-5077; (e-mail) mike.mcnulty@mail.house.gov; (web) www.house.gov/mcnulty.
Office Staff: Chief of Staff/Scheduler, Lana Helfrich; Legis. Dir., James Glenn; Press Secy., Charles Segal.
Committees: Ways & Means (Oversight; Trade).

New York 21st — Capital District — Albany; Schenectady; Troy. The district vote for Bill Clinton was 58% in 1996.

CQ Voting Studies

	1997	1998
Presidential	65%	65%
Party	84%	72%
Participation	97%	83%

Interest Groups

	1997	1998
ADA	80%	75%
ACU	26%	21%
AFL-CIO	100%	n/a
CCUS	30%	23%

Elections

	1996	1998
General	66%	74%
Primary	57%	u/o

Martin T. Meehan (D–Mass.)
Of Lowell • Elected 1992

Born: Dec. 30, 1956, Lowell, Mass.
Education: U. of Massachusetts, Lowell, B.S. 1978; Suffolk U., M.P.A. 1981, J.D. 1986.
Occupation: Lawyer.
Family: Wife, Ellen T. Murphy.
Religion: Roman Catholic.
Political Career: No previous office.

Capitol Office: 2434 Rayburn House Office Building 20515; 225-3411; (fax) 226-0771; (e-mail) martin.meehan@mail.house.gov; (web) www.house.gov/meehan.
Office Staff: Legis. Dir., William McCann; Legis. Dir., Amy Rosenbaum; Press Secy., Nicole Hartburger; Scheduler, Stacey Staniak.
Committees: Armed Services (Military Personnel; Military Research & Development); Judiciary (Crime; Immigration & Claims).

Massachusetts 5th — North Central — Lawrence; Lowell. The district vote for Bill Clinton was 58% in 1996.

CQ Voting Studies

	1997	1998
Presidential	81%	82%
Party	92%	93%
Participation	96%	94%

Interest Groups

	1997	1998
ADA	90%	100%
ACU	20%	4%
AFL-CIO	100%	n/a
CCUS	44%	31%

Elections

	1996	1998
General	u/o	71%
Primary	85%	u/o

Carrie P. Meek (D–Fla.)
Of Miami • Elected 1992

Born: Apr. 29, 1926, Tallahassee, Fla.
Education: Florida A&M U., B.S. 1946; U. of Michigan, M.S. 1948; Florida Atlantic U., attended 1979.
Occupation: Educational administrator; teacher.
Family: Divorced; three children.
Religion: Baptist.
Political Career: Fla. House, 1979–82; Fla. Senate, 1982–93.

Capitol Office: 401 Cannon House Office Building 20515; 225-4506; (fax) 226-0777; (e-mail) www.house.gov/writerep; (web) www.house.gov/meek.
Office Staff: Deputy Chief of Staff, John Schelble; Chief of Staff, Peggy Demon; Legis. Dir., Ken Nealy; Press Secy., Tola Thompson; Scheduler/Office Mgr., Cecilia Morton.
Committees: Appropriations (Treasury, Postal Service & General Government; VA, HUD & Independent Agencies).

Florida 17th — Southeast — Parts of North Dade County; parts of Miami, Carol City. The district vote for Bill Clinton was 85% in 1996.

CQ Voting Studies

	1997	1998
Presidential	71%	80%
Party	82%	86%
Participation	94%	94%

Interest Groups

	1997	1998
ADA	80%	95%
ACU	17%	4%
AFL-CIO	100%	n/a
CCUS	40%	28%

Elections

	1996	1998
General	89%	u/o
Primary	u/o	u/o

Gregory W. Meeks (D-N.Y.)
Of Far Rockaway • Elected 1998

Born: Sept. 25, 1953, Harlem, N.Y.
Education: Adelphi U., B.A. 1975; Howard U., J.D. 1978.
Occupation: Workers' compensation board judge; prosecutor.
Family: Wife, Simone-Marie; two children.
Religion: Baptist.
Political Career: N.Y. Assembly, 1993–98.

Capitol Office: 1710 Longworth House Office Building 20515; 225-3461; (fax) 226-4169; (e-mail) www.house.gov/writerep.
Office Staff: Chief of Staff, Jameel W. Aalim-Johnson; Press Secy., Candace Sandy; Scheduler, Pat Fisher.
Committees: Banking & Financial Services (Domestic & International Monetary Policy; Financial Institutions & Consumer Credit); International Relations (Africa; International Operations & Human Rights).

New York 6th — Southeast Queens — Jamaica; St. Albans. The district vote for Bill Clinton was 85% in 1996.

CQ Voting Studies

	1998
Presidential	79%
Party	86%
Participation	86%

Interest Groups

	1998
ADA	85%
ACU	5%
AFL-CIO	n/a
CCUS	33%

Elections

	1998	1998
General	*56%	u/o
Primary		u/o

*Special election

Robert Menendez (D-N.J.)
Of Union City • Elected 1992

Born: Jan. 1, 1954, New York, N.Y.
Education: St. Peter's College, B.A. 1976; Rutgers U., J.D. 1979.
Occupation: Lawyer.
Family: Wife, Jane; two children.
Religion: Roman Catholic.
Political Career: Union City Board of Education, 1974–82; mayor of Union City, 1986–92; N.J. Assembly, 1987–91; N.J. Senate, 1991–92.

Capitol Office: 405 Cannon House Office Building 20515; 225-7919; (fax) 226-0792; (e-mail) www.house.gov/writerep; (web) www.house.gov/menendez.
Office Staff: Chief of Staff, Michael H. Hutton; Legis. Dir., Jim Datri; Communications Dir., Hal Connolly; Scheduler, Judi Wolford.
Committees: International Relations (International Economic Policy & Trade — ranking member; Western Hemisphere); Transportation & Infrastructure (Aviation; Water Resources & Environment).

New Jersey 13th — Parts of Jersey City and Newark. The district vote for Bill Clinton was 72% in 1996.

CQ Voting Studies

	1997	1998
Presidential	75%	74%
Party	88%	90%
Participation	98%	98%

Interest Groups

	1997	1998
ADA	90%	95%
ACU	13%	12%
AFL-CIO	100%	n/a
CCUS	40%	33%

Elections

	1996	1998
General	79%	80%
Primary	93%	u/o

Jack Metcalf (R-Wash.)
Of Langley • Elected 1994

Born: Nov. 30, 1927, Marysville, Wash.
Education: Pacific Lutheran U., B.A. 1949–51; U. of Washington, attended 1965–66.
Military Career: Army, 1946–47.
Occupation: Teacher; bed and breakfast owner.
Family: Wife, Norma; four children.
Religion: Christian.
Political Career: Republican nominee for Wash. House, 1958; Wash. House, 1960–64; defeated for reelection to Wash. House, 1964; Wash. Senate, 1966–74; Republican nominee for U.S. Senate, 1968, 1974; Wash. Senate, 1980–92; Republican nominee for U.S. House, 1992.

Capitol Office: 1510 Longworth House Office Building 20515; 225-2605; (fax) 225-4420; (e-mail) www.house.gov/writerep; (web) www.house.gov/metcalf.
Office Staff: Admin. Asst., Erik Strom; Chief of Staff, Lew Moore; Legis. Dir., Jeff Markey; Communications Dir., Chris Strow; Scheduler, Rebecca Nichols.
Committees: Banking & Financial Services (Domestic & International Monetary Policy; Financial Institutions & Consumer Credit; Housing & Community Opportunity); Science (Energy & Environment); Transportation & Infrastructure (Aviation; Ground Transportation).

Washington 2nd — Puget Sound — Everett; Bellingham. The district vote for Bill Clinton was 47% in 1996.

CQ Voting Studies

	1997	1998
Presidential	24%	21%
Party	86%	85%
Participation	97%	99%

Interest Groups

	1997	1998
ADA	15%	20%
ACU	88%	80%
AFL-CIO	63%	n/a
CCUS	60%	83%

Elections

	1996	1998
General	49%	55%
Primary	*52%	*51%

*Open primary

John L. Mica (R-Fla.)
Of Winter Park • Elected 1992

Born: Jan. 27, 1943, Binghamton, N.Y.
Education: Miami-Dade Community College, A.A. 1965; U. of Florida, B.A. 1967.
Occupation: Government consultant; real estate investor; congressional aide.
Family: Wife, Pat; two children.
Religion: Episcopalian.
Political Career: Fla. House, 1977–81; Republican nominee for Fla. Senate, 1980.

Capitol Office: 2445 Rayburn House Office Building 20515; 225-4035; (fax) 226-0821; (e-mail) john.mica@mail.house.gov; (web) www.house.gov/mica.
Office Staff: Admin. Asst., Russell Roberts; Legis. Dir./Press Secy., Sharon Pinkerton; Scheduler, Lisa Wandler.
Committees: House Administration; Government Reform (Civil Service; Criminal Justice, Drug Policy & Human Resources — chairman; National Security & Veterans Affairs); Transportation & Infrastructure (Aviation; Ground Transportation).

Florida 7th — Central — Southern Seminole and Volusia counties; Deltona; Port Orange. The district vote for Bill Clinton was 44% in 1996.

CQ Voting Studies

	1997	1998
Presidential	25%	22%
Party	93%	89%
Participation	96%	97%

Interest Groups

	1997	1998
ADA	0%	10%
ACU	100%	92%
AFL-CIO	0%	n/a
CCUS	100%	89%

Elections

	1996	1998
General	62%	u/o
Primary	u/o	u/o

Juanita Millender-McDonald (D–Calif.)
Of Carson • Elected 1996

Born: Sept. 7, 1938, Birmingham, Ala.
Education: U. of Redlands, B.S. 1981; California State U., Los Angeles, M.A. 1988; U. of Southern California, attended.
Occupation: Teacher.
Family: Husband, James McDonald Jr.; five children.
Religion: Baptist.
Political Career: Carson City Council, 1990–92, mayor pro tempore, 1991–92; Calif. Assembly, 1992–96.

Capitol Office: 419 Cannon House Office Building 20515; 225-7924; (fax) 225-7926; (e-mail) millender–mcdonald@mail.house.gov; (web) www.house.gov/millender–mcdonald.
Office Staff: Chief of Staff, Lisa McCalpine; Legis. Dir., Marcus Mason; Press Secy., Heather Brewer; Scheduler, Dianne McNair.
Committees: Small Business (Empowerment — ranking member); Transportation & Infrastructure (Aviation; Ground Transportation).

California 37th — Southern Los Angeles County; Compton; Carson. The district vote for Bill Clinton was 82% in 1996.

CQ Voting Studies

	1997	1998
Presidential	81%	78%
Party	94%	89%
Participation	98%	92%

Interest Groups

	1997	1998
ADA	90%	95%
ACU	12%	4%
AFL-CIO	100%	n/a
CCUS	30%	31%

Elections

	1996	1998
General	85%	85%
Primary	*27%	*61%

*Special election

Dan Miller (R–Fla.)
Of Bradenton • Elected 1992

Born: May 30, 1942, Highland Park, Mich.
Education: U. of Florida, B.S. 1964; Emory U., M.B.A. 1965; Louisiana State U., Ph.D. 1970.
Occupation: Shopping center and restaurant owner; professor.
Family: Wife, Glenda; two children.
Religion: Episcopalian.
Political Career: No previous office.

Capitol Office: 102 Cannon House Office Building 20515; 225-5015; (fax) 226-0828; (e-mail) www.house.gov/writerep; (web) www.house.gov/danmiller.
Office Staff: Chief of Staff, Marty Reiser; Legis. Dir., Danielle Doane; Legis. Correspondent, Martin Baker; Press Secy., Christin Tinsworth; Exec. Asst., Jennifer Gustafson.
Committees: Appropriations (Commerce, Justice, State & Judiciary; Labor, Health & Human Services & Education; Military Construction); Government Reform (Census — chairman; Civil Service).

Florida 13th — Southwest — Sarasota and Manatee counties; Sarasota; Bradenton. The district vote for Bill Clinton was 43% in 1996.

CQ Voting Studies

	1997	1998
Presidential	33%	30%
Party	90%	87%
Participation	99%	97%

Interest Groups

	1997	1998
ADA	20%	10%
ACU	84%	88%
AFL-CIO	25%	n/a
CCUS	100%	76%

Elections

	1996	1998
General	64%	u/o
Primary	u/o	u/o

Gary Miller (R–Calif.)
Of Diamond Bar • Elected 1998

Born: Oct. 16, 1948, Huntsville, Ark.
Education: Mt. San Antonio Community College, attended 1968–70.
Military Career: Army, 1967–68.
Occupation: Real estate developer.
Family: Wife, Cathy; four children.
Religion: Protestant.
Political Career: Diamond Bar City Council, 1989–95, (did not serve 1990–91), mayor, 1993–94; Calif. Assembly, 1995–99.

Capitol Office: 1037 Longworth House Office Building 20515; 225-3201; (fax) 226-6926; (e–mail) www.house.gov/writerep.
Office Staff: Chief of Staff, John Rothrock; District Dir./Press Secy., Bill Blankenship; Legis. Dir., Nelson C. Garcia; Scheduler, Melissa Figge.
Committees: Budget; Science (Energy & Environment; Technology); Transportation & Infrastructure (Aviation; Ground Transportation).

California 41st — Parts of Orange, Los Angeles and San Bernardino counties. The district vote for Bill Clinton was 43% in 1996.

Elections

	1998
General	53%
Primary	*32%

*Open primary

George Miller (D–Calif.)
Of Martinez • Elected 1974

Born: May 17, 1945, Richmond, Calif.
Education: San Francisco State U., B.A. 1968; U. of California, Davis, J.D. 1972.
Occupation: Lawyer; state legislature aide.
Family: Wife, Cynthia; two children.
Religion: Roman Catholic.
Political Career: Democratic nominee for Calif. Senate, 1969.

Capitol Office: 2205 Rayburn House Office Building 20515; 225-2095; (e–mail) george.miller–pub@mail.house.gov; (web) www.house.gov/georgemiller.
Office Staff: Admin. Asst./Press Secy., Daniel Weiss; Legis. Dir., Charles Barone; Personal Secy., Sylvia Arthur.
Committees: Education & Workforce (Early Childhood, Youth & Families; Workforce Protections); Resources — ranking member (Water & Power).

California 7th — Northeastern Bay Area. The district vote for Bill Clinton was 65% in 1996.

CQ Voting Studies

	1997	1998
Presidential	75%	74%
Party	90%	90%
Participation	92%	92%

Interest Groups

	1997	1998
ADA	95%	100%
ACU	4%	8%
AFL-CIO	100%	n/a
CCUS	11%	19%

Elections

	1996	1998
General	72%	77%
Primary	u/o	*76%

*Open primary

David Minge (D–Minn.)
Of Montevideo • Elected 1992
Pronounced: MING-gee (hard G)

Born: Mar. 19, 1942, Clarkfield, Minn.
Education: St. Olaf College, B.A. 1964; U. of Chicago, J.D. 1967.
Occupation: Lawyer; law professor.
Family: Wife, Karen; two children.
Religion: Lutheran.
Political Career: Montevideo School Board, 1989–92.

Capitol Office: 1415 Longworth House Office Building 20515; 225-2331; (fax) 226-0836; (e-mail) www.house.gov/writerep; (web) www.house.gov/minge.
Office Staff: Chief of Staff, Ross Peterson; Legis. Dir., Kimberly J. Overbeck; Press Secy., Jason Kelly; Scheduler, Shelly Zagaros.
Committees: Agriculture (Department Operations, Oversight, Nutrition & Forestry; General Farm Commodities — ranking member); Budget; Joint Economic.

Minnesota 2nd — Southwest — Willmar. The district vote for Bill Clinton was 45% in 1996.

CQ Voting Studies

	1997	1998
Presidential	80%	71%
Party	77%	80%
Participation	99%	99%

Interest Groups

	1997	1998
ADA	70%	85%
ACU	28%	24%
AFL-CIO	75%	n/a
CCUS	70%	56%

Elections

	1996	1998
General	55%	57%
Primary	u/o	u/o

Patsy T. Mink (D–Hawaii)
Of Honolulu • Elected 1990
Also served 1965–77

Born: Dec. 6, 1927, Paia, Maui, Hawaii.
Education: U. of Hawaii, B.A. 1948; U. of Chicago, J.D. 1951.
Occupation: Lawyer.
Family: Husband, John Francis Mink; one child.
Religion: Protestant.
Political Career: Hawaii Territorial House, 1956–58; Hawaii Territorial Senate, 1959; Hawaii Senate, 1962–64; U.S. House, 1965–77; sought Democratic nomination for president, 1972; sought Democratic nomination for U.S. Senate, 1976; State Department official, 1977–78; Honolulu City Council, 1983–87; sought Democratic nomination for governor, 1986; sought Democratic nomination for mayor of Honolulu, 1988.

Capitol Office: 2135 Rayburn House Office Building 20515; 225-4906; (fax) 225-4987; (e-mail) www.house.gov/writerep; (web) www.house.gov/mink.
Office Staff: Office Mgr./Admin. Asst., Helen E. Lewis; Scheduler, Pamela Hayashi.
Committees: Education & Workforce (Early Childhood, Youth & Families; Postsecondary Education, Training & Life-Long Learning); Government Reform (Government Management, Information & Technology; Criminal Justice, Drug Policy & Human Resources — ranking member).

Hawaii 2nd — Suburban and Outer Oahu — "Neighbor Islands". The district vote for Bill Clinton was 57% in 1996.

CQ Voting Studies

	1997	1998
Presidential	72%	83%
Party	93%	93%
Participation	99%	98%

Interest Groups

	1997	1998
ADA	100%	95%
ACU	12%	8%
AFL-CIO	100%	n/a
CCUS	20%	22%

Elections

	1996	1998
General	60%	69%
Primary	60%	90%

Joe Moakley (D–Mass.)
Of South Boston • Elected 1972

Born: Apr. 27, 1927, Boston, Mass.
Education: U. of Miami, attended 1950–51; Suffolk U., J.D. 1956.
Military Career: Navy, 1943–46.
Occupation: Lawyer.
Family: Widowed.
Religion: Roman Catholic.
Political Career: Mass. House, 1953–63; Mass. Senate, 1965–71; sought Democratic nomination for U.S. House, 1970; Boston City Council, 1971–73.

Capitol Office: 235 Cannon House Office Building 20515; 225-8273; (fax) 225-3984; (e-mail) jmoakley@mail.house.gov; (web) www.house.gov/moakley.
Office Staff: Chief of Staff, Kevin Ryan; Legis. Dir., Ellen Williams-Harrington; Press Secy., Karin Walser; Scheduler, Deborah Spriggs.
Committees: Rules — ranking member (Legislative & Budget Process).

Massachusetts 9th — Part of Boston, southern suburbs — Taunton; Braintree; part of Brockton. The district vote for Bill Clinton was 62% in 1996.

CQ Voting Studies

	1997	1998
Presidential	69%	67%
Party	87%	73%
Participation	97%	79%

Interest Groups

	1997	1998
ADA	85%	65%
ACU	8%	13%
AFL-CIO	100%	n/a
CCUS	30%	33%

Elections

	1996	1998
General	72%	u/o
Primary	u/o	u/o

Alan B. Mollohan (D–W.Va.)
Of Fairmont • Elected 1982

Born: May 14, 1943, Fairmont, W.Va.
Education: College of William and Mary, A.B. 1966; West Virginia U., J.D. 1970.
Military Career: Army Reserve, 1970–83.
Occupation: Lawyer.
Family: Wife, Barbara Whiting; five children.
Religion: Baptist.
Political Career: No previous office.

Capitol Office: 2346 Rayburn House Office Building 20515; 225-4172; (fax) 225-7564; (e-mail) www.house.gov/writerep.
Office Staff: Chief of Staff, Liz Hall; Legis. Dir., Sally Gaines; Press Secy., Ron Hudok; Personal Secy., Anne Marie Packo.
Committees: Appropriations (Commerce, Justice, State & Judiciary; District of Columbia; VA, HUD & Independent Agencies — ranking member).

West Virginia 1st — North — Wheeling; Parkersburg; Morgantown. The district vote for Bill Clinton was 49% in 1996.

CQ Voting Studies

	1997	1998
Presidential	55%	63%
Party	69%	70%
Participation	93%	93%

Interest Groups

	1997	1998
ADA	70%	70%
ACU	33%	32%
AFL-CIO	100%	n/a
CCUS	30%	27%

Elections

	1996	1998
General	u/o	85%
Primary	u/o	87%

Dennis Moore (D-Kan.)
Of Lenexa • Elected 1998

Born: Nov. 8, 1945, Anthony, Kan.
Education: Southern Methodist U., attended 1965; U. of Kansas, B.A. 1967; Washburn U., J.D. 1970.
Military Career: Army, 1970.
Occupation: Lawyer.
Family: Wife, Stephene; seven children.
Religion: Protestant.
Political Career: Kan. assistant attorney general, 1971–73; Johnson County district attorney, 1977–89; candidate for Kan. attorney general, 1986.

Capitol Office: 506 Cannon House Office Building 20515; 225-2865; (fax) 225-2807; (e-mail) www.house.gov/writerep.
Office Staff: Chief of Staff, Howard Bauleke; Communications Dir., Chris Esposito; Exec. Asst., Jenny Pechar.
Committees: Banking & Financial Services (Domestic & International Monetary Policy; Financial Institutions & Consumer Credit); Small Business (Empowerment; Regulatory Reform & Paperwork Reduction).

Kansas 3rd — Kansas City region — Overland Park; Lawrence. The district vote for Bill Clinton was 42% in 1996.

Elections

	1998
General	52%
Primary	74%

James P. Moran (D-Va.)
Of Alexandria • Elected 1990

Born: May 16, 1945, Buffalo, N.Y.
Education: College of the Holy Cross, B.A. 1967; City U. of New York, attended 1967–68; U. of Pittsburgh, M.P.A. 1970.
Occupation: Investment broker.
Family: Wife, Mary; four children, one stepchild.
Religion: Roman Catholic.
Political Career: Alexandria City Council, 1979–84, vice mayor, 1982–84; mayor of Alexandria, 1985–90.

Capitol Office: 2239 Rayburn House Office Building 20515; 225-4376; (fax) 225-0017; (e-mail) jim.moran@mail.house.gov; (web) www.house.gov/moran.
Office Staff: Admin. Asst., Paul Reagan; Legis. Dir., Susan Hardesty; Press Secy., Jim McIntyre; Personal Secy./Scheduler, Mary Miller.
Committees: Appropriations (District of Columbia — ranking member; Interior; Defense); Budget.

Virginia 8th — D.C. Suburbs — Part of Fairfax County; Arlington; Alexandria. The district vote for Bill Clinton was 55% in 1996.

CQ Voting Studies

	1997	1998
Presidential	75%	80%
Party	78%	78%
Participation	95%	97%

Interest Groups

	1997	1998
ADA	65%	75%
ACU	13%	8%
AFL-CIO	88%	n/a
CCUS	50%	61%

Elections

	1996	1998
General	66%	67%
Primary	u/o	u/o

Jerry Moran (R–Kan.)
Of Hays • Elected 1996

Born: May 29, 1954, Great Bend, Kan.
Education: U. of Kansas, B.S. 1976, J.D. 1982.
Occupation: Lawyer.
Family: Wife, Robba; two children.
Religion: Protestant.
Political Career: Kansas Senate, 1989–97, vice president, 1993–95; majority leader, 1995–97.

Capitol Office: 1519 Longworth House Office Building 20515; 225-2715; (fax) 225-5124; (e-mail) jerry.moran@mail.house.gov; (web) www.house.gov/moranks01.
Office Staff: Chief of Staff, Tom Hemmer; Legis. Dir., Jon Hixson; Press Secy., Doug McGinn; Scheduler, Becky Banta Kuhn.
Committees: Agriculture (Department Operations, Oversight, Nutrition & Forestry; General Farm Commodities; Risk Management, Research & Specialty Crops); Transportation & Infrastructure (Aviation; Ground Transportation); Veterans' Affairs (Health).

Kansas 1st — Rural West — Salina; Hutchinson; Dodge City. The district vote for Bill Clinton was 28% in 1996.

CQ Voting Studies

	1997	1998
Presidential	27%	29%
Party	95%	90%
Participation	99%	100%

Interest Groups

	1997	1998
ADA	10%	10%
ACU	96%	92%
AFL-CIO	25%	n/a
CCUS	90%	100%

Elections

	1996	1998
General	73%	81%
Primary	76%	u/o

Constance A. Morella (R–Md.)
Of Bethesda • Elected 1986

Born: Feb. 12, 1931, Somerville, Mass.
Education: Boston U., B.A. 1954; American U., M.A. 1967.
Occupation: Professor.
Family: Husband, Anthony C. Morella; nine children.
Religion: Roman Catholic.
Political Career: Candidate for Md. House, 1974; Md. House, 1979–87; sought Republican nomination for U.S. House, 1980.

Capitol Office: 2228 Rayburn House Office Building 20515; 225-5341; (fax) 225-1389; (e-mail) rep.morella@mail.house.gov; (web) www.house.gov/morella.
Office Staff: Chief of Staff, Bill Miller; Legis. Dir., Lisa Boepple; Press Secy., Johnathan Dean; Exec. Asst., Jayne Jordan.
Committees: Government Reform (Civil Service; District of Columbia); Science (Basic Research; Technology — chairman).

Maryland 8th — Montgomery County. The district vote for Bill Clinton was 57% in 1996.

CQ Voting Studies

	1997	1998
Presidential	73%	71%
Party	57%	39%
Participation	97%	98%

Interest Groups

	1997	1998
ADA	65%	65%
ACU	20%	20%
AFL-CIO	38%	n/a
CCUS	90%	56%

Elections

	1996	1998
General	61%	60%
Primary	65%	77%

John P. Murtha (D-Pa.)
Of Johnstown • Elected 1974

Born: June 17, 1932, New Martinsville, W.Va.
Education: U. of Pittsburgh, B.A. 1962.
Military Career: Marine Corps, 1952–55, 1966–67; Marine Corps Reserve, 1967–90.
Occupation: Car wash owner and operator.
Family: Wife, Joyce; three children.
Religion: Roman Catholic.
Political Career: Democratic nominee for U.S. House, 1968; Pa. House, 1969–74.

Capitol Office: 2423 Rayburn House Office Building 20515; 225-2065; (fax) 225-5709; (e–mail) murtha@mail.house.gov; (web) www.house.gov/murtha.
Office Staff: Legis. Dir., Debbie Tekavec; Communications Dir., Brad Clemenson; Exec. Asst., Bill Allen; Schedule Coordinator, Colette Marchesini Pollock.
Committees: Appropriations (Interior; Legislative Branch; Defense — ranking member).

Pennsylvania 12th — Southwest — Johnstown. The district vote for Bill Clinton was 46% in 1996.

CQ Voting Studies

	1997	1998
Presidential	64%	72%
Party	60%	71%
Participation	97%	95%

Interest Groups

	1997	1998
ADA	50%	75%
ACU	32%	21%
AFL-CIO	100%	n/a
CCUS	56%	47%

Elections

	1996	1998
General	70%	68%
Primary	u/o	u/o

Sue Myrick (R-N.C.)
Of Charlotte • Elected 1994

Born: Aug. 1, 1941, Tiffin, Ohio.
Education: Heidelberg College, attended 1959–60.
Occupation: Advertising executive.
Family: Husband, Ed; two children, three stepchildren.
Religion: Evangelical Methodist.
Political Career: Candidate for Charlotte City Council, 1981; Charlotte City Council, 1983–85; sought Republican nomination for mayor of Charlotte, 1984; mayor of Charlotte, 1987–91; sought Republican nomination for U.S. Senate, 1992.

Capitol Office: 230 Cannon House Office Building 20515; 225-1976; (fax) 225-3389; (e–mail) myrick@mail.house.gov; (web) www.house.gov/myrick.
Office Staff: Admin. Asst., Dave Redmond; Legis. Dir., Nina Owcharenko; Press Secy., David Spooner; Scheduler, Dana Graham.
Committees: Rules (Legislative & Budget Process).

North Carolina 9th — Southwest — Gastonia; part of Charlotte. The district vote for Bill Clinton was 37% in 1996.

CQ Voting Studies

	1997	1998
Presidential	24%	18%
Party	94%	92%
Participation	97%	97%

Interest Groups

	1997	1998
ADA	5%	5%
ACU	100%	88%
AFL-CIO	0%	n/a
CCUS	90%	83%

Elections

	1996	1998
General	63%	69%
Primary	u/o	u/o

Jerrold Nadler (D-N.Y.)
Of Manhattan • Elected 1992
Pronounced: NAD-ler

Born: June 13, 1947, Brooklyn, N.Y.
Education: Columbia U., A.B. 1969; Fordham U., J.D. 1978.
Occupation: State legislator; lawyer.
Family: Wife, Joyce L. Miller; one child.
Religion: Jewish.
Political Career: N.Y. Assembly, 1976–92; candidate for Manhattan Borough President, 1985; candidate for New York City Comptroller, 1989.

Capitol Office: 2334 Rayburn House Office Building 20515; 225-5635; (fax) 225-6923; (e-mail) jerrold. nadler@mail.house.gov; (web) www.house.gov/ nadler.
Office Staff: Chief of Staff, Amy Rutkin; Admin. Asst., Brett Heimov; Legis. Dir., John Doty; Press Secy., Joel Finkelstein; Office Mgr./Scheduler, Janice Siegel.
Committees: Judiciary (Commercial & Administrative Law — ranking member; Constitution); Transportation & Infrastructure (Oversight & Investigations; Ground Transportation).

New York 8th — West Side Manhattan; parts of southwest Brooklyn. The district vote for Bill Clinton was 78% in 1996.

CQ Voting Studies

	1997	1998
Presidential	80%	76%
Party	93%	94%
Participation	95%	94%

Interest Groups

	1997	1998
ADA	100%	100%
ACU	4%	8%
AFL-CIO	100%	n/a
CCUS	20%	24%

Elections

	1996	1998
General	82%	86%
Primary	82%	u/o

Grace F. Napolitano (D-Calif.)
Of Norwalk • Elected 1998

Born: Dec. 4, 1936, Brownsville, Texas.
Education: Brownsville H.S., graduated 1954.
Occupation: Regional transportation claims agent.
Family: Husband, Frank; five children.
Religion: Roman Catholic.
Political Career: Norwalk City Council, 1986–92, mayor, 1989–90; Calif. Assembly, 1993–99.

Capitol Office: 1407 Longworth House Office Building 20515; 225-5256; (fax) 225-0027; (e-mail) grace@mail.house.gov.
Office Staff: Chief of Staff, Chuck Fuentes; Legis. Dir., Kate Krause; Press Secy., Michael Torra; Scheduler, Bianca Zinzi.
Committees: Resources (Forests & Forest Health; Water & Power); Small Business (Tax, Finance & Exports).

California 34th — East Los Angeles County suburbs; West Covina. The district vote for Bill Clinton was 64% in 1996.

Elections

	1998
General	68%
Primary	*37%

*Open primary

Richard E. Neal (D–Mass.)
Of Springfield • Elected 1988

Born: Feb. 14, 1949, Worcester, Mass.
Education: American International College, B.A. 1972; U. of Hartford, M.P.A. 1976.
Occupation: Public official; college lecturer.
Family: Wife, Maureen; four children.
Religion: Roman Catholic.
Political Career: Springfield City Council, 1978–84; mayor of Springfield, 1984–89.

Capitol Office: 2236 Rayburn House Office Building 20515; 225-5601; (fax) 225-8112; (e-mail) www.house.gov/writerep; (web) www.house.gov/neal.
Office Staff: Chief of Staff, Ann Jablon; Legis. Dir., Mike Prucker; Press Secy., William Tranghese; Exec. Asst., JoAnn Healy.
Committees: Ways & Means (Oversight; Trade).

Massachusetts 2nd — West Central — Northampton; Springfield; Sturbridge. The district vote for Bill Clinton was 61% in 1996.

CQ Voting Studies

	1997	1998
Presidential	75%	77%
Party	89%	91%
Participation	95%	95%

Interest Groups

	1997	1998
ADA	90%	95%
ACU	25%	12%
AFL-CIO	100%	n/a
CCUS	50%	35%

Elections

	1996	1998
General	72%	u/o
Primary	u/o	u/o

George Nethercutt (R–Wash.)
Of Spokane • Elected 1994

Born: Oct. 7, 1944, Spokane, Wash.
Education: Washington State University, B.A. 1967; Gonzaga U., J.D. 1971.
Occupation: Lawyer; congressional aide.
Family: Wife, Mary Beth; two children.
Religion: Presbyterian.
Political Career: No previous office.

Capitol Office: 1527 Longworth House Office Building 20515; 225-2006; (fax) 225-3392; (e-mail) george.nethercutt–pub@mail.house.gov; (web) www.house.gov/nethercutt.
Office Staff: Chief of Staff, Edward Feddeman; Legis. Dir., Amy Flachbart; Press Secy., Ken Lisaius; Scheduler, Maddie Burns.
Committees: Appropriations (Agriculture, Rural Development, FDA & Related Agencies; Interior; Defense); Science (Space & Aeronautics).

Washington 5th — East — Spokane. The district vote for Bill Clinton was 44% in 1996.

CQ Voting Studies

	1997	1998
Presidential	29%	27%
Party	93%	93%
Participation	98%	98%

Interest Groups

	1997	1998
ADA	5%	0%
ACU	92%	96%
AFL-CIO	13%	n/a
CCUS	100%	89%

Elections

	1996	1998
General	56%	57%
Primary	*51%	*58%

*Open primary

Bob Ney (R-Ohio)
Of St. Clairsville • Elected 1994
Pronounced: NAY

Born: July 5, 1954, Wheeling, W.Va.
Education: Ohio U., attended 1972–74; Ohio State U., B.S. 1976.
Occupation: State health and education program manager; local safety director; educator.
Family: Divorced; two children.
Religion: Roman Catholic.
Political Career: Ohio House, 1981–83; defeated for re-election to Ohio House, 1982; Ohio Senate, 1985–95.

Capitol Office: 1024 Longworth House Office Building 20515; 225-6265; (fax) 225-3394; (e-mail) www.house.gov/writerep; (web) www.house.gov/ney.
Office Staff: Chief of Staff/Press Secy., Neil Volz; Legis. Dir., Maria Robinson; Exec. Asst., Maggie Riith.
Committees: House Administration; Banking & Financial Services (Domestic & International Monetary Policy; General Oversight & Investigations; Housing & Community Opportunity); Transportation & Infrastructure (Ground Transportation; Water Resources & Environment); Joint Printing.

Ohio 18th — East — Steubenville; Zanesville. The district vote for Bill Clinton was 48% in 1996.

CQ Voting Studies

	1997	1998
Presidential	33%	27%
Party	89%	82%
Participation	98%	97%

Interest Groups

	1997	1998
ADA	20%	15%
ACU	71%	80%
AFL-CIO	38%	n/a
CCUS	80%	83%

Elections

	1996	1998
General	50%	60%
Primary	u/o	u/o

Anne M. Northup (R-Ky.)
Of Louisville • Elected 1996

Born: Jan. 22, 1948, Louisville, Ky.
Education: St. Mary's College, B.A. 1970.
Occupation: Teacher.
Family: Husband, Robert Wood Northup; six children.
Religion: Roman Catholic.
Political Career: Ky. House, 1987–96.

Capitol Office: 1004 Longworth House Office Building 20515; 225-5401; (fax) 225-5776; (e-mail) www.house.gov/writerep; (web) www.house.gov/northup.
Office Staff: Chief of Staff, Terry Carmack; Legis. Dir., Kristi Craig; Press Secy., Julie R. Adams; Scheduler, Sharon McBride.
Committees: Appropriations (Labor, Health & Human Services & Education; Treasury, Postal Service & General Government; VA, HUD & Independent Agencies).

Kentucky 3rd — Louisville and suburbs. The district vote for Bill Clinton was 53% in 1996.

CQ Voting Studies

	1997	1998
Presidential	25%	24%
Party	92%	91%
Participation	99%	99%

Interest Groups

	1997	1998
ADA	5%	0%
ACU	88%	88%
AFL-CIO	0%	n/a
CCUS	100%	100%

Elections

	1996	1998
General	50%	52%
Primary	u/o	u/o

Charlie Norwood (R–Ga.)
Of Evans • Elected 1994

Born: July 27, 1941, Valdosta, Ga.
Education: Georgia Southern U., B.S. 1964; Georgetown U., D.D.S. 1967.
Military Career: Army, 1967–69.
Occupation: Dentist.
Family: Wife, Gloria; two children.
Religion: Methodist.
Political Career: No previous office.

Capitol Office: 1707 Longworth House Office Building 20515; 225-4101; (fax) 225-0279; (e-mail) www.house.gov/writerep; (web) www.house.gov/norwood.
Office Staff: Chief of Staff, John S. Walker; Legis. Dir., Christopher Giblin; Press Secy., John Stone; Exec. Asst., Sarah Bass.
Committees: Commerce (Energy & Power; Health & Environment); Education & Workforce (Oversight & Investigations).

Georgia 10th — Northeast — Augusta. The district vote for Bill Clinton was 48% in 1996.

CQ Voting Studies

	1997	1998
Presidential	24%	17%
Party	93%	91%
Participation	97%	93%

Interest Groups

	1997	1998
ADA	0%	5%
ACU	96%	100%
AFL-CIO	0%	n/a
CCUS	90%	83%

Elections

	1996	1998
General	52%	60%
Primary	u/o	u/o

Jim Nussle (R–Iowa)
Of Manchester • Elected 1990

Born: June 27, 1960, Des Moines, Iowa.
Education: Luther College, B.A. 1983; Drake U., J.D. 1985.
Occupation: Lawyer.
Family: Divorced; two children.
Religion: Lutheran.
Political Career: Delaware County attorney, 1986–90.

Capitol Office: 303 Cannon House Office Building 20515; 225-2911; (fax) 225-9129; (e-mail) nussleia@mail.house.gov; (web) www.house.gov/nussle.
Office Staff: Chief of Staff, Rich Meade; Press Secy., Steve Webber; Exec. Asst., Jennifer Eisenbrandt.
Committees: Budget; Ways & Means (Trade).

Iowa 2nd — Northeast — Waterloo; Dubuque. The district vote for Bill Clinton was 53% in 1996.

CQ Voting Studies

	1997	1998
Presidential	28%	27%
Party	92%	89%
Participation	98%	99%

Interest Groups

	1997	1998
ADA	10%	10%
ACU	92%	84%
AFL-CIO	0%	n/a
CCUS	100%	100%

Elections

	1996	1998
General	53%	55%
Primary	u/o	u/o

James L. Oberstar (D–Minn.)
Of Chisholm • Elected 1974

Born: Sept. 10, 1934, Chisholm, Minn.
Education: College of St. Thomas, B.A. 1956; College of Europe (Bruges, Belgium), M.A. 1957.
Occupation: Language teacher; congressional aide.
Family: Wife, Jean; six children.
Religion: Roman Catholic.
Political Career: Sought Democratic nomination for U.S. Senate, 1984.

Capitol Office: 2365 Rayburn House Office Building 20515; 225-6211; (fax) 225-0699; (e-mail) oberstar@mail.house.gov; (web) www.house.gov/oberstar.
Office Staff: Admin. Asst., William G. Richard; Legis. Dir., Chip Gardiner; Communications Dir., Mary Kerr; Office Mgr., Jill Beatty.
Committees: Transportation & Infrastructure — ranking member.

Minnesota 8th — Northeast — Iron Range; Duluth. The district vote for Bill Clinton was 53% in 1996.

CQ Voting Studies

	1997	1998
Presidential	63%	83%
Party	77%	89%
Participation	94%	98%

Interest Groups

	1997	1998
ADA	80%	95%
ACU	17%	13%
AFL-CIO	100%	n/a
CCUS	40%	24%

Elections

	1996	1998
General	67%	66%
Primary	u/o	u/o

David R. Obey (D–Wis.)
Of Wausau • Elected 1969
Pronounced: OH-bee

Born: Oct. 3, 1938, Okmulgee, Okla.
Education: U. of Wisconsin, B.S. 1960, M.A. 1962.
Occupation: Real estate broker.
Family: Wife, Joan; two children.
Religion: Roman Catholic.
Political Career: Wis. Assembly, 1963–69.

Capitol Office: 2314 Rayburn House Office Building 20515; 225-3365; (e-mail) www.house.gov/writerep.
Office Staff: Staff Dir., William Stone; Legis. Dir., Paul G. Carver; Press Secy., Kori Hardin; Exec. Asst./Personal Secy., Carly Burns.
Committees: Appropriations — ranking member (Labor, Health & Human Services & Education — ranking member).

Wisconsin 7th — Northwest — Wausau; Superior; Stevens Point. The district vote for Bill Clinton was 49% in 1996.

CQ Voting Studies

	1997	1998
Presidential	69%	88%
Party	88%	91%
Participation	97%	98%

Interest Groups

	1997	1998
ADA	80%	95%
ACU	21%	16%
AFL-CIO	100%	n/a
CCUS	30%	11%

Elections

	1996	1998
General	57%	61%
Primary	u/o	u/o

John W. Olver (D–Mass.)
Of Amherst • Elected 1991

Born: Sept. 3, 1936, Honesdale, Pa.
Education: Rensselaer Polytechnic Institute, B.S. 1955; Tufts U., M.S. 1956; Massachusetts Institute of Technology, Ph.D. 1961.
Occupation: Professor.
Family: Wife, Rose; one child.
Religion: Unspecified.
Political Career: Mass. House, 1969–73; Mass. Senate, 1973–91.

Capitol Office: 1027 Longworth House Office Building 20515; 225-5335; (fax) 226-1224; (e–mail) john.olver@mail.house.gov; (web) www.house.gov/olver.
Office Staff: Chief of Staff, Jennie Kugel; Legis. Dir., David J. Oliveira; Press Secy./Scheduler, Wendy Frankson.
Committees: Appropriations (Military Construction — ranking member; Transportation).

Massachusetts 1st — West — Berkshire Hills; Fitchburg; Amherst. The district vote for Bill Clinton was 61% in 1996.

CQ Voting Studies

	1997	1998
Presidential	80%	85%
Party	96%	96%
Participation	99%	98%

Interest Groups

	1997	1998
ADA	100%	95%
ACU	4%	0%
AFL-CIO	100%	n/a
CCUS	30%	24%

Elections

	1996	1998
General	53%	72%
Primary	u/o	u/o

Solomon P. Ortiz (D–Texas)
Of Corpus Christi • Elected 1982

Born: June 3, 1937, Robstown, Texas.
Education: Institute of Applied Science, attended 1962; Del Mar College, attended 1965–67.
Military Career: Army, 1960–62.
Occupation: Law enforcement official.
Family: Divorced; two children.
Religion: Methodist.
Political Career: Nueces County constable, 1965–69; Nueces County Commission, 1969–77; Nueces County sheriff, 1977–83.

Capitol Office: 2136 Rayburn House Office Building 20515; 225-7742; (fax) 226-1134; (e–mail) www.house.gov/writerep; (web) www.house.gov/ortiz.
Office Staff: Chief of Staff, Florencio Rendon; Legis. Dir., Marvin E. King; Press Secy., Cathy Travis; Scheduler, Rhiannon Burruss.
Committees: Armed Services (Military Installations & Facilities; Military Readiness — ranking member); Resources (Energy & Mineral Resources; Fisheries Conservation, Wildlife & Oceans).

Texas 27th — Gulf Coast — Corpus Christi; Brownsville. The district vote for Bill Clinton was 57% in 1996.

CQ Voting Studies

	1997	1998
Presidential	55%	66%
Party	61%	72%
Participation	97%	94%

Interest Groups

	1997	1998
ADA	60%	70%
ACU	35%	17%
AFL-CIO	100%	n/a
CCUS	60%	56%

Elections

	1996	1998
General	65%	63%
Primary	70%	u/o

Doug Ose (R–Calif.)
Of Sacramento • Elected 1998
Pronounced: OH-see

Born: June 27, 1955, Sacramento, Calif.
Education: U. of California, Berkeley, B.S. 1977.
Occupation: Real estate developer.
Family: Wife, Lynnda; two children.
Religion: Lutheran.
Political Career: No previous office.

Capitol Office: 1508 Longworth House Office Building 20515; 225-5716; (fax) 226-1298; (web) www.house.gov/ose; (e-mail) doug.ose@mail.house.gov.
Office Staff: Chief of Staff, Marko Mlikotin; Legis. Dir., Mickey Forrest; Press Secy., Peter DeMarco.
Committees: Agriculture (General Farm Commodities; Risk Management, Research & Specialty Crops); Banking & Financial Services (Domestic & International Monetary Policy; Housing & Community Opportunity); Government Reform (Government Management, Information & Technology; Criminal Justice, Drug Policy & Human Resources).

California 3rd — North Central Valley. The district vote for Bill Clinton was 45% in 1996.

Elections

	1998
General	52%
Primary	*30%

*Open primary

Major R. Owens (D–N.Y.)
Of Brooklyn • Elected 1982

Born: June 28, 1936, Memphis, Tenn.
Education: Morehouse College, B.A. 1956; Atlanta U., M.L.S. 1957.
Occupation: Librarian.
Family: Wife, Maria Cuprill; five children.
Religion: Baptist.
Political Career: N.Y. Senate, 1975–83.

Capitol Office: 2305 Rayburn House Office Building 20515; 225-6231; (fax) 226-0112; (e-mail) www.house.gov/writerep; (web) 143.231.11.188/welcome.htm.
Office Staff: Admin. Asst., Jacqueline Ellis; Legis. Dir., Sudafi Henry; Press Secy., Susan Loeb; Exec. Asst., Deborah Aledo-Simpson.
Committees: Education & Workforce (Postsecondary Education, Training & Life-Long Learning; Workforce Protections — ranking member); Government Reform (Government Management, Information & Technology; Postal Service).

New York 11th — Central Brooklyn — Flatbush; Crown Heights; Brownsville. The district vote for Bill Clinton was 90% in 1996.

CQ Voting Studies

	1997	1998
Presidential	75%	83%
Party	93%	95%
Participation	93%	94%

Interest Groups

	1997	1998
ADA	95%	100%
ACU	8%	0%
AFL-CIO	100%	n/a
CCUS	20%	22%

Elections

	1996	1998
General	92%	90%
Primary	u/o	u/o

Michael G. Oxley (R–Ohio)
Of Findlay • Elected 1981

Born: Feb. 11, 1944, Findlay, Ohio.
Education: Miami U. (Oxford, Ohio), B.A. 1966; Ohio State U., J.D. 1969.
Occupation: FBI agent; lawyer.
Family: Wife, Patricia; one child.
Religion: Lutheran.
Political Career: Ohio House, 1973–81.

Capitol Office: 2233 Rayburn House Office Building 20515; 225-2676; (e–mail) mike.oxley@mail.house.gov; (web) www.house.gov/oxley.
Office Staff: Chief of Staff, Jim Conzelman; Legis. Dir., Bob Foster; Press Secy., Peggy Peterson; Office Mgr./Personal Secy., Debi Deimling.
Committees: Commerce (Finance & Hazardous Materials — chairman; Telecommunications, Trade & Consumer Protection).

Ohio 4th — West Central — Mansfield; Lima; Findlay. The district vote for Bill Clinton was 37% in 1996.

CQ Voting Studies

	1997	1998
Presidential	35%	24%
Party	82%	89%
Participation	94%	96%

Interest Groups

	1997	1998
ADA	10%	5%
ACU	68%	96%
AFL-CIO	13%	n/a
CCUS	100%	100%

Elections

	1996	1998
General	65%	64%
Primary	u/o	u/o

Ron Packard (R–Calif.)
Of Oceanside • Elected 1982

Born: Jan. 19, 1931, Meridian, Idaho.
Education: Brigham Young U., attended 1948–50; Portland State U., attended 1952–53; U. of Oregon, D.M.D. 1957.
Military Career: Navy Dental Corps, 1957–59.
Occupation: Dentist.
Family: Wife, Jean; seven children.
Religion: Mormon.
Political Career: Carlsbad School Board, 1962–74; Carlsbad City Council, 1976–78; mayor of Carlsbad, 1978–82.

Capitol Office: 2372 Rayburn House Office Building 20515; 225-3906; (fax) 225-0134; (e–mail) rep.packard@mail.house.gov; (web) www.house.gov/packard.
Office Staff: Chief of Staff/Legis. Dir., Ray Mock; Legis. Dir., Eric Mondero; Communications Dir., Adam Schwartz; Exec. Asst./Scheduler, Eric Joyce.
Committees: Appropriations (Energy & Water Development — chairman; Foreign Operations & Export Financing; Transportation).

California 48th — Part of Orange, San Diego and Riverside counties. The district vote for Bill Clinton was 34% in 1996.

CQ Voting Studies

	1997	1998
Presidential	27%	20%
Party	92%	91%
Participation	99%	97%

Interest Groups

	1997	1998
ADA	5%	5%
ACU	84%	96%
AFL-CIO	0%	n/a
CCUS	100%	100%

Elections

	1996	1998
General	66%	77%
Primary	u/o	*71%

*Open primary

Frank Pallone Jr. (D–N.J.)
Of Long Branch • *Elected 1988*
Pronounced: pa-LOAN

Born: Oct. 30, 1951, Long Branch, N.J.
Education: Middlebury College, B.A. 1973; Tufts U., M.A. 1974; Rutgers U., J.D. 1978.
Occupation: Lawyer.
Family: Wife, Sarah Hospodor; three children.
Religion: Roman Catholic.
Political Career: Long Branch City Council, 1982–88; N.J. Senate, 1984–88.

Capitol Office: 420 Cannon House Office Building 20515; 225-4671; (fax) 225-9665; (e-mail) www.house.gov/writerep.
Office Staff: Admin. Asst., Timothy J. Yehl; Legis. Dir., Steve Guili; Press Secy., Ted Loud; Scheduler, Jeff Carroll.
Committees: Commerce (Energy & Power; Finance & Hazardous Materials; Health & Environment); Resources (Fisheries Conservation, Wildlife & Oceans).

New Jersey 6th — Central — Part of Edison; New Brunswick; Long Branch. The district vote for Bill Clinton was 55% in 1996.

CQ Voting Studies

	1997	1998
Presidential	79%	78%
Party	89%	92%
Participation	97%	99%

Interest Groups

	1997	1998
ADA	95%	100%
ACU	12%	12%
AFL-CIO	100%	n/a
CCUS	30%	28%

Elections

	1996	1998
General	61%	57%
Primary	u/o	u/o

Bill Pascrell Jr. (D–N.J.)
Of Paterson • *Elected 1996*
Pronounced: pas-KRELL

Born: Jan. 25, 1937, Paterson, N.J.
Education: Fordham U., B.A. 1959, M.A. 1961.
Military Career: Army, 1961; Army Reserve, 1962–67.
Occupation: City official; teacher.
Family: Wife, Elsie Marie; three children.
Religion: Roman Catholic.
Political Career: Paterson Board of Education, 1977–81, president, 1981; N.J. Assembly, 1988–97; mayor of Paterson, 1990–97.

Capitol Office: 1722 Longworth House Office Building 20515; 225-5751; (fax) 225-5782; (e-mail) bill.pascrell@mail.house.gov; (web) www.house.gov/pascrell.
Office Staff: Chief of Staff, Ed Farmer; Legis. Dir., David Filippelli; Office Mgr., Margaret Van Tassell.
Committees: Small Business (Regulatory Reform & Paperwork Reduction — ranking member); Transportation & Infrastructure (Ground Transportation; Water Resources & Environment).

New Jersey 8th — North — Paterson. The district vote for Bill Clinton was 58% in 1996.

CQ Voting Studies

	1997	1998
Presidential	68%	70%
Party	79%	85%
Participation	98%	98%

Interest Groups

	1997	1998
ADA	70%	95%
ACU	36%	16%
AFL-CIO	100%	n/a
CCUS	40%	33%

Elections

	1996	1998
General	51%	62%
Primary	u/o	u/o

Ed Pastor (D–Ariz.)
Of Phoenix • Elected 1991
Pronounced: pas-TORE

Born: June 28, 1943, Claypool, Ariz.
Education: Arizona State U., B.A. 1966, J.D. 1974.
Occupation: Teacher; gubernatorial aide; public policy consultant.
Family: Wife, Verma Mendez Pastor; two children.
Religion: Roman Catholic.
Political Career: Maricopa County Board of Supervisors, 1977–91.

Capitol Office: 2465 Rayburn House Office Building 20515; 225-4065; (fax) 225-1655; (e-mail) ed.pastor@mail.house.gov; (web) www.house.gov/pastor.
Office Staff: Admin. Asst./Scheduler, Laura Campos; Legis. Dir., Blake Gable; Press Secy., Maura Saavedra.
Committees: Appropriations (Energy & Water Development; Legislative Branch — ranking member; Transportation); Standards of Official Conduct.

Arizona 2nd — Southwest — Southwestern Tucson; southern Phoenix; Yuma. The district vote for Bill Clinton was 64% in 1996.

CQ Voting Studies

	1997	1998
Presidential	79%	82%
Party	86%	91%
Participation	99%	99%

Interest Groups

	1997	1998
ADA	95%	100%
ACU	8%	4%
AFL-CIO	100%	n/a
CCUS	50%	39%

Elections

	1996	1998
General	65%	68%
Primary	u/o	u/o

Ron Paul (R–Texas)
Of Surfside • Elected 1996
Also served 1976–77, 1979–85

Born: Aug. 20, 1935, Pittsburgh, Pa.
Education: Gettysburg College, B.S. 1957; Duke U., M.D. 1961.
Military Career: Air Force, 1963–65; Air National Guard, 1965–68.
Occupation: Physician.
Family: Wife, Carol Wells; five children.
Religion: Protestant.
Political Career: U.S. House, 1976–77, 1979–85; sought Republican nomination for U.S. Senate, 1984; Libertarian candidate for U.S. President, 1988.

Capitol Office: 203 Cannon House Office Building 20515; 225-2831; (fax) 226-4871; (e-mail) rep.paul@mail.house.gov; (web) www.house.gov/paul.
Office Staff: Chief of Staff, Tom Lizardo; Legis. Dir., Joe Becker; Press Secy., Michael Sullivan; Scheduler, Anamarie Pratt.
Committees: Banking & Financial Services (Capital Markets & Securities; Domestic & International Monetary Policy; General Oversight & Investigations); Education & Workforce (Early Childhood, Youth & Families; Workforce Protections).

Texas 14th — Southeast; Gulf Coast. The district vote for Bill Clinton was 42% in 1996.

CQ Voting Studies

	1997	1998
Presidential	40%	30%
Party	80%	74%
Participation	98%	98%

Interest Groups

	1997	1998
ADA	30%	20%
ACU	80%	88%
AFL-CIO	25%	n/a
CCUS	60%	65%

Elections

	1996	1998
General	51%	55%
Primary	*54%	u/o

*Runoff election

Donald M. Payne (D–N.J.)
Of Newark • Elected 1988

Born: July 16, 1934, Newark, N.J.
Education: Seton Hall U., B.A. 1957.
Occupation: High school teacher; company community affairs director.
Family: Widowed; three children.
Religion: Baptist.
Political Career: Essex County Board of Chosen Freeholders, 1972–78; sought Democratic nomination for Essex County executive, 1978; sought Democratic nomination for U.S. House, 1980; Newark Municipal Council, 1982–88; sought Democratic nomination for U.S. House, 1986.

Capitol Office: 2209 Rayburn House Office Building 20515; 225-3436; (fax) 225-4160; (e–mail) donald.payne@mail.house.gov; (web) www.house.gov/payne.
Office Staff: Admin. Asst./Chief of Staff, Maxine James; Legis. Dir./Press Secy., Kerry B. McKenney; Scheduler, Heather Cooper.
Committees: Education & Workforce (Early Childhood, Youth & Families; Employer-Employee Relations); International Relations (Africa — ranking member).

New Jersey 10th — Parts of Newark and Jersey City. The district vote for Bill Clinton was 82% in 1996.

CQ Voting Studies

	1997	1998
Presidential	72%	82%
Party	87%	88%
Participation	92%	91%

Interest Groups

	1997	1998
ADA	85%	90%
ACU	5%	9%
AFL-CIO	100%	n/a
CCUS	20%	20%

Elections

	1996	1998
General	84%	84%
Primary	82%	92%

Ed Pease (R–Ind.)
Of Terre Haute • Elected 1996

Born: May 22, 1951, Vigo County, Ind.
Education: Indiana U., A.B. 1973, J.D. 1977; Indiana State U., attended 1981–85.
Occupation: College administrator; lawyer.
Family: Single.
Religion: United Methodist.
Political Career: Ind. Senate, 1981–93.

Capitol Office: 119 Cannon House Office Building 20515; 225-5805; (e–mail) www.house.gov/writerep; (web) www.house.gov/pease.
Office Staff: Chief of Staff, Brian Kerns; Legis. Dir., Bill Maxam; Press Secy./District Dir., Brian Kerns; Exec. Asst., David Clark.
Committees: Judiciary (Courts & Intellectual Property; Immigration & Claims); Small Business; Transportation & Infrastructure (Aviation; Ground Transportation).

Indiana 7th — West — Terre Haute; Lafayette. The district vote for Bill Clinton was 35% in 1996.

CQ Voting Studies

	1997	1998
Presidential	28%	23%
Party	93%	91%
Participation	100%	99%

Interest Groups

	1997	1998
ADA	15%	0%
ACU	96%	100%
AFL-CIO	13%	n/a
CCUS	90%	100%

Elections

	1996	1998
General	62%	69%
Primary	30%	83%

Nancy Pelosi (D–Calif.)
Of San Francisco • Elected 1987
Pronounced: pa-LOH-see

Born: Mar. 26, 1940, Baltimore, Md.
Education: Trinity College, A.B. 1962.
Occupation: Public relations consultant.
Family: Husband, Paul Pelosi; five children.
Religion: Roman Catholic.
Political Career: Calif. Democratic Party chairman, 1981–83.

CQ Voting Studies

	1997	1998
Presidential	77%	80%
Party	91%	94%
Participation	93%	94%

Interest Groups

	1997	1998
ADA	100%	95%
ACU	4%	12%
AFL-CIO	100%	n/a
CCUS	20%	33%

Elections

	1996	1998
General	84%	86%
Primary	u/o	*85%

*Open primary

Capitol Office: 2457 Rayburn House Office Building 20515; 225-4965; (fax) 225-8259; (e–mail) sf.nancy@mail.house.gov; (web) www.house.gov/pelosi.
Office Staff: Admin. Asst., Judith Lemons; Legis. Dir., Carolyn Bartholomew; Press Secy., George Papgiannis; Scheduler, Laurel Collins.
Committees: Appropriations (Foreign Operations & Export Financing — ranking member; Labor, Health & Human Services & Education); Select Intelligence (Human Intelligence, Analysis & Counterintelligence).

California 8th — San Francisco. The district vote for Bill Clinton was 74% in 1996.

Collin C. Peterson (D–Minn.)
Of Detroit Lakes • Elected 1990

Born: June 29, 1944, Fargo, N.D.
Education: Moorhead State U., B.A. 1966.
Military Career: Army National Guard, 1963–69.
Occupation: Accountant.
Family: Divorced; three children.
Religion: Lutheran.
Political Career: Minn. Senate, 1977–87; sought Democratic nomination for U.S. House, 1982; Democratic nominee for U.S. House, 1984, 1986; sought Democratic nomination for U.S. House, 1988.

CQ Voting Studies

	1997	1998
Presidential	51%	55%
Party	60%	53%
Participation	99%	99%

Interest Groups

	1997	1998
ADA	65%	60%
ACU	52%	56%
AFL-CIO	88%	n/a
CCUS	70%	56%

Elections

	1996	1998
General	68%	72%
Primary	u/o	u/o

Capitol Office: 2159 Rayburn House Office Building 20515; 225-2165; (fax) 225-1593; (e–mail) tocollin.peterson@mail.house.gov; (web) www.house.gov/collinpeterson.
Office Staff: Admin. Asst./Legis. Dir., Mark Brownell; Press Secy., Allison Myhre; Scheduler, Cherie Slayton.
Committees: Agriculture (Livestock & Horticulture — ranking member); Veterans' Affairs (Health).

Minnesota 7th — Northwest — Moorhead; part of St. Cloud. The district vote for Bill Clinton was 45% in 1996.

John E. Peterson (R-Pa.)
Of Pleasantville • Elected 1996

Born: Dec. 25, 1938, Titusville, Pa.
Education: Titusville H.S., graduated 1956.
Military Career: Army Reserve, 1957–63.
Occupation: Supermarket owner.
Family: Wife, Saundra; one child.
Religion: Methodist.
Political Career: Pleasantville Borough Council, 1969–77; Pa. House, 1977–85; Pa. Senate, 1985–97.

Capitol Office: 307 Cannon House Office Building 20515; 225-5121; (fax) 225-5796; (e-mail) www.house.gov/writerep; (web) www.house.gov/johnpeterson.
Office Staff: Admin. Asst., Bob Ferguson; Legis. Dir., Bob Moran; Press Secy., Jennifer Bennett; Appts. Secy., Wendy Colfer.
Committees: Appropriations (Interior; Legislative Branch; Treasury, Postal Service & General Government); Resources (Forests & Forest Health).

Pennsylvania 5th — Northwest, Central — State College. The district vote for Bill Clinton was 40% in 1996.

CQ Voting Studies

	1997	1998
Presidential	28%	24%
Party	95%	93%
Participation	99%	98%

Interest Groups

	1997	1998
ADA	5%	0%
ACU	96%	96%
AFL-CIO	0%	n/a
CCUS	100%	100%

Elections

	1996	1998
General	60%	85%
Primary	38%	u/o

Tom Petri (R-Wis.)
Of Fond du Lac • Elected 1979
Pronounced: PEE-try

Born: May 28, 1940, Marinette, Wis.
Education: Harvard U., A.B. 1962, J.D. 1965.
Occupation: Lawyer.
Family: Wife, Anne Neal Petri; one child.
Religion: Lutheran.
Political Career: White House aide, 1969–70; Wis. Senate, 1973–79; Republican nominee for U.S. Senate, 1974.

Capitol Office: 2462 Rayburn House Office Building 20515; 225-2476; (fax) 225-2356; (e-mail) tompetri@mail.house.gov; (web) www.house.gov/petri.
Office Staff: Admin. Asst./Legis. Dir., Joseph Flader; Press Secy., Niel Wright; Exec. Asst., John Broehm.
Committees: Education & Workforce (Early Childhood, Youth & Families; Employer-Employee Relations; Postsecondary Education, Training & Life-Long Learning); Transportation & Infrastructure (Aviation; Ground Transportation — chairman).

Wisconsin 6th — Central — Oshkosh; Fond du Lac; Manitowoc. The district vote for Bill Clinton was 45% in 1996.

CQ Voting Studies

	1997	1998
Presidential	29%	30%
Party	83%	85%
Participation	99%	99%

Interest Groups

	1997	1998
ADA	25%	15%
ACU	80%	88%
AFL-CIO	38%	n/a
CCUS	80%	94%

Elections

	1996	1998
General	73%	93%
Primary	u/o	u/o

David D. Phelps (D–Ill.)
Of Eldorado • Elected 1998

Born: Oct. 26, 1947, Eldorado, Ill.
Education: Southern Illinois U., B.S. 1969.
Occupation: Retail business owner; teacher.
Family: Wife, Leslie; four children.
Religion: Baptist.
Political Career: Saline County clerk and recorder, 1980–85; Ill. House, 1985–99.

Capitol Office: 1523 Longworth House Office Building 20515; 225-5201; (fax) 225-1541; (e-mail) www.house.gov/writerep.
Office Staff: Chief of Staff, Robert Griner; Legis. Dir., Kristin Nicholson; Scheduler, Sara Shumard.
Committees: Agriculture (Department Operations, Oversight, Nutrition & Forestry; General Farm Commodities); Small Business (Rural Enterprises).

Illinois 19th — Rural — Southern counties; Decatur. The district vote for Bill Clinton was 47% in 1996.

Elections

	1998
General	58%
Primary	83%

Charles W. "Chip" Pickering Jr.
(R–Miss.)
Of Laurel • Elected 1996

Born: Aug. 10, 1963, Laurel, Miss.
Education: Mississippi College, attended 1981–82; U. of Mississippi, B.A. 1986; Baylor U., M.B.A. 1989.
Occupation: Congressional aide; USDA official.
Family: Wife, Leisha Jane; five children.
Religion: Baptist.
Political Career: No previous office.

Capitol Office: 427 Cannon House Office Building 20515; 225-5031; (fax) 225-5797; (e-mail) c.pickering@mail.house.gov; (web) www.house.gov/pickering.
Office Staff: Chief of Staff, Susan Connell; Legis. Dir., Graham Hill; Press Secy., Quinton Dickerson; Appts. Secy., Marcy Scoggins.
Committees: Commerce (Energy & Power; Health & Environment; Telecommunications, Trade & Consumer Protection).

Mississippi 3rd — East central — Meridian. The district vote for Bill Clinton was 36% in 1996.

CQ Voting Studies

	1997	1998
Presidential	21%	20%
Party	92%	90%
Participation	96%	94%

Interest Groups

	1997	1998
ADA	0%	0%
ACU	92%	100%
AFL-CIO	0%	n/a
CCUS	90%	94%

Elections

	1996	1998
General	61%	85%
Primary	*56%	u/o

*Runoff election

Owen B. Pickett (D–Va.)
Of Virginia Beach • Elected 1986

Born: Aug. 31, 1930, Richmond, Va.
Education: Virginia Polytechnic Institute and State U., B.S. 1952; U. of Richmond, LL.B. 1955.
Occupation: Lawyer; accountant.
Family: Wife, Sybil Catherine Pickett; three children.
Religion: Baptist.
Political Career: Va. House, 1972–86; Va. Democratic Party chairman, 1980–82; Democratic National Committee, 1980–82; withdrew from campaign for Democratic nomination for U.S. Senate, 1982.

Capitol Office: 2133 Rayburn House Office Building 20515; 225-4215; (fax) 225-4218; (e–mail) owen.pickett@mail.house.gov; (web) www.house.gov/pickett.
Office Staff: Admin. Asst./Press Secy., Jeanne Evans; Legis. Dir., Albert A. Oetken; Scheduler, Donna T. Wooten.
Committees: Armed Services (Military Readiness; Military Research & Development — ranking member); Resources (Forests & Forest Health; Water & Power).

Virginia 2nd — Parts of Norfolk and Virginia Beach. The district vote for Bill Clinton was 45% in 1996.

CQ Voting Studies

	1997	1998
Presidential	76%	60%
Party	63%	59%
Participation	97%	98%

Interest Groups

	1997	1998
ADA	65%	55%
ACU	20%	16%
AFL-CIO	75%	n/a
CCUS	80%	78%

Elections

	1996	1998
General	65%	94%
Primary	u/o	u/o

Joseph R. Pitts (R–Pa.)
Of Kennett Square • Elected 1996

Born: Oct. 10, 1939, Lexington, Ky.
Education: Asbury College, A.B. 1961; West Chester U., M.Ed. 1972.
Military Career: Air Force, 1963–69.
Occupation: Nursery owner; teacher.
Family: Wife, Virginia M. Pitts; three children.
Religion: Protestant.
Political Career: Pa. House, 1972–96.

Capitol Office: 504 Cannon House Office Building 20515; 225-2411; (fax) 225-2013; (e–mail) pitts.pa16@mail.house.gov; (web) www.house.gov/pitts.
Office Staff: Chief of Staff, Bill Wichterman; Legis. Dir., Lauren Noise; Press Secy., Tonya Neff; Exec. Asst., Mary Geis.
Committees: Armed Services (Military Personnel; Military Procurement); Budget; Small Business (Empowerment — chairman; Rural Enterprises).

Pennsylvania 16th — Southeast — Lancaster. The district vote for Bill Clinton was 37% in 1996.

CQ Voting Studies

	1997	1998
Presidential	28%	21%
Party	96%	96%
Participation	100%	99%

Interest Groups

	1997	1998
ADA	5%	0%
ACU	96%	96%
AFL-CIO	0%	n/a
CCUS	100%	100%

Elections

	1996	1998
General	59%	71%
Primary	45%	u/o

Richard W. Pombo (R–Calif.)
Of Tracy • Elected 1992
Pronounced: POM-bo

Born: Jan. 8, 1961, Tracy, Calif.
Education: California State Polytechnic U., Pomona, attended 1979–81.
Occupation: Rancher.
Family: Wife, Annette; three children.
Religion: Roman Catholic.
Political Career: Tracy City Council, 1990–93.

Capitol Office: 2411 Rayburn House Office Building 20515; 225-1947; (fax) 226-0861; (e-mail) rpombo@mail.house.gov; (web) www.house.gov/pombo/pombo.htm.
Office Staff: Chief of Staff, Steve Ding; Legis. Dir., Paul Kavinoky; Communications Dir., Mike Hardiman; Scheduler, Amy Taylor.
Committees: Agriculture (Department Operations, Oversight, Nutrition & Forestry; Livestock & Horticulture — chairman); Resources (Fisheries Conservation, Wildlife & Oceans; National Parks & Public Lands; Water & Power).

California 11th — Parts of San Joaquin and Sacramento counties; Stockton; Lodi. The district vote for Bill Clinton was 46% in 1996.

CQ Voting Studies

	1997	1998
Presidential	23%	23%
Party	92%	92%
Participation	95%	99%

Interest Groups

	1997	1998
ADA	0%	10%
ACU	92%	96%
AFL-CIO	0%	n/a
CCUS	60%	89%

Elections

	1996	1998
General	59%	61%
Primary	u/o	*64%

*Open primary

Earl Pomeroy (D–N.D.)
Of Valley City • Elected 1992

Born: Sept. 2, 1952, Valley City, N.D.
Education: U. of North Dakota, B.A. 1974; U. of Durham (England), attended 1975; U. of North Dakota, J.D. 1979.
Occupation: Lawyer.
Family: Wife, Laurie Kirby; two children.
Religion: Presbyterian.
Political Career: N.D. House, 1981–85; N.D. insurance commissioner, 1985–93.

Capitol Office: 1533 Longworth House Office Building 20515; 225-2611; (fax) 226-0893; (e-mail) rep.earl.pomeroy@mail.house.gov.
Office Staff: Chief of Staff, Karen Frederickson; Legis. Dir., Michael Smart; Press Secy., Amy Goffe; Scheduler, Janelle Kempel.
Committees: Agriculture (General Farm Commodities; Risk Management, Research & Specialty Crops); International Relations (Asia & the Pacific; Western Hemisphere).

North Dakota — At large. The district vote for Bill Clinton was 40% in 1996.

CQ Voting Studies

	1997	1998
Presidential	69%	72%
Party	74%	78%
Participation	94%	97%

Interest Groups

	1997	1998
ADA	70%	90%
ACU	38%	21%
AFL-CIO	88%	n/a
CCUS	60%	50%

Elections

	1996	1998
General	55%	56%
Primary	u/o	u/o

John Edward Porter (R–Ill.)
Of Wilmette • Elected 1980

Born: June 1, 1935, Evanston, Ill.
Education: Massachusetts Institute of Technology, attended 1953–54; Northwestern U., B.S., B.A. 1957; U. of Michigan, J.D. 1961.
Military Career: Army Reserve, 1958–64.
Occupation: Lawyer.
Family: Wife, Kathryn Cameron Porter; five children.
Religion: Presbyterian.
Political Career: Republican nominee for Cook County Circuit Court judge, 1970; Ill. House, 1973–79; Republican nominee for U.S. House, 1978.

Capitol Office: 2373 Rayburn House Office Building 20515; 225-4835; (fax) 225-0837; (e-mail) www.house.gov/writerep; (web) www.house.gov/porter.
Office Staff: Admin. Asst., Rob Bradner; Legis. Dir., Julie DeBolt; Press Secy., David Kohn; Scheduler, Lynn Guhse Caperton.
Committees: Appropriations (Foreign Operations & Export Financing; Labor, Health & Human Services & Education — chairman; Military Construction).

Illinois 10th — North and Northwest Chicago suburbs — Waukegan. The district vote for Bill Clinton was 50% in 1996.

CQ Voting Studies

	1997	1998
Presidential	47%	39%
Party	73%	69%
Participation	96%	98%

Interest Groups

	1997	1998
ADA	40%	15%
ACU	46%	46%
AFL-CIO	29%	n/a
CCUS	90%	83%

Elections

	1996	1998
General	69%	u/o
Primary	68%	u/o

Rob Portman (R–Ohio)
Of Cincinnati • Elected 1993

Born: Dec. 19, 1955, Cincinnati, Ohio.
Education: Dartmouth College, B.A. 1979; U. of Michigan, J.D. 1984.
Occupation: Lawyer; White House aide.
Family: Wife, Jane; three children.
Religion: Methodist.
Political Career: White House associate counsel, 1989; White House Legislative Affairs director, 1989–91.

Capitol Office: 238 Cannon House Office Building 20515; 225-3164; (fax) 225-1992; (e-mail) portmail@mail.house.gov; (web) www.house.gov/portman.
Office Staff: Chief of Staff, Bob Schellhas; Legis. Dir., Barbara A. Pate; Communications Dir., Brian R. Besanceney; Scheduler, Melissa Bennett.
Committees: Standards of Official Conduct; Ways & Means (Oversight; Social Security).

Ohio 2nd — Southwest and Eastern Cincinnati and suburbs. The district vote for Bill Clinton was 34% in 1996.

CQ Voting Studies

	1997	1998
Presidential	31%	29%
Party	88%	91%
Participation	97%	98%

Interest Groups

	1997	1998
ADA	20%	5%
ACU	92%	88%
AFL-CIO	0%	n/a
CCUS	90%	78%

Elections

	1996	1998
General	72%	76%
Primary	u/o	u/o

David E. Price (D-N.C.)
Of Chapel Hill • Elected 1986
Did not serve 1995–97

Born: Aug. 17, 1940, Erwin, Tenn.
Education: Mars Hill College, attended 1957–59; U. of North Carolina, B.A. 1961; Yale U., B.D. 1964, Ph.D. 1969.
Occupation: Professor.
Family: Wife, Lisa; two children.
Religion: Baptist.
Political Career: N.C. Democratic Party chairman, 1983–84; U.S. House, 1987–95; Democratic nominee for U.S. House, 1994.

Capitol Office: 2162 Rayburn House Office Building 20515; 225-1784; (fax) 225-2014; (e-mail) david. price@mail.house.gov.
Office Staff: Admin. Asst., Billy Moore; Senior Legis. Asst., Jean-Louise Beard; Communications Dir., Thomas Bates; Exec. Asst., Catherine Clifford.
Committees: Appropriations (Treasury, Postal Service & General Government; VA, HUD & Independent Agencies); Budget.

North Carolina 4th — Central — Durham; Chapel Hill; part of Raleigh. The district vote for Bill Clinton was 51% in 1996.

CQ Voting Studies

	1997	1998
Presidential	73%	77%
Party	84%	86%
Participation	99%	99%

Interest Groups

	1997	1998
ADA	95%	95%
ACU	8%	8%
AFL-CIO	100%	n/a
CCUS	50%	61%

Elections

	1996	1998
General	54%	57%
Primary	u/o	87%

Deborah Pryce (R-Ohio)
Of Dublin • Elected 1992

Born: July 29, 1951, Warren, Ohio.
Education: Ohio State U., B.A. 1973; Capital U., J.D. 1976.
Occupation: Judge; lawyer.
Family: Husband, Randy Walker; one child, one stepchild.
Religion: Presbyterian.
Political Career: Franklin County Municipal Court judge, 1985–92.

Capitol Office: 221 Cannon House Office Building 20515; 225-2015; (fax) 225-3529; (e-mail) pryce@ mail.house.gov; (web) www.house.gov/pryce.
Office Staff: Chief of Staff, Tim Day; Legis. Dir., Will Nordwind; Press Secy., Mindi Boyagian; Exec. Asst., Karla Ganswindt.
Committees: Rules (Legislative & Budget Process).

Ohio 15th — Central — Western Columbus and suburbs. The district vote for Bill Clinton was 44% in 1996.

CQ Voting Studies

	1997	1998
Presidential	40%	26%
Party	86%	70%
Participation	95%	77%

Interest Groups

	1997	1998
ADA	15%	5%
ACU	72%	83%
AFL-CIO	0%	n/a
CCUS	100%	100%

Elections

	1996	1998
General	71%	66%
Primary	86%	u/o

Jack Quinn (R–N.Y.)
Of Hamburg • Elected 1992

Born: Apr. 13, 1951, Buffalo, N.Y.
Education: Siena College, B.A. 1973; State U. of New York, Buffalo, M.Ed. 1973–83.
Occupation: Teacher.
Family: Wife, Mary Beth McAndrews; two children.
Religion: Roman Catholic.
Political Career: Town of Hamburg Council, 1982–84; Hamburg town supervisor, 1985–93.

Capitol Office: 229 Cannon House Office Building 20515; 225-3306; (fax) 226-0347; (e–mail) www.house.gov/writerep; (web) www.house.gov/quinn.
Office Staff: Admin. Asst., Mary Lou Palmer; Legis. Dir., Beth Thompson; Press Secy., Gina Holiday; Scheduler, Libby LeGrice.
Committees: Transportation & Infrastructure (Aviation; Ground Transportation; Water Resources & Environment); Veterans' Affairs (Benefits — chairman).

New York 30th — West — Buffalo. The district vote for Bill Clinton was 57% in 1996.

CQ Voting Studies

	1997	1998
Presidential	36%	30%
Party	80%	74%
Participation	96%	95%

Interest Groups

	1997	1998
ADA	30%	30%
ACU	58%	48%
AFL-CIO	63%	n/a
CCUS	78%	76%

Elections

	1996	1998
General	55%	68%
Primary	u/o	u/o

George P. Radanovich (R–Calif.)
Of Mariposa • Elected 1994
Pronounced: Ruh-DON-o–vitch

Born: June 20, 1955, Mariposa, Calif.
Education: California State Polytechnic U., B.S. 1978.
Occupation: Vintner; bank manager; carpenter.
Family: Wife, Ethie; one child.
Religion: Roman Catholic.
Political Career: Mariposa County Board of Supervisors, 1989–92, chairman, 1991; sought Republican nomination for U.S. House, 1992.

Capitol Office: 123 Cannon House Office Building 20515; 225-4540; (fax) 225-3402; (e–mail) george.radanovich@mail.house.gov; (web) www.house.gov/radanovich.
Office Staff: Chief of Staff/Legis. Dir., John W. McCamman; Exec. Asst., Lisa Ford.
Committees: Budget; International Relations (Africa; International Economic Policy & Trade); Resources (National Parks & Public Lands; Water & Power).

California 19th — Central Valley — Fresno; Madera. The district vote for Bill Clinton was 40% in 1996.

CQ Voting Studies

	1997	1998
Presidential	27%	20%
Party	92%	90%
Participation	96%	93%

Interest Groups

	1997	1998
ADA	0%	0%
ACU	96%	100%
AFL-CIO	0%	n/a
CCUS	80%	94%

Elections

	1996	1998
General	67%	79%
Primary	u/o	*82%

*Open primary

Nick J. Rahall II (D-W.Va.)
Of Beckley • Elected 1976

Born: May 20, 1949, Beckley, W.Va.
Education: Duke U., A.B. 1971; George Washington U., attended 1972.
Occupation: Broadcasting executive; travel agent.
Family: Divorced; three children.
Religion: Presbyterian.
Political Career: No previous office.

Capitol Office: 2307 Rayburn House Office Building 20515; 225-3452; (fax) 225-9061; (e-mail) nrahall@mail.house.gov.
Office Staff: Admin. Asst./Press Secy., Kent Keyser; Legis. Dir., Birdie W. Kyle; Exec. Asst., Mary Sykes.
Committees: Resources (Energy & Mineral Resources; National Parks & Public Lands); Transportation & Infrastructure (Aviation; Ground Transportation — ranking member).

West Virginia 3rd — South — Huntington; Beckley. The district vote for Bill Clinton was 58% in 1996.

CQ Voting Studies

	1997	1998
Presidential	61%	74%
Party	71%	76%
Participation	98%	97%

Interest Groups

	1997	1998
ADA	80%	85%
ACU	21%	24%
AFL-CIO	100%	n/a
CCUS	20%	28%

Elections

	1996	1998
General	u/o	87%
Primary	u/o	82%

Jim Ramstad (R-Minn.)
Of Minnetonka • Elected 1990

Born: May 6, 1946, Jamestown, N.D.
Education: U. of Minnesota, B.A. 1968; George Washington U., J.D. 1973.
Military Career: Army Reserve, 1968–74.
Occupation: Lawyer; professor; congressional and state house aide.
Family: Single.
Religion: Protestant.
Political Career: Minn. Senate, 1981–91.

Capitol Office: 103 Cannon House Office Building 20515; 225-2871; (fax) 225-6351; (e-mail) mn03@mail.house.gov; (web) www.house.gov/ramstad.
Office Staff: Chief of Staff, Dean Peterson; Legis. Dir., Karin Hope; Exec. Asst., Valerie Nelson.
Committees: Ways & Means (Health; Trade).

Minnesota 3rd — Western Twin Cities suburbs — Bloomington; Minnetonka. The district vote for Bill Clinton was 46% in 1996.

CQ Voting Studies

	1997	1998
Presidential	52%	43%
Party	75%	68%
Participation	100%	100%

Interest Groups

	1997	1998
ADA	40%	20%
ACU	64%	60%
AFL-CIO	13%	n/a
CCUS	90%	94%

Elections

	1996	1998
General	70%	72%
Primary	u/o	u/o

Charles B. Rangel (D-N.Y.)
Of Manhattan • Elected 1970

Born: June 11, 1930, New York, N.Y.
Education: New York U., B.S. 1957; St. John's U., LL.B. 1960.
Military Career: Army, 1948–52.
Occupation: Lawyer.
Family: Wife, Alma; two children.
Religion: Roman Catholic.
Political Career: N.Y. Assembly, 1967–71; sought Democratic nomination for N.Y. City Council president, 1969.

Capitol Office: 2354 Rayburn House Office Building 20515; 225-4365; (fax) 225-0816; (e-mail) www.house.gov/writerep; (web) www.house.gov/rangel.
Office Staff: Exec. Asst., Patricia Bradley; Press Secy./Legis. Dir., Emile Milne.
Committees: Ways & Means — ranking member (Trade); Joint Taxation — ranking member.

New York 15th — Northern Manhattan — Harlem; Washington Heights. The district vote for Bill Clinton was 89% in 1996.

CQ Voting Studies

	1997	1998
Presidential	80%	77%
Party	91%	85%
Participation	92%	86%

Interest Groups

	1997	1998
ADA	95%	90%
ACU	16%	9%
AFL-CIO	100%	n/a
CCUS	30%	29%

Elections

	1996	1998
General	91%	93%
Primary	u/o	u/o

Ralph Regula (R–Ohio)
Of Navarre • Elected 1972
Pronounced: REG-you–luh

Born: Dec. 3, 1924, Beach City, Ohio.
Education: Mount Union College, B.A. 1946–48; Ohio State U., LL.B. 1952.
Military Career: Navy, 1944–46.
Occupation: Lawyer; high school teacher; principal.
Family: Wife, Mary; three children.
Religion: Episcopalian.
Political Career: Ohio Board of Education, 1960–64; Ohio House, 1965–67; Ohio Senate, 1967–73.

Capitol Office: 2309 Rayburn House Office Building 20515; 225-3876; (fax) 225-3059; (e-mail) www.house.gov/writerep; (web) www.house.gov/regula.
Office Staff: Chief of Staff/Press Secy., Connie Ann Veillette; Exec. Secy./Scheduler, Sylvia L. Snyder.
Committees: Appropriations (Commerce, Justice, State & Judiciary; Interior — chairman; Transportation).

Ohio 16th — Northeast — Canton. The district vote for Bill Clinton was 43% in 1996.

CQ Voting Studies

	1997	1998
Presidential	39%	28%
Party	86%	86%
Participation	99%	99%

Interest Groups

	1997	1998
ADA	30%	20%
ACU	56%	64%
AFL-CIO	38%	n/a
CCUS	90%	89%

Elections

	1996	1998
General	69%	64%
Primary	84%	84%

Silvestre Reyes (D–Texas)
Of El Paso • Elected 1996
Pronounced: sil-VES-treh RAY-ess (rolled 'R')

Born: Nov. 10, 1944, Canutillo, Texas.
Education: U. of Texas, attended 1964–65; Texas Western College, attended 1965–66; El Paso Community College, A.A. 1977.
Military Career: Army, 1966–68.
Occupation: U.S. Border Patrol agent.
Family: Wife, Carolina Gaytan; three children.
Religion: Roman Catholic.
Political Career: Canutillo School Board, 1968–70.

Capitol Office: 514 Cannon House Office Building 20515; 225-4831; (fax) 225-6015; (e–mail) silvestrereyes@mail.house.gov; (web) www.house.gov/reyes.

Office Staff: Chief of Staff, Enrique L. Gallegos; Legis. Dir., Dian Copelin; Press Secy., Kathleen Martinez; Scheduler, Vicky Mendoza.

Committees: Armed Services (Military Installations & Facilities; Military Research & Development); Veterans' Affairs (Benefits).

Texas 16th — West — El Paso and suburbs. The district vote for Bill Clinton was 63% in 1996.

CQ Voting Studies

	1997	1998
Presidential	69%	73%
Party	77%	81%
Participation	94%	92%

Interest Groups

	1997	1998
ADA	65%	80%
ACU	38%	13%
AFL-CIO	100%	n/a
CCUS	40%	47%

Elections

	1996	1998
General	71%	88%
Primary	*51%	u/o

*Runoff election

Thomas M. Reynolds (R-N.Y.)
Of Springville • Elected 1998

Born: Sept. 3, 1950, Belfonte, Pa.
Education: Springville Griffith Institute, attended; Kent State U., attended.
Military Career: Air National Guard, 1970–76.
Occupation: Real estate and insurance broker; city legislative aide.
Family: Wife, Donna; four children.
Religion: Presbyterian.
Political Career: Concord Town Council, 1974–82; Erie County Legislature, 1982–88, Republican leader, 1987–88; New York Assembly, 1989–99, minority leader, 1995–98.

Capitol Office: 413 Cannon House Office Building 20515; 225-5265; (fax) 225-5265; (e–mail) www.house.gov/writerep.

Office Staff: Chief of Staff, Sally Vistola; Legis. Dir., Sean McLaughlin; Communications Dir., Michael Brady; Scheduler, Melissa Scott.

Committees: Rules (Rules & Organization of the House).

New York 27th — Suburban Buffalo and rural west — Amherst. The district vote for Bill Clinton was 44% in 1996.

Elections

	1998
General	57%
Primary	u/o

Bob Riley (R–Ala.)
Of Ashland • Elected 1996

Born: Oct. 3, 1944, Ashland, Ala.
Education: U. of Alabama, B.A. 1965.
Occupation: Auto dealer; trucking company executive; farmer.
Family: Wife, Patsy; four children.
Religion: Baptist.
Political Career: Ashland City Council, 1972–76; candidate for mayor of Ashland, 1976.

Capitol Office: 322 Cannon House Office Building 20515; 225-3261; (fax) 225-5827; (e–mail) bob.riley@mail.house.gov; (web) www.house.gov/riley.
Office Staff: Chief of Staff, Earl D. Whipple; Legis. Dir., Dan J. Gans; Press Secy., Susan Dryden; Appts. Secy., Debby McBride.
Committees: Agriculture (Livestock & Horticulture; Risk Management, Research & Specialty Crops); Armed Services (Military Readiness; Military Research & Development); Banking & Financial Services (Capital Markets & Securities; Financial Institutions & Consumer Credit).

Alabama 3rd — East — Anniston; Auburn. The district vote for Bill Clinton was 44% in 1996.

CQ Voting Studies

	1997	1998
Presidential	20%	18%
Party	87%	93%
Participation	88%	99%

Interest Groups

	1997	1998
ADA	0%	5%
ACU	95%	100%
AFL-CIO	0%	n/a
CCUS	78%	89%

Elections

	1996	1998
General	51%	58%
Primary	*64%	u/o

*Runoff election

Lynn Rivers (D–Mich.)
Of Ann Arbor • Elected 1994

Born: Dec. 19, 1956, Au Gres, Mich.
Education: U. of Michigan, B.A. 1987; Wayne State U., J.D. 1992.
Occupation: Law clerk.
Family: Husband, Joe; two children.
Religion: Protestant.
Political Career: Ann Arbor Board of Education, 1985–93, vice president, 1986–87, president 1987–91; Mich. House, 1993–95.

Capitol Office: 1724 Longworth House Office Building 20515; 225-6261; (fax) 225-3404; (e–mail) www.house.gov/writerep; (web) www.house.gov/rivers.
Office Staff: Admin. Asst., Gayle Boesky; Exec. Asst., Donna Childers.
Committees: Budget; Science (Basic Research; Technology).

Michigan 13th — Southeast — Ann Arbor; Westland; Ypsilanti. The district vote for Bill Clinton was 57% in 1996.

CQ Voting Studies

	1997	1998
Presidential	83%	76%
Party	89%	89%
Participation	100%	99%

Interest Groups

	1997	1998
ADA	100%	100%
ACU	12%	12%
AFL-CIO	100%	n/a
CCUS	30%	33%

Elections

	1996	1998
General	57%	58%
Primary	u/o	u/o

Ciro D. Rodriguez (D–Texas)
Of San Antonio • Elected 1997

Born: Dec. 9, 1946, Piedras Negras, Mexico.
Education: St. Mary's U., B.A. 1973; Our Lady of the Lake U., M.S.W. 1978.
Occupation: Social worker; social work instructor.
Family: Wife, Carolina Pena; one child.
Religion: Roman Catholic.
Political Career: Harlandale School Board, 1975–87; Texas House, 1987–97.

Capitol Office: 323 Cannon House Office Building 20515; 225-1640; (fax) 225-1641; (e–mail) www.house.gov/writerep.
Office Staff: Chief of Staff, Jeff Mendelsohn; Legis. Dir., Mark Gillman; Press Secy., Diego de la Garza; Exec. Asst., Stephen Hofmann.
Committees: Armed Services (Military Readiness; Military Research & Development); Veterans' Affairs (Health).

Texas 28th — South San Antonio; Zapata. The district vote for Bill Clinton was 62% in 1996.

CQ Voting Studies

	1997	1998
Presidential	74%	78%
Party	87%	88%
Participation	99%	97%

Interest Groups

	1997	1998
ADA	75%	100%
ACU	26%	4%
AFL-CIO	100%	n/a
CCUS	56%	39%

Elections

	1997	1998
General	*†67%	91%
Primary	†46%	76%

*Runoff election
†Special election

Tim Roemer (D–Ind.)
Of South Bend • Elected 1990

Born: Oct. 30, 1956, South Bend, Ind.
Education: U. of California, San Diego, B.A. 1979; U. of Notre Dame, M.A. 1981, Ph.D. 1985.
Occupation: Congressional aide; adjunct professor.
Family: Wife, Sally; three children.
Religion: Roman Catholic.
Political Career: No previous office.

Capitol Office: 2352 Rayburn House Office Building 20515; 225-3915; (fax) 225-6798; (e–mail) tim.roemer@mail.house.gov; (web) www.house.gov/roemer.
Office Staff: Chief of Staff, Mark H. Brown; Legis. Dir., John St. Croix; Press Secy., Chris Mehl; Exec. Asst., Jane Armstrong.
Committees: Education & Workforce (Oversight & Investigations — ranking member; Postsecondary Education, Training & Life-Long Learning); Select Intelligence (Technical & Tactical Intelligence); Science (Space & Aeronautics; Technology).

Indiana 3rd — Northern Tier — South Bend; Elkhart. The district vote for Bill Clinton was 43% in 1996.

CQ Voting Studies

	1997	1998
Presidential	55%	61%
Party	68%	66%
Participation	98%	99%

Interest Groups

	1997	1998
ADA	55%	65%
ACU	32%	44%
AFL-CIO	75%	n/a
CCUS	70%	78%

Elections

	1996	1998
General	58%	58%
Primary	u/o	u/o

James E. Rogan (R–Calif.)
Of Glendale • Elected 1996

Born: Aug. 21, 1957, San Francisco, Calif.
Education: U. of California, Berkeley, B.A. 1979; U. of California, Los Angeles, J.D. 1983.
Occupation: Lawyer.
Family: Wife, Christine; two children.
Religion: Christian.
Political Career: Glendale Municipal Court judge, 1990–94; Calif. Assembly, 1994–97, majority leader, 1996–97.

Capitol Office: 126 Cannon House Office Building 20515; 225-4176; (fax) 225-5828; (e-mail) www.house.gov/writerep; (web) www.house.gov/rogan.
Office Staff: Chief of Staff, Greg Mitchell; Legis. Dir., Dave Joergenson; Press Secy., Jeff L. Solsby; Exec. Asst./Appts. Secy., Leslie Schindel.
Committees: Commerce (Energy & Power; Telecommunications, Trade & Consumer Protection); Judiciary (Courts & Intellectual Property).

California 27th — Northeastern Los Angeles County; Pasadena; Burbank. The district vote for Bill Clinton was 49% in 1996.

CQ Voting Studies

	1997	1998
Presidential	25%	27%
Party	92%	88%
Participation	96%	96%

Interest Groups

	1997	1998
ADA	5%	0%
ACU	92%	100%
AFL-CIO	0%	n/a
CCUS	80%	100%

Elections

	1996	1998
General	50%	51%
Primary	88%	*59%

*Open primary

Harold Rogers (R–Ky.)
Of Somerset • Elected 1980

Born: Dec. 31, 1937, Barrier, Ky.
Education: Western Kentucky U., attended 1956–57; U. of Kentucky, B.A. 1962, LL.B. 1964.
Military Career: National Guard, 1957–64.
Occupation: Lawyer.
Family: Widowed; three children.
Religion: Baptist.
Political Career: Pulaski and Rockcastle counties commonwealth attorney, 1969–79; Republican nominee for lieutenant governor, 1979.

Capitol Office: 2470 Rayburn House Office Building 20515; 225-4601; (fax) 225-0940; (e-mail) www.house.gov/writerep; (web) www.house.gov/rogers.
Office Staff: Admin. Asst., Kevin I. Fromer; Senior Legis. Asst., Will Smith; Communications Dir., Dan DuBray; Office Mgr./Appts. Secy., Julia Casey.
Committees: Appropriations (Commerce, Justice, State & Judiciary — chairman; Energy & Water Development; Transportation).

Kentucky 5th — Southeast — Middlesboro; Pikeville. The district vote for Bill Clinton was 47% in 1996.

CQ Voting Studies

	1997	1998
Presidential	27%	22%
Party	91%	90%
Participation	99%	97%

Interest Groups

	1997	1998
ADA	5%	5%
ACU	80%	92%
AFL-CIO	0%	n/a
CCUS	90%	88%

Elections

	1996	1998
General	u/o	78%
Primary	u/o	u/o

Dana Rohrabacher (R–Calif.)
Of Huntington Beach • Elected 1988
Pronounced: ROAR-ah-BAH-ker

Born: June 21, 1947, Coronado, Calif.
Education: Los Angeles Harbor College, attended 1965–67; California State U., Long Beach, B.A. 1969; U. of Southern California, M.A. 1971.
Occupation: White House speechwriter; journalist.
Family: Wife, Rhonda Carmony.
Religion: Baptist.
Political Career: No previous office.

CQ Voting Studies

	1997	1998
Presidential	20%	26%
Party	92%	90%
Participation	99%	99%

Interest Groups

	1997	1998
ADA	10%	5%
ACU	92%	100%
AFL-CIO	0%	n/a
CCUS	80%	67%

Elections

	1996	1998
General	61%	59%
Primary	u/o	*54%

*Open primary

Capitol Office: 2338 Rayburn House Office Building 20515; 225-2415; (fax) 225-0145; (e-mail) www.house.gov/writerep; (web) www.house.gov/rohrabacher.
Office Staff: Chief of Staff/Legis.Dir., Rick Dykema; Press Secy., Phaedra Baird; Deputy Chief of Staff, Lisa Watson.
Committees: International Relations (Asia & the Pacific; International Economic Policy & Trade); Science (Energy & Environment; Space & Aeronautics — chairman).

California 45th — Coastal Orange County. The district vote for Bill Clinton was 38% in 1996.

Ileana Ros-Lehtinen (R–Fla.)
Of Miami • Elected 1989
Pronounced: il–ee-AH-na ross-LAY-tin–nen

Born: July 15, 1952, Havana, Cuba.
Education: Miami-Dade Community College, A.A. 1972; Florida International U., B.A. 1975, M.S. 1976–86; U. of Miami, attending.
Occupation: Teacher; private school administrator.
Family: Husband, Dexter Lehtinen; two children, two stepchildren.
Religion: Roman Catholic.
Political Career: Fla. House, 1983–87; Fla. Senate, 1987–89.

CQ Voting Studies

	1997	1998
Presidential	32%	27%
Party	84%	76%
Participation	95%	92%

Interest Groups

	1997	1998
ADA	20%	15%
ACU	76%	80%
AFL-CIO	38%	n/a
CCUS	90%	67%

Elections

	1996	1998
General	u/o	u/o
Primary	u/o	u/o

Capitol Office: 2160 Rayburn House Office Building 20515; 225-3931; (fax) 225-5620; (e-mail) www.house.gov/writerep; (web) www.house.gov/ros–lehtinen.
Office Staff: Admin. Asst., Arturo Estopinan; Legis. Dir., Jay O'Callaghan; Press Secy., Juan Cortinas; Scheduler, Lourdes Wydler.
Committees: Government Reform (Criminal Justice, Drug Policy & Human Resources; National Security & Veterans Affairs); International Relations (International Economic Policy & Trade — chairwoman; Western Hemisphere).

Florida 18th — Southeast — Parts of Dade County; part of Miami. The district vote for Bill Clinton was 43% in 1996.

Steven R. Rothman (D-N.J.)
Of Fair Lawn • Elected 1996

Born: Oct. 14, 1952, Englewood, N.J.
Education: Syracuse U., B.A. 1974; Washington U., J.D. 1977.
Occupation: Judge; lawyer.
Family: Divorced; two children.
Religion: Jewish.
Political Career: Mayor of Englewood, 1983–89; Democratic nominee for Bergen County Freeholder, 1989; Bergen County surrogate court judge, 1993–96.

Capitol Office: 1607 Longworth House Office Building 20515; 225-5061; (fax) 225-5851; (e-mail) steven.rothman@mail.house.gov; (web) www.house.gov/rothman.
Office Staff: Admin. Asst., Charles Young; Legis. Dir., Jim Wall; Press Secy., Phil Goldberg; Scheduler, Mary Flanagan.
Committees: International Relations (International Economic Policy & Trade; Western Hemisphere); Judiciary (Crime).

New Jersey 9th — North — Fort Lee; Hackensack. The district vote for Bill Clinton was 60% in 1996.

CQ Voting Studies

	1997	1998
Presidential	77%	80%
Party	87%	84%
Participation	97%	96%

Interest Groups

	1997	1998
ADA	90%	100%
ACU	13%	8%
AFL-CIO	100%	n/a
CCUS	40%	29%

Elections

	1996	1998
General	56%	65%
Primary	79%	u/o

Marge Roukema (R-N.J.)
Of Ridgewood • Elected 1980
Pronounced: ROCK-ah-muh

Born: Sept. 19, 1929, West Orange, N.J.
Education: Montclair State College, B.A. 1951, attended 1951–53; Rutgers U., attended 1975.
Occupation: High school government and history teacher.
Family: Husband, Richard; two children.
Religion: Protestant.
Political Career: Ridgewood Board of Education, 1970–73; Republican nominee for U.S. House, 1978.

Capitol Office: 2469 Rayburn House Office Building 20515; 225-4465; (fax) 225-9048; (e-mail) www.house.gov/writerep; (web) www.house.gov/roukema.
Office Staff: Chief of Staff, Steve Wilson; Press Secy., Craig Shearman; Exec. Asst., Artemis Rentzis.
Committees: Banking & Financial Services (Capital Markets & Securities; Financial Institutions & Consumer Credit — chairwoman); Education & Workforce (Early Childhood, Youth & Families; Employer-Employee Relations).

New Jersey 5th — North and West — Ridgewood. The district vote for Bill Clinton was 43% in 1996.

CQ Voting Studies

	1997	1998
Presidential	55%	34%
Party	67%	74%
Participation	96%	98%

Interest Groups

	1997	1998
ADA	50%	20%
ACU	42%	60%
AFL-CIO	50%	n/a
CCUS	80%	78%

Elections

	1996	1998
General	71%	64%
Primary	75%	53%

Lucille Roybal-Allard (D–Calif.)
Of East Los Angeles • Elected 1992

Born: June 12, 1941, Boyle Heights, Calif.
Education: California State U., Los Angeles, B.A. 1965.
Occupation: Nonprofit worker.
Family: Husband, Edward Allard; two children, two stepchildren.
Religion: Roman Catholic.
Political Career: Calif. Assembly, 1987–93.

Capitol Office: 2435 Rayburn House Office Building 20515; 225-1766; (fax) 226-0350; (e–mail) www.house.gov/writerep; (web) www.house.gov/roybal–allard.
Office Staff: Chief of Staff, Georgina Verdugo; Legis. Dir., Kate Emanuel; Communications Dir., Loretta Gutierrez Nestor; Exec. Asst., Christine Ochoa.
Committees: Appropriations (Commerce, Justice, State & Judiciary; Treasury, Postal Service & General Government); China Investigation.

California 33rd — East-Central Los Angeles. The district vote for Bill Clinton was 80% in 1996.

CQ Voting Studies

	1997	1998
Presidential	83%	80%
Party	98%	91%
Participation	99%	93%

Interest Groups

	1997	1998
ADA	100%	100%
ACU	8%	0%
AFL-CIO	100%	n/a
CCUS	30%	29%

Elections

	1996	1998
General	82%	87%
Primary	u/o	*86%

*Open primary

Ed Royce (R–Calif.)
Of Fullerton • Elected 1992

Born: Oct. 12, 1951, Los Angeles, Calif.
Education: California State U., Fullerton, B.A. 1977.
Occupation: Tax manager.
Family: Wife, Marie.
Religion: Roman Catholic.
Political Career: Calif. Senate, 1983–93.

Capitol Office: 1133 Longworth House Office Building 20515; 225-4111; (fax) 226-0335; (e–mail) www.house.gov/writerep; (web) www.house.gov/royce.
Office Staff: Chief of Staff/Scheduler, Joan Bates Korich; Legis. Dir., Tom Sheehy; Communications Dir., Bryan Wilkes.
Committees: Banking & Financial Services (Capital Markets & Securities; Financial Institutions & Consumer Credit); International Relations (Africa — chairman; Asia & the Pacific).

California 39th — Parts of Orange and Los Angeles counties — Fullerton. The district vote for Bill Clinton was 41% in 1996.

CQ Voting Studies

	1997	1998
Presidential	24%	20%
Party	90%	83%
Participation	98%	92%

Interest Groups

	1997	1998
ADA	10%	5%
ACU	100%	100%
AFL-CIO	0%	n/a
CCUS	80%	71%

Elections

	1996	1998
General	63%	63%
Primary	u/o	*67%

*Open primary

Bobby L. Rush (D–Ill.)
Of Chicago • Elected 1992

Born: Nov. 23, 1946, Albany, Ga.
Education: Roosevelt U., B.A. 1973; U. of Illinois, Chicago, attended 1975–77, M.A. 1994; McCormick Seminary, M.A. 1998.
Military Career: Army, 1963–68.
Occupation: Insurance broker; political aide.
Family: Wife, Carolyn; five children.
Religion: Protestant.
Political Career: Candidate for Chicago City Council, 1975; sought Democratic nomination for Ill. House, 1978; Chicago City Council, 1983–93; candidate for Chicago mayor, 1999.

Capitol Office: 2416 Rayburn House Office Building 20515; 225-4372; (fax) 226-0333; (e-mail) bobby.rush@mail.house.gov; (web) www.house.gov/rush.
Office Staff: Legis. Dir., Carol Richardson; Press Secy., Robyn Wheeler; Scheduler/Exec. Asst., Lenette Myers.
Committees: Commerce (Energy & Power; Finance & Hazardous Materials; Telecommunications, Trade & Consumer Protection).

Illinois 1st — Chicago — South and southwest sides. The district vote for Bill Clinton was 85% in 1996.

CQ Voting Studies

	1997	1998
Presidential	76%	79%
Party	90%	93%
Participation	94%	93%

Interest Groups

	1997	1998
ADA	100%	95%
ACU	4%	8%
AFL-CIO	100%	n/a
CCUS	40%	33%

Elections

	1996	1998
General	86%	87%
Primary	89%	89%

Paul D. Ryan (R–Wis.)
Of Janesville • Elected 1998

Born: Jan. 29, 1970, Janesville, Wis.
Education: Miami U. (Ohio), B.A. 1992.
Occupation: Congressional aide; economic policy analyst.
Family: Single.
Religion: Roman Catholic.
Political Career: No previous office.

Capitol Office: 1217 Longworth House Office Building 20515; 225-3031; (fax) 225-3393; (e-mail) www.house.gov/writerep.
Office Staff: Chief of Staff, John Murray; Legis. Dir., Joyce Yamat Meyer; Press Secy., Doug McGinn; Scheduler, Janet Pike.
Committees: Banking & Financial Services (Capital Markets & Securities; Domestic & International Monetary Policy); Budget; Government Reform (Census; Government Management, Information & Technology; National Economic Growth).

Wisconsin 1st — Southeast — Racine; Kenosha. The district vote for Bill Clinton was 50% in 1996.

Elections

	1998
General	57%
Primary	81%

Jim Ryun (R–Kan.)
Of Jefferson County • Elected 1996

Born: Apr. 29, 1947, Wichita, Kan.
Education: U. of Kansas, B.A. 1970.
Occupation: Motivational speaker; author; product consultant; Olympic athlete.
Family: Wife, Anne; four children.
Religion: Presbyterian.
Political Career: No previous office.

Capitol Office: 330 Cannon House Office Building 20515; 225-6601; (fax) 225-7986; (e–mail) www.house.gov/writerep; (web) www.house.gov/ryun.
Office Staff: Admin. Asst., Daniel Schneider; Legis. Dir., Mark Kelly; Press Secy., Jay Rinehart; Scheduler, Erin Donovan.
Committees: Armed Services (Military Personnel; Military Procurement); Banking & Financial Services (Domestic & International Monetary Policy; Financial Institutions & Consumer Credit); Budget.

Kansas 2nd — East — Topeka; Leavenworth; Pittsburg. The district vote for Bill Clinton was 39% in 1996.

CQ Voting Studies

	1997	1998
Presidential	24%	21%
Party	96%	94%
Participation	99%	98%

Interest Groups

	1997	1998
ADA	5%	0%
ACU	100%	100%
AFL-CIO	0%	n/a
CCUS	100%	100%

Elections

	1996	1998
General	52%	61%
Primary	62%	78%

Martin Olav Sabo (D–Minn.)
Of Minneapolis • Elected 1978

Born: Feb. 28, 1938, Crosby, N.D.
Education: Augsburg College, B.A. 1959; U. of Minnesota, attended 1960.
Occupation: Public official.
Family: Wife, Sylvia Ann Lee; two children.
Religion: Lutheran.
Political Career: Minn. House, 1961–79, minority leader, 1969–73, speaker, 1973–79.

Capitol Office: 2336 Rayburn House Office Building 20515; 225-4755; (fax) 225-4886; (e–mail) martin.sabo@mail.house.gov; (web) www.house.gov/sabo.
Office Staff: Chief of Staff, Michael Erlandson; Legis. Dir., Marjorie Duske; Press Secy., Bethany Young; Scheduler, Bonnie Gottwald.
Committees: Appropriations (Foreign Operations & Export Financing; Defense; Transportation — ranking member); Standards of Official Conduct.

Minnesota 5th — Minneapolis and suburbs. The district vote for Bill Clinton was 64% in 1996.

CQ Voting Studies

	1997	1998
Presidential	87%	88%
Party	92%	89%
Participation	99%	98%

Interest Groups

	1997	1998
ADA	100%	90%
ACU	4%	0%
AFL-CIO	100%	n/a
CCUS	30%	24%

Elections

	1996	1998
General	64%	67%
Primary	u/o	u/o

Matt Salmon (R–Ariz.)
Of Mesa • Elected 1994

Born: Jan. 21, 1958, Salt Lake City, Utah.
Education: Arizona State U., B.A. 1981; Brigham Young U., M.A. 1986.
Occupation: Communications company executive.
Family: Wife, Nancy; four children.
Religion: Mormon.
Political Career: Ariz. Senate, 1991–95.

Capitol Office: 115 Cannon House Office Building 20515; 225-2635; (fax) 225-3405; (e–mail) msalmon@mail.house.gov; (web) www.house.gov/salmon.
Office Staff: Chief of Staff, Michael Paranzino; Legis. Dir., Glenn Hamer; Press Secy., Heather Mirjahangir; Scheduler, Julia Koppius.
Committees: Education & Workforce (Early Childhood, Youth & Families; Employer-Employee Relations); International Relations (Asia & the Pacific; International Operations & Human Rights).

Arizona 1st — Southeastern Phoenix — Tempe; Mesa. The district vote for Bill Clinton was 46% in 1996.

CQ Voting Studies

	1997	1998
Presidential	24%	26%
Party	93%	93%
Participation	98%	97%

Interest Groups

	1997	1998
ADA	10%	5%
ACU	100%	96%
AFL-CIO	13%	n/a
CCUS	70%	83%

Elections

	1996	1998
General	60%	65%
Primary	u/o	u/o

Loretta Sanchez (D–Calif.)
Of Anaheim • Elected 1996

Born: Jan. 7, 1960, Lynwood, Calif.
Education: Chapman U., B.S. 1982; American U., M.B.A. 1984.
Occupation: Financial adviser; strategic management associate.
Family: Husband, Stephen Simmons Brixey III.
Religion: Roman Catholic.
Political Career: Candidate for Anaheim City Council, 1994.

Capitol Office: 1529 Longworth House Office Building 20515; 225-2965; (e–mail) loretta@mail.house.gov; (web) www.house.gov/sanchez.
Office Staff: Chief of Staff, Lee Godown; Legis. Dir., Laura Rodriguez; Press Secy., Sarah Anderson; Scheduler, Shane Skinner.
Committees: Armed Services (Military Personnel; Military Research & Development); Education & Workforce (Early Childhood, Youth & Families; Workforce Protections).

California 46th — Part of Orange County; Santa Ana; Garden Grove. The district vote for Bill Clinton was 49% in 1996.

CQ Voting Studies

	1997	1998
Presidential	68%	71%
Party	78%	86%
Participation	95%	95%

Interest Groups

	1997	1998
ADA	65%	95%
ACU	28%	8%
AFL-CIO	75%	n/a
CCUS	60%	44%

Elections

	1996	1998
General	47%	56%
Primary	35%	*45%

*Open primary

Bernard Sanders (I-Vt.)
Of Burlington • Elected 1990

Born: Sept. 8, 1941, Brooklyn, N.Y.
Education: U. of Chicago, B.A. 1964.
Occupation: Professor; free–lance writer; documentary filmmaker.
Family: Wife, Jane O'Meara Sanders; one child, three stepchildren.
Religion: Jewish.
Political Career: Mayor of Burlington, 1981–89; independent candidate for U.S. Senate, 1972; independent candidate for governor, 1972; independent candidate for U.S. Senate, 1974; independent candidate for governor, 1976, 1986; independent candidate for U.S. House, 1988.

Capitol Office: 2202 Rayburn House Office Building 20515; 225-4115; (fax) 225-6790; (e–mail) bernie@mail.house.gov; (web) www.house.gov/bernie.
Office Staff: Chief of Staff/Legis. Dir., Eric Edwards; Admin. Asst./Scheduler, Ruthan Wirman.
Committees: Banking & Financial Services (Domestic & International Monetary Policy; General Oversight & Investigations — ranking member); Government Reform (National Economic Growth; National Security & Veterans Affairs).

Vermont — At large. The district vote for Bill Clinton was 53% in 1996.

CQ Voting Studies

	1997	1998
Presidential	73%	83%
Party	92%	94%
Participation	96%	98%

Interest Groups

	1997	1998
ADA	100%	100%
ACU	12%	8%
AFL-CIO	100%	n/a
CCUS	20%	18%

Elections

	1996	1998
General	55%	63%
Primary	u/o	u/o

Max Sandlin (D-Texas)
Of Marshall • Elected 1996

Born: Sept. 29, 1952, Texarkana, Texas.
Education: Baylor U., B.A. 1975, J.D. 1978.
Occupation: Lawyer; county judge; fuel company executive.
Family: Wife, Leslie Howell; four children.
Religion: Baptist.
Political Career: Harrison County Democratic party chairman, 1984–86; Harrison County judge, 1986–89; Harrison County Court at Law judge, 1989–96.

Capitol Office: 214 Cannon House Office Building 20515; 225-3035; (fax) 225-5866; (e–mail) www.house.gov/writerep; (web) www.house.gov/sandlin.
Office Staff: Chief of Staff, Paul Rogers; Legis. Dir./Press Secy., Rosemary Addy; Exec. Asst., Danielle Allen.
Committees: Banking & Financial Services (Capital Markets & Securities; Financial Institutions & Consumer Credit); Transportation & Infrastructure (Aviation; Ground Transportation).

Texas 1st — Northeast — Texarkana; Marshall. The district vote for Bill Clinton was 45% in 1996.

CQ Voting Studies

	1997	1998
Presidential	67%	61%
Party	74%	70%
Participation	99%	97%

Interest Groups

	1997	1998
ADA	60%	80%
ACU	36%	40%
AFL-CIO	88%	n/a
CCUS	70%	61%

Elections

	1996	1998
General	52%	59%
Primary	*56%	u/o

*Runoff election

Mark Sanford (R–S.C.)
Of Sullivan's Island • Elected 1994

Born: May 28, 1960, Fort Lauderdale, Fla.
Education: Furman U., B.A. 1983; U. of Virginia, M.B.A. 1988.
Occupation: Real estate investor; investment banker.
Family: Wife, Jennifer; three children.
Religion: Episcopalian.
Political Career: No previous office.

Capitol Office: 1233 Longworth House Office Building 20515; 225-3176; (fax) 225-3407; (e–mail) sanford@mail.house.gov; (web) www.house.gov/sanford.
Office Staff: Legis. Dir., Scott English; Press Secy., Khris Bershers; Exec. Asst./Appts. Secy., Jessica Gonzales.
Committees: Government Reform (National Security & Veterans Affairs; Postal Service); International Relations (Asia & the Pacific; Western Hemisphere); Science (Space & Aeronautics); Joint Economic.

South Carolina 1st — East — Part of Charleston; Myrtle Beach. The district vote for Bill Clinton was 37% in 1996.

CQ Voting Studies

	1997	1998
Presidential	24%	33%
Party	87%	76%
Participation	98%	98%

Interest Groups

	1997	1998
ADA	20%	20%
ACU	88%	72%
AFL-CIO	0%	n/a
CCUS	60%	71%

Elections

	1996	1998
General	96%	91%
Primary	u/o	u/o

Tom Sawyer (D–Ohio)
Of Akron • Elected 1986

Born: Aug. 15, 1945, Akron, Ohio.
Education: U. of Akron, B.A. 1968, M.A. 1970.
Occupation: Teacher.
Family: Wife, Joyce Handler; one child.
Religion: Presbyterian.
Political Career: Ohio House, 1977–83; mayor of Akron, 1984–86.

Capitol Office: 1414 Longworth House Office Building 20515; 225-5231; (fax) 225-5278; (e–mail) www.house.gov/writerep.
Office Staff: Chief of Staff, Mary Anne Walsh; Press Secy., Betsy Cuthbertson; Exec. Asst., Dianne Tomasek.
Committees: Commerce (Energy & Power; Telecommunications, Trade & Consumer Protection).

Ohio 14th — Northeast — Akron. The district vote for Bill Clinton was 53% in 1996.

CQ Voting Studies

	1997	1998
Presidential	87%	88%
Party	94%	93%
Participation	99%	98%

Interest Groups

	1997	1998
ADA	95%	95%
ACU	8%	0%
AFL-CIO	100%	n/a
CCUS	50%	44%

Elections

	1996	1998
General	54%	63%
Primary	80%	u/o

H. James Saxton (R–N.J.)
Of Mount Holly • Elected 1984

Born: Jan. 22, 1943, Nicholson, Pa.
Education: East Stroudsburg State College, B.A. 1965; Temple U., attended 1967–68.
Occupation: Real estate broker; elementary school teacher.
Family: Divorced; two children.
Religion: Methodist.
Political Career: N.J. Assembly, 1976–82; N.J. Senate, 1982–84.

Capitol Office: 339 Cannon House Office Building 20515; 225-4765; (fax) 225-0778; (e–mail) www.house.gov/writerep; (web) www.house.gov/saxton.
Office Staff: Chief of Staff., Mark O'Connell; Legis. Dir., Mark O'Connell; Press Secy., Jeff Sagnip Hollendonner; Scheduler, Holly Price.
Committees: Armed Services (Military Installations & Facilities; Military Procurement); Resources (Fisheries Conservation, Wildlife & Oceans — chairman); Joint Economic.

New Jersey 3rd — South central — Cherry Hill. The district vote for Bill Clinton was 50% in 1996.

CQ Voting Studies

	1997	1998
Presidential	35%	30%
Party	84%	79%
Participation	98%	98%

Interest Groups

	1997	1998
ADA	30%	25%
ACU	68%	63%
AFL-CIO	38%	n/a
CCUS	80%	81%

Elections

	1996	1998
General	64%	62%
Primary	u/o	u/o

Joe Scarborough (R–Fla.)
Of Pensacola • Elected 1994
Pronounced: SCAR-burro

Born: Apr. 9, 1963, Doraville, Ga.
Education: U. of Alabama, B.A. 1985; U. of Florida, J.D. 1990.
Occupation: Lawyer.
Family: Wife, Melanie Hinton; two children.
Religion: Baptist.
Political Career: No previous office.

Capitol Office: 127 Cannon House Office Building 20515; 225-4136; (fax) 225-3414; (e–mail) www.house.gov/writerep; (web) www.house.gov/scarborough.
Office Staff: Chief of Staff, Bart Roper; Legis. Dir./Press Secy., David Stafford; Scheduler, Jennifer LaTorre.
Committees: Armed Services (Military Installations & Facilities; Military Research & Development); Government Reform (Civil Service — chairman; District of Columbia); Judiciary (Commercial & Administrative Law; Immigration & Claims).

Florida 1st — Panhandle — Pensacola; Fort Walton Beach. The district vote for Bill Clinton was 31% in 1996.

CQ Voting Studies

	1997	1998
Presidential	23%	24%
Party	87%	85%
Participation	93%	92%

Interest Groups

	1997	1998
ADA	10%	10%
ACU	100%	96%
AFL-CIO	0%	n/a
CCUS	70%	78%

Elections

	1996	1998
General	73%	u/o
Primary	u/o	u/o

Bob Schaffer (R–Colo.)
Of Fort Collins • Elected 1996
Pronounced: SHAY-fer

Born: July 24, 1962, Cincinnati, Ohio.
Education: U. of Dayton, B.A. 1984.
Occupation: Property manager; marketing executive; congressional aide.
Family: Wife, Maureen; four children.
Religion: Roman Catholic.
Political Career: Colo. Senate, 1987–97; Republican nominee for lieutenant governor, 1994.

Capitol Office: 212 Cannon House Office Building 20515; 225-4676; (fax) 225-5870; (e-mail) rep.schaffer@mail.house.gov; (web) www.house.gov/schaffer.
Office Staff: Chief of Staff, Susan M. Wadhams; Communications Dir., Adrian Plesha; Exec. Asst./Scheduler, Brandi Graham.
Committees: Agriculture (Livestock & Horticulture); Education & Workforce (Early Childhood, Youth & Families; Oversight & Investigations); Resources (Energy & Mineral Resources; Forests & Forest Health).

Colorado 4th — North and east — Fort Collins; Greeley. The district vote for Bill Clinton was 41% in 1996.

CQ Voting Studies

	1997	1998
Presidential	28%	18%
Party	93%	89%
Participation	99%	100%

Interest Groups

	1997	1998
ADA	5%	5%
ACU	96%	100%
AFL-CIO	0%	n/a
CCUS	90%	78%

Elections

	1996	1998
General	56%	59%
Primary	40%	u/o

Jan Schakowsky (D–Ill.)
Of Evanston • Elected 1998
Pronounced: shuh-COW-ski

Born: May 26, 1944, Chicago, Ill.
Education: U. of Illinois, B.S. 1965.
Occupation: Senior citizens group director; consumer advocate; teacher.
Family: Husband, Robert Creamer; three children.
Religion: Jewish.
Political Career: Candidate for Cook County Board, 1986; Ill. House, 1991–99, floor leader, 1994–99.

Capitol Office: 515 Cannon House Office Building 20515; 225-2111; (fax) 226-6890; (e-mail) www.house.gov/writerep.
Office Staff: Chief of Staff, Cathy Hurwit.
Committees: Banking & Financial Services (Domestic & International Monetary Policy; Housing & Community Opportunity); Government Reform (National Security & Veterans Affairs).

Illinois 9th — Chicago — North Side Lakefront and suburbs; Evanston. The district vote for Bill Clinton was 69% in 1996.

Elections

	1998
General	75%
Primary	45%

Robert C. Scott (D–Va.)
Of Newport News • Elected 1992

Born: Apr. 30, 1947, Washington, D.C.
Education: Harvard U., A.B. 1969; Boston College, J.D. 1973.
Military Career: Army Reserve, 1970–74; National Guard, 1974–76.
Occupation: Lawyer.
Family: Divorced.
Religion: Episcopalian.
Political Career: Va. House, 1979–83; Va. Senate, 1983–93; Democratic nominee for U.S. House, 1986.

Capitol Office: 2464 Rayburn House Office Building 20515; 225-8351; (fax) 225-8354; (e-mail) www.house.gov/writerep; (web) www.house.gov/scott.
Office Staff: Chief of Staff, Joni Ivey; Senior Counsel, Vacant; Communications Dir./Scheduler, Larry Dillard.
Committees: Education & Workforce (Early Childhood, Youth & Families; Oversight & Investigations); Judiciary (Crime — ranking member); China Investigation.

Virginia 3rd — Southeast — Parts of Richmond and Tidewater area. The district vote for Bill Clinton was 65% in 1996.

CQ Voting Studies

	1997	1998
Presidential	72%	89%
Party	87%	91%
Participation	98%	100%

Interest Groups

	1997	1998
ADA	90%	95%
ACU	8%	20%
AFL-CIO	100%	n/a
CCUS	40%	28%

Elections

	1996	1998
General	82%	76%
Primary	u/o	u/o

F. James Sensenbrenner Jr.
(R–Wis.)
Of Menomonee Falls • Elected 1978

Born: June 14, 1943, Chicago, Ill.
Education: Stanford U., A.B. 1965; U. of Wisconsin, J.D. 1968.
Occupation: Lawyer.
Family: Wife, Cheryl Warren; two children.
Religion: Episcopalian.
Political Career: Wis. Assembly, 1969–75; Wis. Senate, 1975–79.

Capitol Office: 2332 Rayburn House Office Building 20515; 225-5101; (fax) 225-3190; (e-mail) sensen09@mail.house.gov; (web) www.house.gov/sensenbrenner.
Office Staff: Admin. Asst., Phil Kiko; Legis. Dir., Krista Stark; Press Secy., Gina Carty; Office Mgr./Scheduler, Arlene Davis.
Committees: Judiciary (Courts & Intellectual Property); Science — chairman.

Wisconsin 9th — Milwaukee Suburbs; Part of Waukesha County; Sheboygan. The district vote for Bill Clinton was 37% in 1996.

CQ Voting Studies

	1997	1998
Presidential	32%	22%
Party	85%	84%
Participation	98%	99%

Interest Groups

	1997	1998
ADA	20%	5%
ACU	88%	92%
AFL-CIO	13%	n/a
CCUS	80%	78%

Elections

	1996	1998
General	74%	91%
Primary	u/o	u/o

Jose E. Serrano (D–N.Y.)
Of Bronx • Elected 1990
Pronounced: ho-ZAY sa-RAH-no (rolled 'R')

Born: Oct. 24, 1943, Mayaguez, P.R.
Education: Dodge Vocational H.S., graduated 1961; Lehman College, attended 1961.
Military Career: Army Medical Corps, 1964–66.
Occupation: Public official.
Family: Wife, Mary Staucet; five children.
Religion: Roman Catholic.
Political Career: N.Y. Assembly, 1975–90; sought Democratic nomination for Bronx borough president, 1985.

Capitol Office: 2342 Rayburn House Office Building 20515; 225-4361; (fax) 225-6001; (e–mail) serrano@mail.house.gov; (web) www.house.gov/serrano.
Office Staff: Chief of Staff/Counsel, Ellyn M. Toscano; Admin. Asst./Legis. Dir., Lucy Hand; Press Secy., Ingrid Ortega; Scheduler, Xavier McCombs.
Committees: Appropriations (Commerce, Justice, State & Judiciary — ranking member; Transportation).

New York 16th — South Bronx. The district vote for Bill Clinton was 94% in 1996.

CQ Voting Studies

	1997	1998
Presidential	80%	80%
Party	95%	91%
Participation	96%	95%

Interest Groups

	1997	1998
ADA	95%	90%
ACU	8%	0%
AFL-CIO	100%	n/a
CCUS	30%	25%

Elections

	1996	1998
General	96%	95%
Primary	u/o	u/o

Pete Sessions (R–Texas)
Of Dallas • Elected 1996

Born: Mar. 22, 1955, Waco, Texas.
Education: Southwestern U., B.S. 1978.
Occupation: Public policy analyst; phone company executive.
Family: Wife, Nete; two children.
Religion: United Methodist.
Political Career: Sought Republican nomination for U.S. House (special election), 1991; Republican nominee for U.S. House, 1994.

Capitol Office: 1318 Longworth House Office Building 20515; 225-2231; (fax) 225-5878; (e–mail) petes@mail.house.gov; (web) www.house.gov/sessions.
Office Staff: Chief of Staff, Jeff Koch; Legis. Dir., Vacant; Press Secy., Pam Arruda; Scheduler, Kimberly McClintock.
Committees: Rules (Rules & Organization of the House; Criminal Justice Oversight).

Texas 5th — East Central — Part of Dallas; eastern and southern suburbs. The district vote for Bill Clinton was 46% in 1996.

CQ Voting Studies

	1997	1998
Presidential	25%	20%
Party	95%	97%
Participation	99%	98%

Interest Groups

	1997	1998
ADA	0%	0%
ACU	100%	100%
AFL-CIO	0%	n/a
CCUS	90%	89%

Elections

	1996	1998
General	53%	56%
Primary		u/o

John Shadegg (R–Ariz.)
Of Phoenix • Elected 1994
Pronounced: SHAD-egg

Born: Oct. 22, 1949, Phoenix, Ariz.
Education: U. of Arizona, B.A. 1972, J.D. 1975.
Military Career: National Guard, 1969–75.
Occupation: State prosecutor; lawyer.
Family: Wife, Shirley Lueck; two children.
Religion: Episcopalian.
Political Career: No previous office.

Capitol Office: 430 Cannon House Office Building 20515; 225-3361; (fax) 225-3462; (e-mail) j.shadegg@mail.house.gov; (web) www.house.gov/shadegg.
Office Staff: Chief of Staff, Elise Finley; Press Secy./Legis. Dir., Andrea Miles; Scheduler, Susan Marshall.
Committees: Commerce (Energy & Power; Finance & Hazardous Materials; Health & Environment).

Arizona 4th — Northern Phoenix; Scottsdale. The district vote for Bill Clinton was 44% in 1996.

CQ Voting Studies

	1997	1998
Presidential	24%	22%
Party	94%	97%
Participation	98%	99%

Interest Groups

	1997	1998
ADA	5%	0%
ACU	100%	100%
AFL-CIO	0%	n/a
CCUS	80%	89%

Elections

	1996	1998
General	67%	65%
Primary	74%	u/o

E. Clay Shaw Jr. (R–Fla.)
Of Fort Lauderdale • Elected 1980

Born: Apr. 19, 1939, Miami, Fla.
Education: Stetson U., B.S. 1961; U. of Alabama, M.B.A. 1963; Stetson U., J.D. 1966.
Occupation: Nurseryman; lawyer; prosecutor.
Family: Wife, Emilie; four children.
Religion: Roman Catholic.
Political Career: Fort Lauderdale assistant city attorney, 1968; Fort Lauderdale chief city prosecutor, 1968–69; Fort Lauderdale associate municipal judge, 1969–71; Fort Lauderdale City Commission, 1971–73; vice mayor of Fort Lauderdale, 1973–75; mayor of Fort Lauderdale, 1975–81.

Capitol Office: 2408 Rayburn House Office Building 20515; 225-3026; (fax) 225-8398; (e-mail) www.house.gov/writerep; (web) www.house.gov/shaw.
Office Staff: Chief of Staff, Clint Tarkoe; Legis. Dir., Michael Harrington; Press Secy., Donna Boyer; Exec. Asst., Mary Kay McClure.
Committees: Ways & Means (Social Security — chairman; Trade).

Florida 22nd — Southeast — Coastal Broward, Dade and Palm Beach counties; Fort Lauderdale. The district vote for Bill Clinton was 54% in 1996.

CQ Voting Studies

	1997	1998
Presidential	36%	34%
Party	87%	86%
Participation	99%	98%

Interest Groups

	1997	1998
ADA	10%	10%
ACU	80%	72%
AFL-CIO	25%	n/a
CCUS	100%	100%

Elections

	1996	1998
General	62%	u/o
Primary	u/o	u/o

Christopher Shays (R–Conn.)
Of Stamford • Elected 1987

Born: Oct. 18, 1945, Darien, Conn.
Education: Principia College, B.A. 1968; New York U., M.B.A. 1974, M.P.A. 1978.
Occupation: Real estate broker; public official; Peace Corps volunteer.
Family: Wife, Betsi de Raismes; one child.
Religion: Christian Scientist.
Political Career: Conn. House, 1975–87; Republican candidate for mayor of Stamford, 1983.

Capitol Office: 1126 Longworth House Office Building 20515; 225-5541; (fax) 225-9629; (e-mail) rep.shays@mail.house.gov; (web) www.house.gov/shays.
Office Staff: Chief of Staff, Peter Carson; Legis. Dir., Kristen Miller; Press Secy., Eric Friedman; Exec. Asst., Robert Russo.
Committees: Budget; Government Reform (Criminal Justice, Drug Policy & Human Resources; National Security & Veterans Affairs — chairman).

Connecticut 4th — Southwest — Stamford; Bridgeport. The district vote for Bill Clinton was 51% in 1996.

CQ Voting Studies

	1997	1998
Presidential	55%	57%
Party	66%	58%
Participation	99%	99%

Interest Groups

	1997	1998
ADA	55%	45%
ACU	56%	40%
AFL-CIO	38%	n/a
CCUS	70%	56%

Elections

	1996	1998
General	60%	69%
Primary	u/o	u/o

Brad Sherman (D–Calif.)
Of Sherman Oaks • Elected 1996

Born: Oct. 24, 1954, Los Angeles, Calif.
Education: U. of California, Los Angeles, B.A. 1974; Harvard U., J.D. 1979.
Occupation: Accountant; lawyer.
Family: Single.
Religion: Jewish.
Political Career: Calif. State Board of Equilization, 1991–97.

Capitol Office: 1524 Longworth House Office Building 20515; 225-5911; (fax) 225-5879; (e-mail) www.house.gov/writerep; (web) www.house.gov/sherman.
Office Staff: Chief of Staff/Press Secy., Peter Loge; Scheduler, Erin Stone.
Committees: Banking & Financial Services (Domestic & International Monetary Policy; Financial Institutions & Consumer Credit); International Relations (International Economic Policy & Trade; International Operations & Human Rights).

California 24th — Northwest Los Angeles County suburbs. The district vote for Bill Clinton was 52% in 1996.

CQ Voting Studies

	1997	1998
Presidential	77%	72%
Party	78%	82%
Participation	98%	99%

Interest Groups

	1997	1998
ADA	75%	95%
ACU	32%	20%
AFL-CIO	88%	n/a
CCUS	50%	61%

Elections

	1996	1998
General	50%	57%
Primary	54%	*54%

*Open primary

Donald L. Sherwood (R–Pa.)
Of Tunkhannock • Elected 1998

Born: Mar. 5, 1941, Nicholson, Pa.
Education: Dartmouth College, B.A. 1963.
Military Career: Army, 1964–66.
Occupation: Automobile dealer; bank executive; horse farm owner; forestry equipment company owner.
Family: Wife, Carol; three children.
Religion: Methodist.
Political Career: Tunkhannock Area School Board, 1978–99, president, 1992–98.
Capitol Office: 1223 Longworth House Office Building 20515; 225-3731; (fax) 225-9594; (e–mail) www.house.gov/writerep.
Office Staff: Chief of Staff, John Enright; Press Secy., Jake O'Donnell.
Committees: Armed Services (Military Readiness; Military Research & Development); Resources (Forests & Forest Health; National Parks & Public Lands); Transportation & Infrastructure (Aviation; Water Resources & Environment).

Elections

	1998
General	49%
Primary	44%

Pennsylvania 10th — Northeast — Scranton. The district vote for Bill Clinton was 45% in 1996.

John Shimkus (R–Ill.)
Of Collinsville • Elected 1996
Pronounced: SHIM-kus

Born: Feb. 21, 1958, Collinsville, Ill.
Education: U.S. Military Academy, B.S. 1980; Southern Illinois U., M.B.A. 1997.
Military Career: Army, 1980–86; Army Reserve, 1986–present.
Occupation: High school teacher; Army officer.
Family: Wife, Karen; two children.
Religion: Lutheran.
Political Career: Candidate for Madison County Board, 1988; Collinsville Township Board of Trustees, 1989–97; Madison County treasurer, 1990–97; Republican nominee for U.S. House, 1992.
Capitol Office: 513 Cannon House Office Building 20515; 225-5271; (e–mail) www.house.gov/writerep; (web) www.house.gov/shimkus.
Office Staff: Chief of Staff, Craig Roberts; Legis. Dir., Dan Blankenburg; Press Secy., Steve Tomaszewski; Scheduler, Carren Ann Crossley.
Committees: Commerce (Energy & Power; Finance & Hazardous Materials; Telecommunications, Trade & Consumer Protection).

CQ Voting Studies

	1997	1998
Presidential	28%	24%
Party	94%	91%
Participation	100%	98%

Interest Groups

	1997	1998
ADA	10%	10%
ACU	88%	88%
AFL-CIO	38%	n/a
CCUS	80%	94%

Elections

	1996	1998
General	50%	61%
Primary	51%	u/o

Illinois 20th — West Central — Part of Springfield; Collinsville. The district vote for Bill Clinton was 48% in 1996.

Ronnie Shows (D–Miss.)
Of Bassfield • Elected 1998
Pronounced: rhymes with "cows"

Born: Jan. 26, 1947, Moselle, Miss.
Education: Jones Junior College, attended 1965–66; Southeastern Baptist College, attended 1967–69; U. of Southern Mississippi, B.A. 1969–71.
Occupation: Teacher; coach.
Family: Wife, Johnnie Ruth; four children.
Religion: Baptist.
Political Career: Jefferson Davis County circuit clerk, 1976–80; Miss. Senate, 1980–88; Miss. District Highway Commission, 1988–99.

Capitol Office: 509 Cannon House Office Building 20515; 225-5865; (fax) 225-5886; (e-mail) www.house.gov/writerep.
Office Staff: Chief of Staff, Marshall Lusk.
Committees: Transportation & Infrastructure (Economic Development & Public Buildings; Ground Transportation); Veterans' Affairs (Health).

Mississippi 4th — Southwest — Jackson. The district vote for Bill Clinton was 46% in 1996.

Elections

	1998
General	53%
Primary	57%

Bud Shuster (R–Pa.)
Of Everett • Elected 1972

Born: Jan. 23, 1932, Glassport, Pa.
Education: U. of Pittsburgh, B.S. 1954; Duquesne U., M.B.A. 1960; American U., Ph.D. 1967.
Military Career: Army, 1954–56.
Occupation: Computer industry executive.
Family: Wife, Patricia; five children.
Religion: United Church of Christ.
Political Career: No previous office.

Capitol Office: 2188 Rayburn House Office Building 20515; 225-2431; (e-mail) www.house.gov/writerep; (web) www.house.gov/shuster.
Office Staff: Chief of Staff, Tim Hugo; Legis. Dir., John McAllister; Press Secy., Scott Brenner; Scheduler, Tara Anderson.
Committees: Transportation & Infrastructure — chairman.

Pennsylvania 9th — South Central — Altoona. The district vote for Bill Clinton was 36% in 1996.

CQ Voting Studies

	1997	1998
Presidential	25%	24%
Party	89%	90%
Participation	96%	94%

Interest Groups

	1997	1998
ADA	15%	10%
ACU	84%	96%
AFL-CIO	13%	n/a
CCUS	90%	94%

Elections

	1996	1998
General	74%	u/o
Primary	u/o	81%

Mike Simpson (R–Idaho)
Of Blackfoot • Elected 1998

Born: Sept. 8, 1950, Burley, Idaho.
Education: Utah State U., Logan, B.S. 1973; Washington U. (Mo.), D.D.S. 1977.
Occupation: Dentist.
Family: Wife, Kathy.
Religion: Mormon.
Political Career: Blackfoot City Council, 1980–84; Idaho House, 1985–99, speaker, 1993–99.

Capitol Office: 1440 Longworth House Office Building 20515; 225-5531; (fax) 225-8216; (e-mail) www.house.gov/writerep.
Office Staff: Chief of Staff, Rhonda Sarantis.
Committees: Agriculture (Risk Management, Research & Specialty Crops); Resources (Fisheries Conservation, Wildlife & Oceans; Water & Power); Transportation & Infrastructure (Aviation; Water Resources & Environment); Veterans' Affairs (Health).

Idaho 2nd — East — Pocatello; Idaho Falls; Twin Falls. The district vote for Bill Clinton was 33% in 1996.

Elections

	1998
General	53%
Primary	40%

Norman Sisisky (D–Va.)
Of Petersburg • Elected 1982

Born: June 9, 1927, Baltimore, Md.
Education: Virginia Commonwealth U., B.S. 1949.
Military Career: Navy, 1945–46.
Occupation: Beer and soft drink distributor.
Family: Wife, Rhoda; four children.
Religion: Jewish.
Political Career: Va. House, 1974–82.

Capitol Office: 2371 Rayburn House Office Building 20515; 225-6365; (fax) 226-1170; (e-mail) www.house.gov/writerep; (web) www.house.gov/sisisky.
Office Staff: Chief of Staff, Jan Faircloth; Legis. Dir./Press Secy., Jessica Battaglia; Scheduler, Andrew Wadium.
Committees: Armed Services (Military Procurement — ranking member; Military Readiness); Select Intelligence (Human Intelligence, Analysis & Counterintelligence; Technical & Tactical Intelligence); Small Business (Regulatory Reform & Paperwork Reduction).

Virginia 4th — Southeast — Chesapeake; part of Portsmouth. The district vote for Bill Clinton was 50% in 1996.

CQ Voting Studies

	1997	1998
Presidential	60%	63%
Party	62%	64%
Participation	98%	99%

Interest Groups

	1997	1998
ADA	55%	65%
ACU	28%	28%
AFL-CIO	75%	n/a
CCUS	70%	61%

Elections

	1996	1998
General	79%	97%
Primary	u/o	u/o

Joe Skeen (R-N.M.)
Of Picacho • Elected 1980

Born: June 30, 1927, Roswell, N.M.
Education: Texas A&M U., B.S. 1950.
Military Career: Navy, 1945–46; Air Force Reserve, 1949–52.
Occupation: Sheep rancher; soil and water engineer; flying service operator.
Family: Wife, Mary; two children.
Religion: Roman Catholic.
Political Career: N.M. Senate, 1961–71, minority leader, 1965–71; N.M. Republican Party chairman, 1962–65; Republican nominee for lieutenant governor, 1970; Republican nominee for governor, 1974, 1978.

Capitol Office: 2302 Rayburn House Office Building 20515; 225-2365; (fax) 225-9599; (e-mail) www.house.gov/writerep; (web) www.house.gov/skeen.
Office Staff: Chief of Staff, Suzanne Eisold; Legis. Dir., Bruce Donisthorpe; Press Secy., Selma Sierra; Exec. Asst., Linda Hewitt.
Committees: Appropriations (Agriculture, Rural Development, FDA & Related Agencies — chairman; Interior; Defense).

New Mexico 2nd — South — Little Texas; Las Cruces; Roswell. The district vote for Bill Clinton was 46% in 1996.

CQ Voting Studies

	1997	1998
Presidential	32%	27%
Party	91%	89%
Participation	99%	99%

Interest Groups

	1997	1998
ADA	0%	10%
ACU	76%	84%
AFL-CIO	13%	n/a
CCUS	100%	100%

Elections

	1996	1998
General	56%	58%
Primary	70%	u/o

Ike Skelton (D–Mo.)
Of Lexington • Elected 1976

Born: Dec. 20, 1931, Lexington, Mo.
Education: Wentworth Military Academy, A.A. 1951; U. of Edinburgh (Scotland), attended 1953; U. of Missouri, A.B. 1953, LL.B. 1956.
Occupation: Lawyer.
Family: Wife, Susan; three children.
Religion: Christian Church.
Political Career: Lafayette County prosecuting attorney, 1957–60; Mo. special assistant attorney general, 1961–63; Mo. Senate, 1971–77.

Capitol Office: 2206 Rayburn House Office Building 20515; 225-2876; (e-mail) www.house.gov/writerep; (web) www.house.gov/skelton.
Office Staff: Admin. Asst., Whitney Frost; Legis. Dir./Press Secy., Lara M. Battles; Scheduler, Jennifer Glacel.
Committees: Armed Services — ranking member (Military Procurement).

Missouri 4th — West-Central — Kansas City suburbs; Jefferson City. The district vote for Bill Clinton was 41% in 1996.

CQ Voting Studies

	1997	1998
Presidential	43%	57%
Party	59%	63%
Participation	95%	99%

Interest Groups

	1997	1998
ADA	40%	65%
ACU	52%	36%
AFL-CIO	75%	n/a
CCUS	78%	65%

Elections

	1996	1998
General	64%	71%
Primary	u/o	u/o

Louise M. Slaughter (D-N.Y.)
Of Fairport • Elected 1986

Born: Aug. 14, 1929, Harlan County, Ky.
Education: U. of Kentucky, B.S. 1951, M.P.H. 1953.
Occupation: Legislative aide; market researcher.
Family: Husband, Robert; three children.
Religion: Episcopalian.
Political Career: Monroe County Legislature, 1975–79; N.Y. Assembly, 1983–87.

Capitol Office: 2347 Rayburn House Office Building 20515; 225-3615; (fax) 225-7822; (e–mail) louiseny@mail.house.gov; (web) www.house.gov/slaughter.
Office Staff: Chief of Staff, David D. Stricklin; Legis. Dir./Counsel, Thomas Bantle; Press Secy., Becky Bailey; Scheduler, Amy Dacey.
Committees: Rules (Rules & Organization of the House).

New York 28th — Rochester and most of suburban Monroe County. The district vote for Bill Clinton was 55% in 1996.

CQ Voting Studies

	1997	1998
Presidential	77%	82%
Party	92%	92%
Participation	95%	96%

Interest Groups

	1997	1998
ADA	85%	100%
ACU	9%	8%
AFL-CIO	100%	n/a
CCUS	30%	39%

Elections

	1996	1998
General	57%	65%
Primary	u/o	u/o

Adam Smith (D-Wash.)
Of Kent • Elected 1996

Born: June 15, 1965, Washington, D.C.
Education: Fordham U., B.A. 1987; U. of Washington, J.D. 1990.
Occupation: City prosecutor; lawyer.
Family: Wife, Sara.
Religion: Christian.
Political Career: Wash. Senate, 1991–97.

Capitol Office: 116 Cannon House Office Building 20515; 225-8901; (fax) 225-5893; (e–mail) adam.smith@mail.house.gov; (web) www.house.gov/adamsmith.
Office Staff: Admin. Asst., Jeff Bjornstad; Legis. Dir./Communications Dir., Alixandria Weise; Office Dir., Linda Danforth.
Committees: Armed Services (Military Procurement; Military Readiness); Resources (Fisheries Conservation, Wildlife & Oceans; Water & Power).

Washington 9th — Puget Sound — Tacoma; parts of King, Pierce and Thurston counties. The district vote for Bill Clinton was 51% in 1996.

CQ Voting Studies

	1997	1998
Presidential	83%	79%
Party	83%	83%
Participation	97%	98%

Interest Groups

	1997	1998
ADA	80%	100%
ACU	20%	0%
AFL-CIO	88%	n/a
CCUS	50%	39%

Elections

	1996	1998
General	50%	65%
Primary	*49%	*58%

*Open primary

Christopher H. Smith (R–N.J.)
Of Robbinsville • Elected 1980

Born: Mar. 4, 1953, Rahway, N.J.
Education: Trenton State College, B.A. 1975.
Occupation: Sporting goods executive.
Family: Wife, Marie; four children.
Religion: Roman Catholic.
Political Career: Republican nominee for U.S. House, 1978.

Capitol Office: 2370 Rayburn House Office Building 20515; 225-3765; (fax) 225-7768; (e–mail) www.house.gov/writerep; (web) www.house.gov/chrissmith.
Office Staff: Chief of Staff, Mary Noonan; Legis. Dir., Mark Roselli; Press Secy., Ken Wolfe; Office Mgr./Scheduler, Patricia Coll.
Committees: International Relations (International Operations & Human Rights — chairman; Western Hemisphere); Veterans' Affairs (Health).

New Jersey 4th — Central — Trenton. The district vote for Bill Clinton was 51% in 1996.

CQ Voting Studies

	1997	1998
Presidential	36%	27%
Party	80%	78%
Participation	96%	98%

Interest Groups

	1997	1998
ADA	30%	25%
ACU	64%	72%
AFL-CIO	75%	n/a
CCUS	50%	61%

Elections

	1996	1998
General	64%	62%
Primary	u/o	u/o

Lamar Smith (R–Texas)
Of San Antonio • Elected 1986

Born: Nov. 19, 1947, San Antonio, Texas.
Education: Yale U., B.A. 1969; Southern Methodist U., J.D. 1975.
Occupation: Lawyer; rancher.
Family: Wife, Elizabeth; two children.
Religion: Christian Scientist.
Political Career: Texas House, 1981–82; Bexar County Commissioners Court, 1983–85.

Capitol Office: 2231 Rayburn House Office Building 20515; 225-4236; (fax) 225-8628; (e–mail) www.house.gov/writerep; (web) www.house.gov/lamarsmith.
Office Staff: Chief of Staff, John Lampmann; Legis. Dir., Lisa Means; Communications Dir., Allen Kay; Staff Asst., Michele Rutherford.
Committees: Judiciary (Crime; Immigration & Claims — chairman); Science (Basic Research; Space & Aeronautics); Standards of Official Conduct — chairman.

Texas 21st — South Central — Western Bexar County; Austin suburbs. The district vote for Bill Clinton was 30% in 1996.

CQ Voting Studies

	1997	1998
Presidential	31%	22%
Party	92%	93%
Participation	97%	98%

Interest Groups

	1997	1998
ADA	0%	0%
ACU	88%	92%
AFL-CIO	0%	n/a
CCUS	100%	100%

Elections

	1996	1998
General	76%	91%
Primary	u/o	u/o

Nick Smith (R–Mich.)
Of Addison • Elected 1992

Born: Nov. 5, 1934, Addison, Mich.
Education: Michigan State U., B.A. 1957; U. of Delaware, M.S. 1959.
Military Career: Air Force, 1959–61.
Occupation: Dairy farmer.
Family: Wife, Bonnalyn; four children.
Religion: Congregationalist.
Political Career: Somerset Township Board of Trustees, 1962–66; Hillsdale County Board of Supervisors, 1966–68; Mich. House, 1979–83; Mich. Senate, 1983–93.

Capitol Office: 306 Cannon House Office Building 20515; 225-6276; (fax) 225-6281; (e–mail) www.house.gov/writerep; (web) www.house.gov/nicksmith.
Office Staff: Admin. Asst., Kurt Schmautz; Legis. Dir., Alec Rogers; Communications Dir., Jason Roe; Scheduler, Mary Christ.
Committees: Agriculture (General Farm Commodities; Risk Management, Research & Specialty Crops); Budget; Science (Basic Research — chairman).

Michigan 7th — South Central — Battle Creek; Jackson. The district vote for Bill Clinton was 45% in 1996.

CQ Voting Studies

	1997	1998
Presidential	35%	26%
Party	88%	87%
Participation	97%	98%

Interest Groups

	1997	1998
ADA	15%	20%
ACU	88%	76%
AFL-CIO	0%	n/a
CCUS	90%	83%

Elections

	1996	1998
General	55%	57%
Primary	75%	u/o

Vic Snyder (D–Ark.)
Of Little Rock • Elected 1996

Born: Sept. 27, 1947, Medford, Ore.
Education: Willamette U., B.A. 1975; U. of Oregon, M.D. 1979; U. of Arkansas, Little Rock, J.D. 1988.
Military Career: Marine Corps, 1967–69.
Occupation: Physician; lawyer.
Family: Single.
Religion: Presbyterian.
Political Career: Ark. Senate, 1991–96.

Capitol Office: 1319 Longworth House Office Building 20515; 225-2506; (fax) 225-5903; (e–mail) snyder.congress@mail.house.gov; (web) www.house.gov/snyder.
Office Staff: Staff Dir., Ed Fry; Legis. Dir., Thad Huguley; Press Secy., Rusty Logan; Scheduler, Mary Starr Ross.
Committees: Armed Services (Military Installations & Facilities; Military Research & Development); Veterans' Affairs (Health).

Arkansas 2nd — Central — Little Rock. The district vote for Bill Clinton was 55% in 1996.

CQ Voting Studies

	1997	1998
Presidential	84%	80%
Party	87%	79%
Participation	99%	99%

Interest Groups

	1997	1998
ADA	80%	85%
ACU	20%	16%
AFL-CIO	88%	n/a
CCUS	60%	61%

Elections

	1996	1998
General	52%	58%
Primary	*51%	u/o

*Runoff election

Mark Souder (R–Ind.)
Of Fort Wayne • Elected 1994
Pronounced: SOW (rhymes with "now")-dur

Born: July 18, 1950, Fort Wayne, Ind.
Education: Indiana U., B.S. 1972; Notre Dame, M.B.A. 1974.
Occupation: Congressional aide; furniture company executive; general store owner.
Family: Wife, Diane; three children.
Religion: Evangelical.
Political Career: No previous office.

Capitol Office: 109 Cannon House Office Building 20515; 225-4436; (fax) 225-3479; (e–mail) souder@mail.house.gov; (web) www.house.gov/souder.
Office Staff: Chief of Staff, Christopher Donesa; Communications Dir., Angela Flood; Scheduler, Dawn Gerson.
Committees: Education & Workforce (Early Childhood, Youth & Families; Postsecondary Education, Training & Life-Long Learning); Government Reform (Census; Criminal Justice, Drug Policy & Human Resources; National Security & Veterans Affairs); Resources (Fisheries Conservation, Wildlife & Oceans; National Parks & Public Lands).

Indiana 4th — Northeast — Fort Wayne. The district vote for Bill Clinton was 36% in 1996.

CQ Voting Studies

	1997	1998
Presidential	24%	24%
Party	90%	89%
Participation	95%	96%

Interest Groups

	1997	1998
ADA	5%	15%
ACU	100%	83%
AFL-CIO	0%	n/a
CCUS	80%	76%

Elections

	1996	1998
General	58%	63%
Primary	82%	u/o

Floyd D. Spence (R–S.C.)
Of Lexington • Elected 1970

Born: Apr. 9, 1928, Columbia, S.C.
Education: U. of South Carolina, A.B. 1952, LL.B. 1956.
Military Career: Naval Reserve, 1947–88.
Occupation: Lawyer.
Family: Wife, Deborah Williams; four children.
Religion: Lutheran.
Political Career: S.C. House, 1957–63, served as a Democrat; Republican nominee for U.S. House, 1962; S.C. Senate, 1967–71, minority leader, 1967–71.

Capitol Office: 2405 Rayburn House Office Building 20515; 225-2452; (fax) 225-2455; (e–mail) www.house.gov/writerep.
Office Staff: Chief of Staff/Press Secy., Craig Metz; Legis. Dir., Miriam E.A. Wolff; Exec. Asst., Caroline S. Bryson.
Committees: Armed Services — chairman (Military Procurement); Veterans' Affairs (Oversight & Investigations).

South Carolina 2nd — Central and South — Columbia suburbs; Hilton Head. The district vote for Bill Clinton was 41% in 1996.

CQ Voting Studies

	1997	1998
Presidential	27%	18%
Party	96%	95%
Participation	99%	99%

Interest Groups

	1997	1998
ADA	0%	5%
ACU	88%	100%
AFL-CIO	0%	n/a
CCUS	90%	78%

Elections

	1996	1998
General	90%	58%
Primary	u/o	u/o

John M. Spratt Jr. (D–S.C.)
Of York • Elected 1982

Born: Nov. 1, 1942, Charlotte, N.C.
Education: Davidson College, A.B. 1964; Oxford U., M.A. 1966; Yale U., LL.B. 1969.
Military Career: Army, 1969–71.
Occupation: Lawyer; community bank executive; insurance agency owner; farmer.
Family: Wife, Jane Stacy; three children.
Religion: Presbyterian.
Political Career: No previous office.

Capitol Office: 1536 Longworth House Office Building 20515; 225-5501; (fax) 225-0464; (e-mail) john.spratt@mail.house.gov; (web) www.house.gov/spratt.
Office Staff: Chief of Staff, Ellen Wallace Buchanan; Legis. Dir., Rudy Barnes; Press Secy., Charles H. Fant; Exec. Asst., Marilee C. Sanders.
Committees: Armed Services (Military Procurement; Military Readiness); Budget — ranking member; China Investigation.

South Carolina 5th — North Central — Rock Hill. The district vote for Bill Clinton was 46% in 1996.

CQ Voting Studies

	1997	1998
Presidential	73%	71%
Party	81%	77%
Participation	97%	94%

Interest Groups

	1997	1998
ADA	70%	85%
ACU	17%	17%
AFL-CIO	88%	n/a
CCUS	50%	50%

Elections

	1996	1998
General	54%	58%
Primary	u/o	u/o

Debbie Stabenow (D–Mich.)
Of Lansing • Elected 1996
Pronounced: STAB-uh–now

Born: Apr. 29, 1950, Clare, Mich.
Education: Michigan State U., B.A. 1972, M.S.W. 1975.
Occupation: Leadership training consultant.
Family: Divorced; two children.
Religion: United Methodist.
Political Career: Ingham County Commission, 1975–78, chair, 1977–1978; Mich. House, 1979–91; Mich. Senate, 1991–94; sought Democratic nomination for governor, 1994; Democratic nominee for lieutenant governor, 1994.

Capitol Office: 1039 Longworth House Office Building 20515; 225-4872; (fax) 225-5820; (e-mail) debbie.stabenow@mail.house.com.
Office Staff: Admin. Asst., Teresa Plachetka; Legis. Dir., Bridget Gonzales; Press Secy., Matt Frankel; Scheduler, JoAnne Huls.
Committees: Agriculture (Livestock & Horticulture; Risk Management, Research & Specialty Crops); Science (Space & Aeronautics; Technology).

Michigan 8th — Central — Part of Lansing. The district vote for Bill Clinton was 49% in 1996.

CQ Voting Studies

	1997	1998
Presidential	81%	73%
Party	87%	85%
Participation	98%	97%

Interest Groups

	1997	1998
ADA	95%	100%
ACU	12%	9%
AFL-CIO	100%	n/a
CCUS	50%	61%

Elections

	1996	1998
General	54%	57%
Primary	u/o	u/o

Pete Stark (D–Calif.)
Of Hayward • Elected 1972

Born: Nov. 11, 1931, Milwaukee, Wis.
Education: Massachusetts Institute of Technology, B.S. 1953; U. of California, Berkeley, M.B.A. 1960.
Military Career: Air Force, 1955–57.
Occupation: Banker.
Family: Wife, Deborah Roderick Stark; five children.
Religion: Unitarian.
Political Career: Sought Democratic nomination for Calif. Senate, 1969.

Capitol Office: 239 Cannon House Office Building 20515; 225-5065; (fax) 225-3805; (e-mail) petemail@stark.house.gov; (web) www.house.gov/stark.
Office Staff: Admin. Asst., Anne Raffaelli; Legis. Dir., Debbie Curtis; Scheduler, Joan Godley.
Committees: Ways & Means (Health — ranking member; Human Resources); Joint Economic — ranking member; Joint Taxation.

California 13th — East Bay — Oakland; Hayward; Santa Clara. The district vote for Bill Clinton was 62% in 1996.

CQ Voting Studies

	1997	1998
Presidential	72%	82%
Party	82%	92%
Participation	86%	93%

Interest Groups

	1997	1998
ADA	100%	90%
ACU	4%	8%
AFL-CIO	100%	n/a
CCUS	10%	6%

Elections

	1996	1998
General	65%	71%
Primary	u/o	*69%

*Open primary

Cliff Stearns (R–Fla.)
Of Ocala • Elected 1988

Born: Apr. 16, 1941, Washington, D.C.
Education: George Washington U., B.S. 1963.
Military Career: Air Force, 1963–67.
Occupation: Hotel executive.
Family: Wife, Joan Moore; three children.
Religion: Presbyterian.
Political Career: No previous office.

Capitol Office: 2227 Rayburn House Office Building 20515; 225-5744; (fax) 225-3973; (e-mail) www.house.gov/writerep; (web) www.house.gov/stearns.
Office Staff: Chief of Staff, Jack Seum; Legis. Dir., Veronica Crowe; Press Secy., Paul Flusche; Exec. Asst., Bonnie Matles.
Committees: Commerce (Energy & Power; Health & Environment; Telecommunications, Trade & Consumer Protection); Veterans' Affairs (Health — chairman).

Florida 6th — North Central — Lake and Marion counties; part of Jacksonville. The district vote for Bill Clinton was 39% in 1996.

CQ Voting Studies

	1997	1998
Presidential	25%	18%
Party	93%	91%
Participation	99%	98%

Interest Groups

	1997	1998
ADA	10%	5%
ACU	100%	96%
AFL-CIO	13%	n/a
CCUS	70%	83%

Elections

	1996	1998
General	67%	u/o
Primary	u/o	u/o

Charles W. Stenholm (D–Texas)
Of Abilene • Elected 1978

Born: Oct. 26, 1938, Stamford, Texas.
Education: Tarleton State Junior College, attended 1957–59; Texas Tech U., B.S. 1961, M.S. 1962.
Occupation: Cotton farmer; teacher.
Family: Wife, Cindy; three children.
Religion: Lutheran.
Political Career: No previous office.

Capitol Office: 1211 Longworth House Office Building 20515; 225-6605; (fax) 225-2234; (e-mail) texas17@mail.house.gov; (web) www.house.gov/stenholm.
Office Staff: Chief of Staff/Scheduler, Lois Auer; Legis. Dir./Press Secy., Rebecca Tice; Press Secy., John Haugen; Scheduler, Jayne Schoonmaker.
Committees: Agriculture — ranking member.

Texas 17th — West Central — Abilene. The district vote for Bill Clinton was 39% in 1996.

CQ Voting Studies

	1997	1998
Presidential	52%	49%
Party	52%	49%
Participation	98%	99%

Interest Groups

	1997	1998
ADA	40%	40%
ACU	58%	48%
AFL-CIO	29%	n/a
CCUS	90%	76%

Elections

	1996	1998
General	52%	54%
Primary	u/o	u/o

Ted Strickland (D–Ohio)
Of Lucasville • Elected 1992
Did not serve 1995–97

Born: Aug. 4, 1941, Lucasville, Ohio.
Education: Asbury College, B.A. 1963; U. of Kentucky, M.A. 1966; Asbury Theological Seminary, M.A. 1967; U. of Kentucky, Ph.D. 1980.
Occupation: Professor; psychologist; minister.
Family: Wife, Frances Smith Strickland.
Religion: Methodist.
Political Career: Democratic nominee for U.S. House, 1976, 1978, 1980; U.S. House, 1993–95.

Capitol Office: 336 Cannon House Office Building 20515; 225-5705; (e-mail) www.house.gov/writerep; (web) www.house.gov/strickland.
Office Staff: Chief of Staff, John Haseley; Admin. Asst., Sara Franko; Press Secy., Jess Goode; Scheduler, Elizabeth McGlynn.
Committees: Commerce (Energy & Power; Health & Environment; Oversight & Investigations).

Ohio 6th — South — Portsmouth; Chillicothe; Athens. The district vote for Bill Clinton was 45% in 1996.

CQ Voting Studies

	1997	1998
Presidential	69%	66%
Party	82%	84%
Participation	98%	99%

Interest Groups

	1997	1998
ADA	75%	85%
ACU	24%	32%
AFL-CIO	100%	n/a
CCUS	44%	33%

Elections

	1996	1998
General	51%	57%
Primary	u/o	u/o

Bob Stump (R–Ariz.)
Of Tolleson • Elected 1976

Born: Apr. 4, 1927, Phoenix, Ariz.
Education: Arizona State U., B.S. 1951.
Military Career: Navy, 1943–46.
Occupation: Cotton and grain farmer.
Family: Divorced; three children.
Religion: Seventh-Day Adventist.
Political Career: Ariz. House, 1959–67; Ariz. Senate, 1967–77, president, 1975–77.

Capitol Office: 211 Cannon House Office Building 20515; 225-4576; (fax) 225-6328; (e-mail) www.house.gov/writerep; (web) www.house.gov/va.
Office Staff: Chief of Staff/Legis. Dir./Press Secy., Lisa Jackson; Scheduler, Dolores Dunn.
Committees: Armed Services (Military Installations & Facilities; Military Procurement); Veterans' Affairs — chairman (Oversight & Investigations).

Arizona 3rd — North and West — Glendale; part of Phoenix; Hopi reservation. The district vote for Bill Clinton was 41% in 1996.

CQ Voting Studies

	1997	1998
Presidential	20%	20%
Party	97%	93%
Participation	99%	99%

Interest Groups

	1997	1998
ADA	5%	0%
ACU	100%	96%
AFL-CIO	0%	n/a
CCUS	90%	78%

Elections

	1996	1998
General	67%	67%
Primary	u/o	u/o

Bart Stupak (D–Mich.)
Of Menominee • Elected 1992
Pronounced: STEW-pack

Born: Feb. 29, 1952, Milwaukee, Wis.
Education: Northwestern Michigan Community College, A.A. 1972; Saginaw Valley State College, B.S. 1977; Thomas M. Cooley Law School, J.D. 1981.
Occupation: Lawyer; state trooper; patrolman.
Family: Wife, Laurie; two children.
Religion: Roman Catholic.
Political Career: Mich. House, 1989–91; sought Democratic nomination for Mich. Senate, 1990.

Capitol Office: 2348 Rayburn House Office Building 20515; 225-4735; (fax) 225-4744; (e-mail) stupak@mail.house.gov; (web) www.house.gov/stupak.
Office Staff: Chief of Staff, Scott Schloegel; Legis. Dir., Dave Buchanan; Press Secy., Bob Meissner; Scheduler, Julie Byrom.
Committees: Commerce (Finance & Hazardous Materials; Health & Environment; Oversight & Investigations).

Michigan 1st — Upper Peninsula; northern Lower Michigan. The district vote for Bill Clinton was 47% in 1996.

CQ Voting Studies

	1997	1998
Presidential	71%	73%
Party	82%	80%
Participation	98%	97%

Interest Groups

	1997	1998
ADA	80%	90%
ACU	20%	20%
AFL-CIO	100%	n/a
CCUS	40%	17%

Elections

	1996	1998
General	71%	59%
Primary	u/o	u/o

John E. Sununu (R-N.H.)
Of Bedford • Elected 1996

Born: Sept. 10, 1964, Boston, Mass.
Education: Massachusetts Institute of Technology, B.S. 1986, M.S. 1987; Harvard U., M.B.A. 1991.
Occupation: Corporate financial officer; management consultant; mechanical engineer.
Family: Wife, Catherine; two children.
Religion: Roman Catholic.
Political Career: No previous office.

Capitol Office: 316 Cannon House Office Building 20515; 225-5456; (fax) 225-5822; (e-mail) rep.sununu@mail.house.gov; (web) www.house.gov/sununu.
Office Staff: Chief of Staff, Paul J. Collins; Legis. Dir., Matt Leland; Press Secy., Barbara J. Riley; Scheduler, Sherri Keniston.
Committees: Appropriations (District of Columbia; Treasury, Postal Service & General Government; VA, HUD & Independent Agencies); Budget.

New Hampshire 1st — East — Manchester. The district vote for Bill Clinton was 49% in 1996.

CQ Voting Studies

	1997	1998
Presidential	29%	24%
Party	95%	89%
Participation	99%	98%

Interest Groups

	1997	1998
ADA	5%	0%
ACU	92%	92%
AFL-CIO	0%	n/a
CCUS	100%	94%

Elections

	1996	1998
General	50%	67%
Primary	28%	u/o

John E. Sweeney (R-N.Y.)
Of Troy • Elected 1998

Born: Aug. 9, 1955, Troy, N.Y.
Education: Hudson Valley Community College, A.A. 1978; Russell Sage College, B.A. 1981; Western New England College, J.D. 1991.
Occupation: Gubernatorial adviser; lawyer; county public safety program director.
Family: Divorced; three children.
Religion: Roman Catholic.
Political Career: N.Y. Republican Party executive director, 1992–95; N.Y. labor commissioner, 1995–97.

Capitol Office: 437 Cannon House Office Building 20515; 225-5614; (fax) 225-6234; (e-mail) www.house.gov/writerep; (web) www.house.gov/sweeney.
Office Staff: Chief of Staff, Geoff Gleason; Legis. Dir./Press Secy., Michael Power; Scheduler, Beth Thompson.
Committees: Banking & Financial Services (Capital Markets & Securities; Housing & Community Opportunity); Small Business (Regulatory Reform & Paperwork Reduction; Rural Enterprises); Transportation & Infrastructure (Aviation; Ground Transportation).

New York 22nd — Rural East — Glens Falls; Saratoga Springs. The district vote for Bill Clinton was 45% in 1996.

Elections

	1998
General	55%
Primary	52%

James M. Talent (R–Mo.)
Of Chesterfield • Elected 1992

Born: Oct. 18, 1956, Des Peres, Mo.
Education: Washington U., B.A. 1978; U. of Chicago, J.D. 1981.
Occupation: Lawyer.
Family: Wife, Brenda; three children.
Religion: Presbyterian.
Political Career: Mo. House, 1985–93, minority leader, 1989–93.

Capitol Office: 1022 Longworth House Office Building 20515; 225-2561; (fax) 225-2563; (e-mail) rep.talent@mail.house.gov; (web) www.house.gov/talent.
Office Staff: Admin. Asst., Mark Strand; Legis. Dir., Katherine Kless; Press Secy., Kristin Young; Exec. Asst., Janis Cooper.
Committees: Armed Services (Military Procurement; Military Readiness); Education & Workforce (Employer-Employee Relations); Small Business — chairman.

Missouri 2nd — Western St. Louis County; Eastern St. Charles County. The district vote for Bill Clinton was 41% in 1996.

CQ Voting Studies

	1997	1998
Presidential	27%	20%
Party	94%	93%
Participation	98%	99%

Interest Groups

	1997	1998
ADA	5%	5%
ACU	100%	96%
AFL-CIO	0%	n/a
CCUS	80%	100%

Elections

	1996	1998
General	61%	70%
Primary	u/o	90%

Tom Tancredo (R–Colo.)
Of Golden • Elected 1998
Pronounced: tan-CRAY-doe

Born: Dec. 20, 1945, North Denver, Colo.
Education: U. of North Colorado, B.A. 1968.
Occupation: Think tank president.
Family: Wife, Jackie; two children.
Religion: Presbyterian.
Political Career: Colo. House, 1977–81; U.S. Education Department regional representative, 1981–93.

Capitol Office: 1123 Longworth House Office Building 20515; 225-7882; (fax) 226-4623; (e-mail) www.house.gov/writerep.
Office Staff: Chief of Staff, Jacque Ponder; Legis. Dir./Press Secy., Scott Glast; Scheduler, Michelle Brosnan.
Committees: Education & Workforce (Early Childhood, Youth & Families; Oversight & Investigations); International Relations (Africa; International Operations & Human Rights); Resources (Energy & Mineral Resources).

Colorado 6th — Denver suburbs — Aurora; Lakewood. The district vote for Bill Clinton was 43% in 1996.

Elections

	1998
General	56%
Primary	25%

John Tanner (D–Tenn.)
Of Union City • Elected 1988

Born: Sept. 22, 1944, Halls, Tenn.
Education: U. of Tennessee, B.S. 1966, J.D. 1968.
Military Career: Navy, 1968–72; National Guard, 1974–present.
Occupation: Lawyer; insurance company owner.
Family: Wife, Betty Ann Tanner; two children.
Religion: Disciples of Christ.
Political Career: Tenn. House, 1977–89.

Capitol Office: 1127 Longworth House Office Building 20515; 225-4714; (fax) 225-1765; (e–mail) john.tanner@mail.house.gov; (web) www.house.gov/tanner.
Office Staff: Chief of Staff, Vickie Walling; Legis. Dir., Douglas Thompson; Press Secy., F. Douglass Fleming; Exec. Asst., Kathy Becker.
Committees: Ways & Means (Social Security).

Tennessee 8th — West — Jackson; part of Shelby County. The district vote for Bill Clinton was 51% in 1996.

CQ Voting Studies

	1997	1998
Presidential	59%	55%
Party	66%	65%
Participation	98%	96%

Interest Groups

	1997	1998
ADA	40%	60%
ACU	40%	41%
AFL-CIO	63%	n/a
CCUS	80%	88%

Elections

	1996	1998
General	67%	u/o
Primary	u/o	u/o

Ellen O. Tauscher (D–Calif.)
Of Pleasanton • Elected 1996
Pronounced: TAU (rhymes with "now")-sher

Born: Nov. 15, 1951, Newark, N.J.
Education: Seton Hall U., B.A. 1974.
Occupation: Child care screening executive; marketing executive; investment banker.
Family: Separated; one child.
Religion: Roman Catholic.
Political Career: No previous office.

Capitol Office: 1239 Longworth House Office Building 20515; 225-1880; (fax) 225-5914; (e–mail) ellen.tauscher@mail.house.gov; (web) www.house.gov/tauscher.
Office Staff: Chief of Staff, Katie Merrill; Legis. Dir., Peter Muller; Press Secy., Phil Goldberg; Scheduler, Matthew Sage.
Committees: Armed Services (Military Personnel; Military Procurement); Transportation & Infrastructure (Aviation; Water Resources & Environment).

California 10th — Eastern Contra Costa and Alameda counties. The district vote for Bill Clinton was 48% in 1996.

CQ Voting Studies

	1997	1998
Presidential	79%	77%
Party	87%	79%
Participation	99%	98%

Interest Groups

	1997	1998
ADA	85%	75%
ACU	20%	12%
AFL-CIO	88%	n/a
CCUS	50%	72%

Elections

	1996	1998
General	49%	54%
Primary	75%	*55%

*Open primary

W.J. "Billy" Tauzin (R–La.)
Of Thibodaux • Elected 1980
Pronounced: TOE-zan

Born: June 14, 1943, Chackbay, La.
Education: Nicholls State U., B.A. 1964; Louisiana State U., J.D. 1967.
Occupation: Lawyer.
Family: Wife, Cecile; five children.
Religion: Roman Catholic.
Political Career: La. House, 1971–80; candidate for governor, 1987.

Capitol Office: 2183 Rayburn House Office Building 20515; 225-4031; (fax) 225-0563; (e–mail) www.house.gov/writerep; (web) www.house.gov/tauzin.
Office Staff: Chief Counsel, Wallace Henderson; Legis. Dir., Monica Azare; Press Secy., Ken Johnson; Exec. Asst., Stacy Flynn.
Committees: Commerce (Finance & Hazardous Materials; Telecommunications, Trade & Consumer Protection — chairman); Resources (Energy & Mineral Resources; Fisheries Conservation, Wildlife & Oceans).

Louisiana 3rd — South Central — Houma; New Iberia. The district vote for Bill Clinton was 53% in 1996.

CQ Voting Studies

	1997	1998
Presidential	31%	22%
Party	91%	87%
Participation	96%	93%

Interest Groups

	1997	1998
ADA	15%	5%
ACU	83%	88%
AFL-CIO	0%	n/a
CCUS	100%	100%

Elections

	1996	1998
General	u/o	u/o
Primary	u/o	

Charles H. Taylor (R–N.C.)
Of Brevard • Elected 1990

Born: Jan. 23, 1941, Brevard, N.C.
Education: Wake Forest U., B.A. 1963, J.D. 1966.
Occupation: Tree farmer.
Family: Wife, Elizabeth; three children.
Religion: Baptist.
Political Career: N.C. House, 1967–73, minority leader, 1969–71; N.C. Senate, 1973–75, minority leader, 1973–75; Republican nominee for U.S. House, 1988.

Capitol Office: 231 Cannon House Office Building 20515; 225-6401; (fax) 226-6405; (e–mail) repcharles.taylor@mail.house.gov; (web) www.house.gov/charlestaylor.
Office Staff: Chief of Staff, Roger France; Legis. Counsel, Sean Dalton; Press Secy., Christopher Shields; Scheduler, Frances White.
Committees: Appropriations (Commerce, Justice, State & Judiciary; Interior; Legislative Branch — chairman).

North Carolina 11th — West — Asheville. The district vote for Bill Clinton was 42% in 1996.

CQ Voting Studies

	1997	1998
Presidential	27%	17%
Party	85%	93%
Participation	89%	94%

Interest Groups

	1997	1998
ADA	0%	5%
ACU	91%	96%
AFL-CIO	0%	n/a
CCUS	100%	88%

Elections

	1996	1998
General	58%	57%
Primary	u/o	u/o

Gene Taylor (D–Miss.)
Of Bay St. Louis • Elected 1989

Born: Sept. 17, 1953, New Orleans, La.
Education: Tulane U., B.A. 1976; U. of Southern Mississippi, Gulf Park, attended 1978–80.
Military Career: Coast Guard Reserve, 1971–84.
Occupation: Sales representative.
Family: Wife, Margaret; three children.
Religion: Roman Catholic.
Political Career: Bay St. Louis City Council, 1981–83; Miss. Senate, 1983–89; Democratic nominee for U.S. House, 1988.

Capitol Office: 2311 Rayburn House Office Building 20515; 225-5772; (fax) 225-7074; (e-mail) www.house.gov/writerep.
Office Staff: Chief of Staff, Wayne Weidie; Legis. Dir., Stephen Peranich; Scheduler, Marva Franklin.
Committees: Armed Services (Military Installations & Facilities — ranking member; Military Research & Development); Transportation & Infrastructure (Coast Guard & Maritime Transportation; Water Resources & Environment).

Mississippi 5th — Southeast — Gulf Coast; Hattiesburg. The district vote for Bill Clinton was 35% in 1996.

CQ Voting Studies

	1997	1998
Presidential	33%	33%
Party	45%	41%
Participation	98%	98%

Interest Groups

	1997	1998
ADA	20%	30%
ACU	80%	79%
AFL-CIO	13%	n/a
CCUS	80%	41%

Elections

	1996	1998
General	58%	78%
Primary	94%	u/o

Lee Terry (R–Neb.)
Of Omaha • Elected 1998

Born: Jan. 29, 1962, Omaha, Neb.
Education: U. of Nebraska, B.S. 1984; Creighton U., J.D. 1987.
Occupation: Lawyer.
Family: Wife, Robyn; two children.
Religion: Methodist.
Political Career: Omaha City Council, 1991–99.

Capitol Office: 1728 Longworth House Office Building 20515; 225-4155; (fax) 226-5452; (e-mail) www.house.gov/writerep.
Office Staff: Chief of Staff, Steve Sutton; Legis. Dir., Mark Davis; Press Secy., Carla Martell; Scheduler, Anna Hernandez.
Committees: Banking & Financial Services (Capital Markets & Securities; Housing & Community Opportunity); Government Reform (National Economic Growth; National Security & Veterans Affairs); Transportation & Infrastructure (Oversight & Investigations; Ground Transportation).

Nebraska 2nd — East — Omaha; Sarpy County suburbs. The district vote for Bill Clinton was 38% in 1996.

Elections

	1998
General	66%
Primary	40%

Bill Thomas (R–Calif.)
Of Bakersfield • Elected 1978

Born: Dec. 6, 1941, Wallace, Idaho.
Education: Santa Ana Community College, A.A. 1961; San Francisco State U., B.A. 1963, M.A. 1965.
Occupation: Professor.
Family: Wife, Sharon; two children.
Religion: Baptist.
Political Career: Calif. Assembly, 1975–79.

Capitol Office: 2208 Rayburn House Office Building 20515; 225-2915; (fax) 225-8798; (e–mail) www.house.gov/writerep; (web) www.house.gov/billthomas.
Office Staff: Admin. Asst., Cathy Abernathy; Legis. Dir., Robert S. Winters; Press Secy., Jason Poblete; Scheduler, Rene Edelen.
Committees: House Administration — chairman; Ways & Means (Health — chairman; Trade); Joint Library; Joint Printing — chairman.

California 21st — Kern and Tulare counties — Bakersfield. The district vote for Bill Clinton was 34% in 1996.

CQ Voting Studies

	1997	1998
Presidential	35%	28%
Party	88%	89%
Participation	98%	99%

Interest Groups

	1997	1998
ADA	10%	0%
ACU	80%	92%
AFL-CIO	13%	n/a
CCUS	100%	100%

Elections

	1996	1998
General	66%	79%
Primary	79%	*79%

*Open primary

Bennie Thompson (D–Miss.)
Of Bolton • Elected 1993

Born: Jan. 28, 1948, Bolton, Miss.
Education: Tougaloo College, B.A. 1968; Jackson State U., M.S. 1972.
Occupation: Teacher.
Family: Wife, London; one child.
Religion: Methodist.
Political Career: Bolton Board of Aldermen, 1969–73; mayor of Bolton, 1973–79; Hinds County Board of Supervisors, 1980–93.

Capitol Office: 1408 Longworth House Office Building 20515; 225-5876; (fax) 225-5898; (e–mail) thompsonms02@mail.house.gov; (web) www.house.gov/thompson.
Office Staff: Admin. Asst., Marsha G. McCraven; Legis. Dir., Walter Vinson; Communications Dir., Edward Jackson; Scheduler, Minnie Langham.
Committees: Agriculture (Department Operations, Oversight, Nutrition & Forestry; General Farm Commodities); Budget.

Mississippi 2nd — West central — Mississippi Delta. The district vote for Bill Clinton was 62% in 1996.

CQ Voting Studies

	1997	1998
Presidential	68%	77%
Party	87%	89%
Participation	97%	94%

Interest Groups

	1997	1998
ADA	80%	95%
ACU	16%	13%
AFL-CIO	100%	n/a
CCUS	40%	18%

Elections

	1996	1998
General	60%	71%
Primary	u/o	u/o

Mike Thompson (D–Calif.)
Of St. Helena • Elected 1998

Born: Jan. 24, 1951, St. Helena, Calif.
Education: California State U., Chico, B.A. 1982, M.A. 1996.
Military Career: Army, 1969–73.
Occupation: Vintner; winery maintenance supervisor; Calif. Assembly aide; college instructor.
Family: Wife, Janet; two children.
Religion: Roman Catholic.
Political Career: Calif. Senate, 1990–99.

Capitol Office: 415 Cannon House Office Building 20515; 225-3311; (fax) 225-4335; (e–mail) m.thompson@mail.house.gov.
Office Staff: Chief of Staff/Press Secy., Ed Matovcik; Legis. Dir., David A. Flanders; Scheduler, Fran Bolduc.
Committees: Agriculture (Department Operations, Oversight, Nutrition & Forestry; Risk Management, Research & Specialty Crops); Armed Services (Military Installations & Facilities; Military Personnel).

California 1st — Northern Coast — Eureka. The district vote for Bill Clinton was 48% in 1996.

Elections

	1998
General	62%
Primary	*51%

*Open primary

William M. "Mac" Thornberry
(R–Texas)
Of Clarendon • Elected 1994

Born: July 15, 1958, Clarendon, Texas.
Education: Texas Tech U., B.A. 1980; U. of Texas, J.D. 1983.
Occupation: Lawyer; cattleman; State Department official; congressional aide.
Family: Wife, Sally Adams; two children.
Religion: Presbyterian.
Political Career: No previous office.

Capitol Office: 131 Cannon House Office Building 20515; 225-3706; (fax) 225-3486; (e–mail) www.house.gov/writerep; (web) www.house.gov/thornberry.
Office Staff: Admin. Asst., Clay Sell; Communications Dir., Lou Zickar; Scheduler, Tim Kennedy.
Committees: Armed Services (Military Personnel; Military Procurement); Budget; Resources (Energy & Mineral Resources; Water & Power).

Texas 13th — Eastern Panhandle — Wichita Falls; part of Amarillo. The district vote for Bill Clinton was 39% in 1996.

CQ Voting Studies

	1997	1998
Presidential	32%	23%
Party	94%	92%
Participation	99%	99%

Interest Groups

	1997	1998
ADA	5%	5%
ACU	96%	100%
AFL-CIO	0%	n/a
CCUS	100%	89%

Elections

	1996	1998
General	67%	68%
Primary	u/o	94%

John Thune (R-S.D.)
Of Pierre • Elected 1996
Pronounced: THOON

Born: Jan. 7, 1961, Pierre, S.D.
Education: Biola U., B.S. 1983; U. of South Dakota, M.B.A. 1984.
Occupation: Municipal league executive; congressional aide.
Family: Wife, Kimberley; two children.
Religion: Protestant.
Political Career: S.D. Republican Party executive director, 1989–91; S.D. railroad director, 1991–93.

Capitol Office: 1005 Longworth House Office Building 20515; 225-2801; (fax) 225-5823; (e-mail) jthune@mail.house.gov; (web) www.house.gov/thune.
Office Staff: Chief of Staff, Herb Jones; Legis. Dir., Jafar Karim; Press Secy., Christine Iverson; Scheduler, Amy Mannes.
Committees: Agriculture (General Farm Commodities; Risk Management, Research & Specialty Crops); Small Business; Transportation & Infrastructure (Aviation; Ground Transportation).

South Dakota — At large. The district vote for Bill Clinton was 43% in 1996.

CQ Voting Studies

	1997	1998
Presidential	27%	23%
Party	95%	95%
Participation	99%	99%

Interest Groups

	1997	1998
ADA	5%	5%
ACU	88%	92%
AFL-CIO	13%	n/a
CCUS	90%	100%

Elections

	1996	1998
General	58%	75%
Primary	59%	u/o

Karen L. Thurman (D-Fla.)
Of Dunnellon • Elected 1992

Born: Jan. 12, 1951, Rapid City, S.D.
Education: Santa Fe Community College, A.A. 1970; U. of Florida, B.A. 1973.
Occupation: Teacher.
Family: Husband, John; two children.
Religion: Episcopalian.
Political Career: Dunnellon City Council, 1975–83, mayor, 1979–81; Fla. Senate, 1983–93.

Capitol Office: 440 Cannon House Office Building 20515; 225-1002; (fax) 226-0329; (e-mail) kthurman@mail.house.gov; (web) www.house.gov/thurman.
Office Staff: Chief of Staff, Nora Matus; Legis. Dir., Bob Dobek; Communications Dir., Vacant; Exec. Asst., Scott Sachs.
Committees: Ways & Means (Health).

Florida 5th — Northern West Coast — Part of Pasco county; Alachua County; Hernando County. The district vote for Bill Clinton was 50% in 1996.

CQ Voting Studies

	1997	1998
Presidential	79%	77%
Party	84%	86%
Participation	99%	99%

Interest Groups

	1997	1998
ADA	75%	100%
ACU	24%	8%
AFL-CIO	88%	n/a
CCUS	60%	39%

Elections

	1996	1998
General	62%	66%
Primary	u/o	u/o

Todd Tiahrt (R–Kan.)
Of Goddard • Elected 1994
Pronounced: TEE-hart

Born: June 15, 1951, Vermillion, S.D.
Education: Evangel College, B.A. 1975; Southwest Missouri State U., M.B.A. 1989.
Occupation: College instructor; airline company manager.
Family: Wife, Vicki; three children.
Religion: Assembly of God.
Political Career: Republican nominee for Kan. House, 1990; Kan. Senate, 1993–95.

Capitol Office: 428 Cannon House Office Building 20515; 225-6216; (fax) 225-3489; (e-mail) tiahrt@mail.house.gov; (web) www.house.gov/tiahrt.
Office Staff: Admin. Asst., Matt Schlapp; Legis. Dir., Jeff Kahrs; Scheduler, Scott Margolius.
Committees: Appropriations (District of Columbia; Military Construction; Transportation).

Kansas 4th — South central — Wichita. The district vote for Bill Clinton was 35% in 1996.

CQ Voting Studies

	1997	1998
Presidential	23%	20%
Party	95%	96%
Participation	98%	98%

Interest Groups

	1997	1998
ADA	5%	0%
ACU	100%	100%
AFL-CIO	13%	n/a
CCUS	90%	94%

Elections

	1996	1998
General	50%	58%
Primary	u/o	u/o

John F. Tierney (D–Mass.)
Of Salem • Elected 1996

Born: Sept. 18, 1951, Salem, Mass.
Education: Salem State College, B.A. 1973; Suffolk U., J.D. 1976.
Occupation: Lawyer; chamber of commerce official.
Family: Wife, Patrice.
Religion: Unspecified.
Political Career: Democratic nominee for U.S. House, 1994.

Capitol Office: 120 Cannon House Office Building 20515; 225-8020; (fax) 225-5915; (e-mail) www.house.gov/writerep; (web) www.house.gov/tierney.
Office Staff: Chief of Staff/Press Secy., David Williams; Legis. Dir., Elliott Kaye; Scheduler, Mary Flanagan-Taylor.
Committees: Education & Workforce (Employer-Employee Relations; Postsecondary Education, Training & Life-Long Learning); Government Reform (Criminal Justice, Drug Policy & Human Resources; National Security & Veterans Affairs).

Massachusetts 6th — North Shore — Lynn; Peabody. The district vote for Bill Clinton was 59% in 1996.

CQ Voting Studies

	1997	1998
Presidential	75%	80%
Party	94%	96%
Participation	99%	98%

Interest Groups

	1997	1998
ADA	100%	100%
ACU	12%	4%
AFL-CIO	100%	n/a
CCUS	20%	22%

Elections

	1996	1998
General	48%	55%
Primary	86%	87%

Patrick J. Toomey (R-Pa.)
Of Allentown • Elected 1998

Born: Nov. 17, 1961, Providence, R.I.
Education: Harvard U., B.A. 1984.
Occupation: Restaurateur; investment banker.
Family: Wife, Kris.
Religion: Roman Catholic.
Political Career: Allentown Government Study Commission, 1994–96.

Capitol Office: 511 Cannon House Office Building 20515; 225-6411; (fax) 226-0778; (e-mail) www.house.gov/writerep.
Office Staff: Chief of Staff, Chuck Pike; Legis. Dir., Mark Dion; Press Secy., Angie Orem; Scheduler, Kate Rea.
Committees: Banking & Financial Services (Capital Markets & Securities; Domestic & International Monetary Policy); Budget; Small Business (Government Programs & Oversight; Tax, Finance & Exports).

Pennsylvania 15th — East — Allentown; Bethlehem. The district vote for Bill Clinton was 47% in 1996.

Elections

	1998
General	55%
Primary	27%

Edolphus Towns (D-N.Y.)
Of Brooklyn • Elected 1982

Born: July 21, 1934, Chadbourn, N.C.
Education: North Carolina A&T State U., B.S. 1956; Adelphi U., M.S.W. 1973.
Military Career: Army, 1956–58.
Occupation: Professor; hospital administrator.
Family: Wife, Gwendolyn; two children.
Religion: Baptist.
Political Career: Brooklyn Borough deputy president, 1976–82.

Capitol Office: 2232 Rayburn House Office Building 20515; 225-5936; (fax) 225-1018; (e-mail) www.house.gov/writerep; (web) www.house.gov/towns.
Office Staff: Chief of Staff, Brenda Pillors; Communications Dir., Chandra Tuck; Scheduler/Office Mgr., Gerri Taylor.
Committees: Commerce (Finance & Hazardous Materials — ranking member; Health & Environment); Government Reform (District of Columbia; Criminal Justice, Drug Policy & Human Resources; National Security & Veterans Affairs).

New York 10th — Parts of Brooklyn — Bedford-Stuyvesant; Brooklyn Heights. The district vote for Bill Clinton was 89% in 1996.

CQ Voting Studies

	1997	1998
Presidential	67%	76%
Party	85%	82%
Participation	90%	82%

Interest Groups

	1997	1998
ADA	85%	95%
ACU	9%	9%
AFL-CIO	100%	n/a
CCUS	33%	31%

Elections

	1996	1998
General	91%	92%
Primary	u/o	55%

James A. Traficant Jr.   (D–Ohio)
Of Poland • Elected 1984

Born: May 8, 1941, Youngstown, Ohio.
Education: U. of Pittsburgh, B.S. 1963; Youngstown State U., M.S. 1973, M.S. 1976.
Occupation: County drug program director.
Family: Wife, Patricia Choppa; two children.
Religion: Roman Catholic.
Political Career: Mahoning County sheriff, 1981–85.

Capitol Office: 2446 Rayburn House Office Building 20515; 225-5261; (fax) 225-3719; (e–mail) telljim@mail.house.gov; (web) www.house.gov/traficant.
Office Staff: Chief of Staff/Press Secy., Paul Marcone; Legis. Dir., Dan Blair; Scheduler, DeVonne Richburg.
Committees: Transportation & Infrastructure (Aviation; Oversight & Investigations — ranking member).

Ohio 17th — Northeast — Youngstown, Warren. The district vote for Bill Clinton was 58% in 1996.

CQ Voting Studies

	1997	1998
Presidential	36%	46%
Party	23%	32%
Participation	99%	97%

Interest Groups

	1997	1998
ADA	25%	45%
ACU	76%	64%
AFL-CIO	75%	n/a
CCUS	60%	61%

Elections

	1996	1998
General	91%	68%
Primary	u/o	u/o

Jim Turner   (D–Texas)
Of Crockett • Elected 1996

Born: Feb. 6, 1946, Fort Lewis, Wash.
Education: U. of Texas, B.B.A 1968, M.B.A. 1971, J.D. 1971.
Military Career: Army, 1978.
Occupation: Lawyer.
Family: Wife, Ginny; two children.
Religion: Baptist.
Political Career: Texas House, 1981–84; mayor of Crockett, 1989–91; Texas Senate, 1991–96.

Capitol Office: 208 Cannon House Office Building 20515; 225-2401; (fax) 225-5955; (e–mail) tx02@mail.house.gov; (web) www.house.gov/turner.
Office Staff: Chief of Staff, Elizabeth Hurley; Legis. Dir., Laurie Knight; Press Secy., Jennifer Beltz; Scheduler, Ashley Newell.
Committees: Armed Services (Military Procurement; Military Research & Development); Government Reform (Government Management, Information & Technology — ranking member; Criminal Justice, Drug Policy & Human Resources).

Texas 2nd — East — Lufkin; Orange. The district vote for Bill Clinton was 45% in 1996.

CQ Voting Studies

	1997	1998
Presidential	61%	52%
Party	67%	56%
Participation	98%	97%

Interest Groups

	1997	1998
ADA	50%	65%
ACU	48%	48%
AFL-CIO	75%	n/a
CCUS	80%	72%

Elections

	1996	1998
General	52%	58%
Primary	59%	u/o

Mark Udall (D–Colo.)
Of Boulder • Elected 1998

Born: July 18, 1950, Tucson, Ariz.
Education: Williams College, B.A. 1972.
Occupation: Colo. Outward Bound School executive director.
Family: Wife, Margaret Fox; two children.
Religion: Unspecified.
Political Career: Colo. House, 1997–99.

Capitol Office: 128 Cannon House Office Building 20515; 225-2161; (fax) 226-7840; (e–mail) www.house.gov/writerep.
Office Staff: Chief of Staff, Alan Salazar; Press Secy., Lawrence Pacheco; Scheduler, Marian Goodman.
Committees: Resources (Forests & Forest Health; National Parks & Public Lands); Science (Space & Aeronautics; Technology).

Elections

	1998
General	50%
Primary	44%

Colorado 2nd — Northwest Denver suburbs; Boulder. The district vote for Bill Clinton was 49% in 1996.

Tom Udall (D–N.M.)
Of Santa Fe • Elected 1998

Born: May 18, 1948, Tuscon, Ariz.
Education: Prescott College, B.A. 1970; Cambridge U., B.L.L. 1975; U. of New Mexico, J.D. 1977.
Occupation: Lawyer.
Family: Wife, Jill Cooper; one stepchild.
Religion: Mormon.
Political Career: Assistant U.S. attorney, 1978–81; sought Democratic nomination for U.S. House, 1982; Democratic nominee for U.S. House, 1988; N.M. attorney general, 1991–99.

Capitol Office: 502 Cannon House Office Building 20515; 225-6190; (fax) 226-1331; (e–mail) www.house.gov/writerep.
Office Staff: Chief of Staff, Gerald Gonzalez; Legis. Dir., Damon Martinez; Press Secy., Mo Elleithee; Scheduler, Ramon DeAzua.
Committees: Resources (Forests & Forest Health; National Parks & Public Lands); Small Business (Empowerment; Rural Enterprises).

Elections

	1998
General	53%
Primary	44%

New Mexico 3rd — North and East Central — Farmington; Santa Fe. The district vote for Bill Clinton was 53% in 1996.

Fred Upton (R–Mich.)
Of St. Joseph • Elected 1986

Born: Apr. 23, 1953, St. Joseph, Mich.
Education: U. of Michigan, B.A. 1975.
Occupation: Congressional aide; budget analyst.
Family: Wife, Amey; two children.
Religion: Protestant.
Political Career: No previous office.

Capitol Office: 2333 Rayburn House Office Building 20515; 225-3761; (fax) 225-4986; (e–mail) talk2.fsu@mail.house.gov; (web) www.house.gov/upton.
Office Staff: Chief of Staff, Joan Hillebrands; Legis. Dir., Scott Aliferis; Press Secy., Dave Woodruff; Scheduler, Sharon Dorazio.
Committees: Commerce (Health & Environment; Oversight & Investigations — chairman); Education & Workforce (Early Childhood, Youth & Families).

Michigan 6th — Southwest — Kalamazoo; Benton Harbor; St. Joseph. The district vote for Bill Clinton was 46% in 1996.

CQ Voting Studies

	1997	1998
Presidential	37%	33%
Party	83%	79%
Participation	99%	100%

Interest Groups

	1997	1998
ADA	25%	15%
ACU	80%	56%
AFL-CIO	13%	n/a
CCUS	90%	89%

Elections

	1996	1998
General	68%	70%
Primary	u/o	u/o

Nydia M. Velazquez (D–N.Y.)
Of Brooklyn • Elected 1992
Pronounced: NID-ee–uh veh-LASS-kez

Born: Mar. 22, 1953, Yabucoa, P.R.
Education: U. of Puerto Rico, B.A. 1974; New York U., M.A. 1976.
Occupation: Professor.
Family: Divorced.
Religion: Roman Catholic.
Political Career: N.Y. City Council, 1984–85; defeated for re–election to N.Y. City Council, 1984.

Capitol Office: 2241 Rayburn House Office Building 20515; 225-2361; (fax) 226-0327; (e–mail) www.house.gov/writerep; (web) www.house.gov/velazquez.
Office Staff: Chief of Staff, Michael Bay; Legis. Dir., Catherine Cruz Wojtasik; Press Secy., Dwayne Layler; Scheduler, Mairym Ramos.
Committees: Banking & Financial Services (Capital Markets & Securities; Housing & Community Opportunity); Small Business — ranking member.

New York 12th — Lower East Side of Manhattan; parts of Brooklyn and Queens. The district vote for Bill Clinton was 83% in 1996.

CQ Voting Studies

	1997	1998
Presidential	76%	79%
Party	94%	93%
Participation	96%	94%

Interest Groups

	1997	1998
ADA	95%	95%
ACU	4%	8%
AFL-CIO	100%	n/a
CCUS	20%	33%

Elections

	1996	1998
General	85%	84%
Primary	u/o	u/o

Bruce F. Vento (D–Minn.)
Of St. Paul • Elected 1976

Born: Oct. 7, 1940, St. Paul, Minn.
Education: U. of Minnesota, A.A. 1961; Wisconsin State U., B.S. 1965; U. of Minnesota, attended 1965–70.
Occupation: Science teacher.
Family: Divorced; three children.
Religion: Roman Catholic.
Political Career: Minn. House, 1971–77.

Capitol Office: 2413 Rayburn House Office Building 20515; 225-6631; (fax) 225-1968; (e-mail) vento@mail.house.gov; (web) www.house.gov/vento.
Office Staff: Admin. Asst., Larry Romans; Communications Dir., Erin Sermeus; Office Mgr./Scheduler, Mary Ann Daly.
Committees: Banking & Financial Services (Financial Institutions & Consumer Credit — ranking member; Housing & Community Opportunity); Resources (Fisheries Conservation, Wildlife & Oceans; National Parks & Public Lands).

Minnesota 4th — St. Paul and suburbs. The district vote for Bill Clinton was 58% in 1996.

CQ Voting Studies

	1997	1998
Presidential	84%	85%
Party	98%	97%
Participation	99%	99%

Interest Groups

	1997	1998
ADA	100%	100%
ACU	4%	8%
AFL-CIO	100%	n/a
CCUS	40%	33%

Elections

	1996	1998
General	57%	54%
Primary	u/o	u/o

Peter J. Visclosky (D–Ind.)
Of Merrillville • Elected 1984
Pronounced: vis-KLOSS-key

Born: Aug. 13, 1949, Gary, Ind.
Education: Indiana U. Northwest, B.S. 1970; U. of Notre Dame, J.D. 1973; Georgetown U., LL.M. 1982.
Occupation: Lawyer; congressional aide.
Family: Divorced; two children.
Religion: Roman Catholic.
Political Career: No previous office.

Capitol Office: 2313 Rayburn House Office Building 20515; 225-2461; (fax) 225-2493; (e-mail) www.house.gov/writerep; (web) www.house.gov/visclosky.
Office Staff: Chief of Staff, Charles E. Brimmer; Communications Dir., Chip Lewis; Scheduler, Nicole Gamache.
Committees: Appropriations (Energy & Water Development — ranking member; Defense).

Indiana 1st — Northwest — Gary; Hammond. The district vote for Bill Clinton was 58% in 1996.

CQ Voting Studies

	1997	1998
Presidential	65%	79%
Party	80%	82%
Participation	98%	97%

Interest Groups

	1997	1998
ADA	65%	80%
ACU	29%	12%
AFL-CIO	88%	n/a
CCUS	50%	28%

Elections

	1996	1998
General	69%	73%
Primary	84%	87%

Greg Walden (R–Ore.)
Of Hood River • Elected 1998

Born: Jan. 10, 1957, The Dalles, Ore.
Education: U. of Oregon, B.S. 1981.
Occupation: Radio station owner; congressional aide.
Family: Wife, Mylene; one child.
Religion: Episcopalian.
Political Career: Ore. House, 1989–95, majority leader, 1991–95; Ore. Senate, 1995–97, assistant majority leader, 1995–97.

Capitol Office: 1404 Longworth House Office Building 20515; 225-6730; (fax) 225-5774; (e–mail) www.house.gov/writerep.
Office Staff: Chief of Staff, Bryan MacDonald; Legis. Dir., Lindsay Slater; Communications Dir., Kevin McDermott; Scheduler, Melissa Galvan.
Committees: Agriculture (Department Operations, Oversight, Nutrition & Forestry; Risk Management, Research & Specialty Crops); Government Reform (Government Management, Information & Technology; National Economic Growth); Resources (Energy & Mineral Resources; Water & Power).

Oregon 2nd — East and Southwest — Medford; Bend. The district vote for Bill Clinton was 38% in 1996.

Elections

	1998
General	61%
Primary	55%

James T. Walsh (R–N.Y.)
Of Syracuse • Elected 1988

Born: June 19, 1947, Syracuse, N.Y.
Education: St. Bonaventure U., B.A. 1970.
Occupation: Marketing executive; social worker.
Family: Wife, DeDe Ryan Walsh; three children.
Religion: Roman Catholic.
Political Career: Syracuse Common Council, 1978–88, president, 1986–88; sought nomination for Onondaga County executive, 1987.

Capitol Office: 2351 Rayburn House Office Building 20515; 225-3701; (fax) 225-4042; (e–mail) rep.james.walsh@mail.house.gov; (web) www.house.gov/walsh.
Office Staff: Admin. Asst./Legis. Dir., Art Jutton; Press Secy., James H. O'Connor; Appts. Secy., Jodi Major.
Committees: Appropriations (Agriculture, Rural Development, FDA & Related Agencies; Military Construction; VA, HUD & Independent Agencies — chairman).

New York 25th — Central — Syracuse. The district vote for Bill Clinton was 51% in 1996.

CQ Voting Studies

	1997	1998
Presidential	36%	35%
Party	85%	73%
Participation	98%	98%

Interest Groups

	1997	1998
ADA	35%	30%
ACU	75%	44%
AFL-CIO	38%	n/a
CCUS	80%	89%

Elections

	1996	1998
General	55%	69%
Primary	u/o	u/o

Zach Wamp (R–Tenn.)
Of Chattanooga • Elected 1994

Born: Oct. 28, 1957, Fort Benning, Ga.
Education: U. of North Carolina, attended 1977–78; U. of Tennessee, attended 1978–79; U. of North Carolina, attended 1979–80.
Occupation: Real estate broker.
Family: Wife, Kim; two children.
Religion: Baptist.
Political Career: Republican nominee for U.S. House, 1992.

Capitol Office: 423 Cannon House Office Building 20515; 225-3271; (fax) 225-3494; (e–mail) www.house.gov/writerep; (web) www.house.gov/wamp.
Office Staff: Chief of Staff, Helen Hardin; Legis. Dir., Claire McVay; Press Secy., Dick Kopper; Scheduler, Susan Haigler.
Committees: Appropriations (Commerce, Justice, State & Judiciary; Interior; Legislative Branch); Budget.

Tennessee 3rd — Southeast — Chattanooga; Oak Ridge. The district vote for Bill Clinton was 46% in 1996.

CQ Voting Studies

	1997	1998
Presidential	28%	18%
Party	88%	89%
Participation	97%	98%

Interest Groups

	1997	1998
ADA	5%	15%
ACU	92%	84%
AFL-CIO	0%	n/a
CCUS	80%	76%

Elections

	1996	1998
General	56%	66%
Primary	u/o	93%

Maxine Waters (D–Calif.)
Of Los Angeles • Elected 1990

Born: Aug. 15, 1938, St. Louis, Mo.
Education: California State U., Los Angeles, B.A. 1970.
Occupation: Head Start official.
Family: Husband, Sidney Williams; two children.
Religion: Christian.
Political Career: Calif. Assembly, 1977–91.

Capitol Office: 2344 Rayburn House Office Building 20515; 225-2201; (fax) 225-7854; (e–mail) www.house.gov/writerep; (web) www.house.gov/waters.
Office Staff: Chief of Staff, Rodney Johnson; Press Secy., Rouffin Brown; Scheduler, Joyce Freeland.
Committees: Banking & Financial Services (Capital Markets & Securities; Domestic & International Monetary Policy — ranking member); Judiciary (Constitution).

California 35th — South Central Los Angeles. The district vote for Bill Clinton was 84% in 1996.

CQ Voting Studies

	1997	1998
Presidential	75%	76%
Party	92%	85%
Participation	96%	89%

Interest Groups

	1997	1998
ADA	95%	80%
ACU	8%	0%
AFL-CIO	100%	n/a
CCUS	20%	21%

Elections

	1996	1998
General	86%	89%
Primary	u/o	*87%

*Open primary

Wes Watkins (R–Okla.)
Of Stillwater • Elected 1996
Also served 1977–91 as a Democrat

Born: Dec. 15, 1938, DeQueen, Ark.
Education: Oklahoma State U., B.S. 1960, M.S. 1961.
Military Career: Okla. National Guard, 1960–67.
Occupation: Communications executive; homebuilding contractor; economic developer.
Family: Wife, Lou; three children.
Religion: Presbyterian.
Political Career: Okla. Senate, 1975–77; U.S. House, 1977–91, served as a Democrat; sought Democratic nomination for governor, 1990; independent candidate for governor, 1994.

Capitol Office: 1401 Longworth House Office Building 20515; 225-4565; (fax) 225-5966; (e–mail) wes.watkins@mail.house.gov; (web) www.house.gov/watkins.
Office Staff: Chief of Staff, Leslie Belcher; Legis. Dir., Scott Raab; Scheduler, Angela Kraus.
Committees: Ways & Means (Human Resources; Oversight).

Oklahoma 3rd — Southeast — "Little Dixie." The district vote for Bill Clinton was 47% in 1996.

CQ Voting Studies

	1997	1998
Presidential	24%	23%
Party	93%	93%
Participation	95%	98%

Interest Groups

	1997	1998
ADA	0%	5%
ACU	96%	92%
AFL-CIO	0%	n/a
CCUS	89%	100%

Elections

	1996	1998
General	51%	62%
Primary	79%	u/o

Melvin Watt (D–N.C.)
Of Charlotte • Elected 1992

Born: Aug. 26, 1945, Steele Creek, N.C.
Education: U. of North Carolina, B.S. 1967; Yale U., J.D. 1970.
Occupation: Nursing home owner; campaign manager; lawyer.
Family: Wife, Eulada; two children.
Religion: Presbyterian.
Political Career: N.C. Senate, 1985–86.

Capitol Office: 1230 Longworth House Office Building 20515; 225-1510; (fax) 225-1512; (e–mail) nc12.public@mail.house.gov; (web) www.house.gov/watt.
Office Staff: Chief of Staff, Joyce Brayboy Dalton; Press Secy./Scheduler, Shelley Winters.
Committees: Banking & Financial Services (Domestic & International Monetary Policy; Financial Institutions & Consumer Credit); Joint Economic; Judiciary (Commercial & Administrative Law; Constitution — ranking member).

North Carolina 12th — Central — Parts of Charlotte, Winston-Salem and Kannapolis. The district vote for Bill Clinton was 53% in 1996.

CQ Voting Studies

	1997	1998
Presidential	77%	89%
Party	94%	95%
Participation	99%	98%

Interest Groups

	1997	1998
ADA	100%	100%
ACU	4%	4%
AFL-CIO	100%	n/a
CCUS	30%	28%

Elections

	1996	1998
General	71%	56%
Primary	u/o	84%

J.C. Watts Jr. (R–Okla.)
Of Norman • Elected 1994

Born: Nov. 18, 1957, Eufaula, Okla.
Education: U. of Oklahoma, B.S. 1981.
Occupation: Property management company owner; professional football player; youth minister.
Family: Wife, Frankie; five children.
Religion: Southern Baptist.
Political Career: Okla. Corporation Commission, 1991–95.

Capitol Office: 1210 Longworth House Office Building 20515; 225-6165; (fax) 225-3512; (e–mail) rep.jcwatts@mail.house.gov; (web) www.house.gov/watts.
Office Staff: Chief of Staff, Mike Hunter; Press Secy./Deputy Chief of Staff, Pamela D. Pryor; Legis. Dir., Jack Horner.
Committees: Armed Services (Military Personnel; Military Procurement); Transportation & Infrastructure (Aviation; Economic Development & Public Buildings).

Oklahoma 4th — Southwest; part of Oklahoma City. The district vote for Bill Clinton was 40% in 1996.

CQ Voting Studies

	1997	1998
Presidential	24%	21%
Party	94%	91%
Participation	97%	99%

Interest Groups

	1997	1998
ADA	0%	10%
ACU	100%	84%
AFL-CIO	0%	n/a
CCUS	89%	94%

Elections

	1996	1998
General	58%	62%
Primary	u/o	u/o

Henry A. Waxman (D–Calif.)
Of Los Angeles • Elected 1974

Born: Sept. 12, 1939, Los Angeles, Calif.
Education: U. of California, Los Angeles, B.A. 1961, J.D. 1964.
Occupation: Lawyer.
Family: Wife, Janet; two children.
Religion: Jewish.
Political Career: Calif. Assembly, 1969–75.

Capitol Office: 2204 Rayburn House Office Building 20515; 225-3976; (fax) 225-4099; (e–mail) www.house.gov/writerep; (web) www.house.gov/waxman.
Office Staff: Admin. Asst., Patricia Delgado; Chief of Staff/Press Secy., Philip Schiliro; Office Mgr., Norah Lucey-Mail.
Committees: Commerce (Health & Environment; Oversight & Investigations); Government Reform — ranking member.

California 29th — West Los Angeles County; Santa Monica; West Hollywood. The district vote for Bill Clinton was 67% in 1996.

CQ Voting Studies

	1997	1998
Presidential	85%	84%
Party	92%	94%
Participation	94%	94%

Interest Groups

	1997	1998
ADA	95%	100%
ACU	0%	4%
AFL-CIO	100%	n/a
CCUS	20%	18%

Elections

	1996	1998
General	68%	74%
Primary	u/o	*71%

*Open primary

Anthony D. Weiner (D–N.Y.)
Of Brooklyn • Elected 1998
Pronounced: WEE-ner

Born: Sept. 4, 1964, Brooklyn, N.Y.
Education: State U. of New York, Plattsburgh, B.A. 1985.
Occupation: Congressional aide.
Family: Single.
Religion: Jewish.
Political Career: New York City Council, 1992–99.

Capitol Office: 501 Cannon House Office Building 20515; 225-6616; (fax) 226-7253; (e-mail) www.house.gov/writerep.
Office Staff: Chief of Staff, Kevin Ryan; Chief of Staff, Christopher Bloitti; Legis. Dir., Eric Rosen; Press Secy., Serena Torrey; Scheduler, Lisa Webster.
Committees: Judiciary (Commercial & Administrative Law; Crime); Science (Space & Aeronautics; Technology).

New York 9th — Parts of Brooklyn and Queens — Sheepshead Bay; Forest Hills. The district vote for Bill Clinton was 65% in 1996.

Elections

	1998
General	66%
Primary	29%

Curt Weldon (R–Pa.)
Of Aston • Elected 1986

Born: July 22, 1947, Marcus Hook, Pa.
Education: West Chester State College, B.A. 1969.
Occupation: Teacher; consultant.
Family: Wife, Mary Gallagher Weldon; five children.
Religion: Protestant.
Political Career: Mayor of Marcus Hook, 1977–82; Delaware County Council, 1981–86, chairman, 1982–86; Republican nominee for U.S. House, 1984.

Capitol Office: 2452 Rayburn House Office Building 20515; 225-2011; (fax) 225-8137; (e-mail) curtpa7@mail.house.gov; (web) www.house.gov/cweldon.
Office Staff: Chief of Staff, Michael Barbera; Legis. Dir., Nancy Lifset; Press Secy., Pete Peterson; Exec. Asst./Scheduler, Cara Liberi.
Committees: Armed Services (Military Readiness; Military Research & Development — chairman); China Investigation; Science (Energy & Environment; Technology).

Pennsylvania 7th — Suburban Philadelphia — Part of Delaware County. The district vote for Bill Clinton was 45% in 1996.

CQ Voting Studies

	1997	1998
Presidential	36%	28%
Party	76%	77%
Participation	91%	96%

Interest Groups

	1997	1998
ADA	30%	25%
ACU	60%	60%
AFL-CIO	50%	n/a
CCUS	89%	78%

Elections

	1996	1998
General	67%	72%
Primary	83%	u/o

Dave Weldon (R–Fla.)
Of Palm Bay • Elected 1994

Born: Aug. 31, 1953, Amityville, N.Y.
Education: State U. of New York, Stony Brook, B.S. 1978; State U. of New York, Buffalo, M.D. 1981.
Military Career: Army Medical Corps, 1981–87; Army Reserve, 1987–92.
Occupation: Physician.
Family: Wife, Nancy; one child.
Religion: Christian.
Political Career: No previous office.

Capitol Office: 322 Cannon House Office Building 20515; 225-3671; (fax) 225-3516; (e-mail) fla15@mail.house.gov; (web) www.house.gov/weldon.
Office Staff: Chief of Staff, Dana Gartzke; Legis. Dir., Stuart Burns; Press Secy., Eldon Girdner; Scheduler, Barbara Reynolds.
Committees: Banking & Financial Services (Domestic & International Monetary Policy; Financial Institutions & Consumer Credit); Science (Energy & Environment; Space & Aeronautics).

Florida 15th — Central — Brevard, Osceola and Indian River counties; Palm Bay; Melbourne. The district vote for Bill Clinton was 41% in 1996.

CQ Voting Studies

	1997	1998
Presidential	19%	16%
Party	87%	91%
Participation	92%	95%

Interest Groups

	1997	1998
ADA	0%	0%
ACU	92%	92%
AFL-CIO	0%	n/a
CCUS	67%	89%

Elections

	1996	1998
General	51%	63%
Primary	u/o	79%

Jerry Weller (R–Ill.)
Of Morris • Elected 1994

Born: July 7, 1957, Streator, Ill.
Education: Joliet Junior College, attended 1977; U. of Illinois, B.S. 1979.
Occupation: Congressional aide; state and federal official; hog farmer; sales representative.
Family: Single.
Religion: Christian.
Political Career: Ill. House, 1987–93.

Capitol Office: 424 Cannon House Office Building 20515; 225-3635; (fax) 225-3521; (e-mail) www.house.gov/writerep; (web) www.house.gov/weller.
Office Staff: Admin. Asst., Jim Hayes; Legis. Dir., Bill Hempler; Press Secy., Maggie Lockwood; Exec. Asst., Alan Tennille.
Committees: Ways & Means (Oversight; Social Security).

Illinois 11th — South Chicago Suburbs and exurbs — Joliet. The district vote for Bill Clinton was 51% in 1996.

CQ Voting Studies

	1997	1998
Presidential	28%	26%
Party	92%	86%
Participation	99%	98%

Interest Groups

	1997	1998
ADA	5%	15%
ACU	84%	92%
AFL-CIO	50%	n/a
CCUS	80%	88%

Elections

	1996	1998
General	52%	59%
Primary	u/o	u/o

Robert Wexler (D–Fla.)
Of Boca Raton • Elected 1996

Born: Jan. 2, 1961, Queens, N.Y.
Education: Emory U., attended 1978–79; U. of Florida, B.A. 1982; George Washington U., J.D. 1985.
Occupation: Lawyer.
Family: Wife, Laurie; three children.
Religion: Jewish.
Political Career: Fla. Senate, 1990–97.

Capitol Office: 213 Cannon House Office Building 20515; 225-3001; (fax) 225-5974; (e-mail) www.house.gov/writerep; (web) www.house.gov/wexler.
Office Staff: Chief of Staff/Legis. Dir., Suzanne Stoll; Press Asst., Josh Rogin; Scheduler, Lisa White.
Committees: International Relations (Asia & the Pacific; Western Hemisphere); Judiciary (Courts & Intellectual Property).

Florida 19th — Southeast — Parts of Palm Beach and northern Broward counties; Boca Raton. The district vote for Bill Clinton was 65% in 1996.

CQ Voting Studies

	1997	1998
Presidential	76%	88%
Party	84%	90%
Participation	94%	95%

Interest Groups

	1997	1998
ADA	90%	100%
ACU	17%	0%
AFL-CIO	100%	n/a
CCUS	40%	18%

Elections

	1996	1998
General	66%	u/o
Primary	*65%	u/o

*Runoff election

Bob Weygand (D–R.I.)
Of North Kingstown • Elected 1996
Pronounced: WAY-gend (hard G)

Born: May 10, 1948, Attleboro, Mass.
Education: U. of Rhode Island, B.F.A. 1971, B.S. 1976.
Occupation: Landscape architect; architectural firm executive.
Family: Wife, Frances; three children.
Religion: Roman Catholic.
Political Career: R.I. House, 1985–93; lieutenant governor, 1993–97.

Capitol Office: 215 Cannon House Office Building 20515; 225-2735; (fax) 225-5976; (e-mail) robert.weygand@mail.house.gov; (web) www.house.gov/weygand.
Office Staff: Chief of Staff, James M. Russo; Legis. Dir., Kevin M. Wilson; Press Secy., Gregg Perry; Scheduler, Patrice Croci.
Committees: Banking & Financial Services (Capital Markets & Securities; Housing & Community Opportunity); Budget.

Rhode Island 2nd — West — Western Providence; Warwick. The district vote for Bill Clinton was 59% in 1996.

CQ Voting Studies

	1997	1998
Presidential	65%	73%
Party	84%	87%
Participation	97%	99%

Interest Groups

	1997	1998
ADA	70%	90%
ACU	25%	20%
AFL-CIO	100%	n/a
CCUS	30%	56%

Elections

	1996	1998
General	64%	72%
Primary	48%	u/o

Edward Whitfield (R–Ky.)
Of Hopkinsville • Elected 1994

Born: May 25, 1943, Hopkinsville, Ky.
Education: U. of Kentucky, B.S. 1965; Wesley Theological Seminary, attended 1966; U. of Kentucky, J.D. 1969.
Military Career: Army Reserve, 1967–73.
Occupation: Lawyer; oil distributor; railroad executive.
Family: Wife, Constance; one child.
Religion: Methodist.
Political Career: Ky. House, 1974–75.

Capitol Office: 236 Cannon House Office Building 20515; 225-3115; (fax) 225-3547; (e–mail) www.house.gov/writerep; (web) www.house.gov/whitfield.
Office Staff: Policy Dir., Larry VanHoose; Legis. Dir., Karen Long; Press Secy., Anthony Hulen; Scheduler, Carri Leinger.
Committees: Commerce (Energy & Power; Health & Environment; Oversight & Investigations).

Kentucky 1st — West — Paducah. The district vote for Bill Clinton was 47% in 1996.

CQ Voting Studies

	1997	1998
Presidential	31%	23%
Party	92%	88%
Participation	98%	97%

Interest Groups

	1997	1998
ADA	0%	5%
ACU	96%	96%
AFL-CIO	13%	n/a
CCUS	100%	88%

Elections

	1996	1998
General	54%	55%
Primary	u/o	u/o

Roger Wicker (R–Miss.)
Of Tupelo • Elected 1994

Born: July 5, 1951, Pontotoc, Miss.
Education: U. of Mississippi, B.S. 1973, J.D. 1975.
Military Career: Air Force, 1976–80; Air Force Reserve, 1980–present.
Occupation: Lawyer; congressional aide.
Family: Wife, Gayle; three children.
Religion: Southern Baptist.
Political Career: Miss. Senate, 1987–95.

Capitol Office: 206 Cannon House Office Building 20515; 225-4306; (fax) 225-3549; (e–mail) roger.wicker@mail.house.gov; (web) www.house.gov/wicker.
Office Staff: Chief of Staff, John Keast; Legis. Dir., Chris Pedigo; Admin. Asst./Press Secy., Stovall Witte; Scheduler, Michelle Barlow.
Committees: Appropriations (Labor, Health & Human Services & Education; Military Construction; VA, HUD & Independent Agencies).

Mississippi 1st — North — Tupelo. The district vote for Bill Clinton was 42% in 1996.

CQ Voting Studies

	1997	1998
Presidential	28%	23%
Party	94%	91%
Participation	99%	96%

Interest Groups

	1997	1998
ADA	0%	0%
ACU	80%	96%
AFL-CIO	0%	n/a
CCUS	100%	100%

Elections

	1996	1998
General	68%	67%
Primary	u/o	u/o

Heather A. Wilson (R–N.M.)
Of Albuquerque • Elected 1998

Born: Dec. 30, 1960, Keene, N.H.
Education: Air Force Academy, B.S. 1982; Oxford U., M.Phil. 1984, D.Phil. 1985.
Military Career: Air Force, 1978–89.
Occupation: Management consultant; National Security Council staff member.
Family: Husband, Jay Hone; three children.
Religion: Methodist.
Political Career: N.M. Children, Youth and Families secretary, 1995–98.

Capitol Office: 226 Cannon House Office Building 20515; 225-6316; (fax) 225-4975; (e-mail) ask.heather@mail.house.gov; (web) www.house.gov/wilson.
Office Staff: Chief of Staff, Bobby Carr; Legis. Dir., Jim Stein; Press Secy., Eddie Binder; Scheduler, Ashley Weh.
Committees: Commerce (Energy & Power; Finance & Hazardous Materials; Telecommunications, Trade & Consumer Protection); Select Intelligence (Human Intelligence, Analysis & Counterintelligence; Technical & Tactical Intelligence).

New Mexico 1st — Central — Albuquerque. The district vote for Bill Clinton was 48% in 1996.

CQ Voting Studies

	1998
Presidential	22%
Party	86%
Participation	99%

Interest Groups

	1998
ADA	0%
ACU	83%
AFL-CIO	n/a
CCUS	100%

Elections

	1998	1998
General	*45%	48%
Primary		62%

*Special election

Bob Wise (D–W.Va.)
Of Clendenin • Elected 1982

Born: Jan. 6, 1948, Washington, D.C.
Education: Duke U., A.B. 1970; Tulane U., J.D. 1975.
Occupation: Lawyer.
Family: Wife, Sandra; two children.
Religion: Episcopalian.
Political Career: W.Va. Senate, 1981–83.

Capitol Office: 2367 Rayburn House Office Building 20515; 225-2711; (fax) 225-7856; (e-mail) bobwise@mail.house.gov; (web) www.house.gov/wise.
Office Staff: Admin. Asst., Lowell Johnson; Legis. Dir., Jane Mellow; Press Secy., Steve Cohen; Scheduler, Jodi O'Mear.
Committees: Government Reform (National Security & Veterans Affairs); Transportation & Infrastructure (Economic Development & Public Buildings — ranking member; Ground Transportation).

West Virginia 2nd — Center — Charleston; Eastern Panhandle. The district vote for Bill Clinton was 49% in 1996.

CQ Voting Studies

	1997	1998
Presidential	80%	74%
Party	80%	81%
Participation	96%	96%

Interest Groups

	1997	1998
ADA	80%	80%
ACU	17%	4%
AFL-CIO	100%	n/a
CCUS	40%	33%

Elections

	1996	1998
General	69%	73%
Primary	86%	86%

Frank R. Wolf (R–Va.)
Of Vienna • Elected 1980

Born: Jan. 30, 1939, Philadelphia, Pa.
Education: Pennsylvania State U., B.A. 1961; Georgetown U., LL.B. 1965.
Military Career: Army Reserve, 1962–63.
Occupation: Lawyer; congressional aide.
Family: Wife, Carolyn; five children.
Religion: Presbyterian.
Political Career: Sought Republican nomination for U.S. House, 1976; Republican nominee for U.S. House, 1978.

Capitol Office: 241 Cannon House Office Building 20515; 225-5136; (fax) 225-0437; (e–mail) www.house.gov/writerep; (web) www.house.gov/wolf.
Office Staff: Admin. Asst., Charles E. White; Legis. Dir., Janet Shaffron; Press Secy., Roseanne Dupras; Scheduler, Kristin Erb.
Committees: Appropriations (Foreign Operations & Export Financing; Transportation — chairman; Treasury, Postal Service & General Government).

Virginia 10th — North — Part of Fairfax County; Manassas. The district vote for Bill Clinton was 38% in 1996.

CQ Voting Studies

	1997	1998
Presidential	28%	24%
Party	87%	88%
Participation	98%	99%

Interest Groups

	1997	1998
ADA	15%	10%
ACU	84%	80%
AFL-CIO	25%	n/a
CCUS	90%	72%

Elections

	1996	1998
General	72%	72%
Primary	u/o	u/o

Lynn Woolsey (D–Calif.)
Of Petaluma • Elected 1992
Pronounced: WOOL-zee

Born: Nov. 3, 1937, Seattle, Wash.
Education: U. of Washington, attended 1955–57; U. of San Francisco, B.S. 1980.
Occupation: Personnel service owner.
Family: Divorced; four children.
Religion: Presbyterian.
Political Career: Petaluma City Council, 1985–93.

Capitol Office: 439 Cannon House Office Building 20515; 225-5161; (fax) 225-8714; (e–mail) lynn.woolsey@mail.house.gov; (web) www.house.gov/woolsey.
Office Staff: Chief of Staff, Janice Morris; Legis. Dir., Paul Chatalas; Press Secy., Amy Feinberg; Scheduler, Courtney Bright.
Committees: Education & Workforce (Early Childhood, Youth & Families; Workforce Protections); Science (Basic Research).

California 6th — Northern Bay area; Sonoma and Marin counties. The district vote for Bill Clinton was 57% in 1996.

CQ Voting Studies

	1997	1998
Presidential	80%	84%
Party	96%	95%
Participation	96%	99%

Interest Groups

	1997	1998
ADA	100%	100%
ACU	0%	8%
AFL-CIO	100%	n/a
CCUS	30%	28%

Elections

	1996	1998
General	62%	68%
Primary	u/o	*65%

*Open primary

David Wu (D-Ore.)
Of Portland • Elected 1998

Born: Apr. 8, 1955, Taiwan.
Education: Stanford U., B.S. 1977; Harvard Medical School, attended 1978; Yale U., J.D. 1982.
Occupation: Lawyer.
Family: Wife, Michelle; one child.
Religion: Presbyterian.
Political Career: No previous office.

Capitol Office: 510 Cannon House Office Building 20515; 225-0855; (fax) 225-9497; (e-mail) david.wu@mail.house.gov.
Office Staff: Chief of Staff, Christopher Porter; Press Secy., Mark Kornblau.
Committees: Education & Workforce (Early Childhood, Youth & Families; Employer-Employee Relations); Science (Space & Aeronautics; Technology).

Oregon 1st — Western Portland and suburbs. The district vote for Bill Clinton was 50% in 1996.

Elections

	1998
General	50%
Primary	52%

Albert R. Wynn (D-Md.)
Of Largo • Elected 1992

Born: Sept. 10, 1951, Philadelphia, Pa.
Education: U. of Pittsburgh, B.S. 1973; Howard U., attended 1973–74; Georgetown U., J.D. 1977.
Occupation: Lawyer.
Family: Separated; one child.
Religion: Baptist.
Political Career: Md. House, 1983–87; Md. Senate, 1987–93.

Capitol Office: 407 Cannon House Office Building 20515; 225-8699; (fax) 225-8714; (e-mail) albert.wynn@mail.house.gov; (web) www.house.gov/wynn.
Office Staff: Chief of Staff, Curt Clifton; Legis. Dir., Keith Griffin; Press Secy., Elena M. Temple; Office Mgr./Personal Secy., Norma Collins.
Committees: Commerce (Energy & Power; Telecommunications, Trade & Consumer Protection).

Maryland 4th — Inner Prince George's County; Silver Spring. The district vote for Bill Clinton was 80% in 1996.

CQ Voting Studies

	1997	1998
Presidential	75%	82%
Party	87%	91%
Participation	99%	96%

Interest Groups

	1997	1998
ADA	90%	100%
ACU	4%	4%
AFL-CIO	100%	n/a
CCUS	40%	33%

Elections

	1996	1998
General	85%	86%
Primary	85%	87%

C.W. Bill Young (R–Fla.)
Of Indian Rocks Beach • Elected 1970

Born: Dec. 16, 1930, Harmarville, Pa.
Education: Pennsylvania public schools, attended.
Military Career: National Guard, 1948–57.
Occupation: Insurance executive; public official.
Family: Wife, Beverly; three children.
Religion: Methodist.
Political Career: Fla. Senate, 1961–71, minority leader, 1967–71.

Capitol Office: 2407 Rayburn House Office Building 20515; 225-5961; (fax) 225-9764; (e-mail) www.house.gov/writerep.
Office Staff: Admin. Asst./Press Secy., Harry Glenn; Legis. Dir., Greg Lankler; Scheduler, Rayne Simpson.
Committees: Appropriations — chairman (Labor, Health & Human Services & Education; Defense).

Florida 10th — West — Southern Pinellas County; St. Petersburg. The district vote for Bill Clinton was 51% in 1996.

CQ Voting Studies

	1997	1998
Presidential	27%	20%
Party	84%	77%
Participation	94%	83%

Interest Groups

	1997	1998
ADA	10%	0%
ACU	79%	90%
AFL-CIO	38%	n/a
CCUS	100%	93%

Elections

	1996	1998
General	67%	u/o
Primary	u/o	u/o

Don Young (R–Alaska)
Of Fort Yukon • Elected 1973

Born: June 9, 1933, Meridian, Calif.
Education: Yuba Junior College, A.A. 1952; California State U., Chico, B.A. 1958.
Military Career: Army, 1955–57.
Occupation: Elementary school teacher; riverboat captain.
Family: Wife, Lula Fredson; two children.
Religion: Episcopalian.
Political Career: Fort Yukon City Council, 1960–64; mayor of Fort Yukon, 1964–68; Alaska House, 1967–70; Alaska Senate, 1971–73; Republican nominee for U.S. House, 1972.

Capitol Office: 2111 Rayburn House Office Building 20515; 225-5765; (fax) 225-0425; (e-mail) www.house.gov/writerep; (web) www.house.gov/donyoung.
Office Staff: Admin. Asst., Colin Chapman; Legis. Dir., Levon Boyagian; Communications Dir., Greg Thom; Exec. Asst., Jessica Sweeney.
Committees: Resources — chairman; Transportation & Infrastructure (Aviation; Coast Guard & Maritime Transportation; Water Resources & Environment).

Alaska — At large. The district vote for Bill Clinton was 33% in 1996.

CQ Voting Studies

	1997	1998
Presidential	21%	27%
Party	71%	84%
Participation	73%	94%

Interest Groups

	1997	1998
ADA	5%	20%
ACU	86%	84%
AFL-CIO	38%	n/a
CCUS	80%	78%

Elections

	1996	1998
General	59%	63%
Primary	89%	90%

Donna M.C. Christensen
(D–Virgin Is.)
Of St. Croix • Elected 1996

Born: Sept. 19, 1945, Teaneck, N.J.
Education: St. Mary's College (Indiana), B.S. 1966; George Washington U., M.D. 1970.
Occupation: Physician; health official.
Family: Divorced; two children.
Religion: Moravian.
Political Career: Virgin Is. Democratic Territorial Committee, 1980–97, chairwoman, 1980–82; Virgin Is. Board of Education, 1984–86; Virgin Is. acting commissioner of health, 1993–94.

Capitol Office: 1711 Longworth House Office Building 20515; 225-1790; (fax) 225-5517; (e-mail) www.house.gov/writerep; (web) www.house.gov/christian–christensen.
Office Staff: Admin. Asst., Lorraine Hill; District Dir./Press Secy., James A. O'Bryan; Legis. Dir., Brian Modeste; Public Relations Officer, Loan Sewer; Scheduler/Exec. Asst., Shelley Thomas.
Committees: Resources (National Parks & Public Lands; Water & Power); Small Business (Rural Enterprises — ranking member).

Virgin Islands — At large.

Eni F.H. Faleomavaega
(D–Am. Samoa)
Of Pago Pago • Elected 1988
Pronounced: EN-ee FOL-ee-oh-mav-ah-ENG-uh

Born: Aug. 15, 1943, Vailoatai, Am. Samoa
Education: Brigham Young U., A.A. 1964, B.A. 1966; Texas Southern U., attended 1969; U. of Houston, J.D. 1972; U. of California, Berkeley, LL.M. 1973.
Military Career: Army, 1966–69; Army Reserve, 1983–present.
Occupation: Lawyer; congressional aide.
Family: Wife, Hinanui Bambridge Cave; five children.
Religion: Mormon.
Political Career: Am. Samoa deputy attorney general, 1981–84; Democratic candidate for U.S. House, 1984; lieutenant governor, 1985–89.

Capitol Office: 2422 Rayburn House Office Building 20515; 225-8577; (fax) 225-8757; (e-mail) faleomavaega@mail.house.gov; (web) www.house.gov/faleomavaega.
Office Staff: Admin. Asst./Press Secy., Aliimau Scanlan; Legis. Dir., Martin R. Yerick; Office Mgr./Exec. Asst., Nancy M. Leong.
Committees: International Relations (Asia & the Pacific; International Operations & Human Rights); Resources (Energy & Mineral Resources; Fisheries Conservation, Wildlife & Oceans — ranking member).

American Samoa — At large.

Eleanor Holmes Norton (D–D.C.)
Of Washington • Elected 1990

Born: June 13, 1937, Washington, D.C.
Education: Antioch College, B.A. 1960; Yale U., M.A. 1963, LL.B. 1964.
Occupation: Professor; lawyer.
Family: Divorced; two children.
Religion: Episcopalian.
Political Career: New York City Human Rights Commission, 1971–77; Equal Employment Opportunity Commission chairman, 1977–81.

Capitol Office: 1424 Longworth House Office Building 20515; 225-8050; (fax) 225-3002; (e–mail) www.house.gov/writerep; (web) www.house.gov/norton.
Office Staff: Chief of Staff/Press Secy., Donna Brazile; Legis. Dir., Jon Bouker; Scheduler, Sheila Bunn.
Committees: Government Reform (Civil Service; District of Columbia — ranking member); Transportation & Infrastructure (Aviation; Economic Development & Public Buildings).

District of Columbia — At large. The district vote for Bill Clinton was 85% in 1996.

Carlos A. Romero-Barcelo
(D–P.R.)
Of San Juan • Elected 1992
Pronounced: ro-MARE-oh bar–sell-O

Born: Sept. 4, 1932, San Juan, P.R.
Education: Yale U., B.A. 1953; U. of Puerto Rico, LL.B. 1956.
Occupation: Lawyer; real estate broker.
Family: Wife, Kathleen; four children.
Religion: Roman Catholic.
Political Career: Mayor of San Juan, 1967–77; governor, 1977–85; Puerto Rico Senate, 1986–88.

Capitol Office: 2443 Rayburn House Office Building 20515; 225-2615; (fax) 225-2154; (e–mail) www.house.gov/writerep; (web) www.house.gov/romero-barcelo.
Office Staff: Chief of Staff, Astrid Jimenez; Legis. Dir., Yvonne E.R. Benner; Press Secy., Iris Eden Santiago; Scheduler, Joanne Ferreira-Oda.
Committees: Education & Workforce (Early Childhood, Youth & Families; Employer-Employee Relations); Resources (Fisheries Conservation, Wildlife & Oceans; National Parks & Public Lands — ranking member).

Puerto Rico — At large.

Robert A. Underwood (D–Guam)
Of Baza Gardens • Elected 1992

Born: July 13, 1948, Tamuning, Guam.
Education: California State U., Los Angeles, B.A. 1969, M.A. 1971; U. of Southern California, Ph.D. 1987.
Occupation: Professor; college administrator.
Family: Wife, Lorraine Aguilar; five children.
Religion: Roman Catholic.
Political Career: No previous office.

Capitol Office: 2418 Rayburn House Office Building 20515; 225-1188; (fax) 226-0341; (e-mail) guamtodc@mail.house.gov; (web) www.house.gov/underwood.
Office Staff: Chief of Staff, Ester Kiaaina; Press Secy., Cathy Gault; Scheduler/Personal Secy., Angie Borja.
Committees: Armed Services (Military Installations & Facilities; Military Readiness); Resources (Energy & Mineral Resources — ranking member).

Guam — At large.

APPENDIXES

State Delegations to the 106th Congress

The list below gives the names of senators and representatives of each state delegation for the 106th Congress. The senators are listed by seniority and the representatives by district. Freshmen are in italics.

Alabama
Richard C. Shelby (R)
Jeff Sessions (R)
  1. Sonny Callahan (R)
  2. Terry Everett (R)
  3. Bob Riley (R)
  4. Robert B. Aderholt (R)
  5. Robert E. "Bud" Cramer (D)
  6. Spencer Bachus (R)
  7. Earl F. Hilliard (D)

Alaska
Ted Stevens (R)
Frank H. Murkowski (R)
  AL Don Young (R)

American Samoa
  AL Eni F.H. Faleomavaega (D)

Arizona
John McCain (R)
Jon Kyl (R)
  1. Matt Salmon (R)
  2. Ed Pastor (D)
  3. Bob Stump (R)
  4. John Shadegg (R)
  5. Jim Kolbe (R)
  6. J.D. Hayworth (R)

Arkansas
Tim Hutchinson (R)
Blanche Lincoln (D)
  1. Marion Berry (D)
  2. Vic Snyder (D)
  3. Asa Hutchinson (R)
  4. Jay Dickey (R)

California
Dianne Feinstein (D)
Barbara Boxer (D)
  1. Mike Thompson (D)
  2. Wally Herger (R)
  3. Doug Ose (R)
  4. John T. Doolittle (R)
  5. Robert T. Matsui (D)
  6. Lynn Woolsey (D)
  7. George Miller (D)
  8. Nancy Pelosi (D)
  9. Barbara Lee (D)
  10. Ellen O. Tauscher (D)
  11. Richard W. Pombo (R)
  12. Tom Lantos (D)
  13. Pete Stark (D)
  14. Anna G. Eshoo (D)
  15. Tom Campbell (R)
  16. Zoe Lofgren (D)
  17. Sam Farr (D)
  18. Gary A. Condit (D)
  19. George P. Radanovich (R)
  20. Cal Dooley (D)
  21. Bill Thomas (R)
  22. Lois Capps (D)
  23. Elton Gallegly (R)
  24. Brad Sherman (D)
  25. Howard P. "Buck" McKeon (R)
  26. Howard L. Berman (D)
  27. James E. Rogan (R)
  28. David Dreier (R)
  29. Henry A. Waxman (D)
  30. Xavier Becerra (D)
  31. Matthew G. Martinez (D)
  32. Julian C. Dixon (D)
  33. Lucille Roybal-Allard (D)
  34. Grace F. Napolitano (D)
  35. Maxine Waters (D)
  36. Steven T. Kuykendall (R)
  37. Juanita Millender-McDonald (D)
  38. Steve Horn (R)
  39. Ed Royce (R)
  40. Jerry Lewis (R)
  41. Gary Miller (R)
  42. George E. Brown Jr. (D)
  43. Ken Calvert (R)
  44. Mary Bono (R)
  45. Dana Rohrabacher (R)
  46. Loretta Sanchez (D)
  47. Christopher Cox (R)
  48. Ron Packard (R)
  49. Brian P. Bilbray (R)
  50. Bob Filner (D)
  51. Randy "Duke" Cunningham (R)
  52. Duncan Hunter (R)

Colorado
Ben Nighthorse Campbell (R)
Wayne Allard (R)
  1. Diana DeGette (D)
  2. Mark Udall (D)
  3. Scott McInnis (R)
  4. Bob Schaffer (R)
  5. Joel Hefley (R)
  6. Tom Tancredo (R)

Connecticut
Christopher J. Dodd (D)
Joseph I. Lieberman (D)
  1. John B. Larson (D)
  2. Sam Gejdenson (D)
  3. Rosa DeLauro (D)
  4. Christopher Shays (R)
  5. Jim Maloney (D)
  6. Nancy L. Johnson (R)

Delaware
William V. Roth Jr. (R)
Joseph R. Biden Jr. (D)
   AL Michael N. Castle (R)

District of Columbia
   AL Eleanor Holmes Norton (D)

Florida
Bob Graham (D)
Connie Mack (R)
1. Joe Scarborough (R)
2. Allen Boyd (D)
3. Corrine Brown (D)
4. Tillie Fowler (R)
5. Karen L. Thurman (D)
6. Cliff Stearns (R)
7. John L. Mica (R)
8. Bill McCollum (R)
9. Michael Bilirakis (R)
10. C.W. Bill Young (R)
11. Jim Davis (D)
12. Charles T. Canady (R)
13. Dan Miller (R)
14. Porter J. Goss (R)
15. Dave Weldon (R)
16. Mark Foley (R)
17. Carrie P. Meek (D)
18. Ileana Ros-Lehtinen (R)
19. Robert Wexler (D)
20. Peter Deutsch (D)
21. Lincoln Diaz-Balart (R)
22. E. Clay Shaw Jr. (R)
23. Alcee L. Hastings (D)

Georgia
Paul Coverdell (R)
Max Cleland (D)
1. Jack Kingston (R)
2. Sanford D. Bishop Jr. (D)
3. Mac Collins (R)
4. Cynthia A. McKinney (D)
5. John Lewis (D)
6. Johnny Isakson (R)
7. Bob Barr (R)
8. Saxby Chambliss (R)
9. Nathan Deal (R)
10. Charlie Norwood (R)
11. John Linder (R)

Guam
   AL Robert A. Underwood (D)

Hawaii
Daniel K. Inouye (D)
Daniel K. Akaka (D)
1. Neil Abercrombie (D)
2. Patsy T. Mink (D)

Idaho
Larry E. Craig (R)
Michael D. Crapo (R)
1. Helen Chenoweth (R)
2. *Mike Simpson (R)*

Illinois
Richard J. Durbin (D)
Peter G. Fitzgerald (R)
1. Bobby L. Rush (D)
2. Jesse L. Jackson Jr. (D)
3. William O. Lipinski (D)
4. Luis V. Gutierrez (D)
5. Rod R. Blagojevich (D)
6. Henry J. Hyde (R)
7. Danny K. Davis (D)
8. Philip M. Crane (R)
9. *Jan Schakowsky (D)*
10. John Edward Porter (R)
11. Jerry Weller (R)
12. Jerry F. Costello (D)
13. *Judy Biggert (R)*
14. J. Dennis Hastert (R)
15. Thomas W. Ewing (R)
16. Donald Manzullo (R)
17. Lane Evans (D)
18. Ray LaHood (R)
19. *David D. Phelps (D)*
20. John Shimkus (R)

Indiana
Richard G. Lugar (R)
Evan Bayh (D)
1. Peter J. Visclosky (D)
2. David M. McIntosh (R)
3. Tim Roemer (D)
4. Mark Souder (R)
5. Steve Buyer (R)
6. Dan Burton (R)
7. Ed Pease (R)
8. John Hostettler (R)
9. *Baron P. Hill (D)*
10. Julia Carson (D)

Iowa
Charles E. Grassley (R)
Tom Harkin (D)
1. Jim Leach (R)
2. Jim Nussle (R)
3. Leonard L. Boswell (D)
4. Greg Ganske (R)
5. Tom Latham (R)

Kansas
Sam Brownback (R)
Pat Roberts (R)
1. Jerry Moran (R)
2. Jim Ryun (R)
3. *Dennis Moore (D)*
4. Todd Tiahrt (R)

Kentucky
Mitch McConnell (R)
Jim Bunning (R)
1. Edward Whitfield (R)
2. Ron Lewis (R)
3. Anne M. Northup (R)
4. *Ken Lucas (D)*
5. Harold Rogers (R)
6. *Ernie Fletcher (R)*

Louisiana
John B. Breaux (D)
Mary L. Landrieu (D)
1. Vacant (Rep. Livingston resigned Feb. 28, 1999)
2. William J. Jefferson (D)
3. W.J. "Billy" Tauzin (R)
4. Jim McCrery (R)
5. John Cooksey (R)
6. Richard H. Baker (R)
7. Chris John (D)

Maine
Olympia J. Snowe (R)
Susan Collins (R)
1. Tom Allen (D)
2. John Baldacci (D)

Maryland
Paul S. Sarbanes (D)
Barbara A. Mikulski (D)
1. Wayne T. Gilchrest (R)
2. Robert L. Ehrlich Jr. (R)
3. Benjamin L. Cardin (D)
4. Albert R. Wynn (D)
5. Steny H. Hoyer (D)
6. Roscoe G. Bartlett (R)
7. Elijah E. Cummings (D)
8. Constance A. Morella (R)

Massachusetts
Edward M. Kennedy (D)
John Kerry (D)
1. John W. Olver (D)
2. Richard E. Neal (D)
3. Jim McGovern (D)
4. Barney Frank (D)
5. Martin T. Meehan (D)
6. John F. Tierney (D)
7. Edward J. Markey (D)
8. *Michael E. Capuano (D)*
9. Joe Moakley (D)
10. Bill Delahunt (D)

Michigan
Carl Levin (D)
Spencer Abraham (R)
1. Bart Stupak (D)
2. Peter Hoekstra (R)
3. Vernon J. Ehlers (R)
4. Dave Camp (R)
5. James A. Barcia (D)
6. Fred Upton (R)
7. Nick Smith (R)
8. Debbie Stabenow (D)
9. Dale E. Kildee (D)
10. David E. Bonior (D)
11. Joe Knollenberg (R)
12. Sander M. Levin (D)
13. Lynn Rivers (D)
14. John Conyers Jr. (D)
15. Carolyn Cheeks Kilpatrick (D)
16. John D. Dingell (D)

Minnesota
Paul Wellstone (D)
Rod Grams (R)
1. Gil Gutknecht (R)
2. David Minge (D)
3. Jim Ramstad (R)
4. Bruce F. Vento (D)
5. Martin Olav Sabo (D)
6. Bill Luther (D)
7. Collin C. Peterson (D)
8. James L. Oberstar (D)

Mississippi
Thad Cochran (R)
Trent Lott (R)
1. Roger Wicker (R)
2. Bennie Thompson (D)
3. Charles W. "Chip" Pickering Jr. (R)
4. *Ronnie Shows (D)*
5. Gene Taylor (D)

Missouri
Christopher S. Bond (R)
John Ashcroft (R)
1. William L. Clay (D)
2. James M. Talent (R)
3. Richard A. Gephardt (D)
4. Ike Skelton (D)
5. Karen McCarthy (D)
6. Pat Danner (D)
7. Roy Blunt (R)
8. Jo Ann Emerson (R)
9. Kenny Hulshof (R)

Montana
Max Baucus (D)
Conrad Burns (R)
AL Rick Hill (R)

Nebraska
Bob Kerrey (D)
Chuck Hagel (R)
1. Doug Bereuter (R)
2. *Lee Terry (R)*
3. Bill Barrett (R)

Nevada
Harry Reid (D)
Richard H. Bryan (D)
1. *Shelley Berkley (D)*
2. Jim Gibbons (R)

New Hampshire
Robert C. Smith (R)
Judd Gregg (R)
1. John E. Sununu (R)
2. Charles Bass (R)

New Jersey
Frank R. Lautenberg (D)
Robert G. Torricelli (D)
1. Robert E. Andrews (D)
2. Frank A. LoBiondo (R)
3. H. James Saxton (R)
4. Christopher H. Smith (R)
5. Marge Roukema (R)
6. Frank Pallone Jr. (D)
7. Bob Franks (R)
8. Bill Pascrell Jr. (D)
9. Steven R. Rothman (D)
10. Donald M. Payne (D)
11. Rodney Frelinghuysen (R)
12. *Rush D. Holt (D)*
13. Robert Menendez (D)

New Mexico
Pete V. Domenici (R)
Jeff Bingaman (D)
1. Heather A. Wilson (R)
2. Joe Skeen (R)
3. *Tom Udall (D)*

New York
Daniel Patrick Moynihan (D)
Charles E. Schumer (D)
1. Michael P. Forbes (R)
2. Rick A. Lazio (R)
3. Peter T. King (R)
4. Carolyn McCarthy (D)
5. Gary L. Ackerman (D)
6. Gregory W. Meeks (D)
7. *Joseph Crowley (D)*
8. Jerrold Nadler (D)
9. *Anthony D. Weiner (D)*
10. Edolphus Towns (D)
11. Major R. Owens (D)
12. Nydia M. Velazquez (D)
13. Vito J. Fossella (R)
14. Carolyn B. Maloney (D)
15. Charles B. Rangel (D)

16. Jose E. Serrano (D)
17. Eliot L. Engel (D)
18. Nita M. Lowey (D)
19. Sue W. Kelly (R)
20. Benjamin A. Gilman (R)
21. Michael R. McNulty (D)
22. *John E. Sweeney (R)*
23. Sherwood Boehlert (R)
24. John M. McHugh (R)
25. James T. Walsh (R)
26. Maurice D. Hinchey (D)
27. *Thomas M. Reynolds (R)*
28. Louise M. Slaughter (D)
29. John J. LaFalce (D)
30. Jack Quinn (R)
31. Amo Houghton (R)

North Carolina
Jesse Helms (R)
John Edwards (D)
1. Eva Clayton (D)
2. Bob Etheridge (D)
3. Walter B. Jones Jr. (R)
4. David E. Price (D)
5. Richard M. Burr (R)
6. Howard Coble (R)
7. Mike McIntyre (D)
8. *Robin Hayes (R)*
9. Sue Myrick (R)
10. Cass Ballenger (R)
11. Charles H. Taylor (R)
12. Melvin Watt (D)

North Dakota
Kent Conrad (D)
Byron L. Dorgan (D)
AL Earl Pomeroy (D)

Ohio
Mike DeWine (R)
George V. Voinovich (R)
1. Steve Chabot (R)
2. Rob Portman (R)
3. Tony P. Hall (D)
4. Michael G. Oxley (R)
5. Paul E. Gillmor (R)
6. Ted Strickland (D)
7. David L. Hobson (R)
8. John A. Boehner (R)
9. Marcy Kaptur (D)
10. Dennis J. Kucinich (D)
11. *Stephanie Tubbs Jones (D)*
12. John R. Kasich (R)
13. Sherrod Brown (D)
14. Tom Sawyer (D)
15. Deborah Pryce (R)
16. Ralph Regula (R)
17. James A. Traficant Jr. (D)
18. Bob Ney (R)
19. Steven C. LaTourette (R)

Oklahoma
Don Nickles (R)
James M. Inhofe (R)
1. Steve Largent (R)
2. Tom Coburn (R)
3. Wes Watkins (R)
4. J.C. Watts Jr. (R)
5. Ernest Istook (R)
6. Frank D. Lucas (R)

Oregon
Ron Wyden (D)
Gordon H. Smith (R)
1. *David Wu (D)*
2. *Greg Walden (R)*
3. Earl Blumenauer (D)
4. Peter A. DeFazio (D)
5. Darlene Hooley (D)

Pennsylvania
Arlen Specter (R)
Rick Santorum (R)
1. Robert A. Brady (D)
2. Chaka Fattah (D)
3. Robert A. Borski (D)
4. Ron Klink (D)
5. John E. Peterson (R)
6. Tim Holden (D)
7. Curt Weldon (R)
8. James C. Greenwood (R)
9. Bud Shuster (R)
10. *Donald L. Sherwood (R)*
11. Paul E. Kanjorski (D)
12. John P. Murtha (D)
13. *Joseph M. Hoeffel (D)*
14. William J. Coyne (D)
15. *Patrick J. Toomey (R)*
16. Joseph R. Pitts (R)
17. George W. Gekas (R)
18. Mike Doyle (D)
19. Bill Goodling (R)
20. Frank R. Mascara (D)
21. Phil English (R)

Puerto Rico
AL Carlos A. Romero-Barcelo (D)

Rhode Island
John H. Chafee (R)
Jack Reed (D)
1. Patrick J. Kennedy (D)
2. Bob Weygand (D)

South Carolina
Strom Thurmond (R)
Ernest F. Hollings (D)
1. Mark Sanford (R)
2. Floyd D. Spence (R)
3. Lindsey Graham (R)
4. *Jim DeMint (R)*
5. John M. Spratt Jr. (D)
6. James E. Clyburn (D)

South Dakota
Tom Daschle (D)
Tim Johnson (D)
AL John Thune (R)

Tennessee
Fred Thompson (R)
Bill Frist (R)
1. Bill Jenkins (R)
2. John J. "Jimmy" Duncan Jr. (R)
3. Zach Wamp (R)
4. Van Hilleary (R)
5. Bob Clement (D)
6. Bart Gordon (D)
7. Ed Bryant (R)
8. John Tanner (D)
9. Harold E. Ford Jr. (D)

Texas
Phil Gramm (R)
Kay Bailey Hutchison (R)
1. Max Sandlin (D)
2. Jim Turner (D)
3. Sam Johnson (R)
4. Ralph M. Hall (D)

5. Pete Sessions (R)
6. Joe L. Barton (R)
7. Bill Archer (R)
8. Kevin Brady (R)
9. Nick Lampson (D)
10. Lloyd Doggett (D)
11. Chet Edwards (D)
12. Kay Granger (R)
13. William M. "Mac" Thornberry (R)
14. Ron Paul (R)
15. Rubén Hinojosa (D)
16. Silvestre Reyes (D)
17. Charles W. Stenholm (D)
18. Sheila Jackson-Lee (D)
19. Larry Combest (R)
20. *Charlie Gonzalez (D)*
21. Lamar Smith (R)
22. Tom DeLay (R)
23. Henry Bonilla (R)
24. Martin Frost (D)
25. Ken Bentsen (D)
26. Dick Armey (R)
27. Solomon P. Ortiz (D)
28. Ciro D. Rodriguez (D)
29. Gene Green (D)
30. Eddie Bernice Johnson (D)

Utah
Orrin G. Hatch (R)
Robert F. Bennett (R)
1. James V. Hansen (R)
2. Merrill Cook (R)
3. Christopher B. Cannon (R)

Vermont
Patrick J. Leahy (D)
James M. Jeffords (R)
AL Bernard Sanders (I)

Virgin Islands
AL Donna M.C. Christensen (D)

Virginia
John W. Warner (R)
Charles S. Robb (D)
1. Herbert H. Bateman (R)
2. Owen B. Pickett (D)
3. Robert C. Scott (D)
4. Norman Sisisky (D)
5. Virgil H. Goode Jr. (D)
6. Robert W. Goodlatte (R)
7. Thomas J. Bliley Jr. (R)
8. James P. Moran (D)
9. Rick Boucher (D)
10. Frank R. Wolf (R)
11. Thomas M. Davis III (R)

Washington
Slade Gorton (R)
Patty Murray (D)
1. *Jay Inslee (D)*
2. Jack Metcalf (R)
3. *Brian Baird (D)*
4. Richard "Doc" Hastings (R)
5. George Nethercutt (R)
6. Norm Dicks (D)
7. Jim McDermott (D)
8. Jennifer Dunn (R)
9. Adam Smith (D)

West Virginia
Robert C. Byrd (D)
John D. Rockefeller IV (D)
1. Alan B. Mollohan (D)
2. Bob Wise (D)
3. Nick J. Rahall II (D)

Wisconsin
Herb Kohl (D)
Russell D. Feingold (D)
1. *Paul D. Ryan (R)*
2. *Tammy Baldwin (D)*
3. Ron Kind (D)
4. Gerald D. Kleczka (D)
5. Thomas M. Barrett (D)
6. Tom Petri (R)
7. David R. Obey (D)
8. *Mark Green (R)*
9. F. James Sensenbrenner Jr. (R)

Wyoming
Craig Thomas (R)
Michael B. Enzi (R)
AL Barbara Cubin (R)

Congressional Leadership

SENATE

Republicans
President Pro Tempore — Strom Thurmond, S.C. (224-5972)
Majority Leader — Trent Lott, Miss. (224-6253)
Assistant Majority Leader — Don Nickles, Okla. (224-5754)
Conference Chairman — Connie Mack, Fla.
Conference Secretary — Paul Coverdell, Ga.
Chief Deputy Whip — Judd Gregg, N.H.
Policy Committee Chairman — Larry E. Craig, Idaho
Committee on Committees Chairman — Slade Gorton, Wash.
National Republican Senatorial Committee Chairman —
　Mitch McConnell, Ky.

Democrats
President — Al Gore (244-8391)
Minority Leader — Tom Daschle, S.D. (224-2321)
Minority Whip — Harry Reid, Nev.
Conference Chairman — Tom Daschle, S.D.
Conference Secretary — Barbara A. Mikulski, Md.
Chief Deputy Whip — John B. Breaux, La.
Assistant Floor Leader — Richard J. Durbin, Ill.
Policy Committee Chairman — Tom Daschle, S.D.
Policy Committee Co-Chairman — Byron L. Dorgan, N.D.
Steering and Coordination Committee Chairman — John Kerry, Mass.
Technology and Communications Committee Chairman — John D.
　Rockefeller IV, W.Va.
Democratic Senatorial Campaign Committee Chairman — Robert G. Torricelli,
　N.J.

HOUSE

Republicans
Speaker of the House — J. Dennis Hastert, Ill. (225-0600)
Majority Leader — Dick Armey, Texas (225-7772)
Majority Whip — Tom DeLay, Texas (225-5951)
Conference Chairman — J. C. Watts, Okla.
Conference Vice Chairman — Tillie Fowler, Fla.
Conference Secretary — Deborah Pryce, R-Ohio
Chief Deputy Whip — Roy Blunt, Mo.
Policy Committee Chairman — Christopher Cox, Calif.
Steering Committee Chairman — J. Dennis Hastert, Ill.
National Republican Congressional Committee Chairman —
　Thomas M. Davis III, Va.

Democrats
Minority Leader — Richard A. Gephardt, Mo. (225-2671)
Minority Whip — David E. Bonior, Mich. (225-2106)
Caucus Chairman — Martin Frost, Texas
Caucus Vice Chairman — Robert Menendez, N.J.
Assistant to the Democratic Leader — Rosa DeLauro, Conn.
Chief Deputy Whips — Chet Edwards, Texas; John Lewis, Ga.; Maxine Waters,
　Calif.; Ed Pastor, Ariz.
Policy and Steering Committee Chairman — Richard A. Gephardt, Mo.
Policy and Steering Committee Co-Chairman — Steny H. Hoyer, Md.
Democratic Congressional Campaign Committee Chairman —
　Patrick Kennedy, R.I.

Senate Committees

The standing committees and their subcommittees of the U.S. Senate for the 106th Congress are listed below in alphabetical order; also listed is the Select Ethics Committee. The listing includes the room number, zip code, and telephone number for each committee. Membership is given in order of seniority on the committee. Address abbreviations used are as follows: SD (Dirksen Senate Office Bldg.), SH (Hart Senate Office Bldg.), SR (Russell Senate Office Bldg.), and CAP (Capitol). The telephone area code for Washington is 202.

Agriculture, Nutrition and Forestry
SR-328A 20510; 224-2035

Richard G. Lugar, R-Ind., chairman

Republicans
Jesse Helms, N.C.
Thad Cochran, Miss.
Mitch McConnell, Ky.
Paul Coverdell, Ga.
Pat Roberts, Kan.
Peter G. Fitzgerald, Ill.
Charles E. Grassley, Iowa
Larry E. Craig, Idaho
Rick Santorum, Pa.

Democrats
Tom Harkin, Iowa
Patrick J. Leahy, Vt.
Kent Conrad, N.D.
Tom Daschle, S.D.
Max Baucus, Mont.
Bob Kerrey, Neb.
Tim Johnson, S.D.
Blanche Lincoln, Ark.

Subcommittees

Forestry, Conservation and Rural Revitalization
SR-328A 20510; 224-2035

Republicans
Craig, chairman
Santorum
Coverdell
Fitzgerald
Grassley

Democrats
Conrad
Leahy
Daschle
Baucus

Marketing, Inspection and Product Promotion
SR-328A 20510; 224-2035

Republicans
Coverdell, chairman
Helms
Cochran
McConnell

Democrats
Baucus
Conrad
Kerrey

Production and Price Competitiveness
SR-328A 20510; 224-2035

Republicans
Roberts, chairman
Helms
Cochran
Grassley
Craig

Democrats
Kerrey
Daschle
Johnson
Lincoln

Research, Nutrition and General Legislation
SR-328A 20510; 224-2035

Republicans
Fitzgerald, chairman
McConnell
Roberts
Santorum

Democrats
Leahy
Johnson
Lincoln

Appropriations
S-128 CAP 224-3471

Ted Stevens, R-Alaska, chairman

Republicans
Thad Cochran, Miss.
Arlen Specter, Pa.

Democrats
Robert C. Byrd, W.Va.
Daniel K. Inouye, Hawaii

Senate Committees

Pete V. Domenici, N.M.
Christopher S. Bond, Mo.
Slade Gorton, Wash.
Mitch McConnell, Ky.
Conrad Burns, Mont.
Richard C. Shelby, Ala.
Judd Gregg, N.H.
Robert F. Bennett, Utah
Ben Nighthorse Campbell, Colo.
Larry E. Craig, Idaho
Kay Bailey Hutchison, Texas
Jon Kyl, Ariz.

Ernest F. Hollings, S.C.
Patrick J. Leahy, Vt.
Frank R. Lautenberg, N.J.
Tom Harkin, Iowa
Barbara A. Mikulski, Md.
Harry Reid, Nev.
Herb Kohl, Wis.
Patty Murray, Wash.
Byron L. Dorgan, N.D.
Dianne Feinstein, Calif.
Richard J. Durbin, Ill.

Subcommittees

Agriculture, Rural Development and Related Agencies
SD-136 20510; 224-5270

Republicans
Cochran, chairman
Specter
Bond
Gorton
McConnell
Burns

Democrats
Kohl
Harkin
Dorgan
Feinstein
Durbin

Commerce, Justice, State and Judiciary
S-146A CAP 224-7277

Republicans
Gregg, chairman
Stevens
Domenici
McConnell
Hutchison
Campbell

Democrats
Hollings
Inouye
Lautenberg
Mikulski
Leahy

Defense
SD-122 20510; 224-7255

Republicans
Stevens, chairman
Cochran
Specter
Domenici
Bond
McConnell
Shelby
Gregg
Hutchison

Democrats
Inouye
Hollings
Byrd
Leahy
Lautenberg
Harkin
Dorgan
Durbin

District of Columbia
S-128 CAP 224-2731

Republicans
Hutchison, chairman
Kyl

Democrats
Durbin

Energy and Water Development
SD-127 20510; 224-7260

Republicans
Domenici, chairman
Cochran
Gorton
McConnell
Bennett
Burns
Craig

Democrats
Reid
Byrd
Hollings
Murray
Kohl
Dorgan

Foreign Operations
SD-142 20510; 224-2104

Republicans
McConnell, chairman
Specter
Gregg
Shelby
Bennett
Campbell
Bond

Democrats
Leahy
Inouye
Lautenberg
Harkin
Mikulski
Murray

Interior
SD-131 20510; 224-7233

Republicans
Gorton, chairman
Stevens
Cochran
Domenici

Democrats
Byrd
Leahy
Hollings
Reid

Burns
Bennett
Gregg
Campbell

Dorgan
Kohl
Feinstein

Labor, Health and Human Services and Education

SD-184 20510; 224-7230

Republicans
Specter, chairman
Cochran
Gorton
Gregg
Craig
Hutchison
Stevens
Kyl

Democrats
Harkin
Hollings
Inouye
Reid
Kohl
Murray
Feinstein

Legislative Branch

S-125 CAP 224-8921

Republicans
Bennett, chairman
Stevens
Craig

Democrats
Feinstein
Durbin

Military Construction

SD-140 20510; 224-7204

Republicans
Burns, chairman
Hutchison
Craig
Kyl

Democrats
Murray
Reid
Inouye

Transportation

SD-190 20510; 224-7281

Republicans
Shelby, chairman
Domenici
Specter
Bond
Gorton
Bennett
Campbell

Democrats
Lautenberg
Byrd
Mikulski
Reid
Kohl
Murray

Treasury and General Government

SD-190 20510; 224-7337

Republicans
Campbell, chairman
Shelby
Kyl

Democrats
Dorgan
Mikulski

VA, HUD and Independent Agencies

SD-130 20510; 224-7211

Republicans
Bond, chairman
Burns
Shelby
Craig
Hutchison
Kyl

Democrats
Mikulski
Leahy
Lautenberg
Harkin
Byrd

Armed Services

SR-228 20510; 224-3871

John W. Warner, R-Va., chairman

Republicans
Strom Thurmond, S.C.
John McCain, Ariz.
Robert C. Smith, N.H.
James M. Inhofe, Okla.
Rick Santorum, Pa.
Olympia J. Snowe, Maine
Pat Roberts, Kan.
Wayne Allard, Colo.
Tim Hutchinson, Ark.
Jeff Sessions, Ala.

Democrats
Carl Levin, Mich.
Edward M. Kennedy, Mass.
Jeff Bingaman, N.M.
Robert C. Byrd, W.Va.
Charles S. Robb, Va.
Joseph I. Lieberman, Conn.
Max Cleland, Ga.
Mary L. Landrieu, La.
Jack Reed, R.I.

Subcommittees

Airland Forces

SR-228 20510; 224-3871

Republicans
Santorum, chairman
Inhofe

Democrats
Lieberman
Cleland

Roberts
Allard
Hutchinson

Landrieu
Reed

Emerging Threats and Capabilities

SR-228 20510; 224-3871

Republicans
Roberts, chairman
Smith (N.H.)
Santorum
Snowe
Sessions

Democrats
Bingaman
Kennedy
Byrd
Lieberman

Personnel

SR-228 20510; 224-3871

Republicans
Allard, chairman
Thurmond
McCain
Snowe

Democrats
Cleland
Kennedy
Reed

Readiness and Management Support

SR-228 20510; 224-3871

Republicans
Inhofe, chairman
Thurmond
McCain
Santorum
Roberts
Hutchinson

Democrats
Robb
Bingaman
Byrd
Cleland
Landrieu

Seapower

SR-228 20510; 224-3871

Republicans
Snowe, chairman
McCain
Smith (N.H.)
Sessions

Democrats
Kennedy
Robb
Reed

Strategic Forces

SR-228 20510; 224-3871

Republicans
Smith (N.H.), chairman
Thurmond
Inhofe
Allard
Hutchinson
Sessions

Democrats
Landrieu
Bingaman
Byrd
Robb
Lieberman

Banking, Housing and Urban Affairs

SD-534 20510; 224-7391

Phil Gramm, R-Texas, chairman

Republicans
Richard C. Shelby, Ala.
Connie Mack, Fla.
Robert F. Bennett, Utah
Rod Grams, Minn.
Wayne Allard, Colo.
Michael B. Enzi, Wyo.
Chuck Hagel, Neb.
Rick Santorum, Pa.
Jim Bunning, Ky.
Michael D. Crapo, Idaho

Democrats
Paul S. Sarbanes, Md.
Christopher J. Dodd, Conn.
John Kerry, Mass.
Richard H. Bryan, Nev.
Tim Johnson, S.D.
Jack Reed, R.I.
Charles E. Schumer, N.Y.
Evan Bayh, Ind.
John Edwards, N.C.

Subcommittees

Economic Policy

SD-534 20510; 224-7391

Republicans
Mack, chairman
Bennett
Enzi
Bunning

Democrats
Reed
Dodd
Kerry

Financial Institutions

SD-534 20510; 224-7391

Republicans
Bennett, chairman
Hagel
Mack

Democrats
Bryan
Reed
Schumer

Enzi
Santorum
Bunning
Crapo
Shelby
Allard

Edwards
Johnson
Bayh
Sarbanes

Housing and Transportation
SD-534 20510; 224-7391

Republicans
Allard, chairman
Santorum
Grams
Shelby
Gramm

Democrats
Kerry
Edwards
Dodd
Bryan

International Trade and Finance
SD-534 20510; 224-7391

Republicans
Enzi, chairman
Crapo
Grams
Hagel
Mack

Democrats
Johnson
Kerry
Bayh
Schumer

Securities
SD-534 20510; 224-7391

Republicans
Grams, chairman
Bunning
Shelby
Allard
Bennett
Hagel
Santorum
Crapo

Democrats
Dodd
Schumer
Bayh
Johnson
Bryan
Reed
Edwards

Budget
SD-621 20510; 224-0642

Pete V. Domenici, R-N.M., chairman

Republicans
Charles E. Grassley, Iowa
Don Nickles, Okla.
Phil Gramm, Texas
Christopher S. Bond, Mo.
Slade Gorton, Wash.
Judd Gregg, N.H.
Olympia J. Snowe, Maine
Spencer Abraham, Mich.
Bill Frist, Tenn.
Rod Grams, Minn.
Gordon H. Smith, Ore.

Democrats
Frank R. Lautenberg, N.J.
Ernest F. Hollings, S.C.
Kent Conrad, N.D.
Paul S. Sarbanes, Md.
Barbara Boxer, Calif.
Patty Murray, Wash.
Ron Wyden, Ore.
Russell D. Feingold, Wis.
Tim Johnson, S.D.
Richard J. Durbin, Ill.

Commerce, Science and Transportation
SD-508 20510; 224-5115

John McCain, R-Ariz., chairman

Republicans
Ted Stevens, Alaska
Conrad Burns, Mont.
Slade Gorton, Wash.
Trent Lott, Miss.
Kay Bailey Hutchison, Texas
Olympia J. Snowe, Maine
John Ashcroft, Mo.
Bill Frist, Tenn.
Spencer Abraham, Mich.
Sam Brownback, Kan.

Democrats
Ernest F. Hollings, S.C.
Daniel K. Inouye, Hawaii
John D. Rockefeller IV, W.Va.
John Kerry, Mass.
John B. Breaux, La.
Richard H. Bryan, Nev.
Byron L. Dorgan, N.D.
Ron Wyden, Ore.
Max Cleland, Ga.

Subcommittees

Aviation
SH-427 20510; 224-4852

Republicans
Gorton, chairman
Stevens

Democrats
Rockefeller
Hollings

Burns
Lott
Hutchison
Ashcroft
Frist
Snowe
Brownback
Abraham

Inouye
Bryan
Breaux
Dorgan
Wyden
Cleland

Communications
SH-227 20510; 224-5184

Republicans
Burns, chairman
Stevens
Gorton
Lott
Ashcroft
Hutchison
Abraham
Frist
Brownback

Democrats
Hollings
Inouye
Kerry
Breaux
Rockefeller
Dorgan
Wyden
Cleland

Consumer Affairs, Foreign Commerce and Tourism
SH-425 20510; 224-5183

Republicans
Ashcroft, chairman
Gorton
Abraham
Burns
Brownback

Democrats
Bryan
Breaux

Manufacturing and Competitiveness
SD-245 20510; 224-1745

Republicans
Abraham, chairman
Snowe
Ashcroft
Frist
Brownback

Democrats
Dorgan
Bryan
Hollings
Rockefeller

Oceans and Fisheries
SH-428 20510; 224-8172

Republicans
Snowe, chairman
Stevens
Gorton
Hutchison

Democrats
Kerry
Inouye
Breaux

Science, Technology and Space
SH-428 20510; 224-8172

Republicans
Frist, chairman
Burns
Hutchison
Stevens
Abraham

Democrats
Breaux
Rockefeller
Kerry
Dorgan

Surface Transportation and Merchant Marine
SH-427 20510; 224-4852

Republicans
Hutchison, chairman
Stevens
Burns
Snowe
Frist
Abraham
Ashcroft
Brownback

Democrats
Inouye
Breaux
Dorgan
Bryan
Wyden
Cleland

Energy and Natural Resources
SD-304 20510; 224-4971
Frank H. Murkowski, R-Alaska, chairman

Republicans
Pete V. Domenici, N.M.
Don Nickles, Okla.
Larry E. Craig, Idaho
Ben Nighthorse Campbell, Colo.
Craig Thomas, Wyo.
Gordon H. Smith, Ore.
Jim Bunning, Ky.

Democrats
Jeff Bingaman, N.M.
Daniel K. Akaka, Hawaii
Byron L. Dorgan, N.D.
Bob Graham, Fla.
Ron Wyden, Ore.
Tim Johnson, S.D.
Mary L. Landrieu, La.

Peter G. Fitzgerald, Ill.
Slade Gorton, Wash.
Conrad Burns, Mont.

Evan Bayh, Ind.
Blanche Lincoln, Ark.

Subcommittees

Energy Research, Development, Production and Regulation
SD-308 20510; 224-6567

Republicans
Nickles, chairman
Domenici
Bunning
Gorton
Craig
Fitzgerald
Smith (Ore.)

Democrats
Graham
Akaka
Dorgan
Johnson
Landrieu
Bayh

Forests and Public Land Management
SD-306 20510; 224-6170

Republicans
Craig, chairman
Burns
Fitzgerald
Campbell
Domenici
Thomas
Smith (Ore.)

Democrats
Wyden
Akaka
Johnson
Landrieu
Bayh
Lincoln

National Parks, Historic Preservation and Recreation
SD-354 20510; 224-6969

Republicans
Thomas, chairman
Campbell
Burns
Nickles
Bunning
Gorton

Democrats
Akaka
Graham
Landrieu
Bayh
Lincoln

Water and Power
SD-304 20510; 224-2564

Republicans
Smith (Ore.), chairman
Gorton
Bunning
Craig
Campbell

Democrats
Dorgan
Graham
Wyden
Lincoln

Environment and Public Works
John H. Chafee, R-R.I., chairman
SD-410 20510; 224-6176

Republicans
John W. Warner, Va.
Robert C. Smith, N.H.
James M. Inhofe, Okla.
Craig Thomas, Wyo.
Christopher S. Bond, Mo.
George V. Voinovich, Ohio
Michael D. Crapo, Idaho
Robert F. Bennett, Utah
Kay Bailey Hutchison, Texas

Democrats
Max Baucus, Mont.
Daniel Patrick Moynihan, N.Y.
Frank R. Lautenberg, N.J.
Harry Reid, Nev.
Bob Graham, Fla.
Joseph I. Lieberman, Conn.
Barbara Boxer, Calif.
Ron Wyden, Ore.

Subcommittees

Clean Air, Wetlands, Private Property and Nuclear Safety
SD-410 20510; 224-6176

Republicans
Inhofe, chairman
Voinovich
Bennett
Hutchison

Democrats
Graham
Lieberman
Boxer

Fisheries, Wildlife and Drinking Water
SD-410 20510; 224-6176

Republicans
Crapo, chairman
Thomas
Bond
Warner

Democrats
Reid
Lautenberg
Wyden
Graham

290 Senate Committees

Bennett
Hutchison

Boxer

Superfund, Waste Control and Risk Assessment

SD-410 20510; 224-6176

Republicans
Smith (N.H.), chairman
Warner
Inhofe
Crapo

Democrats
Lautenberg
Moynihan
Boxer

Transportation and Infrastructure

SD-410 20510; 224-6176

Republicans
Voinovich, chairman
Warner
Smith (N.H.)
Bond
Inhofe
Thomas

Democrats
Baucus
Moynihan
Reid
Graham
Lieberman

Finance

SD-219 20510; 224-4515

William V. Roth Jr., R-Del., chairman

Republicans
John H. Chafee, R.I.
Charles E. Grassley, Iowa
Orrin G. Hatch, Utah
Frank H. Murkowski, Alaska
Don Nickles, Okla.
Phil Gramm, Texas
Trent Lott, Miss.
James M. Jeffords, Vt.
Connie Mack, Fla.
Fred Thompson, Tenn.

Democrats
Daniel Patrick Moynihan, N.Y.
Max Baucus, Mont.
John D. Rockefeller IV, W.Va.
John B. Breaux, La.
Kent Conrad, N.D.
Bob Graham, Fla.
Richard H. Bryan, Nev.
Bob Kerrey, Neb.
Charles S. Robb, Va.

Subcommittees

Health Care

SD-219 20510; 224-4515

Republicans
Chafee, chairman
Roth
Jeffords
Grassley
Gramm
Nickles
Hatch
Thompson

Democrats
Rockefeller
Baucus
Breaux
Conrad
Graham
Bryan
Kerrey

International Trade

SD-219 20510; 224-4515

Republicans
Grassley, chairman
Thompson
Murkowski
Roth
Lott
Gramm
Hatch
Chafee
Jeffords

Democrats
Moynihan
Baucus
Rockefeller
Breaux
Conrad
Graham
Kerrey
Robb

Long-Term Growth and Debt Reduction

SD-219 20510; 224-4515

Republicans
Murkowski, chairman
Mack
Chafee

Democrats
Graham
Bryan

Social Security and Family Policy

SD-219 20510; 224-4515

Republicans
Nickles, chairman
Gramm
Lott
Jeffords
Chafee
Thompson

Democrats
Breaux
Moynihan
Rockefeller
Kerrey
Robb

Taxation and IRS Oversight

SD-219 20510; 224-4515

Republicans
Hatch, chairman
Roth
Lott
Nickles
Mack
Murkowski
Grassley
Thompson

Democrats
Baucus
Moynihan
Conrad
Bryan
Robb

Foreign Relations
Jesse Helms, R-N.C., chairman

SD-450 20510; 224-4651

Republicans
Richard G. Lugar, Ind.
Paul Coverdell, Ga.
Chuck Hagel, Neb.
Gordon H. Smith, Ore.
Rod Grams, Minn.
Sam Brownback, Kan.
Craig Thomas, Wyo.
John Ashcroft, Mo.
Bill Frist, Tenn.

Democrats
Joseph R. Biden Jr., Del.
Paul S. Sarbanes, Md.
Christopher J. Dodd, Conn.
John Kerry, Mass.
Russell D. Feingold, Wis.
Paul Wellstone, Minn.
Barbara Boxer, Calif.
Robert G. Torricelli, N.J.

Subcommittees

African Affairs

SD-450 20510; 224-4651

Republicans
Frist, chairman
Grams
Brownback

Democrats
Feingold
Sarbanes

East Asian and Pacific Affairs

SD-450 20510; 224-4651

Republicans
Thomas, chairman
Helms
Coverdell
Hagel
Smith (Ore.)

Democrats
Kerry
Feingold
Wellstone
Torricelli

European Affairs

SD-450 20510; 224-4651

Republicans
Smith (Ore.), chairman
Lugar
Ashcroft
Coverdell
Hagel

Democrats
Biden
Sarbanes
Dodd
Wellstone

International Economic Policy, Export and Trade Promotion

SD-450 20510; 224-4651

Republicans
Hagel, chairman
Thomas
Frist
Lugar

Democrats
Sarbanes
Kerry
Boxer

International Operations

SD-450 20510; 224-4651

Republicans
Grams, chairman
Helms
Brownback
Frist

Democrats
Boxer
Kerry
Feingold

Near Eastern and South Asian Affairs

SD-450 20510; 224-4651

Republicans
Brownback, chairman
Ashcroft
Smith (Ore.)
Grams
Thomas

Democrats
Wellstone
Torricelli
Sarbanes
Dodd

Senate Committees

Western Hemisphere, Peace Corps, Narcotics and Terrorism

SD-450 20510; 224-4651

Republicans
Coverdell, chairman
Helms
Lugar
Ashcroft

Democrats
Dodd
Boxer
Torricelli

Governmental Affairs
Fred Thompson, R-Tenn., chairman

SD-340 20510; 224-4751

Republicans
William V. Roth Jr., Del.
Ted Stevens, Alaska
Susan Collins, Maine
George V. Voinovich, Ohio
Pete V. Domenici, N.M.
Thad Cochran, Miss.
Arlen Specter, Pa.
Judd Gregg, N.H.

Democrats
Joseph I. Lieberman, Conn.
Carl Levin, Mich.
Daniel K. Akaka, Hawaii
Richard J. Durbin, Ill.
Robert G. Torricelli, N.J.
Max Cleland, Ga.
John Edwards, N.C.

Subcommittees

International Security, Proliferation and Federal Services

SH-442 20510; 224-2254

Republicans
Cochran, chairman
Stevens
Collins
Domenici
Specter
Gregg

Democrats
Akaka
Levin
Torricelli
Cleland
Edwards

Investigations

SH-601 20510; 224-2254

Republicans
Collins, chairman
Roth
Stevens
Voinovich
Domenici
Cochran
Specter

Democrats
Levin
Akaka
Durbin
Cleland
Edwards

Oversight of Government Management, Restructuring and the District of Columbia

SH-601 20510; 224-3682

Republicans
Voinovich, chairman
Roth
Gregg

Democrats
Durbin
Torricelli

Health, Education, Labor and Pensions
James M. Jeffords, R-Vt., chairman

SD-428 20510; 224-5375

Republicans
Judd Gregg, N.H.
Bill Frist, Tenn.
Mike DeWine, Ohio
Michael B. Enzi, Wyo.
Tim Hutchinson, Ark.
Susan Collins, Maine
Sam Brownback, Kan.
Chuck Hagel, Neb.
Jeff Sessions, Ala.

Democrats
Edward M. Kennedy, Mass.
Christopher J. Dodd, Conn.
Tom Harkin, Iowa
Barbara A. Mikulski, Md.
Jeff Bingaman, N.M.
Paul Wellstone, Minn.
Patty Murray, Wash.
Jack Reed, R.I.

Subcommittees

Aging

SH-615 20510; 224-0136

Republicans
DeWine, chairman
Jeffords
Hutchinson
Gregg

Democrats
Mikulski
Murray
Dodd

Children and Families
SH-625 20510; 224-5800

Republicans
Gregg, chairman
Frist
DeWine
Collins
Brownback
Hagel

Democrats
Dodd
Bingaman
Wellstone
Murray
Reed

Employment, Safety and Training
SH-608 20510; 224-2962

Republicans
Enzi, chairman
Jeffords
Hutchinson
Hagel
Sessions

Democrats
Wellstone
Kennedy
Harkin
Dodd

Public Health
SD-422 20510; 224-7139

Republicans
Frist, chairman
Gregg
Enzi
Collins
Brownback
Sessions

Democrats
Kennedy
Harkin
Mikulski
Bingaman
Reed

Indian Affairs
SH-838 20510; 224-2251
Ben Nighthorse Campbell, R-Colo., chairman

Republicans
Frank H. Murkowski, Alaska
John McCain, Ariz.
Slade Gorton, Wash.
Pete V. Domenici, N.M.
Craig Thomas, Wyo.
Orrin G. Hatch, Utah
James M. Inhofe, Okla.

Democrats
Daniel K. Inouye, Hawaii
Kent Conrad, N.D.
Harry Reid, Nev.
Daniel K. Akaka, Hawaii
Paul Wellstone, Minn.
Byron L. Dorgan, N.D.

Judiciary
SD-224 20510; 224-5225
Orrin G. Hatch, R-Utah, chairman

Republicans
Strom Thurmond, S.C.
Charles E. Grassley, Iowa
Arlen Specter, Pa.
Jon Kyl, Ariz.
Mike DeWine, Ohio
John Ashcroft, Mo.
Spencer Abraham, Mich.
Jeff Sessions, Ala.
Robert C. Smith, N.H.

Democrats
Patrick J. Leahy, Vt.
Edward M. Kennedy, Mass.
Joseph R. Biden Jr., Del.
Herb Kohl, Wis.
Dianne Feinstein, Calif.
Russell D. Feingold, Wis.
Robert G. Torricelli, N.J.
Charles E. Schumer, N.Y.

Subcommittees

Administrative Oversight and the Courts
SH-308 20510; 224-6736

Republicans
Grassley, chairman
Sessions
Thurmond
Abraham

Democrats
Torricelli
Feingold
Schumer

Antitrust, Business Rights and Competition
SD-161 20510; 224-9494

Republicans
DeWine, chairman
Hatch
Specter
Thurmond

Democrats
Kohl
Torricelli
Leahy

Constitution, Federalism and Property Rights
SD-164 20510; 224-5710

Republicans
Ashcroft, chairman

Democrats
Feingold

Hatch
Smith (N.H.)
Specter
Thurmond

Kennedy
Leahy

Criminal Justice Oversight

SD-161 20510; 224-9494

Republicans
Thurmond, chairman
DeWine
Ashcroft
Abraham
Sessions

Democrats
Schumer
Biden
Torricelli
Leahy

Immigration

SD-323 20510; 224-6098

Republicans
Abraham, chairman
Specter
Grassley
Kyl

Democrats
Kennedy
Feinstein
Schumer

Technology, Terrorism and Government Information

SH-702 20510; 224-4521

Republicans
Kyl, chairman
Hatch
Grassley
DeWine

Democrats
Feinstein
Biden
Kohl

Youth Violence

SD-163 20510; 224-2808

Republicans
Sessions, chairman
Smith (N.H.)
Kyl
Ashcroft

Democrats
Biden
Feinstein
Kohl

Rules and Administration
Mitch McConnell, R-Ky., chairman

SR-305 20510; 224-6352

Republicans
Jesse Helms, N.C.
Ted Stevens, Alaska
John W. Warner, Va.
Thad Cochran, Miss.
Rick Santorum, Pa.
Don Nickles, Okla.
Trent Lott, Miss.
Kay Bailey Hutchison, Texas

Democrats
Christopher J. Dodd, Conn.
Robert C. Byrd, W.Va.
Daniel K. Inouye, Hawaii
Daniel Patrick Moynihan, N.Y.
Dianne Feinstein, Calif.
Robert G. Torricelli, N.J.
Charles E. Schumer, N.Y.

Select Ethics
Robert C. Smith, R-N.H., chairman

SH-220 20510; 224-2981

Republicans
Pat Roberts, Kan.
George V. Voinovich, Ohio

Democrats
Harry Reid, Nev.
Richard J. Durbin, Ill.
Kent Conrad, N.D.

Select Intelligence
Richard C. Shelby, R-Ala., chairman

SH-211 20510; 224-1700

Republicans
John H. Chafee, R.I.
Richard G. Lugar, Ind.
Mike DeWine, Ohio
Jon Kyl, Ariz.
James M. Inhofe, Okla.
Orrin G. Hatch, Utah
Pat Roberts, Kan.
Wayne Allard, Colo.

Democrats
Bob Kerrey, Neb.
Richard H. Bryan, Nev.
Bob Graham, Fla.
John Kerry, Mass.
Max Baucus, Mont.
Charles S. Robb, Va.
Frank R. Lautenberg, N.J.
Carl Levin, Mich.

Senate Committees

Small Business SR-428A 20510; 224-5175
Christopher S. Bond, R-Mo., chairman

Republicans
Conrad Burns, Mont.
Paul Coverdell, Ga.
Robert F. Bennett, Utah
Olympia J. Snowe, Maine
Michael B. Enzi, Wyo.
Peter G. Fitzgerald, Ill.
Michael D. Crapo, Idaho
George V. Voinovich, Ohio
Spencer Abraham, Mich.

Democrats
John Kerry, Mass.
Carl Levin, Mich.
Tom Harkin, Iowa
Joseph I. Lieberman, Conn.
Paul Wellstone, Minn.
Max Cleland, Ga.
Mary L. Landrieu, La.
John Edwards, N.C.

Special Aging SD-G31 20510; 224-5364
Charles E. Grassley, R-Iowa, chairman

Republicans
James M. Jeffords, Vt.
Larry E. Craig, Idaho
Conrad Burns, Mont.
Richard C. Shelby, Ala.
Rick Santorum, Pa.
Chuck Hagel, Neb.
Susan Collins, Maine
Michael B. Enzi, Wyo.
Jim Bunning, Ky.
Tim Hutchinson, Ark.

Democrats
John B. Breaux, La.
Harry Reid, Nev.
Herb Kohl, Wis.
Russell D. Feingold, Wis.
Ron Wyden, Ore.
Jack Reed, R.I.
Richard H. Bryan, Nev.
Evan Bayh, Ind.
Blanche Lincoln, Ark.

Special Committee on the Year 2000 Technology Problem SD-B40 20510; 224-5224
Robert F. Bennett, R-Utah, chairman

Republicans
Jon Kyl, Ariz.
Susan Collins, Maine
Gordon H. Smith, Ore.

Democrats
Christopher J. Dodd, Conn.
Daniel Patrick Moynihan, N.Y.
Jeff Bingaman, N.M.

Veterans' Affairs SR-412 20510; 224-9126
Arlen Specter, R-Pa., chairman

Republicans
Strom Thurmond, S.C.
Frank H. Murkowski, Alaska
James M. Jeffords, Vt.
Ben Nighthorse Campbell, Colo.
Larry E. Craig, Idaho
Tim Hutchinson, Ark.

Democrats
John D. Rockefeller IV, W.Va.
Bob Graham, Fla.
Daniel K. Akaka, Hawaii
Paul Wellstone, Minn.
Patty Murray, Wash.

House Committees

The standing committees and their subcommittees of the U.S. House of Representatives for the 106th Congress are listed below in alphabetical order; also listed is the Select Intelligence Committee. The listing includes the room number, zip code, and telephone number for each committee. Membership is given in order of seniority on the committee. Address abbreviations used are as follows: CHOB (Cannon House Office Bldg.), LHOB (Longworth House Office Bldg.), RHOB (Rayburn House Office Bldg.), OHOB (O'Neill House Office Bldg. at 300 New Jersey Ave. S.E.), FHOB (Ford House Office Bldg. at 2nd and D Sts. S.W.), and CAP (Capitol). The telephone area code for Washington is 202.

Agriculture   1301 LHOB 20515; 225-0029
Larry Combest, R-Texas, chairman

Republicans
Bill Barrett, Neb.
John A. Boehner, Ohio
Thomas W. Ewing, Ill.
Robert W. Goodlatte, Va.
Richard W. Pombo, Calif.
Charles T. Canady, Fla.
Nick Smith, Mich.
Terry Everett, Ala.
Frank D. Lucas, Okla.
Helen Chenoweth, Idaho
John Hostettler, Ind.
Saxby Chambliss, Ga.
Ray LaHood, Ill.
Jerry Moran, Kan.
Bob Schaffer, Colo.
John Thune, S.D.
Bill Jenkins, Tenn.
John Cooksey, La.
Ken Calvert, Calif.
Gil Gutknecht, Minn.
Bob Riley, Ala.
Greg Walden, Ore.
Mike Simpson, Idaho
Doug Ose, Calif.
Robin Hayes, N.C.
Ernie Fletcher, Ky.

Democrats
Charles W. Stenholm, Texas
George E. Brown Jr., Calif.
Gary A. Condit, Calif.
Collin C. Peterson, Minn.
Cal Dooley, Calif.
Eva Clayton, N.C.
David Minge, Minn.
Earl F. Hilliard, Ala.
Earl Pomeroy, N.D.
Tim Holden, Pa.
Sanford D. Bishop Jr., Ga.
Bennie Thompson, Miss.
John Baldacci, Maine
Marion Berry, Ark.
Virgil H. Goode Jr., Va.
Mike McIntyre, N.C.
Debbie Stabenow, Mich.
Bob Etheridge, N.C.
Chris John, La.
Leonard L. Boswell, Iowa
David D. Phelps, Ill.
Ken Lucas, Ky.
Mike Thompson, Calif.
Baron P. Hill, Ind.

Subcommittees

Department Operations, Oversight,   1430 LHOB 20515; 225-0171
Nutrition and Forestry

Republicans
Goodlatte, chairman
Ewing
Pombo
Canady
Hostettler
Chambliss
LaHood
Moran (Kan.)
Cooksey
Walden

Democrats
Clayton
Berry
Thompson (Miss.)
Goode
Phelps
Hill (Ind.)
Thompson (Calif.)
Brown (Calif.)
Minge

General Farm Commodities, Resource   1430 LHOB 20515; 225-0171
Conservation and Credit

Republicans
Barrett (Neb.), chairman
Boehner
Smith (Mich.)

Democrats
Minge
Thompson (Miss.)
Phelps

House Committees

Lucas (Okla.)
Chambliss
Moran (Kan.)
Thune
Jenkins
Ose
Hayes

Hill (Ind.)
Clayton
Pomeroy
Holden
Bishop
Baldacci

Livestock and Horticulture
1432P LHOB 20515; 225-2171

Republicans
Pombo, chairman
Boehner
Goodlatte
Everett
Lucas (Okla.)
Chenoweth
Hostettler
Schaffer
Calvert
Gutknecht
Riley

Democrats
Peterson (Minn.)
Holden
Condit
Dooley
Berry
McIntyre
Stabenow
Etheridge
Boswell
Lucas (Ky.)

Risk Management, Research and Specialty Crops
1741P LHOB 20515; 225-4652

Republicans
Ewing, chairman
Barrett (Neb.)
Smith (Mich.)
Everett
Lucas (Okla.)
Chambliss
LaHood
Moran (Kan.)
Thune
Jenkins
Gutknecht
Riley
Walden
Simpson
Ose
Hayes
Fletcher

Democrats
Condit
Brown (Calif.)
Dooley
Hilliard
Pomeroy
Bishop
Baldacci
Goode
McIntyre
Stabenow
Etheridge
John
Boswell
Lucas (Ky.)
Thompson (Calif.)

Appropriations
H-218 CAP 225-2771
C.W. Bill Young, R-Fla., chairman

Republicans
Ralph Regula, Ohio
Jerry Lewis, Calif.
John Edward Porter, Ill.
Harold Rogers, Ky.
Joe Skeen, N.M.
Frank R. Wolf, Va.
Tom DeLay, Texas
Jim Kolbe, Ariz.
Ron Packard, Calif.
Sonny Callahan, Ala.
James T. Walsh, N.Y.
Charles H. Taylor, N.C.
David L. Hobson, Ohio
Ernest Istook, Okla.
Henry Bonilla, Texas
Joe Knollenberg, Mich.
Dan Miller, Fla.
Jay Dickey, Ark.
Jack Kingston, Ga.
Rodney Frelinghuysen, N.J.
Roger Wicker, Miss.
Michael P. Forbes, N.Y.
George Nethercutt, Wash.
Randy "Duke" Cunningham, Calif.

Democrats
David R. Obey, Wis.
John P. Murtha, Pa.
Norm Dicks, Wash.
Martin Olav Sabo, Minn.
Julian C. Dixon, Calif.
Steny H. Hoyer, Md.
Alan B. Mollohan, W.Va.
Marcy Kaptur, Ohio
Nancy Pelosi, Calif.
Peter J. Visclosky, Ind.
Nita M. Lowey, N.Y.
Jose E. Serrano, N.Y.
Rosa DeLauro, Conn.
James P. Moran, Va.
John W. Olver, Mass.
Ed Pastor, Ariz.
Carrie P. Meek, Fla.
David E. Price, N.C.
Chet Edwards, Texas
Robert E. "Bud" Cramer, Ala.
James E. Clyburn, S.C.
Maurice D. Hinchey, N.Y.
Lucille Roybal-Allard, Calif.
Sam Farr, Calif.

298 House Committees

Todd Tiahrt, Kan.
Zach Wamp, Tenn.
Tom Latham, Iowa
Anne M. Northup, Ky.
Robert B. Aderholt, Ala.
Jo Ann Emerson, Mo.
John E. Sununu, N.H.
Kay Granger, Texas
John E. Peterson, Pa.

Jesse L. Jackson Jr., Ill.
Carolyn Cheeks Kilpatrick, Mich.
Allen Boyd, Fla.

Subcommittees

Agriculture, Rural Development, FDA and Related Agencies
2362 RHOB 20515; 225-2638

Republicans
Skeen, chairman
Walsh
Dickey
Kingston
Nethercutt
Bonilla
Latham
Emerson

Democrats
Kaptur
DeLauro
Hinchey
Farr
Boyd

Commerce, Justice, State and Judicial
H-309 CAP 225-3351

Republicans
Rogers, chairman
Kolbe
Taylor (N.C.)
Regula
Latham
Miller (Fla.)
Wamp

Democrats
Serrano
Dixon
Mollohan
Roybal-Allard

Defense
H-149 CAP 225-2847

Republicans
Lewis (Calif.), chairman
Young (Fla.)
Skeen
Hobson
Bonilla
Nethercutt
Istook
Cunningham
Dickey
Frelinghuysen

Democrats
Murtha
Dicks
Sabo
Dixon
Visclosky
Moran (Va.)

District of Columbia
H-147 CAP 225-5338

Republicans
Istook, chairman
Cunningham
Tiahrt
Aderholt
Emerson
Sununu

Democrats
Moran (Va.)
Dixon
Mollohan

Energy and Water Development
2362 RHOB 20515; 225-3421

Republicans
Packard, chairman
Rogers
Knollenberg
Forbes
Frelinghuysen
Callahan
Latham

Democrats
Visclosky
Edwards
Pastor
Clyburn

Foreign Operations, Export Financing and Related Programs
H-150 CAP 225-2041

Republicans
Callahan, chairman
Porter
Wolf
Packard
Knollenberg
Forbes

Democrats
Pelosi
Lowey
Jackson
Kilpatrick
Sabo

House Committees 299

Kingston
Lewis (Calif.)

Interior
B-308 RHOB 20515; 225-3081

Republicans
Regula, chairman
Kolbe
Skeen
Taylor (N.C.)
Nethercutt
Wamp
Kingston
Peterson (Pa.)

Democrats
Dicks
Murtha
Moran (Va.)
Cramer
Hinchey

Labor, Health and Human Services and Education
2358 RHOB 20515; 225-3508

Republicans
Porter, chairman
Young (Fla.)
Bonilla
Istook
Miller (Fla.)
Dickey
Wicker
Northup
Cunningham

Democrats
Obey
Hoyer
Pelosi
Lowey
DeLauro
Jackson

Legislative Branch
H-147 CAP 225-5338

Republicans
Taylor (N.C.), chairman
Wamp
Lewis (Calif.)
Granger
Peterson (Pa.)

Democrats
Pastor
Murtha
Hoyer

Military Construction
B-300 RHOB 20515; 225-3047

Republicans
Hobson, chairman
Porter
Wicker
Tiahrt
Walsh
Miller (Fla.)
Aderholt
Granger

Democrats
Olver
Edwards
Farr
Boyd
Dicks

Transportation
2358 RHOB 20515; 225-2141

Republicans
Wolf, chairman
DeLay
Regula
Rogers
Packard
Callahan
Tiahrt
Aderholt
Granger

Democrats
Sabo
Olver
Pastor
Kilpatrick
Serrano
Clyburn

Treasury, Postal Service and General Government
B-307 RHOB 20515; 225-5834

Republicans
Kolbe, chairman
Wolf
Forbes
Northup
Emerson
Sununu
Peterson (Pa.)

Democrats
Hoyer
Meek
Price
Roybal-Allard

Veterans Affairs, Housing and Urban Development and Independent Agencies
H-143 CAP 225-3241

Republicans
Walsh, chairman
DeLay
Hobson
Knollenberg

Democrats
Mollohan
Kaptur
Meek
Price

House Committees

Frelinghuysen
Wicker
Northup
Sununu

Cramer

Armed Services
Floyd D. Spence, R-S.C., chairman

2120 RHOB 20515; 225-4151

Republicans
Bob Stump, Ariz.
Duncan Hunter, Calif.
John R. Kasich, Ohio
Herbert H. Bateman, Va.
James V. Hansen, Utah
Curt Weldon, Pa.
Joel Hefley, Colo.
H. James Saxton, N.J.
Steve Buyer, Ind.
Tillie Fowler, Fla.
John M. McHugh, N.Y.
James M. Talent, Mo.
Terry Everett, Ala.
Roscoe G. Bartlett, Md.
Howard P. "Buck" McKeon, Calif.
J.C. Watts Jr., Okla.
William M. "Mac" Thornberry, Texas
John Hostettler, Ind.
Saxby Chambliss, Ga.
Van Hilleary, Tenn.
Joe Scarborough, Fla.
Walter B. Jones Jr., N.C.
Lindsey Graham, S.C.
Jim Ryun, Kan.
Bob Riley, Ala.
Jim Gibbons, Nev.
Mary Bono, Calif.
Joseph R. Pitts, Pa.
Robin Hayes, N.C.
Steven T. Kuykendall, Calif.
Donald L. Sherwood, Pa.

Democrats
Ike Skelton, Mo.
Norman Sisisky, Va.
John M. Spratt Jr., S.C.
Solomon P. Ortiz, Texas
Owen B. Pickett, Va.
Lane Evans, Ill.
Gene Taylor, Miss.
Neil Abercrombie, Hawaii
Martin T. Meehan, Mass.
Robert A. Underwood, Guam
Patrick J. Kennedy, R.I.
Rod R. Blagojevich, Ill.
Silvestre Reyes, Texas
Tom Allen, Maine
Vic Snyder, Ark.
Jim Turner, Texas
Adam Smith, Wash.
Loretta Sanchez, Calif.
Jim Maloney, Conn.
Mike McIntyre, N.C.
Ciro D. Rodriguez, Texas
Cynthia A. McKinney, Ga.
Ellen O. Tauscher, Calif.
Robert A. Brady, Pa.
Robert E. Andrews, N.J.
Baron P. Hill, Ind.
Mike Thompson, Calif.
John B. Larson, Conn.

Subcommittees

Military Installations and Facilities
2340 RHOB 20515; 225-7120

Republicans
Hefley, chairman
Fowler
McHugh
McKeon
Hostettler
Hilleary
Scarborough
Stump
Saxton
Buyer

Democrats
Taylor (Miss.)
Ortiz
Abercrombie
Underwood
Reyes
Snyder
Brady (Pa.)
Thompson (Calif.)

Military Personnel
2340 RHOB 20515; 225-7560

Republicans
Buyer, chairman
Bartlett
Watts
Thornberry
Graham
Ryun
Bono
Pitts
Hayes
Kuykendall

Democrats
Abercrombie
Meehan
Kennedy
Sanchez
McKinney
Tauscher
Thompson (Calif.)
Larson

Military Procurement
2340 RHOB 20515; 225-4440

Republicans
Hunter, chairman
Spence

Democrats
Sisisky
Skelton

Stump
Hansen
Saxton
Talent
Everett
Watts
Thornberry
Graham
Ryun
Gibbons
Bono
Pitts
Hayes

Spratt
Evans
Blagojevich
Allen
Turner
Smith (Wash.)
Maloney (Conn.)
McIntyre
McKinney
Tauscher
Brady (Pa.)

Military Readiness 2117 RHOB 20515; 225-6288

Republicans
Bateman, chairman
Chambliss
Jones (N.C.)
Riley
Hunter
Hansen
Weldon (Pa.)
Fowler
Talent
Everett
Gibbons
Sherwood

Democrats
Ortiz
Sisisky
Spratt
Pickett
Underwood
Blagojevich
Smith (Wash.)
Maloney (Conn.)
McIntyre
Rodriguez

Military Research and Development 2340 RHOB 20515; 225-1967

Republicans
Weldon (Pa.), chairman
Bartlett
Kuykendall
Sherwood
Kasich
Bateman
Hefley
McHugh
McKeon
Hostettler
Chambliss
Hilleary
Scarborough
Jones (N.C.)
Riley

Democrats
Pickett
Taylor (Miss.)
Meehan
Kennedy
Reyes
Allen
Snyder
Turner
Sanchez
Rodriguez
Andrews
Hill (Ind.)
Larson

Banking and Financial Services 2129 RHOB 20515; 225-7502
Jim Leach, R-Iowa, chairman

Republicans
Bill McCollum, Fla.
Marge Roukema, N.J.
Doug Bereuter, Neb.
Richard H. Baker, La.
Rick A. Lazio, N.Y.
Spencer Bachus, Ala.
Michael N. Castle, Del.
Peter T. King, N.Y.
Tom Campbell, Calif.
Ed Royce, Calif.
Frank D. Lucas, Okla.
Jack Metcalf, Wash.
Bob Ney, Ohio
Bob Barr, Ga.
Sue W. Kelly, N.Y.
Ron Paul, Texas
Dave Weldon, Fla.
Jim Ryun, Kan.
Merrill Cook, Utah
Bob Riley, Ala.
Rick Hill, Mont.
Steven C. LaTourette, Ohio
Donald Manzullo, Ill.
Walter B. Jones Jr., N.C.

Democrats
John J. LaFalce, N.Y.
Bruce F. Vento, Minn.
Barney Frank, Mass.
Paul E. Kanjorski, Pa.
Maxine Waters, Calif.
Carolyn B. Maloney, N.Y.
Luis V. Gutierrez, Ill.
Nydia M. Velazquez, N.Y.
Melvin Watt, N.C.
Gary L. Ackerman, N.Y.
Ken Bentsen, Texas
Jim Maloney, Conn.
Darlene Hooley, Ore.
Julia Carson, Ind.
Bob Weygand, R.I.
Brad Sherman, Calif.
Max Sandlin, Texas
Gregory W. Meeks, N.Y.
Barbara Lee, Calif.
Virgil H. Goode Jr., Va.
Frank R. Mascara, Pa.
Jay Inslee, Wash.
Jan Schakowsky, Ill.
Dennis Moore, Kan.

House Committees

Paul D. Ryan, Wis.
Doug Ose, Calif.
John E. Sweeney, N.Y.
Judy Biggert, Ill.
Lee Terry, Neb.
Mark Green, Wis.
Patrick J. Toomey, Pa.

Charlie Gonzalez, Texas
Stephanie Tubbs Jones, Ohio
Michael E. Capuano, Mass.

Independent
Bernard Sanders, Vt.

Subcommittees

Capital Markets, Securities and Government-Sponsored Enterprises

2129 RHOB 20515; 226-0469

Republicans
Baker, chairman
Lucas (Okla.)
Manzullo
Jones (N.C.)
Ryan
Sweeney
Biggert
Terry
Toomey
Roukema
King
Royce
Paul
Cook
Riley

Democrats
Kanjorski
Ackerman
Velazquez
Bentsen
Weygand
Sandlin
Waters
Maloney (N.Y.)
Maloney (Conn.)
Hooley
Mascara
Jones (Ohio)
Capuano

Consumer Credit

2129 RHOB 20515; 225-2258

Republicans
Roukema, chairwoman
McCollum
Bereuter
Castle
Campbell
Royce
Metcalf
Barr
Kelly
Weldon (Fla.)
Ryun
Cook
Riley
Hill (Mont.)
LaTourette

Democrats
Vento
Maloney (N.Y.)
Watt
Ackerman
Bentsen
Sherman
Sandlin
Meeks
Gutierrez
Mascara
Inslee
Moore
Gonzalez

Domestic and International Monetary Policy

B-303 RHOB 20515; 226-0473

Republicans
Bachus, chairman
Paul
Ose
McCollum
Castle
Lucas (Okla.)
Metcalf
Ney
Weldon (Fla.)
Ryun
Ryan
Biggert
Green (Wis.)
Toomey

Democrats
Waters
Frank
Watt
Carson
Meeks
Lee
Kanjorski
Sherman
Inslee
Schakowsky
Moore

Independent
Sanders

General Oversight and Investigations

212 OHOB 20515; 226-3280

Republicans
King, chairman
LaTourette
Bachus
Ney
Barr
Paul

Independent
Sanders

Democrats
Gutierrez
Goode
Gonzalez

Housing and Community Opportunity
B-303 RHOB 20515; 225-6634

Republicans
Lazio, chairman
Ney
Green (Wis.)
Bereuter
Baker
Campbell
Barr
Kelly
Hill (Mont.)
Jones (N.C.)
Ose
Sweeney
Terry
Metcalf

Democrats
Frank
Velazquez
Maloney (Conn.)
Hooley
Carson
Weygand
Vento
Lee
Goode
Schakowsky
Jones (Ohio)
Capuano

Budget
309 CHOB 20515; 226-7270
John R. Kasich, R-Ohio, chairman

Republicans
Saxby Chambliss, Ga.
Christopher Shays, Conn.
Wally Herger, Calif.
Bob Franks, N.J.
Nick Smith, Mich.
Jim Nussle, Iowa
Peter Hoekstra, Mich.
George P. Radanovich, Calif.
Charles Bass, N.H.
Gil Gutknecht, Minn.
Van Hilleary, Tenn.
John E. Sununu, N.H.
Joseph R. Pitts, Pa.
Joe Knollenberg, Mich.
William M. "Mac" Thornberry, Texas
Jim Ryun, Kan.
Mac Collins, Ga.
Zach Wamp, Tenn.
Mark Green, Wis.
Ernie Fletcher, Ky.
Gary Miller, Calif.
Paul D. Ryan, Wis.
Patrick J. Toomey, Pa.

Democrats
John M. Spratt Jr., S.C.
Jim McDermott, Wash.
Lynn Rivers, Mich.
Bennie Thompson, Miss.
David Minge, Minn.
Ken Bentsen, Texas
Jim Davis, Fla.
Bob Weygand, R.I.
Eva Clayton, N.C.
David E. Price, N.C.
Edward J. Markey, Mass.
Gerald D. Kleczka, Wis.
Bob Clement, Tenn.
James P. Moran, Va.
Darlene Hooley, Ore.
Ken Lucas, Ky.
Rush D. Holt, N.J.
Joseph M. Hoeffel, Pa.
Tammy Baldwin, Wis.

Commerce
2125 RHOB 20515; 225-2927
Thomas J. Bliley Jr., R-Va., chairman

Republicans
W.J. "Billy" Tauzin, La.
Michael G. Oxley, Ohio
Michael Bilirakis, Fla.
Joe L. Barton, Texas
Fred Upton, Mich.
Cliff Stearns, Fla.
Paul E. Gillmor, Ohio
James C. Greenwood, Pa.
Christopher Cox, Calif.
Nathan Deal, Ga.
Steve Largent, Okla.
Richard M. Burr, N.C.
Brian P. Bilbray, Calif.
Edward Whitfield, Ky.
Greg Ganske, Iowa
Charlie Norwood, Ga.
Tom Coburn, Okla.
Rick A. Lazio, N.Y.
Barbara Cubin, Wyo.
James E. Rogan, Calif.

Democrats
John D. Dingell, Mich.
Henry A. Waxman, Calif.
Edward J. Markey, Mass.
Ralph M. Hall, Texas
Rick Boucher, Va.
Edolphus Towns, N.Y.
Frank Pallone Jr., N.J.
Sherrod Brown, Ohio
Bart Gordon, Tenn.
Peter Deutsch, Fla.
Bobby L. Rush, Ill.
Anna G. Eshoo, Calif.
Ron Klink, Pa.
Bart Stupak, Mich.
Eliot L. Engel, N.Y.
Tom Sawyer, Ohio
Albert R. Wynn, Md.
Gene Green, Texas
Karen McCarthy, Mo.
Ted Strickland, Ohio

304 House Committees

John Shimkus, Ill.
Heather A. Wilson, N.M.
John Shadegg, Ariz.
Charles W. "Chip" Pickering Jr., M
Vito J. Fossella, N.Y.
Roy Blunt, Mo.
Ed Bryant, Tenn.
Robert L. Ehrlich Jr., Md.

Diana DeGette, Colo.
Thomas M. Barrett, Wis.
Bill Luther, Minn.
Lois Capps, Calif.

Subcommittees

Energy and Power
2125 RHOB 20515; 225-2927

Republicans
Barton, chairman
Bilirakis
Stearns
Largent
Burr
Whitfield
Norwood
Coburn
Rogan
Shimkus
Wilson
Shadegg
Pickering
Fossella
Bryant
Ehrlich

Democrats
Hall (Texas)
McCarthy (Mo.)
Sawyer
Markey
Boucher
Pallone
Brown (Ohio)
Gordon
Rush
Wynn
Strickland
Deutsch
Klink

Finance and Hazardous Materials
2125 RHOB 20515; 225-2927

Republicans
Oxley, chairman
Tauzin
Gillmor
Greenwood
Cox
Largent
Bilbray
Ganske
Lazio
Shimkus
Wilson
Shadegg
Fossella
Blunt
Ehrlich

Democrats
Towns
Deutsch
Stupak
Engel
DeGette
Barrett (Wis.)
Luther
Capps
Markey
Hall (Texas)
Pallone
Rush

Health and Environment
2125 RHOB 20515; 225-2927

Republicans
Bilirakis, chairman
Upton
Stearns
Greenwood
Deal
Burr
Bilbray
Whitfield
Ganske
Norwood
Coburn
Lazio
Cubin
Shadegg
Pickering
Bryant

Democrats
Brown (Ohio)
Waxman
Pallone
Deutsch
Stupak
Green (Texas)
Strickland
DeGette
Barrett (Wis.)
Capps
Hall (Texas)
Towns
Eshoo

Oversight and Investigations
2125 RHOB 20515; 225-2927

Republicans
Upton, chairman
Barton
Cox
Burr
Bilbray
Whitfield
Ganske

Democrats
Klink
Waxman
Stupak
Green (Texas)
McCarthy (Mo.)
Strickland
DeGette

House Committees

Blunt
Bryant

Telecommunications, Trade and Consumer Protection
2125 RHOB 20515; 225-2927

Republicans
Tauzin, chairman
Oxley
Stearns
Gillmor
Cox
Deal
Largent
Cubin
Rogan
Shimkus
Wilson
Pickering
Fossella
Blunt
Ehrlich

Democrats
Markey
Boucher
Gordon
Rush
Eshoo
Engel
Wynn
Luther
Klink
Sawyer
Green (Texas)
McCarthy (Mo.)

Education and the Workforce
Bill Goodling, R-Pa., chairman

2181 RHOB 20515; 225-4527

Republicans
Tom Petri, Wis.
Marge Roukema, N.J.
Cass Ballenger, N.C.
Bill Barrett, Neb.
John A. Boehner, Ohio
Peter Hoekstra, Mich.
Howard P. "Buck" McKeon, Calif.
Michael N. Castle, Del.
Sam Johnson, Texas
James M. Talent, Mo.
James C. Greenwood, Pa.
Lindsey Graham, S.C.
Mark Souder, Ind.
David M. McIntosh, Ind.
Charlie Norwood, Ga.
Ron Paul, Texas
Bob Schaffer, Colo.
Fred Upton, Mich.
Nathan Deal, Ga.
Van Hilleary, Tenn.
Vernon J. Ehlers, Mich.
Matt Salmon, Ariz.
Tom Tancredo, Colo.
Ernie Fletcher, Ky.
Jim DeMint, S.C.
Johnny Isakson, Ga.

Democrats
William L. Clay, Mo.
George Miller, Calif.
Dale E. Kildee, Mich.
Matthew G. Martinez, Calif.
Major R. Owens, N.Y.
Donald M. Payne, N.J.
Patsy T. Mink, Hawaii
Robert E. Andrews, N.J.
Tim Roemer, Ind.
Robert C. Scott, Va.
Lynn Woolsey, Calif.
Carlos A. Romero-Barcelo, P.R.
Chaka Fattah, Pa.
Ruben Hinojosa, Texas
Carolyn McCarthy, N.Y.
John F. Tierney, Mass.
Ron Kind, Wis.
Loretta Sanchez, Calif.
Harold E. Ford Jr., Tenn.
Dennis J. Kucinich, Ohio
David Wu, Ore.
Rush D. Holt, N.J.

Subcommittees

Early Childhood, Youth and Families
2181 RHOB 20515; 225-4527

Republicans
Castle, chairman
Johnson
Souder
Paul
Goodling
Greenwood
McIntosh
Upton
Hilleary
Petri
Roukema
Boehner
Graham
Schaffer
Salmon
Tancredo
DeMint

Democrats
Kildee
Miller
Payne
Mink
Scott
Kucinich
Woolsey
Romero-Barcelo
Fattah
Hinojosa
McCarthy (N.Y.)
Sanchez
Ford
Wu

306 House Committees

Employer-Employee Relations
2181 RHOB 20515; 225-4527

Republicans
Boehner, chairman
Talent
Petri
Roukema
Ballenger
Goodling
McKeon
Hoekstra
Salmon
Fletcher
DeMint

Democrats
Andrews
Kildee
Payne
Romero-Barcelo
McCarthy (N.Y.)
Tierney
Wu
Holt

Oversight and Investigations
2181 RHOB 20515; 225-4527

Republicans
Hoekstra, chairman
Norwood
Hilleary
Schaffer
Tancredo
Fletcher

Democrats
Roemer
Scott
Kind
Ford

Postsecondary Education, Training and Life-Long Learning
2181 RHOB 20515; 225-4527

Republicans
McKeon, chairman
Goodling
Petri
Barrett (Neb.)
Greenwood
Graham
McIntosh
Castle
Souder
Deal
Ehlers
Isakson

Democrats
Martinez
Tierney
Kind
Holt
Owens
Mink
Andrews
Roemer
Fattah
Hinojosa

Workforce Protections
2181 RHOB 20515; 225-4527

Republicans
Ballenger, chairman
Barrett (Neb.)
Hoekstra
Graham
Paul
Johnson
Boehner
Isakson

Democrats
Owens
Miller
Martinez
Woolsey
Sanchez
Kucinich

Government Reform
2154 RHOB 20515; 225-5074
Dan Burton, R-Ind., chairman

Republicans
Benjamin A. Gilman, N.Y.
Constance A. Morella, Md.
Christopher Shays, Conn.
Ileana Ros-Lehtinen, Fla.
John M. McHugh, N.Y.
Steve Horn, Calif.
John L. Mica, Fla.
Thomas M. Davis III, Va.
David M. McIntosh, Ind.
Mark Souder, Ind.
Joe Scarborough, Fla.
Steven C. LaTourette, Ohio
Mark Sanford, S.C.
Bob Barr, Ga.
Dan Miller, Fla.
Asa Hutchinson, Ark.
Lee Terry, Neb.
Judy Biggert, Ill.
Greg Walden, Ore.
Doug Ose, Calif.

Democrats
Henry A. Waxman, Calif.
Tom Lantos, Calif.
Bob Wise, W.Va.
Major R. Owens, N.Y.
Edolphus Towns, N.Y.
Paul E. Kanjorski, Pa.
Patsy T. Mink, Hawaii
Carolyn B. Maloney, N.Y.
Eleanor Holmes Norton, D.C.
Chaka Fattah, Pa.
Elijah E. Cummings, Md.
Dennis J. Kucinich, Ohio
Rod R. Blagojevich, Ill.
Danny K. Davis, Ill.
John F. Tierney, Mass.
Jim Turner, Texas
Tom Allen, Maine
Harold E. Ford Jr., Tenn.
Jan Schakowsky, Ill.

House Committees 307

Paul D. Ryan, Wis.
John T. Doolittle, Calif.
Helen Chenoweth, Idaho

Independent
Bernard Sanders, Vt.

Subcommittees

Census 114 OHOB 20515; 226-1973

Republicans
Miller (Fla.), chairman
Doolittle
Davis (Va.)
Ryan
Souder

Democrats
Maloney (N.Y.)
Davis (Ill.)
Ford

Civil Service B-371C RHOB 20515; 225-6427

Republicans
Scarborough, chairman
Hutchinson
Morella
Mica
Miller (Fla.)

Democrats
Cummings
Norton
Allen

Criminal Justice, Drug Policy and Human Resources B-372 RHOB 20515; 225-2548

Republicans
Mica, chairman
Barr
Gilman
Shays
Ros-Lehtinen
Souder
LaTourette
Hutchinson
Ose

Democrats
Mink
Towns
Cummings
Kucinich
Blagojevich
Tierney
Turner

District of Columbia B-349A RHOB 20515; 225-6751

Republicans
Davis (Va.), chairman
Morella
Horn
Scarborough

Democrats
Norton
Maloney (N.Y.)
Towns

Government Management, Information and Technology B-373 RHOB 20515; 225-5147

Republicans
Horn, chairman
Biggert
Davis (Va.)
Walden
Ose
Ryan

Democrats
Turner
Kanjorski
Owens
Mink
Maloney (N.Y.)

National Economic Growth, Natural Resources and Regulatory Affairs B-377 RHOB 20515; 225-4407

Republicans
McIntosh, chairman
Ryan
Barr
Terry
Walden
Chenoweth
Doolittle

Democrats
Kucinich
Lantos
Kanjorski
Ford

Independent
Sanders

National Security, Veterans Affairs and International Relations B-373 RHOB 20515; 225-2577

Republicans
Shays, chairman
Souder
Ros-Lehtinen
McHugh
Mica
McIntosh
Sanford
Terry
Biggert
Chenoweth

Democrats
Blagojevich
Lantos
Wise
Tierney
Allen
Towns
Schakowsky

Independent
Sanders

308 House Committees

Postal Service
B-349B RHOB 20515; 225-3741

Republicans
McHugh, chairman
Sanford
Gilman
LaTourette
Vacancy

Democrats
Fattah
Owens
Davis (Ill.)

House Administration
1309 LHOB 20515; 225-8281
Bill Thomas, R-Calif., chairman

Republicans
John A. Boehner, Ohio
Vernon J. Ehlers, Mich.
Bob Ney, Ohio
John L. Mica, Fla.
Thomas W. Ewing, Ill.

Democrats
Steny H. Hoyer, Md.
Chaka Fattah, Pa.
Jim Davis, Fla.

International Relations
2170 RHOB 20515; 225-5021
Benjamin A. Gilman, R-N.Y., chairman

Republicans
Bill Goodling, Pa.
Jim Leach, Iowa
Henry J. Hyde, Ill.
Doug Bereuter, Neb.
Christopher H. Smith, N.J.
Dan Burton, Ind.
Elton Gallegly, Calif.
Ileana Ros-Lehtinen, Fla.
Cass Ballenger, N.C.
Dana Rohrabacher, Calif.
Donald Manzullo, Ill.
Ed Royce, Calif.
Peter T. King, N.Y.
Steve Chabot, Ohio
Mark Sanford, S.C.
Matt Salmon, Ariz.
Amo Houghton, N.Y.
Tom Campbell, Calif.
John M. McHugh, N.Y.
Kevin Brady, Texas
Richard M. Burr, N.C.
Paul E. Gillmor, Ohio
George P. Radanovich, Calif.
John Cooksey, La.
Tom Tancredo, Colo.

Democrats
Sam Gejdenson, Conn.
Tom Lantos, Calif.
Howard L. Berman, Calif.
Gary L. Ackerman, N.Y.
Eni F.H. Faleomavaega, Am. Samoa
Matthew G. Martinez, Calif.
Donald M. Payne, N.J.
Robert Menendez, N.J.
Sherrod Brown, Ohio
Cynthia A. McKinney, Ga.
Alcee L. Hastings, Fla.
Pat Danner, Mo.
Earl F. Hilliard, Ala.
Brad Sherman, Calif.
Robert Wexler, Fla.
Steven R. Rothman, N.J.
Jim Davis, Fla.
Earl Pomeroy, N.D.
Bill Delahunt, Mass.
Gregory W. Meeks, N.Y.
Barbara Lee, Calif.
Joseph Crowley, N.Y.
Joseph M. Hoeffel, Pa.

Subcommittees

Africa
705 OHOB 20515; 226-7812

Republicans
Royce, chairman
Houghton
Campbell
Chabot
Tancredo
Radanovich

Democrats
Payne
Hastings (Fla.)
Meeks
Lee

Asia and the Pacific
B-359 RHOB 20515; 226-7825

Republicans
Bereuter, chairman
Leach
Rohrabacher
King
Sanford
Salmon
McHugh
Burr
Gillmor
Manzullo
Royce
Cooksey

Democrats
Lantos
Berman
Faleomavaega
Martinez
Brown (Ohio)
Wexler
Davis (Fla.)
Pomeroy
Ackerman
Hastings (Fla.)

House Committees

International Economic Policy and Trade
702 OHOB 20515; 225-3345

Republicans
Ros-Lehtinen, chairwoman
Manzullo
Chabot
Brady (Texas)
Radanovich
Cooksey
Bereuter
Rohrabacher
Campbell
Burr

Democrats
Menendez
Danner
Hilliard
Sherman
Rothman
Delahunt
Crowley
Hoeffel

International Operations and Human Rights
B-358 RHOB 20515; 225-5748

Republicans
Smith (N.J.), chairman
Goodling
Hyde
Tancredo
Burton
Ballenger
King
Salmon

Democrats
McKinney
Faleomavaega
Hilliard
Sherman
Delahunt
Meeks

Western Hemisphere
2401-A RHOB 20515; 226-7820

Republicans
Gallegly, chairman
Burton
Ballenger
Smith (N.J.)
Ros-Lehtinen
Sanford
Brady (Texas)
Gillmor
Vacancy

Democrats
Ackerman
Martinez
Menendez
Wexler
Rothman
Davis (Fla.)
Pomeroy

Judiciary
2138 RHOB 20515; 225-3951
Henry J. Hyde, R-Ill., chairman

Republicans
F. James Sensenbrenner Jr., Wis
Bill McCollum, Fla.
George W. Gekas, Pa.
Howard Coble, N.C.
Lamar Smith, Texas
Elton Gallegly, Calif.
Charles T. Canady, Fla.
Robert W. Goodlatte, Va.
Ed Bryant, Tenn.
Steve Chabot, Ohio
Bob Barr, Ga.
Bill Jenkins, Tenn.
Asa Hutchinson, Ark.
Ed Pease, Ind.
Christopher B. Cannon, Utah
James E. Rogan, Calif.
Lindsey Graham, S.C.
Mary Bono, Calif.
Spencer Bachus, Ala.
Joe Scarborough, Fla.

Democrats
John Conyers Jr., Mich.
Barney Frank, Mass.
Howard L. Berman, Calif.
Rick Boucher, Va.
Jerrold Nadler, N.Y.
Robert C. Scott, Va.
Melvin Watt, N.C.
Zoe Lofgren, Calif.
Sheila Jackson-Lee, Texas
Maxine Waters, Calif.
Martin T. Meehan, Mass.
Bill Delahunt, Mass.
Robert Wexler, Fla.
Steven R. Rothman, N.J.
Tammy Baldwin, Wis.
Anthony D. Weiner, N.Y.

Subcommittees

Commercial and Administrative Law
B-353 RHOB 20515; 225-2825

Republicans
Gekas, chairman
Bryant
Graham
Chabot
Bachus
Bono
Scarborough

Democrats
Nadler
Baldwin
Watt
Weiner
Delahunt

House Committees

Constitution
H2-362 FHOB 20515; 226-7680

Republicans
Canady, chairman
Hyde
Hutchinson
Bachus
Goodlatte
Barr
Jenkins
Graham

Democrats
Watt
Waters
Frank
Conyers
Nadler

Courts and Intellectual Property
B-351A RHOB 20515; 225-5741

Republicans
Coble, chairman
Sensenbrenner
Gallegly
Goodlatte
Jenkins
Pease
Cannon
Rogan
Bono

Democrats
Berman
Conyers
Boucher
Lofgren
Delahunt
Wexler

Crime
207 CHOB 20515; 225-3926

Republicans
McCollum, chairman
Chabot
Barr
Gekas
Coble
Smith (Texas)
Canady
Hutchinson

Democrats
Scott
Meehan
Rothman
Weiner
Jackson-Lee

Immigration and Claims
B-370B RHOB 20515; 225-5727

Republicans
Smith (Texas), chairman
McCollum
Gallegly
Pease
Cannon
Canady
Goodlatte
Scarborough

Democrats
Jackson-Lee
Berman
Lofgren
Frank
Meehan

Resources
1324 LHOB 20515; 225-2761

Don Young, R-Alaska, chairman

Republicans
W.J. "Billy" Tauzin, La.
James V. Hansen, Utah
H. James Saxton, N.J.
Elton Gallegly, Calif.
John J. "Jimmy" Duncan Jr., Tenn.
Joel Hefley, Colo.
John T. Doolittle, Calif.
Wayne T. Gilchrest, Md.
Ken Calvert, Calif.
Richard W. Pombo, Calif.
Barbara Cubin, Wyo.
Helen Chenoweth, Idaho
George P. Radanovich, Calif.
Walter B. Jones Jr., N.C.
William M. "Mac" Thornberry, Texas
Christopher B. Cannon, Utah
Kevin Brady, Texas
John E. Peterson, Pa.
Rick Hill, Mont.
Bob Schaffer, Colo.
Jim Gibbons, Nev.
Mark Souder, Ind.
Greg Walden, Ore.
Donald L. Sherwood, Pa.
Robin Hayes, N.C.

Democrats
George Miller, Calif.
Nick J. Rahall II, W.Va.
Bruce F. Vento, Minn.
Dale E. Kildee, Mich.
Peter A. DeFazio, Ore.
Eni F.H. Faleomavaega, Am. Samoa
Neil Abercrombie, Hawaii
Solomon P. Ortiz, Texas
Owen B. Pickett, Va.
Frank Pallone Jr., N.J.
Cal Dooley, Calif.
Carlos A. Romero-Barcelo, P.R.
Robert A. Underwood, Guam
Patrick J. Kennedy, R.I.
Adam Smith, Wash.
Chris John, La.
Donna M.C. Christensen, Virgin Is.
Ron Kind, Wis.
Jay Inslee, Wash.
Grace F. Napolitano, Calif.
Tom Udall, N.M.
Mark Udall, Colo.
Joseph Crowley, N.Y.
Vacancy

Mike Simpson, Idaho
Tom Tancredo, Colo.

Subcommittees

Energy and Mineral Resources
1626 LHOB 20515; 225-9297

Republicans
Cubin, chairman
Tauzin
Thornberry
Cannon
Brady (Texas)
Schaffer
Gibbons
Walden
Tancredo

Democrats
Underwood
Rahall
Faleomavaega
Ortiz
Dooley
Kennedy
John
Inslee

Fisheries Conservation, Wildlife and Oceans
805 OHOB 20515; 226-0200

Republicans
Saxton, chairman
Tauzin
Hansen
Gilchrest
Pombo
Jones (N.C.)
Souder
Hayes
Simpson

Democrats
Faleomavaega
Vento
DeFazio
Abercrombie
Ortiz
Pallone
Romero-Barcelo
Smith (Wash.)

Forests and Forest Health
1337 LHOB 20515; 225-0691

Republicans
Chenoweth, chairman
Duncan
Doolittle
Gilchrest
Peterson (Pa.)
Hill (Mont.)
Schaffer
Sherwood
Hayes

Democrats
Kennedy
Kildee
Pickett
Kind
Napolitano
Udall (N.M.)
Udall (Colo.)
Crowley

National Parks and Public Lands
814 OHOB 20515; 226-7736

Republicans
Hansen, chairman
Gallegly
Duncan
Hefley
Pombo
Radanovich
Jones (N.C.)
Cannon
Hill (Mont.)
Gibbons
Souder
Sherwood

Democrats
Romero-Barcelo
Rahall
Vento
Kildee
Christensen
Kind
Inslee
Udall (N.M.)
Udall (Colo.)
Crowley

Water and Power
1337 LHOB 20515; 225-8331

Republicans
Doolittle, chairman
Calvert
Pombo
Chenoweth
Radanovich
Thornberry
Walden
Simpson

Democrats
Dooley
Miller
DeFazio
Pickett
Smith (Wash.)
Christensen
Napolitano

Rules
H-312 CAP 225-9191

David Dreier, R-Calif., chairman

Republicans
Porter J. Goss, Fla.
John Linder, Ga.
Deborah Pryce, Ohio
Lincoln Diaz-Balart, Fla.

Democrats
Joe Moakley, Mass.
Martin Frost, Texas
Tony P. Hall, Ohio
Louise M. Slaughter, N.Y.

312 House Committees

Richard "Doc" Hastings, Wash.
Sue Myrick, N.C.
Pete Sessions, Texas
Thomas M. Reynolds, N.Y.

Subcommittees

Legislative and Budget Process
421 CHOB 20515; 225-1547

Republicans
Goss, chairman
Pryce
Hastings (Wash.)
Myrick
Dreier

Democrats
Frost
Moakley

Rules and Organization of the House
421 CHOB 20515; 225-8925

Republicans
Linder, chairman
Diaz-Balart
Sessions
Reynolds
Dreier

Democrats
Hall (Ohio)
Slaughter

Science
2320 RHOB 20515; 225-6371
F. James Sensenbrenner Jr., R-Wis., chairman

Republicans
Sherwood Boehlert, N.Y.
Lamar Smith, Texas
Constance A. Morella, Md.
Curt Weldon, Pa.
Dana Rohrabacher, Calif.
Joe L. Barton, Texas
Ken Calvert, Calif.
Nick Smith, Mich.
Roscoe G. Bartlett, Md.
Vernon J. Ehlers, Mich.
Dave Weldon, Fla.
Gil Gutknecht, Minn.
Thomas W. Ewing, Ill.
Christopher B. Cannon, Utah
Kevin Brady, Texas
Merrill Cook, Utah
George Nethercutt, Wash.
Frank D. Lucas, Okla.
Mark Green, Wis.
Steven T. Kuykendall, Calif.
Gary Miller, Calif.
Judy Biggert, Ill.
Mark Sanford, S.C.
Jack Metcalf, Wash.

Democrats
George E. Brown Jr., Calif.
Ralph M. Hall, Texas
Bart Gordon, Tenn.
Jerry F. Costello, Ill.
Tim Roemer, Ind.
James A. Barcia, Mich.
Eddie Bernice Johnson, Texas
Lynn Woolsey, Calif.
Alcee L. Hastings, Fla.
Lynn Rivers, Mich.
Zoe Lofgren, Calif.
Mike Doyle, Pa.
Sheila Jackson-Lee, Texas
Debbie Stabenow, Mich.
Bob Etheridge, N.C.
Nick Lampson, Texas
John B. Larson, Conn.
Mark Udall, Colo.
David Wu, Ore.
Anthony D. Weiner, N.Y.
Michael E. Capuano, Mass.
Vacancy

Subcommittees

Basic Research
B-374 RHOB 20515; 225-7858

Republicans
Smith (Mich.), chairman
Boehlert
Smith (Texas)
Morella
Gutknecht
Ewing
Lucas (Okla.)
Biggert

Democrats
Johnson
Etheridge
Woolsey
Larson
Rivers
Doyle

Energy and Environment
Annex 2 FHOB 20515; 225-9662

Republicans
Calvert, chairman
Weldon (Pa.)
Barton
Rohrabacher
Ehlers

Democrats
Costello
Doyle
Hall (Texas)
Barcia
Johnson

House Committees 313

Weldon (Fla.)
Miller
Biggert
Metcalf

Hastings (Fla.)
Lofgren

Space and Aeronautics
2320 RHOB 20515; 225-7858

Republicans
Rohrabacher, chairman
Smith (Texas)
Barton
Calvert
Bartlett
Ehlers
Weldon (Fla.)
Cannon
Brady (Texas)
Cook
Nethercutt
Lucas (Okla.)
Green (Wis.)
Kuykendall
Sanford

Democrats
Gordon
Hall (Texas)
Roemer
Hastings (Fla.)
Lofgren
Jackson-Lee
Lampson
Stabenow
Etheridge
Larson
Udall (Colo.)
Wu
Weiner

Technology
2319 RHOB 20515; 225-8844

Republicans
Morella, chairman
Weldon (Pa.)
Bartlett
Gutknecht
Ewing
Cannon
Brady (Texas)
Cook
Green (Wis.)
Kuykendall
Miller

Democrats
Barcia
Rivers
Stabenow
Udall (Colo.)
Wu
Weiner
Capuano
Gordon
Roemer

Select Intelligence
H-405 CAP 225-4121
Porter J. Goss, R-Fla., chairman

Republicans
Jerry Lewis, Calif.
Bill McCollum, Fla.
Michael N. Castle, Del.
Sherwood Boehlert, N.Y.
Charles Bass, N.H.
Jim Gibbons, Nev.
Ray LaHood, Ill.
Heather A. Wilson, N.M.

Democrats
Julian C. Dixon, Calif.
Nancy Pelosi, Calif.
Sanford D. Bishop Jr., Ga.
Norman Sisisky, Va.
Gary A. Condit, Calif.
Tim Roemer, Ind.
Alcee L. Hastings, Fla.

Subcommittees

Human Intelligence, Analysis and Counterintelligence
H-405 CAP 225-4121

Republicans
McCollum, chairman
Bass
Lewis (Calif.)
Gibbons
LaHood
Wilson

Democrats
Hastings (Fla.)
Pelosi
Sisisky
Condit

Technical and Tactical Intelligence
H-405 CAP 225-4121

Republicans
Castle, chairman
Boehlert
Bass
Gibbons
LaHood
Wilson

Democrats
Bishop
Roemer
Condit
Sisisky

Small Business
2361 RHOB 20515; 225-5821
James M. Talent, R-Mo., chairman

Republicans
Larry Combest, Texas
Joel Hefley, Colo.
Donald Manzullo, Ill.
Roscoe G. Bartlett, Md.
Frank A. LoBiondo, N.J.
Sue W. Kelly, N.Y.
Steve Chabot, Ohio
Phil English, Pa.
David M. McIntosh, Ind.
Rick Hill, Mont.
Joseph R. Pitts, Pa.
Michael P. Forbes, N.Y.
John E. Sweeney, N.Y.
Patrick J. Toomey, Pa.
Jim DeMint, S.C.
Ed Pease, Ind.
John Thune, S.D.
Mary Bono, Calif.

Democrats
Nydia M. Velazquez, N.Y.
Norman Sisisky, Va.
Juanita Millender-McDonald, Calif.
Danny K. Davis, Ill.
Carolyn McCarthy, N.Y.
Bill Pascrell Jr., N.J.
Ruben Hinojosa, Texas
Donna M.C. Christensen, Virgin Is.
Robert A. Brady, Pa.
Tom Udall, N.M.
Dennis Moore, Kan.
Stephanie Tubbs Jones, Ohio
Charlie Gonzalez, Texas
David D. Phelps, Ill.
Grace F. Napolitano, Calif.
Brian Baird, Wash.
Vacancy

Subcommittees

Empowerment
B-363 RHOB 20515; 226-2630

Republicans
Pitts, chairman
English
DeMint
Vacancy
Vacancy

Democrats
Millender-McDonald
Moore
Jones (Ohio)
Udall (N.M.)

Government Programs and Oversight
B-363 RHOB 20515; 226-2630

Republicans
Bartlett, chairman
Bono
Forbes
Toomey
Vacancy

Democrats
Davis (Ill.)
Hinojosa
Gonzalez
Vacancy

Regulatory Reform and Paperwork Reduction
B-363 RHOB 20515; 226-2630

Republicans
Kelly, chairman
Combest
McIntosh
Sweeney
Hill (Mont.)

Democrats
Pascrell
Sisisky
Brady (Pa.)
Moore

Rural Enterprises
B-363 RHOB 20515; 226-2630

Republicans
LoBiondo, chairman
Hill (Mont.)
DeMint
Pitts
Sweeney

Democrats
Christensen
Phelps
Udall (N.M.)
Baird

Tax, Finance and Exports
B-363 RHOB 20515; 226-2630

Republicans
Manzullo, chairman
Chabot
English
Forbes
Toomey

Democrats
McCarthy (N.Y.)
Hinojosa
Gonzalez
Napolitano

Standards of Official Conduct
HT-2 CAP 225-7103
Lamar Smith, R-Texas, chairman

Republicans
Joel Hefley, Colo.
Joe Knollenberg, Mich.
Dave Camp, Mich.

Democrats
Howard L. Berman, Calif.
Martin Olav Sabo, Minn.
Ed Pastor, Ariz.

House Committees 315

Rob Portman, Ohio

Chaka Fattah, Pa.
Zoe Lofgren, Calif.

Transportation and Infrastructure
2165 RHOB 20515; 225-9446

Bud Shuster, R-Pa., chairman

Republicans
Don Young, Alaska
Tom Petri, Wis.
Sherwood Boehlert, N.Y.
Herbert H. Bateman, Va.
Howard Coble, N.C.
John J. "Jimmy" Duncan Jr., Tenn.
Thomas W. Ewing, Ill.
Wayne T. Gilchrest, Md.
Steve Horn, Calif.
Bob Franks, N.J.
John L. Mica, Fla.
Jack Quinn, N.Y.
Tillie Fowler, Fla.
Vernon J. Ehlers, Mich.
Spencer Bachus, Ala.
Steven C. LaTourette, Ohio
Sue W. Kelly, N.Y.
Ray LaHood, Ill.
Richard H. Baker, La.
Charles Bass, N.H.
Bob Ney, Ohio
Jack Metcalf, Wash.
Ed Pease, Ind.
Asa Hutchinson, Ark.
Merrill Cook, Utah
John Cooksey, La.
John Thune, S.D.
Frank A. LoBiondo, N.J.
J.C. Watts Jr., Okla.
Jerry Moran, Kan.
John T. Doolittle, Calif.
Lee Terry, Neb.
Donald L. Sherwood, Pa.
Gary Miller, Calif.
John E. Sweeney, N.Y.
Jim DeMint, S.C.
Doug Bereuter, Neb.
Steven T. Kuykendall, Calif.
Mike Simpson, Idaho
Johnny Isakson, Ga.

Democrats
James L. Oberstar, Minn.
Nick J. Rahall II, W.Va.
Robert A. Borski, Pa.
William O. Lipinski, Ill.
Bob Wise, W.Va.
James A. Traficant Jr., Ohio
Peter A. DeFazio, Ore.
Bob Clement, Tenn.
Jerry F. Costello, Ill.
Eleanor Holmes Norton, D.C.
Jerrold Nadler, N.Y.
Pat Danner, Mo.
Robert Menendez, N.J.
Corrine Brown, Fla.
James A. Barcia, Mich.
Bob Filner, Calif.
Eddie Bernice Johnson, Texas
Frank R. Mascara, Pa.
Gene Taylor, Miss.
Juanita Millender-McDonald, Calif.
Elijah E. Cummings, Md.
Earl Blumenauer, Ore.
Max Sandlin, Texas
Ellen O. Tauscher, Calif.
Bill Pascrell Jr., N.J.
Leonard L. Boswell, Iowa
Jim McGovern, Mass.
Tim Holden, Pa.
Nick Lampson, Texas
John Baldacci, Maine
Marion Berry, Ark.
Ronnie Shows, Miss.
Brian Baird, Wash.
Shelley Berkley, Nev.

Subcommittees

Aviation
2251 RHOB 20515; 226-3220

Republicans
Duncan, chairman
Sweeney
Young (Alaska)
Petri
Ewing
Mica
Quinn
Ehlers
Bachus
LaHood
Bass
Metcalf
Pease
Hutchinson
Cook
Cooksey
Thune
LoBiondo
Watts
Moran (Kan.)

Democrats
Lipinski
Costello
Brown (Fla.)
Johnson
Millender-McDonald
Cummings
Boswell
Baldacci
Berry
Norton
Menendez
Tauscher
McGovern
Lampson
Rahall
Traficant
DeFazio
Danner
Filner
Sandlin

316 House Committees

Doolittle
Sherwood
Miller
DeMint
Kuykendall
Simpson
Isakson

Holden

Coast Guard and Maritime Transportation
507 FHOB 20515; 226-3552

Republicans
Gilchrest, chairman
LoBiondo
Young (Alaska)
Coble

Democrats
DeFazio
Taylor (Miss.)
Baird

Economic Development, Public Buildings, Hazardous Materials and Pipeline
586 FHOB 20515; 225-3014

Republicans
Franks, chairman
Cooksey
Ewing
LaTourette
Watts

Democrats
Wise
Norton
Shows

Ground Transportation
B-376 RHOB 20515; 226-0727

Republicans
Petri, chairman
Franks
Boehlert
Bateman
Coble
Duncan
Horn
Mica
Quinn
Fowler
Bachus
LaTourette
Kelly
LaHood
Baker
Bass
Ney
Metcalf
Pease
Cook
Thune
Moran (Kan.)
Terry
Miller
Sweeney
DeMint
Bereuter

Democrats
Rahall
Clement
Nadler
Danner
Barcia
Filner
Mascara
Sandlin
Pascrell
Holden
Shows
Berkley
Borski
Lipinski
Wise
Brown (Fla.)
Johnson
Millender-McDonald
Cummings
Blumenauer
Berry

Oversight, Investigations and Emergency Management
589 FHOB 20515; 225-5504

Republicans
Fowler, chairman
Terry
Doolittle
Isakson

Democrats
Traficant
Nadler
Berkley

Water Resources and Environment
B-375 RHOB 20515; 225-4360

Republicans
Boehlert, chairman
Sherwood
Young (Alaska)
Bateman
Gilchrest
Horn
Franks
Quinn
Ehlers
LaTourette
Kelly
Baker
Ney
Hutchinson

Democrats
Borski
Taylor (Miss.)
Blumenauer
Baird
Clement
Costello
Menendez
Barcia
Mascara
Tauscher
Pascrell
Boswell
McGovern
Lampson

House Committees

LoBiondo
Doolittle
Bereuter
Kuykendall
Simpson

Baldacci

Veterans' Affairs
Bob Stump, R-Ariz., chairman

335 CHOB 20515; 225-3527

Republicans
Christopher H. Smith, N.J.
Michael Bilirakis, Fla.
Floyd D. Spence, S.C.
Terry Everett, Ala.
Steve Buyer, Ind.
Jack Quinn, N.Y.
Cliff Stearns, Fla.
Jerry Moran, Kan.
J.D. Hayworth, Ariz.
Helen Chenoweth, Idaho
Ray LaHood, Ill.
James V. Hansen, Utah
Howard P. "Buck" McKeon, Calif.
Jim Gibbons, Nev.
Mike Simpson, Idaho
Richard H. Baker, La.

Democrats
Lane Evans, Ill.
Bob Filner, Calif.
Luis V. Gutierrez, Ill.
Corrine Brown, Fla.
Mike Doyle, Pa.
Collin C. Peterson, Minn.
Julia Carson, Ind.
Silvestre Reyes, Texas
Vic Snyder, Ark.
Ciro D. Rodriguez, Texas
Ronnie Shows, Miss.
Shelley Berkley, Nev.
Vacancy
Vacancy

Subcommittees

Benefits

335 CHOB 20515; 225-9164

Republicans
Quinn, chairman
Hayworth
LaHood
Hansen
Gibbons

Democrats
Filner
Reyes
Berkley
Vacancy

Health

335 CHOB 20515; 225-9154

Republicans
Stearns, chairman
Smith (N.J.)
Bilirakis
Bachus
Moran (Kan.)
Chenoweth
McKeon
Simpson
Vacancy

Democrats
Gutierrez
Doyle
Peterson (Minn.)
Carson
Snyder
Rodriguez
Shows

Oversight and Investigations

335 CHOB 20515; 225-3569

Republicans
Everett, chairman
Stump
Spence
Buyer

Democrats
Brown (Fla.)
Vacancy
Vacancy

Ways and Means
Bill Archer, R-Texas, chairman

1102 LHOB 20515; 225-3625

Republicans
Philip M. Crane, Ill.
Bill Thomas, Calif.
E. Clay Shaw Jr., Fla.
Nancy L. Johnson, Conn.
Amo Houghton, N.Y.
Wally Herger, Calif.
Jim McCrery, La.
Dave Camp, Mich.
Jim Ramstad, Minn.
Jim Nussle, Iowa
Sam Johnson, Texas
Jennifer Dunn, Wash.

Democrats
Charles B. Rangel, N.Y.
Pete Stark, Calif.
Robert T. Matsui, Calif.
William J. Coyne, Pa.
Sander M. Levin, Mich.
Benjamin L. Cardin, Md.
Jim McDermott, Wash.
Gerald D. Kleczka, Wis.
John Lewis, Ga.
Richard E. Neal, Mass.
Michael R. McNulty, N.Y.
William J. Jefferson, La.

318 House Committees

Mac Collins, Ga.
Rob Portman, Ohio
Phil English, Pa.
Wes Watkins, Okla.
J.D. Hayworth, Ariz.
Jerry Weller, Ill.
Kenny Hulshof, Mo.
Scott McInnis, Colo.
Ron Lewis, Ky.
Mark Foley, Fla.

John Tanner, Tenn.
Xavier Becerra, Calif.
Karen L. Thurman, Fla.
Lloyd Doggett, Texas

Subcommittees

Health
1136 LHOB 20515; 225-3943

Republicans
Thomas, chairman
Johnson (Conn.)
McCrery
Crane
Johnson
Camp
Ramstad
English

Democrats
Stark
Kleczka
Lewis (Ga.)
McDermott
Thurman

Human Resources
B-317 RHOB 20515; 225-1025

Republicans
Johnson (Conn.), chairman
English
Watkins
Lewis (Ky.)
Foley
McInnis
McCrery
Camp

Democrats
Cardin
Stark
Matsui
Coyne
Jefferson

Oversight
1136 LHOB 20515; 225-7601

Republicans
Houghton, chairman
Portman
Dunn
Watkins
Weller
Hulshof
Hayworth
McInnis

Democrats
Coyne
McNulty
McDermott
Lewis (Ga.)
Neal

Social Security
B-316 RHOB 20515; 225-9263

Republicans
Shaw, chairman
Johnson
Collins
Portman
Hayworth
Weller
Hulshof
McCrery

Democrats
Matsui
Levin
Tanner
Doggett
Cardin

Trade
1104 LHOB 20515; 225-6649

Republicans
Crane, chairman
Thomas
Shaw
Houghton
Camp
Ramstad
Dunn
Herger
Nussle

Democrats
Levin
Rangel
Neal
McNulty
Jefferson
Becerra

Key Votes for 1998

Since 1945, Congressional Quarterly has selected a series of key votes on major issues of the year.

An issue is judged by the extent that it represents:
- A matter of major controversy.
- A matter of presidential or political power.
- A decision of potentially great impact on the nation and lives of Americans.

For each group of related votes on an issue, one key vote usually is chosen — the one that, in the opinion of CQ editors, was important in determining the outcome.

Charts showing how each member of Congress voted on these issues can be found after the vote descriptions.

KEY SENATE VOTES

1. S 1601. Human Cloning Ban. Motion to invoke cloture (thus limiting debate) on the motion to proceed to the bill banning creation of a human embryo through cloning. Motion rejected 42-54: R 42-12; D 0-42 (ND 0-34, SD 0-8). Feb. 11, 1998. Three-fifths of the total Senate (60) is required to invoke cloture. *(Senate vote 10)*

2. S 1663. Campaign Finance Overhaul. Motion to invoke cloture (thus limiting debate) on the McCain, R-Ariz., substitute amendment that would revise financing of federal political campaigns. Motion rejected 51-48: R 7-48; D 44-0 (ND 36-0, SD 8-0). Feb. 26, 1998. Three-fifths of the total Senate (60) is required to invoke cloture. *(Senate vote 16)*

3. S 1768. IMF Funding. McConnell, R-Ky., amendment to provide $17.9 billion for the International Monetary Fund, including $3.4 billion for a new program aimed at preventing global financial crises and $14.5 billion for the U.S. "quota" to the international agency. The amendment would prohibit release of the quota funds unless the IMF agrees to certain conditions, including restricting aid to nations that do not conform to trade agreements. Adopted 84-16: R 41-14; D 43-2 (ND 35-2, SD 8-0). March 26, 1998. *(Senate vote 44)*

4. S 1768. NATO Expansion. Warner, R-Va., amendment to add language to the resolution of ratification that would require the president to certify to Congress that the United States will not support any further NATO expansion for three years from the date Poland, Hungary and the Czech Republic join the alliance. Rejected 41-59: R 24-31; D 17-28 (ND 15-22, SD 2-6). April 30, 1998. A "nay" was a vote in support of the president's position. *(Senate vote 112)*

5. S 1723. Skilled Worker Visas. Passage of the bill to increase the number of so-called H-1B visas, which allow highly skilled immigrants to work in the United States for six years, from the current cap of 65,000 per year to 95,000 for the remainder of fiscal 1998. The measure also would increase the cap on the visas to 105,000 for fiscal 1999 and 115,000 for the following three fiscal years, but would sunset the cap to its original level at the end of fiscal 2002. The bill also would increase the authorization for certain educational grants, authorize funding for an Internet job bank and authorize funding to provide training opportunities in information technology. Passed 78-20: R 51-2; D 27-18 (ND 20-17, SD 7-1). May 18, 1998. A "nay" was a vote in support of the president's position. *(Senate vote 141)*

6. S 1415. Tobacco Restrictions. Motion to invoke cloture (thus limiting debate) on the modified Senate Commerce, Science and Transportation Committee substitute amendment to the bill to increase tobacco restrictions. The substitute would require the tobacco industry to pay $516 billion over 25 years for anti-smoking, education and research programs; raise taxes on cigarettes by $1.10 per pack over five years; and impose penalties on the tobacco industry if youth smoking does not decrease by 60 percent over 10 years. Motion rejected 57-42: R 14-40; D 43-2 (ND 37-0, SD 6-2). June 17, 1998. Three-fifths of the total Senate (60) is required to invoke cloture. A "yea" was a vote in support of the president's position. *(Senate vote 161)*

7. HR 2646. Education Savings Accounts. Adoption of the conference report on the bill to allow individuals to contribute up to $2,000 a year of after-tax funds in tax-sheltered savings accounts that may be used to pay for educational expenses. Adopted (thus cleared for the president) 59-36: R 51-2; D 8-34 (ND 6-28, SD 2-6). June 24, 1998. A "nay" was a vote in support of the president's position. *(Senate vote 169)*

Southern states — Ala., Ark., Fla., Ga., Ky., La., Miss., N.C., Okla., S.C., Tenn., Texas, Va.

8. S 2057. Same-Sex Military Training. Byrd, D-W.Va., amendment to the Gramm, R-Texas, amendment. The Byrd amendment would prohibit the armed forces from housing male and female recruits in the same barracks and would prohibit them from conducting gender-integrated basic training. The Gramm amendment would remove restrictions on recipients of Naval Reserve Officers' Training Corps scholarships. Rejected 39-53: R 31-21; D 8-32 (ND 5-27, SD 3-5). June 25, 1998. (Subsequently, the Gramm amendment was adopted by voice vote.) A "nay" was a vote in support of the president's position. *(Senate vote 180)*

9. S 2159. Economic Sanctions. Stevens, R-Alaska, motion to table (kill) the Lugar, R-Ind., amendment that would revise the process the president and Congress use to impose unilateral economic sanctions by establishing guidelines for future sanctions and setting up procedures for consideration and implementation of sanctions proposals. The amendment would prohibit the president from implementing any unilateral economic sanction without 45 days' notice, and it would express the sense of Congress that all future unilateral sanctions end within two years of their enactment unless extended by law. Motion agreed to 53-46: R 27-28; D 26-18 (ND 22-14, SD 4-4). July 15, 1998. *(Senate vote 201)*

10. HR 1122. "Partial-Birth" Abortion. Passage, over President Clinton's Oct. 10, 1997, veto, of the bill to ban a certain late-term abortion procedure, in which the physician partially delivers the fetus before completing the abortion. Anyone convicted of performing such an abortion would be subject to a fine and up to two years in prison. Rejected 64-36: R 51-4; D 13-32 (ND 9-28, SD 4-4). Sept. 18, 1998. A two-thirds majority of those present and voting (67 in this case) of both houses is required to override a veto. A "nay" was a vote in support of the president's position. *(Senate vote 277)*

11. HR 4328. Fiscal 1999 Omnibus Appropriations. Adoption of the conference report on the bill to provide almost $500 billion in new budget authority for those Cabinet departments and federal agencies whose fiscal 1999 appropriations bills were never enacted. The measure incorporates eight previously separate appropriations bills: Labor-HHS-Education, Interior, Treasury-Postal, Foreign Operations, Commerce-Justice-State, District of Columbia, Agriculture and Transportation. In addition, the bill provides $20.8 billion in "emergency" supplemental spending, including $6.8 billion for military spending ($1.9 billion of it for Bosnia operations), $5.9 billion for relief to farmers, $2.4 billion for anti-terrorism programs, $3.35 billion to address Year 2000 computer problems and $1.55 billion for disaster relief from Hurricane Georges. The measure also contains language to extend expiring tax provisions (at a cost of $9.7 billion over nine years). Adopted (thus cleared for the president) 65-29: R 33-20; D 32-9 (ND 26-9, SD 6-0). Oct. 21, 1998. A "yea" was a vote in support of the president's position. *(Senate vote 314)*

Senate Key Votes	1	2	3	4	5	6	7	8	9	10	11
ALABAMA											
Sessions	Y	N	N	Y	Y	N	Y	Y	N	Y	N
Shelby	Y	N	Y	Y	Y	N	Y	Y	Y	Y	Y
ALASKA											
Murkowski	Y	N	Y	N	Y	N	Y	Y	N	Y	?
Stevens	Y	N	Y	Y	Y	N	Y	Y	Y	Y	Y
ARIZONA											
Kyl	Y	N	N	N	Y	N	Y	Y	Y	Y	N
McCain	Y	Y	Y	N	Y	Y	Y	N	Y	Y	N
ARKANSAS											
Hutchinson	Y	N	Y	Y	N	N	Y	?	Y	Y	Y
Bumpers	N	Y	Y	Y	N	Y	N	Y	N	N	?
CALIFORNIA											
Boxer	N	Y	Y	N	Y	Y	N	N	Y	N	Y
Feinstein	N	Y	Y	Y	Y	Y	Y	N	N	N	Y
COLORADO											
Allard	Y	N	N	N	Y	N	Y	N	N	Y	N
Campbell	N	N	N	Y	Y	N	Y	Y	Y	Y	Y
CONNECTICUT											
Dodd	N	Y	Y	N	Y	Y	N	N	N	N	Y
Lieberman	N	Y	Y	N	Y	Y	Y	N	Y	N	Y
DELAWARE											
Roth	N	N	Y	N	Y	Y	Y	?	N	Y	Y
Biden	N	Y	Y	N	N	Y	Y	N	N	Y	Y
FLORIDA											
Mack	N	N	N	N	Y	N	Y	N	Y	Y	Y
Graham	N	Y	Y	N	Y	Y	N	N	Y	N	Y
GEORGIA											
Coverdell	Y	N	N	N	Y	N	Y	Y	Y	Y	Y
Cleland	N	Y	Y	N	Y	Y	Y	N	N	N	Y
HAWAII											
Akaka	N	Y	Y	N	N	Y	?	?	Y	N	Y
Inouye	N	Y	Y	N	Y	Y	N	Y	Y	N	?
IDAHO											
Craig	Y	N	Y	Y	Y	N	Y	Y	N	Y	Y
Kempthorne	Y	N	Y	Y	Y	N	Y	N	N	Y	Y
ILLINOIS											
Durbin	N	Y	Y	N	N	Y	N	N	N	N	Y
Moseley-Braun	N	Y	Y	N	N	Y	N	N	N	N	Y
INDIANA											
Coats	Y	N	Y	N	Y	N	Y	Y	N	Y	N
Lugar	N	N	Y	N	Y	N	Y	N	N	Y	N
IOWA											
Grassley	Y	N	Y	N	Y	Y	Y	Y	Y	Y	N
Harkin	N	?	Y	Y	N	Y	N	N	Y	N	Y
KANSAS											
Brownback	Y	N	Y	N	Y	N	Y	Y	N	Y	Y
Roberts	Y	N	Y	Y	Y	N	Y	Y	N	Y	Y
KENTUCKY											
McConnell	Y	N	Y	N	Y	N	Y	Y	Y	Y	Y
Ford	N	Y	Y	N	N	Y	N	Y	Y	Y	Y
LOUISIANA											
Breaux	N	Y	Y	N	Y	Y	Y	N	Y	Y	Y
Landrieu	N	Y	Y	N	Y	Y	N	N	N	Y	Y
MAINE											
Collins	N	Y	Y	N	Y	Y	Y	N	Y	N	N
Snowe	N	Y	Y	Y	Y	Y	Y	N	Y	N	N
MARYLAND											
Mikulski	N	Y	Y	N	N	Y	N	N	Y	N	Y
Sarbanes	N	Y	Y	N	N	Y	N	N	N	N	Y

		Democrats	Republicans	
Y	Voted for "yea"		–	Announced against
N	Voted against "nay"		P	Voted "present"
+	Announced for		C	Voted "present" to avoid possible conflict of interest
#	Paired for		?	Did not vote or otherwise make a position known
X	Paired against			

Senate Key Votes	1	2	3	4	5	6	7	8	9	10	11
MASSACHUSETTS											
Kennedy	N	Y	Y	N	N	Y	N	N	Y	N	Y
Kerry	N	Y	Y	N	N	Y	N	N	Y	N	Y
MICHIGAN											
Abraham	Y	N	N	N	Y	Y	Y	Y	N	Y	Y
Levin	?	Y	Y	N	N	Y	N	N	Y	N	N
MINNESOTA											
Grams	Y	N	Y	N	Y	N	Y	Y	N	Y	N
Wellstone	N	Y	N	Y	N	Y	N	N	Y	N	N
MISSISSIPPI											
Cochran	Y	N	Y	N	Y	N	Y	N	N	Y	Y
Lott	Y	N	Y	N	Y	N	Y	Y	Y	Y	Y
MISSOURI											
Ashcroft	Y	N	N	Y	Y	N	Y	Y	Y	Y	N
Bond	Y	N	Y	Y	Y	N	Y	N	N	Y	Y
MONTANA											
Burns	Y	N	Y	Y	Y	N	Y	Y	N	Y	Y
Baucus	N	Y	Y	N	Y	Y	?	?	N	N	N
NEBRASKA											
Hagel	Y	N	Y	N	Y	N	Y	N	Y	Y	N
Kerrey	N	Y	Y	N	Y	Y	N	N	N	N	N
NEVADA											
Bryan	-	Y	Y	N	Y	Y	N	N	Y	N	Y
Reid	?	Y	Y	Y	Y	Y	N	N	Y	Y	N
NEW HAMPSHIRE											
Gregg	Y	N	Y	N	Y	Y	Y	Y	N	Y	Y
Smith	Y	N	N	Y	Y	N	Y	Y	Y	Y	N
NEW JERSEY											
Lautenberg	N	Y	Y	N	Y	Y	N	N	Y	N	Y
Torricelli	N	Y	Y	Y	N	Y	Y	Y	Y	N	Y
NEW MEXICO											
Domenici	Y	N	Y	N	Y	N	+	N	N	Y	Y
Bingaman	N	Y	Y	Y	Y	Y	N	N	Y	N	Y
NEW YORK											
D'Amato	Y	N	Y	N	?	Y	Y	N	Y	Y	Y
Moynihan	N	Y	Y	Y	N	Y	N	Y	N	Y	N
NORTH CAROLINA											
Faircloth	Y	N	N	Y	?	N	Y	Y	Y	Y	Y
Helms	Y	N	N	Y	Y	N	Y	Y	Y	Y	?
NORTH DAKOTA											
Conrad	N	Y	Y	Y	Y	Y	N	Y	N	Y	Y
Dorgan	N	Y	Y	Y	Y	Y	N	N	N	Y	Y
OHIO											
DeWine	Y	N	Y	N	Y	Y	Y	Y	Y	Y	Y
Glenn	N	Y	Y	N	N	Y	N	?	?	N	?
OKLAHOMA											
Inhofe	Y	N	N	Y	Y	N	Y	Y	Y	Y	N
Nickles	Y	N	N	Y	Y	N	Y	Y	Y	Y	N
OREGON											
Smith	N	N	Y	N	Y	Y	Y	N	N	Y	Y
Wyden	N	Y	Y	Y	Y	Y	N	-	Y	N	Y
PENNSYLVANIA											
Santorum	Y	N	Y	N	Y	N	Y	Y	N	Y	N
Specter	N	Y	Y	Y	Y	?	?	?	Y	Y	N
RHODE ISLAND											
Chafee	N	Y	Y	Y	Y	Y	N	N	N	N	Y
Reed	N	Y	Y	Y	Y	Y	N	N	Y	N	Y
SOUTH CAROLINA											
Thurmond	N	N	Y	Y	Y	N	Y	N	Y	Y	Y
Hollings	N	Y	Y	Y	Y	Y	N	Y	Y	Y	?
SOUTH DAKOTA											
Daschle	N	Y	Y	N	Y	Y	N	N	N	Y	Y
Johnson	N	Y	Y	N	Y	Y	N	N	N	Y	Y
TENNESSEE											
Frist	Y	N	Y	N	Y	Y	Y	Y	N	Y	Y
Thompson	Y	Y	N	N	Y	N	Y	N	Y	Y	Y

Senate Key Votes	1	2	3	4	5	6	7	8	9	10	11
TEXAS											
Gramm	Y	N	Y	N	Y	N	Y	N	N	Y	N
Hutchison	Y	N	Y	Y	Y	N	Y	N	N	Y	Y
UTAH											
Bennett	N	N	Y	N	Y	Y	Y	Y	Y	Y	Y
Hatch	Y	N	Y	N	Y	N	Y	Y	Y	Y	Y
VERMONT											
Jeffords	N	Y	Y	Y	Y	Y	N	N	N	N	Y
Leahy	N	Y	Y	Y	Y	Y	N	N	Y	Y	Y
VIRGINIA											
Warner	?	N	Y	Y	Y	N	Y	N	N	Y	Y
Robb	N	Y	Y	N	Y	N	N	N	N	N	Y
WASHINGTON											
Gorton	Y	N	Y	N	Y	N	Y	Y	N	Y	Y
Murray	N	Y	Y	Y	Y	Y	N	N	Y	N	Y
WEST VIRGINIA											
Byrd	N	Y	Y	Y	N	Y	Y	Y	N	Y	N
Rockefeller	N	Y	Y	N	N	Y	?	?	N	N	Y
WISCONSIN											
Feingold	N	Y	N	N	N	Y	N	N	Y	N	N
Kohl	N	Y	Y	Y	Y	Y	Y	N	Y	N	N
WYOMING											
Enzi	Y	N	Y	Y	Y	N	Y	Y	N	Y	N
Thomas	Y	N	Y	N	N	N	Y	N	N	Y	N

	Democrats	*Republicans*
Y	Voted for "yea"	– Announced against
N	Voted against "nay"	P Voted "present"
+	Announced for	C Voted "present" to avoid possible conflict of interest
#	Paired for	? Did not vote or otherwise make a position known
X	Paired against	

KEY HOUSE VOTES

1. HR 2631. Line-item vetoes. Passage, over President Clinton's Nov. 13, 1997, veto, of the bill to disapprove Clinton's line-item vetoes of 38 projects, totaling $287 million, in the fiscal 1998 military construction appropriations bill (HR 2016 - PL 105-45). Passed 347-69: R 197-23; D 149-46 (ND 100-41, SD 49-5); I 1-0. Feb. 5, 1998. A two-thirds majority of those present and voting (277 in this case) of both chambers is required to override a veto. A "nay" was a vote in support of the president's position. *(House vote 10)*

2. HR 2400. Special Transportation Projects. Graham, R-S.C., amendment to strike provisions that provide funds for specified projects, including about $9 billion for highway projects, and other funding for specified transit and bus projects. Rejected 79-337: R 67-152; D 12-184 (ND 6-137, SD 6-47); I 0-1. April 1, 1998. *(House vote 95)*

3. HR 6. Affirmative Action. Riggs, R-Calif., amendment to prohibit any public institution of higher education that participates in any Higher Education Act program from discriminating against, or granting preferential treatment to, any person or group in admissions based in whole or in part on race, sex, color, ethnicity or national origin. Rejected 171-249: R 166-55; D 5-193 (ND 2-143, SD 3-50); I 0-1. May 6, 1998. A "nay" was a vote in support of the president's position. *(House vote 133)*

4. HR 10. Financial Services Overhaul. Passage of the bill to eliminate current Glass-Steagall Act and Bank Holding Company Act barriers against affiliations between banking, securities, insurance and other firms. Passed 214-213: R 153-73; D 61-139 (ND 47-100, SD 14-39); I 0-1. May 13, 1998. *(House vote 151)* A "nay" was a vote in support of the president's position.

5. S 1150. Food Stamps for Legal Immigrants. Adoption of the rule (H Res 446) to dispose of the conference report on the bill to reauthorize agricultural research and education programs through fiscal 2002. The rule would have allowed a point of order to strike $818 million in funding in the conference report to restore food stamps to 250,000 legal immigrants. Rejected 120-289: R 118-98; D 2-190 (ND 1-140, SD 1-50); I 0-1. May 22, 1998. *(House vote 188)*

6. HR 4104. Contraceptive Coverage. Lowey, D-N.Y., amendment to prohibit the Office of Personnel Management from accepting a contract that provides coverage for prescription drugs unless the plan also provides equivalent coverage for prescription contraception drugs. Adopted 224-198: R 48-177; D 175-21 (ND 130-17, SD 45-4); I 1-0. July 16, 1998. *(House vote 290)*

7. HR 4194. Public Housing Overhaul. Lazio, R-N.Y., amendment to overhaul public housing management and allow increased local control over rents and occupancy standards. Adopted 230-181: R 215-4; D 15-176 (ND 8-136, SD 7-40); I 0-1. July 17, 1998. *(House vote 296)*

8. HR 4250. Managed Care Regulations. Passage of the bill to revise managed care and medical insurance regulations. The bill would provide a range of patient protections, create a two-step appeals process for challenging a health plan administrator's decisions and expand the availability of medical savings accounts. Passed 216-210: R 213-12; D 3-197 (ND 2-147, SD 1-50); I 0-1. July 24, 1998. A "nay" was a vote in support of the president's position. *(House vote 339)*

9. HR 2183. Campaign Finance Overhaul. Passage of the bill to ban soft money contributions for federal elections, expand regulations on advertising that advocates a candidate and tighten the definition of what constitutes coordination with a federal candidate. The text of the bill is the Shays-Meehan substitute adopted by the House on Aug. 3. Passed 252-179: R 61-164; D 190-15 (ND 142-9, SD 48-6); I 1-0. Aug. 6, 1998. *(House vote 405)*

10. H Res 525. Release of Starr Report. Adoption of the resolution to provide for the release and distribution of the report from Independent Counsel Kenneth W. Starr regarding allegations of criminal offenses and other misconduct by President Clinton. Under the resolution, the Judiciary Committee will review the materials to determine whether they contain grounds for impeachment. It also requires the committee to immediately release the initial 445-page report, and release other documents to the public on Sept. 28 unless the committee votes not to release certain materials. Adopted 363-63: R 224-0; D 138-63 (ND 102-46, SD 36-17); I 1-0. Sept. 11, 1998. *(House vote 425)*

11. HR 3736. Skilled Worker Visas. Passage of the bill to increase the number of six-year H-1B skill- and profession-based visas for foreign workers from 65,000 to 115,000 in fiscal 1999 and 2000 and 107,500 in fiscal 2001. The bill also would require some employers using H-1B workers to prove they have tried to recruit qualified U.S. workers and have not laid off U.S. workers. Passed 288-133: R 189-34; D 99-98 (ND 66-76, SD 33-22); I 0-1. Sept. 24, 1998. A "nay" was a vote in support of the president's position. *(House vote 460)*

ND Northern Democrats   SD Southern Democrats

12. HR 4328. Fiscal 1999 Omnibus Appropriations. Adoption of the conference report on the bill to provide almost $500 billion in new budget authority for those Cabinet departments and federal agencies whose fiscal 1999 appropriations bills were never enacted. The measure incorporates eight previously separate appropriations bills: Labor-HHS-Education, Interior, Treasury-Postal, Foreign Operations, Commerce-Justice-State, District of Columbia, Agriculture and Transportation. In addition, the bill provides $20.8 billion in "emergency" supplemental spending, including $6.8 billion for military spending ($1.9 billion of it for Bosnia operations), $5.9 billion for relief to farmers, $2.4 billion for anti-terrorism programs, $3.35 billion to address Year 2000 computer problems and $1.55 billion for disaster relief from Hurricane Georges. The measure also contains language to extend expiring tax provisions (at a cost of $9.7 billion over nine years), increase the number of H-1B visas for high-tech foreign workers, impose a three-year moratorium on new taxes on Internet access, implement the Chemical Weapons Convention and extend for six months Chapter 12 of the bankruptcy code, which is designed to help struggling farmers. Adopted 333-95: R 162-64; D 170-31 (ND 120-26, SD 50-5); I 1-0. Oct. 20, 1998. (HR 4328 was originally the fiscal 1999 Transportation appropriations bill.) A "yea" was a vote in support of the president's position. *(House vote 538)*

13. H Res 611. Impeachment of President Clinton/Article I - Grand Jury Perjury. Adoption of Article I of the resolution, which would impeach President Clinton for "perjurious, false and misleading testimony" during his Aug. 17, 1998, federal grand jury testimony about his relationship with former White House intern Monica Lewinsky, his prior testimony in the Paula Jones sexual harassment lawsuit and his attempts to influence others' testimony in both. Adopted 228-206: R 223-5; D 5-200 (ND 1-149, SD 4-51); I 0-1. Dec. 19, 1998. A "nay" was a vote in support of the president's position. *(House vote 543)*

Southern states — Ala., Ark., Fla., Ga., Ky., La., Miss., N.C., Okla., S.C., Tenn., Texas, Va.

House Key Votes	1	2	3	4	5	6	7	8	9	10	11	12	13
ALABAMA													
1 *Callahan*	Y	N	Y	N	N	N	?	Y	N	Y	Y	Y	Y
2 *Everett*	Y	N	Y	N	N	N	Y	Y	N	Y	Y	Y	Y
3 *Riley*	Y	N	Y	N	N	N	Y	Y	N	Y	Y	Y	Y
4 *Aderholt*	Y	N	Y	N	N	N	Y	Y	N	Y	Y	Y	Y
5 Cramer	Y	N	N	Y	N	Y	N	N	Y	Y	Y	Y	N
6 *Bachus*	Y	N	Y	N	N	N	Y	Y	Y	Y	N	N	Y
7 Hilliard	Y	N	N	N	N	Y	N	N	Y	N	N	Y	N
ALASKA													
AL *Young*	Y	N	N	N	N	N	Y	Y	N	?	N	Y	Y
ARIZONA													
1 *Salmon*	N	Y	Y	Y	Y	N	Y	Y	N	Y	Y	N	Y
2 Pastor	Y	N	N	N	N	Y	N	N	Y	Y	Y	Y	N
3 *Stump*	Y	Y	Y	Y	N	N	Y	Y	N	Y	N	N	Y
4 *Shadegg*	Y	Y	Y	Y	Y	N	Y	N	N	Y	Y	Y	Y
5 *Kolbe*	Y	Y	Y	Y	Y	Y	Y	Y	N	Y	N	Y	Y
6 *Hayworth*	Y	Y	Y	Y	N	N	Y	N	N	Y	Y	Y	Y
ARKANSAS													
1 Berry	Y	N	N	N	N	Y	N	N	Y	Y	N	Y	N
2 Snyder	Y	N	N	N	N	Y	?	N	Y	Y	Y	Y	N
3 *Hutchinson*	Y	N	Y	N	N	N	Y	Y	N	Y	N	Y	Y
4 Dickey	N	N	N	N	N	N	Y	Y	N	Y	Y	Y	Y
CALIFORNIA													
1 *Riggs*	Y	N	Y	Y	?	Y	Y	Y	Y	Y	N	N	Y
2 *Herger*	?	N	Y	Y	Y	N	Y	Y	N	Y	Y	Y	Y
3 Fazio	Y	N	N	Y	N	Y	N	N	Y	Y	Y	?	N
4 *Doolittle*	Y	N	Y	Y	Y	N	+	Y	N	Y	Y	Y	Y
5 Matsui	Y	N	Y	N	N	Y	N	N	Y	Y	Y	Y	N
6 Woolsey	Y	N	N	N	N	Y	N	N	Y	N	Y	Y	N
7 Miller	Y	N	N	N	?	Y	N	N	Y	N	Y	N	?
8 Pelosi	Y	N	N	N	N	Y	N	N	Y	N	Y	Y	N
9 Lee[1]			N	N	N	Y	N	N	Y	N	N	N	N
10 Tauscher	Y	N	N	Y	N	Y	N	N	Y	Y	Y	Y	N
11 *Pombo*	Y	N	Y	N	Y	N	Y	N	N	Y	N	Y	Y
12 Lantos	Y	N	N	N	N	Y	N	N	Y	Y	Y	Y	N
13 Stark	N	N	N	N	?	Y	N	N	Y	N	N	?	N
14 Eshoo	?	N	N	N	N	Y	N	N	Y	Y	Y	Y	N
15 *Campbell*	Y	Y	Y	N	N	Y	Y	Y	N	Y	Y	N	Y
16 Lofgren	N	P	N	N	N	Y	N	N	Y	N	Y	Y	N
17 Farr	Y	N	N	N	N	Y	N	N	Y	Y	Y	Y	N
18 Condit	Y	Y	N	Y	Y	Y	Y	N	Y	Y	N	N	N
19 *Radanovich*	Y	N	?	Y	Y	N	Y	Y	N	Y	Y	Y	Y
20 Dooley	N	N	N	N	Y	N	Y	N	N	Y	Y	Y	N
21 *Thomas*	Y	Y	Y	Y	Y	Y	Y	Y	N	Y	Y	Y	Y
22 Capps, L.[2]		N	N	N	N	Y	N	N	Y	Y	Y	Y	N
23 *Gallegly*	Y	N	Y	Y	Y	Y	Y	Y	N	Y	N	Y	N
24 Sherman	N	N	N	N	N	Y	N	N	Y	N	Y	Y	N
25 *McKeon*	+	N	Y	Y	Y	N	Y	Y	N	Y	Y	Y	Y
26 Berman	Y	N	N	N	N	Y	N	N	Y	Y	Y	Y	N
27 *Rogan*	Y	Y	Y	Y	N	Y	N	Y	N	Y	Y	Y	Y
28 *Dreier*	Y	N	Y	N	Y	N	Y	Y	N	Y	Y	Y	Y
29 Waxman	N	N	N	N	N	Y	N	N	Y	Y	Y	Y	N
30 Becerra	+	N	N	N	N	Y	N	N	Y	N	Y	Y	N
31 Martinez	N	N	N	N	N	Y	N	N	Y	N	N	N	N
32 Dixon	Y	N	N	N	N	Y	N	N	Y	Y	Y	Y	N
33 Roybal-Allard	Y	N	N	N	N	+	−	N	Y	N	Y	N	N
34 Torres	Y	?	N	N	?	Y	N	N	Y	N	Y	Y	N
35 Waters	Y	?	N	N	N	Y	N	N	Y	N	?	Y	N
36 Harman	N	N	N	?	?	Y	?	N	Y	Y	Y	Y	N
37 Millender-McD.	Y	N	N	N	N	Y	−	N	Y	Y	Y	Y	N
38 *Horn*	Y	N	Y	Y	Y	Y	Y	Y	Y	Y	N	Y	Y
39 *Royce*	N	?	Y	Y	Y	N	Y	Y	N	Y	N	N	Y
40 *Lewis*	Y	N	N	Y	N	Y	Y	N	N	Y	Y	Y	Y

	Democrats	*Republicans*	**Independent**
Y	Voted for "yea"		− Announced against
N	Voted against "nay"		P Voted "present"
+	Announced for		C Voted "present" to avoid possible conflict of interest
#	Paired for		
X	Paired against		? Did not vote or otherwise make a position known

House Key Votes	1	2	3	4	5	6	7	8	9	10	11	12	13
41 *Kim*	Y	N	Y	N	N	N	Y	Y	Y	Y	Y	Y	Y
42 Brown	Y	N	N	N	N	Y	N	N	Y	N	N	Y	N
43 *Calvert*	Y	N	Y	Y	N	Y	Y	Y	N	Y	Y	Y	Y
44 *Bono, M.*[3]			Y	Y	Y	Y	Y	Y	N	Y	Y	Y	Y
45 Rohrabacher	N	Y	Y	Y	Y	N	Y	Y	N	Y	N	N	Y
46 Sanchez	N	N	N	N	N	Y	N	N	Y	Y	+	Y	N
47 *Cox*	Y	Y	Y	Y	Y	N	Y	Y	N	Y	Y	Y	Y
48 Packard	Y	N	Y	Y	Y	N	Y	Y	Y	Y	Y	Y	Y
49 Bilbray	Y	N	Y	Y	N	Y	Y	Y	Y	Y	Y	N	Y
50 Filner	N	N	N	N	N	#	-	N	Y	N	N	N	N
51 *Cunningham*	Y	N	Y	Y	Y	N	Y	Y	?	Y	Y	Y	Y
52 Hunter	Y	Y	Y	N	Y	N	Y	Y	N	Y	N	Y	Y
COLORADO													
1 DeGette	N	N	N	Y	N	Y	N	N	Y	Y	N	N	N
2 Skaggs	N	Y	-	-	-	Y	N	N	Y	N	Y	N	N
3 McInnis	Y	N	Y	N	Y	N	Y	Y	N	Y	Y	Y	Y
4 Schaffer	Y	Y	Y	N	Y	N	Y	Y	N	Y	Y	N	Y
5 Hefley	Y	N	Y	N	Y	N	Y	Y	N	Y	N	N	Y
6 Schaefer	Y	N	?	Y	Y	N	Y	Y	N	?	Y	Y	Y
CONNECTICUT													
1 Kennelly	Y	N	N	Y	N	?	?	N	Y	Y	?	Y	N
2 Gejdenson	Y	N	N	Y	N	Y	N	N	Y	Y	N	Y	N
3 DeLauro	Y	N	N	Y	N	Y	N	N	Y	Y	N	Y	N
4 *Shays*	N	Y	N	Y	N	Y	Y	Y	Y	Y	Y	N	N
5 Maloney	Y	N	N	N	N	Y	N	N	Y	Y	Y	Y	N
6 *Johnson*	Y	N	N	Y	N	Y	Y	Y	Y	Y	Y	N	Y
DELAWARE													
AL *Castle*	Y	Y	N	Y	N	Y	Y	Y	Y	Y	Y	N	Y
FLORIDA													
1 Scarborough	Y	Y	Y	N	Y	N	Y	Y	N	?	Y	N	Y
2 Boyd	Y	N	N	Y	N	Y	N	N	Y	Y	Y	N	N
3 Brown	Y	N	N	N	N	Y	N	N	Y	N	N	Y	N
4 Fowler	Y	N	Y	Y	Y	N	Y	Y	N	Y	Y	Y	Y
5 Thurman	Y	N	N	N	N	Y	N	N	Y	Y	N	N	N
6 Stearns	Y	N	Y	Y	Y	N	Y	Y	N	Y	Y	N	Y
7 Mica	Y	N	Y	Y	Y	N	+	Y	N	Y	Y	N	Y
8 McCollum	Y	Y	Y	N	Y	N	Y	Y	N	Y	Y	Y	Y
9 Bilirakis	Y	N	Y	Y	Y	N	Y	Y	N	Y	Y	Y	Y
10 Young	Y	Y	Y	Y	Y	N	Y	?	N	Y	Y	Y	Y
11 Davis	N	N	N	N	N	Y	N	N	Y	Y	Y	Y	N
12 Canady	Y	N	Y	Y	N	N	Y	Y	N	Y	Y	Y	Y
13 Miller	N	Y	Y	Y	Y	N	Y	Y	N	Y	Y	N	Y
14 Goss	Y	Y	Y	Y	Y	N	Y	Y	N	Y	+	N	Y
15 Weldon	Y	N	Y	N	N	N	Y	Y	N	Y	Y	N	Y
16 Foley	Y	Y	Y	N	?	Y	Y	Y	Y	Y	Y	Y	Y
17 Meek	Y	N	N	N	N	Y	N	N	Y	N	N	Y	N
18 *Ros-Lehtinen*	Y	?	N	Y	N	N	Y	Y	N	Y	Y	Y	Y
19 Wexler	N	Y	N	Y	N	Y	N	N	Y	N	N	Y	N
20 Deutsch	N	N	N	Y	?	Y	N	N	Y	N	N	Y	N
21 Diaz-Balart	Y	N	N	Y	N	N	Y	Y	N	Y	Y	Y	Y
22 Shaw	Y	N	Y	Y	Y	Y	Y	Y	N	Y	Y	Y	Y
23 Hastings	Y	N	?	N	N	Y	N	N	N	N	Y	Y	N
GEORGIA													
1 *Kingston*	Y	Y	Y	Y	Y	N	Y	Y	N	N	Y	N	Y
2 Bishop	Y	N	N	Y	N	Y	N	N	N	Y	Y	Y	N
3 Collins	Y	N	Y	Y	Y	N	Y	Y	N	N	N	N	Y
4 McKinney	N	N	N	N	N	Y	N	N	Y	N	N	Y	N
5 Lewis	Y	Y	N	N	N	?	?	N	Y	N	N	Y	N
6 *Gingrich*[4]			Y	Y				Y		Y	Y	Y	Y
7 Barr	Y	Y	Y	Y	Y	N	Y	N	N	Y	N	N	Y
8 Chambliss	Y	N	Y	N	N	N	Y	Y	N	Y	Y	Y	Y
9 Deal	Y	Y	Y	Y	Y	N	Y	Y	Y	N	N	N	Y
10 Norwood	Y	N	Y	Y	Y	N	Y	Y	N	N	Y	Y	Y
11 Linder	Y	N	Y	Y	Y	N	Y	?	N	Y	Y	Y	Y
HAWAII													
1 Abercrombie	Y	N	N	N	N	Y	N	N	Y	N	Y	Y	N
2 Mink	Y	N	N	N	N	Y	N	N	Y	Y	N	Y	N
IDAHO													
1 Chenoweth	Y	N	Y	N	N	N	Y	N	N	Y	N	N	Y
2 Crapo	Y	N	Y	Y	N	N	Y	N	N	Y	Y	Y	Y

House Key Votes	1	2	3	4	5	6	7	8	9	10	11	12	13
ILLINOIS													
1 Rush	Y	N	N	N	N	Y	N	N	Y	N	N	Y	N
2 Jackson	Y	N	N	N	N	Y	N	N	Y	N	N	Y	N
3 Lipinski	Y	N	Y	N	N	N	N	N	Y	Y	N	Y	N
4 Gutierrez	N	N	N	N	N	Y	N	N	Y	Y	Y	Y	N
5 Blagojevich	Y	N	N	Y	N	Y	N	N	Y	Y	N	Y	N
6 *Hyde*	Y	Y	Y	Y	N	N	Y	Y	N	Y	Y	N	Y
7 Davis	Y	N	N	N	N	Y	N	N	Y	N	N	Y	N
8 *Crane*	Y	N	Y	Y	Y	N	Y	Y	N	Y	Y	N	Y
9 Yates	N	?	?	?	N	Y	N	?	Y	N	?	N	N
10 *Porter*	+	Y	Y	Y	Y	Y	Y	Y	Y	Y	Y	Y	Y
11 *Weller*	Y	N	Y	Y	N	N	Y	Y	N	Y	Y	Y	Y
12 Costello	Y	N	N	N	N	N	N	N	Y	Y	N	N	N
13 *Fawell*	Y	N	Y	Y	Y	N	Y	Y	N	Y	Y	Y	Y
14 *Hastert*	Y	N	Y	Y	Y	N	Y	Y	N	Y	Y	Y	Y
15 *Ewing*	N	N	Y	N	N	N	Y	Y	N	Y	Y	Y	Y
16 *Manzullo*	Y	N	Y	N	Y	N	Y	Y	N	Y	Y	N	Y
17 Evans	Y	N	N	N	N	Y	N	N	Y	Y	N	Y	N
18 *LaHood*	Y	N	N	N	N	N	Y	Y	N	Y	Y	Y	Y
19 Poshard	Y	N	N	N	N	N	Y	N	Y	?	?	?	N
20 *Shimkus*	Y	N	Y	Y	Y	N	Y	Y	Y	Y	Y	Y	Y
INDIANA													
1 Visclosky	Y	N	N	N	N	Y	N	N	Y	Y	N	Y	N
2 *McIntosh*	Y	?	Y	Y	Y	N	Y	Y	N	Y	Y	N	Y
3 Roemer	Y	N	N	N	N	N	N	N	Y	Y	Y	Y	N
4 *Souder*	Y	Y	N	Y	N	N	Y	Y	N	Y	Y	Y	N
5 *Buyer*	Y	N	N	Y	Y	N	Y	Y	N	Y	Y	Y	Y
6 *Burton*	+	N	Y	Y	N	N	Y	Y	N	+	Y	Y	Y
7 *Pease*	Y	N	Y	Y	N	N	Y	Y	N	Y	Y	Y	Y
8 *Hostettler*	Y	N	Y	Y	Y	N	Y	Y	N	N	N	N	Y
9 Hamilton	Y	N	N	N	N	Y	N	N	Y	Y	Y	Y	N
10 Carson	N	N	-	N	N	Y	N	N	N	N	N	Y	N
IOWA													
1 *Leach*	N	Y	N	Y	N	Y	Y	Y	Y	Y	Y	Y	Y
2 *Nussle*	N	N	N	Y	N	N	Y	Y	N	Y	Y	Y	Y
3 Boswell	N	N	N	N	N	Y	N	N	Y	Y	Y	Y	N
4 *Ganske*	N	N	Y	Y	N	Y	Y	N	Y	Y	Y	Y	Y
5 *Latham*	Y	N	Y	Y	N	N	Y	Y	N	Y	Y	Y	Y
KANSAS													
1 *Moran*	Y	N	N	N	N	N	Y	Y	N	Y	Y	Y	Y
2 *Ryun*	Y	N	Y	N	N	N	Y	Y	N	Y	Y	Y	Y
3 *Snowbarger*	Y	N	N	N	Y	N	Y	Y	N	Y	Y	Y	Y
4 *Tiahrt*	Y	N	Y	N	Y	N	Y	Y	N	Y	Y	Y	Y
KENTUCKY													
1 *Whitfield*	Y	N	Y	Y	Y	N	Y	Y	N	Y	N	Y	Y
2 *Lewis*	Y	N	Y	N	Y	N	Y	Y	N	Y	Y	Y	Y
3 *Northup*	Y	N	Y	Y	N	N	Y	Y	N	Y	Y	Y	Y
4 *Bunning*	Y	N	Y	Y	N	N	Y	Y	N	Y	Y	Y	Y
5 *Rogers*	Y	N	Y	N	Y	N	Y	Y	N	Y	Y	Y	Y
6 Baesler	Y	N	Y	N	N	Y	Y	N	Y	Y	N	Y	N
LOUISIANA													
1 *Livingston*	Y	N	Y	Y	N	N	?	Y	N	Y	Y	Y	Y
2 Jefferson	Y	?	N	N	N	Y	?	N	Y	N	N	Y	N
3 *Tauzin*	Y	N	Y	Y	Y	N	Y	Y	N	Y	Y	Y	Y
4 *McCrery*	Y	P	Y	Y	Y	N	Y	Y	N	Y	Y	Y	Y
5 *Cooksey*	Y	N	Y	Y	N	N	Y	Y	N	Y	Y	Y	Y
6 *Baker*	Y	N	Y	Y	N	N	Y	Y	N	Y	Y	Y	Y
7 John	Y	N	N	Y	N	?	?	?	N	Y	Y	Y	N
MAINE													
1 Allen	Y	N	N	N	N	Y	N	N	Y	Y	Y	Y	N
2 Baldacci	Y	N	N	N	N	Y	N	N	Y	Y	Y	Y	N
MARYLAND													
1 *Gilchrest*	Y	N	Y	N	Y	Y	Y	Y	Y	Y	Y	Y	Y

	Democrats	*Republicans*	**Independent**	
Y	Voted for "yea"		–	Announced against
N	Voted against "nay"		P	Voted "present"
+	Announced for		C	Voted "present" to avoid possible conflict of interest
#	Paired for		?	Did not vote or otherwise make a position known
X	Paired against			

House Key Votes	1	2	3	4	5	6	7	8	9	10	11	12	13
2 Ehrlich	Y	Y	Y	Y	Y	Y	Y	N	Y	Y	Y	Y	
3 Cardin	Y	N	N	N	N	Y	N	N	Y	Y	Y	N	
4 Wynn	?	N	N	N	N	N	N	N	Y	Y	N	Y	N
5 Hoyer	Y	N	N	N	N	Y	N	N	Y	Y	Y	Y	N
6 Bartlett	Y	N	Y	Y	Y	N	Y	Y	N	Y	Y	N	Y
7 Cummings	Y	N	N	N	N	Y	N	N	Y	N	N	Y	N
8 Morella	Y	Y	N	Y	N	Y	Y	N	Y	Y	Y	Y	N
MASSACHUSETTS													
1 Olver	Y	N	N	N	N	Y	N	N	Y	Y	N	Y	N
2 Neal	Y	N	N	Y	N	Y	N	N	Y	N	Y	Y	N
3 McGovern	Y	N	N	Y	N	Y	N	N	Y	Y	Y	Y	N
4 Frank	N	N	N	N	N	Y	N	N	Y	Y	N	Y	N
5 Meehan	N	N	N	N	N	Y	N	N	Y	N	Y	?	N
6 Tierney	Y	N	N	N	N	Y	N	N	Y	Y	Y	Y	N
7 Markey	N	N	N	Y	N	Y	N	?	Y	N	Y	Y	N
8 Kennedy	Y	N	N	N	N	Y	N	N	Y	N	Y	Y	N
9 Moakley	Y	N	N	N	N	Y	?	N	Y	Y	N	Y	N
10 Delahunt	Y	N	N	Y	N	Y	N	N	Y	N	Y	Y	N
MICHIGAN													
1 Stupak	N	N	N	Y	N	N	N	N	N	Y	N	N	N
2 Hoekstra	Y	Y	Y	Y	Y	N	Y	Y	N	Y	Y	N	Y
3 Ehlers	Y	N	N	Y	N	N	N	Y	N	Y	N	Y	Y
4 Camp	Y	N	Y	N	N	N	Y	Y	N	Y	Y	Y	Y
5 Barcia	Y	N	N	Y	N	N	N	N	Y	?	N	Y	Y
6 Upton	N	N	N	Y	N	Y	Y	Y	Y	Y	Y	N	Y
7 Smith	N	Y	N	Y	N	N	Y	Y	Y	Y	N	N	Y
8 Stabenow	Y	N	N	Y	N	Y	N	N	Y	Y	Y	Y	N
9 Kildee	Y	N	N	N	N	N	N	N	Y	Y	N	Y	N
10 Bonior	Y	N	N	N	N	Y	N	N	Y	Y	N	Y	N
11 Knollenberg	Y	N	Y	Y	Y	N	Y	Y	N	Y	Y	Y	Y
12 Levin	Y	N	N	Y	N	Y	N	N	Y	Y	Y	Y	N
13 Rivers	N	N	N	N	N	Y	N	N	Y	Y	N	N	N
14 Conyers	N	N	N	N	?	Y	N	N	Y	N	N	Y	N
15 Kilpatrick	Y	N	N	N	N	Y	N	N	Y	N	N	Y	N
16 Dingell	Y	N	N	Y	N	Y	N	N	Y	Y	N	Y	N
MINNESOTA													
1 Gutknecht	Y	Y	Y	N	N	N	Y	Y	N	Y	Y	Y	Y
2 Minge	N	Y	N	N	N	Y	N	N	Y	Y	Y	N	N
3 Ramstad	N	N	Y	N	N	Y	Y	Y	Y	Y	Y	Y	Y
4 Vento	N	N	N	N	N	Y	N	N	Y	Y	Y	Y	N
5 Sabo	Y	N	N	N	N	Y	N	N	Y	N	Y	Y	N
6 Luther	N	N	N	N	N	Y	Y	N	Y	Y	Y	N	N
7 Peterson	Y	N	N	N	N	N	N	N	N	Y	N	Y	N
8 Oberstar	Y	N	N	N	N	Y	N	N	Y	Y	N	Y	N
MISSISSIPPI													
1 Wicker	Y	N	Y	N	?	N	Y	Y	N	Y	Y	Y	Y
2 Thompson	Y	N	N	N	N	Y	N	N	Y	N	N	Y	N
3 Pickering	Y	N	Y	N	Y	N	Y	Y	N	Y	Y	Y	Y
4 Parker	Y	Y	Y	Y	?	?	?	Y	Y	Y	Y	Y	Y
5 Taylor	Y	N	Y	N	N	N	Y	N	Y	Y	N	N	Y
MISSOURI													
1 Clay	Y	N	N	N	N	Y	N	N	Y	N	N	Y	N
2 Talent	Y	N	Y	Y	N	N	Y	Y	N	Y	Y	Y	Y
3 Gephardt	Y	N	N	N	N	Y	N	N	Y	Y	Y	Y	N
4 Skelton	Y	N	N	N	N	N	Y	N	Y	Y	?	Y	N
5 McCarthy	N	N	N	N	N	Y	N	N	Y	Y	Y	Y	N
6 Danner	Y	N	N	N	N	Y	Y	Y	Y	N	Y	Y	N
7 Blunt	Y	N	Y	N	N	Y	Y	Y	N	Y	N	Y	Y
8 Emerson	Y	N	Y	Y	Y	N	Y	Y	N	Y	N	Y	Y
9 Hulshof	Y	N	Y	N	N	Y	Y	Y	Y	Y	Y	Y	Y
MONTANA													
AL Hill	Y	Y	Y	Y	N	?	?	Y	Y	Y	Y	Y	Y
NEBRASKA													
1 Bereuter	Y	N	Y	N	N	N	Y	Y	N	Y	Y	Y	Y
2 Christensen	Y	Y	?	N	N	N	Y	Y	N	Y	Y	N	Y
3 Barrett	Y	Y	N	N	N	N	Y	Y	Y	Y	Y	Y	Y
NEVADA													
1 Ensign	N	N	N	Y	Y	Y	Y	Y	N	Y	Y	N	Y
2 Gibbons	Y	N	N	Y	Y	Y	Y	Y	N	Y	Y	Y	Y

House Key Votes	1	2	3	4	5	6	7	8	9	10	11	12	13
NEW HAMPSHIRE													
1 Sununu	Y	N	Y	Y	Y	N	Y	Y	N	Y	Y	Y	Y
2 *Bass*	Y	N	Y	Y	Y	Y	Y	Y	Y	Y	Y	Y	Y
NEW JERSEY													
1 Andrews	N	N	N	Y	N	Y	N	N	Y	Y	N	Y	N
2 *LoBiondo*	Y	N	Y	Y	N	N	Y	Y	Y	Y	N	Y	Y
3 *Saxton*	Y	N	N	Y	Y	N	Y	Y	Y	Y	Y	Y	Y
4 *Smith*	Y	N	Y	Y	N	N	Y	Y	N	Y	N	N	Y
5 *Roukema*	Y	N	Y	Y	Y	Y	Y	N	Y	Y	Y	N	Y
6 Pallone	Y	N	N	Y	N	Y	N	N	Y	Y	N	Y	N
7 *Franks*	N	N	Y	Y	N	Y	Y	Y	Y	Y	N	Y	Y
8 Pascrell	Y	N	N	Y	N	Y	N	N	Y	Y	N	Y	N
9 Rothman	N	N	N	N	N	Y	N	N	Y	Y	N	Y	N
10 Payne	N	?	N	N	N	Y	N	N	Y	N	N	Y	N
11 *Frelinghuysen*	Y	Y	Y	Y	Y	Y	Y	Y	Y	Y	Y	N	Y
12 *Pappas*	Y	Y	Y	Y	Y	N	Y	Y	N	Y	N	N	Y
13 Menendez	Y	N	N	Y	N	Y	N	N	Y	Y	Y	Y	N
NEW MEXICO													
1 *Wilson* [5]						Y	Y	Y	N	Y	Y	Y	Y
2 *Skeen*	Y	N	N	N	N	N	Y	Y	N	Y	Y	Y	Y
3 *Redmond*	Y	N	N	N	N	N	Y	Y	N	Y	Y	Y	Y
NEW YORK													
1 *Forbes*	Y	N	N	Y	N	N	Y	N	Y	Y	Y	Y	Y
2 *Lazio*	Y	N	N	Y	N	Y	Y	Y	Y	Y	Y	Y	Y
3 *King*	Y	N	N	Y	?	N	Y	Y	N	Y	Y	N	N
4 McCarthy	Y	N	N	Y	N	Y	N	N	Y	Y	Y	Y	N
5 Ackerman	N	N	N	Y	N	Y	N	N	Y	N	N	Y	N
6 Meeks [6]		N	N	Y	?	Y	N	N	Y	N	N	Y	N
7 Manton	Y	N	N	Y	N	Y	N	N	Y	Y	?	Y	N
8 Nadler	Y	N	N	Y	N	Y	N	N	Y	Y	N	Y	N
9 Schumer	Y	N	N	Y	N	Y	N	N	Y	Y	Y	Y	N
10 Towns	N	N	N	Y	?	Y	N	N	Y	N	N	Y	N
11 Owens	N	N	N	N	N	Y	N	N	Y	N	N	Y	N
12 Velázquez	Y	N	N	N	N	Y	N	N	Y	N	N	Y	N
13 *Fossella*	Y	N	N	Y	N	N	Y	Y	N	Y	Y	Y	Y
14 Maloney	Y	N	N	Y	N	Y	N	N	Y	Y	Y	Y	N
15 Rangel	N	?	N	Y	N	Y	N	N	Y	Y	N	Y	N
16 Serrano	Y	N	N	N	N	Y	N	N	Y	N	N	Y	N
17 Engel	N	N	N	Y	N	Y	N	N	Y	N	N	Y	N
18 Lowey	Y	N	N	Y	N	Y	N	N	Y	Y	Y	Y	N
19 *Kelly*	Y	N	N	Y	N	Y	Y	Y	Y	Y	Y	Y	Y
20 *Gilman*	Y	N	N	Y	N	Y	Y	Y	Y	Y	Y	Y	Y
21 McNulty	Y	N	?	Y	N	?	?	N	Y	Y	N	Y	N
22 *Solomon*	Y	N	Y	N	Y	N	Y	Y	N	Y	Y	Y	Y
23 *Boehlert*	Y	N	N	Y	N	Y	Y	Y	Y	Y	Y	Y	Y
24 *McHugh*	Y	N	Y	N	N	N	N	Y	Y	Y	Y	Y	Y
25 *Walsh*	Y	N	N	N	N	N	Y	Y	Y	Y	Y	Y	Y
26 Hinchey	Y	N	N	N	N	Y	N	N	Y	N	N	Y	N
27 *Paxon*	Y	N	Y	Y	Y	Y	Y	N	Y	Y	Y	Y	Y
28 Slaughter	Y	N	N	N	N	Y	N	N	Y	Y	Y	Y	N
29 LaFalce	Y	N	N	N	N	N	N	N	Y	Y	Y	Y	N
30 *Quinn*	Y	N	N	Y	–	N	Y	Y	Y	Y	Y	Y	Y
31 *Houghton*	Y	N	N	Y	Y	Y	Y	Y	Y	Y	Y	Y	N
NORTH CAROLINA													
1 Clayton	Y	N	N	N	N	?	N	N	Y	N	Y	Y	N
2 Etheridge	Y	N	N	N	N	Y	N	N	Y	Y	Y	Y	N
3 *Jones*	Y	Y	Y	N	Y	N	Y	Y	N	Y	N	Y	Y
4 Price	Y	N	N	N	Y	Y	N	N	Y	Y	Y	Y	N
5 *Burr*	Y	Y	N	Y	Y	N	Y	Y	N	Y	Y	N	Y
6 *Coble*	Y	N	Y	Y	Y	N	Y	Y	N	Y	Y	N	Y
7 McIntyre	Y	N	N	N	N	Y	Y	N	Y	Y	Y	Y	N
8 Hefner	Y	N	N	N	N	Y	N	N	N	Y	N	Y	N
9 *Myrick*	Y	Y	N	Y	Y	N	Y	Y	N	Y	Y	Y	N
10 *Ballenger*	Y	Y	Y	Y	Y	N	Y	Y	N	Y	Y	N	Y

	Democrats	*Republicans*	**Independent**	
Y	Voted for "yea"		–	Announced against
N	Voted against "nay"		P	Voted "present"
+	Announced for		C	Voted "present" to avoid possible conflict of interest
#	Paired for			
X	Paired against		?	Did not vote or otherwise make a position known

House Key Votes	1	2	3	4	5	6	7	8	9	10	11	12	13
11 Taylor	Y	Y	Y	Y	?	N	Y	Y	N	Y	Y	Y	Y
12 Watt	Y	N	N	N	N	Y	N	N	Y	N	Y	Y	N
NORTH DAKOTA													
AL Pomeroy	Y	Y	N	Y	N	Y	N	N	Y	Y	Y	Y	N
OHIO													
1 Chabot	N	Y	Y	Y	Y	N	Y	Y	N	Y	Y	N	Y
2 Portman	Y	N	Y	Y	Y	N	Y	Y	N	Y	N	Y	Y
3 Hall	+	N	N	Y	N	N	N	N	Y	Y	Y	Y	N
4 Oxley	Y	N	Y	Y	N	Y	Y	Y	N	Y	Y	Y	Y
5 Gillmor	Y	N	Y	Y	N	N	Y	Y	Y	Y	Y	Y	Y
6 Strickland	N	N	N	N	N	Y	N	Y	N	Y	N	Y	N
7 Hobson	Y	Y	N	Y	Y	Y	Y	Y	N	Y	Y	Y	Y
8 Boehner	Y	Y	Y	Y	Y	N	Y	Y	N	Y	Y	Y	Y
9 Kaptur	Y	N	N	N	N	Y	N	N	Y	Y	N	N	N
10 Kucinich	Y	N	N	N	N	N	N	N	Y	Y	N	Y	N
11 Stokes	Y	N	N	N	N	Y	N	N	Y	N	N	Y	N
12 Kasich	Y	Y	Y	Y	N	N	Y	Y	N	Y	Y	Y	Y
13 Brown	N	N	N	Y	N	Y	N	N	Y	Y	N	Y	N
14 Sawyer	Y	N	N	Y	N	Y	N	N	Y	Y	Y	Y	N
15 Pryce	Y	N	N	Y	N	Y	Y	Y	N	+	+	+	Y
16 Regula	Y	N	N	Y	N	N	Y	Y	Y	Y	Y	Y	Y
17 Traficant	Y	N	N	N	Y	Y	N	Y	N	Y	N	Y	N
18 Ney	Y	N	N	Y	N	N	Y	Y	N	Y	N	Y	Y
19 LaTourette	Y	N	N	Y	N	Y	Y	Y	Y	Y	Y	Y	Y
OKLAHOMA													
1 Largent	Y	Y	N	N	Y	N	Y	Y	N	Y	Y	N	Y
2 Coburn	Y	Y	Y	N	Y	N	Y	Y	N	Y	Y	N	Y
3 Watkins	Y	N	N	N	N	Y	Y	Y	N	Y	Y	Y	Y
4 Watts	Y	N	N	N	N	N	Y	Y	N	Y	N	Y	Y
5 Istook	Y	Y	Y	N	Y	N	Y	Y	N	Y	Y	N	Y
6 Lucas	Y	N	Y	N	N	N	Y	Y	N	Y	Y	Y	Y
OREGON													
1 Furse	?	N	N	N	?	Y	N	N	Y	?	Y	Y	N
2 Smith	Y	N	Y	N	P	N	Y	Y	N	Y	Y	Y	Y
3 Blumenauer	Y	N	N	N	N	Y	N	N	Y	Y	Y	N	N
4 DeFazio	N	N	N	N	?	Y	N	N	Y	Y	N	N	N
5 Hooley	Y	N	N	N	N	Y	N	N	Y	Y	Y	Y	N
PENNSYLVANIA													
1 Brady[7]					N	Y	N	N	Y	N	N	Y	N
2 Fattah	Y	N	N	N	N	Y	N	N	Y	N	N	Y	N
3 Borski	Y	N	N	N	N	Y	Y	N	Y	Y	N	Y	N
4 Klink	?	N	N	N	N	N	Y	N	Y	Y	N	N	N
5 Peterson	Y	N	Y	N	N	N	Y	Y	N	Y	Y	Y	Y
6 Holden	Y	N	N	N	N	N	N	N	Y	Y	N	N	N
7 Weldon	Y	N	N	Y	N	N	Y	Y	Y	Y	N	Y	Y
8 Greenwood	N	N	Y	Y	Y	Y	Y	Y	Y	Y	Y	Y	Y
9 Shuster	Y	N	?	N	Y	N	Y	Y	N	Y	Y	Y	Y
10 McDade	Y	N	N	Y	N	N	Y	Y	Y	Y	Y	Y	Y
11 Kanjorski	N	N	N	N	N	Y	N	N	Y	Y	N	N	N
12 Murtha	Y	N	N	Y	N	Y	N	N	N	Y	?	Y	N
13 Fox	Y	N	N	Y	N	Y	Y	Y	Y	Y	Y	Y	Y
14 Coyne	Y	N	N	N	N	Y	N	N	Y	Y	N	Y	N
15 McHale	Y	N	N	N	N	Y	N	N	Y	Y	Y	Y	Y
16 Pitts	Y	N	Y	N	Y	N	Y	N	N	Y	Y	Y	Y
17 Gekas	Y	N	Y	Y	N	N	Y	Y	N	Y	Y	Y	Y
18 Doyle	Y	N	?	Y	N	N	N	N	Y	Y	N	Y	N
19 Goodling	Y	N	Y	Y	Y	N	Y	Y	N	Y	Y	Y	Y
20 Mascara	Y	N	N	N	N	N	N	N	Y	Y	N	Y	N
21 English	Y	N	N	Y	N	Y	N	Y	N	Y	Y	Y	
RHODE ISLAND													
1 Kennedy	Y	N	N	N	N	Y	N	N	Y	N	Y	Y	N
2 Weygand	Y	N	N	N	N	Y	N	N	Y	Y	Y	Y	N
SOUTH CAROLINA													
1 Sanford	N	Y	N	Y	Y	N	Y	N	Y	Y	Y	N	Y
2 Spence	Y	N	Y	Y	Y	N	Y	Y	N	Y	N	Y	Y
3 Graham	Y	Y	Y	N	Y	N	Y	Y	Y	Y	Y	N	Y
4 Inglis	Y	Y	Y	Y	Y	N	Y	?	Y	Y	N	Y	
5 Spratt	Y	N	N	Y	N	Y	N	N	Y	Y	Y	Y	N
6 Clyburn	Y	N	N	N	N	Y	N	N	Y	N	N	Y	N

House Key Votes	1	2	3	4	5	6	7	8	9	10	11	12	13
SOUTH DAKOTA													
AL *Thune*	Y	N	Y	N	N	N	Y	Y	Y	Y	Y	Y	Y
TENNESSEE													
1 *Jenkins*	Y	N	Y	N	Y	N	Y	Y	N	+	Y	Y	Y
2 *Duncan*	N	N	Y	N	Y	N	Y	Y	Y	Y	N	N	Y
3 *Wamp*	Y	Y	Y	Y	Y	N	Y	Y	Y	Y	N	N	Y
4 *Hilleary*	Y	Y	Y	N	Y	N	Y	Y	N	Y	N	Y	Y
5 Clement	Y	N	N	N	N	Y	N	N	Y	Y	Y	Y	N
6 Gordon	Y	N	N	Y	N	Y	N	N	Y	Y	Y	Y	N
7 *Bryant*	Y	N	Y	Y	N	N	Y	Y	N	Y	Y	Y	Y
8 Tanner	Y	N	N	Y	N	Y	?	N	Y	Y	Y	Y	N
9 Ford	Y	N	N	Y	N	+	–	–	Y	N	Y	Y	N
TEXAS													
1 Sandlin	Y	N	N	N	N	Y	N	N	Y	Y	N	Y	N
2 Turner	Y	N	N	N	N	Y	N	N	Y	Y	N	Y	N
3 *Johnson, Sam*	Y	Y	Y	N	?	N	Y	Y	N	Y	Y	N	Y
4 Hall	Y	Y	Y	N	N	N	Y	N	N	Y	Y	Y	Y
5 *Sessions*	Y	Y	Y	N	Y	N	Y	Y	N	Y	Y	Y	Y
6 *Barton*	Y	Y	Y	N	Y	N	?	Y	N	Y	Y	N	Y
7 *Archer*	Y	Y	Y	Y	Y	N	Y	Y	N	Y	Y	Y	Y
8 *Brady*	Y	N	Y	N	Y	N	Y	N	N	Y	+	N	Y
9 Lampson	Y	N	N	N	N	Y	N	N	Y	Y	N	Y	N
10 Doggett	N	N	N	N	N	Y	N	N	Y	Y	N	Y	N
11 Edwards	Y	Y	N	N	N	Y	N	N	Y	Y	Y	Y	N
12 *Granger*	Y	N	Y	N	N	N	Y	Y	N	Y	Y	Y	Y
13 *Thornberry*	Y	Y	Y	N	Y	N	Y	Y	N	Y	Y	Y	Y
14 *Paul*	Y	N	Y	N	Y	N	N	N	N	Y	Y	N	Y
15 Hinojosa	Y	N	N	N	N	Y	N	N	Y	Y	Y	Y	N
16 Reyes	Y	N	N	N	?	Y	N	N	Y	Y	Y	Y	N
17 Stenholm	Y	Y	N	N	N	N	Y	N	Y	Y	Y	Y	Y
18 Jackson-Lee	Y	N	N	N	N	Y	N	N	Y	N	Y	Y	N
19 *Combest*	Y	N	Y	N	N	N	Y	Y	N	Y	N	Y	Y
20 Gonzalez	?	?	?	?	?	?	?	?	?	?	N	Y	N
21 *Smith*	Y	N	Y	N	Y	N	Y	Y	N	Y	Y	Y	Y
22 *DeLay*	Y	N	Y	Y	Y	N	Y	Y	N	Y	Y	Y	Y
23 *Bonilla*	Y	Y	N	N	N	N	Y	Y	N	Y	Y	Y	Y
24 Frost	Y	N	N	Y	N	Y	N	N	Y	Y	Y	Y	N
25 Bentsen	Y	N	N	N	N	Y	N	N	Y	Y	Y	Y	N
26 *Armey*	?	N	Y	Y	Y	N	Y	Y	N	Y	Y	Y	Y
27 Ortiz	Y	N	N	N	N	X	–	N	Y	Y	Y	Y	N
28 Rodriguez	Y	N	N	N	N	Y	N	?	Y	Y	N	Y	N
29 Green	Y	N	N	N	?	Y	N	N	Y	Y	N	Y	N
30 Johnson, E.B.	Y	N	N	Y	N	Y	N	N	Y	–	Y	Y	N
UTAH													
1 *Hansen*	Y	N	Y	Y	N	N	Y	Y	N	Y	Y	?	Y
2 *Cook*	Y	Y	Y	Y	N	Y	Y	Y	Y	Y	Y	Y	Y
3 *Cannon*	Y	?	Y	N	Y	N	Y	Y	N	Y	Y	Y	Y
VERMONT													
AL **Sanders**	Y	N	N	N	N	Y	N	N	Y	N	Y	Y	N
VIRGINIA													
1 Bateman	Y	N	+	+	–	N	Y	Y	N	Y	Y	Y	Y
2 Pickett	Y	N	N	N	N	Y	N	N	Y	Y	Y	Y	N
3 Scott	Y	N	N	N	N	Y	N	N	Y	N	Y	Y	N
4 Sisisky	Y	N	N	N	N	Y	N	N	Y	Y	Y	Y	N
5 Goode	Y	N	N	N	Y	N	Y	Y	N	Y	N	N	Y
6 *Goodlatte*	Y	N	Y	Y	Y	N	Y	Y	N	Y	Y	Y	Y
7 *Bliley*	Y	N	Y	Y	Y	N	Y	Y	N	Y	Y	Y	Y
8 Moran	Y	N	N	Y	N	Y	N	N	Y	N	Y	Y	N
9 Boucher	Y	N	N	N	N	Y	N	N	Y	Y	N	Y	N
10 *Wolf*	Y	Y	N	Y	N	N	Y	N	Y	Y	Y	N	Y
11 *Davis*	Y	N	N	N	N	Y	N	N	Y	Y	Y	Y	Y
WASHINGTON													
1 *White*	Y	Y	N	Y	N	N	Y	Y	Y	Y	Y	N	Y

	Democrats	*Republicans*	**Independent**	
Y	Voted for "yea"		–	Announced against
N	Voted against "nay"		P	Voted "present"
+	Announced for		C	Voted "present" to avoid possible conflict of interest
#	Paired for		?	Did not vote or otherwise make a position known
X	Paired against			

House Key Votes	1	2	3	4	5	6	7	8	9	10	11	12	13
2 Metcalf	Y	N	Y	Y	Y	N	Y	Y	Y	Y	N	Y	Y
3 *Smith, Linda*	Y	N	Y	Y	N	N	Y	Y	Y	Y	Y	N	Y
4 Hastings	Y	N	Y	Y	Y	N	Y	Y	N	Y	Y	Y	Y
5 Nethercutt	Y	Y	Y	Y	N	Y	N	Y	N	Y	Y	Y	Y
6 Dicks	Y	N	N	Y	N	Y	N	N	Y	Y	Y	Y	N
7 McDermott	N	N	N	N	N	Y	N	N	Y	N	N	N	N
8 *Dunn*	Y	N	Y	Y	Y	Y	?	Y	N	Y	Y	Y	Y
9 Smith, Adam	Y	N	N	Y	N	Y	N	N	Y	Y	Y	N	N
WEST VIRGINIA													
1 Mollohan	Y	N	N	Y	N	N	N	N	N	N	N	?	N
2 Wise	Y	N	N	Y	N	Y	N	N	Y	Y	N	Y	N
3 Rahall	Y	N	N	Y	N	N	N	N	N	Y	N	Y	N
WISCONSIN													
1 *Neumann*	N	Y	?	Y	Y	N	Y	Y	N	Y	Y	N	Y
2 *Klug*	N	?	N	Y	Y	Y	Y	?	Y	Y	Y	N	Y
3 Kind	N	Y	N	N	N	Y	N	N	Y	Y	Y	N	N
4 Kleczka	Y	N	N	N	N	Y	N	N	Y	Y	N	N	N
5 Barrett	N	Y	N	N	N	Y	N	N	Y	Y	N	N	N
6 *Petri*	N	N	Y	N	Y	N	Y	Y	Y	Y	Y	N	Y
7 Obey	Y	N	N	N	N	Y	N	N	Y	N	N	Y	N
8 Johnson	N	N	N	N	N	Y	N	N	Y	Y	N	N	N
9 *Sensenbrenner*	N	Y	Y	Y	Y	N	Y	Y	N	Y	Y	N	Y
WYOMING													
AL Cubin	Y	Y	Y	Y	Y	N	Y	Y	N	Y	Y	Y	Y

[1] Barbara Lee, D-Calif., was sworn in April 21, replacing Ronald V. Dellums, D-Calif., who resigned Feb. 6.

[2] Lois Capps, D-Calif., was sworn in March 17, replacing Walter Capps, D-Calif., who died Oct. 28, 1997.

[3] Mary Bono, R-Calif., was sworn in April 21, replacing Sonny Bono, R-Calif., who died Jan. 5.

[4] Newt Gingrich, R-Ga., as Speaker of the House, voted at his discretion.

[5] Heather Wilson, R-N.M., was sworn in June 25, replacing Stephen H. Schiff, R-N.M., who died March 25.

[6] Gregory W. Meeks, D-N.Y., was sworn in Feb. 5, replacing Floyd H. Flake, D-N.Y., who resigned Nov. 15, 1997.

[7] Robert A. Brady, D-Pa., was sworn in May 21, replacing Thomas M. Foglietta, D-Pa., who resigned Nov. 11, 1997.

Senate Terms of Office

Term Expires 2000

Abraham, Spencer, R-Mich.
Akaka, Daniel K., D-Hawaii
Ashcroft, John, R-Mo.
Bingaman, Jeff, D-N.M.
Bryan, Richard H., D-Nev.
Burns, Conrad, R-Mont.
Byrd, Robert C., D-W.Va.
Chafee, John H., R-R.I.
Conrad, Kent, D-N.D.
DeWine, Mike, R-Ohio
Feinstein, Dianne, D-Calif.
Frist, Bill, R-Tenn.
Gorton, Slade, R-Wash.
Grams, Rod, R-Minn.
Hatch, Orrin G., R-Utah
Hutchison, Kay Bailey, R-Texas
Jeffords, James M., R-Vt.
Kennedy, Edward M., D-Mass.
Kerrey, Bob, D-Neb.
Kohl, Herb, D-Wis.
Kyl, Jon, R-Ariz.
Lautenberg, Frank R., D-N.J.
Lieberman, Joseph I., D-Conn.
Lott, Trent, R-Miss.
Lugar, Richard G., R-Ind.
Mack, Connie, R-Fla.
Moynihan, Daniel Patrick, D-N.Y.
Robb, Charles S., D-Va.
Roth, William V. Jr., R-Del.
Santorum, Rick, R-Pa.
Sarbanes, Paul S., D-Md.
Snowe, Olympia J., R-Maine
Thomas, Craig, R-Wyo.

Term Expires 2002

Allard, Wayne, R-Colo.
Baucus, Max, D-Mont.
Biden, Joseph R. Jr., D-Del.
Cleland, Max, D-Ga.
Cochran, Thad, R-Miss.
Collins, Susan, R-Maine
Craig, Larry E., R-Idaho
Domenici, Pete V., R-N.M.
Durbin, Richard J., D-Ill.
Enzi, Michael B., R-Wyo.
Gramm, Phil, R-Texas
Hagel, Chuck, R-Neb.
Harkin, Tom, D-Iowa
Helms, Jesse, R-N.C.
Hutchinson, Tim, R-Ark.
Inhofe, James M., R-Okla.
Johnson, Tim, D-S.D.
Kerry, John, D-Mass.
Landrieu, Mary L., D-La.
Levin, Carl, D-Mich.
McConnell, Mitch, R-Ky.
Reed, Jack, D-R.I.
Roberts, Pat, R-Kan.
Rockefeller, John D. IV, D-W.Va.
Sessions, Jeff, R-Ala.
Smith, Robert C., R-N.H.
Smith, Gordon H., R-Ore.
Stevens, Ted, R-Alaska
Thompson, Fred, R-Tenn.
Thurmond, Strom, R-S.C.
Torricelli, Robert G., D-N.J.
Warner, John W., R-Va.
Wellstone, Paul, D-Minn.

Term Expires 2004

Bayh, Evan, D-Ind.
Bennett, Robert F., R-Utah
Bond, Christopher S., R-Mo.
Boxer, Barbara, D-Calif.
Breaux, John B., D-La.
Brownback, Sam, R-Kan.
Bunning, Jim, R-Ky.
Campbell, Ben Nighthorse, R-Colo.
Coverdell, Paul, R-Ga.
Crapo, Mike, R-Idaho
Daschle, Tom, D-S.D.
Dodd, Christopher J., D-Conn.
Dorgan, Byron L., D-N.D.
Edwards, John, D-N.C.
Feingold, Russell D., D-Wis.
Fitzgerald, Peter G., R-Ill.
Graham, Bob, D-Fla.
Grassley, Charles E., R-Iowa
Gregg, Judd, R-N.H.
Hollings, Ernest F., D-S.C.
Inouye, Daniel K., D-Hawaii
Leahy, Patrick J., D-Vt.
Lincoln, Blanche, D-Ark.
McCain, John, R-Ariz.
Mikulski, Barbara A., D-Md.
Murkowski, Frank H., R-Alaska
Murray, Patty, D-Wash.
Nickles, Don, R-Okla.
Reid, Harry, D-Nev.
Schumer, Charles E., D-N.Y.
Shelby, Richard C., R-Ala.
Specter, Arlen, R-Pa.
Voinovich, George V., R-Ohio
Wyden, Ron, D-Ore.

TV Guide to Senate Floor Action

Cable television viewers accustomed to watching the normally fastpaced, well orchestrated action of the House of Representatives have found that the Senate operates quite differently.

In contrast to the 435-member House, where the leadership sets the agenda for the week and usually makes it stick, the Senate often operates at the mercy of its 100 members.

Many of the Senate rules are designed to assure that members who hold minority views have a chance to make their point.

One determined senator can take advantage of the rules to delay action for days or weeks on legislation he or she opposes.

The Senate often meanders through hours of cursory debate and quorum calls, during which a clerk slowly calls the roll. No one answers, not even members who are present.

Proceedings are broadcast by the Cable Satellite Public Affairs Network (C-SPAN).

Typical Day

A typical day in the Senate might go like this:

- The Senate is **called to order** by the presiding officer. The constitutional presiding officer, the vice president, seldom is in attendance. Usually the president pro tempore presides over the opening minutes of the Senate session.

During the course of the day, other members of the majority party take turns presiding over the Senate for an hour at a time. Whoever is in the chair is addressed as Mr. (or Madame) President.

- The Senate chaplain delivers the **opening prayer.**
- The majority leader and the minority leader are recognized for opening remarks. The majority leader usually announces his plan for the day's business, which is developed in consultation with the minority leadership.
- Several senators, usually fewer than half a dozen, who have requested time in advance are recognized for **special orders,** during which they may speak about any topic for five minutes. (Before TV came to the Senate, special orders were fifteen minutes.) Some senators ask for special order time every day.
- After special orders, the Senate usually conducts **morning business.** During morning business — which need not be in the morning — members conduct routine administrative chores. They introduce bills and receive reports from committees and messages from the president.
- After morning business, the Senate begins work on **legislative** or **executive** matters. If the majority leader wants the Senate to begin work on a piece of legislation, he normally asks for unanimous consent to call up the measure.

If any member objects, the leader may make a debatable **motion** that the Senate begin work on the bill.

The debatable motion gives opponents the opportunity to launch a **filibuster,** or extended debate, even before the Senate officially begins work on the bill.

Sponsors of the bill may file a **cloture petition** seeking to shut off debate.

Under normal circumstances, the Senate votes on the petition two days after it is filed. To terminate debate, sixty votes are needed, regardless of how many members are voting.

Even after cloture is invoked, debate on the motion can continue for thirty hours. In addition, opponents can keep a filibuster going by demanding votes on all amendments filed before cloture.

A few measures, such as the budget resolution and conference reports, are privileged and a motion to consider them is not debatable.

After the Senate begins work on a bill, floor debate is generally handled by **managers,** usually the chairman and the ranking minority member of the committee with jurisdiction over the measure.

Some measures are considered under a **time agreement** in which the Senate unanimously agrees to limit debate and to divide the time in some prearranged fashion. Usually, however, legislation is considered with no limit on debate.

In the absence of a time agreement, any senator may seek recognition from the chair, and once recognized, may speak for as long as he or she wishes.

Unless the Senate has unanimously agreed to limit **amendments,** senators may offer as many as they wish. Generally, amendments need not be **germane,** or directly related, to the bill.

Most bills are passed by a voice vote with only a handful of senators present.

Any member can request a **roll call,** or recorded vote, on an amendment or on final passage of a measure. Although Senate rules require a **sufficient second** by at least eleven members, the presiding officer often orders a roll call vote when fewer members second the request.

The Senate leadership tries to schedule roll call votes at a time convenient to members; thus few votes are held on Mondays or Fridays, when members are often in their home states.

Senate roll calls are casual affairs. Few members answer the clerk as their names are called. Instead, senators stroll in from the cloakrooms or their offices and congregate in the well (the area between the front row of desks and the desk occupied by the presiding officer and the other officials of the Senate). When they are ready to vote, senators catch the eye of the clerk and vote, often by indicating thumbs-up or thumbs-down.

Roll call votes are supposed to last fifteen minutes, but some have lasted for more than an hour, as members waited for late-comers to arrive from other appointments.

- Often, near the end of the day, the majority leader and the minority leader quickly move through a **wrap-up** period, during which minor bills that previously had been cleared by all members are passed by unanimous consent.

It is not uncommon for the Senate to pass as many as a dozen bills on the Senate **calendar** in just a few minutes during the wrap-up.

- Just before the Senate finishes its work for the day, the majority leader will seek unanimous consent for his agenda for the next session — when the Senate will convene, which senators will be given special orders and, sometimes, specific time agreements for consideration of legislation.

TV Guide to House Floor Action

The House of Representatives has supplanted soap operas as preferred daytime viewing for millions of Americans.

Since the House opened its chambers to television in 1979, C-SPAN has brought the often rambunctious antics of the 435 members and the representatives of the District of Columbia, Puerto Rico, Guam, American Samoa, and the Virgin Islands to life with far more impact than history books.

Because its membership is so large, the House has developed rigid rules to expedite its business. As a result, the House is actually more manageable and efficient than the Senate, with just 100 members.

There is little "dead" air — no quorum calls or desultory speeches as in the Senate. Members, who usually have less than five minutes to make their points, must get right to the heart of the issue.

In just one or two days, the House can pass major legislation that would take weeks in the Senate.

Typical Day

A typical day in the House might go like this:
- The chaplain delivers the **opening prayer.**
- The Speaker approves the *Journal,* the record of the previous day's proceedings. Often a member will demand a roll call vote on the approval of the *Journal.* The vote gives party leaders an opportunity to find out which members are absent. On days when hotly contested legislation is to be considered, the absence of just a few members might alter the outcome of a vote.
- After some procedural activities — receiving messages from the Senate or the president, granting committees permission to file reports or to meet during the session, etc. — members are recognized for **one minute speeches.**

On a typical day, ten or twenty members come to the well to deliver their brief statements, which can be on any topic — current events, a bill due on the floor that day, a tribute to a prominent constituent, or a Democratic harangue against some action of the Republican leadership.
- The House then turns to its legislative business.

Virtually every major bill is considered under a **rule** that sets forth guidelines for floor action. The rule, which is a resolution reported by the Rules Committee, sets a time limit for general debate on the bill and specifies which, if any, amendments are permitted.

The rule is generally approved with little opposition. However, rules are occasionally defeated by members opposed to the bill, or by members who want a more favorable rule that will allow them to offer their amendments.

Sometimes members approve an **open rule,** which permits unlimited amendments, or a **closed rule,** which permits no amendments. However, most major bills are considered under a **modified open/closed rule,** which permits only specific amendments identified in the rule.

Privileged matters such as conference reports, the budget resolution, and appropriations bills can come to the floor without a rule.

After the rule is adopted, the House resolves into the Committee of the Whole House on the State of the Union (known simply as the **Committee of the Whole**) to consider the bill. The Speaker relinquishes the gavel to a chairman, who presides over the Committee.

The debate time is controlled by the **managers** of the bill, usually the chairman and ranking minority member of the standing committee with jurisdiction over the measure. After time for general debate has expired, amendments that are permitted under the rule can be offered.

Debate on the amendments is conducted under a **five-minute rule:** Supporters and opponents are limited to five minutes. However, members may obtain additional time for debate by offering pro-forma amendments to **strike out the last word.**

Voting is by voice (the usual procedure); division (members stand to be counted); teller (a seldom-used procedure in which members walk past designated tellers); or by electronic device. When members vote electronically, they insert a plastic card into one of the many voting stations on the House floor and press a button to record a "yea," a "nay," or a "present." Their vote is immediately recorded on a big screen on the wall above the Speaker's desk and tabulated, giving a running vote total.

Most electronic votes last fifteen minutes.

Votes cannot technically be taken without a **quorum** (although they often are because no one objects). A point of order that a quorum is not present mandates an electronic vote. A quorum in the Committee of the Whole is 100; a House quorum is 218.

After the amending process is complete, the Committee **rises,** and the chairman reports to the Speaker on the actions taken.

Acting once again as the House, the members vote on final passage of the bill, sometimes after voting on a motion to recommit the bill to its committee of origin.

- On many noncontroversial bills, the House leadership wants to speed up action, bypassing the Rules Committee and the Committee of the Whole.

It can do that by waiving, or **suspending** the rules. Bills under **suspension,** sometimes as many as a dozen at a time, are usually brought up early in the week.

Suspensions cannot be amended. Debate is limited to forty minutes. Then members are asked to vote on whether they want to suspend the rules and pass the bill. A single vote accomplishes both steps. A two-thirds vote is needed to suspend the House rules, making it a gamble sometimes to bring up legislation under suspension.

If a bill is defeated under the two-thirds requirement, it often is brought back to the floor later under regular procedures, where only a simple majority is sufficient.

To accommodate many members who have not returned from their districts on Mondays, recorded votes on suspensions are usually delayed until Tuesday. Roughly half the measures under suspension are passed by voice vote.

- Measures that are even less controversial are placed on the **consent calendar** or are passed by **unanimous consent.** These measures, such as resolutions expressing congratulations to a winning sports team or approving a minor transfer of government land, are cleared through the leadership of both parties. A single objection on the floor can block passage.

- After the House completes its legislative business, members are allowed to speak for up to sixty minutes under **special orders.** They must reserve the time in advance but can speak on any topic. The television cameras record the speeches, which often are made to an almost deserted chamber.

Congressional Bell System

On days Congress is in session, a system of electric lights and buzzers is used to inform members of proceedings on the floor. The clocks in the House and Senate office buildings light up with the respective number of buzzer rings, signaling members of impending votes or other legislative action. In the House, the signals include:

1 ring — teller vote (not a recorded vote).

1 long ring, pause, followed by 3 rings — the start or continuation of a notice quorum call.

1 long ring — termination of a notice quorum call.

2 rings — electronically recorded vote.

2 rings, pause, followed by 2 rings — a manual roll-call vote.

2 rings, pause, followed by 5 rings — first 15-minute vote in a series, where subsequent votes are to be five minutes in length.

3 rings — quorum call.

3 rings, pause, followed by 5 rings — quorum call in the Committee of the Whole, which may be immediately followed by a five-minute recorded vote.

4 rings — adjournment of the House.

5 rings — five-minute electronically recorded vote.

6 rings — recess of the House.

In the Senate, one long ring signifies that a session is convening; one red light on the right-hand side of the clock remains lighted at all times while the Senate is in actual session. In the Senate, the signals include:

1 ring — yeas and nays.

2 rings — quorum call.

3 rings — call of absentees.

4 rings — adjournment or recess.

5 rings — five minutes remaining on yea-and-nay vote.

6 rings — morning business concluded or temporary recess.

Glossary of Legislative Terms

Act. The term for legislation once it has passed both houses of Congress and has been signed by the president or passed over his veto, thus becoming law.

Amendment. A proposal to alter the language or provisions in a bill or in another amendment.

Amendment in the Nature of a Substitute. An amendment that seeks to replace the entire text of a bill or replaces a large portion of it.

Appropriations Bill. A bill that gives legal authority to spend or obligate money from the Treasury. An appropriations bill generally cannot provide more money than has been authorized for a particular program under separate legislation.

Authorization. Basic, substantive legislation that establishes or continues the legal operation of a federal program or agency, either indefinitely or for a specific period of time. An authorization normally is a prerequisite for an appropriation and sets a ceiling for it.

Bills. Most legislative proposals before Congress are in the form of bills and are designated by HR in the House of Representatives or S in the Senate, according to the house in which they originate, and by a number assigned in the order in which they are introduced during the two-year period of a Congress. "Public bills" deal with general questions and become public laws if approved by Congress and signed by the president. "Private bills" deal with such matters as an individual's claim against the government or special immigration request, and become private laws if approved and signed.

Bills Introduced. Any number of members may join in introducing a bill or resolution. The first member listed is the sponsor of the bill; the others are cosponsors.

Bills Referred. When introduced, a bill is referred to the committee or committees that have jurisdiction over the subject of the bill.

Budget. The document sent to Congress by the president early each year estimating government revenue and expenditures for the ensuing fiscal year.

Budget Resolution. A concurrent resolution passed by both houses of Congress, but not requiring the president's signature, setting forth or revising the congressional budget for the following three fiscal years.

By Request. A phrase used when a member introduces a bill at the request of an executive agency or private organization but does not necessarily endorse it.

Calendar. An agenda of business awaiting possible action by the chamber. The House uses five legislative calendars — the Consent, Discharge, House, Private, and Union calendars, according to the type of bill involved. The Senate uses only an executive calendar.

Clean Bill. Frequently after a committee has finished a major revision of a bill, one of the committee members will assemble the changes and what is left of the original bill into a new measure and introduce it as a "clean bill." The revised measure, which is given a new number, then is referred back to the committee, which reports it to the floor for consideration.

Clerk of the House. Chief administrative officer of the House of Representatives.

Cloture. The process in the Senate for ending a filibuster other than by unanimous consent. A petition to limit debate must be signed by sixteen senators, and the motion to invoke cloture then must be agreed to by three-fifths of the Senate's membership.

Committee. A division of the House or Senate that prepares legislation for action by the parent chamber or makes investigations as directed by the parent chamber. Most committees are divided into subcommittees, which study legislation, hold hearings, and report bills to the full committee.

Committee of the Whole. The working title of what is formally "The Committee of the Whole House on the State of the Union." To expedite business, the House resolves itself into the Committee of the Whole to consider amendments to most major bills. The Speaker is supplanted with a "chairman" who presides over debate and voting on amendments. When work on a measure is complete, the Committee "rises," the Speaker returns to the chair, and the full House then votes on passage of the legislation.

Concurrent Resolution. A statement expressing the sense of Congress on some issue. Designated H Con Res or S Con Res, depending on the chamber of origin, it must be adopted by both houses, but it does not go to the president or have the force of law.

Glossary of Legislative Terms 341

Conference. A meeting between selected members of the House and Senate to reconcile differences between the two chambers' versions of the same legislation.

Congressional Record. The daily, printed account of proceedings in the House and Senate, with a substantially verbatim account of debate. Members are allowed to revise their spoken remarks.

Continuing Resolution. A joint resolution to continue appropriations for a department or agency when a fiscal year is beginning and Congress has not enacted the department's regular appropriations bill. Also called "CR" or continuing appropriations.

Division Vote. A vote in which all members present who favor a bill are asked to stand, followed by all those opposed. No record is kept of how members voted (also called "standing vote").

Entitlement Program. A federal program such as Social Security or unemployment compensation that guarantees a certain level of benefits to persons who meet requirements set by law.

Filibuster. A time-delaying strategy of debate, quorum calls, amendments, and other procedures used by a minority to defeat or achieve compromise on a proposition favored by the majority.

Fiscal Year. Financial operations of the government are carried out in a twelve-month period beginning October 1 each year. Fiscal 1999, for example, began October 1, 1998, and will end September 30, 1999.

Five-Minute Rule. A debate-limiting rule of the House that, while the Committee of the Whole sits, allows a member offering an amendment to speak for five minutes in its favor, followed by an opponent who also speaks for five minutes.

Floor Manager. A member who has the task of steering legislation through floor debate and the amending process to a final vote in the chamber. The floor manager is usually the chairman or ranking minority member of the committee that reported the legislation.

Frank. A member's facsimile signature, which is used on envelopes in lieu of stamps, for the member's official outgoing mail. The "franking privilege" is the right to send mail postage-free.

Germane. Pertaining to the subject matter of the measure at hand.

Hearings. Committee sessions for taking testimony from witnesses. The public and press may attend open hearings; the vast majority of hearings are open to the public.

Hopper. Box on House clerk's desk where members deposit bills and resolutions to be introduced.

Joint Resolution. A resolution requiring approval of both the House and Senate. It becomes law if signed by the president or passed over his veto. Differing in no substantive way from a bill, a joint resolution often is used to address a limited matter. A joint resolution also is used for a constitutional amendment, which requires passage by two-thirds of each chamber but does not go to the president.

Law. An act of Congress that has been signed by the president or passed over his veto by Congress. Public bills, when signed, become public laws and are cited by the letters PL and a hyphenated number.

Majority Leader. In the Senate, the majority leader, in consultation with the minority leader, directs the legislative schedule for the chamber. He also is his party's spokesperson and chief strategist. In the House, the majority leader is second to the Speaker and serves as his party's legislative strategist. There also is a minority leader, who is the floor leader for the minority party in each chamber.

Majority Whip. In effect, the assistant majority leader, in either the House or Senate. His job is to help marshal majority forces in support of party strategy and legislation. There also is a minority whip, who performs duties of whip for the minority party.

Marking Up a Bill. Working on legislation in committee or subcommittee; approving, amending, or rejecting each provision and the bill as a whole.

Morning Hour. Time set aside for the conduct of routine business. The House rarely has a morning hour.

Motion. A request by a member to institute any one of a wide array of parliamentary actions. He "moves" for a certain procedure, such as the consideration of a measure.

Nominations. Presidential appointments to government and diplomatic posts that are subject to Senate confirmation.

One-Minute Speeches. Delivered at the beginning of a legislative day in the House, these may cover any topic but are limited to one minute in duration.

Override a Veto. If the president disapproves a bill and sends it back to Congress with his objections, Congress may try to override his veto and enact the bill into law. The override requires a recorded vote with a two-thirds majority in each chamber.

342 Glossary of Legislative Terms

Pair. A "gentleman's agreement" between two lawmakers who are on opposite sides of an issue, made in advance of a vote to cancel out the effects of absences. Notices of pairs are printed in the *Congressional Record*.

Parliamentarian. Each chamber employs several parliamentarians to assist the presiding officer in making rulings and conducting business of the chamber.

Pocket Veto. The act of the president in withholding his approval of a bill after Congress has adjourned.

Point of Order. An objection raised by a member that the chamber is departing from rules governing its conduct of business. The chair then must rule on whether the objection is justified.

President of the Senate. The vice president of the United States presides over the Senate. In his absence, a president pro tempore presides.

President Pro Tempore. The presiding officer of the Senate in the absence of the vice president of the United States.

Previous Question. A motion that, if approved, has the effect of cutting off all debate, preventing further amendments, and forcing a vote on the pending matter.

Quorum. The number of members whose presence is necessary for transaction of business. In the Senate, a majority of the membership comprises a quorum. In the House, a quorum also is a majority of the members, except in the Committee of the Whole House, where it is one hundred members.

Readings of Bills. Traditionally, a bill has to be read three times before passage. In modern practice, a bill is considered to have been read first upon introduction, second upon floor consideration, and third after all floor debate. Seldom are bills actually read aloud in their entirety.

Recommit to Committee. A motion made after a bill has been debated to return it to the committee that reported it. Recommittal usually is a death blow to a bill, unless done with instructions to adopt a particular amendment and report the bill back to the chamber.

Reconciliation. The 1974 budget act provides for a "reconciliation" procedure for bringing tax and appropriations bills into conformity with congressional budget resolutions. Congress instructs its legislative committees to approve measures adjusting revenues and expenditures by a certain amount by a given deadline. The recommendations of these committees are consolidated without change by the Budget committees into an omnibus reconciliation bill, which then must be approved by both houses of Congress.

Reconsider a Vote. A motion to reconsider the vote by which an action was taken has the effect, until disposed of, of putting the action in abeyance. Such a motion can be made only by a member who voted on the prevailing side.

Recorded Vote. A vote on which a public record is kept of each member's stand. In the Senate, this is accomplished through a roll call of the senators. The House uses an electronic voting system, and a recorded vote can be obtained on demand of one-fifth of a quorum (forty-four members) of the full house, or one-fourth (twenty-five) during Committee of the Whole.

Report. Both a verb and a noun as a congressional term. After completing a markup of a bill, a committee reports its recommendations to the chamber along with the measure. It usually publishes a written report containing an explanation of the bill as approved and the committee's reasons for its action.

Resolution. Designated H Res or S Res, a "simple" resolution deals with matters entirely within the prerogatives of one house. It does not require passage by the other chamber or approval by the president, and it does not have the force of law.

Rider. An amendment, usually not germane, that a sponsor offers to a bill to enhance the amendment's chances of enactment.

Rules. The term has two congressional meanings. Both houses of Congress have standing rules governing procedure. In the House, the term also refers to resolutions reported by the Rules Committee, which, upon approval by the full House, govern the length and terms of debate for most bills considered on the floor.

Secretary of the Senate. Chief administrative officer of the Senate.

Speaker. The presiding officer of the House of Representatives.

Strike Out the Last Word. In the House's Committee of the Whole, when debate is limited by the five-minute rule, a member may gain recognition from the chair by moving to "strike out the last word" of the amendment or section of a bill under consideration. The motion is pro forma, requires no vote, and does not alter the measure being debated. Members also use "strike out the requisite number of words."

Supplemental Appropriations Bill. Legislation appropriating added funds for a department during the current fiscal year after its regular appropriations bill has been enacted.

Suspend the Rules. A time-saving procedure used for considering bills in the House under which no amendments may be offered and debate is limited to twenty minutes per side. A two-thirds vote is required for passage under suspension of the rules, a procedure reserved mostly for noncontroversial bills.

Table a Bill. A motion to "lay on the table" effectively kills a bill if approved.

Treaties. Executive proposals, such as arms control proposals, that must be submitted to the Senate for approval by two-thirds of the senators present.

Unanimous Consent. The Senate or House can do almost anything it wishes, regardless of its rules, upon unanimous consent of the chamber. But objection from a single member can block action.

Unanimous Consent Agreement. Also called a time limitation agreement, it is an agreement negotiated by the Senate leadership to govern one or more aspects of action on a measure. In effect, it is similar to a rule in the House.

Veto. Disapproval by the president of a bill or joint resolution. When Congress is in session, the president must veto a bill within ten days, excluding Sundays, after he has received it; otherwise, it becomes law without his signature.

Voice Vote. Members answer "aye" or "no" in chorus, and the presiding officer decides the result. No record is made of how individual members voted.

Yeas and Nays. A recorded vote (see above).

Yield. When a member has been recognized to speak, no other member may speak unless he or she obtains permission from the member recognized. Requests are made in the form, "Will the gentleman yield?"

Save When You Order More Copies of *Who's Who in Congress* for Your Organization

Take advantage of these special discounts on *Who's Who in Congress 1999*:

Number of copies	Cost per copy	Discount
less than 10	$17.95	
10-49	$12.56	30%
50-99	$10.77	40%
100-249	$8.97	50%

Sales at above discount are non-returnable. These discounts are available to organizations only. Call for our retail discount schedule.

❏ I want to save on additional copies of *Who's Who in Congress 1999* (ISBN 1-56802-080-5). Send me____ copies at the special discounted prices above.

❏ Check enclosed for $_____, payable to Congressional Quarterly.

❏ Bill me (Organizations only). Shipping and handling charges will be included in your invoice.
Authorizing signature _____

Shipping charge for prepaid and credit card orders 7% of order total. Minimum shipping charge: $4.50

D.C. addresses please include 5.75% sales tax; VA addresses include 4.5%

Bill to:

Organization _____
Attention _____ - Dept./Room _____
Telephone (required) _____
Street Address _____
City _____ State ____ ZIP ____

Ship to (if different):

_____

Call toll free to order: 1-800-638-1710
In metropolitan D.C. call: 1-202-822-1475
Or FAX your order to: 1-800-380-3810

Additional Discounts & Customized Copies

Discounts for additional quanties available. Also, custom editions of *Who's Who in Congress* are available. Put your organization's name on the cover of this handy guide to Congress. For more information, call Maureen Whelan at 202-887-8501.

Congressional Quarterly Books
1414 22nd Street, NW
Washington, D.C. 20037

L9WWB1

BUSINESS REPLY MAIL
First Class   Permit No. 10182   Washington, D.C.

POSTAGE WILL BE PAID BY ADDRESSEE

Congressional Quarterly Books
Customer Service and Fulfillment, Dept. L9WWB1
1414 22nd Street, N.W.
Washington, D.C. 20077-6778

No Postage Necessary If Mailed In The United States

New from CQ Press

CQ's *Politics in America 2000* gives you complete profiles of every member of the 106th Congress, written by CQ's expert Political Staff.

Profiles of newly elected as well as incumbent members of the 106th Congress look at each member's legislative priorities, personal style and achievements, giving an insider's view of Congress as only CQ can. Accompanying each profile are key facts including: address, phone and fax numbers; e-mail address; biographical data; full committee assignments; election results; key votes; interest group ratings; district votes for president in recent election; campaign finance data, and congressional district profiles.

PLUS Politics in America comes with a FREE CD-ROM that includes all the member information in the book, plus photos and maps. This CD-ROM is compatible with Windows™ and Macintosh® systems.

Send me_____ copies of *Politics in America 2000* with FREE CD-ROM at $98.95. Hardbound. (1-56802-470-3).

Send me_____ copies of *Politics in America 2000* with FREE CD-ROM at $55.95. Paperback. (1-56802-471-1).

❑ Check enclosed for $_____, payable to Congressional Quarterly *(include shipping, see below).*

❑ Charge my (circle one) MasterCard/Visa/AmEx in the amount of $_____, payable to Congressional Quarterly *(include shipping, see below).*
Account # _____Exp. Date _____
Signature _____

Shipping charge for prepaid and credit card orders 7% of order total.
Minimum shipping charge: $4.50

D.C. addresses please include 5.75% sales tax;
VA addresses include 4.5%

❑ Bill me (Organizations only). Shipping and handling charges will be included in your invoice.
Authorizing signature _____

Organization _____
Attention _____ - Dept./Room _____
Telephone (required) _____
Street Address _____
City _____ State _____ ZIP _____

Call toll free to order: 1-800-638-1710
In metropolitan D.C. call: 1-202-822-1475
Or FAX your order to: 1-800-380-3810

To order, detach and mail to:
Congressional Quarterly Books
1414 22nd Street, NW
Washington, D.C. 20037

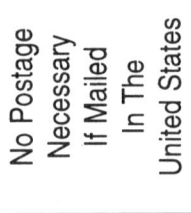

No Postage Necessary If Mailed In The United States

BUSINESS REPLY MAIL
First Class   Permit No. 10182   Washington, D.C.

POSTAGE WILL BE PAID BY ADDRESSEE

Congressional Quarterly Books
Customer Service and Fulfillment, Dept. L9WWB2
1414 22nd Street, N.W.
Washington, D.C. 20077-6778